Uncertain Partners

Uncertain Partners

Stalin, Mao, and the Korean War

Sergei N. Goncharov
John W. Lewis
Xue Litai

STANFORD UNIVERSITY PRESS
Stanford, California

Sources of illustrations: Most of the photographs are courtesy of New China News Agency. The ones of I. V. Kovalev (7) and of the Soviet secret document (22) are from Kovalev's personal archives. The Korean War map (33) is from *KangMei YuanChao Zhanzheng de Jingyan Zongjie (Caoqao)* (Summing Up the Experiences of the War to Resist America and Aid Korea [Draft]).

Stanford University Press
© 1993 by the Board of Trustees of the
Leland Stanford Junior University
Printed in the United States of America

CIP data appear at the end of the book

Original printing 1993
Last figure below indicates year of this printing:
03 02 01 00 99 98 97 96 95

Stanford University Press publications are distributed exclusively by Stanford University Press within the United States, Canada, Mexico, and Central America; they are distributed exclusively by Cambridge University Press throughout the rest of the world.

FOR

LENA

DOROTHY WALTERS

AND

DAVID

Preface

Tolstoy once observed that the origins of major events appear far simpler to those close to them than they appear at the remove of years. "The deeper we delve in search of these causes the more of them we find," he wrote. "Each separate cause or whole series of causes appears to us equally valid in itself and equally false by its insignificance compared to the magnitude of the events, and by its impotence—apart from the cooperation of all the other coincident causes—to occasion the event."

Crucial developments in Soviet-Chinese relations in the 1940s and 1950s long appeared to confirm Tolstoy's insight. The more we learned about them the greater the number of plausible explanations became. After the collapse of the Sino-Soviet alliance, the facile Communist-bloc interpretations of the day soon gave way to a variety of competing accounts of the events of the previous two decades. A classic study by the political scientist Donald Zagoria traces the seeds of the bloc's collapse to the "uneven stages of socio-economic development [of China and the Soviet Union]; their divergent revolutionary expectations and aspirations; [and] the strong element of nationalism and anti-white imperialism in the Chinese Communist revolution." Explanation piled on explanation.

Now, however, we revert to the idea that the history of the Sino-Soviet relationship was above all the product of competing security concepts and national interests and was dominated by the strategic designs and political acuity of Mao Zedong and Joseph Stalin. We begin the study in 1945, when security was of course a foremost concern for both. On August 13, just as the war against Japan was concluding, Mao suggested that questions of weaponry and China's security were being hotly debated within his leadership when he noted, "Can atom bombs decide wars? No, they can't. Atom bombs could not make Japan surrender. . . . Some of our comrades . . . believe that the atom bomb is all-powerful; that is a big mistake." The debate against the weapons-decide-everything school within the Chinese Communist Party signaled a deep division about the future determinants of military victory and national security.

Certainly the preoccupation with war and its instruments did not erase the history of prewar relations between Russia and China, including the Communists, or the bitter personal memories of Mao and his comrades, whose role in the Chinese revolution had been alternately exploited and disparaged by Stalin. It did sufficiently fix their priorities to make political-military questions dominant. As important as other concerns or memories were, the Chinese civil war and the budding Cold War patterned and perpetuated the preoccupation with security. How to find guaranteed security in a world of perpetual conflict was a central concern as the new Chinese state formed in 1949 and as Stalin weighed his options in Asia and the world.

The idea for writing this book about Sino-Soviet security relations and their influence on Korean events was a child of discovery. In the East Asian Collection of the Hoover Institution and in the archives of the Soviet Union, we found untapped collections of documents, both Chinese and Russian. Colleagues in Moscow and Beijing added to this storehouse, and Koreans, Chinese, and Russians and Americans gave us leads on sources and knowledgeable individuals to interview. We quickly came to realize the magnitude of the task before us, but it took critical reviews of early drafts to make us rethink the task and redirect our research. As we read the materials analyzed for this study, we decided that we might have the documentary basis to attempt a reevaluation of a crucial chapter in Chinese politics and to reopen questions on the Sino-Soviet alliance. We were ambitious enough to believe that the result might cast new light on the origins of the Cold War in Asia.

A collection of Mao's manuscripts, speeches, and articles entitled *Jianguo Yilai Mao Zedong Wengao* (Mao Zedong's Manuscripts Since the Founding of the Republic) was our first major discovery, and we joined a host of other scholars eager to mine it for new insights. Volume 1 of this publication, which covers the period from September 1949 to the end of 1950, contains 523 documents, including 364 that had gone unpublished. We have translated some of these materials in the Appendix.

We also found additional Chinese and Korean sources, such as the memoirs of Shi Zhe and Li Yueran (Mao's interpreters during the talks with Stalin and other Soviet leaders), Wu Xiuquan (a senior Chinese diplomat and participant in the Mao-Stalin summit in early 1950), Zhu Zhongli (the wife of the Chinese ambassador at Moscow, Wang Jiaxiang), Chai Chengwen (the Chinese political counselor in Pyongyang at the beginning of the

Korean War and later the PRC negotiator at Panmunjom), Peng Dehuai (commander of the Chinese troops in Korea), Zhou Enlai (the Chinese premier and foreign minister), and Yoo Sung Chul (a former general in the Korean People's Army and head of the Operations Department of the army at the outset of the war). We have interviewed Yoo Sung Chul, Kang Sang Ho (a former deputy head of a provincial branch of the Korean Workers' Party and former vice-minister of the North Korean secret police), and Chung Sang Chin (a former general who served in the Directorate of Ordnance of the North Korean Ministry of Defense). In addition, we wish to acknowledge the generous help of He Di, Shang Lingkui, Wang Jifei, Xing Shugang, Zhu Ruizhen, Song Jiuguang, and Pan Zhenqiang. Several others agreed to be interviewed only on condition of anonymity.

Our second major find was a collection of documents in the personal archive of I. V. Kovalev, Stalin's personal representative to Mao Zedong, whose background we review in Chapter One. We have interviewed him and are grateful to him for his permission to use these invaluable materials. Although there is a continuing paucity of Soviet materials, we have incorporated recent memoirs of eyewitnesses such as Andrei Gromyko, N. T. Fedorenko (Stalin's interpreter), and Soviet military advisers and have interviewed senior Soviet officials such as Ivan Arkhipov, who participated in the negotiations and later served as the chief Soviet adviser in China.

After the defeat of the anti-Gorbachev coup in August 1991, the authorities of the Russian Republic took control of the archives of the Communist Party of the Soviet Union and the KGB, and reportedly the materials will be declassified up to 1961. We have participated in opening up the former Central Committee archive, now called the Center for the Preservation of Contemporary Documents, and understand that materials on the Korean War era do exist. Nevertheless, we believe that it will be some years before these materials will be fully processed and made available to scholars, and we have decided to proceed in the knowledge—and hope—that future scholars will have access to far more documentary sources on Sino-Soviet relations.

In addition to Lieutenant General Kovalev, a number of former officials and scholars in Russia provided invaluable assistance and information. We particularly wish to thank G. Kuzmin, Iu. M. Garushiants, K. V. Shevelev, Iu. A. Ovchinnikov, S. L. Tikhvinskii, R. M. Aslanov, L. P. Deliusin, A. V. Meliksetov, A. M. Grigoriev, A. G. Iakovlev, A. I. Evsikov, A. M. Ledovskii, Iu. S. Peskov, V. S. Miasnikov, A. D. Dubrovskii, V. P. Tkachenko, M. S. Kapitsa, and E. P. Bazhanov. As in China, there was a large group of specialists who preferred to be quoted on the promise of anonymity; we express our special gratitude to them.

To our best knowledge, this is the first book on this topic written jointly by Russian, American, and Chinese authors. In preparing this study, the three of us have had many debates that reveal not only different interpretations of the data but also different scholarly traditions. Although we have tried to write in one "voice," we recognize that sometimes different attitudes toward styles of analysis, documentation, and speculation have surfaced. We have learned to respect these differences, and each of us has had to reexamine his own inherited biases.

Several other "voices" have helped us rethink the discrepancies and provided generous criticism and advice. We wish to thank in this regard Barton Bernstein, Gordon Chang, David Holloway, Melvyn Leffler, and John Merrill. Each read earlier drafts of the manuscript and led us to undertake major revisions. They deserve much of the credit for urging us to search more diligently for Soviet sources, a search that eventually led us to Ivan Kovalev's archive and other troves of knowledge in the new Russia.

We faced the challenge that comes from deciding on what must seem trivial matters. All things Chinese, Russian, and Korean are cited and spelled in many different ways. The official spelling systems in North and South Korea, not just the People's Republic of China and Taiwan, are quite different but take on a certain political significance. Even from the academic perspective, no spelling system is truly adequate, and the several "standard" orthographies all posed problems. With some misgivings and an exception for the names of some well-known figures and place-names (for example, Chiang Kai-shek, Quemoy, and Yangtze) and Chinese people and places under the jurisdiction of Taiwan, we have used standard pinyin and, for Chinese place-names and boundaries, the pinyin gazetteer in *Zhonghua Renmin Gongheguo Fen Sheng Dituji* (Collection of Provincial Maps of the People's Republic of China; Beijing, 1983). For the transliteration of Russian names and places, we have used the Library of Congress system, again with the exception of such well-known figures as Tolstoy and Anastas Mikoyan. Finally, we have rendered Korean places, both North and South, according to the official U.S. army histories of the Korean War, including such volumes as Roy E. Appleman, *South to the Naktong, North to the Yalu* (Washington, D.C., 1961). However, we have used the spelling of Korean names adopted by the individuals themselves, where known, in each part of Korea.

Our combined labors could not have succeeded without the aid of gifted editors, map makers, proofreaders, and manuscript preparers. Here we especially wish to thank Barbara Mnookin and Muriel Bell of the Stanford University Press and Carole Hyde of the Stanford Center for International Security and Arms Control. A special word of appreciation goes to Jacquelyn Lewis, Tamara Karganova, Ryoo Jin-kyu, Gerry Bowman, Douglas Peckler, Lho Kyongsoo, and others in the Center, each of whom significantly helped in bringing this book to completion. We would also like to thank Danyune Zhang, whose eye for detail and care in finding and organizing our research materials proved invaluable. As in so much of our research, Anca Ruhlen, the Center librarian, undertook the quest for references and special scientific materials, a quest in which we were unstintingly assisted by the staff of the Hoover Institution's East Asian Collection.

The generous help that supported our research and writing came from a number of important sources. We wish to thank the Carnegie Corporation of New York, the Columbia Foundation, the Peter Kiewit Foundation, the Henry Luce Foundation, the William and Flora Hewlett Foundation, the John D. and Catherine T. MacArthur Foundation, and the Walter H. Shorenstein Family Fund. We must add the obvious disclaimer that we alone bear the responsibility for this volume, its faults as well as its ideas and judgments.

There were times that each of us felt overwhelmed by the magnitude of the task, particularly when Sergei called from Moscow during the fateful August coup that he was off to man the barricades at the Russian "White House." We know that only our readers have the right to evaluate how successful we were in this endeavor and will do so by what they read. Yet we shall always judge the merit of this effort by the extraordinary affection we have formed for one another. May this book not only betoken personal friendship but in its small way stand as a symbol of genuine international cooperation.

S. N. G.
J. W. L.
X. L. T.

August 1, 1992

Contents

Photographs follow pages 72 and 142

Uncertain Partners

ONE

Stalin, Mao, and the
Chinese Civil War, 1945-1948

Like the imperial Russian rulers before him, Joseph Stalin after the Second World War strove to dominate the periphery of the Soviet Union and to recover lost lands and influence in Asia, as well as in Europe and the Middle East. The postwar antecedents of the Sino-Soviet alliance of 1950 can be traced as much to traditional Russian objectives as to Stalin's policies in 1945. His ambition to annihilate rivals built on an imperial urge to seize buffer zones and thereby fortify the Soviet Union's geopolitical position.[1] Although history might have suggested to him that hatred most often greeted countries pursuing hegemony over neighboring lands, Stalin insisted on the legitimacy and the mutual benefit of that pursuit. Since the Soviet Union had emerged from the war as a world power, the argument ran, ensuring its security would inevitably yield a safer world. Now that Russia's "historic borders" had been restored, southern Sakhalin and the Kurils no longer served as a base for Japanese aggression, and a "free and independent" Poland denied Germany a future springboard for attacking the Soviet Union.[2]

Chairman Mao Zedong, leader of the Chinese Communist Party (CCP), long shared with the Soviet Union the preference for buffer zones beyond his nation's border. This outlook was, after all, in accord with the traditional Chinese view of the just ordering of foreign relations: a stable hierarchy leading from the emperor's rule of the Middle Kingdom to suzerainty over Inner Asia and the outer barbarians, a dominion acknowledged and ritualized in the tribute paid to the emperor.[3] Mao's nationalistic outlook coincided in many ways with Stalin's basic orientation but, of course, with reverse import for Chinese territory.

So it was that the two Communist leaders appraised the implications of external glacis for their own national security. Locked in a mental world of warring armies and aircraft, neither squarely faced the coming of the nuclear age or contemplated the possibilities for peaceful accommodation with the West. They regarded a third world war as probable, for Stalin even inevitable, and likely to replay the gruesome features of the monstrous conflict then just ending. For them, the goal went beyond mere survival; each anticipated in his own way his regime's eventual triumph over hostile forces and daunting odds. The pathway to the future would be paved with the stepping-stones of the past, and the events of 1945 constituted the gateway to the certain confrontations just ahead.

The fundamentals coupling Moscow and the revolutionary Chinese government, established in Beijing on October 1, 1949, thus did not originate at the time of Mao's trip to the Soviet Union that December.[4] As so many scholars and officials have noted, their relationship lay rooted in actions and outcomes years before, and many of the issues the two addressed in Moscow reflected their long history of painful, wrenching encounters. Competing security interests, ideological prejudices, and personality quirks had bounded those issues and their approaches to them. Here, without plunging into the vast literature on the subject, we briefly examine the postwar history of those approaches as a necessary background to the negotiation of the Sino-Soviet treaty of February 14, 1950.[5] For Stalin and Mao, that history constituted the cardinal and vexing reality, not a textbook tale.

The First Sino-Soviet Alliance

On February 11, 1945, Joseph Stalin, Franklin D. Roosevelt, and Winston Churchill, then in conclave at the Crimean port of Yalta, signed an agreement for disposing of Far Eastern questions.[6] Stalin had conditioned the Soviet Union's entrance into the war against Japan on that agreement, which would ensure the expansion of Soviet supremacy in Asia. The accord stated that the status quo in Outer Mongolia (the Mongolian People's Republic) would be preserved, and that the "former rights of Russia violated by the treacherous attack of Japan in 1904" would be restored. In addition to validating various Soviet claims against Japan itself, Yalta gave Moscow extraterritorial rights in China and prescribed the conclusion of a treaty of alliance between Moscow and the Nationalist government in Chongqing (Chungking).[7]

The security equation for Stalin was simple: subordinate the interests of weak states (including China) to those of the powerful, divide the strategic regions of the world into spheres of influence, and widen the buffer zones along the periphery of the Soviet state.[8] His was the diplomacy of imperial Russia.

Chiang Kai-shek, the Nationalist leader of the Republic of China, saw the Yalta accords as a disgrace and a national disaster. Yalta shattered his dream of recovering China's lost lands, and when, in January 1946, the disclosure of the accords in the Chinese press triggered strong public protests, seriously undermining his authority, he sought Washington's backing to thwart Stalin's depredations.[9]

In June 1945, the Kremlin authorized talks to negotiate the treaty of friendship and alliance with the Nationalists, a treaty characterized by most Chinese as a mere appendix to Yalta.[10] Stalin agreed. He started the talks off on a sour note, contemptuously tossing a copy of the Yalta Far Eastern Agreement before the Chinese foreign minister as he highlighted its stipulations regarding future Soviet demands in Asia.

Even as the negotiators sat down at the table in Moscow, Stalin had initiated a dialogue with his chief interlocutor, Foreign Minister T. V. Soong, concerning the Soviet objectives for East Asia.[11] This dialogue continued from June 30 to August 10, which is to say, effectively over the whole of the proceedings. Stalin began by telling Soong, "In the past, Russia wanted an alliance with Japan in order to break up China. Now, we want an alliance with China to curb Japan." A few days later, he spelled out his rationale: "Japan will not be ruined even if she accepts unconditional surrender, like Germany. . . . We are closed up. We have no outlet. One should keep Japan vulnerable from all sides, north, west, south, east; then she will keep quiet." On July 7, Stalin, musing about the future, predicted that Japan "will restore her might in 20, 30 years. [The] whole plan of our relations with China is based on this. Now our preparation in [the] Far East in case Japan restores [her] might is inadequate." He lamented that it would take 40 years to build the Soviet ports and rail systems in the Far East. "Therefore we want [an] alliance," he said. "Mongolia is part of this plan." He told Soong, "We need [the Chinese ports of] Dairen [Dalian] and Port Arthur [Lüshun] for 30 years in case Japan restore[s] its forces. We could strike at her from there." Even after the atomic bombing of Hiroshima, Stalin relayed his fears that Japan would revive rapidly and informed the foreign minister, as their talks ended on August 10, "in case of war we would have to interfere. [The] Chinese will want us to interfere. War may come in 10, 15, 20 years."

Such was the thesis and the tone that Stalin imposed on the deliberations. Although the Soviet and Chinese negotiators could identify some items of consensus, their differences abounded. The most irreconcilable issue was the disposition of the Mongolian People's Republic (Outer Mongolia). Dominion over this inner-Asian land was critical to both nations, but Stalin interpreted the Yalta agreement, which promised that "the status quo in Outer-Mongolia . . . shall be preserved," as meaning its independence from China and permanent inclusion in the Soviet security orbit. This interpretation contradicted Chiang Kai-shek's view of the legal status quo.* More fundamentally, accepting Stalin's terms would tilt the regional power equation to Moscow's advantage and formalize its control of buffer lands inside China. Stalin seized the opportunity and rushed the conclusion of the treaty "under the signboard of jointly fighting against Japanese invasion."

The first and second rounds of the treaty negotiations (June 30–July 13; August 7–14) differed markedly. Between the two rounds, Stalin participated in the Potsdam conference of the great powers.[12] In the first period, Stalin's most potent bargaining chip in the negotiations with the Nationalists was his pending decision on Soviet participation in the war with Japan. The United States considered that participation absolutely vital for saving American lives, a judgment that caused Washington to press the Nationalists to be more obliging in accepting Soviet terms. For this reason, Chiang's team in Moscow had to worry that any resistance to signing the treaty might damage Sino-American relations.[13] Convinced that "Russia's entry into the war depended a great deal upon the outcome of the negotiations," Roosevelt's successor, Harry S. Truman, instructed W. Averell Harriman, his ambassador in Moscow, to keep him "closely informed of the progress of the talks."[14]

Just before the second phase of the talks began, the atomic bomb entered the picture. At the Potsdam meeting, Truman had informed Stalin that the United States possessed an unprecedentedly destructive weapon, and on August 6, the day before the start of the second round of the Sino-Soviet talks, Hiroshima was obliterated.[15]

That event significantly altered the American estimate of the need for Soviet armies to strike against Japan. As a result, Washington shifted tactics. According to Truman, he instructed Harriman to tell Stalin that the Yalta requirements had already been met and to "request that no agreement be made involving further concessions by China." Nevertheless, Truman persisted in urging Chiang Kai-shek to forge ahead with the talks (though not to accept Stalin's terms) in order to ensure the Red Army's entry into the war.[16]

---

*The Chinese traditionally regarded Outer Mongolia as a part of China, but a give-and-take over the area began in 1921, when Soviet forces occupied it. Though Lenin promptly recognized an independent Mongolian People's Republic at that stage, Moscow did a turnabout in 1924, recognizing Outer Mongolia as a part of China in discussions with Beijing on the establishment of diplomatic relations. Stalin later began treating Outer Mongolia as an important buffer zone protecting the Trans-Siberian Railroad, and in 1936 he concluded a treaty of mutual cooperation with the Mongolian People's Republic without informing China. Li Jiagu, "Sino-Soviet Intercourse," p. 117.

Stalin adjusted his policy to the new circumstances. On August 8, his government announced that the Soviet Union would consider itself at war with Japan as of August 9. He launched and then accelerated the Soviet offensive against the Japanese forces in Manchuria and thereby confronted Chiang Kai-shek's negotiators with a probable fait accompli, the Red Army's occupation of China's Northeast.*

In the second phase of the talks, therefore, the Nationalists (led by T. V. Soong and a new foreign minister, Wang Shih-chieh) faced a different and even more serious threat to their bargaining position. They knew, of course, that meeting Stalin's claims would threaten their national interests and domestic power, but they also feared that ruptured relations with Stalin might lead to greater cooperation between the Soviet and Communist forces in Manchuria.[17] Any long-term Soviet armed presence on Chinese territory raised the specter of massive Soviet aid to the Chinese troops under Mao Zedong. On August 10, Stalin warned the Nationalists that they had better sign the treaty quickly, because Mao's forces were then moving into the Northeast. His warning worked; Chiang's diplomats acquiesced to Stalin's terms.[18]

Some aspects of the 1945 treaty and its associated notes particularly favored the Soviet Union and were especially galling to the Chinese. Besides having to commit itself to the results of a plebiscite in Outer Mongolia, the Nationalist government accepted the leasing of the port city of Dalian, the exclusive Sino-Soviet military and commercial use of the naval base at Lüshun, and joint ownership of the main Manchurian railroads (later renamed the Chinese Changchun Railroad), all for a term of 30 years.[19] On each of these agreements, Stalin wrested concessions that met and in some cases exceeded the Yalta mandate.[20]

When the two foreign ministers signed the Treaty of Friendship and Alliance on August 14, 1945, Nationalist China and the Soviet Union embarked on a formal partnership "to render impossible the repetition of aggression and violation of the peace by Japan."[21] By coincidence, the treaty was signed on the same day that Emperor Hirohito bowed to the Allies' call for surrender, weakening the anti-Japanese premise on which it

---

*Manchuria (*Manzhou*) was the name of China's northeastern region until 1949. From late in the Qing Dynasty on, it consisted of three provinces: Liaoning (Fengtien), Jilin (Kirin), and Heilongjiang (Heilungkiang). On March 9, 1932, the Japanese organized Manchuria into the puppet state of Manchukuo. But the Chinese still regularly referred to the region as the Northeast, and that became its official name when the Northeast People's Government was formally established on Aug. 27, 1949. Similar name changes dot the history of many Chinese cities as well as provinces. For example, Fengtien at times was the name of Liaoning Province's capital city as well as the province itself; the city, later known outside China as Mukden, is now called Shenyang.

was based. Tokyo's decision to capitulate, however, did not deter Stalin from his own military program: throughout August, his battalions continued to press forward to the full conquest of Manchuria. Their victory enforced and even extended what his diplomats had gained on August 14.

Stalin did offer phantom carrots along with his quite genuine threats in the talks. He acknowledged that the Nationalists were the sole legitimate government of China, pledged to provide help only to it, and stated that the Communist divisions should be merged into the Nationalist armies.[22] Contemporary evidence, however, suggests that neither the Nationalists nor the Americans believed that Stalin would keep his word. As early as August 17, in response to President Truman's query whether Moscow would abide by the treaty, T. V. Soong (who had resigned as foreign minister but continued as prime minister) replied that Stalin's adherence would only be temporary. Soong indicated that Stalin would surely reverse his policy if the Chiang government remained weak. Truman concurred and promised to offer aid to make Chiang less vulnerable.[23]

Although the treaty legalized an unequal relationship between the two countries, most historians credit the Nationalist Chinese with having staved off even more predatory Soviet demands on China. This may be so, but for our story, it is more relevant that Stalin obviously believed the treaty had ratified a long-term Soviet sphere of influence in Manchuria, Mongolia, and elsewhere, especially Xinjiang.[24] It is that belief that colored the Soviet leader's attitudes toward the rise of communism in China after 1945.

Soviet and Chinese Communist Strategy in the Immediate Postwar Period

In both letter and spirit, the Treaty of Friendship and Alliance collided with some of the most cherished tenets of the Chinese Communist Party. It also undermined Mao's widely publicized pronouncement of 1936 that after the victory of the revolution, Outer Mongolia would "automatically become a part of the Chinese federation, at its own will."[25] But the Chinese Communists were in no position to cross Stalin, and a few days after the treaty was signed, they expressed their official endorsement of it as a measure ensuring cooperation with the Soviet Union and peace in the Far East.[26]

Some Party leaders opposed the clauses of the treaty that compromised China's sovereignty, but they said nothing in public.[27] They privately concluded that the American atomic bomb had frightened Stalin.[28] Moreover, many of them reportedly believed that the Soviet leader was satisfied with his gains from the war and would condone no further expansionism that might unleash a nuclear war or upset the stability needed to rebuild the Soviet economy.[29] As we shall see, Stalin's actual attitude toward the threat of a nuclear war did not match Mao's perception of it, but the Chinese then had no way of ascertaining the Soviet leader's real views.

Japan's decision to surrender in August 1945 immediately raised the prospect of armed conflict between the Nationalists and the Communists. In order to avert renewed civil war, Chiang Kai-shek, allegedly at Washington's behest, invited Mao to the Nationalists' wartime capital in Chongqing to "discuss state affairs."[30] Given the mood of the Chinese people against further fighting, Mao could not refuse the invitation. But the always suspicious Communist leader did not want to go to Chongqing himself and indicated that he would send Zhou Enlai to act on his behalf.[31] Stalin decided to intervene. He twice cabled Mao to urge him to join the negotiations with Chiang.

In the first cable (dated August 22), Stalin said that China must hold to the road of peaceful development, that he believed the Nationalists and Communists should reach a peace accord because a civil war would destroy the Chinese nation, and that, accordingly, he thought both Zhou and Mao should go to Chongqing.[32] After receiving Stalin's cable, an angry Mao remarked, "I simply don't believe that the nation will perish if the people stand up and struggle [against the Nationalist government]."

Some hours later, he received the second cable from Moscow. If Mao persisted, Stalin asserted, his stand would be repudiated in China and abroad. He assured Mao that the United States and the Soviet Union would guarantee his personal safety during his stay in Chongqing. We will never know what went through Mao's mind at that moment, but soon thereafter he decided to fly to Chongqing.[33] At about the same time, Stalin told Politburo members Liu Shaoqi and Gao Gang, who were then in Moscow for urgent consultations, that Mao's talks with Chiang were a necessary tactic: the talks would buy time for the Chinese Communists to regroup and mobilize their armies for the coming battles.[34] Chinese propaganda quickly fell into line. The Nationalist leader, till now routinely called the "reactionary fascist dictator Chiang" became "President Chiang."[35]

Moscow clearly wanted to keep the Chinese revolution in check. The Soviet representative to Yan'an recalls, "Moscow's decision on noninterference [in the conflict between the Communists and the Nationalists] amounted to a refusal to support Mao's adventurist policies, which could have created a situation leading to global conflict."[36] Later, in the 1950s, when Sino-Soviet relations began to deteriorate, Mao privately stated that Stalin in fact had hurt the Chinese revolution, and that if the Chinese Communists had followed Stalin's instructions, they would have been defeated.[37] He did not acknowledge the considerable Soviet assistance that was already flowing to the Communist forces in Manchuria in the late summer of 1945 and that radically affected the outcome of the civil war.

We shall return many times to the complicated relations between Stalin and Mao. The tense and sometimes suspicious nature of the intercourse between the two leaders that summer was driven both by the zero-sum character of their immediate strategic interests and by their bitter recollections of earlier betrayals. This subject is the theme of numerous books and articles, and here we wish only to recall that during the 1940s, frictions between Stalin and Mao had two principal causes. First, Stalin did not consider Mao a true Marxist and always suspected that the Chinese revolution sooner or later would mutate "into something else," meaning something anti-Marxist and anti-Soviet.[38] Mao's 1938 purge of the pro-Moscow faction in the CCP leadership, headed by Wang Ming, fortified that belief.[39]

Equally important but less well known is the fact that there had been a serious rift between the two leaders over the prosecution of the war against Germany. At two momentous periods of Soviet distress—the catastrophic defeats in the summer of 1941 and the battle for Moscow at the end of the year—Stalin had pleaded with Mao to have his troops take the offensive and thereby prevent a probable Japanese assault against the Soviet Far East. Mao refused to commit his troops, stating that he did not want to sacrifice his own armies in a losing engagement against a superior foe. Only in early 1943 did Mao agree to a Soviet request for help by moving some of his units to the vicinity of the Great Wall.[40] Stalin reportedly did not forget or forgive Mao for his lack of support at the moment of truth. Ironically, Stalin's two cables in August 1945 highlighted how much the strategic situation had changed. Now Stalin was trying to curtail Mao's offensive actions, while Mao was eager to sound the battle cry for the men he had kept from combat during the war against Japan. The tactics had changed, but the underlying security game stayed the same.

In any case, Mao had already begun devising his own strategy toward his Nationalist foes long before the defeat of Japan. By August 1944, the CCP leaders had worked out a guiding principle to consolidate their bases in North China and the Central Plains [*gonggu Huabei Zhongyuan*], create new bases oriented toward the South and North [*xiangnanbei liangyi fazhan*], and stress those oriented toward the South [*zhongdian xiangnan*].[41] On the eve of Japan's surrender a year later, Mao received intelligence that Japanese forces (including Japanese-controlled puppet troops) in the Yangtze River valley were exploring ways to avoid punishment for their wartime actions and were considering surrender to the Communists as one alternative. In light of this information, Mao turned away from his

1944 strategy to a policy of "defend toward the north and expand to the south" (*xiangbei fangyu xiangnan fazhan*).[42] He ordered his agents to incite defections among the Chinese puppet soldiers under Japanese command in order to seize the Central China cities of Shanghai, Nanjing, and Hangzhou ahead of the Nationalists.[43] In August 1945, he approved a plan to spark an armed insurrection in Shanghai and appointed his own mayor for the city.[44]

When the predicted uprisings of the puppet troops failed to materialize, however, Mao again shifted direction.[45] He reset his sights on the Northeast and in line with Stalin's instruction, acted to avoid fights with the Nationalists. Up to this point, the Communists had hoped for an opening in the Northeast but understood that the Japanese dominated the region. At the conclusion of the Seventh Party Congress (April–June 1945), for example, Mao had noted, "The Northeast is of primary importance to the immediate future of our Party and the Chinese revolution. Once we occupy the Northeast, we can lay a solid foundation for the Chinese revolution even if we lose all the existing base areas. . . . Now we have not yet laid a solid foundation [for the Chinese revolution]."[46] As a contingency plan, from August 17 to August 20, he dispatched nine regiments to the Northeast and directed Manchurian-born cadres to return home.[47]

But by this time any large-scale entry of CCP armed forces into the Northeast depended on Moscow's acquiescence, and any turn in strategy toward the Northeast had to await clarification of Soviet aims and policies.[48] The Soviets and Nationalists made their treaty of alliance public on August 26. The same day, Mao, uncertain of Stalin's intentions toward the Northeast, wrote, "We cannot include the whole Northeast in the regions we are planning either to occupy or to place under our control." As a hedge, he sent an advance group to Manchuria, but up to late August, he did not reverse the policy to "expand to the south."[49]

Stalin had little interest in clarifying his plans for the benefit of the Chinese Communists. It was presumably because he feared that a rapid buildup of their strength in Manchuria might imperil the conclusion of the treaty with the Nationalists and thereby jeopardize Soviet special rights in China that he did not tell Mao of his resolve to complete the treaty or to enter the war against Japan.[50] Stalin's aim all along was to make Manchuria part of the Soviet security belt in the Far East. To this end, he permitted both the looting of factories in the region and the initiation of negotiations with the Nationalists on "economic cooperation" there.[51] The two actions were taken to buttress Soviet control of China's premier industrial base.[52]

Before his declaration of war on Japan, Stalin had plotted to create pro-Soviet regimes in Manchuria and Korea and ordered groups of Chinese and

Korean Communists in the Soviet Union to move there.[53] On August 11, while the Soviet forces were pushing deeper inside Manchuria, he cabled the Chinese group: "The task of the Soviet Red Army is to liberate the Northeast. Your task is to construct the Northeast. Await orders." Later, Moscow directed this group to join the Red Army's advance into the Northeast and then to expand the local Communist armed forces. Four hundred members of the Chinese group were divided into 57 teams, each assigned to collaborate with the Soviets in setting up a given city's municipal administration. Appointed deputy commanders of the Soviet garrisons of these 57 cities, the team leaders immediately organized not only local governments but also armed constabularies.[54]

At the same time, Stalin's fear of a resurgent U.S. presence in Manchuria with the return of the Nationalists prompted him to step up his sub rosa support for the Communists under Mao.[55] As we have noted, he secretly promoted and unabashedly used the growing Communist strength as a bargaining chip in his treaty negotiations with the Nationalists. The Soviet armies were instructed to shield and aid Mao's units as they swept into the Northeast, but these units were not in any circumstances to operate openly under the banner of his Eighth Route Army.[56]

Still, Stalin worried about the international repercussions of the growth of Communist power in Manchuria. Earlier in August, V. M. Molotov (then a vice-chairman of the Council of Ministers of the USSR) reminded Soviet headquarters in Manchuria that the Chinese Communists' activities there might undermine Moscow's relations with the Allies.[57] Moscow told Marshal Aleksandr M. Vasilevskii, the Red Army's commander in the Far East, to choose one man to go to Yan'an and explore ways to coordinate the military and political activities of the Soviet and CCP forces in the Northeast.[58] Arriving on September 15, this representative informed Yan'an of the policy Moscow proposed to follow: to turn Shenyang (Mukden), Changchun, Harbin, and the railroads over to the Nationalists as required by the treaty and to support Mao's forces in other places.[59]

That night, the Chinese Politburo met in emergency session to review the Soviet policy and decided that it could create a unique opportunity for the Party.[60] The gathered leaders, under the chairmanship of Liu Shaoqi, now adopted a revised strategy of "expand to the north and defend toward the south" (*xiangbei fazhan xiangnan fangyu*).[61] With Manchuria the leading target, the Politburo proposed to have about half of the 50,000 cadres and 200,000 soldiers then moving toward the Central Plains reverse course and converge on Manchuria.[62]

Four days later Mao, who was in Chongqing for peace negotiations with Chiang Kai-shek, approved the Politburo's plan and ordered its execution.

Within months, about 20,000 political cadres, 100,000 enlisted men, and enough officers to run 100 regiments had reached the Northeast; by the end of the year, the number of troops had swelled to 400,000.[63] In addition, Mao transferred 22 members of the Central Committee (including four members of the Politburo), one-fourth of the total, to run the base areas in Manchuria.[64]

On October 10, the Nationalists and Communists signed a statement to put their armed conflict on hold, but Mao dismissed the accord as a temporary expedient. In briefing the Soviet representative to Yan'an on the results of the Chongqing talks, Mao told him that the basic differences with Chiang had not been resolved, and that a civil war was virtually inevitable because of the unremitting Nationalist attacks on his troops.[65] Mao was implicitly disavowing Stalin's earlier judgment that a civil war could be avoided if the Communists participated in peace negotiations. He was also warning Moscow that he should not be blamed for the impending hostilities.

While the Chinese Communist armies were preparing for the coming struggle for Manchuria, Chiang Kai-shek concentrated on liberating the big cities in other parts of the country from the Japanese. He apparently pinned his hope for a solution in the Northeast on Moscow's willingness to abide by the treaty and believed that at some point his troops would simply take over all of Manchuria from the Red Army.[66] Chiang, in short, played directly into Mao's strategy.

In November, needing more time to move his forces into Manchuria, Mao twice directed Peng Zhen, secretary of the CCP Northeast Bureau, to request that the Soviet troops postpone their pullout from the region. Moscow approved the request.[67] Ironically, Chiang's government also needed to buy time to redeploy its own units and form its administration in Manchuria. Facing rising Communist opposition, Nationalist officials there feared for their personal safety and sought Soviet protection. Unaware of Mao's similar request, Chiang asked the Red Army to prolong its stay, even though he had deep misgivings about Stalin's true aims for the region.[68] Stalin indeed had mixed motives. By delaying his army's departure from Manchuria, he could simultaneously ensure the official handover of the region's three big cities and the Chinese Changchun Railroad to the Nationalists and forestall the introduction of U.S. forces into Manchuria.[69]

Meanwhile, the Soviet commanders in Manchuria were at pains to balk Chiang so far as they could. They rebuffed his request to use three ports in the Northeast—Dalian, Huludao, and Yingkou—for off-loading troops and supplies,[70] thereby tolerating if not openly assisting the Communist takeover of Jehol and Chahar provinces. They advised Mao to send additional units to Manchuria and quietly handed over the three Northeast ports to his forces, thereby frustrating the Nationalist plan to transfer troops to Manchuria.[71] And, not least, they allowed the Communists to build a clandestine munitions complex in the Soviet-controlled city of Dalian and to recruit an additional 300,000 servicemen from Dalian and its suburbs.[72] At the end of the civil war, Su Yu, deputy commander of the Third Field Army, acknowledged that the weapons produced by the complex "were very powerful and ensured the victory of the Huai-Hai campaign by our army [the decisive battle for East China and one of the three decisive campaigns in the civil war]."[73]

External events were also affecting policies in the Northeast. Churchill's "Iron Curtain" speech in Fulton, Missouri, on March 5, 1946, for example, activated Stalin's fears of global confrontation with the West and may have modified his attitude toward the Nationalist-Communist conflict over Manchuria.[74] By this time, the Sino-Soviet talks on "economic cooperation" had broken down, adding to Stalin's qualms about working with the Nationalists.[75] In the next two months, Stalin sought to grasp their real aims. He issued several invitations to Chiang to attend a summit meeting in the Soviet Union, but, worried about Washington's reaction, Chiang declined.[76] At about the same time, the Nationalists sponsored anti-Soviet demonstrations in China, and an angry Stalin ordered Soviet diplomats there to cease cooperating with them. From April 6 to May 3, the Red Army withdrew from the Northeast, in a rapid pullout that enabled the Chinese Communist forces to take over most of the former Soviet garrisons.[77]

As the Communists were tightening their control in the Northeast, the civil war erupted. On June 26, 1946, Nationalist forces attacked Communist units at Xuanhuadian, Hubei, and Mao informed one of Stalin's representatives that Chiang had broken the October 10 cease-fire. The Nationalist leader had never kept his word on any agreement, he charged, once again insinuating that Stalin's advice to cooperate with the Nationalists was misguided.[78] Mao's implied criticism seemed to be justified by an action Chiang took a few months later. This action, so seemingly trivial to outside observers, was to have a profound effect on the Kremlin.

On November 4, 1946, in what Stalin interpreted as a move to extend U.S. influence in China, Chiang's government signed a commercial treaty with the United States. Stalin plainly feared that the treaty would undermine the Soviet Union's special rights under the 1945 alliance.[79] On December 27, Moscow countered by signing a "trade" document of its own with the CCP authorities in the Northeast. By this and similar commercial contracts, the Soviets undertook to supply the Communists with explosives, detonators, and blasting fuses for military use.[80]

By this time, the civil war was being waged ever more ferociously, and the Nationalists were on the offensive. In March 1947, as Chiang's troops overran Yan'an, the Communists' capital, they appeared to be on the point of losing. At this moment Mao, we believe, faced a strategic dilemma. Should Stalin conclude that a Communist defeat was in the offing, he might cut a deal with Chiang in order to rescue Mao. The next step would be pressure on Mao to make concessions to the Nationalists and to yield to an action-reaction process beyond his control. Mao thus had to prove that he could prolong the war and eventually achieve victory if he was to avoid a costly compromise. Probably for this reason, a senior Communist leader, Ren Bishi, told the Soviet representative that the evacuation of Yan'an was a tactical move that had been planned to set the stage for a future offensive. Ren appealed to the Soviets not to trust Western reports that Mao's armies were finished.[81]

Mao's approach (and Ren's arguments) apparently persuaded Stalin, who responded by upping Soviet aid to Mao's forces. On May 20, the Soviets signed an accord with the CCP Northeast Bureau providing for greater political and military support. As part of the deal, the bureau agreed to increase the region's exports to the Soviet Union and guaranteed it special transportation rights in Manchuria.[82]

Another dramatic moment occurred in July 1947, when Stalin received news via Paris that the Communists had collapsed, and that Nationalist soldiers had captured several senior Communist figures, including General He Long and Chairman Mao's wife, Jiang Qing. Stalin had no way to verify this news, because his representatives had been evacuated from Mao's headquarters to a safe hideout. Unaware of the true situation, Stalin sent word to Mao offering him sanctuary in the Soviet Union. Soon thereafter, Mao summoned the Soviet liaison officers to his headquarters to assure them that he and his retinue were quite alive if not totally well.[83]

We should note that this was the first time in the postwar years that the question of a visit by Mao to the Soviet Union was raised in earnest. In this case, Mao probably declined to go not only because the ostensible reason for the visit was false, but because he thought he would have to deal with Stalin from a position of weakness and believed the Soviet leader would seize on this to try to exact damaging concessions.

Early that autumn, the battle began to turn in the Communists' favor, and Mao accorded higher priority to rectifying his relations with Stalin. In October, after his forces had defeated the Nationalists throughout the Northwest, he informed Stalin that he was convinced Chiang's troops could no longer sustain large-scale offensive operations there.[84] In December, an even more confident Mao cabled Stalin that the Communist troops had blunted the Nationalist offensive and had launched a general counteroffensive that would lead to victory.[85] His optimism was consistent with evidence that Stalin could confirm: Washington had begun reducing its commitments to China and had withdrawn the Marine divisions that had been stationed there after the war.

By then, Stalin had already decided that it was time to side openly with Mao, though, as we shall see, their relations continued to be complex and problematic. On October 27, the Nationalists signed a relatively obscure relief agreement with the United States, and Moscow used the occasion to communicate a change of line toward China.[86] Faced with the choice of supporting the Chinese Communists or accepting the possibility of a permanent U.S. presence on his borders with a Nationalist victory, Stalin opted to throw in his lot with Mao.[87]

He acted to arm his new Chinese partners. The CCP representatives had restarted talks with the Soviets to take over weapons and equipment stored in Manzhouli, a city in the Northeast.[88] Soviet troops had captured the huge arsenal from the Japanese Guandong Army in Manchuria, and up to this time, the Soviet commanders had refused Chinese Communist overtures to acquire it.[89] The matériel involved, including tanks and heavy artillery, was sufficient to equip 600,000 men. On instructions from Moscow, the Soviets transferred the arsenal to Mao's men.

So it was that between 1945 and late 1947 Soviet and Chinese Communist strategies began to converge. The stage had moved to the battlefield, and Mao's forces prepared for the final offensives. His high command had reached a consensus that Moscow's contribution to the war effort was positive and, in the Northeast, indispensable.[90]

Leaders, Intermediaries, and Advisers

Before we proceed further, let us pause for a brief look at how officials in the two Communist parties interacted, gained information about their counterparts, and distilled that information for their leaders. Although we concentrate on high politics, Stalin and Mao did not make decisions in a vacuum. Others played a critical part, and we must scrutinize their contributions if we are to understand the relations at the top.

During the postwar years, Stalin exercised absolute authority in all foreign policy matters. In searching through the numerous accounts of his talks with the Chinese, we have found no case of a member of the Soviet Politburo uttering anything of significance to the Chinese when Stalin was directly engaged. There is no example, nor can we imagine one, in which others in the Kremlin elite expressed opinions at odds with Stalin's. We have discovered no opposition, no dissent.

While pursuing his strategies in a global context, Stalin fastened on a few countries that he considered focal either as dangerous adversaries, potential allies, or otherwise special actors in the Soviet Union's struggle with the United States. Yet Stalin after all was only one fallible man. He had to rely on input from subordinates at home and abroad, and the people who kept him informed carried substantial political weight.

This was especially true of Soviet policy toward China from 1945 to 1950. For Stalin could not concentrate exclusively on the Middle Kingdom. But he did take personal charge of the most important issues concerning China, and that guaranteed the Soviet bureaucracy's undivided attention to those issues.[91] The Chinese believed that only Stalin and Molotov understood relations with them, and that other members of the Soviet elite simply carried out orders from the very top.[92] But even Molotov was not a man to cross Stalin, especially after the foreign minister's fortunes began to decline in the late 1940s.

So how was Stalin kept informed? We now know that there were a few well-used channels, each quite separate from the others. Because Moscow had official relations with the Nationalist government, it maintained clandestine contact with the CCP through a radio provided by the Comintern, and even after the dissolution of the Comintern in 1943, its transmitter continued to be the main means of direct communication between Mao and the Kremlin for another year.[93]

Stalin also maintained a team of representatives in Yan'an who reported to him via their own radios. From the winter of 1940 to the end of 1942, the team consisted of several military intelligence officers; from May 1942 to October 1945, the chief Soviet representative was TASS correspondent P. P. Vladimirov (Vlasov); and from December 1945 to July–August 1949, Doctors Orlov and Mel'nikov were the top representatives. The Chinese leaders passed these Soviet agents classified information on the situation in the country and the policy of the Party, but they also gathered intelligence on their own and transmitted it to Stalin. Mao frequently had long chats with them, obviously assuming that his ideas and proposals would reach Stalin. To make sure, he often used the Comintern transmitter to deliver his own dispatches to the Soviet capital.[94]

In these years, 1945–49, the Soviet embassy in Chongqing and then in Nanjing was practically excluded from contacts with the Communists and could transmit only official news and what tidbits it got from Nationalist authorities and contacts. As a consequence of this "division of labor," there are no Moscow-Yan'an documents at all in the archives of the Russian Ministry of Foreign Affairs. Only the archives of the Central Committee and the military intelligence services can be expected to contain useful reports.[95]

Besides these routine channels, the Kremlin occasionally commissioned individual agencies to give Stalin news from certain regions or to oversee the implementing of his policies there. Throughout the 1940s and into the early 1950s, for example, other Soviet intelligence services, first the NKVD and then the military's MGB, controlled reporting on Xinjiang. Similarly, from August 1945 until the Red Army's withdrawal in the spring of 1946, Soviet military commanders had a definitive say in the day-to-day affairs of Manchuria. Even after the army withdrew, communications from its headquarters in Lüshun, one of the two enduring Soviet enclaves in the Northeast, continued to be of great value.[96]

But useful as all this traffic from the various defense and intelligence agencies was, it was of secondary importance in Stalin's decision-making on China. It did help him determine how his policies were being monitored and carried out, to be sure, but in devising those policies, what Stalin most prized was news and hearsay concerning the thinking, priorities, and possible reactions of the relevant senior leaders. In the case of Mao, that information could come only from the Soviet representatives in routine and direct contact with the Chairman and his closest lieutenants.

Bureaucratic rituals often complicated the way reportage reached the top. During the first half of the 1940s, the Soviet representatives in Yan'an had little standing in the Moscow hierarchy. Within the bowels of officialdom, they were treated like radio operators whose real job was to send and receive messages, even though Stalin was known to check the contents of the CCP's messages against the accounts of his own people. After the war and as the Communists moved toward victory, this situation changed.

In the postwar years, a new generation of Soviet proconsuls emerged, first in Eastern Europe and then in China. These specially designated agents not only reported on events but also handled daily administration. In Europe, they were instrumental in aligning the satellites' domestic and foreign policy to Stalin's. In the countries the Soviet leader considered crucial, these proconsuls possessed two distinctly different attributes from their predecessors. First, they had high rank within the Soviet bureaucracy and had a good feel for Stalin's personal thinking on grand strategy. These qualities allowed them to make decisions independently in cases of emergency. They did not need to consult Moscow; they were Stalin's men. Second, they had considerable experience in the practical management of state affairs. They could grasp the real situation, act, and take responsibility for their recommendations and actions.

In this and the next two chapters, we shall repeatedly encounter Ivan V. Kovalev, and his archive and memory will enrich the story of the making of the Sino-Soviet alliance. Kovalev was one of Stalin's proconsuls until the Soviet dictator deemed him expendable. He represented a generation of tough, competent bureaucrats in their forties and early fifties who had already had remarkable careers during the war. Other representatives of this generation do not need special introduction. Among them are such notables as A. N. Kosygin, A. A. Gromyko, and D. F. Ustinov. If Kovalev had outlasted Mao's visit to Moscow, he, too, might have joined the ranks of this super elite of the Khrushchev and Brezhnev eras.

For a time, as we shall see, Kovalev did acquire wide-ranging authority from Stalin and spoke or reported directly to him. He treated his mandate with utmost seriousness, and on those occasions when he had to act without consulting Moscow, his recommendations were in explicit congruence with Stalin's directives and vision. Because Kovalev's position and personality made a deep impression on the Chinese, he was able to gain sensitive information from them and convey it directly to the Soviet leader. In his capacity as a conduit, he played an important role in shaping Stalin's perceptions.

As we know from our interviews with him, he drafted his reports in ways that would please Stalin and move him toward conclusions that Kovalev favored. Some documents signed by him were written by his aide, a man named Pavlov who had served as a staff writer for the railroad newspaper *Gudok* (Whistle). Kovalev's team members, individually and collectively, provided Stalin the basic material for decisions made during the crucial months from the spring of 1949 to December, when Mao arrived in Moscow.

Kovalev knew that the Kremlin leader did not wish to model China solely along Soviet lines. He was well aware of the fact that his boss regarded the Middle Kingdom as a special case and did not automatically repudiate Mao's idiosyncrasies as deviations. But in deference to Stalin's little-disguised suspicions of Mao, he lost no chance to recount each questionable remark or quirk of the Chinese leader. His reports often exaggerated Mao's alleged attempts to court the Americans or bourgeois elements within China. As Kovalev knew, Stalin treasured such details, and wartime experience had taught the Soviet representative that any failure to pass along word of Chinese "errors" could mean dismissal and purge.

After late January 1949, when he came to Xibaipo with Anastas Mikoyan, Kovalev, a former railway commissar, migrated from engineering to international politics.* Following the CCP high command's move to Beiping in March, Kovalev practically monopolized Soviet contacts with the Party leaders. Even after the establishment of official relations in October, Soviet diplomats did not enjoy anything like the kind of access Kovalev had to Mao and his associates. Indeed, it was a situation he helped along by playing on the strained relations of Mao and Soviet Ambassador N. V. Roshchin to convince Stalin that no serious issue concerning China could be resolved by the foreign ministry.[97] Stalin certainly relied on information other than Kovalev's, but his took priority up to the end of his career. We demonstrate his unique role in the pages that follow.

Like Soviet representatives before him, Kovalev had his favorites among the senior Chinese leaders, and he sometimes manipulated his relations with them to bolster his own standing. From his documents, memoirs, and interviews, it is clear that he despised Zhou Enlai, considering him to be pro-Western and unreliable. He had a better opinion of Liu Shaoqi but felt much greater empathy for Chen Yun and Lin Biao, with whom he first worked in Manchuria in the summer of 1948.

He felt closest to Gao Gang, the Communist boss of Manchuria, from whom he received especially sensitive information and damning gossip on Mao's inner sanctum. Admittedly, bitterness over his own dismissal and what he perceives to have been Stalin's betrayal of Gao has colored Kovalev's memory of Gao Gang and perhaps others. Nevertheless, his still vivid images of the past help explain the meaning and fill in the gaps of what happened more than four decades ago.

While urging caution, we should still be cognizant of the degree to which Kovalev was kept informed by the Chinese leaders on the most important issues. One of the Chinese who, from August 1949, worked as an interpreter for Kovalev writes, "The CCP Central Military Commission fre-

---

*Ivan Vladimirovich Kovalev, born in 1901, participated in the civil war and then worked as a railroad engineer. He became a director of the strategically important Western Railroad in 1937 and two years later was appointed the head of a department in the People's Commissariat of Transportation. At that time, he went to Mongolia, where he organized transport and other logistics for G. K. Zhukov's armies assigned to fight Japan; the next year, he did the same job during the war against Finland. On the eve of the German invasion, he was made vice-minister of supervision of the USSR. During the war, he served first as head of the Department of Military Transportation of the General Staff and then, from the beginning of 1942, as a member of the Transportation Bureau under the Soviet Defense Committee. In Dec. 1944, he was promoted to the post of People's Commissar of Transportation (Narodnyi Komissar Putei Soobshchenia). As such, he organized Stalin's trip to Potsdam in July 1945 and immediately afterward oversaw the transport of Soviet troops and supplies to the Far East for the war with Japan. Marshal Zhukov in his last interview stated that Kovalev should be named the man who made the greatest contributions to Soviet victory. Kovalev, "Rails of Victory," pp. 40–49; Khlebodarov, "Special Missions"; "Congratulations on the Jubilee."

quently sent a 'leather folder' full of top-secret cables to Kovalev's place; among these were those [cables] reporting on the situation on the battle-field in the South. Even such an interpreter as I had no access to them. They were translated by five interpreters that were brought by Kovalev." Kovalev, we should note, brought his own interpreters and transmitters to China and thought his communications system was secure, but the Chinese had broken his code and were quite aware of what he was telling Moscow.[98]

Mao's situation and requirements for information differed from Stalin's in several respects. Most importantly, though Mao was undoubtedly the recognized leader of his Party, in the first postwar years he had not acquired a total monopoly over foreign policy-making and felt no need to do so. He esteemed and sought the opinions of Politburo members Liu Shaoqi, Zhou Enlai, and, to a lesser extent, Gao Gang on important matters concerning relations with Moscow. Mao had played no role within the Comintern, which made him both suspicious of and partially dependent on its representatives, and on the eve of the Korean War, he had to pay heed to the opinions of his military. Real differences regularly cropped up within the Politburo, and though Mao's vote counted above all the others combined, he still had to act collegially. He felt the need to persuade his colleagues, to invent tactical solutions that would satisfy the Politburo majority, and sometimes to mold his actions to the opinions of others.

Moreover, we should not dismiss the influence of "democratic figures" in Mao's governing circles. They were often sharply critical of his moves toward Moscow, and to him they reflected ideas from not only intellectuals but even a broad stratum of "the masses." In the years of the civil war and the first months of the People's Republic, he could neither ignore their opinions nor suppress them without incurring high costs. Unwilling to pay that price, he acted to formulate and implement his strategy in ways acceptable to the democratic elements within the hierarchy. These elements may have limited his freedom of action, but they had had their uses, providing him with additional ammunition against domestic critics and against Stalin's most humiliating demands.

All of these factors affected Mao's handling of practical foreign policy affairs. Generally, he formulated the broad strategic guidelines and gave Zhou Enlai, his foreign minister, wide latitude in carrying them out. That latitude, as well as the division of labor, became especially evident when the Sino-Soviet treaty was being negotiated.

Another notable difference between Stalin and Mao stemmed from Stalin's overriding interest in China as a factor in the global scheme of things. He was essentially interested in Chinese domestic affairs only to the extent that they might influence Mao's foreign policies and behavior abroad. He had no interest in learning from the Chinese experience or its leaders. By contrast, Mao during the years of our study turned to the Soviet Union as the most important exemplar for his own state, and he treated information on Soviet domestic developments as having practical application at home.

The scope of his information on Soviet affairs differed dramatically from Stalin's on China. The Chairman had no high-ranking representative in Moscow who could inform him regularly and authoritatively on the situation in the Kremlin or the sentiments of Soviet society at large until October 1949. The appointment of Wang Jiaxiang as ambassador improved Mao's access to a certain degree but not decisively so. Stalin was hard to contact and even more difficult to probe for reliable information. With no easy way to gauge Moscow's true intentions, Mao had to fall back on general principles derived from his own experience and reading and on estimates or guesses from the few Sovietologists he trusted.

Among those who constantly briefed Mao on Soviet affairs was a handful of men who had spent years in Moscow and had personal experiences and informed opinions on how things were done there. These included Ren Bishi, Wang Jiaxiang, and Shi Zhe, the last two becoming more and more important during the period under consideration. Also, by the time of the talks on the treaty, Li Fuchun and Wu Xiuquan had become more active in relations with the Soviet Union.

Wang Jiaxiang and Shi Zhe, one high and the other in the middle ranks of the bureaucracy, did not just implement Mao's instructions. In varying ways, they served as intermediaries between the two sides. This role was manifested, for example, during Mao's stay in Moscow, when Wang passed off certain ideas broached to the Kremlin as his own in order to conceal Mao's authorship. For his part, Shi Zhe, whose autobiography and articles constitute a primary source for this study, often exceeded his authority as a "mere translator" and Mao's secretary. On many occasions, Shi saw fit not to translate Mao's rude remarks, and he similarly colored his appraisal of certain Soviet leaders in ways that would shape Mao's thinking. Both Wang and Shi acted independently, unlike their Soviet counterparts (such as N. T. Fedorenko), who tended to confine themselves to their technical roles.

The Soviet intermediary Kovalev outranked Shi Zhe but did not necessarily have greater influence on Stalin than Shi had on Mao. Even more fascinating is the fact that each understood this and developed strong feelings about the other. Their attitude toward each other in turn affected their personal relations and what they said to their bosses. We know this because we now have a unique opportunity to check the accounts of both men, and we conclude not only that their relations were poor but that each actively worked against the other. Years later, their differences bias their memoirs and how they remember the same events.

Kovalev, simply put, detested Shi Zhe. In our interviews with him and in his unpublished memoirs, he recalls that Shi Zhe drank too much and so he plied Shi with liquor to get him to talk. He belittles Shi's qualifications as a translator and remembers him as saying, "I am an old soldier and translate as well as I can." Shi returned the favor, but his dislike for Kovalev was more than personal. Much as he deplored Kovalev's behavior, especially his autocratic and officious style, what he questioned most of all was the Soviet representative's political motives. In December 1949, he learned of a Kovalev report to Stalin that was highly critical of Mao's policies in several fields. This report (which we will consider in due course) complicated the already tense relations between Stalin and Mao, and Shi concluded that this was Kovalev's intent. Like Kovalev, Shi Zhe misses no opportunity to disparage his counterpart. Even though he well knows that Kovalev was a high-ranking Soviet official—he had been a minister for four years when he came to China—Shi identifies him as a vice-minister and goes on to say that Kovalev was of too low a rank to have had meaningful access to top Soviet leaders, and that he did not dare present disagreeable information to Stalin. With some relish, he details Stalin's denunciations of Kovalev in late January 1949, when the Soviet leader, as we shall see, decided to sell out Kovalev in order to impress Mao.[99]

At the time of this writing, Kovalev and Shi have sharply divergent views on Stalin and his stance toward China. Kovalev, during the years of his service in China, had great respect for Stalin, and he expressed no doubts about his policies. He deemed Stalin's moves to block China's opening to the United States and to organize the union of Asian Communist parties as a way of controlling the CCP both natural and appropriate. He strongly backed Stalin's effort to retain the pro-Soviet terms of the Sino-Soviet treaty of 1945 in any new treaty. His memoirs describe all these matters with approval and in detail. What was unacceptable for Kovalev and influenced his later attitude toward Stalin was the way the dictator turned against his subordinates and allies, and this is why the memoirs relate in great detail how Stalin thrice betrayed Gao Gang.

Shi Zhe admiringly calls Stalin one of the "great historic figures" whom he was lucky to meet. Some of this admiration had personal roots. For example, he says that Stalin so trusted his Chinese partners that he sometimes used Shi as his translator without the Soviet interpreter being present.[100] Though Shi does not overlook what he calls Stalin's "improper behavior" toward China, especially his "great-nation chauvinism," he softens his history of the roughest moments during the Moscow talks with stories of Stalin's "positive attitude" toward China and its leaders, and treats these moments as mistakes that had nothing to do with the Soviet leader's fundamental policies or real intentions. Moreover, he deletes certain episodes in his account that could spoil his picture of Stalin's relatively benign attitude toward China, such as his refusal to assist in the invasion of Taiwan, his proposal to organize an Asian Cominform, and his part in Gao Gang's fall.

By examining the roles of the intermediaries and advisers, we have gone some distance in resolving how Mao and Stalin learned about each other, communicated, and were influenced by their subordinates. The recollections and surviving archives of these subordinates offer the best chance of reconstructing some of history's major events and coming closer to the men who made them. Taken together we can calibrate the validity of what they tell us and thus what kind of people influenced the Soviet and Chinese leaders.

Mao's Objectives and Stalin's Response

We now have a somewhat richer and more nuanced notion of how the two highest leaders came to understand and deal with each other as we return to the story of their relations in the immediate postwar years. As we have seen, relations with Moscow posed a ticklish dilemma for Mao and other Party leaders. One of their most prized achievements during the Sino-Japanese war was their emancipation from Moscow's heavy-handed control and from the influence of "dogmatists," represented by Wang Ming, who had stressed absolute obedience to Stalin.[101] Then, after 1945, Mao once again found himself dependent on Soviet assistance and constrained by somewhat dissonant Soviet policies. Though we can only imagine the difficulty and pain of Mao's adjustment, it is not hard to fathom why he so resented Stalin's later actions.

Nevertheless, Mao was prepared to come to terms with his predicament, and he immediately set about drafting a theoretical overview that would locate the Chinese revolution according to Stalin's postwar coordinates and correlate global nuclear politics with the interests of his new China.[102] Mao expressed this overview most cogently in his interview with the American journalist Anna Louise Strong in August 1946.[103]

Briefly stated, Mao elaborated two central ideas, one on the vast zone of competition lying between the superpowers (later to be called the "intermediate zone") and one on nuclear weapons as "paper tigers."[104] At one point in the interview, in an effort to clarify the first concept, Mao placed two teacups on a table, equating them to the United States and the Soviet Union. He then put many small wine glasses between the cups to represent the countries and the "vast zone" lying between the two giants; by implication he was referring to what is now called the Third World.

Mao argued that the Soviet Union constituted the principal obstacle to the establishment of American global hegemony, and because of that, the "U.S. reactionaries rabidly hate the Soviet Union and actually dream of destroying this socialist state." These reactionaries, however, faced a great obstacle: "The United States and the Soviet Union are separated by a vast zone which includes many capitalist, colonial and semi-colonial countries of Europe, Asia and Africa." The United States could not attack the Soviet Union before conquering these countries and would first direct its full force against them. The only viable strategy to avoid a superpower conflict in the long run would have to be a struggle against the United States in that zone. "Before the U.S. reactionaries have subjugated these countries," Mao declared, "an attack on the Soviet Union is out of the question."

Mao subsumed the atomic threat under this "vast zone" concept. Asked what would happen if the United States used the bomb against the Soviet Union, he said: "The atom bomb is a paper tiger that the U.S. reactionaries use to scare people. It looks terrible, but in fact it isn't. Of course, the atom bomb is a weapon of mass slaughter, but the outcome of a war is decided by the people, not by one or two new types of weapon." In the vast zone, American atomic power would have little utility or even relevance to the outcome of the struggle for dominance. The laws of historical development, not the bomb, would determine the fate of the reactionaries, and the United States only appeared strong to some Chinese but in fact was weak.[105]

Mao's theory met Stalin's international axioms head on. It replaced the defense of the Soviet Union with the struggle for national liberation in the vast zone. War could be avoided by intensifying that struggle; war was not inevitable, as Stalin had proclaimed. The dynamic of international politics resided as much in the medium and small states as in the great powers, including the Soviet Union. Since China was part of the intermediate zone, the civil war then just resuming should take center stage in Communist strategic thinking.[106]

Not very subtly, Mao was implying that Stalin, the master strategist, would have to be more resolute and forthcoming in his support for the Chinese revolution. The Soviet fears of a nuclear war with the United States were unjustified if the battleground was going to be confined to China and other parts of the vast zone. Mao was insisting that his revolution was not a card to be played in great-power politics but a principal player in its own right and even a guarantor that the game would be conducted on Communist terms. Any Soviet strategist worth his salt would have to regard the

Chinese Communists as an important asset, not a burden, and as equals, not subordinates.

Not widely recognized is the fact that Stalin's judgments on the potential of the Chinese revolution, whether wittingly or not, did begin to converge with this view in the postwar years. After the Mao-Chiang talks of October 1945 in Chongqing and a belligerent speech by Chiang Kai-shek in January 1946, the Soviet leader began to change his mind. It now appeared that there was little prospect of creating a coalition government, and that Mao's evaluation of the Chinese power equation was not so unrealistic after all.[107] Stalin was coming to the conclusion that a full-scale Chinese civil war was unavoidable, and that the Nationalists would almost certainly be aided by the United States. By 1947, he decided that the Communists had a genuine chance of succeeding because of their ever-widening popular support.

In the main, the military balance proved the most important factor moving Stalin to have second thoughts. His high command closely followed the news from the battlefronts of China, and its conclusions found their way into the Soviet press. When, after Communist setbacks from late 1946 through early 1947, Mao's military fortunes began to develop "in a direction favorable to the people," Moscow revised its estimates of Communist capabilities and endurance.[108] This change was telegraphed by an October 10 article in a Soviet journal heralding Mao's outstanding place as a leader of the Chinese revolution.[109] More important, authoritative Soviet authors step by step advertised the Kremlin's prediction that the Chinese revolutionaries would inevitably conquer China.[110]

With what seemed certain victory in sight, it is understandable why in January 1948 Stalin admitted to the Yugoslav leader Milovan Djilas that he had erred in demanding Communist cooperation with Chiang Kai-shek, and that Mao was right. Stalin's admission is all the more meaningful in the context in which it was made. It came in the midst of a discussion of the Greek civil war, which had just entered a pivotal stage. Stalin argued that the revolution in Greece must be ended because its strategic location made it vital to the West's security. The United States, "the strongest state in the world," he said, would never let the Communists win in Greece.[111]

On the other hand, Stalin indicated, a Communist success in China was probable because "China is a different case, relations in the Far East are different." The implication was that American armed involvement in China was unlikely, a conclusion the Soviet leader may have been led to because Washington's support for the Nationalists was then rapidly waning. Stalin clearly grasped the essence of U.S. foreign policy in the late 1940s, which had made Europe its strategic focus. Even though the Truman administration was still seeking subsidies for the Nationalists, Stalin recognized that the United States had limited capabilities in continental Asia and would have to curb its commitments there.[112] What Stalin does not seem to have grasped was that this reading of the situation was in accord with Mao's theory of the vast zone.

The China-Greek comparison in Stalin's assessment revealed what for him was the key variable: the different capacities of the two revolutions to succeed. Stalin's confidence in the Chinese revolution lay in his conviction that no outside interference could or would stop it. A revolution in Greece, by contrast, would certainly succumb to U.S. power without direct Soviet help, but to provide such assistance was to risk a war with the United States. The difference in capacity also meant that the Chinese revolution would proceed independently of his will, which forced him to treat Mao's China more as an equal than a satellite. One senior Soviet diplomat, M. S. Kapitsa, has characterized Stalin's views on the limits of his influence in these terms: "Proceeding from strategic consideration, Stalin advocated assistance to the Chinese Communists but also understood the limitations on Soviet capabilities to shape the situation in China and to influence its policy. He often said that the Russian and Chinese revolutions were two different matters."[113] By all evidence, then, it seems fair to conclude that by early 1948, Stalin had decided China would be his partner, rarely, if ever, his pawn.

Soviet policy-makers faced two uncertainties. One was the possibility that Washington, caught up in the presidential election campaign of 1948, might reverse its policy and once more fling itself into the Chinese civil war, as the Republican presidential candidate, Thomas E. Dewey, appeared to be advocating. In early fall, just before the elections, Mao launched an all-out offensive in Manchuria and plotted the campaigns that would sweep across North China.[114] Moscow worried that Dewey, whom the U.S. press had picked as the indisputable winner, would order U.S. troops to rush to the aid of the desperate Nationalists.[115]

The second uncertainty was whether a shift in the scene of battle would bring a change in the West's attitudes. Till now, the principal fighting had been concentrated in the North, where the Communists seemed sure to win. But once they moved into Central and South China, they would challenge the traditional bastions of Anglo-American interests. This next stage of the war greatly increased the danger of a Communist-American showdown, for Mao's forces were in fact quite ready to do battle with any U.S. troops they encountered.[116] Stalin could not be sure in advance that no such battles would ever occur.

These considerations no doubt figured in Stalin's decision in the late summer to pass along a letter from Chiang Kai-shek urging talks between his people and the Communists. Mao's high command simply ignored the letter, and Moscow said nothing.[117] The reality was that Mao alone now controlled all consequential contacts with Chiang and could ignore Stalin's overtures, however indirect, to influence the nature of the Nationalist-Communist conflict.

Mao's primacy was further confirmed at the end of 1948, when he cabled the Soviet leader about the new approach he intended to take toward any peace talks with the Nationalists. Mao merely informed the Kremlin that his representatives would hold talks only with those local Nationalist authorities and military commanders who planned to cease fighting or surrender.[118] He was rejecting as irrelevant Stalin's implicit suggestion, in transmitting Chiang's letter, that a comprehensive political settlement should or could be worked out with the central government in Nanjing.

The last Soviet attempt to encourage a political compromise in China was undertaken on January 10, 1949, when Stalin sent Mao a Nationalist memorandum asking for Soviet mediation in the civil war. Stalin solicited Mao's opinion on his draft answer to the memo, in which he again implied an interest in a peaceful solution to the civil war and a concern about American intervention. Mao predictably fired back a cable the next day rejecting the very idea of Soviet mediation.[119]

Hence, by the beginning of 1949, Stalin could no longer exert effective control over Mao's strategy in the civil war and had to accept whatever risks that strategy might entail. The only choice for the Soviet leader was to await the outcome of the war, to avoid premature commitments, and to redouble his agents' efforts to gather information about Mao's policies. Mao now had to be treated as a potential major partner.

Stalin, Titoism, and Mao

Stalin, Milovan Djilas once recalled, "regarded as sure only whatever he held in his fist, and everyone beyond the control of his police was a potential enemy." In Stalin's way of thinking, "Everyone imposes his own system as far as his army can reach."[120] So far as he was concerned, ideological rectitude meant an instant readiness both to obey him without question and to wage battles against his "enemies." His yardstick for measuring ideological purity had no ticks for Marx and Lenin, only for obedience to himself.

Stalin held absolute power and designed his policies to perpetuate it. He judged the Soviet system that he had created to be optimal for his purposes. Yet, in 1945, during talks with Tito, he remarked that socialism could be built even under the British monarchy.[121] Throughout his rule, Stalin dras-

tically twisted ideological dogma to serve political necessity. These ideological turns further complicated the relations between China and the
USSR.

For the most part, Mao believed in the model of the Bolshevik revolution
and socialist construction in Russia, and saw his own revolution as part of
the world revolution.[122] But at the same time, he advocated "unifying
Marxism with the practice of the Chinese revolution" and was bent on acting independently of Moscow and its orders.[123] This was anathema for Stalin, of course. To him, the Zunyi conference in 1935, the watershed in
Mao's rise to supreme commander, had brought "nationalistic forces" to
power in the Chinese Party, reason enough to be wary of the Chairman.
But Stalin had more immediate reasons for distrusting Mao in 1945.[124]
Simply put, the revolutionary leader appeared to be courting the Americans. On several occasions during the war, Moscow advised Yan'an to oust
the U.S. representatives there, but Mao paid no attention.[125]

Stalin's fear of Chinese Communist independence was not unjustified,
to be sure, as even a cursory reading of Mao's interview with Anna Louise
Strong indicates. Furthermore, the theme of independence emerged even
more clearly in several well-publicized articles written by Mao's theorists
before September 1947, when the Cominform was created. For example,
one Party theorist in mid-1946 virtually dismissed the U.S.-Soviet contradiction as not being "the most pressing and acute" and emphasized instead
the contradictions between the United States and the peoples of colonial
and semicolonial countries, between the capitalist countries, and between
the "American reactionaries and the American people."[126] Similar ideas
were expressed in a major *Jiefang Ribao* piece in January by Lu Dingyi,
the head of the CCP Propaganda Department.[127] In none of these or similar
articles did the Chinese mention the primacy of the Soviet-led fight against
American imperialism.

Evidence of Stalin's doubts about Mao's reliability can be seen in the Soviet leader's cultivation of a special relationship with Gao Gang, the Communist leader in China's Northeast. Moscow treated Gao as a true "internationalist," even though he had been criticized several times by Mao for
his opposition to the Chairman and his loyalty to the Soviet Union. After
the war, Soviet representatives stayed in regular contact with Gao in Manchuria. In July 1947, he made a secret trip to Khabarovsk in the Far East
for talks with Marshal R. Ia. Malinovskii, commander of the Far Eastern
military district. There Gao confidentially reported on the "nationalistic
and anti-Soviet" attitudes within the Chinese Communist leadership.[128]
Mao, who was reportedly aware of Gao's special (and unauthorized) ties

with Moscow and knew that the Soviet Union was milking Gao for intelligence and using him to influence the CCP Central Committee, would have quite naturally resented Gao's tactics and Stalin's duplicity.[129]

The question of reliability was not one-sided. For Mao had reason, at least early on, to doubt the authenticity of Stalin's anti-imperialist policies. The exigencies of war had pressed the Soviet leader to cooperate with his Western allies, and for a short while afterward, he considered it expedient to be flexible and to work with democratic political leaders in the governments of the "new democratic countries." Even as he brought down the iron fist in Eastern Europe in the first postwar years, he advocated caution and cooperation in dealing with the West and asked the leaders of the Communist parties of Italy and France to disarm and to participate in coalition governments.

With the steady development of the Cold War, accommodation with the West vanished, and Stalin made war on the slightest heresies, heretofore tolerated, within the satellites. The turning point in this process was the late spring of 1947, when Secretary of State George C. Marshall proposed what became the European Recovery Program. Stalin understood that the economic assistance proffered by the Marshall Plan would appeal to his East European allies, and that the Soviet Union had no comparable enticement of its own. His answer was rejection, and he moved to expand and exploit his dominance over these states.[130] In September, he created the Information Bureau of the Communist and Workers' Parties (Cominform) as his answer to the Marshall Plan and redefined his strategies to compete in a world of two hostile camps.

Having drawn the East-West line, Stalin became obsessed with hidden enemies inside his own camp and with clinching his mastery over it. The test case was Yugoslavia, and practical politics, not ideology, mandated Stalin's decision to target Josip Tito.[131] He selected the Yugoslavs to teach others a "lesson," because they (and the Chinese) had made revolution without the intervention of the Soviet Red Army. This history had made them independent and, Stalin held, unreliable.

Stalin apparently also believed that the Yugoslavian Party contained many disciplined Communists who would obey Stalin in the same way the Russian Communists had slavishly confessed to nonexistent crimes "in the interests of the Party." This time he was mistaken, and Stalin, to the horror of his other allies, became enraged. The trials of "traitors and spies" throughout Eastern Europe ensued. Stalin's mania for subservience defined the "ideological dimension" of his perception of the Chinese revolution.

Mao, too, could use ideology tactically. In December 1947, three months after the organization of the Cominform, the Chairman endorsed the concept of the two-camps struggle, though he concentrated on the struggle in the area between the two camps (the intermediate zone, which he did not regard as a separate camp).[132] He thereby accepted the idea of absolute Soviet leadership in the battle against imperialism. This acceptance was reflected in the CCP's revised official slogan, to "struggle against Chiang Kai-shek and the United States and for [the Chinese people's] unity with the Communist Party and the Soviet Union." As Mao later revealed, it had not been easy to adopt this slogan, especially since some "democratic personages" feared American power and doubted the strength of the Party and "the people . . . to defeat all enemies at home and abroad."[133] Only after some debate did the Chinese adopt the new rallying cry. By this decision, Mao pressed Stalin to choose between Mao's past history of disobedience and ideological independence and his current endorsement of the Kremlin's line.

The decision was later linked to Mao's proposal to visit Moscow. Sometime in early May 1948, several weeks after his arrival in Fuping County, Hebei Province, he informed Stalin of his intention to travel via Mongolia to the Soviet Union in secret and hold talks with the Soviet leader.[134] With his armies on the offensive, the timing was right to meet Stalin. This episode is murky at best, but Mao apparently believed that the shift in line in December reinforced his proposal.

At this point, Chiang Kai-shek's collapse was becoming increasingly assured. Because of Washington's uninterrupted support for the Nationalists in the immediate postwar years, Mao had abandoned his earlier hope for cooperation with the United States.[135] With victory in sight, he needed to ensure the diplomatic recognition of the future Communist government by the socialist bloc, and he saw the visit to Moscow as achieving this purpose. Mao told at least one confidant, "I want to visit the Soviet Union and ask Stalin to take the lead in recognizing our new government"; this was particularly crucial because the United States, with its policy of underwriting Chiang Kai-shek, "won't support us."[136] He also said, "We will meet big problems if foreign countries do not recognize our regime within three days after its founding."[137] A meeting with Stalin and his commitment on recognition could help avert those problems.

Stalin thought otherwise and refused Mao's request. The Soviet ruler replied "that the revolutionary war in China is in its decisive phase, and that Chairman Mao, as its military leader, would do better not to leave his post." If serious matters came up, Stalin would then send an emissary from among his Politburo colleagues to discuss them with Mao. "Hopefully," Stalin said, "Chairman Mao will reconsider his intentions."[138] To Mao, Stalin's ever-so-polite letter was a rebuke. As Communist military commander, he could be presumed to know much better than Stalin if this was a good time for a journey to Moscow, and he needed no instruction on the matter.

We have an alternative account of this same event. Marshal Nie Rong-zhen, a senior military commander close to Mao, recollects Mao's telling him that Stalin had invited him to Moscow for treatment of an illness and asking Nie's opinion on whether he should go. Nie recommended that Mao delay his acceptance because the war had entered a climactic phase and because it would be difficult to guarantee his safety en route.[139]

Can these two versions of the reasons for postponing the visit to Moscow be reconciled? The first version states that "only a very limited number of people" knew about the proposed trip to Moscow, and it seems likely that Nie Rongzhen knew only part of the story. According to Shi Zhe, Mao was in "excellent" health during his stay in Huashan.[140] Consequently, it is probable that Mao concocted the story of his illness to save face if Stalin refused.[141] Whatever the truth, this small episode suggests the complexities that plagued the relations between the two leaders well before Mao's victory.

At a more general level, several interrelated factors helped mold Stalin's attitude toward the Chinese revolutionary leaders. As we review that attitude, it must be kept in mind that Europe, especially the future of Germany, weighed most heavily on Stalin's mind. He was deeply concerned about China, but it was not his first priority. Moreover, the United States was in the midst of a presidential election campaign, and Stalin could not rule out that a new administration in Washington might reverse the weakening U.S. commitment to the Nationalists.

At this time, he could not be sure when and at what price Mao would unify China. How willing would Mao be to accede to Soviet interests after victory, and what concessions could still be wrenched from the Nationalists before their final collapse? With these questions uppermost in his mind, Stalin considered it still too early to give the Chinese revolutionary commander any serious and binding promises concerning his relations with the future Chinese government, especially promises about the regions of China falling within the Soviet security zone.

Moreover, Mao was asking to come to Moscow at the very moment Stalin had decided to punish Tito for his Party's alleged deviations by expelling the Yugoslavs from the Cominform.[142] The coming showdown in June sharply decreased Stalin's tolerance for insubordination but complicated his tactics toward Mao. As it turned out, the reply to Mao's May proposal to visit the Soviet Union was conditioned by Stalin's twin desires: to denounce Tito and to enlarge Moscow's dominance over those left within the

Cominform. Making ready his blow against Tito, Stalin could ill afford either to blast or to bless another headstrong ally, especially when that ally had just publicly endorsed his major policy line. Mao had placed the Soviet master politician on the horns of a dilemma, and the best Stalin could do was procrastinate.

Nevertheless, it had by now become evident to him that the two needed each other, and that the likely Communist conquest of China required an upgrading of their relations. So it was that the contacts between Stalin and Mao acquired a new and more positive character.

In mid-May 1948, while awaiting Stalin's response to his request to visit Moscow, Mao cabled the Soviet leader that the civil war in China had entered its final stage, and that the Chinese Party had acquired substantial experience in armed struggle. At the same time, Mao acknowledged that he and his colleagues had no experience in managing complicated economic matters or in governing big cities. He asked the Soviet Politburo for expert help to solve China's economic problems, especially the repair of railroads in the Northeast.[143]

Stalin agreed and assigned I. V. Kovalev, the People's Commissar of Transportation, to the mission.* Kovalev, whom we met earlier in this chapter, had played a decisive role in organizing rail transport during the war, and Stalin was reaching for one of the best when he dispatched his commissar to China. The fact of the nomination itself is perhaps the most eloquent testimony to the high status Stalin now attached to Mao. We would argue that from this moment on, the Chinese Communist Party had become an essential part of Stalin's strategic equation and a strong pillar in his foreign policy.[144]

In a first meeting with Kovalev, Stalin handed him Mao's cable and told him: "We definitely will render all possible assistance to the new China. If socialism is victorious in China and other countries follow the same road, we can consider the victory of socialism throughout the world to be guaranteed. No unexpected events can threaten us. Because of that, we must not spare any effort or resources in assisting the Chinese Communists."

On the very eve of Kovalev's departure to China, Stalin again spoke to him. At this meeting, Stalin grasped a volume of Lenin's works and read a

---

*In his memoirs, Nikita Khrushchev writes: "Stalin appointed a railroad expert who'd been a people's commissar during the war. I forget his name, but I remember that after the defeat of the Japanese in northern China, Stalin sent this man to supervise the reconstruction of the Manchurian railroads and act as our plenipotentiary representative in Manchuria. We had confidence in him. Stalin considered him his personal trusty." Khrushchev, *Khrushchev Remembers: Last Testament*, pp. 242–43. Khrushchev is obviously speaking about Kovalev, and not, as the publishers of the Khrushchev volume mistakenly suggest, A. S. Paniushkin.

sentence from it on the centrality of the Chinese revolution for the global triumph of communism. He was ordering Kovalev to play a pivotal role in history's turning point. One interesting feature of Stalin's statements was that they demonstrated that he was still not absolutely sure of the CCP victory. Nor was he fully satisfied that a victorious China would follow the same road as the Soviet one. He still had considerable doubts about Mao's true ideological stance and his attitude toward the Western powers.

Thereafter, every detail in the relations with China was under Stalin's personal supervision. No one, not even Kovalev, dared to interfere in this highly sensitive domain. Kovalev recalls: "Stalin kept everything related to China in his own hands. Even the most local and insignificant requests from Mao were addressed only to [Stalin]. For example, in the beginning of 1949, I communicated with Molotov and Vyshinskii concerning several questions. Instead of an answer, both of them sent me cables stating, 'From now on, in all matters concerning China communicate only with comrade Filippov' [Stalin's code name in the ciphered cables to China]." Kovalev came the closest to understanding China, but he is the first to say that Stalin kept much about China to himself.

Kovalev reached China in June 1948 with a small team of engineers; others quickly followed, for a contingent of some 300 railroad specialists and workers. His official title was Representative of the USSR Council of Ministers for the Affairs of the Chinese Changchun Railroad. As this suggests, Kovalev's broader role was cloaked in secrecy, though his assistance to the reconstruction of the railroads was by no means just a cover. By the end of the year, the Soviet team had helped repair about 1,300 kilometers of railroads and 62 bridges in the Northeast.[145] By making a valuable contribution to Communist military victory in the strategically important Northeast, Kovalev had established his credentials as a credible go-between in Mao's eyes.

Stalin had a much more important mission in mind for Kovalev. Given the timing, the rail representative was told to stay in close touch with Mao and to keep Stalin informed about all developments in China. Kovalev's immediate task was to ascertain the Chinese leader's position on Yugoslavia and his policy toward the United States.

Despite the rapidly improving ties between the Kremlin and the CCP, the Cominform's adoption of the anti-Tito resolution in June created a problem for the Chinese Communists. They had no dispute with the Yugoslavs, indeed, felt great sympathy, almost a kindred affection, for them. The Chinese and Yugoslavs had fought similar revolutions against great odds and without receiving decisive or unequivocal Soviet support.[146] All this, of course, was irrelevant. Approval of the Cominform resolution was the inescapable price the Chinese had to pay to advance their relations with the Soviet Union.

The task of announcing the CCP's new policy fell to Politburo member Liu Shaoqi. In a November 1948 article, "On Internationalism and Nationalism," written for the Cominform bulletin *For a Lasting Peace, for a People's Democracy!*, Liu (and, of course, Mao) explicitly condemned Yugoslavia and praised the Soviet Union, "leader of the anti-imperialist forces of the world."[147] The revised line involved more than rejecting the principle of Titoism. It also required abandoning the Yan'an policy that stressed Maoism and equated Mao to Marx, Engels, Lenin, and Stalin.[148] Liu and Mao still had the problem, however, of balancing apparent obeisance to the Soviet Union with their insistence on dominance at home. In his own article for the issue of the Cominform bulletin, Mao made no mention of Yugoslavia even as he once again and even more resolutely affirmed the two-camps line and the leading role of the Soviet Union.

These mixed signals probably did not escape Stalin's attention. In any case, it is clear that a month after the new Chinese line was announced, he was still not sure of Mao's actual attitude toward Tito. In December, Stalin summoned Kovalev to Moscow for a report on the situation in China. During their conversation, the Soviet leader directly inquired about the Chinese position on the "Yugoslav issue" and demanded to know whose side the Chinese had taken.[149] We do not know Kovalev's answer at the time, but we do have his report to Moscow written some months later. Here he stressed that in 1947 Mao had sent two top lieutenants, Lu Dingyi and Liu Ningyi, to Yugoslavia and inferred from this that Mao wanted to understand "how Yugoslavia, which had declared itself to be a socialist country, might find a way, under the conditions of severe struggle between the camps of socialism and imperialism, to establish friendly relations with the imperialist countries, the United States and England."[150] Given this later appraisal of Mao's motives, we can at least guess what he told Stalin in December 1948; namely, that Mao could not be trusted.

By then, Sino-American relations had come to the forefront of Stalin's attention, triggered by the Chinese Communists' apparent willingness to do business with Angus Ward, the U.S. consul general in Shenyang (Mukden). At the beginning of November 1948, when the city came under Communist control, the new officials met Ward several times. During their conversations, Ward expressed his interest in cooperating with the new authorities and in strengthening ties with them. The Communist officials reciprocated by indicating their own interest in cooperation and friendship.[151]

This conciliatory posture ran counter to Stalin's objectives. Even before the occupation of Shenyang, the revolutionary leaders asked for Kovalev's ideas on how to deal with the foreign consulates in the city. The Russians had reports that the American consulate had a powerful radio transmitter and was an important intelligence center. Moreover, many U.S. military aides in the consulate had acted as advisers to the Nationalists in battles against the Communists. Kovalev had no special instructions on how to deal with the consulate but gave the Chinese strong advice as his "personal opinion." He advised:[152]

> Isolate the U.S. consul general and do not let his employees go outside [the consulate];
> Strictly limit the right of all the employees of other consulates to go outside [their consulates], and if they do go out, provide an escort for them;
> If the Chinese comrades are certain there are radio transmitters at any location that are continuing to operate, confiscate them.

In all probability, it was after the Communists received this advice that they decided to stiffen their treatment toward Consul General Angus Ward. In any case, on November 20, People's Liberation Army troops blockaded the consulate.* Charging the American diplomats with spying, the Communists cut off electricity and water to the consulate and demanded that Ward hand over the U.S. radio transmitter. Ward refused and was placed under house arrest. The Ward affair provoked a strong reaction in Washington and would prove to be an additional obstacle impeding American recognition of the new Chinese regime.[153]

Although Mao had followed Kovalev's recommendations concerning Ward and his consulate, the Chinese leader was reluctant to go further, fearing that harsher actions might ruin any hope for rapprochement with Washington. Sometime in December, Mao cabled Stalin, saying that he had followed Kovalev's advice but had trepidations about actually entering the consulate to seize its radio transmitter. Stalin asked Kovalev, who was then in Moscow, for details, and after hearing the reply, approved the steps Kovalev had recommended.

But Stalin also had a question for Kovalev: why had he not given specific instructions concerning the radio transmitter at the Shenyang consulate? Kovalev answered, "I have detected an interesting tendency among the Chinese comrades. They don't want to quarrel with the Americans; they want us to quarrel with them. Personally, if I were in their place, I would handle the American consulate in Mukden just like enemy headquarters

---

*The name People's Liberation Army (PLA) was not formally approved for all Communist army military units until Nov. 1, 1948. But it had been adopted by some CCP military units as early as 1945–46. Academy of Military Science, *Zhongguo Renmin Jiefangjun Liushi Nian Dashiji*, pp. 440–41.

are treated during wartime. But I did not want to give this advice to the Chinese because later they would quote it." Stalin laughed in approval and did not reply to Mao's cable.

During this same meeting, Kovalev told Stalin that, generally speaking, the Chinese were too delicate in dealing with the Americans. He still recalls his impression that they had done nothing to expel the American navy from Qingdao and pretended to overlook the U.S. military presence in their territorial waters and on their soil. Kovalev was telling Stalin what he expected to hear and thereby fed his fears. There was to be no hint of Sino-American normalization after the Communist takeover. China had become a centerpiece in Stalin's grand design, and he wanted a guarantee that all Chinese contacts with his global foe, the United States, would be strictly controlled.

Furthermore, by the end of 1948, the Chinese Communists had moved closer to Moscow, and Stalin had responded. Although the war lasted for many more bloody months, Mao's victory appeared increasingly certain, and for the Kremlin the course of the armed struggle in China had a direct bearing on its own international conflict with the United States and with Tito. The policies that would dominate the Cold War and dictate Soviet-Chinese relations for the next decade had begun to crystallize.

TWO

Prelude to Negotiations

In late 1948, as it became obvious that military victory would be Mao's, Stalin finally decided that he would have to deal with the Chairman as the leader of the Asian giant. Stalin apparently perceived that he had to grasp the nature of the revolutionary state and its domestic and foreign policy, and to ready alternative policies of his own to cope with the problems the "changing of the dynasty" would bring.

But Moscow's China policy still lagged behind the swiftly moving events in China itself. The simple fact was, Stalin could not shake his doubts about Mao's long-term intentions toward the Soviet Union and the West. When the Soviet leader at last turned his full attention to China, he fastened on the report Mao had presented to the Seventh Party Congress of the Chinese Communist Party in April 1945, in which he set out his basic ideas for the new state. Since this policy statement had not been replaced at an official Party meeting, it remained authoritative in Stalin's mind.[1]

In that report, "On Coalition Government," Mao advocated the creation of a "new democracy" based on an alliance of workers, peasants, and bourgeois elements. He envisioned a state in which the citizens could "freely develop their individuality" and a private capitalist economy, and a government that would "protect all appropriate forms of private property." This state would exist in China for a long period, and Mao did not delineate any obvious pathway for its transformation to socialism.[2]

Although Mao's report was in harmony with the postwar Soviet policies concerning "people's democracies" in Europe and the need for a coalition with the Nationalists in China, it did not fit Stalin's thinking by 1949. Mao seems to have foreseen this early on, as suggested by his caution to Anna Louise Strong in the course of their conversations in 1946–47 to bypass Moscow on her next trip to China. His warning was reportedly based on his appreciation that Maoism differed markedly from Stalinism, and his prophesy of peril proved to be accurate when Stalin's police arrested Strong in early 1949 for propagating Mao's ideas in Moscow.[3]

After the Marshall Plan of 1947 and especially after the break with Tito in 1948, Stalin's policies toward the people's democracies of Eastern Europe became characterized by extreme rigidity and by measures to force them toward "true socialism." In this environment, Mao's theory of new democracy could be used as evidence of his heretical leaning and was thus no longer to be tolerated. By the late 1940s, Soviet specialists confidentially assessed the full implications of the theory and judged it to be a deviation from the most important ideas of Marxism-Leninism, such as the political hegemony of the proletariat and the transformation of the bourgeois-democratic revolution into a socialist one. These specialists even supposed that Mao's unorthodox policies could pave the way for the preservation of bourgeois privileges and status in China.[4]

Stalin's dilemma, of course, was that he could ill afford to treat Mao like Tito and urgently needed to know Mao's long-term aims. It was in this mood that he summoned Kovalev to Moscow in December 1948 to report on the situation in China. On the basis of Kovalev's information, the Soviet dictator convened a special Politburo meeting to review alternative actions toward China. The stage was being set for some landmark decisions in 1949.[5]

For Mao, the need to signal his intentions to Stalin was equally if not more acute. By early January 1949, Mao recognized that the Americans had begun to shy away from their support of Chiang Kai-shek, but by this time Mao could only ascribe sinister motives to changes in U.S. policy. He confided to his Politburo colleagues that the rapidly approaching victory of the Chinese revolution had diminished the Truman administration's willingness to come to the aid of the Nationalists; the United States might even grant diplomatic recognition to his government. He warned, nonetheless, that the Americans had merely altered tactics and were bent on sabotaging the Chinese revolution from within. The Chairman urged the Politburo to heighten its vigilance to cope with the next phase of U.S. machinations.[6] The anti-American direction of his policy had become irreversible.

By the last half of 1948, moreover, the goal of forging a coalition with the Nationalists had become irrelevant, and the anti-imperialist and anti-landlord mood among his cadres and soldiers had soared. Thus Mao had pressing reasons to draft a replacement program that would satisfy both Stalin and his own supporters, and he made several attempts to convey to Stalin personally the outlines of his "new thinking" on the future Chinese regime and to win his backing. At a Politburo meeting in September, Mao stated, "The Soviet Union will assist us in preparing for the transition from the completion of the new democracy to socialism, and first of all it will help us develop the economy."[7]

On September 28, he sent Stalin a report on the Politburo meeting, saying that he had many issues to discuss directly with the Soviet leader. He proposed to visit Moscow in November, a request that he repeated on October 16. In the second request, Mao stressed that he wished to consult with Stalin on matters related to the creation of the post-victory government. When the November visit did not materialize, Mao on December 30, 1948, informed Stalin that he had called a meeting of some of his chief lieutenants to map out the year ahead, and that they had decided to hold a second plenum of the seventh Central Committee in the spring after a visit to Moscow. Mao was telling Stalin that the Chinese would formulate the guidelines for their state and governmental systems only after consulting the Soviet leader and taking into account his recommendations. He implied that the future guidelines would replace those of 1945 and put to rest Soviet fears about any Chinese deviations. Stalin again refused to approve a visit.

One senior CCP leader, Bo Yibo, recollects that the failure to organize Mao's visit to Moscow at this time was caused by poor communications from China and the Chinese leader's preoccupation with directing great offensives against the Nationalists.[8] In the telling of Mao's secretary, however, the preoccupation was Stalin's, not the Chairman's. According to Shi Zhe, Anastas Mikoyan, who had arrived in China in late January 1949, told Mao that Stalin had disapproved the visit not only because of poor communications but because he wanted Mao to exercise personal leadership at this crucial moment in the civil war.[9]

For Mao, this was unwelcome news. Even as the civil war was nearing the end, he still had no way to predict Stalin's reaction to his political platform and would still have to wait for broader and more substantive agreements for future cooperation from the Soviet side. Mao's uneasiness was probably lessened only by the fact that Stalin had begun to treat him seriously enough to fulfill at last the Soviet leader's promise to send a member of his Politburo for discussions, eight months after the promise had been made. Whatever their limitations, these talks were to become a turning point in Sino-Soviet relations.

The Mikoyan Visit of 1949

How the Mikoyan visit was organized sheds light on Soviet thinking at the time.[10] In the first place, Moscow insisted on keeping the visit secret, lest it complicate relations with the United States.* Nevertheless, Stalin seems finally to have concluded that a Communist victory was inevitable and the possibility of U.S. involvement in the civil war remote, so that the risk of a U.S.-Soviet confrontation over China was minimal.

On January 31, Mikoyan, accompanied by Kovalev, arrived at Mao's temporary headquarters in Xibaipo, Hebei Province, for a one-week stay. On his arrival, Mikoyan presented a piece of wool to Mao as Stalin's gift. He had "brought only his ears" to listen to his Chinese comrades, he declared, and would report what they said to Stalin. The implication was that Stalin considered it imperative to study the Chinese leader and his policies before meeting him. Mikoyan met three times with Mao, Zhu De, Liu Shaoqi, Zhou Enlai, and Ren Bishi—all members of the Party Central Secretariat.[11] Of all the meetings, the most important took place over a three-day period, February 1–3, when Mao delivered a detailed report on his present and future policies.[12] The Soviet staff meticulously took notes on the report and later passed them to Stalin.[13]

We now have a Chinese version of this document.[14] Here we shall highlight those parts of it that could affect relations between the two states. First, Mao predicted an early Communist victory. He reasoned that the high morale of the troops, the support of the majority of the population, and the correctness of the Party's course ensured success. Mao believed that the most difficult tasks ahead were the crossing of the Yangtze River and the seizure of Nanjing (Nanking) and Shanghai. Once his armies had accomplished those tasks, Chiang's resistance would collapse.

Further, Mao virtually dismissed the possibility of direct American intervention in the civil war. He forecast that the Americans would limit their assistance to providing Chiang transport and war matériel. The U.S. reluctance to intervene, he argued, constituted one of the most decisive conditions for the victory of the Chinese revolution.[15]

Tibet and Taiwan, Mao reported, were the places of greatest challenge to the PLA. In the case of Tibet, the problems were only technical, such as poor communications, but Taiwan was a different proposition because it

---

*Shi Zhe writes: "Several times en route Mikoyan demanded that the car stop and [that he be allowed] to go to people's houses to have a look. For security considerations, we asked him not to do so. Mikoyan answered, 'Anyway people will know about my visit and the news will rapidly spread all over the world. People will say, the Soviet devil came to China to engage in sabotage. Thus it is impossible to ensure secrecy.'" Shi Zhe, "With Chairman Mao," p. 153. Years later, Mikoyan was amazed that there had been no leaks about his visit. Kovalev noted in his diary that Stalin ordered Mikoyan to keep the visit secret and to say he was making an inspection tour of the Party committees in Omsk, Novosibirsk, Krasnoiarsk, and Khabarovsk. During stopovers in these cities, Mikoyan did organize meetings with local Party leaders to bolster his cover story.

fell "under the protection of American imperialism." For that reason, the liberation of Taiwan would "require more time" than the liberation of Tibet. These estimates, it should be noted, directly addressed questions of priority interest to Stalin. Especially pressing was the question of American intervention.

Proceeding on to the nature of the future Chinese state, Mao declared that it would be "a people's democratic dictatorship based on the worker-peasant alliance; in fact, it would be a proletarian dictatorship." He emphasized that even though the coalition government would include some "democratic parties" (mostly non-Communist opponents of the Nationalists), it would be totally dominated by the Communist Party.

Carefully attuned to Stalin's dogma at the time, these statements demonstrated a marked shift from new democracy toward a Soviet-style system. The same could be said of the state's planned economy. Mao avowed that the new China would adhere to the Soviet experience during the process of reconstruction and would utilize Soviet economic aid. All the same, he made no attempt to conceal his ideas on some non-Stalinist features of his proposed state system. He spoke of cooperation with the national bourgeoisie and overseas Chinese and of land reform without collectivization.

Of greatest interest to Mikoyan were Mao's views on foreign policy. The Chairman characterized that policy as "inviting guests after cleaning house." He planned first to eradicate all traces of imperialism in China and then to begin establishing diplomatic relations on an equal footing. He defined "cleaning house" as the thorough elimination of the privileges enjoyed by the imperialists in China, the repayment of all the debts owed to it, and the complete exodus of all foreign troops and police forces. His one compromise was his decision to defer the seizure of the colonial bastions of Hong Kong and Macao because of their economic value to China. He acknowledged that even taking into account that compromise, his overall foreign policy could bring serious economic and security problems and delay recognition by some states. Nevertheless, Mao insisted, that policy was needed to restore the nation's dignity.

Continuing, Mao indicated his readiness to align with Moscow in the struggle against imperialism and to recognize such friends as the Soviet Union even before "the house would be cleaned." He expressed a desire for the Soviet Union to become the first power to recognize his government.

Mikoyan responded, somewhat indirectly to be sure, that once that government was founded the Kremlin would grant it diplomatic recognition, and we can surmise that this pledge manifested a certain satisfaction with Mao's presentation.[16] Further, from Mao's later remarks in a speech to a

Party plenum in March tying his hope for the rapid reconstruction of China after liberation to Soviet assistance, it is reasonable to suppose that Mikoyan had also promised him extensive economic cooperation.[17] Stalin's own pleasure with the results of the visit was manifested in the form of two cables, to Kovalev and Mao, after Mikoyan returned home, expressing general support for Mao's line toward the national bourgeoisie, for his proposal to use Hong Kong as a base for foreign trade, and for his guidelines for state building.[18]

On the other hand, Stalin could not shed his doubts concerning Mao's policy in almost every other significant realm. Once Mikoyan was back in Moscow, Stalin was often heard to complain that the Chinese leader, his emphasis on proletarian dictatorship notwithstanding, gave insufficient attention to the Chinese workers and relied too heavily on the peasantry.[19] Even during the visit, Mikoyan reminded the Chinese Party leaders that it was a mistake to distribute all the land confiscated from the landlords and rich peasants to the poorer peasants. The rural cadres should instead organize the peasants into collective farms. Mao replied that distributing land to peasants had ensured their active participation in the revolution and had proved necessary for the Communist victory.[20]

Even more serious obstacles arose when bilateral relations were addressed. After outlining the main elements of his pro-Soviet foreign policy, Mao told Mikoyan:

We think that as our liberation war makes more and more victorious progress, we will need more and more friends. Here I speak about genuine friends. . . . Friends are divided into genuine and false ones. Genuine friends are sympathetic to us, support and assist us, and demonstrate sincere and honest friendship. False friends are friendly on the surface. They tell you one thing but do another, or even devise some evil designs; they fool the people and afterwards take joy in the people's disasters. We should be alert on this point.

This statement so astonished Mikoyan that he became visibly embarrassed, not knowing what message Mao was trying to communicate.[21] To the Soviet official, apparently, the words could only have been aimed at Moscow.

That Mao in fact had his doubts about Stalin's sincerity in supporting the Chinese revolution was demonstrated by other questions he raised in his conversations with Mikoyan. At one point, for example, Mao quoted a certain "lady, who was a leader of the revolutionary wing of the Kuomintang," probably referring to Madame Sun Yat-sen. She had said that many of her colleagues believed China should demand the unconditional return of the Soviet share in the Chinese Changchun Railroad and of the Mongolian People's Republic. Mikoyan replied that he was not authorized to comment on such matters, and Kovalev recalls his own impression that Mao's quotes from the "lady" reflected his own opinion.[22] By raising the issue of the railroad and Mongolia, Mao was touching on the core contradiction between his interest in national revival and Stalin's determination to create a buffer zone on Chinese soil.

In the end, though, what counted most was the Soviet assessment of the Communists' chances of military success. Although that assessment had become more optimistic by the end of 1948, if we can go by the significant jump in news about Communist victories in the Soviet press from then on, Stalin still did not share Mao's confident belief that the United States would never intervene militarily in the civil war.[23] While Mikoyan was in China, the PLA, having defeated the Nationalists in the North, was making ready to cross the Yangtze in the final phase of the war. Mikoyan naturally fixed on Chinese accounts of these preparations, and herein lies one of the most controversial aspects of the visit.

In the late 1940s and well into the 1950s, Mao and other Chinese Party leaders repeatedly contended that Mikoyan had recommended that the PLA not cross the Yangtze. That advice they charged up primarily to three reasons. First of all, the Soviets had simply erred in their estimate of the PLA and believed it could not defeat the Nationalists. Marshal Nie Rongzhen comments that Stalin, lacking confidence in the military power of the Chinese Communists, "was somewhat like the ancient man of Qi who was worried that the sky might fall anytime."[24] Fear that the crossing would raise the danger of U.S. armed intervention was the second reason, and, third, Stalin wanted to split China in half, creating conflicting "Northern and Southern Dynasties," the better to control the Communist half.[25]

But this widely reported and widely believed story of the Soviets urging the Communists to stop at the Yangtze may be false. Shi Zhe, Mao's personal secretary who attended the meetings, quotes Mikoyan as "expressing the congratulations of Stalin and all the Politburo members and their best wishes for the achievement of a quick victory and the final liberation of the whole nation." According to Shi, the "Northern and Southern Dynasties" question only arose on the Party's agenda in April 1949, in response to a Nationalist proposal that seemed to suggest the division of the country between the two sides.[26] By the time Mikoyan had completed his Xibaipo visit, he had covered more than 20 topics related to future cooperation, and his own notes make no mention of any recommendation against advancing into the South. Any hint of settling for a division of the country at this point would have ruined the conversations.[27]

Chinese scholars who have now had a chance to examine the archives in Beijing on the Mikoyan visit and have interviewed Party veterans about it write that they have learned nothing to substantiate the allegation that Stalin advised Mao to stay north of the Yangtze. They insist that there is considerable evidence for the very opposite. By the beginning of 1949, they say, it was clear to all that the Nationalists were finished, and only a fool would have advised a Communist halt. They conclude that it would have been impossible for Stalin to give such counsel.[28]

Still, are we to believe that Mao, Zhou Enlai, and others simply invented this story in an effort to discredit Stalin and blunt his influence? According to Marshal Nie Rongzhen, Mikoyan was indeed interested in assessing the military balance. Nie had the impression that Mikoyan had doubts about the PLA's capability to pursue its offensive drive because of recent heavy losses.[29] Quite possibly, given the existing tensions with Moscow, Mao and Zhou looked for a hidden meaning behind these doubts and read into them a recommendation to stop fighting.[30] Whatever the truth of the matter, Mikoyan's visit illustrated the tense and complicated nature of Moscow's relations with Mao's Party, even as the two sides tried to reconcile at least some of their basic interests.[31]

A lengthy cable from Stalin to Mao following Mikoyan's visit sheds some light on this affair. Sometime in April 1949, shortly before the PLA crossed the Yangtze on the 20th, Stalin sent the Chinese his own estimate of the military picture in China. He began by stating that although the PLA's victories to date were dramatic, the war was far from over. Further movement by the PLA toward countries in Southeast Asia might activate their colonial masters. He warned that the British, French, and Americans might resort to military measures to preserve their foreign holdings, and that Mao should consider the possibility of enemy landings to seize Chinese ports and attack the PLA from the rear.[32]

Stalin made three recommendations to the Chinese:

a. Do not hurry; prepare seriously for the PLA offensive in the South in order to reach the borders of neighboring countries.

b. Select two good armies from the main forces of the PLA moving southward and redeploy them to the vicinity of the ports; provide them reinforcements and keep them in a state of combat readiness for blocking the moves of the enemy.

c. For the time being, do not cut the ranks of the PLA.[33]

As the recipient of these concrete guidelines from Stalin, Mao was undoubtedly reminded of the disastrous Soviet advice in the 1920s to seize and hold well-fortified cities, which almost destroyed the revolution. However, Stalin may well have had something else in mind. He may have been drawing on his own wartime experience in 1943, when the Red Army in an offensive near Kharkov had suffered one of its most calamitous defeats because it had not adequately guarded its flanks and rear.

If Stalin here clearly signaled that he did not oppose a PLA offensive to the South, other Soviet actions were undoubtedly conveying a different message to Mao. Only a short time before, Mao apparently believed, Stalin had tried to mediate an end to the civil war; as late as the spring, Stalin was still expressing the hope that the peace talks between the Communists and Nationalists would succeed.[34] Furthermore, unlike most of the other foreign ambassadors in the Nationalist capital of Nanjing, Soviet Ambassador N. V. Roshchin had moved to Guangzhou with Chiang Kai-shek's army.[35] Adding to his suspicions, Mao presumably knew that the Soviet side was holding talks with Nationalist authorities in Xinjiang on matters of air transportation.[36] For Mao, all these actions may well have suggested that Stalin wanted to keep China divided, enabling him to play one part against the other.

Although these Chinese suspicions, ill-founded or not, led to some contentious exchanges during the Mao-Mikoyan talks, the visit on balance was rated a success by both sides. The Soviet decisions relayed by Mikoyan were breakthroughs in Soviet–Chinese Communist relations, and his visit marked the first practical step leading to Mao's journey to Moscow in December. Nevertheless, the visit indicated that Soviet distrust of Mao survived, and that the commitment to him remained conditional.

Mikoyan's visit was the first in which Moscow addressed the Chinese Communists not as a party in opposition but as potential rulers. The discussions with Mao demonstrated the future pattern of almost all high-level Sino-Soviet talks. Most were to aim for a total convergence of interests, and each subsequent breakthrough toward this goal produced a new round of complications. All thereafter highlighted the simple truth that those interests might be periodically adjusted but would never be made one.

Leaning to One Side

On June 30, 1949, Mao declared in his article "On the People's Democratic Dictatorship" that "all Chinese without exception must lean either to the side of imperialism or to the side of socialism." He said, "the twenty-eight years' experience of the Communist Party have taught us to lean to one side, and we are firmly convinced that in order to win victory and consolidate it, we must lean to one side. . . . Sitting on the fence will not do, nor is there a third road." He had made his choice to lean to the Soviet side. "Internationally, we belong to the side of the anti-imperialist front headed by the Soviet Union," he declared, and so set the direction for his future government's foreign policy.[37] We turn now to the origins of that policy.

From the earliest years, the common bonds of Marxism-Leninism drew the Communist parties of China and the Soviet Union together even as culture and political interest pulled them apart. For the Chinese after the anti-Japanese war, the question was not whether to lean toward Moscow but in what degree. As early as 1946, Zhou Enlai told the special U.S. envoy (and former army chief of staff) George C. Marshall, "We will certainly lean to one side. However, the extent [of our leaning to the Soviet side] depends on your policy toward us."[38]

Zhou's statement is hardly surprising. From the 1920s on, the Soviet Union had exerted great influence over the Chinese revolution. Both parties saw themselves on the same path in the world revolution. At this point, moreover, the CCP leaders had few realistic alternatives to a partnership with Moscow. The United States had placed the full weight of its support behind the Nationalists, or so Mao thought. Whatever his personal views, Mao could not act alone, and many of his colleagues on the Politburo strongly favored an alliance with Moscow. Finally, Mao recognized he could not walk a neutral road. Stalin's actions against Tito forced an either/or decision on the Chinese Communists.[39]

A month after Mikoyan returned home, another memorable event occurred in the village of Xibaipo. This was the second plenum of the Seventh Central Committee (March 5–13, 1949), at which the Party redefined its post-takeover program. It was at this meeting that Mao publicly announced the policies discussed with Mikoyan.[40] These policies marked a fundamental shift away from the program adopted at the Party congress in April 1945, which had committed the Communists to "a united-front democratic alliance based on the overwhelming majority of the people, under the leadership of the working class."[41]

At the March plenum, Mao spoke of creating a transitional polity and society to facilitate the movement toward socialism. He provided neither a timetable for attaining socialism nor a clear-cut definition of it but stressed the cardinal political conditions for success. The Party must work with the cooperative elements of the national bourgeoisie and "revolutionary intellectuals" in a "people's democratic dictatorship, led by the proletariat and based on the worker-peasant alliance." The center of gravity of the Party's work, he said, had become the city.[42]

This evident change in Mao's political course complicated things for the Soviets. Stalin from now on could not afford to cause a breach with the Chinese Communists, and Mao had removed any basis for valid criticism on ideological grounds. With the painful Tito case emblazoned in his memory, Stalin had no choice but to endorse, if not embrace, Mao's chosen course. Mao had placed Stalin in the uncomfortable posture of dealing with a partner that had proven armed strength and an autonomous political will.

More and more Soviet articles now glorified the Chinese revolution. One writer quoted Politburo member Dong Biwu as saying that the character of political power in the liberated areas was the same as that in Eastern Europe; others stressed the Chinese Party's leading role in the PLA's victories and called the defeat of the Nationalists inescapable.[43] Moscow, after years of silence on the matter, made the Chinese revolution the exemplar for the peoples of Asia.[44] The Communist revolutionaries had once again gained a prestigious standing in Moscow's worldview.

Amid all this positive tone and optimism, there was one glaring omission: the Soviet press made virtually no reference to Mao. The authoritative magazine *Novoe Vremia* merely mentioned Mao as *a* leader of the revolution, totally overlooking his role as the creator of the program adopted at the second plenum and his contributions to Marxism-Leninism. A later *Novoe Vremia* editorial on the founding of the People's Republic managed to avoid naming Mao at all; the plenum was said to be the realization of the "genius predictions" of Stalin.[45] The comparable *Pravda* editorial quoted Mao just once, picking up his statement that the victory of the Chinese revolution would have been impossible without Soviet influence and assistance.[46] Only later, as we shall see, were Mao's contributions, stature, and ideas routinely acknowledged. After the signing of the Sino-Soviet treaty in February, he was publicly named in the Soviet Union as *the* "leader of the Chinese people."[47]

Again, Stalin's preoccupation with global politics shaped his stance toward the Chinese. After Tito's expulsion from the Cominform in June 1948, U.S. tactics in dealing with Sino-Soviet relations changed significantly. Taking encouragement from U.S. contacts with the Chinese Communists in Yan'an in 1944, Washington now sought to stimulate a Yugoslav-type split between Mao and Stalin. Several Americans who had met Mao at the time concluded that he was a nationalist and an agrarian reformer of a sharply different ideological orientation from the Soviets; the more sophisticated view in Washington was that over time, the United States might well be able to drive a wedge between Moscow and the Chinese Communists.[48] Stalin appears to have recognized the shifting U.S. tactics after mid-1948 and grew even more suspicious of Mao.

Stalin could have certified Mao's credentials as a true Marxist only if Mao had been willing to totally subsume his interests under those of the Soviet Union. Mao was not, and the inner circle of the Soviet Politburo sneered at his best efforts to please Moscow then and even after the founding of the People's Republic of China in October 1949.[49] Stalin's hostility in turn generated a self-confirming response within the Kremlin and throughout the Cominform. Reports detailing Mao's errors and heresies poured onto the Soviet leader's desk.[50] Mao's fears that Stalin saw him as a potential Tito were well founded.[51]

It was in this climate of mutual distrust that the Chinese Communists, during the spring and summer of 1949, undertook the task of defining their future government's foreign relations. The task was completed in two stages, the first in March and April and the second from April to June. The process began at the Central Committee's second plenum, where the Chinese began formulating their basic national goals within the developing international context. That done, they then moved to the second stage—determining their policies toward the Soviet Union. Despite an unfortunate paucity of reliable data that allows us to do little more than sketch our general thinking on this matter, we feel strongly that some understanding of Chinese attitudes toward foreign relations is essential to appreciating Mao's situation prior to his arrival in Moscow on December 16.

Like the Nationalists before them, the Communists most wanted to restore what they perceived as China's rightful place in the world. This article of faith rested on the conviction that China was unique, its countless people destined for world power status. They believed that this birthright had been wrenched from them during the "epoch of national shame," the years from the mid-nineteenth century on, when China began suffering defeats and exploitation at the hands of foreigners. Western powers had crushed China into semicolonial dependency, imposing unequal treaties and demanding special privileges. Virtually all patriotic Chinese related national revival to the abolition of those treaties and the humiliating privileges they had accorded the "foreign devils." The authority of any legitimate government required the abrogation of the treaties and a firm stance on the principle of equality.

The Nationalist government had achieved some significant successes in this realm. In 1942–43, the unequal treaties with Great Britain and the United States were abolished and replaced by equal ones.[52] But later, during the civil war, when the Nationalists found themselves in increasing need of American assistance, they signed agreements with the United States that could be interpreted by their opponents as unequal, and Chiang's reputation suffered accordingly.[53] The Communists, not surprisingly, pounced on these treaties for propaganda purposes, but in so doing, they restricted the kinds of arguments Mao could legitimately employ later in negotiations with the Soviet Union. Although Mao was not above acting in ways he had previously assailed, the issue of equality was too sensitive to justify such an obvious volte-face at the onset of his rule.

Mao understood the delicate task of enunciating his policy line on treaties and the status of foreigners during the Central Committee's second plenum that March.[54] He defined the first principles of his foreign policy in terms of "systematically and completely destroying imperialist domination in China." In practice, the implementing of these principles would entail four things:

> Nonrecognition of the "legal status of any foreign diplomatic establishments and personnel" from the Nationalist period*
> Refusal to recognize "all the treasonable treaties" from that period
> Abolition of foreign "propaganda agencies" in China
> Assumption of Chinese control over the entire foreign trade and customs system

Mao urged his comrades not to be in a hurry to gain diplomatic recognition from the "imperialist countries" but to be willing to establish relations with "all countries on the principle of equality."[55] Although Mao made only brief mention of the Soviet Union by name in this speech, he was coming close to announcing the policy of "leaning to one side." He apparently believed that Mikoyan had conveyed Moscow's commitment, albeit one not made fully explicit, to recognize the People's Republic, and he no longer worried about the future isolation of his government.

Mao's tone at the second plenum may have sounded tough, but in fact he was enunciating a more flexible position toward establishing diplomatic relations with "all countries" than the one he had presented to Mikoyan. He had told Mikoyan that any formal relationship with the Western powers would be out of the question until "the house would be cleaned." Now, though opposing haste, he allowed for the possibility of recognition on the condition of equality. Here we see the difference between Mao's positions intended for a Soviet audience and those formulated for domestic consumption.

Mao had to tread lightly because many of his non-Communist supporters, the so-called "democratic figures" who were cooperating with the Communists, did not want to break ties with the United States. In April, shortly after Mao moved to Beiping,[56] the opinions of these democratic elements found expression in conversations between Mao and his long-time

---

*As early as Nov. 23, 1948, Zhou Enlai had told the CCP Northeast Bureau that the Chinese Communists would not recognize the "diplomatic relations established between the Nationalists and the United States, Britain, France, and others." But Chinese scholars and official histories credit the policy to Mao, citing the note he appended to the "Directive of the CCP Central Committee on Foreign Affairs" (Jan. 19, 1949), where he identified "rebuilding the oven" or "making a fresh start" (i.e., the nonrecognition of all foreign diplomatic missions from the Nationalist period) as the first of the "three guiding principles" of his early foreign policy. The other two, as noted earlier, were "inviting guests after cleaning house" and "leaning to one side." Li Ping and Fang Ming, *Zhou Enlai Nianpu*, pp. 799–800; Han Nianlong, *Dandai Zhongguo Waijiao*, p. 3; Chi Aiping, "Mao Zedong's Strategic Guidance," p. 33; "Mao's Four Talks," p. 27.

friend Zhang Zhizhong, who headed a Nationalist delegation that had come to the city for peace talks. Zhang pointed out that Chiang Kai-shek's close ties with the United States had been an underlying cause for the Nationalist defeat and advised Mao not to become involved in the global struggle between Washington and Moscow. Nevertheless, he said, the West had greater economic potential and might do more for China's revival than the Soviet Union. Mao's government could play a pivotal role in international relations if it adopted neutrality but established normal relations with the West. Mao, of course, could not accept Zhang's advice, but he knew that Zhang had alerted him to an important political quandary.[57]

On April 17, Zhou Enlai, then the Communist leader in charge of foreign affairs, explained the Party's diplomatic line to a meeting of "democratic personages" in Beiping. The new government would be "very careful" in dealing with "treasonable treaties," he told them. Some treaties would have to be abrogated but some could stand with revision and others could be retained. He did not mention the Sino-Soviet treaty of 1945 or any other treaty, leaving himself room for later maneuver. "No country can any longer interfere in China's domestic affairs," he said. "To this end we have struggled for more than a hundred years!" Though he welcomed foreign aid that would be advantageous to China, the country should not depend on it. "We should not even depend on the Soviet Union and the new democracies."[58]

If Mao and Zhou were moving closer to the Soviet Union, both men also appreciated the folly of totally alienating the United States. As the de facto leaders of much of mainland China, they had already begun to come to terms with the nation's fundamental interests and were attempting to devise a policy that would lessen U.S. hostility toward their regime. Beyond this, sensitive though they were to Stalin's attitude toward such a policy, they still had questions about his ultimate aims and were uncertain about any forthcoming assistance from Moscow.[59]

At about this time, Zhou spelled out his goals: "The Chinese Communist Party should have an ally. If Chiang Kai-shek and the reactionaries form an alliance with the United States, the Chinese Communist Party must align itself with the Soviet Union. It is a fond dream of the United States to split China from the Soviet Union. However, the Chinese Communist Party cannot afford to make enemies on both sides; no force can prevent it from having two friends or even more." The government of the People's Republic might not be able to have close relations with the United States but could, for example, conduct trade with it. Trade could deepen mutual understanding and lead to an exploration of diplomatic ties on the basis of equality.[60]

This policy, it should be noted, stemmed in part from Mao's uncertainties about how Washington would respond to the coming Communist offensive into South China. His plan was to occupy the coastal areas and port cities as quickly as possible, thus denying the Americans an easy way to reintroduce their military forces. Whether by coincidence or design, this strategy coincided with Stalin's advice in his lengthy April cable. By holding out the possibility of trade and future ties, Mao apparently hoped to delay any U.S. armed response until it was too late.[61] He could not know that at this point, the Truman administration had no inclination to intervene in the Chinese civil war.

Although the Mao-Zhou statements may have clarified the Communists' broad goals, they did not specify how far the leaders would go to achieve their goals in practice. The burning question on the unequal treaties concluded by the Nationalists was the fate of the Sino-Soviet treaty of 1945. Mao had made no secret in the past about his contempt for the treaty, but what would he do about it now that the power to dispose of it would be his? Many Communists at the time believed that Moscow's policy toward China could not be distinguished from Washington's, and that the Kremlin was bent on exploiting and subjugating China.[62]

If Mao's basic goal was to free China of the legacy of the inequities and injustices, he would have to answer his critics by shedding this legacy in his relations with the Soviet Union as well as the West. As he apparently saw the matter, Mao had several plausible and somewhat overlapping choices: repudiate the 1945 treaty and demand a new type of relationship with Moscow; adopt policies fully independent of Moscow and risk Stalin's hostility; align with Moscow and use the treaty to fortify China's security vis-à-vis the United States and other capitalist countries; accept a close relationship with the Soviet Union in "form" but struggle to change its essence toward greater equality.

Even before the second plenum in March, as we have noted, Mao chose the last two options in modified form. This choice not surprisingly placed him in the predicament of appearing to imperil his foreign policy goal of making a clean break with China's humiliating past. Answering his critics, and there appeared to have been many, the Chairman made the most of a weak case. Then and later (in 1956), he repeated his endorsement of Stalin's argument that the postwar conflicts had split the world into two antagonistic camps, leaving China no room for flexibility. On the eve of victory, the fledgling state had to stand with one side or the other, and Washington's actions in the civil war had ended any realistic possibility of aligning with the U.S.-led camp. China, as Mao saw it, needed help against a growing American threat. Such help could only come from the Kremlin, and the Soviet Union would only uphold states within its own camp.[63]

Mao reevaluated his own power in light of the coming PLA victory. He understood that the triumph of his revolution altered Stalin's calculus. Especially with the signing of the North Atlantic Treaty on April 4, 1949, Mao believed, the Soviet leader had no alternative but to treat China as a vital asset in the Cold War.[64] That event, Mao knew, increased Stalin's obsession with buffer zones all along the Soviet borders and, ipso facto, would heighten Soviet interest in Xinjiang and Manchuria, where the Russian presence was already strong. Mao's tactical dilemma was how to take advantage of this added interest without perpetuating Chinese dependency. He understood that, if security belts were so important to Moscow, he might be able to exact a price for them and discredit the charges of bowing meekly to Stalin's demands. Erasing the odious terms of the 1945 treaty would have to be delayed. Making the case that Mao's foreign policy, despite strong evidence to the contrary, marked out a staunchly independent path for China took priority, and the selling job fell to the foreign minister—designate, Zhou Enlai.[65]

Although Mao decided on this course even before the second plenum, he apparently implemented the policy line of leaning to one side in two stages. The first had come at the plenum itself. He informed the Central Committee of that part of the policy that would accord with the national consensus: the revival of the nation in the quest for equality and independence. Only in the inner sanctum of the top elite did he first share his thoughts on the second stage, about leaning to one side in alliance with and temporary dependence on the Soviet Union. His declaration on June 30 ended both the months of secrecy and the open debate within the Party and among its "democratic" (that is, non-Communist) supporters on new China's foreign policy line.

Tactics

Mao's leaning-to-one-side policy was thus intended primarily to serve his goal of national revival, not fundamentally to align his foreign policy with "proletarian internationalism" or the will of Moscow. For this reason, the policy did not preclude attempts to establish limited relations with the United States or other Western nations. Still, these attempts now had to fit within the leaning-to-one-side framework, and Mao had to monitor closely Stalin's reactions to any moves toward the West. The Angus Ward case months before had demonstrated Stalin's opposition to the normalization of Chinese Communist relations with the United States, and Mao had to act guardedly.

On the other hand, the momentum of China's revolution and its centrality in Stalin's global calculus meant that he could not just impose his will on the Chinese. He, too, had to act with discretion. On March 15,

1949, for example, Stalin cabled Kovalev in response to a question by a senior CCP leader on how to deal with local capitalists and how to maintain economic relations with the capitalist countries.[66] Stalin recommended that steps be taken to win the cooperation of the national bourgeoisie (that is, pro-Communist capitalists) as a force that could "assist in the struggle against imperialism."

Two considerations apparently motivated Stalin's response. One was his unwillingness or inability to assume the total burden of economic aid to China. This unwillingness, as we shall see, was to become fully manifest during the later negotiations on a Soviet loan to China. Additionally, Stalin believed that China was not ready for a "proletarian dictatorship" but had only reached the transitional stage of a "people's democracy" with a large bourgeoisie.

On the question of China's political relations with the United States and other Western countries, Stalin was unalterably negative. In mid-April, Zhou Enlai told Kovalev that the American ambassador, Leighton Stuart, was seeking to establish contacts with the Chinese Communists "for purely business purposes." Kovalev, who naturally assumed that Zhou was acting on Mao's instructions and recalls wondering why Mao would risk jeopardizing his relations with the Soviet Union by pursuing dubious contacts with the United States, said in response: "It is your internal matter, . . . but I have several questions for you. In particular, how does the Chinese leadership evaluate the attempts of the United States to rescue Chiang Kai-shek's regime? And to dismember China into several Chinas? How can you harmonize your contacts with them with the preparations for a final blow against Chiang Kai-shek's forces? What does the CCP expect from the meeting with the American businessmen while the armed struggle against Chiang Kai-shek is proceeding? Perhaps, the Americans will subsidize your struggle?" Zhou said nothing in reply and with a wave of his hand changed the subject. Several days later, the matter came up again, and Kovalev gave the same response.[67]

Kovalev quickly informed Stalin of these conversations, and in the long and important April cable that Stalin sent to Mao just before the Communist armies crossed the Yangtze, the Soviet leader specifically referred to the question of contacts with the United States. The Chinese Communists must not reject the possibility of establishing political relations with the capitalist countries, including the United States, he said, but they should do so only on the condition that they officially break all political, military, and economic ties with the Nationalists. The main aim of U.S. policy, he contended, was to split the country into three regions with three different governments, the South with its capital in Guangzhou, Central

China with its capital in Nanjing, and the Northeast under the Communists. Washington could then initiate relations with all three and pit them one against the other—the same divide-and-conquer tactic that Mao had once attributed to the Soviet Union. Concluding, Stalin implied that if Mao truly wanted to mold a unified China under his own leadership, he should not establish relations with the United States.[68]

In this and similar messages, Stalin avoided ideological arguments in urging Mao not to deal with the Americans. Instead, he once more stressed how relations with Washington would endanger China's unification. He appears to have assumed, moreover, that no U.S. president would break relations with the Nationalists at this time, and that the Chinese Communists must see how little was to be gained from modest contacts with the Americans compared with what a dramatic improvement in their relations with Moscow would bring.

In all of these exchanges, Stalin was relying on Kovalev to keep him fully up to date on any steps Mao took to repair his relations with the United States. The Chinese leaders, well tuned to the Kremlin's sensitivities on the question of ties with the West, decided that it would be folly to hide their intentions from Kovalev. An example of their deliberate openness came on April 24, when Mao told the Soviet representative: "The Americans have reduced the number of security guards at their embassy in Nanjing from 40 to six men. Generally speaking, America has recently begun to behave more cautiously. Britain has not yet made any contact with the Communist Party and because of that, is doing foolish things." The two ambassadors had stayed on in Nanjing, he pointed out, not because they wished to establish contacts with the Communist Party, but because their countries' major interests were there and in Shanghai.[69] In a somewhat roundabout way, Mao was telling Stalin that the possibility existed for an opening to the United States.

In April, at about the time of the Zhou-Kovalev conversations, the Communists told the U.S. consul general in Beiping that they would like to develop trade relations with the United States and Japan. Further, through an informant, they leaked the idea that they could mediate the Cold War between the United States and the Soviet Union.[70] On April 28, Mao told his military officers, "The U.S. side has entrusted some people to request the establishment of diplomatic relations with our side. The British side is doing its best to do business with us. We may consider the issue of establishing diplomatic relations with the United States (and Britain), provided they cut off relations with the Nationalist regime."[71] This proviso, of course, echoed the condition Stalin had set down for improved Sino-American political relations.

The first significant test of future U.S.-China relations came after the Communist takeover of the Nationalist capital of Nanjing on April 23. On learning that a quarrel had erupted when a PLA battalion commander arrived at Ambassador Stuart's residence, Mao sent orders to all PLA units to handle disputes with foreign diplomats and citizens more judiciously.[72] U.S. and British diplomats were to be put under special protection so as not to give their governments a pretext to intervene in the civil war.[73] On June 28, Huang Hua, head of the Foreign Affairs Office of the Military Control Committee in Nanjing, contacted Stuart with an oral invitation from Mao and Zhou to visit them in Beiping. Only a directive from "the highest level" prevented Stuart from accepting, and he understood that his rejection of the visit had caused Mao and Zhou to lose face.[74]

Stuart stayed in Nanjing until August 2, and his contacts with Communist representatives from May to July offered the last chance for tolerable relations between the two countries. During this period, their communications were subtle and complicated.[75] Although mixed signals from the Communists may well have reflected internal differences in the Chinese high command as well as pressure from Moscow, they appear from hindsight to have been carefully orchestrated by Mao. For example, by telling an American diplomat that his leaning toward Moscow did not rule out improved relations with Washington, a message he knew would reach Stalin via Kovalev, Mao could silence his critics in the Party and remind Stalin of China's potential (and more ominous) alternatives in pursuing its own goals.[76]

Although all these political games were important, Mao and Zhou understood that winning Stuart over was the key to the American stance. According to Chinese accounts, Mao's emissary gave the American ambassador a note on July 9 filling him in on the Party's leaning-to-one-side policy, which had been made public on June 30. Mao explained that the policy did not exclude the possibility of establishing economic and diplomatic ties with the United States. He urged Stuart to pay attention to the "difference between the [Party's] political line and the stand of a state," but Stuart was not impressed.[77] Whether such a meeting in fact took place is unclear, but one thing is certain: Mao's leaning-to-one-side declaration had taken its toll, and U.S.-China relations would not begin to recover for more than two decades.

Adding to Mao's frustration was the fact that the contacts with the U.S. ambassador not only failed to produce results but also threatened to offend Moscow. Accordingly, the Communists had no incentive to persevere once they had been soundly rebuffed by Stuart and the U.S. administration.[78] They began taking an openly hostile attitude toward the Americans soon after Stuart informed them of Washington's disapproval of his visit to Beiping.[79]

Simultaneously, Mao moved to allay Stalin's suspicions and win his trust. He knew that delay would be fatal. Stalin's mood of suspicion and intolerance after the Cominform's passage of the anti-Tito resolution had made it imperative for Mao to pay deference to the Soviet Union immediately and unambiguously. Party leader Deng Xiaoping quotes Mao as saying, "It is better to lean to one side on our own initiative than to do it passively."[80]

Though some sources have argued that Moscow forced Mao to reveal his intentions, we believe that the leaning-to-one-side declaration of June 30, 1949, was the logical outcome of the policies—national revival and alliance with the Communist bloc—that Mao had been developing in stages since the March plenum.[81] Stalin was a factor in the political calculus, but only one.

At the end of September, Mao's basic ideas became law in the transitional constitution, the Common Program.[82] On September 21, a few days before adopting the program, Mao proclaimed that the Chinese people had "now stood up," and he added, "We must unite . . . first of all with the Soviet Union and the New Democracies, so that we shall not stand alone in our struggle."[83]

War and the Changing Global Equation

At the same time as the Chinese Communist leaders were calibrating their future relations with the Soviet Union and the West, they began to define China's place in the international strategic structure. They were searching for ways to establish cooperation with the Soviet Union on the most favorable possible terms, and to this end they had to ascertain Stalin's strategy and China's part in it, a quest to which we now turn.

We have already remarked on Stalin's firm belief in the inevitability of a third world war and the Soviet Union's ultimate victory. Molotov quotes him as saying: "The First World War tore one country away from capitalist slavery. The Second World War created the socialist system, and the Third World War will finish imperialism forever."[84] In the early postwar years, preparations for this final third-round showdown became the core of all Soviet policies, both domestic and foreign. Although some scholars have argued that toward the end of his life Stalin was adopting a more compromising or benign view of the global situation and threats to Soviet security, the documents now in hand lead to the opposite judgment.[85]

Stalin believed that war would break out within the coming 20 or so years, as we noted in the previous chapter, and that Germany would again be the instigator.[86] In getting ready for war, it was critical for Stalin to create the most advantageous conditions for entering it. In contrast to the just-ended world war, the Soviet Union would enter the next one fully prepared, with reliable allies and at a time and place of its own choosing. To make the needed preparations, it would have to buy time. Meanwhile, Stalin would avoid high-risk conflicts and compute the limits of his external actions. Molotov in particular recalls how Stalin constantly modulated his moves in terms of their potential for causing resistance or other reactions from the West. He was especially leery of actions that could provoke an enemy counterstrike at a moment or place of Soviet weakness.[87] These concerns characterized Stalin's overall approach both in general and toward China.

A central issue in that approach was the possible role of nuclear weapons. The Chinese leaders, as we have noted, had already concluded that the U.S. nuclear arsenal had frightened Stalin and had caused him to work with Chiang even at their expense. They correctly grasped the constraints underlying Stalin's strategy and appreciated that he did not want to become involved in a fight with the Americans as a result of provocative behavior on their part. Nevertheless, we now have evidence that the Chinese had an exaggerated view of Stalin's nuclear fears.

According to Molotov, for example, Stalin kept calm when President Truman at Potsdam in August 1945 tried to surprise or even intimidate him with the mention of a superweapon. Molotov remarks: "We understood that for the time being they were unable to unleash a war. They only had one or two bombs; after they blasted Hiroshima and Nagasaki, no more remained. But even if some remained, they could not play a significant role."[88] One reason for this calmness, Molotov notes, was Stalin's determination to accelerate the building of his own nuclear weapons and the means of their delivery.[89] By the spring of 1949, that program was nearly completed; the Soviet Union exploded its first bomb on August 29, 1949.

Perhaps another reason for his response at Potsdam and shortly thereafter was his continued adherence to a prenuclear doctrine that stressed the role of "permanently operating factors."[90] In the emerging nuclear environment, Stalin thought he could counter the U.S. threat with conventional arms, though these were obviously the only weapons at his disposal until the summer of 1949 in any event.[91] But Soviet realism about the atomic bomb grew steadily as the U.S. nuclear arsenal expanded and was deployed ever closer to Soviet territory.[92]

Stalin came to believe that a nuclear war was becoming possible, even likely, and he began to consider how to delay the war or guarantee victory in it. Specifically, he asked, how could the Soviet Union counteract the effect of American forward deployments? A search for answers to this question gradually introduced the nuclear element into Stalin's thinking about the necessity of an expanded buffer along the Soviet borders. In time, that thinking culminated in his ideas on nuclear encirclement and counterencirclement, in which China gained a prominent place.[93]

More generally, as we have said, the emerging Cold War, marked by such events as Churchill's Fulton speech in March 1946 and the proclamation of the Truman Doctrine in the spring of 1947, forced Stalin to alter his ideas on China and to shift his support to Mao. These changes in turn fed into his evolving ideas on encirclement and China's potential role in offsetting it. Up to early 1946 at least, Stalin had clung to the hope that the American military could be excluded from the buffer region in China through agreements with Chiang Kai-shek. In December 1945, he had told Chiang's son: "You absolutely cannot let the United States send one soldier to China; it will be very difficult to solve the Northeast problem if even one American soldier comes to China."[94] But Chiang had not acceded to Stalin's demand and had allowed the U.S. Marines to come ashore in China, and after the Fulton speech, Stalin's hope evaporated.

We have a hint of the Kremlin's appraisal of the world situation toward the end of 1946 in a report by the Soviet ambassador to the United States, which is said to reflect Molotov's views.[95] In it he stated that the United States had already abandoned its wartime course of cooperation among the "big three" and now sought world domination. The growing network of American bases in the Pacific, as well as the Atlantic, was intended for the coming war against the Soviet Union. The diplomat evaluated the American military presence in China within this more threatening context.

Although "encirclement" had not yet reentered the Soviet vocabulary (having been actively used in the prewar years to mean general capitalist encirclement), the basic principles of the concept were already evident. Interestingly, though China was being treated as an important element in the concept, it was of much less importance than either Japan or Germany. Moreover, China was not mentioned as part of the Soviet counterstrategy; only the Soviet Union and the "new democratic states" in Europe rated that status in 1946.

Less than a year later, in July 1947, the same Soviet diplomat drafted a new report in light of the Truman Doctrine and the initial steps toward the Marshall Plan. This time the concept of encirclement was made explicit:

The realization of all these measures [in America's foreign policy] would enable it to create a strategic ring around the Soviet Union, in the West running through West Germany and the Western European countries, in the North through the network of bases on the northern islands in the Atlantic as well as through those in Canada and Alaska, in the East through China and Japan, and in the South through the countries of the Middle East and Mediterranean.[96]

Again, in this second report, China figured as part of the encirclement but not as a factor in the strategy of counterencirclement, and the ambassador specifically characterized the Soviet Union's eastern flank as secondary to Europe.[97]

But by the following February there seems to have been at least some shift away from relegating China to a lesser position, for that is when we find Stalin telling Milovan Djilas that he had mistakenly assessed the prospects for the Chinese revolution and now accepted the possibility of Mao's victory.[98] This may have been one of the earliest times for China to be mentioned, however indirectly, as part of Stalin's thinking about counterencirclement. The indirectness may have resulted from his unshakable disquietude about the U.S. presence in China and his irritation over CCP contacts with American representatives. In any case, the change was modest at best. Stalin still considered China of limited importance in any plan of counterencirclement. His wariness, we may surmise, resulted more from his preoccupation with European affairs than from his misgivings about Mao. Asia was a decidedly secondary theater for the Soviets. During the prolonged Berlin crisis from June 1948 through May 1949, Stalin was riveted by the possible inclusion of West Germany in the developing American alliance structure. That move would greatly enhance the West's potential for encirclement, and he sought to block it at all costs.[99]

The Soviet preoccupation with events in Europe was, of course, not news to the Chinese. Yet they kept hoping for a change because Stalin's Eurocenteredness restricted the amount of attention and support they could receive from Moscow. It led him to caution the Chinese Communists against intensifying the struggle with the Nationalists, and that, too, constrained Mao's freedom of maneuver. The Chinese Communists resented being dealt with as lifeless participants by Stalin and longed to become his active allies in a sphere of responsibility of their own. That desire had surfaced as early as Mao's interview with Anna Louise Strong in August 1946.

For all these reasons, the Chinese went to elaborate lengths to persuade Stalin of their centrality. They selected February-March 1949 to make their move. This was the eve of the PLA's southern offensive, and the Party needed clear-cut Soviet backing. Internationally, these months followed the first signs of easing tensions around Berlin and the beginning of the Kremlin's intensified campaign to block the creation of NATO.

At this time, a CCP intelligence agent visited Kovalev and asked him if he wanted to be briefed on top-secret information from Chiang's headquarters, which had only recently been obtained by a reliable source in Shanghai. Kovalev naturally said yes, and he and the agent met in extreme secrecy on the outskirts of Shenyang in the Northeast. Later, in the 1950s and early 1960s, that agent, Liu Xiao, served as Beijing's ambassador to the Soviet Union.[100]

Liu told Kovalev that he had acquired an American war plan for the launching of a third world war from Asia. In a three-way military alliance, the United States would send some 2,000,000–3,000,000 troops into China's North and Northeast, the Japanese would resurrect their imperial army, and Chiang would mobilize additional millions. A general offensive against the Soviet Union would be preceded by a preemptive nuclear strike against 100 targets in Manchuria and the Soviet Far East. After annihilating the PLA and the Soviet forces in the Far East, the offensive would move westward toward the Urals.

Whatever the American plans may have been at this time, they did not remotely include anything resembling the plan Liu Xiao had sketched.* On the other hand, we do know that during this time Chiang persistently declared that the civil war in China was the first stage in a third world war already under way.[101] What the Nationalists wanted, of course, was direct U.S. intervention in their war, and the plan that reached Liu Xiao may have been of their devising. It is also possible that this was a pure invention of the Chinese Communists themselves. After all, if they could sell Moscow on this "American scheme," they would have had a strong argument for increased Soviet assistance for their own southern offensive, since this could now be construed as a preemptive strike in defense of the Soviet Union. Mao ipso facto would have become Stalin's strategic partner.

Whatever Kovalev's personal opinion of Liu's disclosure, he promptly transmitted the plan to Stalin. According to Kovalev, the Soviet leader was uncharacteristically slow to react and did not reply "for a long time." Even then, the response came only after Kovalev several times gave Stalin information similar to Liu Xiao's that had been passed to him by other Chinese

---

*In May 1948, the U.S. Joint Chiefs of Staff approved a war plan called Halfmoon, which assumed the Soviet Union would begin hostilities, and which, among other things, called for U.S. forces to withdraw from Korea and China, to defend Japan, and, if possible, to provide aid to the Nationalists. Several other plans followed Halfmoon, and on Jan. 28, 1949, the JCS completed Plan Trojan, which dealt with the first year of a global war and primarily with an atomic attack on the Soviet Union. Throughout this period, the JCS "faced the dismal prospects of limited military resources, a declining budget, and a growing Soviet threat." After the creation of NATO, the JCS wrote Plan Offtackle, which contemplated "a strategic offensive in Western Eurasia and a strategic defensive in the Far East." Ross, *American War Plans*, pp. 90, 92, 96, 103. See also Condit, *History of Joint Chiefs of Staff*, Chaps. 13–14.

sources. Clearly, the Chinese Communists had set in motion a coordinated effort to persuade the Kremlin that an Asian war plan was in place.

Stalin's response to Mao (via Kovalev) best capsulizes his reasoning—or his rationalization—at the moment, and we quote it here in full:

> War is not favorable for the imperialists. Their crisis has begun; they are not ready to fight. [They] are threatening [us] with the atom bomb, [but] we are not afraid of it.
> Now, there are no material conditions for the assault, for the starting of a war.
> Now, the situation is such that America is less ready to strike than the USSR is ready to strike back. Things are like this from the point of view of normal people—objective [ones].
> However, in history there are abnormal people. The American secretary of defense, [James V.] Forrestal, suffered from hallucinations.
> We are ready to strike back.[102]

Stalin's reference to the U.S. atomic threat may have reflected his anxieties about the rapid development of U.S. nuclear weapons then being tested in the Pacific.[103] Though rare, this reference to the atomic threat may be enough to adumbrate Stalin's state of mind on the American nuclear advantage.

Undoubtedly, he had put off answering Kovalev's cable until he could check on the Chinese intelligence through his own channels. We do not know what he learned, but he certainly did not get strong confirming evidence. Instead, he fell back on the familiar argument that the West's economic crises impaired its readiness to wage war, and he reiterated his confident attitude toward the atomic bomb. Although all this was old hat, Stalin's reply did contain a new message: the Soviets were gaining on the Americans and were more ready than they to strike back in retaliation.

This fearless posture might be explained by the steady progress in the Soviet nuclear project but more likely reflected Stalin's normal public stance in the face of adversity. A breakthrough in the project was still months away, and the American atomic stockpile was growing. Given the low probability of an American attack, Stalin could strike a heroic pose even while fearing the resurgence of American power. This pose cost him nothing; only later, when asked to back Mao's invasion plans for Taiwan, were his true views unmasked.

The increase in American weaponry was only one of Stalin's worries. Kovalev's information was sent in early March, and Stalin's cable was drafted sometime on the eve of or just after the formation of NATO in April 1949. That event was clearly a great setback for Stalin. No longer could he count on the sharpening of Anglo-American tensions (which he had considered the most serious problem for the West), and even the Western-occupied zones of Germany were being aligned with a hostile military alliance. Stalin was trying to put a good face on a solid defeat, or at the very least he wanted to convey an upbeat message to the Chinese.

Indeed, China was the one bright spot on an otherwise gloomy strategic landscape for the Soviet dictator. The PLA's offensive had brought it to the banks of the Yangtze, poised for a direct challenge to British and American interests in the South. Stalin was on the verge of changing his view of the CCP's international status and military potential.

An event near the end of April proved decisive in this respect. During the crossing of the river, PLA artillery damaged several British warships and forced them to retreat.[104] Kovalev recalls that Moscow paid close attention to a special meeting of the British Parliament, in which the Conservatives demanded that Britain punish the Chinese Communists by sending marines in and bombing Beiping. Moscow reportedly believed that many American officials backed these calls for retaliation, and from the tone of the cables from his capital, as well as from the mood in China, Kovalev surmised that war might be imminent. The Soviet Pacific Fleet and troops on the Liaodong Peninsula in the Northeast were put on alert.[105]

In the end, however, the British and Americans did nothing. This outcome apparently strengthened Stalin's belief that his two bitter foes were not yet ready for a large-scale war and his conviction that the PLA could stand up to them. So it was that by the summer of 1949, Stalin was ready to assign Communist China a profoundly different role in his global strategy. Events on the battlefields of China, when compared with the inauspicious developments in Europe, were forcing him to acknowledge Mao's China as an effective and vital confederate. The pressing task was to translate his new appreciation of China into a common understanding for joint cooperation. The visit of the Party leader Liu Shaoqi to Moscow in July–August 1949 provided the opportunity to do just that.

Liu Shaoqi's Mission to Moscow

Beginning in April 1949, Mao frequently lectured Kovalev on the history of intra-Party struggle and emphasized that the result was often the ouster of Party leaders and sweeping purges. Kovalev got the impression that Mao was trying to assure him that he had not personally hurt any CCP leaders who had been close to Moscow. Moreover, during each of these conversations, Mao "joked" about being a person who lacked Stalin's trust, who was considered a "right opportunist," and who was branded an enemy of the "Moscow group," headed by Wang Ming. By all of these comments, Mao was betraying his anxieties about his later and by now inevitable face-to-face encounter with Stalin.[106]

But Mao was also using these occasions to underscore that he was a stranger to the Soviet high command, that he alone among the Chinese Party leaders had never been to Moscow or met any Soviet Politburo member except Mikoyan. Despite his obvious misgivings, Mao knew he would have to go, and at the end of April 1949, while the Yangtze crossings were proceeding, Mao told Kovalev that he was ready to fly to Moscow.

Kovalev dutifully transmitted Mao's request, and again Stalin turned him down: "You must not hurry to visit Moscow. You cannot now leave China and your leadership over affairs because of the complicated situation in the South and because China in fact has no government, and that [circumstance] is linked with some danger to the course of the revolution." Although this answer superficially appears to be the same as the one Stalin had given Mao in May 1948, the message this time was quite different and was so received by Mao. He responded with relief, almost joy. He raised his hands and three times exclaimed, "Long live Comrade Stalin!"

Kovalev instantly discerned that Mao's exclamations were motivated by Stalin's explicit recognition of him as the leader of China and the inference that Stalin would not try to force him from power just as the final chapter of the Chinese civil war was coming to a close. With Stalin's response in hand, the Chairman decided to send a delegation to Moscow headed by Liu Shaoqi, the second highest leader in the Chinese Party hierarchy.[107]

Stalin's cable, moreover, was but one in a series of communications between the two leaders that resulted in their agreement on a number of outstanding issues. On March 10, for example, Mao had informed Stalin of his directive to install border markers along the Amur River and expressed his willingness to comply with any border rules preferred by the Soviet side.[108] This was a significant breakthrough in light of the history of clashes between Soviet and Nationalist border units during the 1920s and 1930s and was to serve as the basis for a later (1951) agreement on navigation rules for the Sino-Soviet boundary rivers. Although the question of these rivers is contentious to this day, Mao at the beginning was trying to get started on the right foot.

In the summer, just before Liu's visit, Mao touched on another tender area affecting Chinese relations with the Soviet Union—Xinjiang. Since that western region provided the shortest and most secure route from the Soviet Union into China, he told Kovalev, it would be strategically important in case of a "new war with imperialists." In passing, Mao remarked that the PLA planned to expel the Nationalists from the area in 1950–51.

Mao obviously knew of Stalin's years-long struggle to bring Xinjiang under Soviet control and could be certain that Stalin would not take his plan lightly. Mao was telling Kovalev—and through him Stalin—that his aims were consistent with Soviet interests, and that Xinjiang could become a base for bilateral military cooperation. We have no record that Stalin voiced any objections to Mao's war aims in the region, and during Liu's visit, Mao's advance warning became a starting point for significant agreements on Xinjiang.

Furthermore, before Liu's visit, Mao and Stalin reached an accord on several items relating to the future Chinese Communist state. Mao reportedly welcomed Stalin's advice, conveyed in his April 1949 cable, to hasten the creation of central and local organs of power, not to model them on Soviet organizations, and to give more attention to the development of industry. Moreover, with the direct participation of Kovalev and his team, the two sides hammered out a preliminary agreement on the scope and form of Soviet economic and technological aid to China.[109]

There were matters on which Mao and Stalin could not agree, though the issues involved were somewhat clarified in advance of Liu's visit. The future of Mongolia was one sticking point. Mao had questioned Mikoyan on Mongolia in February, and the Chinese often raised the same topic with Kovalev thereafter. In one discussion on administrative structures for China's national minorities, Mao asked Kovalev, "Why not undertake the unification of Inner and Outer Mongolia under [the condition of] autonomy but incorporated into the Chinese Democratic Republic?" The Soviet adviser replied that he was not authorized to treat such questions because they dealt with the internal affairs of the Mongolian People's Republic, but said he thought the Mongolians were unlikely to accept such "autonomy."[110]

The possibility of a Soviet loan to China was another unresolved subject. In his April cable, Stalin declared his readiness to arrange barter trade with China but said he could not react to Mao's request for a loan right away because any loan had to be approved by the Supreme Soviet. He indicated that he was not rejecting the idea of a loan outright but was unwilling to approve it before the details could be worked out.[111]

Stalin had his own list of questions for the Chinese, and he was not shy about probing Mao to get answers. During Mikoyan's visit, Mao had raised the possibility of China acquiring gratis the Soviet shares in the Chinese Changchun Railroad, and thereafter Stalin many times asked Kovalev to sound out the Chinese on their real stance toward the 1945 railroad agreement. Stalin was especially keen to know if the Chinese leaders considered the agreement mutually beneficial. When Kovalev talked the matter over with Gao Gang and Chen Yun, both insisted that the agreement was equal and satisfactory. Nonetheless, Kovalev offered Stalin his personal opinion that the Chinese secretly wanted total control of the railroad and in practice were doing their best to wrest the management of the line from Soviet personnel.[112]

Hence, Liu Shaoqi flew to Moscow with the knowledge of which issues had been agreed on in principle and could be thrashed out in detail and which remained fundamentally unresolved. The border regime, cooperation in Xinjiang, trade, and assistance on state building, for example, fell in the first category. The future of Mongolia and the Chinese Changchun Railroad came under the second category, a category that would be left for a later Mao-Stalin summit. And there was a gray area, including such topics as a loan, that might be explored during Liu's visit or left alone until the summit.

The resolution to send the delegation headed by Liu Shaoqi to Moscow was affirmed by the Chinese Politburo in May 1949. Three main tasks were set for it. First, Liu would supply the Soviets details about the Chinese revolution, giving emphasis to the Chinese experience of armed struggle. Second, he would explain the Party's views on the relationship between the Chinese and world revolutions and the influence of China's revolution on the colonial and semicolonial states. Finally, his foremost task would be to elicit Soviet understanding and sympathy and to gain the USSR's assistance and international support for China after the PLA's victory.[113]

Taking into account the caliber of the visit, the Chinese were eager to get started at once on the preparations for it. The work was put in the charge of a top Party leader, Wang Jiaxiang, a future ambassador to the Soviet Union, one of the Sovietologists we met in the previous chapter. The delegation departed from Beiping on July 2, 1949, and arrived in the Soviet capital approximately a week later.[114] It left Moscow on August 14.[115]

Wang was in the midst of the final preparations when Mao issued his leaning-to-one-side declaration on June 30. Mao's statement, published in *Pravda* on July 6, set the tone for Liu's arrival in Moscow a few days later.[116] The weight Stalin attached to the talks can be seen from the fact that he met with the Chinese delegation six times.[117] Right up to the eve of Liu's arrival, Stalin was repositioning China in his strategic equation and reaching the decision that it would become his number one ally, with a sphere of responsibility of its own.

Soon after Liu's team arrived, Stalin held a reception in its honor at his dacha in Kuntsevo, and all the most senior Soviet leaders showed up. On their return from the reception, the Chinese set about preparing an advance statement of their views on all the significant subjects they wanted to cover, so Stalin would be prepared to reply point by point to all their requests and questions. This document has apparently not survived, but we have a summary of it from a Chinese participant in the talks and will examine its relevant parts here.[118] As might be expected, the delegation elected to describe the nature of the Chinese revolution and the future Chinese state in much the same language as Mao used in his report to Mikoyan and his speech to the second plenum.

Of great moment to Stalin, the statement updated the Chinese leaders' conclusion on the probability of U.S. intervention in the revolution, noting that "it seems that any large-scale armed interference, with the imperialists dispatching a million-man army to China, is impossible." In any event, such "armed interference of imperialism," should it come, "could only delay the moment of victory of the Chinese revolution; it cannot destroy or stop the Chinese revolution." Echoing Stalin's long April cable, the Chinese stated that imperialists could send an army of "one or two hundred thousand" in a campaign to occupy some large ports or strike surprise blows but added, "we have already made preparations for this." Such an assessment obviously diverged from Mao's talks with Mikoyan, in which he had totally excluded the possibility of an American intervention.

One of the key topics addressed in the document was the international impact of the Chinese revolution on other states and revolutionary movements. It said that the Chinese experience applied to other semicolonial and colonial countries. That experience included the encirclement of cities by the countryside and the use of illegal and armed struggle combined with legal means of struggle. By focusing on this unique history, the Chinese were demonstrating their aspiration to act independently in world affairs and their hope, if not determination, to become the leader of the colonial and semicolonial states. Talks about a division of labor in the world constituted a focal point in the Stalin-Liu exchanges.

In its review of foreign policy, the document basically reiterated the line taken in Mao's report to the second plenum (as against his more rigid statements to Mikoyan). The question of the recognition of the People's Republic by foreign countries was treated in some depth. China would never agree to any recognition that would "tie our hands and feet," but "if the imperialist states choose a policy of recognition of the new government of China, then we shall be prepared to establish diplomatic relations with them; at this time we hope that the Soviet Union will recognize China ahead of these states."

Turning to the matter of the treaties and other agreements concluded by the Nationalist government, the Chinese stated, "we are ready to examine them anew and to solve any issues on a case-by-case basis. The principle will be: we are ready to recognize and inherit everything that is favorable to the interests of the Chinese people as well as [in the interests] of peace and democracy in the world."

There was nothing surprising in this formula on the Nationalists' treaties, but there were two important points of added nuance. The first was
the requirement that existing treaties must be in "the interests of the
Chinese people." This qualification was in accordance with the Party's official line; without exception, the CCP would not honor any treaty that it
considered unequal and humiliating. That line seemed to require changes
in the Sino-Soviet treaty of August 1945.

The second point is to be found in the statement that the Party was ready
to "recognize and inherit" all Nationalist agreements it judged to be in the
interest "of peace and democracy in the world." To understand the implication of this phrase, we must recall that in the Communist jargon of the
period, the Soviet Union was "the leader of the camp of peace and democracy." The Chinese were telling Stalin that they might be willing to preserve
some clauses of the 1945 treaty and other agreements he had concluded
with Chiang Kai-shek that the Soviet Union considered essential to its interests. Again, this change reflected the shift in March and April toward
greater realism and flexibility.

That change in fact had been the basis of Mao's leaning-to-one-side policy. He would align with Moscow and, with its assistance, blot out all remnants of inequality in China's foreign relations. To do so, he was prepared
to pay the price of temporary concessions to Soviet interests while striving
for greater equality with Moscow at the least possible cost. This dual position underlay the Liu document.

The document had a separate section devoted to that position, in which
the delegation reviewed such issues as the 1945 alliance with the Nationalists, the Soviet military presence in Lüshun, and the independence of
Mongolia and stated, "Mao Zedong is prepared, when China and the Soviet Union establish diplomatic relations, to undertake an open visit to the
Soviet Union and is hoping that the Soviet Union will consider the timing
and format [of the visit]."

We do not know how or even whether the document treated the thor-
niest issues. Though the author of the summary was present at the talks,
his book barely touches on these matters. He merely notes that in the end
Liu Shaoqi expressed his government's readiness to accept the independence of Mongolia, a significant concession made only after repeated probing of Moscow's position on the matter.[119]

Late on July 11, Stalin received the Chinese delegation in the Kremlin.
By this time, he had read the Chinese document and was prepared to discuss it in depth.[120] He began by expressing approval in principle of the
CCP's domestic policy line and then said, "As soon as the new China is
established, the Soviet Union will recognize it. The Soviet-Chinese treaty

was signed in 1945 because at that time we were dealing with the Nationalists and could not do otherwise. After the creation of the new China, Mao Zedong can immediately come to Moscow. We shall solve this problem [of the treaty] after he arrives in Moscow."[121] These were the messages the Chinese most wanted to hear. They were of enormous consequence to them and went a long way toward satisfying their basic national aims while leaving all the hard bargaining of details to Mao.

But Stalin was not willing to accommodate them in everything and noted which Chinese proposals fell out of bounds, though in a somewhat backhanded way. "The Soviet troops deployed in Lüshun are the freedom force that is deterring the military forces of America and Chiang Kaishek," he told them. "By protecting the Soviet Union, they are also protecting the interests of the Chinese revolution." They must be content with that for the time being, he gave them to understand, adding that "as soon as the peace treaty with Japan is signed and the United States withdraws its troops from Japan, the Soviet Union can immediately withdraw its forces from Lüshun. If the Chinese comrades demand it, the Soviet Army can be withdrawn right away. The political power in Dalian must be unified with that of the Northeast. At present, the port of Dalian must be used jointly by China and the Soviet Union. That is the real situation."

Kovalev records Stalin's statement in virtually the same words, though with some additional nuance: "Our government considers that after the withdrawal of American troops from Japan, the Soviet Union can consider withdrawing our own troops from Port Arthur [Lüshun]. But if the Chinese Communist Party considers it necessary to have an immediate withdrawal of the Soviet troops from Port Arthur, then, in order to provide political gains for the Chinese Communist Party, the USSR is ready to withdraw from Port Arthur immediately."[122]

What is evident in both versions is the polemical nature of Stalin's remarks. They were obviously directed toward a Chinese proposal for "immediate withdrawal" from Lüshun, and Stalin was suggesting two options to the Chinese. One would allow for a transitional period, which he wanted, and the other would produce the prompt withdrawal that Mao sought. The Soviet diplomat M. S. Kapitsa has described the disparity between the two approaches this way: "One of the most serious reasons for Stalin's distrust of Mao was Lüshun, Dalian, and the Chinese Changchun Railroad. Mao was very much encouraged by his overall victory and because of that, wanted to have everything returned immediately. Stalin was asking Mao to look at the international situation and at the desperate state of affairs in China and to evaluate correctly the American threat. Because of that he emphasized the necessity for a transitional period."[123]

Stalin was casting the Lüshun problem in the global context. He considered the naval base an indivisible part of his security belt in the confrontation with the United States and as a point of leverage against Japan. Concessions on such a weighty matter were out of the question. Consequently, the option to withdraw forthwith from Lüshun was made more as a threat than a true offer to the Chinese. If they took this choice, Stalin would have deduced that they could not be treated as a reliable partner and would have dealt with them accordingly.[124] Probably for this reason, after Stalin's remarks, Liu Shaoqi refrained from giving an answer even though the option for immediate withdrawal clearly met the stated Chinese objectives.

Just how acutely global strategic problems affected the resolution of bilateral matters was demonstrated during the next meeting of the Chinese delegation with Stalin, on July 27.[125] During this round of negotiations, Gao Gang suggested that the Soviet Union strengthen its military presence in China by stationing more troops in Lüshun and sending warships to the naval base at Qingdao to counter the American threat. In an account disputed by Shi Zhe, Kovalev recalls that Gao ended by floating a proposal to make Manchuria the seventeenth republic of the Soviet Union.[126] Although most of the Soviet Politburo members enthusiastically applauded Gao's idea, Stalin apparently realized that he was speaking without authority. Fixing his eyes on Gao for a few awkward moments of silence, Stalin responded by addressing him as "Comrade Zhang Zuolin," the name of a famous Manchurian warlord. He waved aside the proposal as specious and prejudicial.[127]

Gao's colleagues then turned on him. Angered by his audacious action, Liu Shaoqi called him a traitor. When the meeting broke up, Liu reported the incident to Mao, who ordered Gao home without delay.[128] Stalin tried to soften his blow to Gao by arranging a farewell banquet for him where he goaded the other Chinese into drinking to their disgraced colleague.*

Gao had obviously been trying to heighten his status by currying Stalin's favor, and the attempt had backfired. In fact, he had gone well out on a limb, now that Stalin had revealed his attitude toward "immediate withdrawal." Gao had not only agreed with Stalin's position; his proposal went

*When Gao Gang learned that Mao had summoned him back to Beiping, he went to Kovalev and, speaking in Russian, said that he wanted to have a private talk through the Russian interpreter. His purpose, he said, was to tell the Russians about the anti-Soviet, "rightist-Trotskyite" tendencies of Mao and his allies in the Chinese Communist Party. When this information was passed on to Stalin, he ordered Kovalev not to talk with Gao about these matters because he (Kovalev) had to return to China and must not be known there as someone tainted by the CCP's inner-Party struggles. Kovalev, "Stalin's Dialogue," 1: 89.

much further. The Manchurian leader, it seems, had decided to gamble on his bold initiative only after he understood how seriously Stalin regarded the perpetuation of Soviet dominance in the Northeast. Stalin's behavior in this matter merits some attention as well. He began by criticizing Gao Gang and wound up shielding him, at least temporarily, from purge, thus demonstrating in effect how much he valued Gao's loyalty and the good intentions of his proposal.

There were other sensitive but less contentious subjects on the international part of the agenda for the talks. During the meeting on July 11, Stalin told the Chinese, "You must not worry about getting recognition from the imperialist countries, even less about their attitude toward you. You have a good line for [your] behavior—trade with the imperialist countries. Their economic crises have already begun. I think that [their crises] will accelerate [their] recognition."[129]

This remark was an obvious answer to the passage in Liu's document that the Communist-led state would be ready to establish diplomatic relations with any country willing to offer recognition on equitable terms. Stalin once again demonstrated that he would not welcome the early establishment of diplomatic ties between the Chinese and Moscow's main adversaries. Bent on incorporating China into his international strategy, he wanted to keep its ties with the "imperialist countries," especially with the United States, under his own taut leash.

The Soviet dictator also showed the Chinese that he would not permit them to upset his strategic calculations. That became evident when Liu Shaoqi raised the issue of the "liberation of Taiwan" on July 11. According to Kovalev, the Chinese had already asked Moscow for military aid to "liberate Taiwan" but had not received a positive response.[130] When Liu now renewed the request, Stalin rejected the idea out of hand.[131] Soviet military assistance for the invasion of Taiwan would risk a fight with the U.S. Navy and Air Force and provide a pretext for unleashing a world war. Despite the bold words in his earlier cable to Mao that war was "not favorable for the imperialists" and "we are not afraid of it," he now told the Chinese that as the result of the war, the Soviet Union had suffered countless losses, and nothing could justify that risk. Betraying his real feelings about war, Stalin added, "If we, the leaders, undertake this, the Russian people would not understand us. Moreover, they could chase us away. For underestimating all the wartime and postwar efforts and suffering. For taking it too lightly."

As intended, the Chinese could not argue against the constraints Stalin was under to avoid actions that might provoke the West. Stalin's resistance to the Chinese request for military assistance might even have been reinforced by Liu's appraisal that the possibility of U.S. intervention in the Chinese civil war was greater than zero.

Stalin proposed to turn the matter of aid over to an expanded Politburo meeting, which would bring together senior military leaders and some ministers. On July 27, he invited the Chinese delegation to the Central Committee's headquarters, and Liu Shaoqi, Gao Gang, and Wang Jiaxiang attended.[132] In addition to all the Soviet Politburo members, Marshals Nikolai Bulganin and Aleksandr Vasilevskii took part.[133] Stalin reiterated the arguments he had advanced earlier and offered the Chinese no opening. On the conclusion of his speech, Liu announced that the request for support was withdrawn and the issue was closed.[134]

When, as this incident reveals, Stalin deemed his priorities to be at risk, he could be tough and uncompromising. Conversely, when his strategic designs coincided with those of the Chinese, he could become charming and cooperative. He was to reveal his better self in the matter of Xinjiang, a subject that was also raised in the July 11 talks. At this meeting, Stalin told Liu Shaoqi that, according to his intelligence sources, the United States and Britain were actively promoting ethnic unrest in Xinjiang as a pretext for expanding their presence there.[135] Stalin recommended that the PLA speed up its liberation of China's western regions to block any further Western penetration and promised material help for the task.[136]

On receiving Liu's report, Mao decided to advance the date for the occupation of Xinjiang and instructed the delegation's political secretary, Deng Liqun, to go to Yining in Xinjiang as soon as possible.[137] There, Deng received Soviet support in organizing communications with Mao's headquarters, providing intelligence, and identifying and meeting reliable local leaders. Thanks to this assistance, Xinjiang was taken over swiftly and relatively peacefully later in the year.[138]

All these examples illustrate the dominant approaches of the two leaders to the most pressing bilateral issues. Both were governed by larger strategic considerations. Their ability to meet each other's interests was shaped by the congruence of their global outlooks and their perceptions concerning how any partnership could help fulfill their long-term goals. Their deliberations on strategy were tightly coupled to their exchanges on bilateral issues. By reaching understandings on the most salient world problems, they were setting the terms for possible compromises on the most contested specific questions. Absent those understandings, even the simplest problems proved intractable.

During their talks on July 11, Liu asked Stalin for his views on the probability of a third world war, worldwide trends, and changes in the Communist and labor movements.[139] All three topics raised interrelated questions, and Stalin's answers revealed his vision of the global framework within which Soviet-Chinese relations had to evolve. Still sanguine about international peace, he repeated his thesis that there was little possibility of a world war for at least 15 or 20 years. As he had told Mao in an earlier cable, that war could start only if "a madman" should come to power in the West. Concluding that the years of peace had to be devoted to developing one's own economy, he added that the main factor preventing war would be the struggle of the peoples of the world against a new war.

This emphasis on preventing war in no way meant that Stalin had forsworn his belief in the inevitability of a future global showdown. He said, "If we can secure a twenty-year period of peaceful construction and development, then the probability of war will become smaller—if only the warmongers do not want to be annihilated. After that period they could be annihilated at any moment." Obviously, for Stalin "prevention of war" had a broad meaning. It meant guaranteeing a period of peace long enough to ensure the nation's development and its superiority over its adversaries. It further implied a striving to ensure the conditions under which the Soviet Union either could dictate terms to its adversaries or could be certain of their annihilation. Prevention of war was a process of gaining the absolute initiative for securing lasting victory.

Progress in the Soviet nuclear program reinforced Stalin's confidence that global war could be prevented. Kovalev recalls that Liu asked to tour Soviet nuclear installations, but Stalin refused.[140] As a substitute, Stalin arranged a showing of a documentary film on the purported testing of a Soviet nuclear device "somewhere in a deserted area near the Arctic Circle." After the showing, Stalin boasted about breakthroughs in science and technology and the Soviet Union's capability of producing even more formidable weapons very soon.[141] Since the first Soviet nuclear test did not come until a few weeks later, in late August, we do not know what the film actually depicted. Nevertheless, the film led Stalin to say to Liu Shaoqi: "The Soviet Union is sufficiently strong now not to be afraid of the nuclear blackmail of the United States."[142]

Another pillar in Stalin's war-prevention program was China itself. During the talks on July 11, Stalin proclaimed that the Chinese revolutionary experience had a positive value of its own, that the center of world revolution had gravitated from Europe to East Asia, and that the Chinese Communist Party must fulfill its revolutionary destiny in Asia:

You have to understand the importance of your position and that you are fulfilling a historic mission of unprecedented significance. . . . Let's add to China's population of 475 million, the populations of India, Burma, Indonesia, [and] the Philippines. If the people of these countries listen to you, the Japanese probably also will listen to you. . . . The peoples of Asia are looking to you with hope. There is no other Party in the world that has such far-reaching prospects. You have numerous disciples.[143]

This was truly a milestone, indicating the most profound change in Stalin's global outlook—or so the Chinese assumed. This was the first time he had openly declared that the Chinese Communist state would be his strategic partner or that the Asian theater was becoming as important as Europe. He had put his stamp of approval on Mao's revolutionary experience and his Party's leading role in Asia.

We also have to analyze Stalin's statements from the point of view of his own global strategy. In Europe, any expansionist move would lead to confrontation with the United States and its allies; and toward the West he had to have 20 peaceful years in order to gain strength. Later Stalin, in explaining the situation to Mao, complained that many countries were reluctant "to follow the road of socialism." He cited the example of Austria, where despite the Soviet military presence, the capitalists had gained power. He concluded, "Europe is still not ready for socialism."[144]

Asia was quite a different story. The spheres of influence there were still unsettled, and many Asian nations were "ready for socialism." Moreover, the rise of Communist China presented the opportunity for energetic, offensive blows that need not involve the Soviet Union directly. In such an environment, the Chinese experience of armed struggle for power, if duplicated throughout Asia, could hand Stalin tremendous political-military gains.

Devising the global tactics to maximize this potential advantage in turn required an institutional framework, and Stalin conveyed his vision of it to Liu's group when the Chinese asked Stalin if they could become a member of the Cominform. The Soviet leader answered that this was not feasible because of the fundamental differences between Europe and Asia.[145] He suggested that the Chinese should instead craft a union of Asian Communist parties and play the leading role in it.[146] He added that the Soviet Union, being an Asian as well as a European country, would join this union.

The outlines of the new global role Stalin envisioned for China were becoming manifest. The Chinese would have a sphere of responsibility and influence of their own but would act under the all-embracing control of Moscow and in ways that would not jeopardize its aims. The Chinese were being encouraged to become more active and aggressive in Asia but only to the degree that they did not inadvertently implicate Moscow. The basis was being laid for Sino-Soviet joint planning and the actions that were to lead to the Korean War.

1. Soviet troops entering Harbin, Manchuria, Aug. 1945

2. Chongqing cease-fire negotiations, 1945. From left to right, U.S. Ambassador Patrick Hurley, Chiang Ching-kuo, Chiang Kai-shek, Zhang Qun, Wang Shijie, Mao Zedong.

3. Zhou Enlai with General George C. Marshall on his mission to China to mediate a Nationalist-Communist armistice, 1946

4. (*above*) Zhou Enlai being greeted by (from the left) Mao, Zhu De, Liu Shaoqi, and Peng Dehuai on his return to Yan'an from negotiations with the Nationalists in Chongqing, Jan. 1946

5. (*left*) The American journalist Anna Louis Strong and Liu Shaoqi in Yan'an, 1946

6. Mao in Yan'an, 1946

7. Lt. Gen. Ivan V. Kovalev in 1944, when he was People's Commissar of Transportation. In 1948 Stalin sent him to China as his personal representative.

8. The first train across the Songhua River bridge, rebuilt with Soviet aid by the late summer of 1948

9. Anastas Mikoyan, Mao's interpreter Shi Zhe, and the Chairman at Xibaipo, Hebei Province, in early 1949

10. (*left*) Mao at the Second Plenary Session of the CCP Seventh Central Committee held in Xibaipo, March 1949

11. (*below*) Mao entering Beiping, March 1949

12. PLA advance units crossing the Yangtze River,
April 20, 1949

13. Mao and his wife,
Jiang Qing, in Beiping,
spring, 1949

14. PLA cavalry marching into Shanghai, May 25, 1949

15. Liu Shaoqi during his visit to Moscow, July 1949

16. Mao proclaiming the establishment of the Central People's Government at the founding ceremony of the PRC, Oct. 1, 1949

17. Soviet Ambassador N. V. Roshchin presenting his credentials to Mao, Oct. 16, 1949. Zhou Enlai is at the left.

18. Mao (left) being greeted at Moscow's Yaroslavl Railroad Station by Politburo members V. I. Molotov (center) and Nikolai Bulganin (right), Dec. 16, 1949

19. Stalin's 70th birthday celebration, Dec. 21, 1949. From left to right, front row: Mao Zedong, V. Ulbricht (East German Party leader), Stalin, and Nikita Khrushchev.

ДА ЗДРАВСТВУЕТ ВЕЛИКИЙ ВОЖДЬ И УЧИТЕЛЬ
КОММУНИСТИЧЕСКОЙ ПАРТИИ И СОВЕТСКОГО НАРОДА
ТОВАРИЩ И. В. СТАЛИН !

20. Mao (second from left) at Stalin's 70th birthday celebration in
Moscow with Soviet and East European Party leaders, Dec. 21

21. Stalin, Mao, and Politburo member G. M. Malenkov during Mao's
visit to Moscow, Dec. 1949. Malenkov's picture was patched in later to
increase his prestige.

Товарищу СТАЛИНУ

Докладываю Вам об условиях деятельности концес-
сионных и полностью принадлежащих капиталистическим
странам предприятий, в Китае.

Т.т. Мао Цзе-дун, Лю Шао-ци и Чень Юн (Председа-
тель Финансово-Экономического Комитета Правительства),
с которыми я неоднократно разговаривал, заявляли и за-
являют, что демократическое правительство Китая еще не
создало аппарата для учета всего хозяйства страны, поэ-
тому оно не имеет почти никаких данных об иностранных
капиталистических предприятиях, в том числе и концес-
сионных, как и не располагает данными, на каких условиях они работают. Больше того, правительство до сих
пор не установило предприятий, принадлежащих четырем
крупнейшим капиталистическим семействам Китая, а также
предприятий бюрократического капитала, подлежащих, в
соответствии с декларацией правительства, национализа-
ции. К учету капиталистических предприятий и об"ему их
деятельности они лишь собираются приступить.

Все иностранные капиталистические предприятия,
концессии и торговые фирмы продолжают действовать на
прежних условиях кабальных для Китая соглашений, заклю-
ченных с ними чанкайшистско-гоминдановскими властями.

22. Kovalev's copy of his report to Stalin in January 1950. The report,
marked "Top Secret," is translated in the Appendix as Doc. 31.

23. (*top*) Zhou Enlai signing the Sino-Soviet Treaty of Friendship, Alliance, and Mutual Assistance, Feb. 14, 1950

24. (*bottom*) A. Ia Vyshinskii, Soviet foreign minister, signing the treaty

For the Chinese, Stalin's vision brought benefits as well as challenges. They were obviously pleased to acquire at last an independent and indispensable role in the Soviet strategy; they could only welcome Stalin's recognition of the universal character of their revolution. At the same time, as later events would show, they were not happy about being so definitively absorbed into the Soviet global design.

Stalin's recognition of China as a principal collaborator in his global policies influenced his approach toward most of the delicate issues that surfaced during the talks. His attitude was manifested not only in the substance of the conversations but also in the atmosphere in which they proceeded. For example, on July 27 Stalin, in a wholly uncharacteristic confession of fallibility, admitted that he was not "too well versed" in Chinese affairs and may have caused obstacles in the Chinese revolution. The Chinese side assigned special meaning to the statement.[147] They interpreted the admission as signifying that Stalin had finally come to appreciate the full potential and legitimacy of their revolution.[148]

Stalin seemed to persist in this accommodating manner during another talk with Liu Shaoqi, when he declared that "the Chinese Party is a mature Party, and the Chinese cadres are mature cadres with good training."[149] Soviet participants have recalled that the Moscow hosts were especially attentive and courteous toward the delegation.[150]

From what followed it appears that Liu had come prepared to encounter a quite different Stalin. The Chinese may even have feared that the Soviet leader was planning to denounce them as Titoists, for Liu at this point conveyed Mao's instruction that henceforth the Chinese Communist Party would abide by all Soviet Party resolutions. Stalin disavowed the need for such obedience, commenting:

For us, it seems strange [that] the Communist Party of one state would abide by the decisions of the Communist Party of the other state. There never were things like this, and this is not permissible. Both parties have to carry the responsibility for their own people, mutually consult on some issues, mutually help each other, and, if difficulties arise, unify firmly. This is true. Look, today's Politburo meeting with your participation is a specific form of linkage between [our] two parties. It must be like this.[151]

This statement, however disingenuous, reinforced the delegates' conviction that Stalin would treat them as peers.

Stalin was most helpful and forthcoming when practical matters of cooperation, especially those concerning the emerging strategic accord, were raised. At the July 27 meeting, Liu Shaoqi gave Stalin a document requesting assistance in modernizing China's armed forces and defense industry on a long-term basis. The document, which made no reference to Taiwan, was studied by Stalin and the Soviet high command, and Stalin accepted its recommendations.[152] Soviet military advisers began arriving in China within a few weeks. Stalin also acceded to the Communists' requests for priority assistance in building their air force.[153] In response to still another request, he ordered air force units from Lüshun to Shanghai; these Russian-piloted fighters successfully ended the air raids of the Nationalists on Shanghai and other cities.[154]

Furthermore, the two sides agreed to cooperate in the intelligence and counterintelligence fields. Soon after Liu's group arrived in Moscow, Kovalev informed Stalin that Gao Gang and Liu Shaoqi had complained to him about the activities of Soviet intelligence bodies in China. They had been recruiting some agents without consulting the Chinese, they charged, and even those who were engaged after consultations were removed from the CCP's supervision. One problem, Gao and Liu said, was that a large part of the Soviet intelligence network in China had become unreliable and was working for the Americans and Chiang Kai-shek. They called for these uncontrolled spy activities to cease.[155] Stalin complied, saying, "The situation requires us to unify the efforts of our intelligence bodies, and we are ready to start this immediately. . . . Let us act as a united front!"[156] One Chinese participant in the meetings recalls the effect of the change:

Previously some people, proceeding from an internationalist ideology, were conducting intelligence work for the Soviet Union. [Now] all of them had to tell the Party organizations about [this work] on their own initiative, and the Party organizations were lenient toward them.[157]

Stalin also seemed eager to speak about the plans the Chinese were making for their government. Liu Shaoqi told him of the preparations then being made and noted that Mao planned to declare the founding of the People's Republic on January 1. After pondering this for a bit, Stalin voiced his opposition to the date. He did not concur, he said, because foreigners could use the absence of an official Communist government in China as a pretext for interference. No state could exist so long without an official government, and he recommended that Mao move the timetable up. His recommendation was cabled to Beiping, where the Central Committee promptly decided to set the date up three months, to October 1, 1949.[158]

Getting practical, Stalin agreed to assist in the formation of the organs of state power and set in motion plans for 90 Soviet specialists on political institutions to leave for China on the same train with Liu's delegation. Other specialists departed for China a few days later.[159] The Soviets would help devise the bureaucratic structure of the central government and work out the details of the revised legal system. Some of the specialists would help the Chinese repair and begin operating selected large enterprises.

During Liu's stay in Moscow, another pact was concluded on the principles of barter trade between the two countries. Stalin offered concrete advice on how to reconstruct Chinese industry and promised extensive economic and technical assistance.[160] Gao Gang, the head of the trade delegation of the Northeast, acting on behalf of the Chinese leadership, signed an agreement on a Soviet loan, and news of the agreement was published in the press.[161]

In accordance with Stalin's pledge to establish diplomatic relations as soon as the new state was officially proclaimed, both sides began to undertake practical preparations to this end. As a result, Ge Baoquan, a famous expert in Russian language and literature, was named head of a small group that stayed on in Moscow after Liu's departure to discuss arrangements for a future PRC embassy.[162]

Issue by issue, the Soviets and Chinese had worked out the dimensions and myriad details of a viable Sino-Soviet strategic framework. The Stalin-Liu talks had ranged from broad theory to state administration and the minutiae of intelligence cooperation. Ideas about a model for revolution in Asia had been exchanged, along with proposals for China's Northeast and Northwest, trade, and military assistance. Some serious differences had emerged, but these had not proved especially contentious. These differences would be grist for the coming Mao-Stalin summit. Most notably, Liu left confident that the summit would have a global and lasting impact.

By all his actions during the visit, Stalin had done his best to persuade the Chinese that their leaning-to-one-side decision had been wise and in China's interests. He had dealt positively with almost all of Liu's requests.[163] Yet Stalin had made no irreversible commitments. He had laid the basis for the coming talks with Mao but not much more, and he could reverse course easily if Mao proved unreceptive to later Soviet demands. The gestures were his, and now it would be China's turn to reciprocate. Settling the terms of that reciprocity would await Mao's arrival in Moscow.

THREE

The Making of the Alliance

On October 2, 1949, the day after the founding of the People's Republic of China, the Soviet Union became the first state to establish diplomatic relations with Beijing and to sever ties with the Nationalist government.[1] The response to this event differed conspicuously in the two countries. Chairman Mao Zedong heralded Soviet recognition and personally rewrote routine documents concerning Beijing's relationship with the leading socialist state.[2] The Soviet government, however, failed to send even a congratulatory message to the Chinese leaders, and reportedly Mao and his colleagues were deeply offended. This lapse was more than a gaffe in protocol. It symbolized Stalin's continuing ambivalence about the new Chinese state and his misgivings about the future of Sino-Soviet relations.[3]

We open this chapter with an analysis of the reasons for that ambivalence and its relevance to the Mao-Stalin deliberations that began in December. We argue that concerns about the United States, not China in itself, heightened Stalin's uneasiness about his new ally in the months after his meetings with Liu Shaoqi and determined his initial attitude toward the negotiations that ended with the Sino-Soviet alliance of February 14, 1950. When interpreted by the Soviet representative I. V. Kovalev to Stalin, Chinese actions toward the West and toward Soviet interests in China added to these concerns and helped generate a mood of tension on the eve of Mao's departure for Moscow.

Stalin's Anxieties and Mao's Actions

On September 25, a week before the official announcement of the People's Republic, the Soviet news agency TASS broadcast that the Soviet Union had "the atomic weapon at its disposal."[4] The first Soviet fission bomb had been tested on August 29. Although the Kremlin's official organs welcomed the test and expressed satisfaction that the U.S. nuclear monopoly had been broken, Stalin's worries about Soviet security appear to have become deeper than ever.

As we have remarked, Stalin's fears of encirclement and of U.S. forward-deployed forces had already been magnified by the formation of the North Atlantic Treaty Organization earlier in 1949. He realized that, temporarily at least, the nation's nuclear capability had put it at greater risk of an American preemptive strike at a time when it lacked the means to launch a retaliatory blow against the continental United States.[5] Despite all the progress in reaching understandings with the Chinese Communists during the past year, Stalin's attention stayed fastened on the shifting security equation with his chief rival.

This is not to say that he in any way dismissed the significance of the Chinese or was turning his back on the previous agreements with them. With the Liu visit behind them, the Soviets had indeed begun to promulgate the concept of a partnership with Mao's China. In November, for example, the Politburo member G. M. Malenkov declared that the victory of the Chinese revolution had upset the plans of the United States "to turn China into a crucial component of [its] encirclement of the Soviet Union."[6] Soviet newspapers signaled China's position as a ranking ally by naming it first on their list of countries that had sent Moscow congratulations on the thirty-second anniversary of the Russian October Revolution (November 7).[7]

Nevertheless, behind the headlines and the speeches lay Stalin's lingering doubts about China's proper place in the new nuclear-strategic context. Indirect evidence for these doubts can be found in the Soviet attitude toward the formation of the German Democratic Republic (GDR) the week after the proclamation of the PRC. Because Moscow held total sway over East Germany and could count on its unqualified contribution to the Soviet Union's defense, the Soviet press treated the founding of the GDR as the most notable event in the postwar era.[8] Stalin sent the satellite German state a personal telegram of congratulations, something he had studiously avoided with the People's Republic of China.[9]

Stalin's concerns about Beijing's possible relations with the West and about the future course of Chinese foreign policy in general may have been partially responsible for his suspicions of Mao. Kovalev and others were still feeding Stalin's fears that the Chinese might normalize their ties with the West and as a consequence undermine his counterencirclement strategy and the possibility of effective security cooperation. His mind could hardly have been put to rest, for example, by what Kovalev told him in a report filed on the eve of Mao's arrival in the Soviet capital. Despite Stalin's advice about avoiding political contacts with the West, Kovalev ventured, the

Chinese leaders still hoped to establish diplomatic relations with the United States and Great Britain soon. Indeed, they had already made some anticipatory moves in this direction, he alleged. Zhou Enlai, for example, had opposed sending Soviet specialists to Tianjin and Shanghai lest their presence be seen as threatening to American and British interests there. Similarly, Liu Shaoqi and Li Lisan had opposed inviting delegates from Japan, India, and other countries "dependent upon the Anglo-American bloc" to the upcoming Asian trade union conference in Beijing so as not to imperil the normalization of relations with the United States and Britain.[10] Although Kovalev explicitly laid the blame for such moves to the influence of "capitalist elements" inside China, he strongly hinted that Mao himself was at fault.

Throughout these early months of the People's Republic, Kovalev stressed Mao's quest for independence. When, after Liu's visit, it seemed clear to Kovalev that the Chinese, gratified as they were by Stalin's positive appraisal of their revolutionary experience and strategic role, were going to ignore his proposal to create a union of Asian Communist parties, the Soviet representative used the occasion of the conference of Asian trade unions to make his point.[11] At the opening day of this meeting, November 21, Liu Shaoqi delivered a speech in which he argued that the Chinese revolutionary history of armed struggle and of encirclement of the cities by the countryside applied more generally to Asia.[12] Kovalev, who had received a text of the speech some 15 days in advance, had sent it in code to Moscow, along with his own condemnation of Liu's theme as clear evidence of the Chinese Communists' desire for hegemony in the region.

Since Moscow did not respond to this cable, the Soviet representative then took it on himself to criticize Liu openly at the conference itself. When Stalin heard of this, he fired off a message to Kovalev repudiating the delegate's remarks.[13] The matter was also discussed at a special meeting attended by Mao where the Soviet delegate confessed his error. Mao then sent word to Stalin requesting that the man be pardoned. In his unpublished memoirs, Kovalev charges Stalin with acting in this case just as he had toward Gao Gang during Liu's visit in the summer—ready to sacrifice a trusted confederate in the name of preserving Mao's loyalty.[14]

Although Stalin may well have disagreed with Liu (and did not permit the speech to be published in *Pravda* until January 4), the Soviet leader had far more on his mind than an address to a trade union gathering. Stalin was troubled most about the confrontation with the United States. Accordingly, he endorsed Chinese military actions that were consistent with Soviet interests but would not provoke a hostile U.S. response. We have seen this dualism in his handling of Xinjiang during the Liu visit. In the same vein, he was quite forthcoming in sanctioning the Communist seizure of Tibet because the Indian government (which had influence in Tibet and opposed its seizure by the PLA) was deemed to be reactionary and the likelihood of a direct American involvement there seemed remote.[15]

By contrast, Stalin was flatly against a PLA invasion of Taiwan, a position that he had made crystal clear to Liu in July. Despite Stalin's warnings, Mao had proceeded with his plans. That very month, he had ordered the Third Field Army to prepare for landing operations on the island and had declared that the "Taiwan issue ought to be settled during the summer of 1950."[16] The next month, he gave his senior naval officers the "assignment to liberate Taiwan."[17]

In Mao's mind, Quemoy (Jinmen), the Nationalists' stronghold off the Fujian coast, had to be taken first, and the PLA's disastrous attempt to land on that island at the end of October 1949 demonstrated the folly of an amphibious assault without Soviet military help.[18] But this debacle did not weaken Mao's resolve to occupy Taiwan. It was merely a setback, to be studied as an object lesson in preparing for a subsequent invasion attempt.[19] Using conclusions drawn from the Quemoy fiasco, Mao delayed the planned Taiwan operation and gave highest priority to the buildup of the navy and air force.[20] That buildup, he knew, depended on a massive infusion of Soviet economic and military aid, a factor that might have given Stalin a potential veto over the operation. But Mao was not to be deterred. Intense preparations for the landing progressed, and it was assumed in the West that the attack would probably come in the spring of 1950.[21]

Moreover, Stalin could not be sure that once Mao had consolidated his rule over a unified nation, he would honor those provisions of the 1945 Sino-Soviet treaty that the Soviet leader considered essential to his nation's defense. Once more, Stalin used not-so-subtle indirection to make his point. He did so right away by announcing the appointment of N. V. Roshchin, the man who had been Moscow's ambassador to China during the last years of Chiang's regime, as his first envoy to the PRC. Mao was furious, but he got the point.[22] At the same time, the Soviet press intimated that the territorial arrangements reached with Chiang were final and could not be renegotiated.[23]

Mao's immediate priorities differed markedly from Moscow's. The Chinese leader urgently needed Soviet economic assistance to revive the economy so badly damaged by the long years of warfare. He also needed the umbrella of a military alliance with Moscow that could deter foreign interference and aggression as the PLA concentrated on suppressing the surviving pockets of internal resistance and on achieving national unification.[24]

Mao understood when he formulated the leaning-to-one-side policy that Stalin would not meet these needs without some kind of quid pro quo. During the first months after the founding of the PRC, he appears to have anticipated the range of compromises that would probably be required. One Chinese author quotes people who were close to the Chairman as saying: "In 1949, when [China] was operating under the condition of a tight blockade by world capitalism and when [Mao] had no other choice but to go to Moscow, he had to make many concessions against his will in order to achieve the security of the long northern border, to get guarantees of support for China's confrontation with the United States and Japan, and to get credits of $60 million a year."[25]

As noted, Moscow had helped the Chinese Communists to extend their rule to Xinjiang after Stalin had become convinced that Xinjiang constituted a strategic region of common interest in case of a "new war with imperialists." As a result, the Soviet Union's influence in Xinjiang was considerably diminished, but Mao knew that he would have to modify his own bid for total sovereignty there as well. In Manchuria, the regional leader (and senior Politburo member) Gao Gang continued to flaunt his pro-Soviet allegiance, and for the time being, Mao would not, or could not, do much about it.[26]

Mao's sensitivities about his status vis-à-vis Stalin were also beginning to surface. Mao had been informed that Gao Gang had ordered portraits of Stalin to be displayed throughout Manchuria but that Mao's were nowhere to be seen. In September, Mao summoned Gao to Beijing, and at an emergency Politburo meeting devoted to the hanging of portraits, Liu Shaoqi and Zhou Enlai accused Gao Gang of shaming China and reminded him of his treasonous proposal in July to make Manchuria a Soviet republic. The Politburo thereupon passed a resolution that Stalin's portraits should be taken down except at Soviet garrisons, units where Soviet specialists were working, and other specially designated places. When Kovalev told Stalin of the Politburo's action, the Soviet leader again backed Mao.[27]

All the same, it was obvious to the Chinese that Stalin would not budge on issues critically affecting Soviet national interests. The independence of Outer Mongolia was one of those issues.[28] Above all, Mao, having closely studied Stalin's security views, appreciated that he would have to be extremely cautious in developing any closer, let alone independent, ties with the West.[29] Mao knew his limits and adjusted his preferred policies in preparation for the concrete concessions he knew he would have to make in his deliberations with Stalin.

Getting Ready

So it was that during the first weeks after the PRC was established, Mao Zedong adopted a course of action aimed at demonstrating his allegiance to Stalin and his willingness to comply with the paramount Soviet demands. He wanted most of all not to spoil the atmosphere for the coming summit and to buy time for working out his negotiating tactics without adding to Stalin's anxieties or his demands. At the same time, the Chairman realized that he had to disabuse Stalin of any notion that China could be treated as a Soviet satellite. As delicate as the situation was, he had to exploit every opportunity to demonstrate his independence and his adeptness.

Mao had a chance to prove his balancing skills soon enough. On October 16, he established diplomatic relations with the Mongolian People's Republic (Outer Mongolia), making good Liu's promise three months before. This move infuriated many Chinese as a "sellout of national interests" but was a step patently taken to appease Stalin.[30] Yet in a speech three weeks later saluting the Russians on the anniversary of their October Revolution, he took care to stress the uniqueness of China's conditions and strongly implied that the PRC would not be totally subservient to the Kremlin and its policies.[31] Mao was testing the tactics of political tightrope walking that he would have to employ during his coming showdown with Stalin.

Appeasing Stalin was only one test of Mao's political balancing skills. He also had to tread a tightrope domestically, both within the Party and outside it. In November, Mao briefed the leading members of the left wing of the Nationalist Party, the Democratic League, and other non-Communist parties on his planned trip and asked for their opinions on it. Their replies were harsh and negative. Some critics denounced the visit as a violation of Chinese tradition: the Chinese emperor never traveled to meet the barbarians; he received them and their tribute in the imperial court. Others mentioned their concern that the trip would surely jeopardize relations with the West and any prospects for Western economic aid.[32] We will see his response to these critics as his tactics developed for the talks and in his later actions in Moscow.

It was a pro forma gesture, in any case, for by then the preparations for the visit were well in hand. In October, Mao had appointed a group of experts to assemble background materials and analyses for the trip and assigned Premier Zhou Enlai to work personally with him in supervising the group.[33] A more immediate concern was the imminent departure of

Ambassador Wang Jiaxiang, and the instructions given to Wang graphically illustrate how the plans for the negotiations were evolving.[34]

In a letter to Stalin on the day Wang set out, October 20, Mao pointed out that Wang would serve concurrently as ambassador to Moscow and as the PRC vice–foreign minister in charge of "day-to-day matters in the diplomatic relations with the new democratic countries of Eastern Europe."[35] What Mao was trying to convey to Stalin was his willingness to coordinate Beijing's East European policies with Soviet actions and objectives toward the West. This move was obviously intended to please the Soviet leader, who had earlier denied Liu's request for China to enter the European Cominform. As the Chinese saw it, Stalin had signaled his wariness of any potential competitor for influence in Europe, and they would honor his wishes.

Mao also noted that Wang would wear still another hat: as the representative of the CCP Central Committee he would provide liaison to the Soviet Communist Party's Central Committee. By this act, Mao indicated his intention to treat Party-to-Party relations from the point of view of China's state interests and tried to show that he would not allow petty dogma or Cominform edicts to dominate the Beijing-Moscow agenda. What he was proposing differed sharply from the Soviet practice toward China: Ambassador Roshchin represented the state, and Kovalev represented the Party, with Kovalev being absolutely dominant. These were subtle indicators, to be sure, but such communications lay bare the character of Mao's delicate machinations and his confidence that his message was getting through.

In November, the CCP Politburo met to settle the basic approach to the forthcoming meetings with Stalin. It agreed on three central points.[36] First, the overriding aim would be to "negotiate a treaty," indicating a firm resolve to do away with the humiliating Sino-Soviet treaty of 1945. Second, Mao would set out the replacement treaty in broad outline, but Zhou Enlai, the premier and foreign minister, would negotiate the details.[37] Mao knew quite well that he would be pressed to cut deals in Moscow, and that by making Zhou responsible for the concrete negotiations (and for signing the final accord), he could later hold that he personally had not compromised on principle. Mao assumed that later historians in China would get the point: when the prime minister, not the emperor, signed a potentially damaging treaty, imperial principles and face remained inviolate. Finally, the Politburo decided that the official pretext for Mao's visit would be to attend the celebrations for Stalin's seventieth birthday, and that after the celebrations, the Chairman would simply stay on "for a rest." By this ruse,

Mao would have a face-saving way to depart gracefully if the plans for a renegotiated treaty fell through.[38]

Mao realized that the composition of the delegation could also communicate his objectives for the visit. Accordingly, he decided that only a small group of personal aides would accompany him.[39] On cue, the Kremlin interpreted Mao's decision not to include experts as showing his resolve to discuss only general principles with Stalin, at least at the outset. Kovalev believed that Mao was attempting to restrict the number of eyewitnesses in case things went wrong.[40]

The Politburo then discussed the exact schedule for Mao's visit. It decided that the trip should last three months. Meetings with Stalin would take one month, after which Mao would travel for a month in Romania, Czechoslovakia, and Poland. The third month would be one of rest and recuperation in the Black Sea resort of Sochi. Kovalev reported the proposed schedule to Moscow, which presumably approved the itinerary. In any case, Mao assumed this would be his schedule when he departed Beijing; as it turned out, the East European and Sochi visits were scrubbed.

Meanwhile, Kovalev was keeping Stalin fully informed, and his dispatches were helping to guide preparations for the itinerary in Moscow. Since Mao had told him that his purpose in going to Moscow was to conclude a new Sino-Soviet treaty, he reported, the Chinese expected Stalin to put this matter high on the agenda.

The various tactics Mao employed before his departure unmistakably show that he was aware of his position of weakness in bargaining with Stalin and was making no effort to mask it. He communicated that weakness in an October cable to Stalin somewhat desperately asking for medical help to halt an epidemic of plague in the North and in later requests for loans.[41] This position was a familiar one for Mao, who in the years of combat had repeatedly fought against far stronger foes: in politics as in war, his was the art of reaching temporary and partial accommodations with a superior opponent for the sake of the long term. He had long preached the merits of concentrating forces in order to strike at the weakest point in an adversary's armor and of seizing the initiative under the most adverse circumstances.[42]

The Chinese soon began to put their tactical tenets into practice. On November 9, the Central Committee sent a cable to Wang Jiaxiang advising him that Kovalev had been asked to inform Stalin that Mao Zedong could depart for Moscow in early December, and that it awaited Stalin's decision on Mao's proposal to have Zhou Enlai come to Moscow later.[43] In this way, Mao was baiting a small trap for the Soviet leader, for the gist of the request for Zhou's follow-up trip was that the second part of the Chinese visit would be devoted to more concrete deliberations. Since Stalin had already indicated to Liu Shaoqi that he would never again impose his will on his Chinese comrades, Mao could be quite certain that he would accede to their wishes in so seemingly trivial a matter as the timing of Zhou's arrival in Moscow.[44] As Mao anticipated, Stalin agreed that he could come without Zhou.[45] Only later, as we shall see, did Stalin understand the full implications of the Chinese request and his acceptance of it.

Stage One: Principles, Secrets, and the Home Audience

On the cold and bright morning of December 6, with all the preparations completed and the gifts for Stalin's birthday celebration on board, Mao departed Beijing by train.[46] Mao's eldest son, Anying, and Luo Ruiqing and Li Kenong (the heads of the security and intelligence agencies, respectively) accompanied him to the Soviet border.[47] According to one eyewitness, Mao was apprehensive about being received with appropriate honors in the Soviet capital but was worried above all about his ability to carry out the Central Committee's sweeping political and economic agenda.[48]

Concerns about his personal comfort and security exaggerated Mao's nervousness even as he passed the time smoking and playing mah-jongg.[49] Within China, Mao traveled in an armored railcar captured from Chiang Kai-shek. Designed for weather in South China, it had an inadequate heating system, and throughout this leg of the journey, Mao suffered from the cold. Safety was even more on his mind. He ordered the PLA to protect his route through China, and sentries were posted every hundred meters along the rail line.[50] The soldiers arrested a man "with a pack of explosives" near the Tianjin railway station, but Chinese officials quickly downplayed the incident. Soviet advisers were told that the suspect was only a peasant carrying firecrackers.[51]

When the special train arrived in Shenyang, the largest city in the Northeast, Mao unexpectedly toured the city. He was more interested in seeing how many of his portraits were in evidence than in sightseeing. He quickly discovered that Gao Gang had not complied with the Politburo directive: Stalin's face was everywhere, Mao's far less so. Returning to the train, Mao ordered that the baggage car carrying gifts for Stalin from Gao and Lin Biao be decoupled, and the gifts returned to them. The delegation's gifts represented all of China, he explained, remarking that as he understood it, the Northeast was still part of the country.[52] By having to assert his authority vis-à-vis Stalin on his home ground, he was reminded of the pervasiveness of the Kremlin's influence in the PRC and the difficult task that lay ahead in the Soviet Union.

Leaving the discomfort of his car at the border, Mao boarded a Soviet train for Moscow. On his arrival at Yaroslavl Railway Station at noon on December 16, he was met by two members of the Politburo, V. M. Molotov and Nikolai Bulganin.[53] But this moment of high drama foreshadowed the tensions that would plague the mission. The Chinese had prepared an elaborate luncheon of greeting for the Soviet reception party. The Chairman personally placed the plates of delicacies on the banquet table in his railcar. When Molotov and Bulganin entered the car, Mao invited them to sit and enjoy a small cup of liquor. Molotov refused on the grounds of protocol, ignored the elaborate table setting, and marched out with Bulganin. After the welcoming ceremony on the platform, Mao several times asked the two Soviet leaders to accompany him to the residence where he was to stay but received the same rebuff.[54]

Chinese sources simply note that the welcoming ceremony was curtailed. Because of the cold weather, the Soviets asked Mao to give them a copy of his arrival speech for publication and not to deliver it at the station.[55] There is no doubt that the reception itself was very cold.

Mao's text began by praising the Soviet leadership for abolishing "the unequal treaties of the imperialist Russian period" and for its help to the Chinese revolution. He did not mention the Sino-Soviet treaty of 1945, leaving unstated his attitude toward the accords reached in the Nationalist period. He then spoke about strengthening relations between the two countries and clearly implied that China wanted to be treated as an equal, a point especially noted by the American ambassador in Moscow.[56]

His intentions partially declared but not spoken, Mao then rode by limousine from the railway station to his dacha in the suburbs of Moscow. He was told to rest before having his first meeting with Stalin at six o'clock that evening. Mao welcomed the chance to relax after the ten-day train ride and to contemplate his coming introduction to the Soviet leader. He believed that this first meeting would define the direction and contents of all their subsequent conversations and negotiations.[57]

Then it was off to the Kremlin and Stalin's embrace. We have several Soviet and Chinese accounts of the meeting, but we note that the documents emerging from the official Soviet-era archives tell a different story from the one recalled by the Chinese. The essential difference is that the Chinese emphasize Mao's deviousness and tactical astuteness, whereas the Soviet archival documents stress Mao's directness and the businesslike conversation between the two leaders. Despite the vividness of the Chinese account that follows, for example, the Soviet minutes of the first Mao-Stalin encounter show that Mao began by stating his goal of replacing the 1945 treaty with a new one and that Stalin immediately refused, pointing out that such an action might jeopardize the basic Yalta understandings.

According to the Chinese version, right after the two leaders exchanged greetings, Mao began by telling Stalin, "For a long time I was mistreated and pushed aside and had nowhere to complain. . . ." Although Mao was plainly fishing for an apology for past insults (like the one Stalin had made to Liu Shaoqi), Stalin cut him short. He quipped that victors are never blamed and immediately changed the subject.[58] For Stalin, apologizing to the Chinese Communist Party during Liu's visit five months before was a far different matter from apologizing to Mao himself.

Mao restarted the dialogue with a detailed description of the outstanding features of the Chinese revolution, and Stalin responded by congratulating him for the Party's hard-won victory. The pleasantries out of the way, the Soviet leader asked the Chinese: "You have come from afar, and it is not good for you to return empty-handed. . . . What should we do now? Do you have any ideas or wishes?" Mao answered, "We have come here this time to complete a certain task. A certain thing has to be done, and it must be both beautiful and tasty." Stalin looked absolutely nonplused.

Sure that the obviously bewildered Soviet leader did not grasp the meaning of Mao's words in Russian translation, Shi Zhe, Mao's secretary and interpreter, tried to elaborate on them: "Beautiful means of good shape and imposing; tasty means pleasant and substantial in content." Mao thought for a moment and said, "What is called beautiful is something beautiful in the eyes of the people of the world; what is called tasty is something practical in content."[59] Still mystified, Stalin tried to fathom what was really on Mao's mind. Mao answered somewhat obliquely that he would like to send for Zhou Enlai, his premier and foreign minister, an obvious reference to his interest in a new treaty.[60] Now pretending to wonder what Mao really wanted, Stalin said: "If we cannot establish what we must complete, why call for Zhou Enlai?"

Stalin wanted to break through the verbal haze and put the issue plainly. He could hardly affect to be unaware of the Chinese intention to renegotiate the treaty: Mao knew that Liu Shaoqi had told him as much, after all, and perhaps knew too, that Kovalev, on the eve of Mao's departure, had reminded Stalin that this was Mao's primary goal. It seems clear that Stalin was signaling his desire to have Mao personally sign a new treaty with him, and that Mao was determined to avoid signing the potentially damaging document. At any rate, Mao pled the case for Zhou to come by saying that since Stalin was the head of the Council of Ministers and he was not, they were not of equal rank. Interpreting this remark as an insult, Stalin saved his revenge for the banquet celebrating the treaty in February, where in response to a request for "instructions" by the visiting Vietnamese revolutionary Ho Chi Minh, he said within Mao's hearing, "How can you ask for my instructions? I am the chairman of the Council of Ministers, and you are the chairman of the state. Your rank is higher than mine; I have to ask for your instructions."[61]

In the awkwardness of the moment at the first meeting, several interpretations of what was happening were imaginable, though somewhat strained. Shi Zhe recalls thinking that Stalin wanted a treaty all right, but one signed by him and Mao; yet he did not want to pressure Mao because of the legacy of Soviet miscalculations concerning the Chinese revolution and Mao in particular. He himself grasped Stalin's intent, but "as for Chairman Mao, he had either failed to understand Stalin's delicate hints or did not want to be the one to sign the treaty."[62]

Zhu Zhongli, the wife of Ambassador Wang Jiaxiang, had a contrary impression of the moment. She writes that, "because the question was not studied and prepared in advance, the Soviet side for a period of time did not understand [Mao's] intentions."[63] The diplomat Wu Xiuquan, who participated in the subsequent treaty negotiations, simply concluded that Mao did not want to show his hand prematurely.[64] Given the many communications via Kovalev, this conclusion seems somewhat farfetched.

While all these memoirs contain elements of truth about the befuddlement of this opening round, Liu Xiao, later the ambassador to the Soviet Union, probably comes closest to sensing what was really at stake this first evening. He remarks that in the course of the conversation, Stalin made it abundantly clear that he was unwilling to alter the Soviet sphere of influence defined at Yalta.[65] Mao later stressed that Stalin had not wanted to conclude a new treaty and did so only after two months of hard bargaining.[66] Obviously, the Soviet leader would not have wanted to write a document that jeopardized his basic strategic and security interests or the gains won via the treaty of 1945. He was not about to refer explicitly to the possibility of a new treaty until Mao did, which would put the Chinese in the position of suppliants.

Could it be that what Stalin really wanted was to personally conclude and sign a treaty with China? Putting his name to such a document would have given it extraordinary significance. Previously, he had signed only the most momentous international documents, such as the Yalta accords with Roosevelt and Churchill, and his signature on a treaty with China would have elevated the Sino-Soviet relationship above all other foreign policy ties. If Stalin did hope to sign the accord with China himself, we can imagine how infuriated he would have been by Mao's obvious unwillingness to state forthrightly that he was prepared to go along. In any case, Stalin must have been angered now that he saw how difficult it would be to deal with Mao and understood that he had been trapped into a two-stage negotiation by accepting the Chinese proposal to leave Zhou Enlai at home. Consequently, the first meeting between Stalin and Mao ended in an uneasy and somewhat tense stalemate. The war of nerves between the two overweening egos had begun.

After this initial exchange, Stalin, probably disappointed and impatient, phoned Mao and asked him to clarify his intentions but again received only an elusive reply.[67] For the next five days, they did not meet; until December 21, Stalin's birthday, the two leaders marked time and tried to figure out what to do next.

Mao was not left entirely to his own devices, though, for Molotov, Bulganin, Mikoyan, and other important Soviets did go to his dacha on the first few days. But the conversations were brief and formal. Mao was given no chance to engage them in a discussion of the fundamental bilateral issues—problems of theory, global strategy, and international Communist policy—on which he had so studiously prepared before leaving Beijing. The Chinese recall that Molotov had little interest in hearing Mao's views and just kept nodding without comment.[68]

Stalin was naturally briefed on these visits, and in at least one case, Molotov passed on his appraisal of Mao. He remembers telling Stalin that Mao "was a clever man, a peasant leader, something like the Chinese Pugachev [a famous Russian peasant revolutionary]. Of course, he is far from being Marxist—he confessed to me that he had never read *Das Kapital* by Marx." Still, Molotov recommended that Stalin meet with Mao soon.[69] Kovalev, too, told Stalin about Mao's grievances and advised an early meeting with him. Stalin said, "Many foreign guests have come to us [for the birthday celebration]. We must not treat Comrade Mao differently from them."[70]

On December 19, Mao cabled Liu Shaoqi (who was in charge of Party and state affairs while Mao was in Moscow) and Zhou Enlai to say that "everything is all right with us here; the last few days we have been resting."[71] In fact, by then his "rest" was complete isolation. As Nikita Khrushchev recalls, "Since Stalin neither saw Mao nor ordered anyone else to entertain him, no one dared go see him."[72] It was perhaps during this period that Mao began to perceive the visit as a zero-sum contest and geared himself for combat.[73] This change was manifested in the tit-for-tat game he then tried to play with Stalin. On one occasion, for example, he refused to meet Soviet Ambassador Roshchin who, evidently on instructions from Stalin, had asked for an audience "in order to discuss matters relating to the Japanese Communist Party."[74] This refusal was a dangerous step, for

Stalin was giving ever more serious attention to Japan and eventually would link developments there to the treaty itself.*

Despite the cool reception, Mao continued to find a few pluses in his situation. Well informed about the Western commentaries on his visit, the Chinese leader capitalized on the widespread belief that a Sino-Soviet treaty was a foregone conclusion in order to strengthen his hand in his relations with key non-Communist countries. Soon after arriving in Moscow, he cabled Zhou concerning the conditions on which the PRC would establish relations with Burma and in broader terms exposed his attitude toward relations with all non-Communist countries. Mao stressed that China, linked to Soviet power, should be able to establish diplomatic relations with those states from a position of strength, and that from now on, it would only recognize countries that would first break their diplomatic ties with the Nationalists and send special delegations to Beijing for talks. Official relations would be established only if China deemed the results of those talks satisfactory.[75]

Having achieved no tangible results after a full four days in Moscow, Mao concluded that the time had come to end the fencing, and that he would have to be the first to give way. He would have to tell Stalin exactly what he wanted.[76] On December 20, Mao invited Kovalev to his dacha for this purpose, and he got right to the point.[77] He laid out two approaches to the talks: a general discussion leading to a treaty or a general discussion with no treaty.† Under the first course, the two leaders would deal with

---

*By this time, U.S. diplomatic preparations for a separate peace treaty with Japan were well under way, and the American "reverse course" policy was emasculating many of the occupation reforms for that nation. It was no secret that the treaty, which was completed in 1951, would be accompanied by an arrangement to ensure America's continued use of military bases in Japan and would open the way for the development of Japanese defense forces. On Jan. 6, the *Cominform Bulletin* published a directive for the Japanese Communist Party to shift tactics and resort to violent means against the U.S. defense proposals. The literature on the U.S. "reverse course" policy is extensive, and scholars differ sharply on what was involved. See, for example, Kolko and Kolko, *Limits of Power*, Chap. 19; Reischauer, *United States and Japan*, Chaps. 11–13; Schaller, *American Occupation*, Chaps. 7, 9, 10; Schonberger, "Cold War"; and Schonberger, "Japan Lobby." For a discussion of Moscow's directive to the Japanese Communist Party, see Shulman, *Stalin's Foreign Policy*, pp. 142–43; and Kennan, *Memoirs*, pp. 44–45.

†A knowledgeable Chinese specialist has presented evidence that the Kremlin may also have proposed two alternative ways to conduct the talks, though he does not date the proposal. He writes, "The Soviet Union proposed two options. The first was that the Soviet Union would withdraw its forces from [China's] Northeast [Manchuria], and the old treaty would be preserved. The other was that a new treaty would be signed but the rights of the Soviet Union in the Northeast would be temporarily preserved. At this time, Chairman Mao stated that he preferred the second option, not the first." Rong Zhi, "On Postwar Soviet Policies," p. 103. If this proposal came before Mao's meeting with Kovalev, the Chairman was bound to have concluded that the Soviet Union was

outstanding bilateral issues and come to an agreement on a new alliance treaty and a loan accord. This would require bringing Zhou to Moscow to negotiate and sign the actual documents. Mao added that the establishment of diplomatic relations with Burma, which was still very much on his mind, should be on the agenda, since this would be a model for all future relations between the PRC and nonsocialist nations. If the Soviets preferred the second course, the same issues would be covered but no agreements would be signed. Zhou would not come to Moscow, though he might make a trip eventually.

In presenting his alternatives, Mao's demeanor was tough and resentful. He demanded to meet Stalin on December 23 or 24. He hinted that he was irate at his treatment thus far. He said that he wanted "to visit and have talks" with Soviet Politburo members and to travel to Stalingrad and Leningrad. Clearly, the Chinese leader had little confidence at this time that he could accomplish his chief mission: achieving a new type of alliance with Moscow.

The atmosphere seemed to improve somewhat on the 21st, Stalin's birthday. The presence at the birthday celebration of the victorious leader of the world's most populous nation could only enhance Stalin's standing as head of the international Communist movement and one of the most powerful rulers in the world. Moreover, from the Soviets' point of view, the solemnities could be expected to impress Mao on the eve of their working meetings and deepen his respect for Stalin.[78] The Kremlin leader fully understood that such gains from Mao's presence depended on convincing the world that his relations with Mao were excellent.[79] Perhaps for this reason, Stalin himself supervised the detailed preparations for his birthday jubilee. He specially arranged for Mao to sit at his right hand, the most prestigious place on the reviewing stand, and called on him to deliver the first speech by a foreign guest.[80]

Mao reveled in these honors and played his lead part like a veteran. His speech, he believed, was well received, and with obvious pride he cabled Beijing, "Three times everybody stood up and applauded for a long time."[81] Nonetheless, Mao was still apparently feeling put upon. Seated between Stalin and the Hungarian Communist leader, who tried to engage him in conversation, the Chairman was gloomy and unresponsive.[82]

Although Mao's triumphant appearance may have salved his wounded ego to a degree, there was the embarrassing fact that he no longer had a face-saving pretext for extending his stay in Moscow. His status with Stalin

---

intent on preserving as many of the gains acquired under the 1945 treaty as possible. On the other hand, it would have indicated that Stalin was willing to discuss replacing the old treaty.

was becoming more delicate by the day as uncertainties about a future treaty persisted. Without a resolution of the treaty question, Mao's frustrations increased.

Revealingly, the very next day he cabled the Central Committee to say that China should prepare for trade with other socialist countries, as well as "Britain, Japan, the United States, India, and other states [that] are already doing business with us or will begin to do so pretty soon," even though the Soviet Union, "of course," still occupied the first place in China's foreign trade. He instructed his colleagues that "when preparing the trade agreement with the Soviet Union, you should proceed from a point of view that takes into account the whole situation."[83] Although Mao had long expressed a desire to diversify China's foreign trade, he now appeared to be saying that the scale of economic cooperation with Moscow would depend in the final analysis on the outcome of political agreements with it. For the moment, he was unsure what agreements, if any, would result from the Moscow trip, and he thus stressed the likely need to attract other trading partners.

Immediately after reporting Mao's two options to Stalin and before the Soviet leader could respond, Kovalev made matters worse. The Soviet representative had brought along a report that he had begun drafting some two weeks before Mao's departure for the Soviet capital and finished on the train to Moscow. That report, "Some Policies of the CCP Central Leadership and Practical Problems," was highly critical of Mao's policies, and Kovalev, well aware that it could get him into trouble, asked the diplomat N. T. Fedorenko to co-sign it. After several days, Fedorenko refused, and on December 24, barely a week after Mao's arrival in Moscow, Kovalev submitted the report on his own.[84]

The report, which we cited earlier as indicative of Soviet views on Mao's attitude toward relations with the West, had a chilling effect on Stalin. In censorious prose, Kovalev accused the Chinese leaders of deviating from Stalin's recommendations on domestic policy and committing serious mistakes. As the visitors soon learned, the report "made a very bad impression" on Stalin because it "falsely reflected the political life of our Party's top leadership." Although Mao's conversation with Kovalev on December 20 did produce an invitation to meet with Stalin at least three times over the next ten days—on December 23 or 24, 25, and 30, Kovalev's report had so poisoned the atmosphere that no immediate progress on the problem of the treaty was likely.[85]

In these three sessions, the two leaders dealt with several practical matters. For example, Stalin responded positively to Mao's petition for Soviet teachers to come to the People's University in Beijing and for Soviet help in repairing the Xiaofengman hydroelectric station.[86] Questions of Soviet economic cooperation and loans were raised but treated in a general manner.[87] Unaware at this time of the damage done by Kovalev, an impatient and increasingly ill-tempered Mao could not understand why Stalin was simply dealing with trivia. Thus, at the end of the year, the two were still locked in uneasy stalemate.

In a cable dated January 2, Mao recorded his resentment at his treatment over the previous ten days or so: "Up to now, I have had no chance to go out to speak face to face with any [of the Soviet leaders] alone."[88] Later, in November 1956, the Politburo member Peng Zhen recollected that Mao had characterized this period of his Moscow stay as a time when "he had nothing else to do except eating, sleeping, and visiting the bathroom."[89] Mao's bodyguard remembers him ranting about the Russian food.[90]

Kovalev recalls meeting a pained, peevish Mao who was shouting "Bu hao, bu hao!" (Bad, bad!) and pointing his finger toward Moscow. When asked what he meant, Mao answered that he was angry at the Kremlin, not Kovalev. Kovalev said that no one had the right to denounce "the Boss," and that he would have to make a report.[91]

To complicate the situation, rumors had begun to spread in the Western press that Mao was being mistreated and might even be under house arrest.[92] These rumors, as it turned out, helped Mao. Although they would work against him back home, they were his ally in Moscow. They cast Stalin in an unfavorable light and potentially colored whatever gains he might get from any partnership with China.

To counteract the rumors, and perhaps to put the meetings on a more productive plane as well, a conference was organized between representatives of the two sides on January 1, 1950. Both agreed that Mao Zedong had to inform the world about the true purposes of his visit to Moscow. The rumors had to be dispelled.[93] An "interview" with a correspondent from the Soviet news agency TASS was hastily arranged for January 2, and this interview proved to be a turning point in the visit.[94] As was so often true of TASS interviews, the questions and answers were framed by the interviewee alone—in this case Mao and his aides.[95] The essential message was summarized in one of Mao's "responses": "the problems of the first importance [under consideration] are the existing Sino-Soviet Treaty of Friendship and Alliance, the Soviet loan to the People's Republic of China, [and] trade and a trade pact between the two countries."[96] Here the Chinese were not just characterizing their aims for the negotiations, but implying that some critical decisions on the substance and direction of the deliberations had been reached with Moscow.

By mentioning the "existing" treaty alone as a subject of talks, however,

Mao revealed that no agreement had yet been reached on the conclusion of a new treaty, a revelation calculated to put pressure on Stalin. If in the worst case no agreement could be reached, Mao could quote his interview as early proof that Stalin wanted only to preserve the existing treaty, and that the talks had ended fruitlessly because of the unreasonable behavior of the Soviet side. Beyond that, the reference to the 1945 treaty put Stalin in an awkward position, raising a subject that neither side had in fact brought up in their talks.[97] Finally, in response to another question, Mao indicated that the length of his stay in Moscow would depend on the time needed for resolving the outstanding issues, his way of saying how difficult the talks had become. Moreover, he appeared to be protesting his isolation by stating his desire to visit several places in the Soviet Union.

The interpretations of the interview's content varied from country to country. The PRC press stressed that it proved that a new Sino-Soviet treaty would be signed soon and would enhance bilateral cooperation even more than the 1945 treaty had done.[98] This interpretation at that stage in the deliberations was pure propaganda, though it turned out to be correct. Much of the Western press cited the interview as unmistakable proof that a replacement treaty would be signed soon, but this speculation mostly reflected the belief that the terms of the treaty had been worked out in advance.[99] Some quite recent Chinese articles have called the interview a communiqué and cite it as evidence that negotiations of a new treaty had gotten under way.[100] In fact, no negotiations were being conducted at the time.

Stage Two: Setting Up the Negotiations

Although the real meaning of Mao's answers to TASS was little understood in the outside world, the message was not lost on Stalin. On January 2, immediately after being informed about the contents of the interview, he gathered the most prominent members of his leadership to consider how to respond. In the end, Stalin decided to make a positive reply to Mao's agenda, and that evening Molotov and Mikoyan went to Mao's residence to convey the news. When, in the course of the conversation, the Soviets asked Mao for his "opinions on the Sino-Soviet treaty and other matters," he was quick to answer, having fully prepared his response beforehand.[101]

Taking the same line he had taken with Kovalev on December 22, he formulated three possibilities. The first, obviously his preference, was a new treaty. This course offered several advantages: "in China, workers, peasants, intelligentsia, and the left wing of the national bourgeoisie will be greatly inspired, so that we can isolate the right wing of the national bourgeoisie; and internationally we can acquire more political capital to counter the imperialist states and to look into the treaties that were concluded by China with the imperialist powers in the past." Both parts of Mao's argumentation—domestic and international—demonstrated a nuanced understanding of Stalin's perceptions of China. By stressing that a new treaty would isolate the right wing of the national bourgeoisie, Mao implied that it would otherwise not be isolated, and that as a result, China could be driven into taking a more anti-Soviet and pro-Western direction. Since Kovalev's reports had focused on the importance of the "national bourgeoisie" in China, Stalin would have accorded considerable weight to this side of Mao's argument. By emphasizing that a new treaty would "counter the imperialist states," Mao implied that the struggle with the West might be impeded should the treaty negotiations fail.

As a second possibility, Mao proposed publishing a statement to the effect that the two states had exchanged views on a new treaty and had agreed on its essentials. All mention of details would be omitted. For the record, Mao merely stated that this choice would delay the treaty for several years, but he obviously knew that this face-saving variant would betoken weakness and be as unacceptable to the Soviet side as it was to him. It would deal a serious blow to China's leaning-to-one-side policy and might even tempt a Mao regime grown stronger in the interim to establish closer relations with the West.

Mao's third alternative was by far the worst from Stalin's point of view. It foresaw publishing a joint statement that would set out "the most important points in [our] bilateral relations, but it won't be a treaty." This choice would acknowledge failure in the negotiations and expose a serious rift in Sino-Soviet relations. It would fail even as a face-saving device. Mao could almost see Stalin grimace as he listened to this option.

The range of choices Mao was offering indicates his apprehension that the treaty negotiations might collapse or at least not be wrapped up during his visit. In the best bargaining tradition, the Chairman was communicating his readiness to leave Moscow without a deal if Stalin's demands should prove excessive.[102] Moreover, by pointedly stating that both the second and third choices would preclude bringing his prime minister to Moscow for talks, Mao made Zhou Enlai a knight in his chess game, the outcome of which would be a new, more equitable treaty or an open rift in the relationship.

Although Mao's arguments may have been intended to help Molotov and Mikoyan understand the Chinese objectives and even their logic, the two men already had a fairly good idea of his views from his conversation with Kovalev on December 22. They were thus ready to respond to anything Mao might say. Stalin, too, played political chess, and his game was as well thought out as Mao's. After the Chinese leader had finished his presentation, Molotov quickly accepted Mao's first alternative and said Zhou Enlai should leave for Moscow. Mao still wanted confirmation of the Soviet interpretation of this alternative, and he asked if Molotov truly meant that the treaty of 1945 would be replaced. Molotov said yes.

A breakthrough had been made, and the two sides quickly settled the practical details. They agreed that Zhou should come to Moscow on January 20, and that the talks should be finished by the end of the month. The question of Mao's personal itinerary in the Soviet Union was resolved in response to the Chairman's plea to visit a number of cities and localities in the Soviet Union. All this was worked out with Molotov and Mikoyan, and Mao cabled home the good news at eleven o'clock that night.

A few hours later, at 4:00 A.M., following a phone conversation with Stalin, Mao sent another cable, with more details on the new treaty.[103] Its basic clauses would be the same as in the 1945 treaty: defense against aggression by Japan and its allies and recognition of the independence of Outer Mongolia (the Mongolian People's Republic). There would be a "partial change" on the status of Lüshun and Dalian, "but the concrete contents still have to be discussed." By this time, the Chinese had concluded that Stalin's offer to Liu Shaoqi in July had been mere posturing. Stalin did not want to withdraw Soviet troops from Lüshun and would do his best to hang on to the port and the Chinese Changchun Railroad as long as he could.[104]

The last provisions, we may note, coincided with a proposal that Stalin had allegedly put forward in earlier talks with Mao. At that time, according to one reliable Chinese source, he had offered Mao the option of signing a treaty that permitted Soviet forces to stay temporarily in the Northeast.[105] Knowing from his earlier talks with Liu Shaoqi that Mao had agreed to this option, Stalin's ultimate approval of a shortening of the Soviet lease on Lüshun and Dalian from the 30 years allowed in the 1945 treaty attests to the success of Mao's tactic. But a lease of any length also posed a domestic political problem because of the demand of influential Chinese for a total revision of the existing treaty.

Mao also reported that the Soviet Union had agreed to provide China with U.S. $300 million in credits (confirming that the dollar would be used in all bilateral financial matters) over the next "few years." Mao had proposed this somewhat modest sum because "at present and for several years it will be better for us to borrow less than to borrow more." Finally, he indicated that agreements on barter trade and civil aviation would be signed.[106]

Having outlined what the two sides had agreed to in principle, Mao then concluded with a review of the arguments the Central Committee should present to the Central People's Government Council, which had to approve Zhou Enlai's visit to Moscow: "You should stress that this move [the conclusion of a new treaty] will enable the People's Republic to gain an even more favorable posture. It will press the capitalist countries to play by the rules that we ourselves will set, it will be favorable for the unconditional recognition of China by various countries, [it will lead to] the cancellation of the old treaties and the conclusion of new ones, and it also will deter the capitalist countries from reckless undertakings."

Mao was clearly using altogether different arguments to sell his colleagues on the treaty from those he had made to Molotov and Mikoyan. For the Soviets' benefit, for example, he had contended that the accord would enable China to "counter the imperialist states," but for his domestic audience he stressed quite the opposite, that the treaty would heighten China's power and enable it to establish relations with all countries, including the capitalists, as an equal. Putting the emphasis wholly on the "cancellation of the old treaties and the conclusion of new ones," Mao chose not to mention the controversial provisions of the proposed treaty or any other possible agreements.

With the basic principles worked out, Mao now shifted his attention to the forthcoming talks with Zhou Enlai. In a cable sent at 6:00 A.M. on January 5, apparently after another late-night meeting with senior Soviet officials, he informed the Central Committee that the top government and Party leaders of Xinjiang had to accompany Zhou Enlai on the trip to Moscow.[107]

From this and other instructions, it is clear that Mao wanted to demonstrate to Stalin that Beijing now effectively controlled Xinjiang and also Manchuria and would have to approve any deals concerning them. He recognized that the Soviet side was striving to expand its influence in these two regions and ordered his negotiators to make ready for hard bargaining. Not only must they be prepared to "deliver [detailed] presentations, explaining clearly our point of view," he told the Central Committee, but the committee itself should "continue investigating [the crucial problems] after Zhou Enlai's departure and report its opinions at any time." Although the Chairman realized that Zhou's team would be pressed to make some unpleasant compromises, he wanted his representatives to fight for their proposals even when the Soviets were the most unyielding. He later described the prescribed style of the negotiations as one in which, if the Soviet side "should propose a clause to which we could not agree, then we should argue; if [it] should categorically insist on this clause, then we should acquiesce."[108]

That evening (January 5), Mao sent new instructions to the Central

Committee: "Before Zhou with more than ten people departs [Beijing] or during their travel [to Moscow], it will be necessary to assemble all these people and to tell them that it is imperative to adhere to discipline, that undisciplined words and actions are prohibited, and that on every matter they must obey orders."[109]

While Mao was forced into the uncomfortable position of trying to protect himself from any backlash caused by his concessions thus far, Stalin was obviously content with his bargaining hand and with the substantial progress of the night of January 2. Thereafter, *Pravda* regularly published news on domestic developments in China in the upper right-hand corner of the first page, the most prized spot for any news story. The reasons for Stalin's unvarnished satisfaction undoubtedly mirrored the reasons for Mao's distress. The Soviet leader had made some material concessions, to be sure, but the prejudicial ones had been Mao's. Stalin was pleased, and he expressed his satisfaction in a marked change of attitude toward Mao.[110]

This satisfaction was manifested in Stalin's typical devious way. In late January, he sent Mao Kovalev's report of December 24 (as well as secret information he had received from Gao Gang), apparently in an attempt to gain the Chairman's confidence. Khrushchev simply states, "God only knows what Stalin thought he was doing. He justified it as a friendly gesture."[111] Stalin told Mao, "Kovalev wrote this [report] on his own. We did not authorize him to do so." In "explaining" Kovalev's behavior, he said, "Kovalev is a railroad engineer. He neither understands politics nor has political experience. He is entirely uninitiated in politics. If he burrows into politics, he is like a mouse caught in a pair of bellows."[112] With this action, Stalin both ended Kovalev's career and put Gao's in greater jeopardy than ever. The list of Gao's transgressions was expanding, though more than four years would pass before he was purged.

With the main business out of the way, the delegations then marked time until Zhou's group arrived on January 20, and the next phase of the Moscow summit could begin. On January 11, Mao paid a visit to the chairman of the Presidium of the Supreme Soviet to talk over arrangements for the rest of his stay as discussed with Molotov and Mikoyan. The following day, he visited the Lenin mausoleum and, on January 15–16, he made a short trip to Leningrad.[113] Mao Zedong's isolation was at an end.

Stage Three: Drawing the Line

Until the breakthrough of January 2, the two sides had concentrated almost wholly on bilateral issues, but after mid-January, they turned to international matters. By the time Zhou and his team arrived in Moscow a new element had cropped up that was to strongly influence the direction of the Sino-Soviet talks. U.S. policy toward Chiang Kai-shek's regime on the island of Taiwan had now become the object of vigorous public debate in Washington. Powerful Republican congressmen, arguing that communism had to be contained not only in Europe but all over the world, and insisting on Taiwan's strategic importance to America, were loudly demanding that the administration come to the aid of the embattled Nationalists. The administration, for its part, insisted that the United States should not fight on the side of a regime that was plainly corrupt and ineffectual, and argued that in any case Taiwan had little strategic value. This hands-off policy, one product of a bitter debate within the government, had been formalized in a top-secret National Security Council document, NSC 48/2, on December 30, and announced by President Harry Truman in a press conference on January 5. The NSC document repeated the judgment of the Joint Chiefs of Staff that "the strategic importance of Formosa [Taiwan] does not justify overt military action," and Truman said bluntly, "The United States Government will not provide military aid or advice to Chinese forces on Formosa."[114]

As Mao saw it, Washington's announced policy of staying clear of the Chiang regime was an invitation to accelerate the preparations for the "liberation of Taiwan." Stalin, however, saw the same realities through a quite different lens. Any "Chinese" solution of the Taiwan problem without American interference, if linked to normalizing U.S.-PRC relations, constituted a serious danger to the agreements being transacted in Moscow. That solution could destroy the basis for China's willing acceptance of the Soviet security zone and could provide Mao with an excuse to seek a reconsideration of the most controversial sections of the proposed treaty of alliance.

Stalin's calculus was further complicated on January 6, when the British government announced its decision to establish diplomatic relations with the PRC.[115] Congressional conservatives in the United States promptly denounced the action and demanded that sanctions be imposed against London.[116] But many officials in the Department of State thought the United States should follow suit. Nonrecognition, it was argued, could only push Beijing closer to Moscow, whereas a normalization of Sino-American relations could help divide the two Communist giants.[117]

Meanwhile, the Chinese made no visible move that might have added to Stalin's suspicions. The PRC press continued to stress the primacy of the "struggle against imperialism" and the Soviet Union's leading role in it.[118] British recognition was cited as proof of ever-deepening Anglo-American contradictions and of the failure of the U.S. policy of diplomatically isolating the People's Republic.[119] It may have been a mere coincidence that Beijing began confiscating American consular property in the capital eight days after the United Kingdom's announcement, but the action would not have escaped Stalin's notice.[120] The British action undoubtedly pulled Stalin's mind in one direction, the confiscation in the other.

In any event, so far as Stalin was concerned, Chinese behavior was of less importance than Chinese intentions. Thanks to Kovalev's report of a conversation he had with Mao in early January, Stalin was more suspicious than ever of the PRC's real attitude toward the West. Mao had indicated that he wanted to admit foreign missions into China once he had concluded the treaties with Moscow: "Relying on the treaties with the Soviet Union, we could immediately begin to renegotiate and annul the unequal treaties concluded by the Chiang Kai-shek government with the imperialist states." In his report to Stalin, Kovalev added his own opinion that Mao was preoccupied with early recognition by the United States. Moreover, he said, Mao intended to force the Soviet Union to abandon its interests in China; this is what he meant by renegotiating or annulling the treaties with Chiang. Finally, Kovalev noted, Mao had failed to say anything about countries breaking with Chiang as a precondition for establishing diplomatic relations.[121]

In the circumstances, it is no wonder that soon after the acknowledged breakthrough in early January, Stalin took steps to draw his own line of division, one separating China from the West. As a result, there is good, if indirect, evidence that the Kremlin now deemed the preservation of Chiang's regime on Taiwan to be an imperative in the Soviet alliance with Mao. From January 5 on, *Pravda* began regularly publishing articles about American schemes to occupy Taiwan, about secret contacts between Washington and Taipei, and about Nationalist air raids against the mainland with U.S. support.[122] Such reports were intended to show that the American hands-off policy toward Taiwan was pure fiction.

Of greater consequence, Stalin now changed course and encouraged the PRC's plan to seize Taiwan. In a complete turnaround from 1949, when he had refused to provide air and naval cover for Mao's planned attack on Taiwan, the Soviet press firmly supported the PRC's legitimate right to seize not only Tibet but Taiwan and Hainan as well, and Moscow began to help Mao upgrade his air force.[123]

With Stalin's change of mind, China was no longer barred from using the $300 million Soviet loan for military purposes. In secret, the Chinese won Soviet consent to devote half the money to the purchase of Soviet equipment for their navy.* The Kremlin was giving tangible support for the invasion of Taiwan.[124] Stalin had little to lose in supplying this aid and much to gain if the invasion provoked the predicted U.S. military reaction. Open Soviet support for action against Taiwan, Stalin must have known, would almost certainly strengthen the position of Chiang's American sympathizers.

Stalin took an even more direct step to thwart the normalization of Beijing-Washington ties: he encouraged Mao to seize Hong Kong. Chinese sources make clear that the Soviet leader was pressing Mao to occupy Hong Kong because "there are a lot of imperialist agents in this city." In his answer, Mao not only was evasive but went so far as to disagree with Stalin on the need to seize the colony.[125] Stalin was adopting a more aggressive stance because a PLA offensive against Hong Kong would serve his central purpose.[126] It would help block the normalization of Sino-American relations. In all likelihood, the conversation about Hong Kong (not Shanghai) recalled by Khrushchev occurred sometime shortly after Britain's recognition of the PRC, which Stalin considered a possible precursor to American recognition. The offer of military support for the occupation of Taiwan stemmed from this same Soviet objective.

At one o'clock in the morning on January 7, probably immediately after the Kremlin leadership had analyzed the stories about London's recognition of Beijing, Foreign Minister A. Ia. Vyshinskii went to Mao's residence. The Soviet official proposed that China should publish a statement denouncing the legitimacy of Nationalist China's United Nations' representative and added that the Soviet Union would support China by boycotting the Security Council. Mao accepted the idea. At six o'clock that morning, he sent a cable directing the Central Committee to so inform the United Nations by telegram on January 8 or January 9, and at midnight, he followed up with his own draft of the statement.[127] After the formal notification reached Lake Success (New York) on January 8, Soviet representatives began walking out of all UN organs.[128]

Although the Soviets had begun condemning the continued Nationalist representation in the United Nations in mid-December 1949, this more active ploy of walking out directly coincided with the Soviet change of tactics following the British recognition of the PRC. Interestingly, some Western

* At the then official exchange rate of U.S. $1 = 4 rubles, the full loan would have amounted to R1,200 million. We now know that between 1950 and 1955, the duration of the loan, Soviet military deliveries to China were worth exactly R1,200 million, strongly suggesting that the entire amount was used for military support. The figures are from a document in the archives of a senior Soviet diplomat who was stationed in this period in China.

journalists who observed the Soviets' behavior during this phase concluded that Moscow in reality wanted the walkout to fail politically and the Nationalists to stay seated at the UN. One newsman calculated that a failure to oust the Nationalists would make the West the enemy of Mao's China and the USSR its only friend, putting Stalin in a position to wring additional concessions from the Chinese.[129] These observers, at least, plainly saw through the walkout to Stalin's hidden aim of drawing a sharp line between China and the West, an aim that mirrored Washington's own hope of fostering discord between Moscow and Beijing.

That hope was manifested in a speech by Secretary of State Dean Acheson at the National Press Club on January 12. This presentation, which was quickly sent on to Moscow, was carefully studied by Stalin and had a significant impact on his thinking.[130] In fact, the speech was designed to do just that. When Acheson categorically declared that the Soviet Union was acting to annex parts of China, a "process that is complete in outer Mongolia . . . [and] nearly complete in Manchuria,"[131] his intended audience was not the Americans present but disgruntled Chinese, whose passions he sought to enflame, and Stalin, whom he wanted to check. As we will later show, Acheson was close to the truth when he spotlighted Stalin's designs on Manchuria and Xinjiang, a fact that undoubtedly did enrage Stalin and perhaps even caused him to wonder about leaks in his own hierarchy.[132] To make matters worse from Stalin's perspective, Acheson appeared to reiterate the hands-off policy toward Taiwan that Truman had announced the week before.

Whether wittingly or not, Acheson had struck a raw nerve that would significantly influence the Mao-Stalin talks. For obvious reasons, Stalin wanted Mao to join him in a forceful indictment of the speech and thereby demonstrate their unbreakable unity. Mao had no choice but to agree. It was not simply that he did not want to ruin the atmosphere of the talks on the eve of Zhou's arrival. Acheson had portrayed Mao as a weak leader who allowed himself to be used as a puppet. Mao could not let stand the accusation that he was abdicating the sacred mission of national unification.

On the other hand, Acheson's confirmation of the U.S. hands-off policy came as welcome news to Mao. In December, Mao himself had anticipated this policy, though only vaguely so.[133] But an internal publication that month had concluded that a mere minority of Americans favored noninterference in Taiwan.[134] After the speech, the Chinese concluded that U.S. policy-makers would let the Communists take Taiwan and not come to the island's defense.[135] Mao had reason to believe that the hands-off policy represented a shift in American opinion. This judgment was reflected in an analysis prepared by the designated commander of the Taiwan invasion force.[136]

Stalin would have had the opposite reaction to this change in American policy and the Chinese assessment of it. Indeed, he might even have read it as proof of an emerging tacit understanding between Beijing and Washington on the "liberation" of Taiwan in exchange for the normalization of Sino-American relations. This would have been Stalin's worst nightmare come true.

We can identify several key decisions made by the two leaders immediately after Acheson's speech and, perhaps, partially as a result of it. On January 13, in a same-day reply, Mao approved Liu Shaoqi's proposal to requisition most of the foreign military barracks in Beijing, to confiscate the goods of the U.S. Economic Cooperation Administration in Shanghai, and to begin preparations for the shutdown of all the U.S. consulates.[137] Whatever the motive, Mao's firm and immediate reply, coming within hours of the Acheson speech, would have simultaneously helped quell Soviet fears of Chinese Titoism and reinforced Mao's standing as a staunch nationalist for his domestic audience.

The Americans reacted as if on cue. When Beijing confiscated the Marine Legation barracks on January 14 and ordered the Americans out, the Department of State immediately recalled all U.S. diplomatic personnel, and the American press observed that the growing strains in U.S.-China relations would introduce new obstacles to the seating of the PRC in the United Nations and American recognition of Beijing.[138] In response to this not altogether unexpected reaction, Mao hurried to damp down any discontent among intellectuals and bourgeoisie in China who feared a total break with the United States. On January 18, the day after his return from Leningrad, he instructed Liu Shaoqi to explain to "democratic figures suffering from the fear-of-the-United States illness" that the exodus of the U.S. diplomatic personnel was a favorable development and wholly in the interests of the country.[139]

Mao's dilemma was how to dispel Stalin's suspicions while still indicating his willingness to deal with the capitalist countries, though from a condition of national sovereignty and equality. In the same message, Mao told his colleagues to pay close attention to the pending discussions with the British about official recognition and to keep him fully informed during his stay in Moscow.[140]

Even as Mao was maneuvering to resolve this dilemma, Stalin was pursuing his goal of sharpening the divisions between Beijing and the West. On January 13, the day after Acheson's speech, Foreign Minister Vyshinskii had come to Mao to persuade him to redouble his efforts to gain admission to the United Nations. He suggested that Mao nominate the PRC representative to the UN, and Mao agreed.[141] Five days later, Mao sent Liu Shaoqi a draft of a cable to be sent to the UN, in which he put his demand for the expulsion of "the illegitimate delegates of the Chinese Nationalist reactionary remnant clique" in the most offensive and categorical language.[142] Given the negotiations at hand and the Soviet reaction to Acheson's accusations, Mao's problem was how to accent his stand against the United States, not how to send his own man to the United Nations. By now, Mao knew that the seating issue would not be resolved soon and could only serve as a surrogate in the tortuous tactics affecting Sino-Soviet-American relations.

On the very evening that Mao returned from Leningrad (January 17), Molotov and Vyshinskii went to his residence. After a preliminary exchange on the PRC's approach to establishing diplomatic relations with capitalist countries, Molotov proceeded to the main order of business: a proposal that the Soviet Union, China, and Mongolia issue "official statements" against the "shameless lie" of the U.S. secretary of state.[143]

Mao treated his response with extreme seriousness. He took personal charge of drafting the Chinese statement and sent a copy to Liu Shaoqi with instructions to give it "careful scrutiny" before releasing it for publication.[144] There is little doubt that he and Stalin coordinated their replies to some extent. The Chinese and Soviet denunciations of the Acheson speech were both published on January 21, for example.[145] And both covered many of the same points and even used identical quotations and data.[146] But there were also some decided differences. For instance, the two leaders had agreed to increase the impact of the statements by issuing them under the name of senior officials but had failed to settle on any specific rank.[147] As a result, the Soviets made their foreign minister their spokesman, whereas the Chinese statement, to Stalin's chagrin, was signed by the head of the PRC's News Department. Furthermore, there was a significant difference in tone: rudeness and insults, so typical of Vyshinskii, characterized the Soviet statement; the Chinese were relatively more restrained. As it turned out, American criticism of the two replies to Acheson zeroed in on Vyshinskii's statement, virtually ignoring the Chinese document.[148]

Vyshinskii's emotional language, not surprisingly, convinced many Americans that Acheson had been right on the mark. The Department of State promoted this idea with the press, keeping up a drumbeat that had begun a day after the speech, when the *New York Times*, in a detailed analysis of the Stalin-Mao talks, called attention to the rumored strains between the two leaders.[149] The writer emphasized Mao's effort to counter Stalin's schemes to control Manchuria and Xinjiang and Soviet worries concerning China's demand for economic assistance. By design, the United States was attempting to play a role, perhaps as a spoiler, in the deliberations then about to enter a new phase.

The International Context

Zhou Enlai's contingent arrived in Moscow on January 20, an event interpreted by American China watchers as a sure sign that the meetings were entering a decisive stage and as justification for moving the Department of State into high gear.[150] On January 25, the secretary of state cabled the ambassador in France, instructing him to provide information to selected journalists in Paris concerning the Moscow talks.[151] The department also seized the moment to publish "proof" of the Soviet moves to detach territories from China.[152] This proof fell far short of the facts, though State's paper grasped the essence of Stalin's strategy toward China and his plans for Xinjiang and Manchuria.

Zhou could have not been encouraged when, shortly after his arrival, he and Mao were invited to the Kremlin for a private chat with Stalin and Molotov.[153] The purpose, as it turned out, was to take the Chinese to task for breaking the agreement to have senior officials sign the critiques of the Acheson speech. Molotov, patently speaking on Stalin's instructions, accused Mao of "undermining the trust" between the two sides and said that the head of an information department could not credibly represent his government. Stalin was more conciliatory but stressed that the Chinese behavior "provided a crack that the enemy could penetrate."

Stalin's resentment was further confirmed by *Pravda*'s treatment of the Chinese statement. Undoubtedly on his say-so, the official news organ relegated it to the last page and headlined it in small type. The *Pravda* article on the Acheson speech did not even mention the Chinese rebuttal.[154] In a convoluted way, the United States had become the invisible third partner in the Stalin-Mao dialogue.

At the purely personal level, the exchange about the press release rekindled the animosity between Stalin and Mao. Mao was so enraged that he became visibly sullen and made no response. Sensing his mood, Zhou muttered a brief and guarded explanation about the Chinese statement. The chill continued as the two leaders drove together from the Kremlin to Stalin's dacha. The silence was broken only when the Chinese translator, Shi Zhe, asked Stalin if he still planned to come to Mao's residence. Stalin said yes. Shi told Mao what he had said, and Mao replied, "Swallow your words. Don't invite him." Silence settled in again for another 30 minutes. Stalin tried to retrieve the situation when the car reached the dacha. He asked the Chinese in to attend a dance, but Mao declined and left in a huff.

Although this was not the first or last time that divergent approaches to grand strategy—in this case the handling of Acheson's speech—helped to sour the personal relationship between the two leaders, the incident did alert Stalin to the potential costs of such strains and to anticipate them. He thereafter repeatedly complimented the Chinese Communists and their leaders and attempted to restore cordiality. These attempts perhaps did bear some fruit, but malice drifted close to the surface and reemerged with almost every new disagreement: besides, the Chinese knew Stalin's true attitude toward them; no amount of flattery could disguise that.

What seems to have worried Stalin most was the power of Chinese nationalism. In 1957, Mao recalled that during the Moscow talks, Stalin had frankly characterized Chinese communism as nationalistic and predicted that this nationalism would lead to dangerous results.[155] Stalin translated "nationalism" as any unwillingness of the Chinese (or any other foreigner) to conform to his wishes. It seems clear that his accusation about nationalism was made during the stalemate of the talks; that is, sometime between December 22 and January 2, before Mao had become more accommodating. After the breakthrough had been achieved, the Soviet ruler ordered the magazine *Bol'shevik* to publish Mao's articles, and formally, the order was tantamount to accepting Mao as a Marxist theorist.[156] Nevertheless, Stalin still had serious reservations. After reading Russian translations of Mao's theoretical articles, Stalin exclaimed, "What kind of Marxism is this! It is feudalism!"[157] Probably for this reason, he willingly responded to Mao's request to send the Marxist scholar P. F. Yudin to China to "edit" the Chairman's selected works.[158]

Still, Stalin was ready to accept Mao's non-Marxist and nationalist ideas so long as the Chinese willingly complied with his global strategy. Though Liu Shaoqi's visit had produced an understanding on the division of labor in the world, the modalities still had to be thought out. Beginning in January, the two leaders made it their business to do just that.

On January 4, *Pravda* published Liu's November address to the trade union meeting, in which he had hailed the Chinese strategy of revolutionary armed struggle and proclaimed that it might "become the main path toward the liberation of other people in the colonial and semicolonial countries where similar conditions exist."[159] The next day, *Pravda* openly endorsed the Chinese strategy. It was given a further seal of approval later that month, when a prominent ideologist of the Soviet Communist Party wrote that the Chinese revolution had proved that American imperialism, despite its might, could not halt the liberation struggles in Asia.[160] Many in the United States interpreted this article as a sign of Moscow's backing of these revolutions and its confidence in their victory.[161]

Where before Mao had refused to discuss issues related to Japan with Soviet Ambassador Roshchin, now the two sides examined a coordinated strategy. The Cominform *Bulletin* had published an article on January 6 exhorting the Japanese Communist Party to resist with violence the use of their soil for U.S. defense purposes. This article strongly criticized Nosaka Sanzo, who had spent the war in Yan'an and was known as a faithful supporter of Mao, for his alleged emphasis on the peaceful path to power and his assertion that U.S. forces in Japan were favorable to Japanese democratization.[162] Soon thereafter, Stalin solicited Mao's endorsement of the denunciation, and in response Mao asked Hu Qiaomu to prepare a *Renmin Ribao* editorial castigating Nosaka.

In fact, Stalin was not so subtly calling on Mao to repudiate the nationalist thrust of his own revolution, and he timed this call to coincide with the just-released Acheson speech, which had directly challenged Mao's nationalist credentials. Stalin was testing Mao's fidelity by forcing him to choose sides on a most sensitive issue and at an especially tense moment in U.S.-China relations. It therefore is quite understandable why Mao on January 14, just hours before he left for Leningrad, fired off a cable to his News Department, complaining "I still have not received the draft of the *Renmin Ribao* editorial and the resolution of the Politburo of the Japanese Communist Party. If you are inclined to wait until I can read [the editorial], then I shall only be able to respond to you by cable on [January] 17; if not, then it can be published after Comrade [Liu] Shaoqi has read it."[163] When *Renmin Ribao* printed the editorial on Nosaka (January 17), the tone of the criticism, if judged by Cominform standards, was relatively mild, and quite understandably so.[164]

Two days later, Mao informed his colleagues that he was preparing a translation of the editorial for Stalin.[165] Once Mao proved himself in this way, Stalin must have felt more relaxed on the subject of Chinese nationalism, for not long after, on January 27, the Cominform *Bulletin* published an article lauding Mao's ideas and denouncing the leadership of the Indian Communist Party, which had condemned those ideas.[166]

This small episode of the Nosaka affair exemplifies the Soviet leader's style of repeatedly testing Mao's intentions and exacting his obedience. Simultaneously, it shows the Chairman's skills in appearing to yield in such a way that Stalin, too, found it necessary to make compromises and to recognize the autonomy of his negotiating partner.

The complicated character of the Mao-Stalin relationship and its close linkage to general international developments are further illuminated by another item that moved up on the Sino-Soviet agenda—the recognition of the Democratic Republic of Vietnam. On January 15, the Ministry of Foreign Affairs of the PRC received a cable from the Vietnamese foreign ministry with a proposal to formalize their diplomatic ties. Two days later, Mao asked Liu Shaoqi to send the Vietnamese an immediate positive answer. Liu did so the next day (January 18).[167] Mao's prompt approval was motivated by several noteworthy factors such as the history of close ties between the Chinese and Vietnamese revolutionary leaders. Even as Mao was cabling Liu, Ho Chi Minh was secretly getting ready to depart for Beijing, where he was to request Chinese aid.[168]

Mao believed in revolutionary solidarity as part of his own theory of international class struggle, but he had a special interest in Ho's total victory in the Vietnamese civil war because of his own quest to complete the unfinished Chinese revolution.[169] There was after all the need to exterminate the large force of Nationalist troops concentrated on the Sino-Vietnamese border, and Mao feared they might gain logistical support from the French colonial administration.[170]

At Mao's behest, the Chinese Ministry of Foreign Affairs passed along the Vietnamese request for recognition to Moscow.[171] That request put the Kremlin on the spot because for the first time the Soviet Union had to choose between recognizing a bona fide Communist revolutionary regime and adhering to a treaty of friendship, in this case with France, patron of a government that was then engaged in a civil war with the armies of Ho Chi Minh. Stalin's desire to draw a line between Mao and the West was suddenly being matched by Mao's move to draw a line between the Soviet Union and France.

The Chinese leader was taking a big chance. At this time, France held the key to U.S. plans for building NATO and aligning West Germany solidly with the Western alliance. Even more central to Stalin, France opposed German rearmament. In January, rumors of U.S. plans for a rearmed Germany were tightly linked to bringing it into NATO, a prospect that "terrified the French." Attacking French interests in Indochina at such a pivotal moment would have struck Stalin as half-witted.[172]

Stalin faced the dilemma by pussyfooting. He did not want to be directly involved in the Vietnamese revolution, he told Mao. The Soviet Union could assist, but the heaviest burden would have to fall on China.[173] On the other hand, Stalin did not want to be left out. On January 31, almost two weeks after Beijing's recognition, the Soviet Union finally did recognize Ho Chi Minh's government, but the tone of the Soviet commentaries explaining the act was decidedly defensive.[174] The same reluctance to provide active support for Ho's revolution surfaced again when the Vietnamese leader secretly visited Moscow in February. On the 16th, at a banquet honoring the signing of the treaty of alliance with China, Ho somewhat casually asked Stalin to negotiate a similar document with him, but Stalin equivocated.[175]

The Vietnam example illustrates the kind of division of labor that began to take shape in the course of Mao's visit. Stalin would press for China's acceptance of his country's prerogatives within the Soviet-defined security framework and for the right to dictate Beijing's policies toward the West. Stalin would reciprocate by acknowledging Mao's preeminent role in Asia even when Chinese policies might clash with Soviet interests.

Stalin's willingness to accept Beijing's role in Asia, of course, was not just pure tactics. That role contributed to his strategy of deepening the divisions between his Asian comrades (especially China) and the West, a point not lost on the Western press when Washington and London recognized the Western-oriented Bao Dai government on February 7.[176] On the same day, the Department of State recommended a "strong American effort against the penetration of China southward."[177] Simultaneously, the PRC's chances of being seated in the United Nations greatly diminished.[178] Stalin was having it both ways: Asia, now ever more polarized, was becoming a main battleground in the global struggle with the West. On February 10, the U.S. Congress, reversing its previous stand, passed an aid package for Taiwan and South Korea.[179] Stalin's objective of magnifying the confrontation between Beijing and Washington was being realized.

By "drawing the line" in Asia, Stalin was carrying out his ideas on how to prepare for a third world war. Obviously, this was the most sensitive part of the Stalin-Mao talks, and we have only spotty evidence on what was said. The Soviet leader had nothing to gain by clarifying the connection between Taiwan or Korea and his larger strategic aims. During the talks, Stalin instead told Mao that a "confrontation with the United States is inevitable, but for us it would be favorable to delay its beginning. At present, war is not feasible, because we have just tested the atomic bomb, the country is exhausted, and the people of the USSR would not understand and support such a war."[180] Stalin was simply restating his consistent view. He was relating what was feasible and favorable for the Soviet Union. Yet he also had to assess the intentions of the United States and shape his strategy in response to them. It was this assessment that caused an overall shift in Soviet military strategy at about this time.

The political scientist David Holloway has revealed the dimensions of the Soviet military buildup that began toward the end of 1949 and has cited Stalin's statements in 1950 about the Soviet advantage in Europe and the opportunity for offensive military operations there in the near future. Holloway concludes that Stalin had decided that the maximum danger of an American strike would come around 1954, and that the Soviet Union might be wise to back, though not wage, a preemptive war before then.[181] Stalin's statement to Mao suggests that Stalin was leaning toward what might be called a limited preemptive conflict.

To the extent that Stalin truly expected war to erupt soon, he was becoming more disposed to loosen his strategic constraints on the Chinese and to test America's willingness to use force in Asia's "marginal" areas before it had the backup threat of a hydrogen bomb. Certain that the Soviet Union "was not ready for war" itself, Stalin could authorize more militant Chinese actions only if they would not directly involve the Soviet Army or the leading region of contention, Europe. His changing assessment of the U.S. threat and China's role in meeting it may well help explain his later decisions in the planning of the Korean War.

FOUR

End Game

On January 22, two days after his arrival in Moscow, Zhou Enlai had his first publicly announced meeting with Stalin.[1] Because the most basic and general principles of the accords had already been affirmed by the two highest leaders, Zhou asked that the two sides get started on the exact wording at once. Assenting, Stalin said that Mikoyan and Vyshinskii would negotiate the language with Zhou.[2] That same day, the Chinese delegation broke into two working groups, with Zhou heading the one assigned to write the treaty and Li Fuchun (deputy director of the powerful Finance and Economics Commission) running the group to draft the other agreements. Mao Zedong attended the Zhou-Stalin meeting but thereafter quietly distanced himself from the substantive deliberations.*

Stalin still did not know for sure which Chinese would sign the treaty of alliance, and after the meeting, he phoned Mao to get a straight answer. He wanted Mao to sign and thereby take full responsibility for the pact. Mao, as we have seen, had already handed Zhou the job of negotiating and signing the treaty, and conveyed his decision to Stalin.[3] Nevertheless, despite this tactic of putting Zhou out front, it was plain to all that Mao ran things behind the scenes. To make the point, he occasionally dropped in on the talks. A few days after his arrival, Zhou moved to Mao's residence in order to maintain uninterrupted contact with him on the progress of the formal sessions.[4]

Though the treaty talks made quick headway, the bargaining took the

---

*During the late stages in the publication of this study, the Russian Ministry of Foreign Affairs declassified the files on the treaty negotiations discussed in this chapter. The main arguments in the chapter are based principally on Chinese sources, including documents, memoirs, and interviews. The new Russian archival materials from Russia add a new dimension of understanding but do not appreciably change the general line of argument concerning the treaty. The authors will discuss the new materials in a forthcoming article.

parties past the original end-of-January timetable. On February 9, Stalin, Mao, and Zhou reviewed the developments to date and substantially agreed on the language of all the documents.[5] On February 10, Mao cabled Liu Shaoqi in Beijing, instructing him to prepare for the publication of the agreements. But even at this late hour, he could not give an exact date for the signing. It was to take four more days to thrash out the last nagging questions.

The central document signed on February 14 was formally called the Treaty of Friendship, Alliance, and Mutual Assistance.[6] In this chapter, we concentrate first on that treaty and other open documents and then deal with some of the secret accords.

Open Agreements

The negotiating process, or what we call the end game, began on January 22, when Stalin and Mao talked over the precise terms of the treaty for the first time. Mao Zedong opened the proceedings by saying that cooperative relations between the Soviet Union and China had to be formalized, and that the treaty should promote cooperation between the two states in all fields "in order to prevent the resurgence of Japanese imperialism and renewed aggression by Japan or states that would align with Japan."[7] In these introductory remarks, Mao reiterated the agreed position reached on January 2 that the treaty of 1945 should be replaced.

The target of Mao's reference to "renewed aggression" and "states that would align with Japan" was the United States. Everyone present knew this and recognized that the American connection would give the treaty global strategic significance. The emphasis on the Japanese threat reflected a long-term security consideration for China and simultaneously laid the groundwork for perpetuating the Soviet military presence in Lüshun. During Liu Shaoqi's visit the previous summer, Stalin had linked that presence to the need to deter Japan and the United States.

Concurring with these introductory remarks, Stalin enumerated the topics to be addressed: the treaty of alliance; the agreements on the Chinese Changchun Railroad, Lüshun, and Dalian; trade and a trade agreement; loans; and cooperation in civil aviation. Stalin, it was clear, was ready to settle the entire range of issues that the Chinese had come to negotiate. He had endorsed the framework for the negotiations in early January, and the rest was simply a matter of straightforward bargaining.

Mao recommended covering three of the topics—the Chinese Changchun Railroad, Lüshun, and Dalian—in a single agreement. In 1945, the Nationalists and Soviets had dealt with these three matters in separate documents, but Mao now wanted a package settlement.[8] Because

Mao had already indicated that he would not demand the immediate and complete Soviet withdrawal from Lüshun and Dalian or the early return of the railroad, the proposal to treat them in a single document implied that only partial changes would be introduced in the 1945 clauses. Separate documents would have been required if Mao was seeking a radical change. He was not, and Stalin knew it.

Additional proof of Mao's conciliatory approach toward the treaty of 1945 is provided in his statement to Kovalev on January 9, 1950. At that time, Stalin was preoccupied with "drawing the line" between China and the West, and Mao was trying to dispel his fears. The Chairman told Kovalev: "In all cases, when reconsidering treaties," he would "abide by the decisions that were endorsed by the Soviet side at the Teheran, Yalta, and Potsdam conferences."[9] Was this Mao's total capitulation to Moscow? The answer is no, but the logic is complex. On the night of January 2, Mao learned that the Soviets were prepared to accept those "partial changes" in the 1945 accords that would not jeopardize their national interests. In this statement to Kovalev, he demonstrated to Stalin that China recognized how essential it was for the Soviet leader to preserve his wartime gains. Mao's statement, we believe, was a tactical move. He was offering Stalin more than he demanded but, within the context of the January 2 understandings, pressuring the Soviet leader to make compromises without his having to beg for them. The ancients had a proverb for the occasion: "make concessions for the sake of future gains" (*yuqu guyu*).

In answering Mao, Stalin proved to be equally shrewd. "The Sino-Soviet treaty must be a new treaty; the Yalta agreement should not determine it [the treaty]," he said. "The methods for solving the Lüshun problem are as follows. One is to return Lüshun [to Chinese jurisdiction] after a fixed period and to pull out the troops after the conclusion of a peace treaty with Japan. Another is to withdraw the troops now, but the form of the previous treaty temporarily must not be changed."

Stalin had obviously grasped Mao's thinly disguised message. The Soviet leader recognized that dealing with Lüshun, Dalian, and the Chinese Changchun Railroad in a single document was intended to confirm the 1945 accords, initially delineated at Yalta, though with some revisions. He was breaking the formal link between the new treaty and Yalta but, as we shall see, retaining the actual bond between the two. The Soviet leader knew the Chinese hated the Yalta provisions, and he had already told Liu Shaoqi that the treaty of 1945 was unequal. By formally divorcing the new treaty from Yalta, Stalin sought to demonstrate that the agreements then being worked out would result from China's voluntary compliance and could never be legitimately overturned as an alleged "continuation of Yalta."

By dissociating the agreements from Yalta, Stalin was making another point, and one that fit his earlier statements to Mao that he was willing to put his own name on the new document. He was demonstrating not only that allying with Mao's China would become the heart of his global strategy but also that this alliance had the same level of importance as the wartime cooperation between the Big Three (which he also had personally endorsed). At the same time, Stalin's unwillingness to change "the form of the previous treaty" implied strict limits on how far he would deviate from the treaty of 1945.

Moreover, Stalin was offering Mao the same two choices for resolving the fate of Lüshun as he had proposed to Liu Shaoqi in July 1949. He appears to have reiterated these options to Mao earlier in January. From the Chinese responses then, the Kremlin leader could be confident that Mao would accept Soviet control of Lüshun for a transitional period. His confidence was not misplaced. Mao said he was willing to postpone the removal of Soviet personnel from the naval base until after the conclusion of a peace treaty with Japan.

In these brief but complex exchanges, the two leaders had come to an understanding that eliminated the chief stumbling blocks. They had solved main questions of principle on the way toward an alliance. And, they had settled on a style in their dialogue that suited their personalities. That style should not be confused with trust or friendship. Each could use words that were meant to imply as well as to obscure motives, and each waited for the other to reveal his hidden agenda or expose his weaknesses. Their behavior reminds one of two ancient emperors of the East.

Their compromises resulted from a convergence of interests and their common strategic objective to confront the United States and its allies. Every practical arrangement was produced by a process of mutual, though not always reciprocal, adjustments that had started after August 1945. Now, with the essentials out of the way, the time had come to turn concepts and compromises into precise text language.

The Soviet side, as was its custom in most of its postwar treaties, wrote the first draft.[10] The Chinese then prepared their own text on the basis of that document. Zhou Enlai ordered the Chinese delegation, as well as members of the Chinese embassy, to study the Soviet version "item by item, sentence by sentence, word by word." Zhou himself "mulled over and over again" the details and meaning of the draft, which ran less than a thousand words. In the end, "no changes were made on matters of principle, but a lot of revision went into the wording of the final draft."[11] The negotiations were conducted on the basis of this Chinese text.

The essence of the revisions become clear if we compare the final version with the treaties the Soviet Union concluded with Bulgaria (March 18, 1948), Hungary (February 18, 1948), and Romania (February 4, 1948).[12] The differences between these treaties and the Sino-Soviet document are instructive. For a start, the 1948 treaties emphasized the bilateral rather than the international dimension of the relationship with the USSR. From Moscow's perspective, its connections with the three Central European countries could not decisively affect the global power equation. Accordingly, the preambles of the three treaties stressed bilateral, especially economic ties.

By contrast, the Sino-Soviet treaty's preamble said the two governments were concluding the treaty

to prevent jointly, by strengthening friendship and cooperation between the People's Republic of China and the Union of Soviet Socialist Republics, the revival of Japanese imperialism and the resumption of aggression on the part of Japan or any other state that may collaborate in any way with Japan in acts of aggression; [and were] imbued with the desire to consolidate lasting peace and universal security in the Far East and throughout the world in conformity with the aims and principles of the United Nations.[13]

Understandably, the term "alliance" was used to characterize this treaty but not the treaties with Bulgaria, Hungary, and Romania.

Both sides took care also to stress the alliance's global dimensions in their subsequent propaganda statements. No sooner had the treaty been signed than a series of Soviet speeches and essays were published hailing the nation's attainment of spatial security, or buffers, that gave it the most defensible power base in its history.[14] Molotov at the beginning of March declared: "Only quite recently did it become obvious that the most important result of the victory of allied nations over German fascism and Japanese militarism was the triumph of the national liberation movement in China."[15] With the conclusion of the treaty, Mao's victory in China had been elevated to the most significant postwar event to date.[16]

Mao Zedong, too, stressed the security factor in his speech to the Central People's Government Council just before its vote of ratification. "In what circumstances did we find ourselves at the time we signed this treaty?," he asked. It was a perilous time, he went on in answer, for though "we defeated the reactionaries inside the country, overthrowing the reactionary clique of Chiang Kai-shek supported by the reactionaries abroad, [and] also expelled the foreign reactionaries from the territory of our country;

[that is,] basically expelled them, . . . other reactionaries still exist in the world, and these are the foreign imperialists."[17] An editorial, which was written by Chen Boda (the deputy head of the CCP Central Committee's Propaganda Department) and amended by Mao, asserted that the treaty's main essence was directed "against aggression."[18]

The Chinese even more forcefully than the Soviets emphasized that in correlating the forces of the two nations, the treaty had brought about definitive changes in the world power structure in favor of the Soviet-led camp. Zhou Enlai's speech at the signing ceremony accented the "unity of the nearly 700 million people of the two countries, China and the Soviet Union," and their invincibility, a theme found far less frequently in the Soviet press.[19] Predictably, the Chinese seldom mentioned how the treaty contributed to the creation of a buffer zone along the Soviet borders. They knew the zone infringed their sovereignty, and the less said about that the better.[20]

To return to our comparative discussion, the global significance of the new alliance made itself felt in the clause defining the scope of the Sino-Soviet bilateral relationship. The Soviet-Bulgarian treaty, like its Romanian and Hungarian counterparts, stated that the two sides would "consult with each other on all the important international questions connected with the interests of both countries."[21] Strictly speaking, this might be interpreted to mean that the three countries would have to consult with Moscow on only those international problems affecting the interests of the Soviet Union and themselves. Obviously, the Soviet reading ran in just the opposite direction: the three would have to consult the Soviet Union on all important foreign policy problems, which by definition were connected to the "interests of both countries," and consultation equaled acquiescence to Moscow. Indeed, the narrower interpretation of this clause was a primary reason for Yugoslavia's split with the Soviet Union; Tito was unwilling to inform Moscow about some aspects of his policy toward Albania.[22]

In the treaty with the People's Republic of China, the clause on consultation read differently: "Both Contracting Parties, in the interests of consolidating peace and universal security, will consult with each other in regard to all important international problems affecting the common interests of China and the Soviet Union."[23] The negotiators, presumably the Chinese, had inserted the word "common" before "interests" and thus changed the thrust of the entire clause. Since consultations would be confined to "international problems affecting the common interests" of the two nations, the language implied that there could be conflicting and disconnected interests on these problems, in which case no consultations would be required. Although this possibility might not have loomed large on February 14, 1950, it was to become an ever higher probability within a few months, as the next chapters will show.

This provision plainly echoed Mao's desire to preserve as much freedom of action and flexibility as possible in foreign policy matters even while leaning to one side. It also reflected the Chinese leaders' belief that Beijing might well feel pressed to take independent stands in pursuit of its goals in Asia and thereby come into conflict with the Kremlin.[24] In such cases, the treaty gave Mao license to operate on his own, and Stalin must have known this.

Both sides attached great significance to the principles of state-to-state relations embodied in the treaty, and these, too, differed markedly from the list of principles found in the Soviet treaties with Bulgaria, Hungary, and Romania. In the latter, "respect for independence and state sovereignty [and] noninterference in the internal affairs" were standard. The list was shorter even than that found in the Soviet-Chinese treaty of 1945, where "territorial sovereignty" was included. But in fact the China of 1945, for all its deficiencies, enjoyed far greater freedom than did the European states under Soviet dominion in 1948.

The Sino-Soviet treaty of February 1950 contained a much more complete and detailed set of principles on bilateral relations:

equality, mutual benefit, and mutual respect for the national sovereignty and territorial integrity and noninterference in the internal affairs of the other Contracting Party.[25]

This list of principles demonstrated the unusual character of the Soviet Union's relations with China and Stalin's special treatment of Mao. Their incorporation in the treaty constituted a success for Chinese diplomacy.

One of the Chinese present at the negotiations recalls that the original Soviet draft of the treaty was entitled "Treaty of Friendship and Alliance," and that the words "and Mutual Assistance" were added at Zhou Enlai's suggestion.[26] Although this suggestion was consistent with the titles of the other Soviet treaties, the Chinese regarded the change as a minor victory, symbolizing in their minds their having reached equality with the Soviet Union.[27] In all likelihood, this was also the reason why Zhou and his team insisted on the inclusion of the additional principles in the treaty (a change, we may note, that foreshadowed the "five principles of peaceful coexistence" that became the hallmark of Chinese foreign policy and treaty-making in the mid-1950s).

The February treaty also departed from both the 1945 treaty and the

Soviet–Central European treaties on the key question of security obligations. It provided that

in the event of one of the Contracting Parties being attacked by Japan or any state allied with her and thus being involved in a state of war, the other Contracting Party shall immediately render military and other assistance by all means at its disposal.[28]

The comparable clause in the 1945 Soviet-Chinese treaty stated the obligation as follows:

In the event of one of the High Contracting Parties becoming involved in hostilities with Japan in consequence of an attack by the latter against the said Contracting Party, the other High Contracting Party shall at once give to the Contracting Party so involved in hostilities all the military and other support and assistance with the means in its power.[29]

Though it is evident that fears of Japanese militarism remained high, the new treaty clearly reflected the changed political circumstances of the time. In 1945, Japan alone was held up as the possible aggressor; in 1950, the threat was Japan and "any state allied with her." Everyone on both negotiating teams, as we have said, understood that the "any state" was the United States.

At first glance, the parallel clause in the 1948 treaties with Bulgaria, Hungary, and Romania (where German aggression was of course substituted for Japanese aggression) seems much the same as in the new Sino-Soviet treaty. But there is one critical change in wording. In the three European treaties (as well as in the Soviet-Chinese treaty of 1945), the obligation to render assistance would be triggered if either party found itself involved in a "military engagement" with the aggressor. The triggering clause in the 1950 treaty confined the obligation to "being involved in a state of war." That condition was to have a fundamental impact on the outcome of the Korean War.

"Military engagement" could be interpreted broadly according to the situation at hand, but "being involved in a state of war" had a precise, legal definition. As a result, the Soviet Union was committed to come to the aid of its East European allies (and vice versa) in almost any kind of military conflict but could remain on the sidelines, absent an official declaration of war, even if China should become embroiled in a major conflict with Japan or its allies. The problem of undeclared war that was to so plague the American body politic over the Korean and Vietnamese conflicts arose first between Moscow and Beijing.

Lying behind these legal nuances was Stalin's knowledge that, barring a preemptive strike by the West (which he considered unlikely), any military engagement between his allies and West Germany (and its allies) could begin only at Soviet initiative. Consequently, Moscow's presumed obligation to come to the aid of its allies would add a certain bonus to the Soviet deterrent in Europe while ensuring the Kremlin's control over the circumstances requiring it to honor that obligation. In Europe, Stalin could have it both ways, but China presented a quite different case.

Wu Xiuquan, who participated in the negotiations, states that the original treaty draft contained this clause: "In the event of an invasion of one of the signatory countries by a third country, the other signatory country shall render assistance." Zhou Enlai thought this language was not strong enough and suggested adding after "shall render assistance" the words "with all means at its disposal." This Chinese proposal was accepted by the Soviet side only after "quite some time" and heated debate.[30]

At first glance, the Soviet reluctance to incorporate these additional words in the treaty seems odd. Why would the Kremlin omit a phrase that it had insisted on writing into the treaties with Bulgaria, Hungary, and Romania only two years before? The important difference was that, in accepting the phrase "all means at its disposal" in 1948, the Soviet Union committed itself to a conventional response, whereas now, a few months after it had exploded its first atomic bomb, the phrase could obligate it to wage a nuclear war on China's behalf. In the hazardous era of only starting to build a nuclear arsenal and so soon after Truman had announced the decision to build thermonuclear weapons, the Soviet reluctance to resort to "all means at its disposal" is quite comprehensible.

A second and related reason for the initial Soviet omission of these words goes back to the point made just above. Whereas Stalin and his colleagues could be certain that none of their European partners would dare start a conflict with West Germany or its allies without their blessing, they knew from long experience that Mao was inclined to take risks, even risks that promised to run counter to Soviet interests.

After the Soviet negotiators had become convinced that the Chinese would not drop their insistence on the words "by all means at its disposal," they agreed to the change. Stalin's fallback position was then to hedge the conditions under which the obligation to enter any conflict would be activated. By substituting "state of war" for "military engagement," the obligation would no longer be automatic, though he would still have to worry that China might at some point declare war on its own.

Later events were to show that, although the Soviets had insisted on the substitution and found the wording an effective barrier to their participation in Korea and other Asian conflicts, the Chinese, too, found it useful. Even the possibility of a declaration of war, now linked to the treaty, could have a deterrent effect. To anticipate the argument of the next chapter, the

Chinese believed that one of the reasons why the United States did not extend the Korean conflict to Chinese territory was the existence of the Sino-Soviet treaty.[31]

The other accords that accompanied the treaty were also the product of intricate negotiations. We shall not attempt to analyze these documents in detail here, but treat only those aspects that directly affected the core interests of the two states.

As Mao proposed, the Chinese Changchun Railroad, Lüshun, and Dalian were covered in one accord but with separate articles for each.[32] Article 2 on Lüshun adhered to but went beyond Stalin's formula to withdraw Soviet troops after the conclusion of a peace treaty with Japan. The final text put a time limit on the occupation no matter what: the Soviets were to withdraw "not later than the end of 1952." This stipulation represented an obvious victory for the Chinese. But they were unable to extract the same concession on Dalian. In article 3, Stalin managed to put off any consideration of the Soviet Union's use of the port until the completion of the peace treaty with Japan.

The Soviets insisted on inserting a clause in article 2 that committed the Chinese government to "compensate the Soviet Union for expenses it has incurred in restoring and constructing installations [in Lüshun] since 1945." Later, some Chinese considered this provision to be quite disadvantageous to China, but one diplomat present during the negotiations, Wu Xiuquan, sees nothing particularly offensive in it. He comments that this commitment should be judged by its price, and that the price was governed by the overall bargain.[33]

It was a bargain for which Stalin too was seemingly willing to pay a substantial price. In agreeing to withdraw from Lüshun "not later than the end of 1952," he appeared to be abandoning the idea of acquiring an additional naval base in the Far East, his goal from the moment of the meeting at Yalta. But article 2 did not make the pullout absolute or final. During the "period pending the withdrawal of Soviet troops," there would be ample opportunity to renegotiate the agreement and prolong their stay. This in fact is what happened. In 1952, when the Korean War was far from over, the Chinese government on its own initiative asked Moscow to keep its troops in Lüshun. Agreement on the timing of their withdrawal was reached only after the Korean armistice was signed, and the troops did not leave until 1955, well after Stalin's death.[34]

Of even greater importance was a clause in that article providing for the joint use of Lüshun as a military base should either side be attacked by Japan or any countries aligned with it. The clause provided for mutual concurrence on this point, but did not stipulate any time limit—the PRC was to initiate the move, and the USSR could agree or not. The Soviets thus acquired a qualified right to the base even after 1952 in case of "Japanese" aggression. We should recall that Stalin had coveted Lüshun precisely because of its deterrence value against Japan.

During the high-level talks on January 22, at which Mao was present, Zhou Enlai told Stalin that the PRC was preparing to publish a statement on Mongolian independence. Apparently shocked by this news, the Soviet dictator became tense and blurted out, "Haven't we already solved the Mongolian problem? There is absolutely no problem, so what statements are needed? Besides that, the Mongolian comrades are not present. How can we discuss the problem of Mongolia? What right do we have to discuss the fate of other peoples?"[35] In this way, during the final period of the talks, the conversation moved beyond the agreement on the facilities in Manchuria to Mongolian independence.

Here we find Stalin, who never hesitated to discuss or even to seal "the fate of other peoples" in their absence, at his demagogical best. His outburst in this case presumably stemmed from his belief that the issue had already been disposed of in his talks with Liu Shaoqi the previous summer and especially in view of the PRC's recognition of the Mongolian People's Republic in October. Zhou quickly tried to soothe Stalin by saying that the statement Beijing intended to publish would confirm that recognition.[36] After further conversation, the two sides agreed to include the following language in the final official communiqué on the results of their talks: "both governments affirm that the independent status of the Mongolian People's Republic is fully guaranteed as a result of the plebiscite of 1945 and the establishment with it of diplomatic relations by the People's Republic of China."[37]

As in many other cases, this Chinese step was reciprocated by a Soviet one. The same communiqué stated that the foreign ministers of the two countries "exchanged notes on the decision of the Soviet government to transfer without compensation to the government of the People's Republic of China the property acquired in Manchuria from Japanese owners by Soviet economic organizations, and also on the decision of the Soviet government to transfer without compensation to the government of the People's Republic of China all the buildings in the former military compound in Peking."

The return of the Manchurian property was more symbolic than practical, however, because most of the property involved, equipment captured by the Red Army, had already been removed to the Soviet Union.[38] Most of that equipment was never returned. But the return of "Cossack Town," the compound located near the old Russian embassy in Dongjiaomin

Xiang, west of the Forbidden City, was a political must for the Chinese. The Tsarist government had built the compound, and the Soviet government had continued to enjoy the rights of extraterritoriality in its turn. Upon returning home, Mao had to be able to say that in "cleaning house" and making a break with the country's sorry past, he made exceptions for no one.

The text of the treaty and accompanying agreements appeared to represent a complicated network of mutual concessions and fixed positions based on differing security and strategic considerations. For Mao, there were some real gains compared with what had been agreed to in 1945. Soviet control over Lüshun—and the Chinese Changchun Railroad— would now end in 1952, not 1975. He had won valuable economic aid from Stalin and had bargained with him from a stronger and more equitable position than Chiang Kai-shek had enjoyed in 1945. As we have shown, the treaty not only served to deter the aggression of "Japan or any state allied with her," but also provided for checks and balances on military actions by either party. Those checks and balances in turn steadily reduced the practical security value of the treaty for both sides.

From the West's point of view, on the other hand, the treaty appeared to have welded together an awesome coalition for aggression, a perception that strongly influenced U.S. decision-making at the outbreak of the Korean War.[39] A clear product of the early Cold War, the treaty reflected the interests of the two Communist powers just as the Soviet Union began acquiring its nuclear arsenal and Mao's China was bringing its revolutionary war to a close. Both needed to blunt what they perceived as a mounting threat from the United States, and with great fanfare they fashioned their partnership for mutual defense and national ends.

The Additional Agreement and Other Secret Protocols

On February 14, simultaneously with the conclusion of the treaty of alliance and other documents, China and the Soviet Union signed the "Additional Agreement to the Soviet-Chinese Treaty of Friendship, Alliance, and Mutual Assistance Between the Government of the USSR and the Central People's Government of the People's Republic of China" (hereafter Additional Agreement). This secret protocol (whose existence was hinted at over the years but not confirmed until 1989[40]) declared that "in the interests of ensuring the defense of both countries," China agreed not to allow the citizens of third countries to settle or to carry out any industrial, financial, trade, or other related activities in Manchuria and Xinjiang, and the Soviet Union would impose comparable restrictions on the Soviet Far East and the Central Asian republics.

Although this secret accord appeared to subject both parties to the same restraints, in reality it greatly favored the Soviet side. Moscow had long banned any consequential foreign presence in Central Asia and the Soviet Far East; in 1938–39, most Chinese and Koreans had been forcibly relocated from the Far East on Stalin's orders. At the same time, the exclusion of third-party nationals from Manchuria and Xinjiang ensured that the already legislated Soviet presence there (via aid, advisers, and access to the facilities in the Northeast) would not face any direct foreign competition.

The Additional Agreement concretely reflected Stalin's concept of territorial security. It reinforced a buffer along a significant part of the Soviet border and fitted well the Kremlin's penchant for secret diplomacy. All things considered, the agreement bore Stalin's personal imprint. From his point of view, he had already made a major concession in agreeing to evacuate the Northeast after a set period. Stalin undoubtedly saw the Additional Agreement as a guarantee of a neutral security zone after his armies had pulled out. One hand was taking back what the other was giving away.

The agreement reminded the Chinese of the unequal treaties of the past, and Liu Shaoqi in October 1956 seems to have had it in mind when he told Soviet leaders that in 1950 "in order to make a common struggle against imperialism, China had made concessions on some problems."[41] The Chinese regarded the agreement as so mortifying that it was kept absolutely secret even during the Cultural Revolution, when radical groups routinely plastered confidential documents on campus walls or published them in unauthorized collections. But we have since learned that as early as April 1956, Mao told Mikoyan the secret deals on Xinjiang and Manchuria were "two bitter pills" that Stalin forced him to swallow, and the next year he complained to Gromyko that "only imperialists" would think of imposing such a deal on China.[42] Indeed, in his contempt for the agreement, Mao came close to giving the game away in 1958, when he spoke of "two 'colonies' [in China], the Northeast and Xinjiang, where the people of third countries were not permitted to settle down."[43]

The contents of the Additional Agreement were discussed at least as early as January 22, when Stalin, Mao, and Zhou began translating their previous understandings into more concrete form. Mao's interpreter recollects that Stalin "proposed that the citizens of third countries not be allowed to come to live in the Chinese Northeast [Manchuria] and Xinjiang. Because that question had arisen unexpectedly, some coolness emerged in the conversation."[44]

Zhou Enlai reacted sharply. "Many people of Korean nationality live in the Northeast," he said. "Should we consider them to be citizens of a third country? This is all the more true of the Mongolians who came [to the

Northeast] from foreign countries." Stalin was apparently puzzled by this rejoinder and did not answer. Later, he explained that his proposed agreement was intended to prohibit the activities in the Northeast of people "from the United States, Japan, Britain, and other imperialist countries." This did not appease the Chinese, who felt that even by going so far as to raise the issue, Stalin "had interfered in our internal affairs."

As we have seen, Stalin's scheme to put such restrictions on China alone fell through, for the final agreement made the restrictions at least formally reciprocal. A tentative explanation of how this change came about is provided by the following statement of the diplomat M. S. Kapitsa, who was a participant in the meetings. In the course of our interview with him in 1992, he said: "Stalin wanted to totally exclude the American presence in Manchuria and Xinjiang. The question of the 'Additional Agreement' was raised on his initiative. At first, Stalin wanted an agreement of broader scope, but finally its scope was narrowed and he permitted the conditions to be made mutual. Mao was extremely dissatisfied with the document. The 'Additional Agreement' is crucial for understanding Soviet and Chinese interests at this moment."[45]

Two points deserve attention in Kapitsa's statement. First, it seems likely that what Stalin had in mind by "broader scope" was an agreement that covered more of China or imposed further commitments on the Chinese, or both. In that case, the shrinking of these demands would surely have been a result of objections put forward by Mao and Zhou. Second, it is clear from Kapitsa's statement that Stalin was originally talking only about one-sided constraints on the Chinese and had to accede to their insistence on reciprocal obligations.

The bitter irony of the moment for the Chinese was that the preliminary discussion of this matter took place only a day after they had joined the Soviets in officially repudiating Acheson's characterization of Soviet policy as aimed at "detaching" Xinjiang and Manchuria from China. Mao and Zhou must have been galled indeed by the cynicism of Stalin, who was creating spheres of influence on Chinese territory within hours after self-righteously disavowing such ambitions. The Chinese themselves had declared to the world that Moscow had no evil designs on Xinjiang and Manchuria and, by doing so, had inadvertently weakened their bargaining position just before Stalin's disclosure of those very designs. Though Mao and Zhou managed to wrestle some concessions on the contents of the secret protocol, they had no cause for celebration. The Additional Agreement was to be an enduring source of trouble and embarrassment for the Chairman in the succeeding years.

On February 10, after the basic work on all the accords had been finished, Mao Zedong informed Liu Shaoqi that Chen Boda had written an editorial eulogizing the treaty, and that he, Mao, would cable it to China the next day, after he had reviewed its contents. Mao instructed Liu and Hu Qiaomu to publish the editorial, along with the texts of the treaty and other agreements.[46]

On February 12, Mao sent Liu a cable of instructions for restricted distribution to high-level Party organs. Party officials must take care to see that no "inappropriate opinions" were expressed in the meetings called to discuss the treaty and must strictly "adhere to the position" of the Chen Boda editorial.[47] Mao was treating the editorial as an official directive.

It was in this context that Mao, on the eve of the treaty-signing ceremony, mulled over whether to publicize the Additional Agreement. At five o'clock in the morning on February 14, only hours before the official signing, he sent a priority cable to Liu and Hu instructing them to make a number of deletions in Chen's editorial, "A New Epoch of Sino-Soviet Cooperation," and then to broadcast it, along with the treaty, that night.[48] Mao had decided to keep the Additional Agreement secret.*

However, Mao's changes reveal more than just a sensitivity about the protocol. The one detailed reference to the agreement that was excised fell within a description of how the Sino-Soviet treaty had crushed the aggressive plans of the American and Japanese imperialists and had guaranteed a prolonged era of peace in East Asia. This placement suggests that from Mao's point of view, the Additional Agreement had military and strategic implications and constituted an integral component of the just-concluded security arrangements. But the fact that he wanted it kept secret also suggests that he knew it infringed China's sovereignty and placed much of its security in the hands of Stalin.

It is not hard to fathom why Mao had second thoughts about disclosing the Additional Agreement. Apart from the fact that it would almost certainly arouse popular discontent, it could be used against China by Washington and Taipei; it also revealed more details about the security arrangements than Mao would have wanted to divulge. It was too late, however, to keep the pact totally secret. By then a few senior Chinese officials already knew about it, and it had even been referred to in some publications.

---

*The editorial had made specific mention of the agreement twice. Mao's changes deleted both, to wit, the "17 characters 'The Additional Agreement to the Sino-Soviet Treaty of Friendship, Alliance, and Mutual Assistance,'" in paragraph 1, where it was listed among the documents signed on February 14, and the "entire ninth paragraph; that is, the 53 characters 'The Additional Agreement to the Sino-Soviet Treaty of Friendship, Alliance, and Mutual Assistance is a necessary measure for guaranteeing the defense interests of the two states, and [the realization of] this measure will be beneficial both for China and the Soviet Union.'"

In any case, whether or not to keep the agreement confidential was not a matter for Mao alone to decide. This was after all part of a treaty that Stalin wanted to publicize to the fullest possible extent. Mao's cable of February 14 deleting all mention of the protocol in the editorial was sent at 5:00 A.M., which suggests that Mao and senior Soviet officials had just finished one of their nocturnal meetings. It seems likely that these officials, too, had focused on the reasons why publishing the Additional Agreement would weaken the positive impact of the Sino-Soviet accords and thus not be in the interests of the Soviet Union. The Soviets agreed to keep it secret.

Mao was sufficiently worried about the changes he wanted in the editorial that he made Liu Shaoqi and Hu Qiaomu personally "responsible for proofreading it in strict accordance [with what I have written]." It probably was one of the very few occasions in the history of the PRC when a top Party leader was ordered to proofread a newspaper article before its release and publication.[49]

Despite all these precautions, some Westerners either heard about the document's existence or guessed correctly that there would be some such agreement. For example, from the start of the Sino-Soviet talks, U.S. State Department officials had presumed that the agreements most damaging to China would be concealed in "secret protocols."[50] Similarly, though perhaps by coincidence, the American press referred to "secret codicils" to the treaty in articles that spoke of Soviet advisers moving into authoritative posts in the Chinese army, the secret police, and the Communist Party.[51] The Chinese press denounced all these Western press reports about hidden deals as groundless, which most were, but Mao and a few other Chinese knew that revelations about the Additional Agreement could make each and every one of these allegations seem painfully true.[52]

The Additional Agreement was not the only secret protocol to come out of the Stalin-Mao talks. We are aware of several other such agreements, and still more may come to light once the Soviet Union's Party and state archives are fully opened and canvassed. A senior Soviet diplomat interviewed in August 1992 has revealed one such protocol related to the Additional Agreement's provisions on Xinjiang. It stipulated the terms of future Sino-Soviet cooperation in exploring for and exploiting strategic minerals in the region. The protocol obligated China to sell a specific quota of these minerals to the Soviet Union and forbade their sale to third countries without Moscow's permission. We also know from Shi Zhe that the terms Stalin stipulated for Soviet specialists assigned to the PRC degraded China's sovereignty. The most demeaning of his demands was that a Soviet citizen in China who committed a crime could not be tried before a Chinese court but would be dealt with by the Soviets under their own laws.

Shi Zhe, upon learning of the Soviet demand, uttered in disgust, "Stalin had inherited the guiding principle of Western imperialist countries on providing assistance to foreign countries, revealing great-nation chauvinism."[53] Though resentful, the Chinese had no choice but to bow to Stalin's demands.

Another secret compact was an appendix to the open agreement on the Chinese Changchun Railroad. We must give some background to this document. During the January 22 talks, the Chinese disclosed that they did not intend to change the system of joint management for the railway. They knew that the PRC did not have the resources or qualified personnel to operate the line efficiently and desperately required Soviet participation and help. Nonetheless, Mao wanted China to be the dominant partner. He put forward three demands to ensure its commanding position:

   1. Shorten the period of joint management (in the 1945 agreement it was 30 years)
   2. Change the Chinese and Soviet shares in the railroad from the current 50-50 to 51-49 in favor of China
   3. Make a Chinese general manager

The Soviet team agreed to abridge the period of joint management but refused to alter the ratio of shares and proposed to have Chinese and Soviet nationals rotate as general managers and vice-managers.[54] These Soviet terms were written into the open agreement.[55]

We should not underestimate the importance to China of the shortening of the period of joint management. In this case, unlike that of Lüshun, the Soviet Union was committed to relinquishing all rights to the use of the railroad by the end of 1952 at the latest. If this were the whole story, then the Chinese could consider the victory complete and would have been fully satisfied. But it was not. Again, Stalin in secret offset a concession made in public.

In another protocol signed on February 14, the Chinese essentially reaffirmed the provisions of the Nationalists' 1945 agreement on the Chinese Changchun Railroad.[56] Like that agreement, this one guaranteed the Soviet Union's right to move troops and military equipment via the railroad without notifying the Chinese side in advance; gave it the authority to introduce its troops and military equipment into the Northeast and to send them across the region at the same tariff rates enjoyed by the Chinese military; and exempted it not only from paying any customs duties or taxes for military shipments to Port Arthur (Lüshun), but even from submitting those shipments to the scrutiny of Chinese customs officials. The protocol contained no time limit and thus could continue until officially terminated. China got nothing in return. Stalin rejected Zhou Enlai's demand that

Chinese troops be granted the same rights of movement over Soviet rail lines. This protocol to a large extent reflected the spirit of Kovalev's recommendation in his January report that the existing arrangements on the railroad be preserved intact.[57] Mao obviously had a great deal to conceal.

At least one accord was kept secret not because it was humiliating, but because of the nature of the activities it covered: espionage. Again according to Shi Zhe, Stalin suggested a cooperative arrangement in which the Soviets would provide the money and technical equipment for intelligence gathering, and the Chinese the necessary personnel; all the information acquired would be shared equally. Stalin stressed that for the Soviets the sphere of foreign intelligence in Asia and elsewhere was "quite limited," and the environment for it extremely hostile. This was not the case, he said, for the Chinese. "You have favorable opportunities for your [clandestine activities] abroad" because "people pay less attention to your activities and do not impede them." By "favorable opportunities," he obviously meant the human resources of the overseas Chinese and may have been exposing traces of racism. Mao and Zhou accepted Stalin's suggestion and issued instructions for their specialists to work out a detailed plan.[58] This agreement (which has not yet come to light) went far beyond the intelligence accord reached during Liu Shaoqi's Moscow visit in the summer of 1949. That agreement had merely curtailed uncontrolled Soviet spying on Chinese territory; this one involved intelligence gathering on a global scale.

All of these behind-the-scenes machinations help explain why Mao showed signs of anxiety and fatigue during the last days of his stay in Moscow and on his way back home. It is tempting to put this down to his ambivalence about the results of the negotiations, but he might merely have been showing the wear and tear of the nonstop schedule he had maintained over the past two months. In any case, according to eyewitness reports, both Mao and Stalin were visibly tense and sullen during the banquet given by the Chinese to celebrate the conclusion of the treaty.[59] Stalin made matters worse when, quite unexpectedly, he devoted the bulk of his banquet speech to vilifying Titoism and Yugoslav treachery.[60]

This tense mood is consistent with Mao's ideas on how he should be received when he returned home. For example, as he was making his way out of the Soviet Union he sent Liu Shaoqi and Gao Gang a stern set of instructions. On the stops in the Northeast, Gao Gang was "to inform responsible comrades in each place to maintain secrecy and to permit only a small number of the responsible cadres to be present at the receptions, not allowing many people to know and especially not to publish any news." Likewise, when the entourage arrived in Beijing, "only a small number of

people from the Party and from outside the Party (approximately 100 individuals) need to be at the station to participate in the meeting. Do not
allow too many people to know; the news must be published only after our
arrival in Beijing. Please arrange everything according to this cable."[61] But
these strictures were not out of worries about his own safety (even though
Nationalist agents were on his trail).* Mao did not complain about the
Soviet press's detailed reports on his travels through Siberia and the Soviet
Far East, and there is no evidence that he wanted to hide his general itinerary.[62] Mao's recurrent concern was his image, and his cable was not the
message of a leader returning in triumph.

A strangely symbolic episode on the way home illustrates Mao's perception of what he had just been through and what was most on his mind.
When his train reached Ulan Ude, a town south of the Siberian city of Irkutsk, the local Party bosses came to his railcar and invited him to tour
their town as he had done on other stopovers. Mao refused. His interpreter
believes that the Chairman regarded this land as Chinese from ancient
times, and that his refusal "probably had a deeper meaning."[63] Weighing
Mao's views on the unification and revival of the nation against the results
of his negotiations with Stalin, we must agree with the interpreter. Mao
did not want to legitimate by even the smallest action what he considered
to be a loss for the Chinese nation. In this somewhat petty way, he could
protest the accords and assert his independence.

This same interpreter, Shi Zhe, recounts another minor incident that de-
livers the same message. He recalls that when he asked Mao why the treaty,
originally set to run for 20 years, was changed to 30, the Chairman casually answered, "I do not know when it was changed." Mao, Shi Zhe concludes, was totally unconcerned about the duration of the treaty.[64] One reason for this flip response was Mao's firm belief that the most troublesome
clauses of the treaty would not endure even 20 years, let alone 30, and time
would prove him correct.[65]

In April, Mao's apprehensions about his reception at home surfaced
once more as he prepared to bring the Moscow documents before his colleagues in the Central People's Government Council for ratification. Since
at least some of the 170 or so participants at the meeting knew about the
Additional Agreement, Mao set out to ensure that no information on it

---

*To ensure Mao's safety on his return trip, the CCP Politburo ordered thousands of
security agents to the Northeast. They turned up a Nationalist-planted time bomb under
a rail near the Changchun Station only minutes before it was to go off. Despite the extraordinary security precautions, both of the automobiles Stalin had given Mao as a gift
were stripped of parts during the journey. Ling Hui, "Description of Yang Qiqing," pp.
14–15.

would leak out or come up in the deliberations. To that end, he took care to have Zhou Enlai's report on the treaty printed and distributed to all the participants, and to allow only the most reliable people to make speeches in support of it.[66] Nothing was left to chance. There would be no lapses in discipline.

Mao was the last to speak on the treaty on the day of its ratification, April 11, and he, too, had to be careful how he presented the treaty to the meeting. Even in the classified collection of documents at hand, Mao's speech contains extensive deletions, and the Chinese editors write at length about how he personally edited the filmed version of his presentation before its release.[67]

Mao began by stressing that "unity with friends abroad" was one of the conditions for "strengthening the victory of the revolution." The Moscow agreements, he said, reinforced Sino-Soviet friendship and gave China "a staunch ally." He based his case for the agreements on the threats from "reactionaries" at home and "foreign imperialists," adding, "in circumstances such as this, we need to have a friend" and "if the imperialists are preparing to strike at us, then we can invite [the help of] a good supporter."

The rationale out of the way, Mao made his pitch: "This treaty is a patriotic treaty. Comrades were saying this a few moments ago, and this is right. This treaty is also an internationalist treaty; it is internationalism." Here, we believe, Mao was speaking to those who had heard about the Additional Agreement. Who else would question the patriotism of the Moscow documents? He was arguing that his concessions were necessary and did not truly damage China's integrity or sovereignty. That argument was not only bought by most of his listeners but is still accepted by some senior Chinese officials.[68]

There was a final touch of irony. When Mao called for the vote on the treaty and stood to observe the raised hands, he did not raise his own in approval.[69]

FIVE

The Decision for War in Korea

On June 25, 1950, less than five months after the signing of the Sino-Soviet treaty, war shattered the uneasy peace in Korea. Move by countermove the war escalated, and in mid-September, when the United Nations forces launched their counteroffensive at Inchon, a few miles west of Seoul, Beijing increased its commitment to backstopping the North Korean regime.

As we shall see, senior leaders in both Moscow and Beijing knew at least as early as the end of 1949 that the North Korean leader Kim Il Sung was aiming to attack the South, though none of the principals, including Kim himself, then had in mind the precise timing or conditions of the assault.[1] Khrushchev remembers that during Mao Zedong's visit to Moscow, Stalin asked the Chinese Chairman "what he thought about the essence behind such an action [by the North Koreans]. . . . Mao answered with approval and also expressed the opinion that the United States wouldn't interfere in an internal matter which the Korean people would decide for themselves." A Chinese source quotes Mao as saying, "We still should help 'Xiao' Kim. Korea now faces a complicated situation."[2]

After providing some new information on the rise of Kim Il Sung, we will analyze how Soviet and Chinese views on Korea were affected by the just-concluded Sino-Soviet negotiations on the alliance and broader strategic goals. In doing so, we will be revisiting as well as adding to the many explanations of the origins of the war. We do not seek to develop an entirely original account of the genesis of the war or to deal systematically with the major (and still conflicting) interpretations of other scholars.[3]

Any specialist writing on this topic is immediately confronted by the scarcity of reliable sources. Because of extreme secrecy, even the head of the Soviet secret police learned nothing about Kim's decision to cross the 38th Parallel. During a meeting of the Central Committee in mid-1953, Minister of Internal Affairs Kruglov acknowledged that "we were not aware of the decision on the Korean problem."[4]

However, the documentary gap is partially filled by eyewitness accounts, and we expect the opening of the many Russian archives to produce new troves of information over the coming years.[5] Hundreds of articles and memoirs by Chinese, Soviet Koreans, and Russians have been published since 1989, and a handful of these, we believe, are reasonably reliable (though it should be kept in mind that virtually all sources on the war are biased in varying degrees). Moreover, many high-ranking participants are now willing to share their knowledge and have done so with us on the promise of anonymity. We will use these sources, both old and new, in an attempt to present a coherent and consistent version of the chain of events leading to the North Korean assault on the South that fateful Sunday in June. We recognize, however, that the full story of those events is yet to be told.

Over the past four decades, the genesis of the Korean War has been examined from quite contrasting vantage points. At first, attention was focused on high-level politics, on the contacts between Stalin, Kim Il Sung, and Mao. Later, the focus shifted to analyzing the domestic Korean and Cold War factors that contributed to the outbreak of the conflict.[6] Our own evidence indicates that we need to concentrate once again on high politics.

The Soviet Union and Korea

The search for the origins of the decision to start the war leads inexorably back to the relationship between the Soviet Union and Kim Il Sung's Korea. Throughout the early postwar years, Kim was wholly dependent on Moscow, and North Korea can be justly called a Soviet satellite.[7] The history of that relationship has been extensively treated and is not directly relevant to this study.[8] Here, we simply wish to introduce the Soviet sources that shed additional light on it.

Sometime in 1939 or 1940, Kim Il Sung arrived in the Soviet Far East and was assigned to the Khabarovsk Infantry Officers School. In the summer of 1942, the Soviet General Staff ordered the creation of the 88th Brigade, consisting of four battalions: one Chinese, one of the local peoples of the Far East, one Russian, and one Korean.[9] Stationed in the village of Viatskoe in the Khabarovsk district, the Korean battalion was specifically tasked to train cadres for a future Korean People's Army (KPA). Kim Il Sung was given the rank of captain in the battalion and appointed its commander. He quickly gained a reputation for discipline; Soviet officers recall his strict rules against heavy drinking.[10]

Even at this early date, Kim shared his vision of a future Korea with his brigade comrades. One of them recalls that the new battalion commander "never believed in peaceful unification; he never had such an idea. He only stuck to the idea of armed unification." During his five years in Khaba-rovsk, Kim "prepared himself" for the coming battle, and though he "did not speak to us explicitly about armed unification, . . . he was telling us that we were future generals and would fight together."[11]

On October 10, 1945, the Russian cargo ship *Pugachev* carried Kim and the 66 officers of the 88th from Khabarovsk to the port of Wonsan. These officers were to serve as the core of the North Korean high command throughout the coming decades. Later, after Stalin agreed to the ouster of the local popular leader Cho Man-sik,[12] Kim, then still only in his mid-thirties, became the Soviet commanders' choice for national leader. Stalin thoroughly approved of the selection. For him, Kim's experience in the USSR and training under Soviet commanders made him much more trust-worthy than any potential rivals.[13] Kim himself was less certain and at first refused the assignment. But he finally relented after Col. Gen. Ivan Chis-tiakov, commander of the Soviet 25th Army, urged him strongly to recon-sider.[14]

As all this suggests, the Soviets were by this time firmly in the saddle in North Korea. But earlier, in 1945, just as Stalin's troops were entering the country, Mao had made his own attempt to establish a foothold on the peninsula, ordering a Yan'an-controlled Korean detachment fighting the Japanese in North China to break off and head for Korea.[15] Now he sum-moned some ten or so prominent Koreans who were serving in his revo-lutionary army and informed them of his decision to send them to Korea. "Kim Il Sung has said that Korea was liberated by the Soviet army," he told them. "If Soviet headquarters does not nominate reliable people, it would be bad." As members of the so-called Yan'an faction, some of these men eventually rose to prominence in the North Korean hierarchy. Neverthe-less, virtually all the dominant positions and the real power remained in the hands of Soviet-oriented Koreans and their Soviet advisers.[16]

But this is not to say that the Soviets had things all their own way. Al-though Stalin may have regarded Kim as a puppet, the reality turned out to be far more complex. In fact, Kim was able to use Stalin's trust for his own aims even as Stalin was using him.

The emerging Cold War had a direct bearing on their relations. In his memoirs, V. I. Petukhov, a well-informed Soviet diplomat, describes the at-mosphere of profound distrust that surrounded the work of the Soviet-American commission on Korea in 1947. On the Soviet side, even the most innocent American actions, he writes, were interpreted as a provocation.[17] The Russians very quickly concluded that their interests on the peninsula were irreconcilable with those of the United States; the Americans had by then already drawn the same conclusion.

The two sides were most at odds about which political parties or organizations should participate in a government for a unified Korea. Though Kim Il Sung and the South Korean leader Syngman Rhee were both claiming to have the broad support of the Korean people, the Soviets were convinced that Kim was correct in his assertions that the "progressive forces" in the South were powerful, and that the "revolutionary situation" there was ripe.[18] In any case, even without the evidence of their own eyes in the mounting uprisings, protests, and strikes against the Seoul government, the Soviets could be expected to side with Kim and support his claim to national leadership.[19]

Over time, Soviet reports on the South became interchangeable with the reports Stalin was receiving from Kim himself. All optimistically assessed the South's "revolutionary readiness."[20] The Soviet ambassador to Pyongyang, Terentii Shtykov, embraced Kim's claims. He invariably accompanied Kim on his trips to Moscow and helped him persuade Stalin of the validity of his assessments.[21] Skillfully playing on the firm Soviet commitment to his regime and on the ever more bitter U.S.-Soviet global hostilities, Kim managed to make Moscow see the situation on the peninsula through his own eyes. His success in this regard was to have a profound effect on the developments in Korea thereafter. By 1949, the contrived similarity of Soviet and Korean views helped set the context for the process that led to the Korean War.

While Soviet troops were still stationed in Korea, the formation of the Republic of Korea (ROK) in August 1948 and of the Democratic People's Republic of Korea (DPRK) that September formalized the de facto division of the peninsula at the 38th parallel. Each state claimed to represent the entire nation and remained adamantly antagonistic to the other. From then on, each worked to unite Korea on its own terms and with the assistance of its principal foreign patron.

In Kim's case, that assistance included massive amounts of military hardware, for when the Soviet 25th Army, then numbering more than 120,000 men, pulled out at the end of the year, it handed over all its weapons to the newly formed Korean People's Army (KPA). Additionally, the KPA inherited the armaments seized from Japan's defeated 34th and 58th armies.[22] According to a Soviet source, Moscow's military assistance to the KPA in the late 1940s and early 1950s exceeded that given to Mao's PLA during the same period.[23]

This conspicuous difference in Stalin's treatment of China and the DPRK had much to do with their respective positions in the Soviet orbit. During most of this period, the Chinese were still in the throes of a life-and-death civil war, whereas North Korea was well on the way to building a Com-

munist regime under Soviet tutelage. Direct Soviet involvement in the rise
of Kim Il Sung and the formation of the DPRK helped mold both Stalin's
stance toward the need for combat on the peninsula and Kim's view of the
irrelevance of China in his own sphere of operations.

In fact, the Chinese and Korean Communists did not engage in any serious talks until August 1948, and even then these discussions, between the
representative of the People's Government of the Northeast, Li Fuchun of
the CCP Central Committee's Northeast Bureau, and members of Kim's
government, concentrated solely on economic matters of bilateral interest.[24] The Northeast government did not station a full-fledged trade representative in Pyongyang until the spring of 1949.[25] Despite the arguments
put forward by some Western scholars, China was a bit player in the drama
being played out on the Korean Peninsula until a few months before the
war began.[26]

Nevertheless, relations between the Chinese and Korean Communists
were quite close. When Kim left Manchuria for the Soviet Union, probably
in 1940, he was a member of the Chinese Communist Party, though, at
heart, Kim remained Korean.[27] At the end of 1946, as Lin Biao's forces fell
back before the Nationalists' offensive in South Manchuria, most of the
families of the Communist troops from the region fled to North Korea. Kim
Il Sung ordered special camps built to house them until it was safe to return
to China. The Chinese Communists, including Mao, often expressed their
personal gratitude for this assistance. Moreover, the Northeast Field Army
(predecessor of the Fourth Field Army) recruited thousands of soldiers of
Korean nationality living in Northeast China, and most of these were sub-
sequently transferred to the North Korean army.[28]

These ties influenced Kim as well as the Chinese, but not always in a
positive way. Even as he ordered the local Korean authorities to provide
sanctuary to the Chinese, he told these officials, "We will help them, but
we don't have to give them full support. We'd better help them properly.
These Chinese are too sluggish. If I had only one division, I could destroy
the Central [Nationalist] army right now."[29] During the period preceding
the Korean War, personal relations and experiences affected the Sino-
Korean relationship in notable but often complex ways.

As influential as these experiences and relations were, the main story was
unfolding within Korea itself. Despite the North Koreans' distinct military
advantage after the Soviet evacuation, and the widespread discontent
against Rhee's government, Kim apparently did not consider the time ripe
for war. He could not be sure of victory in an all-out conflict because he
had no assurance of Soviet support, and there were still U.S. troops in the
South.

Still, Stalin was not averse to egging Kim on when the two got together for talks in the spring of 1949.[30] According to Stalin's interpreter, in the course of their meetings, "Stalin asked: 'How is it going, Comrade Kim?' 'Everything will be all right,' [Kim said, but] he complained, 'Only the southerners are making trouble all the time. They are violating the border; there are continuous small clashes.' Stalin became gloomy: 'What are you talking about? Are you short of arms? We shall give them to you. You must strike the southerners in the teeth.' After thinking for a while, he repeated, 'Strike them, strike them.' "[31]

Stalin's response must be understood in the context of the overall situation of the moment. Kim was talking only about "small clashes" and how he should cope with them. Stalin's puzzlement stemmed from his knowledge that Kim had ample arms to counter virtually any southern incursion; the scale of Soviet military assistance to Kim had been immense, as both knew. Their conversation was not about an all-out offensive against the South, and Stalin did not give Kim the go-ahead for one.[32] Stalin, as we have so often remarked, remained cautious so long as the possibility of a major conflict with the United States existed. With U.S. troops still on station in the South, Stalin would not risk a move that would engage them.

After Kim returned home, the essence of Stalin's advice or at least its general spirit leaked to the top Soviet military advisers in Korea. Picking up on the idea of "striking the southerners in the teeth," they began exhorting Kim to take more aggressive action along and below the 38th parallel. The resulting clashes, they forecast, would undermine the morale of Rhee's government and help ensure Kim's ascendancy.[33] Kim gladly complied.

In short order, "large, well-equipped guerrilla bands, trained at the camp near the Korean capital [Pyongyang], infiltrated into the South to establish bases in the rugged mountains along the ROK's eastern coast."[34] Kim clearly hoped that these bands would overthrow the Seoul regime and unify the country under his rule. His target date was the fall of 1949.[35] Although this guerrilla struggle was organized and supported from the North, Kim in public was calling for unification by peaceful means and eschewing all overt military action.[36] His strategy was fully in accord with the guidelines laid down in his conversation with Stalin.

Initially, Kim's strategy of provoking border clashes and employing guerrilla tactics appeared to succeed. In glowing reports to Moscow, Soviet military advisers held up the KPA's performance in a battle in July 1949 near Kaesong as evidence of the winning spirit of the North.[37] But on both the political and the military front, the tide soon turned against Kim. Though the fighting continued, the guerrillas failed to take a single city, let alone rally the majority of the South's people to their side. By the winter of 1949–50, the core guerrilla bands were suffering serious defeats and defections, though many survived to fight in the South after the war broke out.[38] One former North Korean general concludes, "I know that Kim Il Sung pinned his hopes on the guerrilla movement in the South. But, by this time, December 1949, Syngman Rhee had effectively subdued the guerrillas."[39]

Consequently, Kim now faced some hard choices. Political negotiations and the guerrilla option had failed, and Rhee's government was gaining vitality. If he was going to unite the country under Communist rule, Kim would have to resort to a full-scale offensive, and soon. To do this, he needed Stalin's consent and pledge of support. But even with the advantage of his proven loyalty to the Soviet leader, it would take all his talents of persuasion to convince the Kremlin that the South would erupt in rebellion if the North itself attacked. An American specialist on Korea has concluded that the intensifying of guerrilla activity after Kim returned to Pyongyang in April and the exaggeration of the guerrillas' achievements may have been designed to deceive or convince Stalin.[40]

What Kim could not have known, however, was the degree to which Stalin's strategic calculus regarding Asia had changed. Mao now occupied a principal place in Stalin's security thinking. After his talks the previous July with Liu Shaoqi on a global division of spheres of responsibility, Stalin would not take any serious decision in Asia without at a minimum consulting Mao, even though Korea still fell within Moscow's orbit. During the late summer and fall of 1949, the Soviet leader was busily preparing for the Sino-Soviet summit, and with that foremost in mind, he would not have contemplated authorizing any moves toward war by Kim on his own.

Consultations for War

Many chroniclers of the events leading up to the war state that before its outbreak on June 25, Kim Il Sung secretly visited Moscow for talks with Stalin "more than once."[41] If few agree on the dates or details of actual visits,[42] solid evidence exists that Pyongyang, Moscow, and Beijing actively exchanged views and proposals in the year preceding the war.*

* In 1966, the Soviet Ministry of Foreign Affairs prepared a top secret report for General Secretary L. I. Brezhnev and Prime Minister A. N. Kosygin on events leading up to and through the Korean War. Written at a time of heightened Sino-Soviet tensions, the document, while biased, substantiates all major points raised in this and the following chapter on those events but differs on some important details. It states that Kim and other North Korean leaders as early as 1948 sought to unify the peninsula by military means and disregarded proposals for peaceful reunification. By Jan. 1950, the North was adding to its force of 110,000 men. It also concluded that the United States would not enter the war. Kim actively sought the backing of Stalin and Mao for his war aims,

The only visit Kim Il Sung made to Moscow after his tour in March–April 1949 came in late March of the following year. In addition, Kim followed up this visit with a trip to Beijing in May (not on his way home from Moscow in April as is sometimes reported).[43] These consultations were integral to the process leading up to the war. Although many sources dwell on other reported visits by Kim to Moscow between April 1949 and March 1950,[44] we now know from an August 1992 interview with a senior Russian diplomat who has thoroughly canvassed the Soviet-era archives that these trips did not occur. It seems likely that the active flow of communications between Moscow and Pyongyang at this time has been misinterpreted as Kim-Stalin meetings. What matters is the evolution of the exchanges, not whether specific visits did or did not occur.

Nevertheless, we will review here the accounts of the oft-cited visits by Kim to Moscow in December 1949 and February 1950. We do so partly to suggest the kinds of information that appear to have been exchanged between Moscow and Pyongyang in these months (on which the archives do have significant documents) and partly to indicate how pseudohistory can become widely accepted in efforts to explain the origins of one of history's tragedies.

---

but Stalin stressed the need for greater preparation and only approved Kim's ideas in principle. Finally, the Soviet leader approved the plans "during Kim's visit to Moscow in March–April 1950," and began to supply all needed military aid. During Kim's visit to Beijing "in May," Mao also gave the nod and stressed that the Americans would not intervene to save "such a small territory." Mao promised to send men and matériel north "in case the Japanese entered the war," a contingency given by the document as the reason for Mao's movement of troops after June 25. Continuing, the document states that Kim proposed a three-stage approach to war: massing troops at the 38th parallel, proposing a peace plan, and attacking when the plan was rejected. The final operations plan envisaged a North Korean advance of 15–20 km per day and victory in 22–27 days. After the U.S. landing at Inchon in September, Mao, fearing U.S. attacks on China, rebuffed Kim's plea for aid. Stalin pressured the Chairman to intervene, but Mao sent Chinese troops, the "volunteers," only when China itself was threatened. For their part, Soviet advisers took part in all phases of the operations and helped turn the tide after October. "O Koreiskoi Voine 1950–1953 gg. i Peregovorakh o Peremirii" [On the Korean War, 1950–1953, and the Armistice Negotiations], Aug. 9, 1966; document from TsKhSD [Center for the Storage of Contemporary Documentation (former Central Committee Archives)], F. 05, Op. 58, d. 45, pp. 122–25. The authors are grateful to David Holloway for providing his notes on this document.

We should note that the former head of the Korean Section of the CPSU Central Committee's International Department states that no minutes were taken during the secret Kim-Stalin talks. Interview with Vadim P. Tkachenko, March 30, 1992. Assessments of Moscow's role in decisions concerning the Korean War differ sharply; few of these assessments have dealt with Kim's visits to the Soviet Union. See, for example, Shi Zhe, *Zai Lishi*, pp. 506, 511; Sun Lizhong, *Peng Zhong Zai Guowai*, p. 22; Cumings, *Origins of the Korean War*, 2: Chaps. 10, 18; Merrill, *Korea*, Chap. 1; Simmons, *Strained Alliance*, Chap. 5; and Stueck, "Soviet Union."

We turn first to accounts of the December 1949 visit. To repeat, the reader should keep in mind that this visit did not in fact occur. Allegedly arriving in Moscow on the eve of Mao's visit, Kim had in mind something quite different from the ideas Stalin had suggested in the spring. He had already told Soviet advisers in Pyongyang that Korea was not a suitable place for guerrilla warfare and now sought Soviet sanction for a full-scale conventional attack against the South.[45] As two Chinese authors put it, Kim Il Sung had gone to Moscow to press Stalin on "his idea of military unification of Korea."[46] It was logical for Kim to put forward this proposal at the moment of his disillusionment with the prospects for the guerrilla struggle in the South. A conventional invasion remained his only viable option.

A passage in Khrushchev's account (in the original Russian version) appears to relate to this first visit. He quotes Kim as telling Stalin that the North Koreans "wanted to touch the South with the point of a bayonet. . . . After the first impulse from North Korea, there would be an internal explosion and the people's power would be established, which means the same power as exists in North Korea."[47] The head of the KPA Operations Directorate in 1950 recalls "an atmosphere of envy within the KPA's hierarchy" over the fact that Mao's armies had defeated the Nationalists and were unifying their country, and this theme undoubtedly was part of Kim's case for action.[48] In reply, Stalin expressed his general sympathy toward Kim's intentions, a response that Khrushchev finds quite natural in a convinced Communist like Stalin, who was bound to see the battle for the South as an internal matter for the Korean people.

The one purportedly direct account we have of this alleged meeting, by a senior Soviet diplomat, generally coincides with the above but adds some detail: "After October [1949], the Koreans were inspired by the Chinese victory and by the fact that the Americans had fled from mainland China completely; they were sure that the same could be accomplished in Korea quite quickly. They came with such a proposal to Moscow in November–December 1949. . . . During this late 1949 visit, Stalin responded to Kim in the following way: 'The Americans abandoned China because they had been dealing with the problems of this country for a long time. They well understood how enormous the task was to rescue Chiang Kai-shek and the limitations of their potential to accomplish it. Korea is a quite different case. The Americans will never agree to be thrown out of there and because of that, to lose their reputation as a great power. The Soviet people would not understand the necessity of a war in Korea, which is a remote place outside the sphere of the USSR's vital interests.' "[49]

Despite the obvious erroneous dating of this account, we see here what was to become a recurrent pattern in the exchanges between Stalin and Kim before the war. The Korean leader, usually via the Soviet ambassador in Pyongyang, would present his case for completing "the task of national liberation," and Stalin would express his general sympathy for reunification but, until April 1950, refuse to sanction an all-out attack. He feared any conflict that might provoke an American confrontation with the Soviet Union.*

At the same time, Stalin's reluctance to support Kim's proposal, however it may have reached the Korean leader, may have been tempered to some extent by Stalin's growing preoccupation with drawing a line between China and the West. He also could see some merit in the proposal within the framework of his earlier decision to facilitate those offensive actions toward Asia that could succeed but would not implicate the Soviet Union. The conquest of South Korea would enable him to widen the buffer zone along his eastern frontier, to acquire political leverage against Japan or, perhaps, a springboard for an attack against it, to test American resolve and capabilities, and to divert American power away from Europe. All these were pluses so long as the Soviet Union could appear to remain aloof.

For all these reasons, the Soviet leader found Kim's reunification ideas interesting enough to discuss them with Mao later in the month. But the very fact that Stalin had not yet met Mao undoubtedly caused him to avoid giving Kim a firm yes or no. In essence, the Soviet leader put all Korean war planning on hold and told Kim to return after the Soviet-Chinese summit had ended and Mao had left. The summit, he was suggesting, would provide the basis for further deliberations on the feasibility of a quick military victory in Korea. Though we have no information about the nature of the Mao-Stalin exchanges on the Korean problem beyond the statement of two Chinese authors that "Mao was more cautious than both Kim and Stalin. He raised the possibility of American military intervention during his talk with Stalin in Moscow,"[50] this statement fits well what we know of Mao's thinking at that moment. Even assuming that Acheson and Tru-

---

*Molotov relates that "it seemed that [the Korean War] was not needed by us. The Koreans themselves had forced it on us. Stalin was saying that we cannot avoid the national question concerning a unified Korea." Lee Sang Jo, who was a North Korean ambassador to the Soviet Union and defected to it, states, "There, of course, were consultations with Stalin, but the initiative still came from Kim Il Sung, who persuaded the Soviet leader of the success of the plan for a 'national liberation war' personally devised by himself. Although Stalin worried about the possibility of Washington's interference, he at last gave his approval." According to Gen. Dmitrii Volkogonov, Stalin had long been wary of any "aggravation of the situation on the Korean Peninsula [and] did whatever he could to avoid a direct confrontation between the USSR and the U.S.A." *Sto Sorok Besed s Molotovym*, p. 104; Makhov, "Stalin Had Approved"; Volkogonov, *I. V. Stalin*, 2.2: 107–8.

man had announced the new U.S. position toward Korea and Taiwan before he and Stalin ever mentioned Korea, the Chairman could hardly be expected to take the U.S. pullback in aid on faith.[51] The possibility of becoming involved in a shooting war with the Americans in Korea in itself would have given Mao pause. But beyond that, he had just obtained the promise of Soviet assistance for the invasion of Taiwan and would not have wanted an Asian rival for that aid. One Soviet official recalls learning from the Chinese leadership that Mao's negative response to Kim's proposals for war was dictated by the need to recover from the devastation of the civil war and to liberate Taiwan.[52]

Despite their wary attitude toward Kim's ideas for attacking the South, Stalin and Mao, one former DPRK general says, did respond to Kim's appeal for troops. Even though he and his generals knew quite well that Syngman Rhee's army was far weaker than the KPA, Southern-initiated border clashes and the militant speeches of the South Korean military calling for Korean unification by force gave Kim the evidence he needed to stress the "threat from the South."[53] Stalin appears to have been taken in by this evidence. A senior official in Moscow recalls seeing documents at the very end of the 1940s expressing Stalin's "great doubts that the North Korean regime could be preserved and would not fall."[54]

The specter of a northern collapse undoubtedly made Stalin more receptive to Kim's request for troops. Mao learned of the request while he was in Moscow, suggesting that Stalin raised the matter directly with him. The idea was simple: transfer some 14,000 Korean Chinese from the PLA to the North Korean army.[55] The Soviet leader was thereby backing the Korean enterprise but distancing himself from any direct involvement.

Everyone seems to have realized that Kim's need for additional manpower hinged on his plan to invade the South. Marshal Nie Rongzhen recalls that the KPA had been armed with Soviet weapons but was unable to recruit enough men to "sustain a large-scale war." "Therefore," he writes, "in January 1950, Comrade Kim Il Song sent Kim Kwang Hyop [commander of the KPA Second Army] and other comrades to China requesting the return of 14,000 soldiers of Korean nationality, most of whom had joined our . . . Fourth Field Army." Kim Kwang Hyop asked the Chinese to arm these soldiers from China's own arsenals, since to "negotiate again with the Soviet Union . . . would lose much time." On January 22, Mao ordered Nie to arrange for the return of the Koreans and to provide them weapons. Nie remarks, the "Korean comrades were quite satisfied."[56]

These troops, many of them battle-hardened, were merged into the KPA units being readied for the coming offensive. An officer who was later to become deputy director of North Korea's NKVD recalls: "They could not send the Chinese army, so they just sent [ethnic] Koreans and made them wear Korean army uniforms. And they were deployed at the 38th parallel. They were all from China's Yanbian area, where there are a lot of Koreans. Kim Il Sung kept everything secret, and he was very good at it, so that the ordinary Koreans had no idea that these people were from China. In the trains, all these people were wearing North Korean army uniforms, and they said that they were just trained there [in China]. They played a very important role in the attack on South Korea."[57]

Let us now turn to the reported February 1950 meeting. Again, it did not occur, though the exchanges attributed to the alleged encounter suggest the nature of the communications traffic between Moscow and Pyongyang. The only bit of direct information we have on an alleged visit at this point comes from two Soviet military historians, who say that Kim Il Sung talked with Stalin for two and a half hours that month, and that Molotov and the interpreters of the two sides were also present.[58] For obvious reasons, the former head of the Korean section of the International Department of the CPSU's Central Committee has no record of a February meeting,[59] but the second part of Khrushchev's well-known account is sometimes said to relate to it. Khrushchev mentions that he attended a reception in honor of Kim at Stalin's dacha, and that after the talks with Kim, Stalin telegraphed Mao in Beijing, asking for his opinion on Kim's proposals in writing.[60] If Mao was now back home, this reception must have been held sometime between his departure on February 17 and his arrival in Beijing on March 4.[61] Had this meeting occurred, it would have helped explain the complex relations then developing between the Soviets, Koreans, and Chinese.

We are left to guess at what kind of proposals Mao was supposed to react to, but Kim may well have conveyed some new thinking in those early months of 1950. A retired North Korean general recalls that about this time he heard Kim say "he placed great hope on the uprising of 200,000 members of the South Korean Workers' Party [the counterpart to the Korean Workers' Party in the North and now under Pyongyang's control]. He also directly stated that we placed great hope on the guerrilla movement in Chirisan [Chiri Mountain in the Sobaek Mountains in the southern part of the peninsula]."[62]

All this echoed Kim's messages to Moscow in December, but according to another former North Korean general, there was a vital new element in Kim's views at that moment. Kim and his colleagues were now persuaded "that the Americans would never participate in the war. We were absolutely sure in this. . . . The argument was the following: the Americans had not participated in the civil war in China. America was losing the giant,

China, but still had not intervened. America would not participate in such a small war on the Korean Peninsula."

Washington's recent policy statements apparently did much to encourage this view. In the words of one senior North Korean official, after Truman and Acheson had appeared to exclude Korea from the U.S. defensive perimeter, Kim "was convinced that 'the U.S. would not enter the Korean War,' or 'even if they did enter the war, they would not hold sway over the destiny of the war.'"[63] Although considerable controversy surrounds Pyongyang's reaction to Acheson's speech, we believe that Kim used the speech to bolster his case with Stalin irrespective of what his "true" attitude to the speech may have been.[64]

Kim presumably considered one more argument at about this time. A senior Soviet diplomat recalls that during one of Kim's secret visits in 1950 (which can only mean the one in March–April, not February), the Koreans stated that the Americans would be deterred from intervening by the Soviet-Chinese alliance.[65] This argument would have flowed naturally in March, when the treaty had just been concluded.

Despite such Korean assurances and arguments, Stalin could not shake his serious doubts about the use of force on the peninsula, and we should recall that he had already cautioned Kim, "The Americans will never agree to be thrown out of [Korea and] lose their reputation as a great power." Still, according to Khrushchev, when Kim Il Sung reported to Stalin in Moscow, the Korean "was absolutely sure of success. . . . As I remember, Stalin then was expressing his doubts; his worry was whether America would become involved or would disregard [*propustit' mimo ushei*] it [the North's attack on South Korea] completely. [Kim and Stalin] were inclined to think that if [the war] would come quickly (and Kim Il Sung was sure that it would be ended quickly), then the USA's involvement already would be excluded."[66] Stalin wanted to box any conflict on the peninsula between the extremes of escalation into a global conflict and Washington's total dismissal of the matter as irrelevant to its interests.

Simply put, Kim Il Sung was merely a pawn in Stalin's grand chess game. Stalin was principally interested in how a war in Korea would affect his relations with the United States. Only if that war would promote his larger schemes would he agree to it. Kim's assertions that a rebellion would follow a shock invasion of the South would have been a positive factor for Stalin in this regard. Although he welcomed the idea that direct U.S. involvement would be excluded, Stalin was ambivalent about the potential value of the conflict should Washington "disregard" it. The trick was how to keep the Americans out while making them appear to be the loser.

25. Chinese poster of Mao and Stalin celebrating the Moscow visit after Mao's return to Beijing

26. (*above*) The Sixth Session of the Central People's Government, held in Beijing in April 1950. From left to right: Zhou Enlai, Liu Shaoqi, unidentified man, Mao, Zhu De, Peng Dehuai, and Lin Biao.

27. (*left*) Mao speaking to the Central People's Government Council in his call for full preparations to meet the U.S. actions in the Taiwan Strait and Korea, June 28, 1950

28. (*right*) The North Korean leader Kim Il Sung speaking after the UN counteroffensive at Inchon, Sept. 1950

29. (*left*) Zhou Enlai at the meeting of the Chinese People's Political Consultative Conference where he issued China's warning against sending U.S. troops north of the 38th parallel, Sept. 30, 1950

30. Zhou Enlai and Soviet Ambassador N. V. Roshchin exchanging instruments of ratification on the Feb. 14 treaty and agreements, Beijing, Sept. 30, 1950. Standing at left, back row, is N. T. Fedorenko, counselor of the Soviet embassy and translator at the Mao-Stalin talks.

31. Chinese delivering provisions and ammunition to North Korea across the frozen Yalu River, Oct. 1950

32. War matériel being trucked to North Korea, Oct. 1950

33. Chinese map with unit designators in Russian. The map shows the military positions of both sides before the first Chinese campaign, Oct. 25, 1950.

34. Chinese People's Volunteers taking an oath before entering Korea, Oct. 1950

35. CPV troops crossing the Yalu River, Oct. 1950

36. CPV soldiers moving into position in Korea, Oct. 1950

37. CPV Commander Peng Dehuai inspecting the front line positions, 1951

38. Korean women placing a wreath at the tomb of Mao Anying, Mao's oldest son, killed in a U.S. air raid in North Korea, Nov. 1950

39, 40. Kim Il Sung (right) and Peng Dehuai meeting in North Korea, Oct. 1950 and Sept. 1951

41. Left to right, CPV Chief of Staff Xie Fang, Peng Dehuai, and CPV First Deputy Commander Deng Hua in the CPV's cave headquarters in Korea, early 1952

42. Mao and Kim Il Sung at war consultations in Beijing, date uncertain

Because Stalin did not want to commit the Soviet Union itself to an action that could result in war with the United States, he sought to induce Mao to back the North Koreans. His desire to draw China into the decisions on Korea was undoubtedly intensified after Acheson's speech on January 12 and as part of his quest to draw a line between Beijing and the West. Khrushchev recalls that in answer to Stalin's request for an opinion on probable U.S. reactions to a North Korean attack, Mao ventured "that the USA, perhaps, would not be involved, because this was an internal question that would be solved by the Korean people themselves."[67] This exchange took place shortly after Mao's departure from Moscow. Because Mao had earlier expressed his doubts about how the United States would react to Kim's attack, it was quite natural for the Soviet leader to have raised the matter again.

The very fact that Kim had not yet received a definite yes or no from Stalin forced him to make a secret visit to the Soviet capital from March 30 to April 25.[68] The Korean leader had used the early months of 1950 to mobilize convincing evidence for his arguments that the victory of his proposed blitzkrieg was assured.

In the spring, the KPA undertook combat reconnaissance missions in the region of Ongjin Peninsula and to the north of Kaesong. From the interrogation of the many southerners taken prisoner in these actions, the North Korean high command concluded that Kim's forces enjoyed overwhelming superiority in tanks and airplanes, and that the South's state of military readiness was poor. The optimism seems justified, for as three former high officials in the DPRK state, "Kim Il Sung had already prepared everything for this attack. There was a 100,000-man army, tanks, airplanes, artillery—everything was ready."[69] Stalin was known to prefer solid facts over "empty talk," and facts like these obviously resonated in his mind.

A former high-ranking North Korean diplomat has provided the most detailed account of the April meeting, which took place in Stalin's so-called "near" dacha and included Pak Hon Yong, the leader of the South Korean Communists. When Stalin asked about events in Korea, "Kim Il Sung answered that the situation was not bad, and that the North and South were getting ready for unification." But he could not predict how the Koreans would respond to "decisive measures," he said. This did not seem to bother Stalin much. People were like Panurge's flock, he replied: "they would follow the leading ram wherever he might go." Pak Hon Yong then spoke up. He described in glowing terms the conditions of the resistance movement against the regime of Syngman Rhee. He said that a "200,000-strong detachment of Communists in South Korea was ready to rebel at the first signal from the North, and that the population of the South was waiting for land reform and other democratic transformations such as those already conducted in the North."[70]

According to Yoo Sung Chul, who was present at the meeting, Kim recognized that his main task was to calm Stalin's fears of U.S. intervention. To this end, "he made four points to persuade Stalin that the United States would not participate in the war: (1) it would be a decisive surprise attack and the war would be won in three days; (2) there would be an uprising of 200,000 Party members in South Korea; (3) there were guerrillas in the southern provinces of South Korea; and (4) the United States would not have time to participate. Stalin bought the plan."[71]

After listening to the Koreans' presentations, Stalin remarked that "the Korean friends should not expect great assistance and support from the Soviet Union, because it had more important challenges to meet than the Korean problem." Stalin stressed his preoccupation with "the situation in the West" and urged the Koreans to consult with Mao because he had "a good understanding of Oriental matters." The Soviet leader was bluntly telling the Koreans that China was now first among equals within the revolutionary movement in Asia.[72]

Another former North Korean official expands on this last point. Bombarded by Kim's "persistent assertions and requests," he writes, Stalin "reluctantly consented" to his proposals for the attack. Stalin "could not find any excuse for refusal," since Kim had insisted that "he would liberate the people groaning under the dictatorship of Syngman Rhee." Still, Stalin told Kim that even if the United States participated in the war, the Soviet Union had no intention of joining the fray.[73] "Consented," it must be emphasized, did not mean final approval. Stalin was giving a nod to the general idea of an invasion but had made consultations with Mao a condition for his unequivocal assent to any future detailed plan of action.

We find something of the same kind of sliding out from full responsibility in Kim's cautious response to Stalin's question about the situation in the South. Kim could not argue against his own earlier prediction that a "southern rebellion" would result from a shock offensive from the North, but he feared the consequences if that prediction should prove wrong. He thus assigned Pak Hon Yong the task of replying to Stalin, making his colleague the likely scapegoat if the rebellion failed. Less than three years after the end of the war, Pak was tried and executed, though he was not publicly charged with misleading Kim on the revolutionary readiness of the South, for that might have reflected badly on Kim's own judgment and be taken as an admission that Kim had started the war.[74]

Just as Kim was making Pak accountable, so too was Stalin making Mao responsible for the outcome in case of Kim's catastrophic failure. He had to obligate the Chinese, and this is why he told the Koreans to consult Mao. As Stalin evidently judged the Korean situation, Beijing's involvement there would be perceived quite differently in the West from a PLA invasion of Taiwan. If required, Chinese military actions in Korea had the best chance of sharpening the line between China and the West, and Stalin now put a more Machiavellian construction on his earlier prediction that the Americans would "never agree to be thrown out" of Korea or to lose "their reputation as a great power." Later, this American obsession with reputation would fall under the heading of "credibility," and Stalin had thought of a way to use it against them.

When he emphasized that he was mainly preoccupied with the West, and that he would never fight the Americans in Korea, Stalin was reiterating his consistent stance on the matter. This posture excluded any possibility that he would personally give Kim the green light for the invasion. Instead, the Soviet leader told Kim, "'Since I alone cannot decide, I will pass your war plans and military assistance request on to the Party political committee [Politburo] for decision.' Accordingly, Kim Il-song simply returned [home to Korea]."[75] During his final conversation with Kim in April, Stalin once again urged Kim to consult Mao and gave him at least a tacit but still conditional go-ahead before they parted. The Soviet leader said, "If you should get kicked in the teeth, I shall not lift a finger. You have to ask Mao for all the help."[76]

Stalin here maneuvered himself into the enviable position of having everything to gain and nothing to lose. By forcing Mao to affirm Kim's scheme, Stalin forever after could say that he had left the decision to Mao. Fully aware of Mao's determination to seize Taiwan, Stalin could be reasonably sure of Mao's assent and could be confident that the onus for the attack, whether successful or not and regardless of the U.S. reaction, would rest solely on Mao (and Kim).

This was the background to Kim's visit to the PRC after returning home from Moscow. Despite some Soviet and Korean skepticism about whether the Beijing meeting actually took place, Shi Zhe has said that Kim stayed in his house during the visit.[77] Other knowledgeable sources, Soviet as well as Chinese, bear him out. The authors of a recent Chinese account of China's decision to enter the war flatly state, "In April 1950, Kim Il Sung paid a secret visit to Beijing on his way back from Moscow," though we now know that Kim flew from Pyongyang to see Mao from May 13 to 16.[78]

But much as Stalin had badgered Kim about the need to persuade Mao and to get his guarantee of support for the coming war, these authors say that the Korean leader "only informed Mao of his determination to reunify his country by military means during the visit and released no details of his military plan, let alone the date of the action."[79] In fact, it could hardly have been otherwise, for no officially approved plan yet existed. Before Kim could proceed further in his planning, he needed the approval of Stalin, who in turn was awaiting the results of Kim's approach to Mao.

Some five years later, Marshal Peng Dehuai recalled that Mao disagreed with Kim's proposed action but had no way of opposing or stopping it, and a senior Soviet diplomat with knowledge of the archives has told us that Mao at first expressed considerable skepticism when Kim told him that Stalin had reassessed the North's potential for a successful assault on the South.[80] Still, the Chinese were pursuing the unification of their own country and could not deny the Koreans the chance to do the same. Mao offered various arguments in the hope of getting Kim to reconsider, but the Korean would not listen and "did not take [them] seriously."[81] He kept guaranteeing that the KPA could "solve the Korean problem" on its own.

A Soviet diplomat recalls that throughout the multiple bilateral talks on Kim's proposals for war, the Soviets knew that the Chinese Politburo opposed the idea.[82] This stands in seeming contradiction to Mao's positive though noncommittal answer to Kim's request for backing. The contradiction disappears, however, if we take into account Mao's preoccupation with Taiwan at this time. By now, the Chinese leader had secured a promise of Soviet support for the invasion of Taiwan. He could not express his fears of American intervention in Korea without admitting to Stalin the likelihood of the same U.S. involvement in Taiwan, thereby jeopardizing that support. Mao had to be positive.

But the Chairman did raise the question of U.S. intervention in Korea with Kim, and this time in a way that did not exclude the possibility. Mao asked him whether he would like China to send troops to the Sino-Korean border if the Americans did become involved. Kim answered that he would achieve victory within a month, and that the United States could not deploy its forces before then. He rejected the need for sending Chinese troops to the border and appeared confident that the Soviet assistance in hand or in the pipeline was all that would be needed.[83]

Stalin was not long in adding his blessing to Mao's for Kim's war objectives. We may never know the exact details of the series of bilateral conversations among the three leaders, but what is obvious even from the material at hand is how skillfully Kim had achieved his ends by playing on the complicated relations between Stalin and Mao. We would predict that if any transcripts of conversations turn up, they will reveal a pattern of Kim exaggerating Stalin's support to Mao, and vice versa. In the process, Kim

Value of Soviet Military Assistance to North Korea, 1949–1951
(in 000s of rubles)

Year	General[a]	Specific recipients		
		Air force	Armored force	Chief Artillery Department
1949	249,962	195,293	n.a.	51,388
1950	869,677	347,757	1,238	383,164
1951	2,612,822	1,182,044	179,253	881,585

SOURCE: Soviet General Staff document in the possession of G. Kuzmin [pseud.].
[a]The total of all military aid, including assistance to the air force, armored force, and Chief Artillery Department, plus other unspecified recipients.

was restricting his own future options and his ability to hedge against failure.

Moreover, even before Mao gave his "approval" of Kim's intentions, the Soviet leader began to act. According to the North Korean general who headed the Ordnance Directorate of the North's Ministry of Defense, "After [Kim's] April meeting with Stalin, Moscow . . . began to send additional weapons. As soon as Kim Il Sung returned home, the weapons began to arrive in huge numbers at the [DPRK] port of Chongjin. The quantities were obviously bigger than before. This was a final stage in the preparations for war. On arrival, the weapons were immediately distributed among the troops deployed along the 38th parallel."[84]

Two sets of data suggest the scale of this Soviet assistance and, to a limited extent, the timing of its delivery. The ruble value of the shipments for the years 1949, 1950, and 1951 is shown in the accompanying table. The Russian original on which it is based is titled "Actual Deliveries in Industrial Prices," but neither the table nor the surrounding text explains how to convert the prices into foreign currency equivalents. Nor do we know what the prices of Soviet armaments were in this period, though we assume the figures were for internal use and not charges to the North Koreans. It is clear, for all this, that Soviet military deliveries to North Korea jumped dramatically after 1949, and the bulk of these were reportedly put in train soon after Kim's return to Korea in April 1950.

Exactly what was shipped, and when, are unknown, but our second set of figures shows that the KPA was well equipped to go into battle. On the eve of the war, it possessed 258 T-34 tanks (under the 105th Tank Brigade), 178 warplanes, roughly 1,600 artillery pieces and mortars, and several detachments of naval vessels. According to Soviet estimates, the North had a decisive advantage over the South in tanks, personnel, artillery and mortars, and planes. The South had the edge in only one category, naval vessels.[85] But that edge bore little on the land battle being planned, and the overall superiority of the North corresponded to the level prescribed in Soviet military doctrine for a successful offensive.[86]

Mao's Target: Taiwan

Meanwhile, through this whole period of consultations, Mao had been concentrating on his own invasion plans. On February 4, while he was still in Moscow, he had ordered the army to organize the paratroop units needed for an assault on Taiwan; a week later, he approved a report from the Third Field Army designating four divisions to train for the landing operations. On March 11, following his return to Beijing, Mao endorsed the efforts of a former Nationalist general, Zhang Zhizhong, to bring Taiwan under Beijing's control through negotiations—the so-called path of peaceful liberation—as part of the propaganda preparations for the armed attack that Mao regarded as inevitable. At the end of the month, he set in motion plans for an assault on the Zhoushan Islands off Zhejiang Province as a prelude to a landing on Quemoy. After Quemoy, Taiwan would be next.[87]

As the phased plan for the invasion of Taiwan was coming together, Mao, on April 21, sanctioned a major demobilization of the People's Liberation Army. We may never know the full reasoning behind this decision, which stayed in force even after Kim's visit later in the month and, even more incredibly, until after the war had begun. Was the Chairman so confident that the civil war, including the occupation of Taiwan, would come to a successful conclusion? Was he so reassured by Kim's predictions of a quick victory and lack of interest in a pledge of backup troops that he could dismiss Korea as China's problem? Or, was Mao simply positioning himself to stay outside the conflict on the peninsula if it got out of hand? Chinese scholars consider the first question the most relevant one in citing three reasons for Mao's decision: the elimination of most of China's ubiquitous bandits, the limited troop requirements for the invasion of Taiwan and Tibet, and the overriding need to cut military expenses and convert to a civilian economy.[88]

Whatever his thinking, Taiwan was the main target. On April 29, Mao directed Liu Shaoqi to rewrite a report on the situation at home and abroad "in a more tactical way" and to deemphasize China's role in the worldwide struggle between socialism and imperialism so as not to irritate the United States.[89] Although fierce anti-American propaganda continued to fill the pages of Chinese newspapers, Beijing made modest conciliatory gestures toward Washington, including the release of three captured American airmen and minor diplomatic initiatives.[90] On the other hand, on May 11,

Mao severely criticized the Political Department of the 32nd Corps for permitting contacts between its officers and American missionaries in Fujian Province opposite Taiwan.[91] By this time, the PLA had begun assembling the invasion force along the coast, from Shandong to Fujian provinces, and Mao feared that news of these preparations would reach Taipei via the Americans.

The timing of this buildup was hardly coincidental. Once Mao was certain of the imminence of war on the Korean Peninsula, he accelerated his own battle plans. In late April, around the time Kim was in Moscow, Premier Zhou Enlai sent a cable to the Soviet defense minister, Nikolai Bulganin, requesting a speed-up in the delivery of such naval requisitions as ships, airplanes, and coastal artillery. Zhou, who among his other duties was to play a major role in creating China's defense industry, now wanted a guarantee that these items would be delivered by the summer of 1950, and no later than the following spring.[92]

Simultaneously, the CCP Central Committee issued an instruction proclaiming "the liberation of Taiwan . . . the most important task for the entire Party" and ordering Party organizations in East China specifically to provide all necessary assistance in preparation for the Third Field Army to cross the Taiwan Strait. Tacitly, a race had begun between Mao and Kim. Each rushed to fire the first volley, an act that could doom the other's plans. Neither leader would have acted differently even if he had foreseen that outcome.

The Decision

For Stalin, Kim had obeyed his request to consult Mao, and Mao had not opposed the plan for war. Yet Stalin had acted before Mao's response.

Shortly after Kim's return to Pyongyang from Moscow, he received confirmation of Stalin's attitude toward an invasion of the South. The "confirmation" came in the form of a team of Soviet advisers sent to oversee the preparations for war. They included Major General Vasiliev (a battle veteran and hero of the Soviet Union who recently had replaced Major General Smirnov as head of the advisory group), Major General Postnikov (adviser to the KPA General Staff), and Major General Marchenko (an adviser to the KPA General Political Bureau). At this time, a bilateral working group was formed to consider how to proceed. The Korean members included Kim Il Sung, Kang Kon (chief of the KPA General Staff), Kim Chaek (deputy commander of the KPA), and Ho Ka I (or A. I. Hegai, a leader of the Soviet Koreans and member of the Politburo of the Korean Workers' Party). It was "almost certainly" in the course of a meeting of this working group that Kim Il Sung "declared his final resolution to start a war."[93]

Yoo Sung Chul, who as head of the KPA Operations Directorate was in on all the proceedings, provides a revealing picture of the decision-making process. According to him, the new Soviet advisers were chosen for their combat experience; all were from the Soviet General Staff in Moscow:

I did not know, but I thought, that when they sent the advisers, they would have had to consult first in Moscow how to start the war. But they arrived empty-handed. They didn't bring any written order with them. . . . After the May 1st celebrations, Postnikov summoned me. I went to him, and he asked me if we had a plan in our staff. I answered yes. Every army, of course, has an operations plan. We had composed ours on our own. I translated it from Korean into Russian.

Postnikov said, no, this plan is no good. He did not like the way we treated co-ordination between different branches of troops. Moreover, our plan was a defensive one, and he did not like it. He said that they [the Soviet military advisers] would draft one themselves. After a few days—I do not remember, three or four days—they drafted a combat order and passed it to Kang Kon, the chief of staff. Kang Kon summoned me and told me that it was top secret. He ordered me to translate it [from Russian into Korean]. I translated it and passed it to Kang Kon. Kang Kon gave this plan to Kim Il Sung. We did not send it to Stalin for approval, though probably the advisers sent it [to Moscow] themselves.

When they were writing this operations plan, they did not consult with anybody. They did everything themselves. They did not study the terrain and did not know it. . . . Because of that, they made a lot of mistakes. . . .

[This operations plan] was an order for a counterattack and included movement and combat orders for each unit. Another document concerned the coordination between the different branches of the armed forces, among the army, navy, air force, artillery, etc. Besides that, there was a document on engineering support. These were separate documents. There also was a document concerning logistics, on providing supplies from the rear. . . . The draft in Russian was entitled "Preemptive Strike Operations Plan." Presumably, at this same time, the advisers rushed their plan to Stalin for his approval. This top secret plan was then and forever after referred to as a "counterattack" plan, even though it included a "plan to conceal the preparations for a southern invasion as military exercises."

Other sources agree that both the Soviet and the Korean drafters knew the plan involved an attack, not a counterattack. The idea was to use the turmoil and guerrilla struggle in the South and the continuing border skirmishes along the 38th parallel as a "pretext." As Yoo says, "Even after Kim Il Sung dies, you won't be able to find any legal document about an attack; it was a counteroffensive. The meaning of this was (and that was stated there) that South Korea was attacking us and that we would counterattack. . . . It was a fake, disinformation to cover ourselves."

The Soviet role in drafting the plan causes us to examine in some detail Stalin's shift of position on Kim's project, from a wary endorsement of the invasion to an evident willingness to participate in the planning. As one senior Soviet diplomat puts it, "Up to April 1950, Stalin was always cautioning Kim Il Sung concerning his plans for military action, but after that he for some reason changed his mind and began to push for a military solution very actively."[94] One reason for this change of heart relates to the broader strategic framework that so preoccupied Stalin. During April–May, the American hands-off policy, especially toward Korea, was receiving ever closer scrutiny in the Kremlin. Stalin may have been impressed, for example, by the statement of Tom Connally, chairman of the Senate Committee on Foreign Relations, that Korea was not an indispensable part of the U.S. defense strategy and that the Communists could overrun Korea whenever they "take a notion" to do so.[95] It certainly impressed Syngman Rhee, who chastised Connally on May 10 for extending "an open invitation to the Communists to come down and take over South Korea." While some scholars have concluded that statements like Connally's finally convinced Stalin that the Americans would not oppose the North's invasion, we believe his reasoning was far more complex.[96]

March and April had marked a noticeable hardening of American policy toward China. On March 15, Acheson publicly denounced the Sino-Soviet treaty as "an evil omen of imperialistic domination," and the Chinese leadership for having sold out China to the Soviets.[97] His words seemed to be given force a month later, when the Communists invaded Hainan Island on April 16. As if to demonstrate the accuracy of the CIA's estimate that the Chinese possessed "the capability of carrying out their frequently expressed intention of seizing Taiwan during 1950,"[98] the PLA defeated the Nationalist forces in about two weeks. This estimate came only three days after the President received NSC 68, a report on U.S. objectives and programs for national security that, according to the historian Gordon Chang, strengthened the military point of view on China within the U.S. administration.[99] More and more senior officials and analysts advocated stepping in to ensure the Nationalists' hold on Taiwan. Enough signs of a broad behind-the-scenes review of the administration's Asian policies had surfaced in the press that experts in Moscow could not have missed it, though only solid intelligence could have given them a complete and accurate picture.[100]

Stalin would have concluded from press reports and intelligence that, though the Americans might want to aid Taiwan or even South Korea, it would take them many months to amass and get that aid to the western Pacific. The timing was on Kim's side if he moved quickly and decisively. In the worst case, U.S. intervention would lead to a clash between Beijing and Washington and a denial of Taiwan to the Chinese Communists. The resulting rise in Sino-American hostilities would only increase Mao's reliance on Stalin.

Furthermore, Stalin was well aware that the United States would be most reluctant to go to war with the Soviet Union over Korea. With an army that had been sharply reduced after World War Two, it could not run the risk of Soviet retaliation against Western Europe or Japan. Moreover, the Soviet leader reportedly minimized the danger of any such escalation because he had bought Kim Il Sung's argument that a North Korean attack would touch off a revolution in the South, making for a quick and easy consolidation of control.*

Thus, we would argue, it was a mixture of short- and long-term estimates of the U.S. posture in Asia, as of April 1950, that finally led Stalin to become directly involved in Kim's military designs. In doing so, as we have remarked, the Soviet dictator would be pursuing his goals on several levels—to expand the buffer zone along his border, to create a springboard against Japan that could be used during a future global conflict, to test the American resolve, to intensify the hostility between Beijing and Washington, and, finally and foremost, to draw U.S. power away from Europe.

For Mao, meanwhile, these matters were still of little concern. He had a new problem to contend with. The massive buildup of forces opposite Taiwan that he had envisioned was taking longer than expected. Thus, in early June the Central Military Commission postponed the attack on Taiwan itself until the summer of 1951. The planning for the seizure of key intermediate islands was ordered to proceed.[101]

This change in the invasion timetable helps explain why on June 15, only ten days before the outbreak of the conflict on the Korean Peninsula, Mao instructed the acting chief of the General Staff, Nie Rongzhen, to integrate Nationalist defectors into the regular PLA divisions and to develop agricultural units to make the army more self-sufficient. Mao ordered the large-scale demobilization of the PLA to go forward and approved plans for an ideological indoctrination campaign after the troop reductions had been completed later in the year.[102]

With the Taiwan invasion on hold, Mao could proceed with operations to consolidate his grip on the mainland and did not even hint at the necessity of heightening the level of military preparedness or beefing up his forces on the Korean border in anticipation of the war. Just the opposite. On June 23, the then deputy commander of the units chosen for the invasion of Taiwan, Su Yu, asked the Central Military Commission to trans-

---

*The best proof that the Soviets really believed in these optimistic estimates is the fact that the battle plan, which they initially drafted, scheduled the first stage of the military operations to end with the occupation of Seoul after just three or four days of combat. The plan was predicated on the assumption that uprisings throughout the South would result in a lightning victory within about a month. We shall return to the battle schedule when we review the initial stage of the war. See above, footnote to p. 136.

fer three or four corps (*jun*) to East China as a reserve force for the later campaign in the Taiwan Strait. Mao approved this proposal.[103] Riveted to the long-term preparations for that campaign, Mao paid no special attention to Korea, where the conflict would break out 48 hours later.

Mao, as we have shown, was aware of Kim's preparations for military action because he had dispatched ethnic Korean troops and weaponry to the KPA in January, communicated with Stalin on the issue in February, and had relevant conversations with the Korean leader in May. At the same time, there are good reasons to accept the conclusion of Korean and Chinese authors that Mao was not informed about the details of the Korean plans or the timing of the assault.[104] His low priority for China's military preparedness on the very eve of the war is perhaps the best justification for this conclusion.

Keeping Mao out of the picture was Kim's intention. A striking fact about the two months before the war is that the North Koreans—and the Soviets—took steps to keep the Chinese in the dark about their military preparations. According to Yoo Sung Chul, for example, members of the pro-Chinese Yan'an faction "who had entered various military positions were excluded" from helping to draft the operations plan in part "because we had to maintain security."[105] And a former senior North Korean supply officer vividly recalls that before the outbreak of the war, all Soviet weapons were transported to the DPRK by sea instead of by rail through Chinese territory for the specific purpose of denying the Chinese any hard intelligence about the North's preparations. Another retired North Korean officer confirms that purpose.[106] Mao's endorsement had not won Kim's trust.

The PLA's generals were thus in the worst possible position. They knew that an attack was coming in Korea but not when or how. Their armies were being demobilized even as they were supposed to be readying them for a major invasion far to the south. Their leader anticipated an American response to the North's action in Korea, but, as we shall see, they could adopt only modest countervailing measures (such as strengthening the Strategic Reserve).* Mao had spoken, and they could only fall in step behind him.

For these reasons, a mood of apprehension permeated the Chinese high command in the two months before June 25. At least some PLA com-

---

*In the winter of 1949, Mao had removed the Thirteenth Army (made up of the 38th and 39th corps) from the Fourth Field Army to form a support force for local PLA units in times of emergency. The following May, against the possibility of crises in Taiwan, Korea, or Vietnam, Mao added the 40th corps, then on Hainan Island, to this so-called Strategic Reserve. The unit was based in Henan Province. Xu Yan, *Diyi Ci*, p. 16; Du Ping, "Wise Decision," p. 8; Sun Mei, "Introduction to the Various Armies," p. 21.

manders feared that Pyongyang's attack on the South might endanger the young Chinese state. Nonetheless, they could not impede Kim's plans or even appear to be disapproving. Their lack of precise knowledge of the North's timetable was obviously Kim Il Sung's doing, and for this reason, it is not surprising that "on the very eve of the war, relations between the PRC representatives in Pyongyang and DPRK authorities were very tense. Sometimes the Soviet embassy even had to mediate, stressing to the Koreans that the Chinese were their comrades, brothers, and natural allies."[107]

Allies they may have been, but after the war, Chinese leaders, behind closed doors, still voiced their bitterness at having been excluded from the final decision-making on the war. In the mid-1950s, Peng Dehuai and Chen Yi fumed that Kim's "surprise attack" was designed solely by him and Stalin, without consultations with Beijing but at a terrible price for China.[108] As one indicator of the Chinese attitude toward that "surprise attack," we may note that from June to October of 1950—until the Chinese troops entered the war—Beijing did not send any substantial assistance to its "Korean brothers."[109]

The War Begins

The timing of the attack for 4:00 A.M. on Sunday, June 25, was Kim's decision. The fighting began on the Ongjin Peninsula in the west, an area of recurrent border incidents, and then spread along the parallel. The approved operations plan had not specified a date or time. Behaving in his usual manner, Kim consulted with only a handful of senior Koreans. He "simply made up his mind and went ahead. But he normally made up his mind after listening to the Russian advisers." One knowledgeable Korean general adds, "June 25th was proposed by the advisers. It was Sunday, and they may have used the experience of war with Germany, when Hitler attacked Russia on June 22, also a Sunday."[110]

General Kang Sang Ho, who attended the cabinet meeting that rubberstamped the decision for war, notes that it was held only an hour before the invasion began:

Even there, Kim was talking about a counterattack, about South Korea attacking. According to the Constitution, only the cabinet could decide questions of war and peace. Kim said that the South Koreans were already attacking. So as commander-in-chief, Kim ordered a counterattack. He said, "Now war and peace should be determined by the cabinet. I order the war to begin. Do all of you agree?" Everyone did.[111]

We now return to the question of the Soviet–North Korean plan for prosecuting the war. Scheduled to last about a month, the war was to proceed down the peninsula in stages, and the outcome, it was stated, would hinge on the first few days of battle. It is in this sense that Yoo Sung Chul, one of the retired North Korean generals we interviewed, recalls, "The Korean War was planned to last only a few days, so we did not plan anything in case things might go wrong. If you fight a war without preparing for failures, then you are asking for trouble." Another, General Chung Sang Chin, explains that with the conquest of Seoul, "We thought that Syngman Rhee would capitulate, and that the Americans would not intervene. After three days we reorganized the army. The Soviets drafted a new battle plan. We started to assign orders to the units but communications were very poor, and U.S. aircraft were taking a very heavy toll." Finally, an officer of the KPA engineering unit that occupied Seoul laments, "After the occupation of Seoul there were no further preparations. . . . We had to reorganize our communications. We organized two new corps, the first occupied Seoul and the other fought in the east. Communications between divisions, corps, and armies were disconnected. Each unit moved on its own, and each had its own plan."[112]

The Korean and Soviet generals we have interviewed concur that the stages planned to follow the conquest of Seoul never occurred. Improvisation was necessary because communications and coordination among North Korean echelons and units were poor and because the predicted grand uprising in the South never materialized, though there was some serious fighting by guerrillas and infiltrators. But Kim's passion for secrecy had made it impossible to organize opponents of the Rhee regime sufficiently to even attempt a nationwide rebellion. One former North Korean general notes, "Kim supposed that Pak Hon Yong would take care of the guerrilla and Party members [for the uprising in the South], but he failed."[113]

If the southern guerrillas did not get the word, it is no wonder that Washington was caught totally by surprise. Within hours of the North's early-morning assault, Washington received reports of what was clearly an all-out offensive, and Department of State intelligence specialists promptly concluded that the "move in Korea was decided only after the most minute examination [by the Kremlin] of all factors involved in the Far Eastern situation." Moscow, it was believed, had acted to liquidate the South Korean government "on ground militarily most favorable to the Soviet Union" and to back "possible Chinese moves in support of Ho Chi Minh [in Indochina], Burmese Communists, or Malayan Communists."[114]

Department policymakers had definite views on the proper U.S. response, including an urgent request for a meeting of the UN Security Council.[115] Although they were uncertain about China's precise role in Kim Il Sung's decision to launch the attack, they believed that, at the very least, China had not opposed the strike. As they saw it, if the United States did not make a strong reply, there might be "a defeat for U.S. policy in Korea," and this in turn might "cause Chinese Communist leaders to adopt more bold and militant tactics in their attempts to promote Communism in other parts of Asia." Conversely, not only would a powerful U.S. response "produce a marked psychological reaction" on these leaders, but "the prestige of the Chinese Communist regime would suffer" and "the relative weakness or ineptness of the USSR in its Korean adventure" would be exposed. Such an outcome, so the argument went, would weaken Beijing's ties to Moscow.[116]

At dinner that evening at his temporary residence, Blair House, President Truman listened to his military and political lieutenants assess the unfolding crisis and then "emphasized the importance of making the survey of possible next moves by the Soviet Union."[117] The President apparently concurred with senior Department of State officers that if the Soviets "could get away with this move they would probably move in other areas."[118]

It was these other moves that were of paramount concern. In the case of the People's Republic of China, the worry in these and related conversations was not Chinese intervention but whether Taiwan would survive an invasion from the mainland. There was no mention of Korea at all, for example, in a memo that Gen. Douglas MacArthur, Commander-in-Chief, Far East, approved on June 14. Only eleven days before the outbreak of the war, it warned that "the strategic interests of the United States will be in serious jeopardy if Formosa [Taiwan] is allowed to be dominated by a power hostile to the United States" (meaning the PRC).[119]

As for the Soviet Union, once the war started, many U.S. officials concluded that it would stay out of the war. They could adduce no evidence of Soviet intentions to intervene directly on the Korean Peninsula. Such senior Soviet specialists as George Kennan and Charles E. Bohlen expressed the opinion that Moscow would instead do its utmost to "get the United States involved with Asiatic troops, particularly Chinese."[120] Even after the beginning of the all-out Chinese offensive in late November, Secretary of Defense George C. Marshall argued that the United States should not become "involved in a general war in China with the Chinese Communists. To do this would be to fall into a carefully laid Russian trap."[121]

The U.S. and South Korean fortunes on the battlefield steadily deteriorated until mid-August, when U.S. air power and armor began to take their toll on the overextended North Korean forces.[122] During this time, news from the war zone absorbed Washington; neither China nor the Soviet Union, whatever their ultimate intentions, was of comparable concern.[123] In any case, U.S. leaders felt reasonably confident about their initial assessments of the Chinese and Soviet unwillingness to risk war with the United States.

Nevertheless, on June 27 the President took the precaution of ordering the U.S. Seventh Fleet to prevent all military action in the Taiwan Strait, thereby bringing U.S. military power to the salvation of the Nationalists on Taiwan and into direct opposition to Beijing. Given the preponderance of naval forces on the American side, China had no military means to reply, and intercourse between Washington and Beijing quickly degenerated into a war of words.

But as the exchanges flew back and forth, analysts in Washington were somewhat mystified that, in public at least, Beijing did not appear to assign a high priority to the war.[124] There is no evidence that they took special note of a Chinese editorial of July 6 implying that since the United States would be unlikely to concede defeat, the war could be a prolonged affair.[125] Despite warnings from the Indian government "against dismissing lightly" Beijing's allegations that the U.S. actions in the Taiwan Strait constituted aggression against China and were a harbinger of direct military action against China, Washington had no way of judging such statements and added them to a long list of things that might go wrong.[126]

In fact, China had good reason not to assign much priority to Korea. For the moment, its immediate problem was coping with the ominous reality that Truman had committed naval units to the Taiwan Strait. For the moment, the significance of that reality put any thought of coming to Kim's defense on the back burner. Mao's overriding concern with China's own predicament came across most tellingly in his remarks at a meeting of the Central People's Government Council on June 28:

The U.S. invasion of Asia can only touch off the broad and resolute opposition of Asian people. On January 5, Truman said in an announcement that the United States would not intervene in Taiwan. Now his conduct proves that what he said was false. Moreover, he shredded all international agreements related to the American commitment not to intervene in China's internal affairs. The United States thus reveals its imperialist nature in its true colors. It is very advantageous to the Chinese people and the people of Asia [to draw a lesson from the U.S. policy toward Taiwan]. The United States is unable to justify in any way its intervention in the internal affairs of Korea, the Philippines, and Vietnam. The sympathies of the Chinese people and the vast people of the world lie with the countries that have been invaded, and by no means with American imperialism. . . . People throughout the nation and the world, unite and make full preparations for frustrating any provocation of American imperialism.[127]

The Chinese leader considered the U.S. actions toward Taiwan tantamount to a declaration of war.[128] His speech was published in *Renmin Ribao* on June 29 and was evidently intended for a Washington audience.

The most striking fact is that Mao did not make a point of U.S. interference in Korean affairs. He directed his anger instead mainly at American policy toward Taiwan. In a twinkling, Mao's dream of realizing China's complete unification was shattered. His announcement that "it is useful for the Chinese people" to draw a lesson from the U.S. policy toward Taiwan, we believe, demonstrated his anger and appeared to be an omen of how he would later act.

For a time, however, Mao remained determined to put into effect the decision to reduce the strength of the PLA by 1,500,000.[129] On June 30, the Central Military Commission and the Government Administration Council (replaced by the State Council in 1954) agreed to create a body called the Central Demobilization Commission, with Zhou Enlai as head, to oversee this troop reduction.[130] Moreover, as late as July 12, the Chinese high command proceeded with the first stages of the stretched-out Taiwan invasion plan by authorizing assaults on several offshore islands.[131] As we shall see, the schedule for the attack in the summer of 1951 was not finally scrapped until early August.

In this, Mao at last acknowledged that the outbreak of the Korean War had dramatically altered China's strategic position. Beijing was now compelled to face challenges in two directions at once, Taiwan and Korea. Mao's strategic doctrine had long called for concentrating forces in only one direction, and he had to choose.[132] As early as June 30, Zhou Enlai told the head of the navy, Xiao Jingguang: "The change in the situation adds difficulties to our plan to attack Taiwan. . . . The present plan for our armed forces [to cope with the changed situation] is to continue demobilizing the ground forces, strengthen the navy and the air force, and postpone the schedule for attacking Taiwan."[133] The decision communicated to Xiao reflected Mao's first doubts about where his priorities lay. The earlier order to put off the attack on Taiwan was now extended to include the intermediate offshore islands.

Mao waited for Washington's response to what he saw as China's forbearance to no avail. Slowly and not without reluctance, the Chairman began to change his mind. In the middle of July 1950, the Central Military Commission for the first time cited the Korean fighting as the reason for postponing the liberation of Taiwan for the time being.[134] On August 11, it formally delayed the invasion until 1952, and at the end of September, Mao banned the use of slogans promising liberation by a definite date from the National Day celebration.[135] With the Taiwan invasion on long-term hold and the war in Korea escalating, Mao began to concentrate on countering the American threat at hand.[136]

Beijing Prepares for War

In the eyes of the Chinese leaders, the Korean conflict was a revolutionary war and could not be used to justify the "American armed invasion of Taiwan."[137] Thus, when weighing their own future conduct, two questions reportedly preoccupied them: why was Washington's response to the Korean crisis so swift, and why did the United States drastically change its policy toward Taiwan?[138]

To Mao, the answer to both seemed plain: he quickly concluded that the real U.S. aim was to threaten China itself, and he began to act accordingly. His first move shortly after the fighting broke out was to secure his own border by ordering Chinese anti-aircraft units stationed in Andong (now Dandong) to cross the Yalu River to the Korean city of Sinuiju with the objective of protecting the bridges there (see the map on p. 160).[139]

Mao had no doubts about who had launched the war or why. For him, this was a revolutionary war, a struggle for liberation, and he had already blessed Kim Il Sung's aims.[140] But whether because of what seemed to be an early and growing obsession with the minutiae of the Korean conflict or for some other reason, he clearly had doubts about the outcome. The war was barely weeks along when he predicted that the North probably could not achieve an early conquest and began to weigh the potential impact of a massive U.S. intervention on China's security.[141] On July 7 and 10, Premier Zhou Enlai, who was Mao's deputy and the person in charge of daily affairs at the Central Military Commission,* called its senior members into emergency session to examine the PLA's options in dealing with the mounting conflict.[142] At the July 7 meeting, these officers decided to transfer crack units from the Fourth Field Army to the Northeast, near the Korean border.[143] They then passed a major five-part resolution, which an official Chinese source has briefly summarized as follows:[144]

  1. [Concerning] the movement and deployment of troops: by the end of July, four corps and three artillery divisions will be deployed at Andong, . . . Ji'an, and Benxi [in Northeast China];
  2. [Concerning] the organization of headquarters: Su Yu is appointed com-

---

*Zhou was in charge of the commission's day-to-day operations from Oct. 19, 1949, to July 1952, when Mao, disgruntled by Zhou's increasing stature within the military establishment, removed him from that role and named Peng Dehuai as his replacement. Four years later, in 1956, Mao ruptured the tie altogether by removing Zhou from the post of commission vice-chairman. Based on Deng Lifeng, *Xin Zhongguo*, pp. 7, 262; and Qi Shengping, "Description of Marshal Liu Bocheng," p. 3.

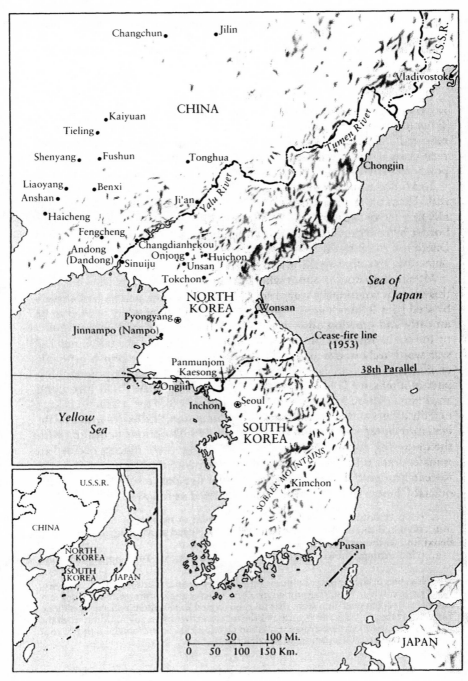

Korea and Adjacent Areas

mander and political commissar of the Northeast Frontier Force Command, and Xiao Hua is appointed deputy political commissar;

3. [Concerning] preparations for [adequate] logistic support;

4. [Concerning] preparations for bringing up (the related military units) to full strength: the General Logistics Department [of the Central Military Commission] is charged with formulating relevant plans for implementation by the prescribed time; and

5. [Concerning] political mobilization: in general, political mobilization should be conducted under the slogan of defending national security. The General Political Department [of the commission] is made responsible for working out a directive with concrete plans.

Mao signed the commission's resolution at midnight on the 7th and directed the acting chief of the General Staff, Nie Rongzhen, to implement it. The resolution was the first high-level decision to prepare for China's entry into the Korean War.

It was passed the same day as the Security Council authorized the creation of a UN command for Korea under a U.S. general.[145] Since the Soviet representatives had not yet ended their walkout, this resolution, like the earlier ones of June 25 and June 27 branding North Korea an "aggressor," went through without a veto. Although Soviet, Chinese, and Korean authors have called the Soviets' absence "a mistake," it was by no means inadvertent. Indeed, the decision was taken at the Politburo level.[146] Andrei Gromyko recalls that he advised Stalin to order the Soviet representative, Iakov Malik, to return to the Security Council and use the veto to defeat any resolution hostile to North Korea or the Soviet Union. But Stalin merely responded, "In my opinion, the Soviet representative must not take part in the Security Council meeting." Gromyko even argued that the Soviet absence would allow the Security Council to dispatch the forces of other countries to South Korea as "United Nations troops." Stalin was unmoved by this argument.[147]

There are two reasonable explanations for Stalin's behavior. First, he may still have believed at this point that the war would go according to the approved operations plan. In that case, the UN decisions would be irrelevant. The second (but not mutually exclusive) explanation is connected with the Sino-Soviet treaty. On the very day the war began, it became clear that the United States would intervene. Given Stalin's long-held policy of avoiding a Soviet-American clash, we believe that he would have reasoned as follows. Should the situation deteriorate to the point that China felt it had to become involved, one side or the other might formally declare "a state of war." That would activate the treaty, thereby obligating Moscow to "immediately render military and other assistance [to Beijing] with all means at its disposal" (Art. 1). Stalin would have been appalled at the prospect, and he would have welcomed the thought that the United States would not declare war with its troops operating under a UN banner. Not surprisingly, the Soviet vice–foreign minister stated at this time that the Soviet Union would not interfere in Korean affairs, and that other countries should not intervene as well, a statement that Chinese officials privately characterized as a "precious jewel" for Truman.[148] The record shows that both Mao and Stalin knew where the other stood on the issue of overt Soviet support.

At the meeting of July 10, the Central Military Commission decided to send the Strategic Reserve to the Northeast, to supplement what was by then a thoroughly thinned-out PLA force.[149] With the wind-down of the civil war, more and more troops had been transferred to South and Southwest China, to the point where only the 42nd Corps and local security units, a total of 170,000 men, with five infantry divisions as the main force, remained in the Northeast Military Region opposite Korea.[150] These divisions represented only one twenty-seventh of the PLA strength.[151]

On July 13, the Central Military Commission ordered the new and old deployments consolidated into a new command, the Northeast Frontier Force (NFF). Su Yu was appointed commander and political commissar and Xiao Jingguang deputy commander. It is clear from the appointment of the two generals who had been responsible for the attack on Taiwan, that Mao had now singled out the Northeast as the principal area of military concern.* The initial troop strength of the NFF—consisting of the Strategic Reserve (i.e., the Thirteenth Army, or the 38th, 39th, and 40th corps), the 42nd Corps (from Qiqihar, Heilongjiang Province), and three artillery divisions (the 1st, 2nd, and 8th)—would total 255,000 men.[152]

Two days later, the commission ordered the entire Thirteenth Army and the 42nd Corps to set off for the Sino-Korean border. By the end of the month, these forces had taken up position in Andong, Fengcheng, Ji'an, Tonghua, Liaoyang, Haicheng, Benxi, Tieling, and Kaiyuan, all close to the frontier.[153] Over the next two months, the troops underwent intensive combat training with the U.S. army as their postulated enemy. Their commanders ordered ex-Nationalist officers and soldiers, especially those who

---

*Su Yu, deputy commander of the Third Field Army, had been in overall charge of the plan to occupy Taiwan, and Xiao Jingguang, commander of the navy, was responsible for transporting the PLA invasion forces. Zhou Jun, pp. 67, 72. The commission's "Decision on Strengthening the Frontier Defense of the Northeast and Creating the Northeast Frontier Force" also ordered Deng Hua and Huang Yongsheng, commanders of the Fifteenth and Thirteenth armies, to swap posts. But only this part of the plan was carried out. No Northeast Frontier Force headquarters was ever formally established; Gao Gang, who headed the Northeast Military Region, assumed command of the NFF units. Du Ping, "Wise Decision," p. 9; Huang Yi, "Zhou Enlai," 1: 9; "Frontier Force."

had fought alongside U.S. soldiers in Burma, to lecture on American tactics.[154] By then, the Chinese leaders were confronting the very real possibility of an enlargement of the war.

At the outset, as the North Korean forces surged toward the southern tip of the peninsula and appeared on the verge of total victory, the war had caused concern in China, but it did not receive priority attention.[155] Apart from ordering the Northeast People's Government in Shenyang to provide some arms and economic and medical aid to North Korea,[156] China's leaders continued to be preoccupied with the problem of economic reconstruction. As July wore on, bringing increased U.S. involvement, however, the central government in Beijing began to have second thoughts about Kim Il Sung's power to win a quick decision. As Zhou Enlai was to reveal some weeks after the fact, Mao had concluded in late July that the military "situation already suggested that the war might turn into a protracted war."

According to Nie Rongzhen, after analyzing the situation in early August, when the North Korean troops had reached the point of their farthest advance, Mao "and the Central Committee thought that there would probably be complications and a reversal of the situation, because . . . the U.S. imperialists might launch a counteroffensive . . . and because [the North Korean] troops had advanced too far in isolation, leaving their rear area vulnerable."[157] Mao had expressed the same fears to Yoo Sung Chul, the director of the KPA Operations Bureau, when Yoo briefed him in August or early September.* Probably at this same time, Deng Hua, the commander of the Thirteenth Army, asked to send observers to Korea. The request was rejected by the Koreans.[158] Still positive about his ultimate victory, Kim preferred to keep the Chinese at arm's length. Mao's warnings were relayed to Kim and Stalin. Neither took them seriously.[159]

On August 5, Mao contacted Gao Gang, who had taken command of the units deployed as the Northeast Frontier Force units the previous month.[160] Responding to a telegram from Gao, Mao gave Gao authority to redeploy these units as necessary and declared that they were "unlikely" to be assigned any "operational tasks" before the end of August.

Although the order establishing the NFF indicates that its mission was

---

*According to Lim Un, *Founding of a Dynasty*, pp. 187–88, Mao told Yoo: "It is excellent that the Korean people have driven the enemy into the southern sea. But if you push them hard into a corner and lay siege to them for a long time, they will unite tightly like clenched fists. . . . It is difficult to attack the enemy once it is united closely. On such an occasion, it is not so bad for you to retreat to some extent and untie the enemy. Then they will dissolve their union as they stretch bended fingers. . . . By doing this, you can dissipate their strength by cutting off their fingers one by one. . . . From a tactical point of view, sometimes retreat is better than an attack. . . . Your enemy is not an easy one. Don't forget you are fighting with the boss of imperialism. Be prepared for the worst all the time and examine seriously the possibilities of retreat."

originally conceived as a defensive one,[161] Gao was now clearly being told to get it combat ready, and quickly. He was specifically ordered to

position these units for battle by the first ten days of September. . . . Please convene a meeting of cadres at the corps and division levels in the second ten days of the month and there instruct them on the purpose and significance of the operation and its general direction. By the end of the month, various units should make full preparations and await orders to set off. You must solve [in time] the ideological problems of the troops so as to keep up their morale and have everything in a state of readiness.

On the same day, August 5, Nie Rongzhen, in accordance with Mao's decision, issued orders to the same effect: the NFF was to "complete all preparations within this month and stand by for action pending further orders."[162] By late August, U.S. and Taiwanese intelligence had noticed these troops on the move.[163]

August was also the time that the Chinese came to grips with the prospect that American atomic weapons might be used if the PLA entered the war. As they weighed their choices in confronting the United States in Korea, China's top commanders met many times both in Beijing and in the Northeast, and this issue was to come up in both meetings and private conversations. Although abundant evidence has come to light that the United States did consider the nuclear option in Korea, virtually all of the conclusions on the Chinese assessment of the situation have been based on indirect evidence.[164] Because of the importance of this issue to broader strategic considerations in the Sino-Soviet alliance, we must consider how the Chinese dealt with the prospect of an American nuclear response to any PLA intervention.

Beijing's public position, as we have seen, was that the Soviet Union had broken the U.S. nuclear monopoly and "boosted the courage of the revolutionary people."[165] This propaganda line served China well so long as war was a remote contingency. Facing a direct confrontation with the United States in combat, however, had a way of clearing the mind of propaganda. The Chinese high command had to reexamine the validity of its position on the bomb as it weighed its choices for and against direct intervention. At the end of this process, these leaders concluded that the United States would probably not use atomic bombs against China or their forces in Korea.[166]

Beijing's reexamination was prompted in part by scare stories sweeping throughout China. Ironically, these stories may have originated from some government publications in July that had deliberately raised the specter of "the menace of the atomic bomb."[167] Rumormongers, some of them agents of the Nationalists, had fanned a doomsday mood by spreading tales about the power of atomic weapons and promoting popular alarm that they might be used.[168] Atomic panic even seized a fraction of the Thirteenth Army. Reportedly, 10 percent of its officers and men dreaded both the U.S. army and the atomic bomb, and called the Yalu River bridge the "gates of hell."[169] To offset the rumors and fears, the Party launched a campaign to restore morale and confidence in the military's ability to protect the Chinese people.[170]

Despite these reassurances, the leadership itself continued to debate the odds of Washington's using nuclear weapons against China. General MacArthur, in a visit to Taiwan in late July, had appeared to sanction a nuclear first strike, and after the visit, Chiang Kai-shek issued a statement "indicating that the talks [with MacArthur] laid the foundations for a joint defense of Formosa and Sino-American military cooperation."[171] At a meeting in early August, He Long, a member of the Central Military Commission, is said to have bluntly asked, "Is there any chance of the Americans using the atomic bomb?" Nie Rongzhen answered reassuringly: "They might use it, but remember that the United States no longer enjoys an atomic monopoly. . . . So they may be less eager to use it nowadays." But Ye Jianying, Su Yu, and some of the other senior commanders there could not shed their anxieties so easily and kept on asking about Washington's nuclear intentions.[172]

In another high-level meeting, the Politburo studied the argument that U.S. planes might drop atomic bombs on advancing troops in order to defeat human-wave assaults, a tactic then under consideration if China entered the war. The majority of Party leaders reasoned that this would be most unlikely, but even if the bomb were employed on the front lines, Chinese troops would not face a catastrophe. They could devise tactics to minimize the danger to themselves and bring the U.S. defenders within their range of damage.[173]

These conclusions on both the strategic and the battlefield use of nuclear weapons were based on several different arguments. At the most general level, the advocates for action held to the precepts of People's War and its line that only men, not a weapon of mass destruction, could determine the outcome of any war. Moreover, what the Americans would later call a nuclear umbrella had been extended to China by the terms of the Sino-Soviet alliance. The Americans would be deterred, a word never used but clearly implied.[174]

The advocates further argued that the nation's industry and cities could not be effectively targeted by the small number of nuclear weapons then assumed to be in the U.S. arsenal. The industrial base was underdeveloped, mostly small-scale, and scattered, and the urban population was less than

10 percent of the country. A nuclear strike against China would be highly destructive but not decisively so. All these views found official expression throughout the next decade.

The Politburo deduced that Washington might want to select the PLA's bases and troop concentrations in the Northeast as the priority targets for a U.S. nuclear strike. The Soviet Union had vital interests in the Northeast, thanks to the secret agreements concluded in February, and Moscow would have to retaliate in order to protect its own bases in Lüshun and other places. The high command restated its conviction that the Americans would have to weigh possible Soviet retaliation when they pondered the pros and cons of a nuclear strike against China.

The foregoing arguments mostly concerned an attack on China proper, but the advocates of action also argued that the United States would not resort to nuclear weapons in Korea either. The Chinese forces were experienced in mobile and guerrilla warfare; they could scatter and hide, as indeed they did prior to their massive intervention in October. After entering Korea, they could take cover in strong, concealed fortifications, and the Chinese believed that the role of tactical nuclear weapons in the mountainous battlefields of Korea would be limited. Finally, the Chinese and UN forces would be confronting each other in what was called "jigsaw pattern warfare" (*quanya jiaocuo de zhanzheng*). In this confusing and ever changing battlefield, the Americans could not avoid hitting themselves.

These arguments proved compelling to the Politburo. Party and military leaders used only a minimum of time debating the likely conditions or consequences of the use of atomic weapons, even as they pursued a political campaign to ease fears in the public and the army about the bomb's effects. A typical instance of this campaign occurred on August 13 when commanders of the Thirteenth Army convened a meeting of officers at the division level and above in Shenyang to discuss how to accelerate preparations for war. When the possible U.S. use of nuclear weapons came up on the agenda, the arguments were familiar and well rehearsed: the atomic bomb could not decide the outcome of war; any war must ultimately be determined by the soldiers on the ground; the battlefield use of atomic bombs would destroy not only Chinese, but also U.S. troops; the Americans would have to think twice before employing a weapon that was universally opposed by the people of the world. The basic tone of the meeting was that the Americans would almost certainly not resort to the bomb in Korea. By this time, no one was seriously offering counterarguments, and the mood of confidence was dutifully transmitted to the skeptical but reticent soldiers.[175]

Nonetheless, there were some quiet dissenters in the high command. In his capacity as commander of the Fourth Field Army, Lin Biao, for example, let slip his anxieties about the devastation that could be wrought by atomic weapons. It should be stressed that accusations against Lin on this matter long predated his purge and denunciation. Mao had originally picked Lin to command the Chinese forces in Korea. On September 30, Mao discussed the appointment with Lin, who underscored the U.S. possession of the bomb and the terrible consequences it could inflict on China. Allegedly, when Mao persisted, Lin refused the assignment on the excuse of poor health.[176]

Six days later, at a meeting of the Central Military Commission to discuss how to ensure Soviet assistance to Chinese forces in Korea, Lin Biao again voiced his concerns about the bomb. After listing the many problems the leadership was facing in its efforts to consolidate the new regime and reconstruct the warworn country, he said, "We have a certainty of success in defeating the Nationalist troops. The United States is highly modernized. In addition, it possesses the atomic bomb. I have no certainty of success [in fighting the U.S. army]. The central leadership should consider this issue with great care."[177]

We will never know whether Lin Biao was speaking only for himself or voicing what other Chinese generals, such as the earlier skeptics He Long, Ye Jianying, and Su Yu, may have felt but had been unwilling to say openly. Lin was at least repeating what many in the populace and the army ranks were grumbling about: the great gamble of making war on a nuclear-armed nation. In the final analysis, as expected, Mao's unwavering stand on the nuclear issue ended the argument. Within days, the time for decision arrived, and at the moment of truth in early October, no one raised the nuclear question.

SIX

China Enters the Korean War

Weeks before the UN launched its counteroffensive at Inchon on September 15, Mao Zedong had deployed his forces for battle. Whether and how they would be employed would depend on the fortunes of war on the peninsula.

Mao had a bit of breathing space as he watched and waited, for as the political scientist Allen S. Whiting notes in his analysis of the Chinese decision to enter the conflict, during the six-week interval from early August, when the Soviets resumed their seat on the Security Council, to mid-September, the Korean situation was characterized by a military stalemate at the front and a diplomatic impasse in the UN debates. Despite Moscow's propaganda tirades, the Soviets appeared stunned by the speed and tenacity of the U.S. response and, as Stalin had forewarned Kim Il Sung, conspicuously detached from the action.[1] The world waited for a breakthrough.

With the completion of the extensive deployments of PLA units to the Northeast and the fighting in a temporary lull, Mao weighed two high probability outcomes to the struggle for Korea. The first would be a North Korean victory. Under this eventuality, any UN counterattack following the South's defeat would take months to mount, and the Northeast Frontier Force (NFF) would not be needed in Korea. The second possible outcome would be the North's failure to attain a knockout blow and becoming bogged down in a protracted struggle. U.S. and South Korean forces might hold fortified positions on the tip of the peninsula and, when reinforced, launch a counteroffensive. In this case, the NFF would be standing by to save the Democratic People's Republic of Korea.[2]

Uncertain about the next turn of events, the Chinese had to be ready for a crisis decision and the deployment of their armies in Korea. We now turn to the story of that decision.

Washington's Calculus

We begin our story by considering the policies of the United States just as the lull was ending and the UN divisions shifted to the offensive. Those policies were shaping Chinese and Soviet perspectives and molding their responses. During this period, the United States had the opportunity to determine the scope of the war and attempted to communicate its limits to Beijing and Moscow. As it turned out, neither capital was sensitive enough to discern Washington's objectives or to accept them as valid if they did see them. One reason for these failed communications is that the tide of battle was just beginning to turn, complicating the ability of both sides to formulate, let alone transmit, unambiguous war aims.

As early as June 29, the U.S. Joint Chiefs of Staff had directed General MacArthur to take special care as he attacked military targets above the 38th parallel "to insure that operations in North Korea stay well clear of the frontiers of Manchuria [Northeast China] or the Soviet Union."[3] By its actions in July, the United States had tried to assure China of its intention to contain the arena of conflict, though the restraints were the subject of periodic review. In mid-August, for example, the Central Intelligence Agency was asked to assess the "factors affecting the desirability of a UN military conquest of all Korea."[4]

At the same time, the bombing of Najin, a town in northeastern Korea near the Soviet border, on August 12, raised questions within the Cabinet about how the U.S. restraints were being conveyed to China and the Soviet Union.[5] Nevertheless, by September 1, when the National Security Council presented a draft report on the proposed course of the war to the Cabinet, Washington had apparently concluded that Moscow and Beijing understood that the battle for Korea would be confined to the peninsula.[6] In any event, the NSC draft stated that "neither the Soviet Union nor the Chinese Communists are ready to engage in general war at this time for this objective."*

In a curious way, U.S. planners sought to signal the war's limits more by actions the U.S. military did not take than by those it did. PRC sources reveal that China either did not interpret these nonactions as deliberate

---

*Approved in final form on Sept. 11 as NSC 81/1 (FRUS, 7: 712–21), "United States Courses of Action with Respect to Korea" recommended that "action north of the 38th parallel should not be initiated or continued, and if any U.N. forces are already north of the 38th parallel they should prepare to withdraw" (pp. 716–17). Though contingency plans were being set in motion at this time against an occupation of the North, 81/1 advocated restraint in the Korean "province bordering the Soviet Union [and] in the area along the Manchurian border" (p. 719). For a discussion of the competing war aims of the Truman administration, see Bernstein.

signals or chose to make its worst-case estimates based on U.S. and South Korean behavior alone—behavior, for example, like that of President Syngman Rhee, who in a highly publicized press conference on September 10 purposefully muddied the message of restraint by calling for a UN advance north that "must not stop until [the] Reds [are] driven entirely out of Kor[ea]." The timing of Rhee's message appeared to be particularly ominous when UN amphibious forces landed at Inchon, west of Seoul, five days later and began a dramatically successful offensive to recapture the South.[7]

Simultaneously, Washington elevated the question of China's involvement to a matter of paramount concern for the first time.[8] U.S. planners understood that the likely Sino-Soviet response to the counteroffensive at Inchon was either "(1) Soviet or Chinese Communist direct intervention, or (2) a suit for peace or an armistice by the North Koreans."[9] At this time, the government of India was actively trying to assure the Chinese that the UN armies constituted no threat to the PRC and to persuade Beijing not to become more involved. The Indian ambassador to China reported that in his meetings with Zhou Enlai, the premier had displayed "no interest [in Korea] beyond [an] expression of sympathy." To be sure, Zhou had intimated that his government would take action "if a world war starts as a result of U. N. forces passing beyond [the] 38th parallel and [the] Soviet Union deciding directly to intervene," but the ambassador felt confident that "China by herself will not interfere in the conflict and try to pull others' chestnuts out of the fire." He reported his additional belief, based on first-hand (though faulty) observations, that on balance "there is no evidence of military preparations" in Manchuria.[10]

Although a raging debate on the future course of the conflict preoccupied Washington and the United Nations as September wore on, nothing surfaced to overturn the basic Western analysis concerning Chinese and Soviet intentions. Even though the inadvertent bombing of Chinese territory on September 24 had raised the level of its uncertainty, official Washington, though worried, proceeded on the assumption that the Chinese and the Soviets would not intercede to save the North Koreans.[11]

But Washington's worries deepened on September 26, when the U.S. embassy in Moscow reported a "momentous decision," revealed in speeches by Mao Zedong and senior Chinese military officials. By proclaiming that the PRC's "foremost task" was "to build up [a] strong army," they were now clearly giving military concerns priority over economic reconstruction.[12] Still more ominous was a report out of New Delhi on September 27 pointing to the "real danger [that] Peking might intervene if UN Forces should cross [the] Parallel."[13] As it happened, Truman was just then in the act of approving a directive permitting military operations in the North, forcing the issue. Washington now had to decide which way the Chinese would jump.[14] British officials, for their part, believed that Beijing would not intervene and urged the Americans not to take Indian misgivings about China's intentions "too seriously," for their source, the Indian ambassador in Beijing, was a "volatile and an unreliable reporter."[15]

Reports from U.S. analysts in Washington and elsewhere offered other intelligence tidbits that reinforced the British assessment. The conclusion that the Chinese would not cross the Yalu thus remained largely intact, though subject to constant review.[16] On September 29, the Joint Chiefs of Staff approved MacArthur's plan for a two-pronged northward offensive that foresaw the Eighth Army proceeding along the western coastal corridor to capture the North Korean capital of Pyongyang and amphibious landings by the U.S. 10th Corps at Wonsan on the east coast.[17]

Mao's Contingency Planning

Western memoirs and U.S. government documents on the August–September phase of the war give extensive attention to the debate concerning Beijing's UN representation and to the government of India's mediation efforts.[18] By August, however, Mao had come to consider the political-diplomatic front of secondary importance. Once a quick North Korean victory was no longer in the cards, Beijing never took its eyes off the drama of the fighting in the South.

The Chairman had already predicted that the main struggle lay ahead, and that China's military involvement was inevitable. In early August, he ordered Zhou Enlai to prepare a contingency plan outlining Chinese and American vulnerabilities. From the 10th on, Mao began paying attention to the Americans' massive buildup of troops in Japan and the concentration of U.S. warships in Asian waters, including amphibious units.[19] Eight days later, after learning from the NFF's deputy commander that the Force could not be brought up to full military readiness on schedule, Mao sent Gao Gang a telegram extending the deadline to September 30. Acting Chief of the General Staff Nie Rongzhen confirmed this change in a cable to Deng Hua, who had replaced Huang Yongsheng as commander of the Thirteenth Army earlier that month.[20]

Meanwhile, Zhou Enlai, pursuing his charge to study all contingencies, assigned Lei Yingfu, head of a section of the General Staff, to simulate map exercises and forecast U.S. military operations.[21] Within days, Lei relayed his judgment that a U.S. counteroffensive would come by sea at one of six Korean ports, and that MacArthur would probably choose Inchon.[22] On the morning of August 23, Zhou handed Lei's prediction to Mao, who immediately summoned Lei for a personal briefing. Persuaded by Lei's findings, Mao ordered Zhou to pass the information along to Kim Il Sung.[23] Zhou did so. Mao also told Lee Sang Jo, Kim Il Sung's representative in Beijing, that Inchon was the most probable landing spot for a U.S. counteroffensive.[24] The same alarm was sounded by the KPA's Soviet advisers, who strongly cautioned that the Americans would be fools not to attack behind enemy lines to cut the North's communications.[25] None of these warnings impressed Kim.

Mao's haste in July to deploy the troops of the NFF was not matched by any concrete arrangements for their logistical support. Technically, the responsibility for coping with the buildup was Gao Gang's, but he had to turn to Beijing for help.[26] On the evening of August 23, Zhou Enlai chaired a meeting to confer about this help and to settle the relevant assignments and responsibilities.[27]

At this point, the Chinese leaders, increasingly anxious about a reversal on the Korean battle front, took another hard look at their contingency planning. On August 27, Mao cabled the vice-chairman of his military commission, Peng Dehuai, then commander and political commissar of the First Field Army and of the Northwest Military Region, that the four corps then deployed in the Northeast were inadequate, and that "we must now assemble [a total of] 12 corps for emergency use."* He tempered the tone of emergency by stating that the decision on these deployments could wait till "the end of September, when we will invite you to Beijing for face-to-face discussions."[28] Beyond this, Nie Rongzhen issued urgent instructions to the NFF to step up its study of publications on MacArthur's combat experiences and the history of the U.S. Eighth Army's amphibious operations.[29]

On August 26, Zhou Enlai led a meeting to review the preparations for war and circulated Lei's report on possible U.S. landing sites for a counterattack. This produced a series of actions five days later, when another conference chaired by Zhou adopted Nie's proposal to add the Ninth and Nineteenth armies to the NFF (for a total of 10 corps, including the four in the Thirteenth Army). The conference passed several emergency measures to set up hundreds of additional field hospitals and first-aid stations

---

* At this time, the military was organized into four numbered field armies (*yezhanjun*) under the Central Military Commission. Below these were a varying number of *bingtuan*, or armies, each of which normally comprised three corps (*jun*). Three divisions (*shi*) made up a corps, three regiments (*tuan*) a division, and three battalions (*ying*) a regiment. As the military historian William W. Whitson notes (*Chinese High Command*, p. xxiii), the conventional Western usage, which makes *bingtuan* "army group" and *jun* "army," is incorrect. For these and other Chinese military terms, see Song Shilun, *Zhongguo Dabaike Quanshu Junshi*, 1: 49; 2: 925–26, 1035, 1159, 1174–75.

in the Northeast, and ordered 100,000 soldiers from the Fourth Field Army held on stand-by as reinforcements for front-line units. The participants in the meeting estimated that the front-line units would suffer some 200,000 casualties in the first 12 months of fighting.[30]

With mobilization on the border in high gear, Mao then looked to Washington and the United Nations for clues to what would happen next. On September 1, the Security Council voted down a Soviet motion for a cease-fire in Korea. Mao, obviously misjudging both the Americans' resolve and their unwillingness to negotiate from weakness, viewed this as a lost opportunity to negotiate peace on the peninsula. Why, Mao asked, did Truman reject negotiations? What did Truman want: to end the war or to extend it?[31]

A few days after the UN vote, the Ministry of Foreign Affairs recalled Chai Chengwen, the political counselor in China's embassy in Pyongyang, for consultations. In a meeting on the 7th, Zhou Enlai asked him what difficulties the Chinese would meet if they had to send troops because of a sudden change in the war situation. Chai replied: "The biggest problems will be caused by inadequate transportation means and the lack of [Korean- and English-language] interpreters. Railroad transportation is not secure. Highways are in bad shape and too narrow. Moreover, it will be impossible [for our troops] to acquire local supplies because there is no available food or munitions. Nor can we seize enough from the enemy to sustain large-scale operations [as the PLA had done in the civil war]."[32] Zhou passed this gloomy assessment on to Mao.

All the same, pursuant to the decision of August 31, the reinforcements began receiving their marching orders. The 50th Corps in Hubei Province received instructions on September 6 to entrain immediately for the Northeast.[33] Two days later, Mao ordered the Ninth Army, then garrisoned near Shanghai, to take up station at embarkation depots along the Tianjin–Pukou Railroad by the end of October; he put the Ninth under the "direct administration" of the Central Military Commission; that is, under his personal control.[34] About this same time, Mao gave the Nineteenth Army in Northwest China the green light to head for areas adjacent to the Lanzhou–Xuzhou Railroad. The two armies were told to await orders to travel to the Korean border area in case they were needed. This was how matters stood when the U.S. counterattack came at Inchon on the 15th.

Yet even as Mao was ordering his armies to the front, leading Party members still questioned whether they ought to take on "the world's foremost imperialist power." Nie Rongzhen recalls that some of his comrades held that China needed a period of rest and recuperation after years of warfare. "To fight or not to fight: This was a question that Comrade Mao Zedong himself had pondered deeply for a long time and from different angles before he finally made up his mind. At that time, our troops were already on the banks of the Yalu River and Comrade Deng Hua's advance party was ready for the crossing." Via Nie, Mao ordered Deng, commander of the NFF, to stand fast "because additional and even more careful consideration would be necessary."[35]

The amphibious attack at Inchon ended the debate for the moment, and the Chinese concentrated on setting their combat plans in motion. Right after the attack, Mao wrote Gao Gang in Shenyang, "Apparently, it won't do for us not to intervene in the war. You must accelerate preparations [for our intervention]."[36] In a report delivered to the Central Military Commission on August 31, the NFF Command had proposed to send an advance team to North Korea to survey the local topography.[37] Zhou Enlai had sat on the report when it was passed on to him, but with the Inchon landing, he put his seal on it and, on September 17, directed the immediate dispatch of a five-man team to Korea. On their arrival, the team members started mapping the land that was to become their battleground a month later.

Meanwhile, the PLA made ready for general war. The Central Military Commission called for the formulation of a nationwide plan to counter U.S. air strikes. It approved proposals to transfer industrial equipment, petroleum, munitions, and other supplies from South Manchuria to North Manchuria, farther from the Yalu.[38] For the time being, the final decision to intervene was left on hold, and the NFF was kept guessing about its fate.[39]

For their part, the North Koreans could not afford the luxury of delay. After the American landing, Kim Il Sung dispatched two of his top lieutenants, Pak Il U and Pak Hon Yong, to Beijing to ask for emergency help.[40] As they quickly learned, the Chinese had still not determined their own course of action, and dodging any firm commitment, simply replied, "We vow to be a powerful supporter of the Korean people."

A shocked Stalin added his own urgent plea to the North Koreans'. According to one possibly reliable source, immediately after the landing, he sent a cable to Mao, bluntly stating that China had to save Kim Il Sung. Stalin added, somewhat gratuitously, that if the PLA were defeated, he would intervene himself.[41] According to Chinese sources, the Soviet leader promised to provide air cover for the PLA troops.[42]

Stalin's anxiety, in all probability, was based on the information he was receiving from Gen. M. V. Zakharov, the deputy chief of the Soviet General Staff, who was then in Pyongyang as head of a special mission to Korea. Sizing up the situation, the general had been pressing Kim to request

Chinese troops and send his own most badly battered units to
east for rebuilding. Soon after the Inchon invasion, Zakharov w
barovsk to organize rescue measures for Moscow's crumbling a

Mao understood quite well that the threat to China had now
measurably. He could not risk offending Stalin just when he might most
need his military backing. But even with the promise of Soviet air support,
the decision to send PLA divisions to war was a difficult one for Mao. Most
importantly, he was not sure whether Stalin would really commit troops to
save China if the PLA should be defeated in Korea.[44] Mao had to worry,
moreover, that if it came down to an open war with the United States, all
hope of conquering Taiwan would vanish indefinitely, and his dependence
on Stalin would grow.[45] Zhou Enlai reportedly shared this worry and cited
the need to unify the country and to avoid a U.S. declaration of war to
justify his opposition to the move.[46] Mao's policies and the consensus
within his Politburo had become questionable, and he had to calculate the
dangers from many different angles.

It appears, for example, that like Zhou and Stalin, Mao was acutely
aware of the importance of avoiding a formal declaration of war. Ever since
the creation of the NFF on July 13, Mao had fretted about the name of the
force to be sent to Korea. He resisted calling it the People's Liberation Army
because this would make the Chinese expeditionary troops official and
could be interpreted as tantamount to the formal declaration that he
sought to avoid. Such a declaration would trigger the provisions under the
Sino-Soviet alliance that required the Soviet Union to render China assistance "by all means at its disposal." Direct Soviet involvement in the conflict, Mao believed, would carry the potential of touching off a third world
war. With all this in mind, he first had the idea of referring to the men as
"support troops" but in the end accepted the recommendation to call them
"volunteers."[47]

Beijing chose this moment, September 30, to issue a public warning to
the Americans not to cross the 38th parallel. Nie Rongzhen says, "While
the General Staff was busy making dispositions, Premier Zhou Enlai declared to the world, . . . 'The [Chinese] people absolutely will not tolerate
foreign aggression, nor will they supinely tolerate seeing their neighbors
being savagely invaded by the imperialists.' "[48]

On the very day of Zhou's speech, September 30, General MacArthur
told the secretary of defense that he regarded "all of Korea open to our
military operations," and advance patrols of the South Korean 3rd Division crossed the 38th parallel. In an interview with the Chinese ambassador the following night, Kim Il Sung frantically requested that Mao send
the NFF into Korea.[49] Kim and Pak Hon Yong also fired off a cable to the

Chairman to the same effect: "If the enemy continues its attacks against areas north of the 38th parallel, we cannot meet the crisis [by ourselves]," they said. "Therefore, we must request that you provide special assistance. We hope the Chinese People's Liberation Army will embark directly to support our army's operations in case the enemy continues attacking the areas north of the 38th parallel."[50] The cable had the desired effect: convinced that Kim's regime was on the verge of collapse, Mao called the Politburo into session.

First Decision, October 2

At 3:00 P.M., October 2, the Politburo held the first of a series of enlarged meetings to formulate China's rejoinder.[51] Handing Kim's telegram to Gao Gang, who had just arrived from Shenyang, Mao remarked, "The situation in Korea has become serious. Now it is not a question of whether or not we should send troops, but a question of dispatching troops immediately. Sending troops one day earlier or later will be crucial to the development of the entire war situation. Today we shall discuss two urgent questions: first, the schedule for sending troops; second, who should be appointed commander of the troops."[52]

Gao asked Mao, "Isn't it correct that you have given the assignment to Chief [Zong] Lin [Biao]?"[53] In fact, he had originally considered Su Yu the best person for the appointment, Mao replied, but "Su Yu is really sick and is now recuperating in Qingdao. I have written a letter telling him just to get better and not to worry."[54] Gao had got it right, however, for as we have seen, Mao had originally thought of putting Lin in command of the Chinese troops because he had previously led most of the men assigned to the NFF. Simply put, Lin had refused to go.[55]

Somewhat abruptly, Mao then announced, "It is my opinion that Chief Peng [Dehuai] is the most appropriate person, since the ailing Lin Biao can't accept the assignment." Zhu De, commander-in-chief of the PLA, exclaimed, "After all, Old Peng is more reliable!" Without dissent, the participants agreed to the choice.

On the same day, the Politburo passed a resolution to "send troops under the name of volunteers to cross into Korea to fight the armies of the United States and the American lackey Syngman Rhee" and set October 15 as the date for the move.[56] As he and his comrades pondered the coming struggle, Mao devised the slogan, "Resist U.S. aggression and aid Korea, protect our homes, and defend the motherland." Although Politburo members praised the way the slogan combined "internationalism with patriotism," the decision to fight was not without controversy, as the next few days would reveal.[57]

The Politburo's resolution of October 2 was Beijing's first decision to intervene. It put China directly on the path to war with the United States. Under the terms of the Sino-Soviet alliance, Mao felt obliged to inform Stalin of the action, and he cabled him that day. Without explicitly saying as much, he wanted to remind the Soviet leader of his promise to provide air cover for Chinese troops entering Korea.[58] Because this cable was responding to the one Stalin sent in mid-September, it seems incomplete on some points. Even so, the full text is instructive:[59]

1. We have decided to send some of our troops to Korea under the name of [Chinese People's] Volunteers to fight the United States and its lackey Syngman Rhee and to aid our Korean comrades. From the following considerations, we think it necessary to do so: the Korean revolutionary force will meet with a fundamental defeat, and the American aggressors will rampage unchecked once they occupy the whole of Korea. This will be unfavorable to the entire East.

2. Since we have decided to send Chinese troops to fight the Americans in Korea, we hold that, first, we should be able to solve the problem; that is, [we are] ready to annihilate and drive out the invading armies of the United States and other countries. Second, since Chinese troops are to fight American troops in Korea (although we will use the name Volunteers), we must be prepared for a declaration of war by the United States and for the subsequent use of the U.S. air force to bomb many of China's main cities and industrial bases, as well as an attack by the U.S. navy on [our] coastal areas.

3. Of these two problems, the primary problem is whether or not the Chinese troops can annihilate the American troops in Korea and effectively resolve the Korean issue. Only when it is possible for our troops to annihilate the American troops in Korea, principally the Eighth Army (an old army with combat effectiveness), can the situation become favorable to the revolutionary camp and to China, although the second problem (a declaration of war by the United States) is still a serious one. This means that the Korean issue will be solved in reality along with the defeat of American troops (in name it probably will remain unsolved because the United States most likely will not admit Korea's victory for a considerable period of time). Consequently, even if the United States declares war on China, the war will probably not be of great scope or last long. The most unfavorable situation, we hold, would result from the inability of the Chinese troops to annihilate American troops in Korea and the involvement of the two countries' troops in a stalemate while the United States publicly declares war on China, undermines the plans for China's economic reconstruction, which has already begun, and sparks the dissatisfaction of [China's] national bourgeoisie and other segments of the people (they are very afraid of war).

4. Under the current situation, we have reached a decision to order the 12 divisions stationed in advance in South Manchuria to set off on October 15. They will be deployed in appropriate areas in North Korea (not necessarily reaching to the 38th parallel). On the one hand, they will fight the enemies who dare to cross the 38th parallel. At the initial stage, they will merely engage in defensive warfare to wipe out small detachments of enemy troops and ascertain the enemy's situation; on the other hand, they will wait for the delivery of Soviet weapons. Once they are [well] equipped, they will cooperate with the Korean comrades in counterattacks to annihilate American aggressor troops.

5. According to our intelligence to date, an American corps (composed of two

infantry divisions and a mechanized division) has 1,500 guns of 70mm to 240mm caliber, including tank cannons and anti-aircraft guns. In comparison, each of our corps (composed of three divisions) has only 36 such guns. The enemy dominates the air. By comparison, we have only just started training pilots. We shall not be able to employ more than 300 aircraft in combat until February 1951. Accordingly, we do not now have any certainty of success in annihilating a single American corps in one blow. Since we have made the decision to fight the Americans, we certainly must be prepared to deal with a situation in which the U.S. headquarters will employ one American corps against our troops in one [of the Korean] theaters. For the purpose of eliminating completely one enemy corps with a certainty of success, we should in such a situation assemble four times as many troops as the enemy (employing four corps to deal with one enemy corps) and firepower from one-and-a-half times to twice as heavy as the enemy's (using 2,200 to 3,000 guns of more than 70mm caliber to deal with 1,500 enemy guns of the same caliber).

    6. In addition to the above-mentioned 12 divisions, we are moving 24 divisions from south of the Yangtze River and from Shaanxi and Gansu provinces to areas along the Xuzhou–Lanzhou, Tianjin–Pukou, and Beijing–Shenyang railroad lines. We plan to employ these divisions as the second and third groups of troops sent to aid Korea in the spring and summer of next year as the future situation requires.

Several points in this telegram deserve analysis. First, Mao justified the sending of troops to Korea not on the basis of China's security but on the basis of the threat to the "entire East." Stalin would not have considered the danger to China alone sufficient reason for providing extensive assistance. An overall change in the "correlation of forces" in Asia in the wake of an American victory in Korea would be a much more powerful argument for the Soviet leader.

Even more telling is Mao's reference to the possibility of a declaration of war by the United States. We have often spoken of how Stalin had insisted on conditioning his promise of all-out assistance to his new Asian ally on a formal state of war. Stalin had seen this provision as a way to protect the Soviet Union from conflicts with the United States, nuclear or otherwise, that might result from Chinese adventurism. It is clear that Mao fully understood the Soviet leader's thinking and was trying to present his arguments accordingly. He was emphasizing that the war might not be contained if substantial help was not quickly forthcoming. In that event, the United States might declare war on China, and Moscow, like it or not, would have been obligated to render assistance "by all means at its disposal." At the same time, he was reassuring Stalin that China would not declare war because it would be impossible for Beijing to do so against the United Nations. He underscored this point by stressing that his troops would go to Korea under the name of the Chinese People's Volunteers. As one aide recalls, Mao said, "The [Chinese] people are volunteering to go to the aid of the Korean people. It is not a confrontation between two countries [China and the United States]."[60]

Mao's statement that a U.S. declaration of war would spark the "dissatisfaction of [China's] national bourgeoisie and other segments of the people (they are very afraid of war)" was also designed to strike a chord with Stalin, who was seriously concerned about and closely monitored the stability of the year-old Communist regime in China. Moreover, Mao was hinting that if Soviet aid proved to be insufficient, China could be humbled or badly wounded by the United States. Should either happen, Mao could legitimately declare the Soviet Union an unreliable ally and alter its policy of leaning to one side.

Finally, Mao came close to blackmailing Stalin when he said that at the initial stage the Chinese troops would only engage in defensive warfare and "wait for the delivery of Soviet weapons." No weapons, no action. Only when the "volunteers" were well equipped would they "cooperate with Korean comrades in counterattacks." Mao was using strong arguments, and we know from a Soviet source that Stalin received Mao's cable with considerable agitation.[61] Moreover, Stalin's state of mind did not improve when, in the next few days, the matter of providing air cover for Chinese troops assigned to Korea was raised.

But Stalin's reaction was not Mao's immediate problem at this point. The Chairman was facing some nasty choices that kept him riveted on Korea, not the Soviet Union. Even as the engine of war began to speed up, he hesitated. He introduced a pause in the preparations to give the Americans a last chance to halt at the 38th parallel. Moreover, Mao needed to convince some wavering Politburo members of the necessity of sending Chinese troops to Korea. Accordingly, he elected to stand pat, neither informing Kim II Sung of the Politburo's October 2 decision nor issuing an implementing order for the military to move.[62]

Early on October 3, Zhou Enlai communicated a secret warning to Washington via the Indian ambassador: "The U.S. troops are going to cross the 38th parallel in an attempt to extend the war. If the U.S. troops really do so, we cannot sit by idly and remain indifferent. We will intervene. Please report this to the prime minister of your country."[63]

Debates in the Politburo

In fact, the "decision" of October 2 was not the final say, for even as the Kremlin and North Korea kept pushing Mao toward war, the CCP Politburo kept tugging him back. Mao several times used a metaphor of three horses drawing a cart to describe his dilemma. He said, "When two horses are pulling in one direction, how can this horse of ours pull in a different one? In this way it is very hard to change the direction, and the only thing left is to proceed together with others." Once while using this metaphor,

Mao was interrupted and informed that a high-ranking Soviet representative wanted to meet him. Mao left the room and when he returned, said, "Look how much the two horses want us to pull in this direction. So, what can we do?" Stalin and Kim were two horses to his one.[64]

That there was considerable opposition to entering the war became evident as the PRC leaders huddled together in conclave in the succeeding days to weigh the pros and cons of that decision. Among those who are definitely known to have attended—Mao Zedong, Zhu De, Liu Shaoqi, Zhou Enlai, Ren Bishi, Chen Yun, Kang Sheng, Gao Gang, Peng Zhen, Dong Biwu, Lin Boqu, Deng Xiaoping, Zhang Wentian, Peng Dehuai, and Li Fuchun—PLA commanders and political commissars from various military regions were called to participate in these deliberations.[65]

At least three critical meetings took place from October 4 to October 8. On the 4th, Peng Dehuai, then in Xi'an, was ordered to fly forthwith to Beijing. He had been forewarned by Mao's August 27 cable. When he arrived at the convention hall a few minutes after 4:00 P.M., he found himself in the middle of a Politburo dispute. Years later, Peng remembered, "Some comrades [at the meeting] told me that Chairman Mao had asked those attending . . . to list the disadvantages involved in dispatching troops to Korea. Chairman Mao then said: 'Your arguments have reason. But all the same, once another nation is in a crisis, we'd feel bad if we stood idly by.'" Peng did not speak because he had arrived late and thought it wise to listen to the lines of debate in progress. When the meeting resumed the next day, Peng had made up his mind: "The tiger wanted to eat human beings; when it would do so would depend on its appetite. No concession could stop it. . . . We should dispatch troops to Korea."[66]

It was a minority view, for from the October 2 meeting on, a majority of the Politburo members and senior military officers expressed reservations about the decision to enter the war.[67] Among the most outspoken were Zhou Enlai, Ren Bishi, Chen Yun, and Lin Biao.[68] Their arguments— that priority ought to be given to overcoming such forbidding obstacles as a huge fiscal deficit and a high rate of unemployment; that China needed a long period of recuperation after years of warfare and had to complete its land reform; that several border provinces and many coastal islands had yet to be "liberated"; that more than a million bandits were still roaming the countryside; and that in the final analysis, the PLA's outdated arsenal would be no match for the U.S. army[69]—echoed sentiments then being voiced nationwide against warlike actions that could only "stir up trouble" and "draw fire against ourselves."[70]

Nie Rongzhen was stoutly in the other camp, berating those who believed that "it would be better not to fight this war except as a last resort."[71]

Mao, too, stood his ground. For years, as if fixed to the polar star, he had watched for signs of a powerful U.S. armed intervention in China. It was his recurring nightmare.[72] Even after the U.S. pledges not to bail out the Nationalists on Taiwan, he had put little faith in America's long-term declarations to stay out of China's internal affairs, and when the Korean War began, he donned his military uniform to symbolize his sense of crisis and his personal feelings about the inevitable.[73]

Mao and his supporters had no doubts that it had become imperative for China to send troops to Korea, and the arguments they mustered would be repeated often during the next days.[74] Mao's backers recalled his prophecy that a Sino-American military conflict was coming, and that the United States had illegally blocked the conquest of Taiwan. U.S. actions toward Taiwan in themselves were a casus belli.[75] Like Mao, they suspected that Washington was bent on subverting the Communist regime and planned to target China after attaining victory in Korea.[76] The conquest of Korea would release U.S. troops for action against China from two directions, Taiwan to the east and Vietnam to the south. Because the situation then would be still more precarious, the Chinese should accept the U.S. challenge on a field of battle chosen by themselves.

Korea would be the best place to make a stand.[77] Mao reasoned that a U.S. occupation of North Korea would jeopardize the Soviet security zone in Asia, and Moscow would have to provide support to block it. The mountains of Korea, moreover, would immobilize or at least impede the U.S. mechanized columns, while logistical support for the Chinese armies lay just across the border. Taiwan and Vietnam offered none of these advantages.[78]

The advocates of action further held that the domestic situation required a strong response. More than three million people were acting against Communist rule, and some were in open revolt.[79] Rumors were spreading throughout China: "U.S. troops will land at various mainland ports"; "the Third World War will take place immediately"; "Chiang Kai-shek will fight [his way] back to the mainland."[80] Encouraged by the successes of the UN forces, which were approaching the Sino-Korean border, opponents of the government were staging armed uprisings, wrecking communication lines, and assassinating government sympathizers.[81] There had been more than 150 cases of sabotage against the rail system in the previously calm Northeast between July 12 and August 11.[82] The turmoil was even reaching areas near Beijing.[83] The government had to act to overcome the perception of weakness. As Mao put it, "If we do not send troops [to Korea], the reactionaries at home and abroad would be swollen with arrogance when the enemy troops press to the Yalu River border."[84]

Furthermore, Mao had to neutralize the pressure from Moscow or maximize the chances of its support should the American threat grow. "If we do not intervene in the Korean War," he told his colleagues, "the Soviet Union will not intervene either . . . once China faces a disaster."[85]

Mao may have felt some sense of obligation to save a nation that was traditionally close to China. After the war broke out, General He Long asked Politburo member Zhu De, "The Democratic People's Republic of Korea was a Soviet responsibility. . . . Why should China become involved [in the Korean War]?" He replied with an ancient Chinese saying about the relationship of two close partners: "When the lips are destroyed, the teeth feel cold [*chunwang chihan*]."[86] Historically speaking, the Chinese emperor regarded Korea as his exclusive domain and attached great importance to his influence there. He treated it as part of China's natural security perimeter.

Finally, and surely not least, Mao and his supporters were confident that the war could be kept limited and nonnuclear. They believed that the alliance treaty and the Soviet presence in the Northeast would deter the Americans from bombing China's industrial centers there.* Indeed, they were convinced that the United States, absorbed as it was with events in Europe, would not make a total commitment to the war in Korea, and that if the conflict dragged on for any length of time, Washington would come under increasing pressure from its European allies to terminate its engagement in what they considered a peripheral region.[87]

Besides, the proponents of action were sure that they could far outlast their opponents on the battlefield. Mao sniffed at the combat capability of the South Korean army, satisfied that no "puppet" troops could fight hard or well.[88] As for the Americans, it was a matter of breaking their will. In the words of Liu Shaoqi, "The key [to concluding the war successfully] lies in the number of the Americans we can kill." These deaths would raise the question of national priorities to high policy, forcing Washington to end the war early and on Chinese terms.[89]

Although time would show how disastrously Mao had miscalculated both his own and U.S. capabilities, it would take six months of fighting to expose the flaws in his arguments.[90] In the end, the essence of the debate within the Politburo turned on grand strategy and the persuasiveness of bravado. When wavering Politburo members argued that an early Sino-American conflict would be disadvantageous to China ("We had better

---

* As a measure of the PRC's confidence in the security of the Northeast, Moscow had undertaken in 1950 to help China build 47 industrial enterprises; the bulk of these, 36, were to be built in that area, and there was no attempt during the war to change away from this heavy concentration of new industrial capacity in the region. Peng Min, *Dangdai Zhongguo de Jiben Jianshe*, pp. 14–17.

wait three or five years to fight the United States"), Mao and his supporters scoffed at the logic. It was obvious that China could not rebuild its industrial base or manufacture more modern arms for war in three to five years, and why, Mao asked, should the government construct such a base only to have it destroyed in a later U.S.-China showdown?[91]

When all the pros and cons were heard, Mao announced his decision. The Chairman had dutifully listened, but he had made up his mind days before. China would fight.

The Creation of the CPV

When the Politburo met the afternoon of the 5th, the newly arrived Peng Dehuai, who had held his tongue during the previous day's debate, now spoke up to tell his colleagues of his conclusion: "It is necessary to dispatch troops to aid Korea. If China is devastated in war, it only means that the liberation war will last a few years longer." Hearing his private choice for commander of the expeditionary force voice such a resolute endorsement, Mao formally announced his decision, and Peng accepted the assignment. Peng merely recalls that, as the meeting broke up, someone said, "You don't seem to be resigned to your advanced age" (an odd comment since Peng was only fifty-two).[92]

That evening, Mao had Peng, Zhou Enlai, and Gao Gang to dinner. "I am an enthusiast [for the campaign] to resist America and aid Korea," Mao told Peng. "You support me wholeheartedly. Now it seems that we have to fight a war." He gave Peng until October 15 to finish all preparations for moving his troops to Korea. Meanwhile, Zhou Enlai would fly to Moscow and solicit Soviet military aid. Also at the dinner, Mao announced his decision to send his eldest son, Mao Anying, to serve as interpreter (from Russian) at Peng's headquarters.[93]

The decision to send Zhou to the Soviet Union was formally approved at a supreme military conference the next morning. At this meeting, chaired by Zhou, the military high command decided that Lin Biao should go along with Zhou, and that the two should specifically seek a guaranteed supply of Soviet arms. In addition, the officers took up the practicalities of the task ahead: the plans for combat operations, the replacement of old weapons and military equipment, the logistical problems, and the formation of Peng's headquarters.[94]

The next day, October 7, patrols of the U.S. 1st Cavalry Division crossed the 38th parallel. As the Chinese saw it, China's last warnings had been disregarded.[95] Its Rubicon had been crossed, and the threat had become direct and immediate. The emergency cleared Mao's mind of all but the essentials. For him, that meant saving the Northeast. South Manchuria,

China's principal industrial base, consumed one-third of its power supply; Shenyang's 2,000 plants accounted for the bulk of its machine-building capacity; Anshan and Benxi produced 80 percent of its steel; and Fushun was the site of its largest coal mine. All these industrial centers were less than 200 kilometers from the Yalu. Furthermore, the Suiho Hydroelectric Station, the largest of its kind in Asia, and other smaller stations were on the south bank of the river. The loss of these plants, which supplied most of the power to the key industrial facilities in South Manchuria, would severely impair the whole of China's industry.[96]

Worse still, in the Chinese view, the permanent presence of a hostile army on the border would put a lasting lien on Chinese power and could eventually cripple it.[97] Gao Gang, the Northeast's boss, summed up the danger this way: "If North Korea is occupied by the U.S. and South Korea, we could not avoid an antagonistic confrontation with the U.S. and the fruit of our economic efforts might be destroyed. There are no grounds for the assertion that it would be more prudent to be destroyed after economic construction is completed."[98] The threat to China's industrial heartland was immediate, the need to fight compelling.

On October 8, Mao issued the official order to enter the war:[99]

1. In order to support the Korean people's war of liberation and to resist the attacks of U.S. imperialism and its running dogs, thereby safeguarding the interests of the people of Korea, China, and all the other countries in the East, I herewith order the name of the Northeast Frontier Force changed to the Chinese People's Volunteers and order the Chinese People's Volunteers to march speedily to Korea and join the Korean comrades in fighting the aggressors and winning a glorious victory.

2. The following units are put under the jurisdiction of the Chinese People's Volunteers: the 38th, 39th, 40th, and 42nd corps of the Thirteenth Army, and the headquarters of the Artillery Command of the [Northeast] Frontier Force and the 1st, 2nd, and 8th artillery divisions. The foregoing units should immediately get everything in readiness and await orders to set off.

3. Comrade Peng Dehuai is appointed commander and political commissar of the Chinese People's Volunteers.

4. The Northeast Administrative Region is to be the general rear base for the Chinese People's Volunteers. Comrade Gao Gang, commander and political commissar of the Northeast Military Region Command, is responsible for handling affairs relevant to offering logistic support and aid to the Korean comrades.

5. While in Korea, the Chinese People's Volunteers must show fraternal feelings and respect for the people, the People's Army, the democratic government, the Workers' Party (namely, the Communist Party), and other democratic parties of Korea, as well as Comrade Kim Il Sung, the leader of the Korean people, and strictly observe military and political discipline. This is a most important political basis for ensuring the fulfillment of your military task.

6. You must fully anticipate possible and inevitable difficulties and be prepared to overcome them with great enthusiasm, courage, care, and stamina. At present,

the international and domestic situation as a whole is favorable to us, not to the aggressors. So long as you comrades are firm and brave and good at uniting with the people there and at fighting the aggressors, final victory will be ours.

Mao addressed the order to the senior military commanders in charge of the operation: Peng Dehuai, Gao Gang, He Jinnian (the deputy commander of the Northeast Military Region), Deng Hua (commander and political commissar of the CPV Thirteenth Army, the former Strategic Reserve), Hong Xuezhi (first deputy commander of the Thirteenth Army), and Xie Fang (chief of staff of the Thirteenth Army).[100] (The military chain of command in October 1950 is shown in the accompanying figure.)

Mao also sent a telegram to his ambassador in Pyongyang with a message for Kim Il Sung: "In view of the current situation, we have decided to send volunteers to Korea to help you fight against the aggressors."[101] The ambassador, Ni Zhiliang, handed the telegram to Kim Il Sung that very night, October 8. As if a heavy load had been lifted, Kim clapped his hands and shouted, "Well done! Excellent!"[102]

In this telegram, Mao set out for Kim the command structure he was putting in place; the next day, Mao's lieutenants translated these decisions into a concrete directive and transmitted it to the CPV command. This was the key operational order for the troops. Following up, Mao cabled Ni Zhiliang and notified him that he had "already assigned comrade Gao Gang to be in charge of all the affairs regarding aid to the Korean comrades" and endorsed Ni's idea of relocating the Chinese embassy north to Huichon, closer to the Yalu.[103]

A day later, Mao cabled Kim Il Sung and Peng Dehuai with his assessment of the military situation:[104]

Currently, massive enemy troops are advancing northward. The enemy rear is weakly defended. I suggest that the [Korean] People's Army units that cannot withdraw to the north should remain in South Korea and open another front in the enemy's rear areas. . . . It will be very helpful to the operations in the north if 40,000–50,000 troops of the [Korean] People's Army could remain in South Korea to undertake the assignment.

Also on the 10th, the CCP Central Committee ordered a nationwide campaign launched to suppress "counterrevolutionaries." As Mao saw it, war justified doing whatever it took to end domestic opposition and unrest, and Beijing warned its cadres never to be soft on any "hostile elements."[105] The result was a round of mass arrests and executions.[106]

By this time, Zhou Enlai and Lin Biao had left for the Soviet Union. The delegation, which departed on the 8th, included Shi Zhe, the interpreter; and Kang Yimin, a confidential secretary of the CCP Central Committee's Administration Office.[107] Before their flight, Mao must have discussed with

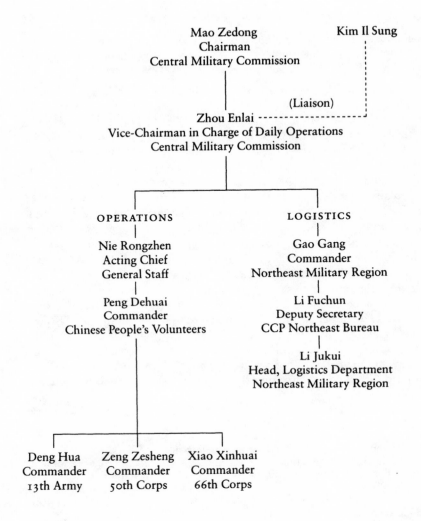

The Chinese military chain of command, October 1950. Contrary to statements in most Western sources, Zhu De (Chu Teh) was the commander of the People's Liberation Army in name only and did not play a significant role in the Korean War.

Zhou the appropriate negotiating strategy for securing Soviet military support.

As Zhou flew west, the PLA hastened to implement Mao's combat order of the 8th.[108] That very day, Peng Dehuai flew to Shenyang to take charge of operations. There he was greeted by another urgent message from Kim Il Sung requesting even more desperately the rapid dispatch of the CPV to Korea.[109] The next day Mao, through Nie Rongzhen, directed the Thirteenth Army to make preparations for battle and the Ninth Army to board trains northward.[110] On the 11th, Li Fuchun and Li Jukui, two key figures in charge of logistics for the CPV, ordered munitions and equipment rushed to several military supply depots in North Korea.[111] By October 19, when Peng's armies crossed the Yalu, the department had moved substantial quantities of matériel into the North, but in the process, American air strikes had destroyed 200 trucks, almost half of Li's inventory.

Stalin Reneges

For Peng Dehuai, the first order of business was to consult with his field commanders. On October 9, the day after his arrival in Shenyang, he and Gao Gang co-chaired a meeting to sound out the views of officers of corps commander rank and above from the Thirteenth Army. Peng's initial proposal, to introduce the CPV in waves, with a first force of six divisions (two corps) making the crossing on the 15th, drew little support.[112] Deng Hua among others argued that two corps were far from enough: the great strength of the UN forces plainly demanded the simultaneous engagement of all four corps assigned to the CPV. Persuaded by their assessment, Peng sent a cable on the 10th to Mao asking for a change in his instructions. Instead of sending in only two corps and two artillery divisions as planned, he said, he and his commanders had decided that they should "amass all our force south of the Yalu River, lest the river bridge [at Andong] be destroyed, which would make it difficult for us to concentrate a superior force and thus rob us of the chance for a successful battle." The decision, if approved, would mean committing the entire force then mobilized on the Chinese side of the Yalu River.[113]

Peng sent another cable to Mao after a quick trip to Andong on October 11, relaying the recommendation of the officers there that the Ninth and Nineteenth armies be activated ahead of schedule and their worries that the simultaneous dispatch of all four corps would leave the rear echelons exposed. We do not have Mao's exact response to this cable, but he plainly concurred with his military's worries, for less than two weeks later, on the 23rd, he ordered the 66th Corps to move out from Tianjin to the Sino-Korean border to serve as a rear guard.[114]

He also concurred with the change of tactics. In an October 11 cable to Peng, Gao Gang, and Deng Hua, he said, "I agree with your idea of dispatching four corps and three artillery divisions and assembling them in the areas you have selected, to await opportunities to annihilate the enemy." Significantly, he went on to note that an anti-aircraft regiment was to be dispatched from Shanghai on October 14, but that the Soviet air force could not "set off for the time being."[115]

Mao did not tell his battlefield commanders why the Soviet planes were not going to "set off." He had learned only a few hours before that Stalin had reneged on his promise to supply air cover for the CPV troops. Sometime in the afternoon (Moscow time), Zhou Enlai had sent him word that the "Soviet side cannot provide aircraft and pilots [*kongjun*]" for operations because it had not made them ready.[116] As Chinese supplies began pouring across the Yalu on the 11th, Stalin had flinched. The CPV, alone and exposed, faced the military showdown with the United States on the peninsula.

Because this story provides a primer of Kremlin politics in action, we will concentrate on the Soviet side of things here and defer the Chinese part of the account to the next section. When Zhou Enlai and his party caught up with Stalin at his villa on the Black Sea on October 10, the Soviet leader, after a brief disquisition on the North's deteriorating military position and Kim's underestimation of the "enemy's might," turned the floor over to Zhou, saying, "Today we want to listen to the opinions and thinking of the Chinese comrades."[117]

Zhou began by reminding Stalin of China's many difficulties: lack of money, weapons, and transport. The Chinese in fact thought that it was inappropriate for China to dispatch troops to Korea, he told Stalin. "We face many difficulties in the supply of weapons and equipment for our army. We cannot regard war as child's play. How can we get out of the war if we are caught in a whirlpool and cannot escape for several years? Moreover, this war probably will involve other fraternal countries if it becomes protracted." Zhou concluded by saying, "We therefore think it better not to send troops."[118] Then he added, almost as an afterthought, that China would not enter the war because "the Americans will declare war on us."[119]

Even as he spoke, of course, as he—and perhaps even Stalin—knew, Chinese supplies and advance units were on the move. It seems likely that in this obvious bit of obfuscation Zhou was acting on Mao's orders to accentuate the CCP Politburo's views on the risks of war. He and Mao may even have contrived a scheme to use their reluctance to enter the war as a negotiating strategy for obtaining Soviet military assistance.

Stalin's response came in two parts. In the first, he explained why the

Soviet Union could not enter the war, and in the second, why China should. He said, "for you [Chinese] it is possible to help the Korean people, but for us it is impossible because as you know the Second World War ended not long ago, and we are not ready for the Third World War. . . . The Americans cannot wage a war on two fronts. The two fronts are the wars in Korea and China. Because of that, there will be no war with China. Therefore, right now it is possible for you to help."[120]

Stalin then enumerated the dire consequences of China's staying out of the war. Since Korea could only be preserved "for at most one week" if it did not have reinforcements, Stalin said, "we must take into account all contingencies and devise concrete countermeasures and plans." The "we" was rhetorical, it seems, for it was plain that the countermeasures were to be China's alone. With a smile, Stalin indicated what would befall the Chinese if the Americans decided to deploy their armies along the Yalu and Tumen rivers: "The economic recovery of the Northeast probably will be out of the question. Thereafter, [the Americans] at will could harass [you] from the air, land, and sea."[121] For the Chinese, the message was clear: fight in Korea or fight in the Northeast.

Stalin continued, "We had better make a commitment to provide sanctuary for our Korean comrades in case they can no longer carry on on their own. . . . Let them redeploy their main forces, weapons and equipment, and some staff members and cadres to Northeast China, and let them move the old, weak, sick, disabled, and wounded to the Soviet Union." The northerners should remove whatever resources of men and matériel they had left to China against the day they reentered Korea, Stalin argued, for "it is far simpler for them to enter Korea from Northeast China than from the Soviet Union." Without a blush, he finished: "In short, our two countries have to bear the burden."

These stark conclusions so shocked Zhou that he gasped. Stalin had outmaneuvered him. Clearly, the Soviet leader had washed his hands of the war. Lin Biao tried to salvage the situation, saying, "It is unnecessary to withdraw the main force of the Koreans. They should remain in Korea where there are many mountains and forests. They can go into the mountains and forests and wage protracted guerrilla warfare. They can continue to fight successfully throughout Korea and bide their time."[122]

Stalin brushed Lin's proposal aside. He pointed out, "Perhaps the enemy will not permit the guerrillas to exist and will wipe them out soon. Since you do not intend to send troops, we should work out concrete plans to provide shelter for our Korean comrades and their troops . . . and enable them to await their opportunity [to return]."

He then reverted to his main topic. "We have considered how to help our

Korean comrades. . . . However, it is hard for our troops to reenter Korea [all of which had been pulled out by the end of 1948] because such an action would mean war with the United States. So, we think China can send a certain number of troops [to Korea] with Soviet-supplied weapons and equipment." Appearing to acknowledge China's concerns about air support, Stalin said, "We can send a certain number of aircraft to offer cover [for the Chinese forces operating in Korea]; however, our air force can only be used in [your] rear and front-line positions. In order to avoid any damaging effects from world opinion, our air force should not be employed behind the enemy's rear so as to guarantee that our aircraft will not be shot down and our pilots captured."

Zhou asked whether the Soviets would immediately deliver weapons and equipment should the Chinese elect to fight in Korea. Stalin replied: "China intends to reorganize its troops and to regularize, integrate, and modernize its various armed services. This is entirely correct and reasonable. In our experience, however, it is quicker, better, and more effective to upgrade and replace equipment during actual combat than during peacetime. While engaged in actual combat, the [Chinese] troops can easily ascertain their shortcomings and make improvements." In any event, the situation was too urgent to hold off until the CPV could be upgraded. As to the replacement of weapons and equipment, Bulganin would make all the necessary arrangements.

The terms of a deal were slowly emerging. The Chinese would send troops to Korea in return for substantial military aid. Stalin and Zhou agreed to send a joint telegram the next day (October 11) to the CCP Central Committee. It was to state that Moscow "can entirely meet China's requirements for the supply of artillery, tanks, and other equipment" for the CPV that was to set off for Korea.

With the mission accomplished, Stalin invited the Chinese to a grand banquet. One Chinese recalls that only Lin Biao left sober.[123] The next morning, Zhou caught an early flight for Moscow, where he could use his embassy's facilities to communicate directly and in code with Beijing.[124]

Arriving in Moscow at 3:00 P.M., Zhou had no sooner submitted his cable to the embassy's code clerks than Molotov, who had flown separately to Moscow, called with startling news. "Now, we do not agree with the decision to send in your troops," he told Zhou, "and we also will not offer you military equipment." Zhou in a fury asked Molotov, "How can you cancel a plan that we settled just a few hours ago?"[125] He had to alert Mao that the joint cable, which had just gone off, was no longer valid. Zhou rushed to relay Molotov's dismaying message to Beijing (where the time was five hours later). It was at this point that Mao learned that his troops would fight without air cover.

What explains Stalin's sudden reversal and renewed ambivalence? We should recall that Stalin had waited for more than a fortnight for a reply to his post-Inchon emergency cable to Mao. During that period, Stalin's ambassador in Beijing had been repeatedly quoting Mao as saying that the Soviet Union, "the stronghold of world socialism," should be shielded, and that China should wage the war on its own, though with Soviet military assistance. But significantly, even as the ambassador relayed Mao's words, he introduced a note of skepticism, suggesting that Mao was really trying to push Stalin to war and was manipulating the Politburo meetings to impede China's entry. He reported, erroneously, that Mao never participated in the actual deliberations but only listened.[126]

Because Stalin would have observed China's warnings to the Americans during this period, he may well have accepted his diplomat's assessment that Mao wanted to delay going to war, and thus would have seen Mao's procrastinating as an attempt to draw Moscow into the conflict. In such case, the Soviet leader obviously had to counter the Chinese tactics and to do so firmly.

Stalin had good reason for his second thoughts and the reversal of his initial commitment to Zhou Enlai. Khrushchev recollects:

Our ambassador was writing very tragic reports concerning Kim Il Sung's state of mind. Kim Il Sung was already prepared to go into the mountains to pursue guerrilla struggle again. When the threat [after Inchon] emerged, Stalin became resigned to the idea that North Korea would be annihilated, and that the Americans would reach our border [that is, the North Korean–Soviet border]. I remember quite well that in connection with the exchange of opinions on the Korean question, Stalin said: "So what? Let the United States of America be our neighbors in the Far East. They will come there, but we shall not fight them now. We are not ready to fight."[127]

Khrushchev goes on to remark that Stalin was both distressed and disappointed. But Stalin was not distressed. When he cabled his representatives in Korea, "Upon receipt of this cable, do not become involved in affairs connected with the Korean War,"[128] he was demonstrating that he would never change his mind about fighting the Americans until he was ready and would certainly not fight them in Korea even if Kim Il Sung's regime should collapse. Moreover, an American conquest of the Korean Peninsula, while not to be welcomed, had its plus side. It would inevitably make Mao more dependent on Moscow and lead to the long-term stationing of Soviet troops in China's Northeast.

Back in Beijing, Mao read Zhou Enlai's message about Stalin's decision in amazement.[129] Mao obviously faced a serious dilemma. He needed to delay the CPV's entry into the war.

For the Chairman, it was clear from the very outset that the Soviet leader was pursuing his own strategic aims and would not willingly pay a high price for assistance to China. Mao apparently believed that the drastic reversal following Inchon had driven Stalin to the conclusion that MacArthur should be checked but that a direct Soviet-American conflict should be averted.[130] Mao was right.

It had been some ten months since Stalin and Mao had concluded the Sino-Soviet treaty in Moscow, and now Mao would put its value to the test. In their discussions, Mao and his lieutenants had shared their misgivings about Stalin but, in the desperation of the moment, they still badly wanted to believe that the Soviet dictator could be persuaded to keep at least some of his promises, if not immediately, then soon after they unleashed their armies across the Yalu.

The Final Decision, October 13

As all hope for immediate Soviet support for the Korean War effort waned, Mao reluctantly had second thoughts of his own.[131] After October 11, he spent a sleepless 70 hours mulling over his options. Nothing in his past experience quite prepared him for a full-scale conflict with the most powerful nation in the world.[132]

At 8:00 P.M., October 10, Peng had cabled Mao to say that he was going to Tokchon, the temporary North Korean capital, the next morning to "discuss with Kim Il Sung many concrete affairs." Some 24 hours later, Zhou's alarming message of Stalin's reversal reached Beijing, and Mao appears to have hesitated. He ordered Nie Rongzhen to phone Peng and tell him to cancel his trip. When Nie got through to Peng at 1:00 A.M., he is quoted as telling him: "The original plan has changed! There is a change! The Chairman asks you and Gao Gang to return to Beijing tomorrow. The central leadership needs to discuss important issues."[133]

Yet, as we have noted, even after Zhou's bad news reached him, Mao had sent a cable to Peng, Gao Gang, and Deng Hua approving the military's plans. Early the next day, with the same resolve, Mao wired Chen Yi, commander of the East China Military Region, with instructions to get the Ninth Army moving northward immediately.[134] Nevertheless, Mao was clearly agonizing. At his direction, the Politburo simultaneously postponed the implementation of the October 9 order to move China's armies into Korea.[135] October the 12th was the time for pulling back from the brink.

Mao sent an order that night to Peng Dehuai, Gao Gang, Deng Hua, and the other top commanders in the Northeast: "For the time being, do not carry out the order issued on October 9. Various units of the Thirteenth Army should remain for training in the places where they originally were stationed. Do not set off [for North Korea]."[136] Rao Shushi and Chen Yi at the East China Military Region Command headquarters received similar orders: "For the time being, do not carry out the order issued on October 9," and the Ninth Army should also remain in place and not move out, as ordered in the directive of the 9th.[137]

That telegram, like the other, was sent on the night of the 12th, as Zhou Enlai waited in Moscow for the Politburo's final decision. In considering the events of this fateful day, the most likely explanation is that Mao wanted to give Zhou ammunition for his next go-around with the Soviet leaders: the Chinese leader was threatening to keep aloof and let the North Korean regime go down to defeat. This explanation is consistent with one other possibility: that he was attempting to condition China's entry into the war on Soviet air support.

Even while he was plagued by ambivalence, doubts, and competing scenarios, the Chinese leader yielded to no one on the Politburo as the most avid advocate of intervention. Several members were apprehensive about the prospects of going it alone in Korea and openly questioned why China should become involved without Stalin's help; if the Soviet Union would not provide air cover and modern equipment, then China should not send in its troops. The old arguments were also raised about China's unpreparedness and the need to stay clear of any large-scale conflicts with the United States for at least three, and preferably five, years.[138] By agreeing to a delay on the 12th, Mao could appear to appease these doubting Thomases. The Soviets' obstinacy provided the basis for a Politburo consensus on the decision for a postponement. At the same time, Mao was bent on keeping the decision secret. In his cable countermanding the order of the 9th, he had cautioned his East China commanders not to "give new explanations to the cadres and democratic personages."[139]

The real test of his will came on the afternoon of the next day, when Mao convened the Politburo in emergency session. Both Peng Dehuai and Gao Gang had flown in to participate.[140] The session was short and to the point. Mao had already made up his mind, for he had concluded that the Americans would not stop short of the Yalu or even at the Yalu, as some of his associates believed. Less than two weeks later, on October 24, Zhou Enlai officially reported Mao's assessment of the ultimate aim of the American military operations in North Korea: "Our intelligence is that [the Americans] planned first to cross the 38th parallel without provoking China and then to direct their spearhead at China. We saw through their tricks. . . . Nehru told me that [the UN forces] would stop 40 miles short of the Yalu

River after crossing the 38th parallel. . . . Obviously, this was the second time [for them] to fool us. If we did nothing, the aggressive enemy would surely continue its advance up to the Yalu River and would devise a second scheme [against China]."[141]

Convinced by intelligence assessments, ideology, a history of conflict, and the statements of some U.S. commanders that the UN juggernaut would not halt at the Yalu, Mao believed that a confrontation with the United States was inescapable, and that it would be better to enter the war before Kim Il Sung retreated into China with his government in exile. The Chinese leader paid no attention to Kim's bravado that the North Koreans would "never lay down our arms or surrender, we will resist to the end."[142] In his view, this was the last chance to intervene in Korea before the war ended in an American victory. The CPV had to move soon.[143]

On the evening of October 13, he telegraphed Zhou Enlai, once again giving the "reasons for our army to enter the Korean War":[144]

1. After discussion with comrades on the Politburo, we have reached a consensus that the entry of our army into Korea continues to be to our advantage. In the first phase, we can only fight the puppet [Republic of Korea] army. With a certainty of success in dealing with the puppet army, we can establish a base in the large mountain area to the north of the Wonsan–Pyongyang line and thus encourage the Korean people. The Korean situation would change to our advantage if we could wipe out several divisions of the puppet army in the first phase.

2. The adoption of our active policy mentioned above is favorable to China, Korea, the East, and the world. If we do not send troops [to Korea], the reactionaries at home and abroad would be swollen with arrogance when the enemy troops press on toward the Yalu River. Consequently, it would be unfavorable to various parties and especially unfavorable to Northeast China. [In such a situation,] the entire Northeast Frontier Force would be tied down and the power supplies in South Manchuria would be controlled [by hostile parties].

In short, we hold that we should enter the war. We must enter the war. Entering the war is greatly to our advantage; conversely, it is greatly to our disadvantage if we do not enter the war.

Meanwhile, back in Moscow, Zhou Enlai had not lost hope that Stalin might change his mind, and persisted in his efforts to gain Soviet military assistance for the CPV. At this point, Stalin was still in residence at the Black Sea villa, so that all Zhou's dealings with him had to go through Molotov. Accordingly, when Mao's cable of the 13th came in, Zhou quickly had it translated and sent to Molotov. That evening, Zhou met with Molotov and asked him to solicit Stalin's reaction. Though Molotov said that he had no official reply for Mao, he had obviously received new instructions from Stalin. He stated that there should be no problem with the guaranteed supply of the Soviet weapons and equipment and then turned to such specifics as the assembly and delivery of that matériel and ways to protect it from U.S. air strikes.[145]

Stalin made known his personal views the next day. When reading Mao's cable, Stalin, so the Chinese were told, said, "The Chinese comrades are so good. The Chinese comrades are so good." The aging dictator, it was said, looked on the point of tears.[146] On the 14th, Stalin approved sending 16 air regiments of fighter planes to China for use in Korea.

Encouraged, Zhou sent a cable directly to Stalin, asking whether it was possible to send bombers to Korea for joint operations with the Chinese troops. He also sought Stalin's advice on how to coordinate the combat operations of the Chinese and Korean forces. At the end of the wire, Zhou appended a detailed list of artillery and related equipment that the CPV needed urgently.[147] Stalin consented to providing air cover but only after the CPV had moved into Korea. He also signed off on sending the critically needed weapons and equipment right away but made no mention of the requested bombers.

The situation was complicated for Stalin. He undoubtedly wanted Mao to go to war, but under what conditions? He knew quite well that he would have to provide China with military assistance; otherwise, as Mao had implied in his cable of October 2, either the Beijing regime might founder or the alliance could be fundamentally impaired. Indeed, Soviet assistance for the defense of China was already forthcoming. His answer to Zhou Enlai may thus have had two ulterior aims: to obtain additional guarantees from China that it would never openly involve the Soviet Union in the conflict and to extract the highest possible political (and perhaps material) price for Moscow's aid.

But at this stage, trying to figure out Stalin's state of mind was a luxury Mao could not afford; U.S. military operations were becoming a direct and immediate threat to China.[148] Accordingly, orders again flowed to shift the forces in East China to the Northeast.[149] Mao telegraphed Chen Yi on the 14th to get the Ninth Army ready to embark.[150] He also sent off two cables to Zhou Enlai, giving him a detailed order of battle on the eve of the war. With Stalin's agreement to provide massive aid, Mao wanted Zhou to inform Stalin that the time for honoring his pledge had come and to give him a preliminary briefing on the coming operations.

Mao's first instinct was to use his troops as a show of force. He wanted to blunt any UN offensive without going on the attack himself for several months, provided that the Americans and South Koreans remained at a line of advance running from Pyongyang to Wonsan. In his second cable to Zhou on the 14th, he said, "Our troops will continue improving [their] defense works if they have enough time. If the enemy tenaciously defends Pyongyang and Wonsan and does not advance [north] in the next six months, our troops will not attack Pyongyang and Wonsan. Our troops will attack Pyongyang and Wonsan only when they are well equipped and trained, and have clear superiority over the enemy in both air and ground forces. In short, we will not talk about waging offensives for six months."

Nevertheless, Mao anticipated the worst and began to revert to his revolutionary war mentality. He spent the whole day of the 14th with Peng Dehuai going over the plans for engagement.[151] In a series of telegrams, Mao began to shift his approach from grand strategy to the tactics of the counteroffensive. It was a transition that he had made before, in the mid-1930s. Soon after the end of the Long March, he had summed up the experiences of the struggle for the abandoned southern base area, called the Jiangxi Soviet. In his essay "Problems of Strategy in China's Revolutionary War" (December 1936), the revolutionary commander concentrated on the "problem of the 'initial battle' or 'prelude.'" As he reviewed the five major engagements with Chiang Kai-shek's forces to defend the Jiangxi Soviet, Mao analyzed, place by place, the deployments of the opposing divisions. His assessment was simple: "The first battle must be won. The plan for the whole campaign must be taken into account. And the strategic stage that comes next must be taken into account. These are the three principles we must never forget when we begin a counter-offensive, that is, when we fight the first battle."[152] These principles, to be sure, would guide Mao in the post-1945 campaigns, but in that case, too, Mao on the eve of battle felt most in his element focusing on the tactical picture. Attention to detail, he believed, had brought victory in the landmark North China Liaoxi-Shenyang, Huai-Hai, and Beiping-Tianjin-Zhangjiakou campaigns in the winter of 1948–49.[153] Roughly two years later, these experiences reverberated in his memory, and apparently he thought that history could repeat itself in the battle for Korea.

On October 15, Mao sent Gao Gang and the commanders of the Thirteenth Army a telegram advising them, "It has been decided that on October 18 or 19 at the latest, our People's Volunteers will begin crossing the [Yalu] River and moving forward."[154] He was almost certainly awaiting Zhou Enlai's return from Moscow to set the specific time and date. Meanwhile, he sent them a second telegram with further details: "One advance corps of our troops had better set off [*zuihao . . . chudong*] on the 17th and arrive at Tokchon on the 23rd. In order to hold its positions and await the fatigued enemy, the corps should start building defense works on the 25th, after one day of rest. A second corps will set off on the 18th. Other units will set off successively thereafter. All of the units will cross the river within about ten days."[155] Mao had worked all night on the decision, and it was 5:00 A.M. by the time he finished.

Peng Dehuai returned to Andong on October 15, fully expecting to act on the Politburo's decision of the 13th.[156] He immediately started things rolling by summoning officers of division-commander rank and above from the Thirteenth Army to a meeting in Andong the next day.* The same day, the 16th, Peng moved up Mao's suggested timetable and ordered the 372nd Regiment of the 42nd Corps to cross the Yalu beginning that night. The next afternoon, Peng flew back to Shenyang.[157] So far as he and the soldiers of the 42nd were concerned, the war had begun.

That afternoon (the 17th), Mao cabled Peng, Gao Gang, and others to have "everything in readiness" for the rest of the two advance corps to set off on the 19th. The formal order would be issued on the 18th, he advised. With Zhou coming home the same day, Mao also asked Peng and Gao to fly back to Beijing. They caught a plane that day.[158]

Meanwhile, the anxieties of Deng Hua and Hong Xuezhi, the commander and first deputy commander of the Thirteenth Army, had been refreshed. Their fear of the UN forces, if anything, had grown. On the 17th, soon after Peng's return to Shenyang, they cabled him: "We can carry out the original order as scheduled, provided the delivery of new [military] equipment is guaranteed within two or three months (the introduction of the air force is especially important). Otherwise, a postponement of the departure schedule [of the CPV] deserves attention." Peng rejected their plea for caution, arguing that another change in the schedule would put the Chinese in a passive military and political posture.[159]

On the evening of the 18th, the Politburo met to debrief Zhou Enlai, after which Mao made his final decision: "[The CPV] will cross the river according to the original plan," he declared, adding, "We cannot postpone the timing [for the troops to set off] any longer."[160] A Soviet source, quoting unnamed "Chinese comrades," states, "before the close of the meeting, Mao Zedong showed a cable from I. V. Stalin and said: 'The Old Man [*Starik*]—the usual way the Chinese leaders in their inner circle referred to Stalin—writes that we have to act.' None of the participants in the meeting dared speak against it, and thus the question of sending Chinese volunteers to Korea was finally settled."[161]

---

*Mao left it to Peng to present the reasons for going to war to the senior CPV cadres. In a long "mobilization speech" to the assembled officers, the CPV commander echoed the arguments for intervention, rebutted the opposition, and in general Maoist terms laid out the course to victory. It was a commander's call to battle, and we reproduce it in full in the Appendix as Doc. 77. Though Peng gave the speech on the 16th (see Zhang Xi, "On the Eve," p. 153), it was actually written in Beijing on the 14th. It is clear from Doc. 78 that Peng remained in the capital till at least one in the morning of the 15th.

A Korean team headed by Pak Hon Yong attended this meeting, and one member recollects that after Mao told the gathering he had decided to send five corps to Korea, he urged the Koreans to cooperate with Peng Dehuai and Gao Gang, and said it would be necessary to set up a Korea-China Joint Command. Whether this would be headed by Peng, with Pak Il U as his deputy, or vice versa, was up to the Koreans: "we leave this matter in your hands." When the Joint Command was created in December, Peng was designated its commander and political commissar.[162]

The reader may recall that a couple of months before, in August, Mao had described to a Korean delegation how he would cut off the enemy's "fingers." This time he adopted his enemies' legs for his metaphor. He told the Koreans that the "important purpose" of the KPA would be to dissipate the strength of the South Korean army as much as possible, "because the South Korean Army and U.S. Army are monsters with two legs and one body. If you cut off one leg of the monster, [you] have nothing to fear if the U.S. has only one leg." Mao dramatized his message by "jumping up and down on one leg."[163]

At 9:00 P.M., Mao sent the following telegram to Deng Hua, Hong Xuezhi, Han Xianchu, Xie Fang, and He Jinnian:

We are determined to move on schedule four corps and three artillery divisions to the northern part of Korea and commence military operations. Tomorrow evening, the 19th, [the first units] will start crossing the Yalu River between Andong and Ji'an. To keep the operation absolutely secret, the troops should start crossing the river every day at dusk and stop at 4:00 A.M. By 5:00 A.M., the troops should have taken cover, and you should keep a close watch on this [*qieshi jiancha*]. To gain experience, you should plan for two or three divisions to cross the river on the first night (the night of the 19th), and for more or less [the same number of] troops to cross the river on the second night. Thereafter, handle the matter at your own discretion. Gao Gang and [Peng] Dehuai will fill you in on the details face to face.[164]

The units in question were the 38th, 39th, 40th, and 42nd corps of the Thirteenth Army and its artillery detachments. Presumably similar orders went to the commander of the 50th Corps, which Mao was then committing to Korea.

The following day, October 19, Mao informed the Party heads around the country of the decision to go to war and set out the line they were to follow with respect to the CPV: For the time being, it was to be "only action and no talk":

In order to defend China and aid Korea, we have decided to dispatch the Volunteers today to the northern part of Korea still under control [of the DPRK]. There they will first get a firm foothold and then wait for opportunities to wage mobile warfare in support of the continued struggle of the Korean people. For several months, we will resort *only to action and no talk*, and we shall not reveal any information in the newspapers for propaganda purposes. We can only inform senior leading cadres within the Party of the matters [they need to know] to carry out [their] job assignments. Various central bureaus should make a point of this. [Italics in the original.]¹⁶⁵

Peng Dehuai returned to Andong that day, and at about 5:30 P.M., after an urgent meeting with Pak Il U on reinforcements for North Korea's collapsing armies, he and his staff crossed the Yalu and headed for the village of Taeyudong, northwest of Onjong. There Peng established his first headquarters, in a mineshaft. Later that evening, the Thirteenth Army began to move out from its positions: the 38th and 42nd corps from Ji'an, and the 39th and 40th from Andong and Changdianhekou. The army's headquarters moved from Andong to Korea four days later.¹⁶⁶ On October 25, two additional corps, the 66th and 50th, were ordered to protect the Thirteenth's right flank and crossed the Yalu.¹⁶⁷

At ten o'clock in the morning of the 25th, two CPV regiments ambushed and destroyed a South Korean battalion near the village of Pukjin northwest of Unsan. The Chinese then pulled back. Small skirmishes occurred over the next days as the CPV prepared for the all-out offensive.¹⁶⁸ More than a month would elapse before General Douglas MacArthur understood that he was in an entirely new war. Mao had known it for weeks. The deepening tragedy of Korea had long passed the point of no return.

The War and the Alliance

The Chinese conventionally divide the battles that followed into five major campaigns.¹⁶⁹ The first dated from October 25 to November 5; the second from November 24 to December 24; the third from December 31 to January 8; the fourth from January 25 to April 21; and the fifth from April 22 to June 10.¹⁷⁰ After mid-1951, the war settled into protracted slaughter near the 38th parallel. Cease-fire talks began on July 10, 1951, and concluded with the armistice signed at Panmunjom on July 27, 1953.

The Chinese had entered the war without Soviet air cover, and when the heavy battles began, they suffered devastating losses from American air strikes. In November, North Korea and China again jointly appealed to Stalin to send jet fighters to Korea, and this time Stalin complied. The pilots of the 64th Independent Fighter Air Corps flew their first combat missions from their Andong air base sometime in the last half of the month.¹⁷¹

Reportedly, Stalin's decision was triggered by an incident in late October, when two American planes in clear weather bombed the Soviet Sukhaia Rechka airfield not far from Vladivostok. Concern about Soviet security, as well as Stalin's certainty about the Chinese regime's commitment to the war, had moved him to send his fighters, but he would not allow them to fly offensive missions and ordered them to keep far north of the frontlines in Korea.[172] The planes gave minimal help to ground operations, and the Soviet pilots made no effort to coordinate their sorties with those operations.[173]

Still, once China entered the war, Stalin did authorize some measures to guarantee his ally's security. Between October and December, he sent 13 air divisions to the Northeast and the coastal areas. This force, the 67th Air Corps, included bombers as well as fighters; besides the air defense of China, it had the mission of training Chinese pilots.[174] On November 3, the Soviet Union, in accordance with the spirit (but not the letter) of the Sino-Soviet alliance treaty, sent ten tank regiments to four cities in Northeast, North, and East China.[175] From this point on, Mao could proceed in the knowledge that the "rear area," China's homeland, would be protected. For the Chinese, this was the most tangible evidence of the treaty's reliability and deterrent value.

Ultimately, China's resort to arms in Korea had three major consequences for the Sino-Soviet alliance. First, the Chinese decision to fight without substantial Soviet assistance in hand and with the understanding that Stalin would try to prevent the war from engulfing the Soviet Union hardened the idea of limits embodied in article 1. Some analysts in Washington feared that the operations of American forces working out of Japanese bases could activate the obligation for Moscow to join China in warding off Japan "or any other state that may collaborate with Japan directly or indirectly in acts of aggression."[176] But in fact there was no chance of this happening; Stalin had determined that not even an attack by Japan-based forces against China itself could activate that obligation.

A second consequence of the Chinese decision to go to war was to convince Stalin that Mao and his government would not compromise with the United States and would stand by the Communist cause even against staggering odds. A senior Soviet military historian has noted: "The Korean conflict strengthened Stalin's trust in Mao and thereby the overall relations between the USSR and the PRC."[177] Never again would the relationship be, as Mao once characterized it, that of "father and son" and "cat and mouse."[178] China reached a historic turning point in its quest for equality the moment its troops crossed the Yalu. From then on, the Kremlin was more forthcoming and flexible in direct support of the war effort. China's conduct during the war placed it firmly on the path to equal status and shared interests with the Soviet Union.

The bonds between the two partners became ever more tangible. Stalin not only committed his own forces to China's defense, but also stepped up his direct military aid to Mao's armies.[179] Over time, Moscow sent the

Chinese enough arms for 64 infantry divisions and 22 air divisions. The CPV also got most of its replacement munitions from the USSR, for China's own munitions industry was unable to meet more than a tenth of the force's requirements during the war.[180] Most of the imported arms were purchased on credit and at bargain prices, though the shipments included many used weapons and leftovers from the U.S. supplies to the Soviet Union under World War II Lend-Lease.[181]

Oddly, after Stalin agreed to provide additional credit to China for the purchase of weapons and equipment from the Soviet Union, the question of whether or how China should repay the money was never formalized.[182] As a result, reimbursement tended to be hit or miss. The Chinese did pay substantial sums for the arms, but in some instances, Stalin lessened the burden on them. For example, when he learned that China had outfitted two Korean divisions (in addition to the two divisions of ethnic Koreans sent to join North Korea's forces in early 1950), he waived the costs for 20 of the 64 infantry divisions the Soviet Union outfitted during the war.[183] The Chinese paid for the rest of the armaments in installments; all loans, which were repaid at an annual rate of about one billion yuan, were settled by the end of 1965.

Chinese aircraft entered the war in a significant way for the first time in the fourth campaign (January 25–April 21, 1951), and thereafter the PLA rotated ten (out of a total of 22) fighter divisions assigned to the conflict.[184] At the outset, Soviet officials would consent to sell China only MiG-9 fighters, even though a large number of MiG-15s had by now been added to the Soviet inventory. When the Chinese protested that obsolete MiG-9s were no match for the most advanced American planes, the officials accused them of denigrating the USSR's weapons. But when the issue finally reached Stalin, he decreed that China should get 372 MiG-15s.[185] The partnership grew stronger as the months passed, so much so that in 1960 Premier Zhou Enlai was prompted to note that Stalin's suspicions of China had vanished during the course of the war.[186]

Finally, as a third consequence, the war was the first test of Mao's strategic view concerning the "vast zone" of competition that lay between the United States and the Soviet Union and of the relevance of the alliance to China's security interests. The Chinese leader concluded from the war that confrontation with U.S. military power would persist and probably intensify. Given the terrible toll of the war, which Mao only vaguely anticipated in October 1950, China would have to construct a strong defense-industrial base and draw heavily on Soviet support to create it. He would have to compromise China's sovereignty long enough to accomplish his plans in this regard—but no longer than that. "The war," we have noted elsewhere, "introduced Mao's China to advanced armaments and techniques. . . . To survive in the modern world, China would have to have modern arms."[187] In summing up the war, the Chinese military particularly stressed deficiencies in the air force, air defenses, and logistics. On the other hand, the officers took considerable pride in the fact that for all the army's terrible losses, China had nevertheless been able to fight the American army to a standstill.[188]

From the short-term Soviet viewpoint, Stalin emerged as the net winner from the Korean War. A bloody line had been drawn between China and the United States, and the possibility of their reconciliation had all but disappeared. North Korea had survived as a socialist state within the Soviet security zone. In the final count, the USSR's casualties were low, and its forces, when introduced, had gained substantial experience in modern warfare. Over the long run, however, the real interests of the Soviet state were badly served. The war provoked an unprecedented buildup of American nuclear forces and militarized the Cold War. Soviet security declined, and the USSR's economic and intellectual isolation in a hostile world was to shackle all its modernization efforts for decades to come.

SEVEN

Summing Up

The course of Sino-Soviet history that we have traveled begins just as the Second World War was ending and the Cold War beginning. On the eve of victory over Japan and renewed civil war with Mao's revolutionary armies, Chiang Kai-shek's representatives negotiated an alliance with the Soviet Union. These negotiations bared Moscow's security objectives in Asia and its designs on its neighbor.

From 1945 to 1949, Soviet security concepts adapted to the uncertain environment of the early Cold War and steadily evolved. Stalin's global strategies, proceeding from the need to prepare for a remote but inevitable world conflict, converged relentlessly on the power of the United States. The United States dominated Stalin's views on national defense and the place of the Soviet Union in the postwar order.

The driving forces behind these strategies and perspectives were tangled and often dimly or inaccurately comprehended by the principals in Moscow. Operating in a Byzantine milieu of violence and cynical manipulation, Stalin lived by the sword but miscalculated the nuclear revolution and the ties between domestic economic development and modern military technology. For all his talk about universal aims and the future, Stalin remained imprisoned by the Russian past.

Decades of combat also left scars on Mao's mind. The revolution was his classroom, and as he emerged victorious he saw little need to contemplate or embrace doctrines or visions inconsistent with its lessons. While demanding change in practice, he resisted any tinkering with his basic ideas. "I have developed my career by summing up historical experiences [wo kao zongjie jingyan chifan]," he once said. He turned constantly to the past, including ancient strategists, as he adapted to the post-takeover challenges.[1] Though history's teachings and his own experiences may have served him well in domestic warfare, they more often than not warped his foreign policies. His strategic principles in coping with Moscow and Washington were the ancient ones of "playing one barbarian off against the other" (*yi yi zhi yi*) and "unite and divide by political manipulation" (*zongheng baihe*).[2]

Some in China could see the flaws in Mao's strategic doctrines, but he ignored or outmaneuvered them and held basically firm to his convictions. Nothing could shake his dream of recovering China's proper place in the world. He believed that his historic mission was to rebuild the Middle Kingdom's power and status. He never doubted that the cultural and moral superiority of China would lead to its triumph over the legions of barbarians, including those to the north.

Yet even as his grand strategy endured, Mao was forced—slowly and grudgingly—to adjust his revolutionary-era tactics to the swiftly moving postwar world. In the initial stage of Soviet-PRC relations, Mao acted on the basis of two assumptions. First, the new state had to align itself with one of the two world blocs in order to ensure its safety against the other as it proceeded toward national unification and centralized rule. Although he regarded this alignment as conditional and temporary, he also assumed that he would have to surrender some of the nation's sovereignty to his more powerful partner.

The contacts between Stalin and Mao in 1949–50 and their deliberations on the terms of their relations demonstrated how Mao grappled with these two assumptions and how he treated the final accords of February 14, 1950. They indicate, moreover, that Mao worried about a domestic backlash to his concessions severe enough to shake his standing as a patriot and his legitimacy as supreme leader. He shied from revealing the shame of the Additional Agreement, which had compromised the nation's independence, and put Zhou Enlai in political harm's way as the treaty's negotiator and signer. Mao lacked the political courage to stand by his actions publicly as his colleagues voted on the results of his deals with Stalin.

Within eight months, Mao no longer tiptoed on the tightrope of suspect assumptions or hid behind others. He set aside the memory of Moscow and moved on. The Korean War put his national vision on trial and taught him the scope and character of Stalin's own worldview as it affected Asia and the security of China. The timing of the war, perhaps not by coincidence, served Stalin's chief purpose of thwarting the restoration of Sino-American relations. For Mao, U.S. actions toward Taiwan in June 1950 and his subsequent decision to send his armies into Korea indefinitely interrupted his plans for the final reunification of the country and deflected the course of national development.

We now attempt to sum up the drama and the struggle that produced the alliance and to reflect on the nature of the relationship that emerged. As we look back to its origins, we can more readily detect the flaws that brought the alliance to an end within a decade, and Asia to war within a year.

Becoming Partners

The Chinese Communists' preoccupation with war and its instruments did not blot out the history of their prewar contacts with Russia or expunge the bitter personal memories among those who had been betrayed by Stalin. It did dominate Mao's policy agenda and make security questions paramount. Both the previous history and its legacies are the subject of a vast literature in the West, which explains and confirms the importance of earlier wounds to contemporary politics.[3] Within the Communist world, however, the Chinese civil war and the emerging Cold War temporarily stifled the most painful memories. As both the Soviet Union and the warring Chinese factions contemplated their optimal tactics, virtually all matters of importance became encrusted in the security dilemma.

During the postwar revolutionary years in China, 1946–49, the supreme goal of Mao and his comrades was total victory. That goal could not be attained without adjusting the Chinese Communist Party's policies to the international situation and counterbalancing the competing interests of the major powers present in the country. The comparative weakness of the CCP at the onset of the renewed civil war and the combined might of Mao's domestic enemies and their foreign friends forced him to accept compromise and to adjust his tactics, even while not losing sight of his ultimate objectives.

Mao had to accommodate Soviet designs for China. During the first months after Japan's capitulation in the fall of 1945, he had to bow to Stalin's insistence on Chinese Communist participation in peace talks with the Nationalists. Later, while the fighting proceeded, the Chinese Communists had to maneuver between the Soviet leader's meddling and his implied threats to abandon them. They only faintly understood that his repeated attempts to mediate a truce in the civil war were intended to exclude any possibility of a Soviet clash with the United States in Asia.

Nevertheless, Mao kept his sights firmly fixed on his ultimate goal: to build a unified and powerful Chinese state that could cast off the legacy of past wrongs and, freed from inherited agonies, achieve equal status in a world system of hostile powers. The resolve to attain total victory at home not only sharpened the confrontation with the Nationalists; it also forced the United States to commit to Chiang Kai-shek, or so it seemed to Mao. The appearance of a growing bond between the Nationalists and Washington in turn strained and eventually ruptured the relations between Stalin and Chiang. Although the Truman administration's support of Chiang was often tentative and always the subject of controversy among policymakers, it did deepen the animosity of China's future Communist rulers toward the United States. These changes, coupled with the PLA's military successes, led inexorably to closer contacts between Moscow and Mao and helped infuse Cold War politics into Asian developments.

By mid-1948, it was becoming ever more obvious how power and future conflicts would be configured in East Asia after the defeat of the Nationalists on the Chinese mainland. Overly conditional and halfhearted as Stalin's military and economic backing may have seemed to Mao, in the Northeast it proved enough to tip the balance toward their closer ties. As the sides were being formed, no one could accurately predict the exact shape of the future political-military system in East Asia or how the interests within it would crystalize.

In 1949, the United States began detaching itself from Chiang as his government neared collapse and his fate was plain for all to see. It made a few faltering attempts to probe potential openings to Mao, but these were either misperceived or bungled. Stalin, too, began to prepare to deal officially with a Communist regime in China, but he delayed giving any unequivocal commitment that would reveal his hand or check his bargaining position. The Kremlin leader, moreover, wanted to maintain the fiction of his noninvolvement in the civil war as long as possible and to extract the last ounce of flesh from the perishing Nationalist government. Mao earnestly sought maximum Soviet support in these final days of the war but resisted making irreversible concessions. He obliquely attempted to use a conceivable rapprochement with the United States as a bargaining chip with Stalin.

By the summer of 1949, events had narrowed Mao's strategic options even further. He faced America's intransigence in reaching a modus vivendi and simultaneously feared Stalin's wrath if the Chinese Communist Party appeared eager to work with Washington. This was the moment the Chairman chose to proclaim his leaning-to-one-side policy and to prepare for the alliance with Moscow. He reluctantly concluded that only the Soviet Union could assure his fledgling government protection from external threats and sufficient help to facilitate its economic rebirth.

Mao did not intend to allow China to become Moscow's satellite. In line with his grand design, he exploited China's strategic value to Stalin in order to build toward a position of equality and to substantiate the case for revoking the worst features of the treaty between Stalin and Chiang. From

Mao's point of view, his alliance with the Soviet Union would only be a first step toward establishing China's rightful position in the world.

On Stalin's side, what mattered most was the coming confrontation between communism and capitalism, the inevitable Third World War that would deliver the death blow to world imperialism. He wanted to enter this war with maximum military readiness and reliable allies. His central priority was to create the conditions under which only Moscow could determine the time and place of the showdown. As a result, during the immediate postwar years, he did everything possible to avert a direct clash with the United States over China. For him, the time and place were wrong. While paying close attention to China, Stalin regarded Europe as the main battleground.

Perpetuating the tradition of Tsarist diplomacy, Stalin held that a necessary condition for his control of the timing and outcome of a future global conflict was the creation of a security belt along his borders. The concessions that he had extracted from the Nationalists in the treaty of 1945 satisfied this prerequisite in the East, and Stalin's dilemma during the next years was how to keep these gains if the Communists won the civil war. The CCP victories, coupled with the sharpening of the Cold War in Europe, gradually caused Stalin to rethink his Asian policies. Although the Soviet leader was still loath to cancel the most offensive terms of the 1945 accords as he moved closer to Mao, he came to view China under communism as a force for countering the U.S. "encirclement" of the Soviet empire. He redefined those terms to fit his concept of partnership.

In order to turn China into a true knight in his counter-encirclement game, Stalin considered two conditions absolutely essential. First of all, he needed to control Mao's relations with the Americans; only then could Mao's power be employed against the United States and coordinated with Soviet actions. In addition, he needed to ensure that the Soviet buffer zone in China would be preserved. Despite his appraisal of China's role as a strategic asset, Stalin was well aware that this role carried hidden perils and could present future obstacles to his policies.

Liu Shaoqi's visit to Moscow in July–August 1949 highlighted the myriad complexities in correlating Soviet and Chinese interests on the eve of the Communist victory in China. The visit served as a rehearsal for the coming Stalin-Mao summit and in large measure shaped its general content and direction. Moreover, it bore directly on the overall Communist approach to East Asia and the idea of dividing the world into spheres of strategic responsibility.

After the formation of NATO in April 1949, Stalin was faced with stalemate in Europe in the immediate future and possible permanent military inferiority over the long term. This new environment suddenly gave the Asian theater added significance. By stressing that the center of the world struggle against the United States had shifted to East Asia and by assigning the Chinese a major leadership role in the competition, Stalin unveiled a shift in strategy. The Chinese could open up a new anti-American front to the East, where the United States and its allies were dramatically retreating and where they could not fight, let alone win, without weakening their stronghold in Europe. China offered the Soviet leader a way to recapture the strategic initiative.

Stalin understood that a Chinese endorsement of Moscow's strategic outlook would require his acknowledgment of the global significance of Mao and his revolution. The Soviet leader would have to accept the need for mutual concessions in dealing with the Chinese and would be forced to provide them extensive economic and military assistance. He found a way to make these adjustments in a manner that would not sacrifice his most cherished objectives, or so he appears to have believed. During his talks with Liu Shaoqi, he unambiguously implied that China's actions in East Asia must be in harmony with Soviet interests (through the creation of a union of Asian Communist parties with Soviet participation), and that Mao would have to abandon any thought of normalizing his relations with Washington. Stalin stated quite bluntly that he would never risk a conflict with the United States over Taiwan and pressed the Chinese to put off their planned "liberation" of the island.

Stalin's views on Taiwan during the summer of 1949 can be traced to his anxieties about nuclear war. The talks with Liu Shaoqi were conducted on the eve of the first Soviet atomic blast. Though politically and psychologically the test was an important event for Moscow, enabling it to unleash a propaganda campaign about "the end of the American atomic monopoly," the possession of the bomb raised serious issues for Soviet defense. Stalin had to keep in mind the possibility of an American preemptive strike before the Soviet Union acquired the means to retaliate against the U.S. homeland. Although the Soviet leader did not consider the U.S. nuclear edge fatal for his plans, he had to be especially cautious until he could complete his preparations for the decisive engagement some decades down the road.

The Chinese leaders undoubtedly relished Stalin's high appraisal of their revolution. They were pleased that the Soviet dictator had at last admitted his many mistakes in dealing with them. Having long striven to become the Soviet Union's strategic partner and to have a sphere of responsibility of their own, they welcomed Stalin's granting them their dream and his recognition that East Asia was no less critical for Soviet security than Europe was. The Kremlin pledge to provide military and economic support for the conquest of Xinjiang demonstrated that Sino-Soviet interests were converging. The time had come to negotiate the terms of the alliance.

Stalin's actions convinced the Chinese that to a limited extent they could resist and channel Moscow's demands. Yet they would have to temporarily accept the Soviet presence and influence and to recognize the fact that the elimination of Soviet special rights in China would take time and great political finesse. They were not in danger of becoming the Kremlin's puppet, but neither were they truly independent. Because of that and adhering to Stalin's advice, they quickly formulated a revolutionary line for Asia in which they would play a leading role. At the same time, they ignored Stalin's other recommendations on establishing a union of Asian Communist parties with Soviet participation and postponing the invasion of Taiwan.

They would use Stalin as much as he used them. The Chinese high command had immense respect for the Soviet experience but no more than it had for its own revolutionary history. Mao never hesitated to underscore the uniqueness of his nation and its needs or to point out the deficiencies of the Soviet blueprint for East Asia as a whole.

The cables and other exchanges between the Chinese and Soviet leaders throughout 1949 alerted both to the complexities and potential difficulties in forming a legal partnership. These impediments governed the subject matter and the limits for their talks in December and January and shaped alternative negotiating strategies. Beyond this, both sides entered the talks much clearer about their bottom-line positions and how hard they would fight for them. Stalin in particular had done his best to demonstrate to the Chinese the value of the cards that he was holding.

As a result, Soviet influence in Xinjiang and in the Northeast weighed on Mao's mind. Stalin had demonstrated his willingness to cooperate with the Chinese Communists in strengthening their control in these crucial territories, but he could easily reverse his policies should Mao prove unwilling to comply with his basic demands. Each was the uncertain partner of the other.

The PLA's failure at Quemoy in late October 1949 came at a particularly bad moment for the Chinese, engaged as they were in the planning for the summit. The debacle served as a powerful proof of the PRC's need for Soviet military and economic assistance. Aid did begin to pour into China, but it provided Moscow greater leverage just as the talks began. Moscow could reduce or even withdraw that aid at any point, a sword that Beijing knew hung over its head.

Moreover, Stalin was ready to extend what we would now call assured deterrence to China only in the framework of his global strategy. He added the condition that the Chinese not draw him into any conflicts with the United States, but he promoted those confrontations that would divide Washington from Beijing. The Soviet leader was worried by reports from his representatives in Beijing that the PRC leaders were attempting to improve relations with the West, were bent on achieving a hegemonic role in East Asia, and were determined to proceed with the "liberation" of Taiwan. If the Chinese were unwilling to act within the boundaries set by Moscow on any of these key strategic policies, Soviet security guarantees were sure to be drastically compromised.

Thus on the very eve of the Moscow summit between Stalin and Mao, cooperative interests became mixed with basic differences in the perceived need for and approaches to common action. Moreover, when the two leaders met in December, they had sharply contrasting mind-sets. Stalin, the leader of an emerging superpower, was trying to preserve what he had already won through conquest and to use China for making further advances. China, by contrast, had yet to be accepted as a legitimate state, let alone a leading player in world politics. For Beijing, the relationship with Moscow involved a paradox: the need to accept inequality in order to achieve equality. Only clever tactics on Mao's part could prevent a temporary contradiction from becoming permanent subservience.

In our discussion of the negotiations between Stalin and Mao, we discerned two distinct stages. During the first of them, lasting from Mao's arrival in the Soviet capital on December 16, 1949, until January 2–3, 1950, the two leaders strove unsuccessfully to define and agree on the basic principles of their relations. Stalin did his best to preserve key aspects of the treaty of 1945 in order to safeguard the Soviet Union's security belt, and Mao spared no effort in restricting them in order to restore China's self-esteem and sovereignty.

During this phase of the talks, Stalin and Mao waged a war of nerves. It was a contest that exposed the unparalleled ruthlessness and arrogance of both, especially so of Stalin. The senior Russian translator recalls, "The very room where the talks were held was like a stage where a demonic show was being acted out. When Stalin walked in, everyone seemed to stop breathing, to freeze. He brought danger. An atmosphere of fear arose." Mao struck the translator as a "loyal follower," whose words delivered in coarse Hunan dialect seemed "somehow crumbly."[4] Time and again, high politics gave way to a test of wills between two pugnacious egos.

With basic interests at stake, they played out a classic zero-sum game, in which common interests and diplomatic niceties fell by the wayside. Neither leader was used to giving way, and both bargained as if there could be no accord at all. Within this surrealistic drama, however, the two central actors had no doubt about the absolute requirement for a treaty. Even as they tested each other's will, they knew that they could not cast the game board aside. The breakthrough in the early days of January was as foreordained as it was essential.

That breakthrough ushered in the next stage of the negotiations. Stalin was profoundly disturbed by Britain's recognition of China and considered it the forerunner of a Sino-American normalization that would ruin all his strategic calculations. Truman and Acheson's announced hands-off policy toward Taiwan provided additional grounds for Stalin's suspicions. Suddenly the tables were turned. The Americans' seeming willingness to tolerate a PLA seizure of the island might well lay the basis for a Beijing-Washington rapprochement. Since the Soviet dictator could not openly oppose the invasion of Taiwan, he had only one recourse: to take stronger measures to separate China from the West. At this point, Mao did not have to do anything more than stand on Stalin's side of the dividing line.

The Chinese Chairman was of two minds. He could be gratified by the fact that, in exchange for submitting to Stalin's demands, he had extracted important pledges from the Kremlin to assist China in its military buildup for the Taiwan invasion. On the other hand, all the subsequent agreements—secret and public, formal and informal—resulted from compromises from which Stalin emerged the clear winner.

There were many examples of this imbalance. Stalin did accept the withdrawal of Soviet forces from the Northeast sooner than stipulated in the 1945 treaty, but the price was the secret Additional Agreement barring "the citizens of third countries" from living or working in Manchuria and Xinjiang and the accord on the movement of Soviet troops via the Chinese Changchun Railroad. The two protocols consolidated Moscow's security zone in China's far west and Northeast. Stalin further manipulated Mao into exerting pressure on the Japanese Communist Party and taking a more hostile stand toward the West, though, at Mao's insistence, he recognized the revolutionary regime of Ho Chi Minh. Most significantly, Stalin promised to defend China against aggression by the United States "by all means" at his disposal but hedged his bets by conditioning the Soviet obligation on the declaration of "a state of war."

Both leaders, of course, had cause for satisfaction as a result of their meeting. The alliance was a reality. Nonetheless, each left the talks more suspicious and more uncertain than when they began. The treaty and accompanying agreements, as we remarked, had many more pluses for Stalin than for Mao, and some of the provisions reminded the Chinese of the unequal treaties of the past. The Additional Agreement was the most vivid manifestation of this fact, and Mao returned to Beijing dedicated to over-turning it at the earliest possible moment. He was more determined than ever to revitalize China and restore its sovereignty.

Stalin's judgments on the talks ran in the opposite direction to Mao's. He appears to have understood quite clearly the Chinese abhorrence of the Additional Agreement. The Soviet leader realized that Mao would demand more equality in the relationship as soon as he could overcome China's most acute domestic problems and would try to establish relations with the West from a position of strength. A successful takeover of Taiwan could remove the most serious obstacle in the relations between Beijing and Washington and thus would create the circumstances for the acceleration of this process. Thus, Stalin had to worry that his military aid for the as-sault against the island would in fact bolster China's power and weaken its hostility toward the United States. Should this train of events come to pass, Mao Zedong would undoubtedly call for a renegotiation of the bilateral arrangements of February 1950.

How fundamental these concerns would be only time would tell. More-over, the concerns were lessened by the understandings reached at the sum-mit on the outlines of the global power struggle. The talks had touched on the problems of war and peace and elaborated a rationale for a serious re-evaluation of the confrontation with the West. After the conclusion of the treaty, the Soviet and Chinese leadership and press consciously filled in the general outlines and reiterated common themes derived from the summit. They jointly boasted about the basic shift in the "correlation of forces" in favor of socialism. The alliance, they emphasized, had put the United States on the defensive and reduced its ability to check the development of revolutions in Asia. The "forces of socialism" had now gone on the march worldwide.

After late 1949, Stalin became more assertive in his strategic planning. The period from the inauguration of NATO to the completion of the West's buildup in Europe provided a window of time to fortify his country and to get ready to fight. Truman's rush to reverse the course of reform and de-mocratization in Japan and his announcement in January 1950 of his de-cision to build the H-bomb added to the urgency of Moscow's planning.

We now know that this was the period in which the Soviet Union halted its military cutbacks and initiated a massive arms buildup. Circumstantial evidence suggests that Stalin's agreements with Mao on the assignment of spheres of responsibility gave the Soviet leader new confidence in his ability to thwart U.S. power. Stalin had begun to believe that the Third World War would erupt not in 20 or 30 years but by the middle of the 1950s. He would have to be ready either to break an early American assault or to wage a preemptive blitzkrieg before the Americans were ready.

Mao could help. His task would be to promote revolutionary struggle in Vietnam and Southeast Asia, threaten to attack Taiwan, and assist Kim Il Sung in his takeover of South Korea. Korea was important for Stalin not only because it was part of the security belt on his eastern flank but also because it provided him with a springboard for an invasion of Japan in case of war. A more aggressive China would cause the United States to split its forces and to face combat on two global fronts.

The toughening of the Soviet-Chinese partnership was closely watched by Washington. From February to March 1950, the debates in the Truman administration explored the grounds for reevaluating its cautious policy toward Taiwan and Korea and for a more resolute global military posture to counter the Communist offensive. NSC 68 of April 14, 1950, was a landmark document in this process and helped draw East Asia into the Cold War.

What part the Stalin-Mao talks played in the outbreak of the Korean War a half year later is hard to pin down, for whether by design or not, the two leaders did not go into the issue of Kim Il Sung's charted invasion of the South. Although both Stalin and Mao endorsed Kim's concept of a "revolutionary war against the lackeys of American imperialism," they had not yet refined their stand on how, beyond military and economic aid, they would support it. We have described the complicated intercourse among the three leaders that led to the final decision to attack and the Soviet part in devising the plan of operations.

On the other hand, the facts now available do clearly call into question the arguments that Kim was driven to war by the South's recurring provocations or that his decision was taken solely on his own initiative. Kim began lobbying for a Soviet-backed invasion of the South as early as March 1949. He proposed it, fought for it, and with a Soviet army battle plan to guide him, executed it. The invasion of June 25, 1950, was pre-planned, blessed, and directly assisted by Stalin and his generals, and reluctantly backed by Mao at Stalin's insistence. Mao knew that preparations for the invasion were under way and, in general, upheld the idea of Korean unification under Kim's rule. But he also expressed reservations about Kim's assumptions and was deliberately kept in the dark on the details of the North's preparations, including the timing of the attack. He acted to reduce his armies and proceed with the invasion of Taiwan even after Kim launched the attack, and the PLA command could only watch in dismay and obey.

In our view, the decision to go to war cannot be laid alone to Stalin's pressure, or to Kim's adventurism, or to a Soviet–North Korean (let alone Sino–North Korean) conspiracy. In fact, the decision came in bits and pieces and was never coordinated or even thoroughly scrutinized by the three states. It was reckless war-making of the worst kind. Each of three Communist leaders was operating on premises that were largely concealed and facts that were fabricated or at best half true. The process was partially driven by Soviet and Chinese policies and perceptions that had nothing to do with Korean reunification as such. The alliance had not provided any mechanisms for joint analysis and joint decision-making, and in any case had not included North Korea.

Kim Il Sung had decided on the need for an invasion by conventional forces because his guerrilla tactics, approved by Stalin in March 1949, had miscarried. Kim presented his case for the invasion on the grounds that these tactics would somehow succeed in the wake of a full-scale attack, but he never fully apprised Stalin of the reasons behind the earlier failures. To win Stalin's backing, he relied on his position of faithful supporter and the basic Soviet interest in a bolder Asian challenge to the West. During his secret visit to Moscow, Kim Il Sung did his best to persuade Stalin that a popular uprising in the South would be triggered by the invasion, that victory would come quickly, and that the Americans would remain on the sidelines until it was too late.

Stalin had no incentive to question Kim's arguments, but he gave the go-ahead on the basis of Soviet interests and on the condition that Mao agree. We have examined his general beliefs that Kim's victory would enlarge the Soviet security zone, provide a vital springboard against Japan, and force a diversion of U.S. forces from Europe to Asia. These were all positive factors for the Soviet dictator. On the other hand, Stalin was willing to support Kim only if the possibility of a Soviet-American clash in Korea would be excluded. He determined that the way to do this was to implicate Mao in the decision and thereby make him bear the full burden for ensuring Kim's survival if the Americans intervened. A Sino-American war, should it erupt in Korea, would have the added benefit of widening the break between Beijing and the West.

Mao could not deny his Korean comrades the very opportunity for unifying their country that the Chinese had demanded for themselves. At the same time, he explicitly worried that Kim's action would provoke a U.S. response, threaten China's security, and preclude the seizure of Taiwan. But he had to minimize the likelihood of American intervention in the Korean conflict when Stalin asked about this possibility in January. He could not claim the opposite for Korea without calling his own assurances into question. Mao was being hoisted by his own petard. All he could do was to accelerate the preparations for the Taiwan operation and hope that the battle for Korea would not spoil his own plans.

In May 1950, Stalin finally gave Kim the signal to proceed. We argue that this decision must be understood against the background of general Soviet calculations about American policy. Although the United States was still avowedly committed to Truman's hands-off approach, signs of a hardening of the U.S. stance toward Asia had surfaced and suggested to Stalin that Washington might reverse course. Appreciating that there would be a window of opportunity as the United States translated its new policy into a substantial military buildup on the ground, Stalin presumably judged that for Kim it was now or never. A more belligerent American attitude toward Asian communism enlarged the chances of U.S. interference in Korea after Kim's assault, to be sure. But Stalin was satisfied that he could maintain the appearance of neutrality if Mao carried the burden of direct military involvement.

Given the sloppy decision-making, misperceptions, and perverted objectives, it is small wonder that the invasion was a disaster. The outbreak of the war was a fatal blow to Mao's plans for Taiwan. Although he proclaimed that Truman had betrayed his word to keep U.S. hands off, the Chinese leader simply misjudged the nature of American decision-making and the mood in Washington. When he learned that the American Seventh Fleet had moved into the Taiwan Strait, Mao pronounced the action tantamount to a declaration of war. He knew, nonetheless, that his government could not declare war without antagonizing Stalin and jeopardizing its alliance with the Soviet Union.

After the war began, Mao postponed his plans for the Taiwan invasion and turned his attention to the defense of the Northeast and possible intervention in Korea. Stalin, on the other hand, took steps to exclude Soviet participation in the war. By preventing the Soviet representative from returning to the Security Council meeting that put the Korean "police action" under UN command, he effectively precluded any formal declaration of war by either the Chinese or the American side and so avoided activating the Sino-Soviet treaty.

The period from the landing at Inchon on September 15 to mid-October, when the first "volunteer" detachments crossed the Yalu, provides an unparalleled opportunity to assess Chinese decision-making in action. Immediately after Inchon, Stalin urged Mao to come to Kim's rescue, promising air cover for the Chinese troops and direct Soviet involvement in case the Chinese were defeated. Mao understood quite well that the danger to China's security had now grown immensely, and he accelerated the deployment of his best armies along the Yalu frontier.

At the same time, both Mao and his comrades were uneasy about Stalin's promise to dispatch Soviet troops in the event of a Chinese defeat. Moreover, many Politburo and military leaders resisted going to war before their own rule had been consolidated. The Chinese economy lay in shambles, and the task of national reunification was far from complete. Mao had to deal with dissent at home, as well as the high probability of war with the United States. As his military commanders hastily set about upgrading the Northeast Frontier Force, his chief foreign policy lieutenant, Zhou Enlai, twice warned the Americans not to cross the 38th parallel and strike north.

By October 8, when the Chinese warnings were ignored and American units had punched across the parallel, the Chairman, not without hesitation and recurrent debate with his colleagues, made up his mind to send in the Chinese People's Volunteers. The threshold between war and peace had been crossed. The motives behind the decision were mixed: the menace that would result from an American presence on the border with the Northeast, the rising unrest throughout the country as the enemy advanced toward the Yalu, and Mao's obviously increasing dependence on an ally that was bent on China's entering the war. In the mountains of Korea, the numerical superiority of the Chinese People's Volunteers could offset American firepower, particularly if reinforced by Soviet arms, and it was Mao's conclusion that American nuclear weapons would not be used there. Korea was the place to take a stand.

When Stalin reneged on his promise to provide air cover for their forces, the Chinese momentarily flinched. The price of war had suddenly gone up. The Soviet dictator, relying on reports of his representatives in Beijing, as well as on his own perception of Mao's intentions, saw the Chinese delay in answering his call for military action as a deliberate ploy to force his hand on Soviet assistance and participation. Stalin held firm, and thereby demonstrated his determination not to face the United States in Korea. The Pyongyang regime could be destroyed, but he would not go to war to rescue it.

For Mao, the die had been cast. He had to proceed even without Soviet air cover in order to save, not North Korea, but China. That bold decision in turn persuaded Stalin to modify his position somewhat and to provide the PLA Soviet weapons and equipment. On the night of October 18–19, after Zhou had briefed the Politburo on the results of his talks in Moscow, the final orders were issued to cross the Yalu. Only after Stalin was certain that the Chinese were fully engaged in the fighting did he secretly introduce fighter planes and send his troops to China. For a time, the uncertainty of the alliance evaporated.

Mao knew that the decision to go to war immeasurably strengthened Stalin's trust in him and dispelled his suspicions. After the Chinese armies struck, Stalin became much more willing to provide assistance to China and to end the most notorious manifestations of inequality in his relations with it. This willingness and, after Stalin's death in 1953, Khrushchev's downgrading of buffer zones and satellite regimes created the conditions for the "golden age" in Sino-Soviet relations that lasted until about 1958.

The Alliance in Retrospect

A close examination of Sino-Soviet relations from September 1945 through October 1950 strips away much of the simplicity that one sometimes finds in analyses of these relations. We have found no evidence that suggests the absolute domination of Stalin or the unlimited servility of Mao Zedong. All of the outcomes of their ties resulted from complicated calculations and compromises, with bilateral considerations often held hostage to domestic or unilaterally defined global requirements.

Although Stalin usually (but not always) got more from the relationship than Mao did, it was at the cost of certain concessions that worked fundamentally to China's benefit over the next decade. Stalin realized that if the Chinese could extract commitments when they were weak and vulnerable, they could become very tough partners indeed as their power grew.

Although we have focused on the history of bilateral Sino-Soviet relations, the United States was always an invisible third partner. Its "presence" at the negotiating table during the talks between Stalin and Mao added to the complexity and uncertainties of the alliance. In fact, both leaders made repeated estimates of how Washington might respond to their actions and statements, and the American factor was a constant in alliance decision-making. The "great strategic triangle" shaped the conduct of Soviet-Chinese relations perhaps no less (but less visibly) in the 1950s than it did in the 1970s. The triangular relationship, in different forms, repeatedly infiltrated the political agendas in Moscow and Beijing over the coming decades.

There is no evidence that in the period of our study the Chinese and Soviets ever attempted to analyze in any serious detail how each perceived the American threat or proposed to cope with it. Indeed, with so many aspects of the alliance unspoken and ambiguous, it is not difficult to see why the unresolved misinterpretations and fundamental disagreements would later lead to a deepening rift.

Their superficial discursion into topics touching the United States should have alerted them to the risks of silence. Even tangential issues that related to perceptions of U.S. power or minor tactics toward it fueled mini-confrontations between Stalin and Mao, and a full-blown quest for common approaches to that power might have brought the talks to a halt. Without raising and addressing major unanswered questions about policies toward the United States, the two Communist leaders could never come to a meaningful accord about the nature of the alliance itself.

The two allies did not discuss whether their relationship could or should be one of political equality. Given the power imbalance favoring the Soviet Union, perhaps China should have accepted a political (and ideological) status consistent with its lesser military and economic power. It did not. Although the Kremlin gave lip service to the need for equality, its attitude throughout the early period of cooperation was that Beijing's real political status was an inferior one. Moscow never accepted the idea that Mao's ideological pretensions were anything more than that.

We see here a lack of any clear, mutually understood, and accepted "basic principles of relations" that could guide cooperation and resolve disputes. Among the questions that should have been posed by the two parties, but were not, several come immediately to mind: What were the political (as opposed to technical) issues that could be legitimately raised and genuinely aired? How should policy differences and real grievances be handled procedurally? What were the external threats facing the alliance itself (as opposed to either nation) and how should they be met? Under what conditions would one side go to war (rather than not go to war) on behalf of the other, and how would the terms of assistance be worked out? What weight should be given to reciprocity, and how would the value of each quid pro quo be determined? Who had the final say? If neither (because of their equality), how would a meeting of minds be reached? Without explicit answers to these questions, the only recourse in a crisis would be the adoption of ad hoc and probably self-serving principles and procedures that each side would try to impose on the other.

Neither leader appears to have fully understood or appreciated the inherent hazards and folly of leaving so much unexplored. In their pursuit of untarnished unity, they perpetuated their differences on security—which were to become so central to the eventual rupturing of the alliance—as well as on other critical issues of perceived common interest.

Built on distrust and forced concessions, the alliance contained the seeds of its own destruction. Its creation had an important impact on the West, but herein lay the fundamental contradiction. The terms of the partnership were inequitable, but in operation the alliance, when facing West, required Moscow to treat China as an equal and to assist its quest for global standing. Stalin needed a dependent ally but promised to help create a powerful and independent one. For Stalin, a more robust China would erase the line between itself and the West and the buffer zone created by the Additional Agreement. Building a stronger China, one objective of the alliance, would also lessen the external security threats that justified the treaty's very existence. From opposing perspectives, neither Stalin nor Mao expected—or in Mao's case wanted—the partnership to last.

In analyzing the foreign policies of Stalin and Mao, we have raised indirectly another question that should now be answered. What mattered most to them when they formulated their grand strategies and tactics, ideology or realpolitik? We shall long debate the possible approaches to this question, and it seems clear that an unqualified choice of one or the other would be wrong. On balance, a striking feature of Mao and Stalin *in camera* is that neither was motivated by the ideology that so characterized their public declarations of the period.

Their private communications mostly carried a message of naked military-political interests and a priority for national security. The concept of security, of course, combines and oversimplifies a host of complex and interrelated realities. National culture, historical experience, leadership ambition and style, military potential and attitudes toward power, and recent memories of war and upheaval all can and did enter into the concept's definition in both nations. In practice, the two leaders typically avoided making precise distinctions when reaching and promulgating their most important decisions and often, for political purposes, couched their security policies in deceptive language. More commonly in Communist societies than others, perhaps, ideology provides the framework for projecting a broad internationalist vision based on pure nationalism and naked power.

Ideology, we find, played a secondary role, despite the apparent similarities between their socioeconomic systems, bureaucratic doctrines, Kafkaesque institutions, and avowed adherence to Marxism-Leninism. On the surface, ideology served as an important link during the creation of the alliance and on some later occasions, but again the documents deflate ideology's significance. This is not to discount the influence of ideology on the foreign policies of the two nations altogether but simply to suggest that it carried far less weight than other facets of the essential dynamics shaping their foreign policy decisions.

True enough, both Mao and Stalin gave ideology pride of place in their foreign policy statements and public pronouncements on domestic questions. It is also true that Marxist-Leninist quotations provided a reliable conceptual framework for discussions within their inner circles. Nevertheless, the two leaders' actions were almost always guided by far more mundane considerations. Ideological declarations could serve power politics but not determine it. Motives found deeply rooted in national traditions far outweighed Marxism-Leninism in practice.

Ideology was extremely important for them on the most general level, to be sure, especially in the selection and treatment of enemies. In their thinking, imperialism was essentially evil, communism good; the final aim of all their political activities was the annihilation of the "imperialist" states. Ideology also had a clear impact on another sphere of foreign policy: the analysis of the domestic situations in other countries, where class concepts often proved crucial. When it came to their face-to-face deliberations on particular external policy issues, however, the ultimate concern on both sides was not class struggle, but state interests (though the arguments were sometimes couched in revolutionary terms). In the final analysis, realpolitik governed their thinking and strained their relations. Time and again, issues of security—general assessments of the American threat, peaceful coexistence, nuclear war, national liberation struggles, and, above all, military cooperation—were the triggers that brought Stalin and Mao into verbal combat and, in the early years, temporary agreement. They were bound to come to grief on these issues in the end, given the profound differences in their strategic outlook and perceptions of their own vital security interests.

Both leaders demonstrated a Machiavellian ability to formulate long-term strategies for their states and to implement them through the persistent application of well-articulated tactics. This does not mean that the two dictators were unusually shrewd or farsighted. They basically failed to credit the prudence or cunning of their adversaries or to make allowance for luck, basic ignorance, and misinformation. They were crippled by outmoded doctrines, and they stuck to tactics that unwittingly undercut their national interests.

The classic dilemma of all who crudely hold that the ends justify the means is that the means become the ends. Both Mao and Stalin assumed that all men were either their subordinates or their foes, and that every weakness of their adversaries should be exploited. "We must not show the slightest timidity before a wild beast," Mao had said of his enemies. "Either kill the tiger or be eaten by him—one or the other."[5] People so defined and so treated responded in kind but brought to the combat a very large stick. Moreover, in believing that their own people were expendable in attaining ultimate goals, they turned potential friends into enemies and steadily depleted the ranks necessary for victory. In the final analysis, the Soviets and

Chinese not only dealt with the "imperialists" in this way; they so treated each other.

The emphasis on state interests and realpolitik inevitably led Stalin and Mao to share the strategic perspectives of their imperial predecessors. Geography, culture, and the nature of authoritarian systems dictated continuities in their outlook and actions. As they stood on the Kremlin wall or Tiananmen at the Forbidden City, the two leaders were consciously affirming their ties to the past, their debt to tradition. Their manner was imperial and imperious.

The relations between Stalin and Mao reveal a variety of idiosyncratic features. Their encounters were intense and direct. Their conversations melded straight talk on explosive and delicate topics with almost subliminal messages conveyed with deviousness and equivocation. The atmosphere was both electric and indeterminate, with both leaders in a constant state of alert, searching out hidden meaning and potential traps in even the most innocent remarks of the other. We know that the auditors and translators who attended these meetings were bewildered and alarmed, and the same may well have been true of the two leaders, since neither was accustomed to being engaged by such blunt interlocutors.

The technique of typing states according to organizational and bureaucratic theories so favored by political scientists is of little use in this case, for organizational processes and bureaucratic rivalries, though clearly present, were held in check by the Soviet and Chinese high commands. Opposition and factionalism emerged from time to time but were soon crushed. As the supreme rulers in their systems, Mao and Stalin achieved and exercised enormous power; they invariably prevailed on issues that mattered to them. They dominated political action in virtually all major decisions, especially those affecting national strategy and foreign policy, and destroyed any vibrant and enlightened opposition that might have helped them refine their policies. The problems that bedeviled Mao and Stalin stemmed from a lack of wisdom, not a lack of power, a lack of informed vision, not a lack of international reach. And in the end, both brought ruin to their nations.

In the years under review, Mao more than Stalin recognized the need for more complete and unwelcome information and preferred to rely on consensus rather than blind obedience. Mao used the public opinion of his people not only to bolster his domestic position, but also to bargain effectively with the Soviets. In comparison, Stalin acted in the name of the Soviet people or the Supreme Soviet for purely demagogical purposes and as a tactic.

No leader, of course, can work purely in a vacuum or on his own. Even dictators need advisers and underlings to bring them information and carry out their will, and there was no want of clever subordinates on either side. Often these intermediaries played on their leader's egotism for their own ends, as we have shown in our discussion of Ivan Kovalev and Shi Zhe. Both leaders needed accurate data and clear analysis, and the officials who provided these at least indirectly influenced the final decisions. Kovalev was a master in this regard. When his information conformed to Stalin's prejudices and predilections, Kovalev could achieve significant autonomy in his own spheres. The conversations of Kim Il Sung with Stalin in the year leading up to the war offers another example of the weak manipulating the strong.

The nature of the Chinese and Soviet political systems required personal contacts between the supreme leaders for major decision-making, and Sino-Soviet summitry became legitimized under Stalin and Mao and persisted through the rule of Nikita Khrushchev. This special mode of intercourse between the bosses of the Kremlin and the Chinese nerve center at Zhongnanhai contributed to the fragility of the Sino-Soviet strategic bond. Their relationship was both personal and distant, but it was the cement that kept the alliance together.

When Stalin died, the strongest bond between the Russian and Chinese leaderships went with him. Ivan Arkhipov, the top Soviet economic adviser in China for most of the period from 1950 to 1958, believes that the chemistry between the two Politburos changed with the passing of Stalin, and that by the end of the period, it was "above all the character of the leaders of both countries" that destroyed the alliance.[6]

What Mao had yielded to Stalin as leader of the international Communist movement he could not grant to Stalin's successors, lesser figures who had little hold over that movement and over China. Although the relations between Mao and Stalin had always been contentious, they had a grudging respect for each other and lived within rules that forced them to cooperate. They accepted the logic of an alliance within the context of global confrontation, inevitable war, and threats from a common enemy. As the world moved toward "peaceful coexistence" after Stalin's death, the logic vanished, and for Mao, only the bitterness of his treatment in Moscow endured.

Below the top echelons, officials on both sides had to accept at face value high-level statements on the importance of the partnership, and as a result, the Soviets and Chinese who carried out the bilateral accords functioned as if they were in fact equals. The bureaucrats of the respective international liaison departments of the two central committees, the military and intelligence staffs, and the ministry-level personnel served together remarkably well.[7] Arkhipov has stressed that the working levels of the two countries carried out the agreed programs "on a sound basis of cooperation and mutual assistance" from 1950 to 1957, but indicates that the "principles of mutual trust" had begun to weaken by the end of his tenure.

The personal ties between Mao and Khrushchev became antagonistic, lacking, in Arkhipov's words, "self-control and restraint, . . . tolerance, and . . . mutual concessions."[8] Arkhipov's account grasps the outward manifestations of all the growing complexities in Mao's attitude toward Stalin, Khrushchev, and the Soviet Union in general. The roots of these complexities lay in the early contacts between the two sides and in the fact that personal politics could never truly reconcile divergent national interests.

Despite these problems, Sino-Soviet relations during the years treated in this study had a lasting impact on the two states. The greatest influence was on Mao, because Stalin died before him and the successors in the Kremlin consciously tried to break with his legacy. Mao lived on for another quarter of a century or so and did not forget. For him, the formative months of the alliance and the trauma of the Korean War remained alive and symbolized the dark side of the alliance. The incongruity between Mao's bitter memories and Khrushchev's clean slate made their rivalry inevitable.

Mao believed that the alliance had deterred America's resort to nuclear weapons in the Korean War, but uppermost in his mind were China's sacrifices in the war and the punishment it had inflicted on the West. The latter, he believed, had the most lasting deterrent value. Moreover, Stalin's reluctance to provide direct and immediate assistance to the Chinese in Korea raised Mao's suspicions on the reliability of the Soviet deterrent for China under the terms of the treaty.[9]

Mao's conversations with Stalin did reveal an essential convergence on the role of nuclear weapons in the postwar world. Both had genuine respect for the bomb. It did have tactical implications, which loomed ever larger in Stalin's military thinking and later in Mao's. Both leaders reached roughly the same conclusion, that nuclear weapons had not fundamentally changed the nature of war, and Mao reiterated this view in his conversations with Stalin's successor. Khrushchev, not impressed, began to redefine Soviet security interests and military doctrines in light of nuclear weapons and their long-range delivery systems.[10]

The alliance and the Korean War reassured Stalin about Mao's loyalty and fortitude in the face of U.S. threats, and the Soviet leader's fear that an independent China would challenge the USSR's hegemony abated during his lifetime. For his part, the staggering human and material losses in Korea imbued Mao with a fierce commitment to building the nation's independent military and political power and caused him to reevaluate the Soviet tie.

Most of all, the war in Korea had proved how badly the Chinese military needed upgrading. Taking into account these twin considerations, the Chairman pursued a dual course. He sought to obtain the maximum possible help from the Soviet Union as he developed his own military. His ultimate goal was to achieve China's independent deterrent and to break free of the alliance restraints.

But Mao faced something of a problem here, for his own generals, off their experiences in Korea, were convinced that the combination of Chinese troops and Soviet weapons was unbeatable. They in fact placed a considerably higher value on the Soviet nuclear umbrella than Mao did. In 1956 Peng Dehuai told the Politburo, "If war breaks out, we will send troops and the Soviet Union will provide the atomic bomb."[11] The generals studied the war and quietly rewrote their tactical handbooks. They also embraced Soviet military doctrines and welcomed Soviet military advisers throughout the PLA. An unintended consequence of the war for Mao was that his army was coming under the influence of a foreign power. It took him five years from the signing of the armistice, until 1958, to remove the cancer.[12]

The years of combat within the framework of the alliance taught Mao and Stalin very different lessons. Both the way the alliance was negotiated and the process of entering the Korean War sowed the seeds of discord between the two states and propelled them onto quite different paths. That is a fundamental finding of this study.

Before the war, Mao had set his mind on "liberating" Taiwan. This was his priority task, and the Korean War made the attainment of that goal impossible. Mao had accepted the Soviet demands to forgo political relations with the United States and then to aid North Korea. In doing so, he had sacrificed all hope of normalizing ties with Washington for the foreseeable future. When the war ended, Mao returned to his priority task, and he clearly expected the Soviet Union to support him. At the very least, he felt that Moscow was obliged not to undertake any steps that would infringe on this goal or any other central Chinese interests. But from the outset, the Kremlin had never taken its eye off its chief foe, and its actions toward Washington were little influenced by what the Chinese may have wanted or thought their due.

The alliance with Stalin was Mao's first experience with a junior partnership at the international level. He had tried partial alliances or "united fronts" with Chiang Kai-shek in earlier years and had gained certain benefits from them as long as they lasted. The partnership with Moscow, despite its advantages, particularly galled him, and he would never again choose to be the subordinate partner of a foreign power, even in the face of a common enemy. He—and his successors—would shy away from any formal agreements with other strong states, especially the two superpowers.

In all probability, Stalin was the only man Mao ever feared. Yet he had personal respect for the Soviet leader as a man who managed to transform his country into a superpower in a limited period of time and who had achieved victory in a great war. We may suppose, too, that Mao was particularly impressed by and admired Stalin's notorious deviousness and secretive nature. Stalin's pretensions to be a philosopher and his willingness to make judgments on all aspects of scholarship and life also would have appealed to the Chinese leader. He undoubtedly felt the Soviet ruler to be a kindred spirit in matters of the mind.

The meeting with Stalin had enormous symbolic meaning for Mao. After the Soviet dictator's death three years later, in March 1953, the Chairman could claim the mantle of leadership over the world revolutionary movement. Stalin's words that the center of revolution had switched to Asia justified Mao's perception that the mandate was now his. The claim had much in common with the Chinese notion of "legitimate inheritance of the throne" (*zhengtong*), according to which the Mandate of Heaven was transmitted from one dynasty to another.

That the fate of a historic alliance should turn so much on personality and outdated perceptions is one of the great ironies of the Cold War and of communism in practice. Beyond the theories of politics and conflict, we discover emperors disrobed and men both heroic and petty. Their uncertain alliance failed and caused so much suffering not because of its systemic flaws—and there were many—but because of their inability to curb their nationalistic aims and to turn with the same passion to their nations' needs.

Within a decade, the alliance fashioned and tested in 1950 had collapsed. Its heritage of power corrupted survived.

Appendix

Documents on the Sino-Soviet Alliance and the Korean War

Most of the documents in this Appendix are from Mao Zedong, *Jianguo Yilai Mao Zedong Wengao Diyi Ce (1949.9–1950.12)* [Mao Zedong's Manuscripts Since the Founding of the Republic, Vol. 1 (September 1949–December 1950)] (Beijing, 1987), cited as JY in the source notes. We have made some deletions in the text. These are indicated by a bracketed note: [translators' omission]. Ellipses show cuts made by the compilers in the original. We have dropped some number of the footnotes. For example, where a note merely provided a person's full name, we have supplied the information in brackets in the text. We have also deleted the many redundant references to the same man and his title; in most cases, we retain this information only at first mention. Finally, we have dropped a few notes that added little or no information to the text. When given, the times in the documents have been translated by the 24-hour day. We have made some trivial grammatical and spelling changes to documents from English-language sources to conform to the style used throughout this book and have consistently translated *zhongyang* as Central Committee, though it can mean central leadership, "center," the Politburo, or the Central Secretariat.

Most of the other documents are from the archive of Stalin's chief advisor on China, I. V. Kovalev. Some have been published in his two-part article, "Stalin's Dialogue with Mao Zedong," *Problemy Dal'nego Vostoka* [Problems of the Far East] (Moscow), No. 6, 1991, and No. 1-3, 1992; we cite this work simply as Kovalev. Others are from Kovalev's memoirs, the full text of which was in press at this writing.

We often use the abbreviations CCP, PRC, and USSR in places where they are spelled out.

* * *

Doc. 1. Excerpt from Soviet Assessment of U.S. Foreign Policy, Sept. 1946

U.S. policy in China is aimed at fully bringing that country under the economic and political control of American monopoly capital. In pursuing this policy, the

U.S. government goes so far as to interfere in China's internal affairs. Over 50,000 U.S. troops are stationed in China today. In some cases, American marines have directly participated in combat against the people's liberation troops. The so-called "mediation" mission of General [George C.] Marshall is only a cover for actual interference in the internal affairs of China.

How far the American government's policy toward China has already gone is seen in its current attempts to control the Chinese army. Recently, the U.S. government submitted to Congress a draft law on military aid to China, under which the Chinese army would be totally reorganized, trained by American instructors, and supplied with American weaponry and ammunition. To implement this program, a mission of American advisers—army and naval officers—is to be sent to China.

China is gradually turning into a bridgehead for American military forces. American air force bases are situated all over its territory. The major ones are at Beiping, Qingdao, Tianjin, Nanjing, Shanghai, Chengdu, Chongqing, and Kunming. Qingdao is the major American naval base in China. The headquarters of the Seventh Fleet is also stationed there. Besides this, more than 30,000 marines are concentrated in Qingdao and its vicinity. Measures taken by the American army in China demonstrate that it expects to remain there for a long time.

SOURCE: [Nikolai V. Novikov], "Veshniaia Politika SShA v Poslevoennii Period" [The Foreign Policy of the USA During the Postwar Period], AVP SSSR [Archive of Foreign Policy of the USSR], File 06, Entry 08, Folder 45, Case 759 (Sept. 27, 1946).

Doc. 2. Mao Cable to Stalin re Markers on the Border Rivers, March 10, 1949

On March 10, 1949, Mao drafted the following cable in response to a request from Moscow:

Concerning the installation of the markers on the Amur River. Agree with the opinion of the friendly side and ask [it] to send technicians; expenses will be on the Chinese side and the markers will be the property of the Chinese side. The markers would be on both banks—ask the friendly side to establish what rules should be followed by both sides; the Chinese side undertakes to abide strictly by them. Please convey via Comrade Kovalev.

SOURCE: Kovalev, 2:87.

Doc. 3. Stalin Cable to Kovalev re Trade with Capitalist Countries, March 15, 1949

[This is] the response of Comrade F(ilippov) [the code name of Stalin] to Minister of Economic Affairs of Manchuria Chen Yun:

Convey to C[omrade] Chen that we Russian Communists hold that the Chinese Communists must not drive away the national bourgeoisie but should draw them to themselves as a force that is able to assist in the struggle against imperialism. Because of that, [we] advise promoting the trade activities of the national bourgeoisie inside China, as well as abroad. Let us say, trade with Hong Kong and other capitalist countries. The Chinese Communists have to decide for themselves what goods to buy and sell.

SOURCE: Kovalev, 2:81.

Doc. 4. *Stalin Cable to Mao re the Principles of Establishing Relations with the United States, April 1949*

We think that the democratic government of China must not reject establishing official relations with some of the capitalist countries, including the United States, if these states officially abandon [their] military, trade, and political support of Chiang Kai-shek's Nationalist government. This condition is necessary because of the following considerations.

At the present time, the policy of the United States is aimed at splitting China into the south, middle, and north, with three [distinct] governments. Meanwhile, the United States is supporting Nationalist governments in southern and central [China]—it seems that it does not even oppose supporting the democratic [i.e., Communist] northeastern government—so that these governments will fight against each other and weaken each other, to the profit of the United States. Accordingly, we think that if you want to have a unified China headed by Communists, you ought to establish relations with only those capitalist governments that officially abandon [their] support of the Nanjing and Canton [Guangzhou] groups [in the middle and south].

We think that you should not reject foreign loans and trade with the capitalist countries on certain conditions. The main thing is that the loans and trade must not impose any economic and financial conditions on China that could be used to limit the national sovereignty of the democratic state and to strangle [its] domestic industry.

SOURCE: Kovalev's unpublished memoirs.

Doc. 5. *Stalin Cable to Mao re a Soviet Loan to China, April 1949*

Concerning the question of a loan from the side of the USSR, we have to inform you of the following:

We are conducting and will conduct trade with China on the principle of goods for goods. For that, no special permission of the USSR Supreme Soviet is required. Concerning a loan, the government cannot make a decision on this problem by itself because the matter of a loan has to be decided by the Supreme Soviet; the latter does not oppose a loan to China in principle but must have a document, signed by the representatives of the state, applying for assistance. Without it, the USSR Supreme Soviet cannot approve the loan.

SOURCE: Kovalev's unpublished memoirs. Excerpt (part of the same cable as Doc. 4).

Doc. 6. Kovalev Notes re Stalin's Conversation with the Liu Shaoqi Delegation on the Importance of the Chinese Revolution, July 1949

[Stalin] said: "I never did like people who are flatterers, and when people pay me too many compliments, I feel disgusted with them. The things I am telling you about the successes of the Chinese Marxists, about the necessity for the Soviet people and the peoples of Europe to learn from you—absolutely does not mean that I am [trying to] buy your sympathy or giving you compliments.

Because of the arrogance of the leaders of the European revolutionary movements after the death of Marx and Engels, the social-democratic movement in Europe began to lag behind in its development. The center of the revolution [then] shifted from the West to the East, and now it has shifted to China and East Asia.

I am saying that you are already playing a significant role now, and you, of course, must not be arrogant. But at the same time, I assert that the responsibility that has been laid on you has grown even greater. You must fulfill your duty toward the revolutions in the countries of East Asia.

Perhaps, on the general theoretical questions of Marxism, we, the Soviet people, are somewhat stronger than you. But if one speaks about the practical application of Marxist principles, then you have such great experience that we must learn from you. In the past, we have already learned a lot of things from you.

One people should learn from the other. Even if it is a small people—it always has many such things that we can learn."

SOURCE: Kovalev, 2:78.

Doc. 7. Stalin Remarks to Liu Shaoqi re Creating a Union of Asian Communist Parties, July 1949

Answering Liu's question if China could become a member of the Cominform, Stalin stated: "It can. But I consider that this is not so necessary. Why? Because there is a basic difference between the situations of the new democratic countries of Eastern Europe and China. Because of that, the policy that is carried out must not be the same in the two cases. In my opinion, there are two points that make China different from the countries of Eastern Europe.

First point. China for a long time has been under the yoke of imperialism, which, I think, has still not abandoned its threats against China.

At present, China has to put in an enormous effort to resist the pressures from imperialism. This is the most characteristic feature of today's situation in China. This point is not characteristic of the new democratic countries [of Eastern Europe].

Second point. The bourgeoisie of China and the bourgeoisie of the East European countries are not the same. The bourgeoisie of the East European countries discredited itself by collaborating with the fascists during the period of fascist occupation and then had to evacuate along with the fascists. Because of that, the proletariat was able to establish its dictatorship and had every reason to confiscate the enterprises that belonged to the bourgeoisie. After that [the proletariat] quickly stepped onto the path of socialism.

In fact, what the countries of Eastern Europe have are not proletarian dictatorships but people's democracies—parliaments and people's fronts are the organs running them.

There is an entirely different situation in China. The Chinese bourgeoisie during the period of the Japanese occupation did not surrender to the Japanese and did not evacuate with them. When the Chinese people stood up in the struggle against America and Chiang Kai-shek, [the bourgeoisie] did not collaborate with the Americans or Chiang Kai-shek. Because of that, the Chinese revolutionary government had no grounds to act against the national bourgeoisie or to take over its enterprises [and put them] under [the government's] own management.

In China, it is still not possible to establish the revolutionary power of a proletarian dictatorship. The revolutionary power that exists in China today is in fact a democratic dictatorship of workers and peasants, and the united national front and the Political Consultative Council are the forms in which it is manifested. That is basically different from the proletarian dictatorship that in fact exists in the countries of Eastern Europe [and that] manifests itself in the form of people's democracy, parliaments, and people's fronts.

The two above-mentioned points require that there be some not so small differences between the policies realized in China and the countries of Eastern Europe. For this reason, the CCP's entrance into the Cominform does not fit the moment.

The situation in the countries of East Asia has a lot in common with the situation in China and creates the possibility for organizing a Union of East Asian Communist Parties. That would be more necessary and timely than the CCP's entrance into the Cominform.

It may still be premature at this time to organize the Union of East Asian Communist Parties. Because the USSR is a country situated in both Europe and in Asia, it would take part in the Union of East Asian Communist Parties."

SOURCE: Kovalev, 2: 79–80.

Doc. 8. Excerpt from Kovalev Transcript for Stalin re Kovalev's Conversation with Liu Shaoqi and Gao Gang on Intelligence and Counterintelligence Work, July 7, 1949

Comrades Gao Gang and Liu Shaoqi . . . stressed that they would like to have closer contact in the work of the Soviet and Chinese [intelligence] organs and [to have] a unified program of action against the imperialists and reactionaries. . . . They emphasized that many people who had been recommended by the CCP for work in the Soviet information bodies, as well as those who were recruited by the Soviet bodies independently, had been cut off from the Party's supervision, had been corrupted, and in some cases had been recruited by American and Kuomintang intelligence. Because of that, we have to undertake a joint effort to purge such persons. . . . Comrade Gao Gang offered the example of Manchuria, where 300 radio transmitters had been uncovered and confiscated by Chinese intelligence, among which 40 were formally supposed to be Soviet but were in fact working for the interests of the Kuomintang and the United States. That was made possible by the lack of sufficient contact between the Chinese and Soviet information and intelligence organs.

SOURCE: Kovalev's unpublished memoirs.

Doc. 9. *Xinhua Agency Press Release re the Establishment of Diplomatic Relations Between China and the Soviet Union, Oct. 3, 1949*

On the afternoon of the 1st of this month, Foreign Minister of the Central People's Government of the People's Republic of China Zhou Enlai sent a memorandum containing the proclamation of Chairman Mao Zedong to the governments of all states.[1] After receiving this proclamation, the Soviet government at 2145 on [Oct.] 2 cabled Minister Zhou Enlai a note signed by [Vice–Foreign Minister Andrei] Gromyko, which stated: "The Soviet government has decided to establish diplomatic relations between the Soviet Union and the PRC and to exchange ambassadors." The full text of Gromyko's note is as follows:

Beijing, to the foreign minister of the Central People's Government of the People's Republic of China, Mr. Zhou Enlai:

The government of the Union of Soviet Socialist Republics has received the memorandum of the Central People's Government of the People's Republic of China, dated October 1, wherein it is proposed that diplomatic relations be established between the PRC and the USSR. The Soviet government, after studying the proposal of the Central People's Government of the PRC, proceeding from the constant desire to establish genuine friendly relations with the Chinese people and firmly believing that the Chinese Central People's Government represents the will of the overwhelming majority of the Chinese people, is specially informing Your Excellency: The Soviet government has decided to establish diplomatic relations between the Soviet Union and the PRC and to exchange ambassadors.

On behalf of the Soviet government,
Vice-Minister of Foreign Affairs, Andrei Gromyko, 2145

SOURCE: JY, pp. 17–18.

[1][For the text of Mao Zedong's "Proclamation of [the] Central People's Government" (Oct. 1, 1949), see *China Monthly Review*, Oct. 1950, supplement, p. 1. The proclamation stated: "This Government is willing to establish diplomatic relations with any foreign government which is willing to observe the principles of equality, mutual benefit and mutual respect for territorial integrity and sovereignty." On the same day, Zhou Enlai became premier of the Government Administration Council (the cabinet—known as the State Council from 1954) and concurrently minister of foreign affairs.—TRANS.]

Doc. 10. Mao Speech After Receiving the Credentials of Soviet Ambassador to China N. V. Roshchin, Oct. 16, 1949

Mr. Ambassador Roshchin:

With great pleasure, I have received the credentials from the Presidium of the Supreme Soviet of the Union of Soviet Socialist Republics submitted by the esteemed ambassador, and sincerely thank the esteemed ambassador for his congratulations. Almost immediately after the founding of the People's Republic of China, we were honored by the fact that the Soviet government was the first to establish diplomatic relations with our state. I believe that the friendship between China and the Soviet Union will be increasingly developed and strengthened because of this decision of your esteemed government. I warmly welcome the nomination of the esteemed ambassador to be the first ambassador extraordinary and plenipotentiary of the Soviet Union to the PRC. I believe that because of the efforts of the esteemed ambassador, the cooperation between your esteemed state and our state will become closer and closer, and that it will at the same time be beneficial for our common struggle for the lasting world peace. Here I sincerely wish prosperity for your esteemed state, well-being to its people, and health to the leader of your state!

SOURCE: JY, p. 71.

Doc. 11. Mao Letter to Stalin re the PRC's Ambassador, Oct. 20, 1949

Comrade Stalin:

Here, let me introduce to you Comrade Wang Jiaxiang. The purposes of Comrade Wang Jiaxiang's stay in the Soviet Union are as follows. He will be the ambassador of our country to the Soviet Union, and concurrently in his capacity as a vice–foreign minister of our country, he will take charge of general affairs in the diplomatic relations with the new democratic countries of Eastern Europe. In addition, as a representative of the CCP Central Committee (he is a member of the Central Committee of our Party), he will maintain contacts on questions concerning links between the two Parties, with you, and with the Central Committee of the Communist Party of the Soviet Union [CPSU]. Let me ask you and the comrades from the CPSU Central Committee to adopt the stance of comrades in giving him continuing advice so that he can achieve comparatively numerous and good results in his work. Let me here express my thanks to you in advance.

With comradely greetings!

SOURCE: JY, p. 81.

Doc. 12. Cables to Stalin re Soviet Plague Relief, Oct. 28, 30, 1949

I

Comrade Filippov [Stalin]:

Black Death has broken out in the region north of Zhangjiakou, with 60 people dead. It has already spread to Zhangjiakou, where four people have died, and is now threatening Beiping [Beijing] and Tianjin. Let me ask you to consider the possibility of transporting by air 4,000,000 units of vaccine and 100,000 units of serum for use in Beijing. We shall order the Chinese government to pay all the necessary expenses by way of barter trade.

Besides this, [let me inform you that] an anti-epidemic unit, comprising more than 30 people and headed by Doctor Maisky,[2] who was sent by your government to China some time ago, has accomplished the work of preventing Black Death in the Northeast with great success. The people of the Northeast and the Chinese public health workers all express their greatest gratitude. Right now, [this unit] is on its way back to the Soviet Union. If it is possible, let me ask you to consider sending a similar anti-epidemic unit again to Beijing for work in Zhangjiakou to help us prevent and cure Black Death. If you should do us the honor of agreeing, we will be deeply grateful!

2

Comrade Filippov:

The October 29 cable has been received. I am very grateful for your agreeing to send to Beijing medical specialists, an anti-epidemic unit, and a large quantity of medicine.

SOURCE: JY, pp. 98–99.

Doc. 13. PRC Central Committee Cable to Ambassador Wang Jiaxiang re Mao Zedong's Departure for Moscow, Nov. 9, 1949

Comrade Jiaxiang:

We have asked [Soviet representative I. V.] Kovalev to inform Comrade Stalin that we are asking him for a decision on the time of Chairman Mao's departure for Moscow. We are of the opinion that Chairman Mao can depart for Moscow at the beginning of December. We are also asking Stalin to decide whether Comrade [Zhou] Enlai should accompany Chairman Mao to Moscow or whether and when Enlai should come after Chairman Mao's arrival in Moscow.

SOURCE: JY, p. 131.

Doc. 14. Mao Cable to Stalin re I. V. Kovalev Accompanying Him, Nov. 12, 1949

Comrade Filippov:

Thank you for welcoming my trip to Moscow. I am preparing to depart during the first ten days of December. At the same time, let me ask your permission to have Comrade Kovalev accompany me. He has already made all the necessary arrangements concerning the work of the Soviet specialists, so his departure cannot disrupt [their] work.

SOURCE: JY, p. 135.

[2]During this period, Maisky, a Soviet doctor, headed the Soviet section of the anti-epidemic unit composed of Chinese and Soviet medical personnel.

Doc. 15. Mao Cable to Stalin re Ren Bishi Coming to Moscow for Treatment, Nov. 21, 1949[3]

Comrade Filippov:

A member of the CCP Politburo, Comrade Ren Bishi, has a very serious illness. Soviet doctors are of the opinion that he should go to Moscow for treatment, and we agree with this opinion. [We] don't know if it is possible and are asking you for an answer.

SOURCE: JY, p. 148.

Doc. 16. CCP Central Committee Cable to the Shandong Branch re Gifts for Stalin's Birthday, Dec. 1, 1949, 1700

Shandong Branch Bureau:

On December 21 this year, Comrade Stalin will celebrate his seventieth birthday. The Central Committee has decided to send gifts of Chinese cabbages, radishes, green onions, and pears grown in Shandong. Within three days after receiving this cable (that is, before December 4), please purchase 5,000 *jin* of each category, all in all 20,000 *jin*, for the Central Committee to send from Jinan by air. The airplane will arrive in Jinan on December 4. Please note the time. When purchasing all these goods (Chinese cabbages, radishes, green onions, and pears), please take care to select the very best.

SOURCE: JY, p. 172.

Doc. 17. Mao Speech at the Railway Station on His Arrival in Moscow, Dec. 16, 1949

Dear comrades and friends:

The fact that I have a chance to visit the capital of the first great socialist country in the world at this time is a very joyful event in my life. A deep friendship exists between the peoples of the two great countries of China and the Soviet Union. After the October socialist revolution, the Soviet government, in accordance with the policy of Lenin and Stalin, was the first to abrogate the unequal treaties of the imperialist Russian period. Over the course of almost 30 years, the Soviet people and government have several times extended their support to the liberation cause of the Chinese people. The fact that in times of hardship and trouble the Chinese people have received brotherly help from the Soviet people and government can never be forgotten.

Nowadays, the important tasks are strengthening the world peace-loving front headed by the Soviet Union; struggling against the warmongers; strengthening state-to-state relations between the two great countries of China and the Soviet Union; and developing friendship between the Chinese people and the Soviet

[3][Ren Bishi went to Moscow in early 1950, returned to China in the summer, and died a few months later, on Oct. 27.—TRANS.]

people. I believe that because of the victory of the people's revolution in China and the founding of the People's Republic of China, because of the joint efforts of the new democratic states and peace-loving people all over the world, because of the common aspirations and close cooperation between the two great countries of China and the Soviet Union, and especially because of the correct international policy of Generalissimo Stalin, all these tasks will be completely fulfilled with excellent results.

Long live Sino-Soviet friendship and cooperation!

SOURCE: JY, p. 189.

Doc. 18. Mao Cable from Moscow re Establishing Diplomatic Relations with Burma, Dec. 19, 1949

Comrades [Liu] Shaoqi, [Zhou] Enlai:

1. As to the question of the Burmese government's request to establish diplomatic relations, in a return cable you should ask the government whether it is willing to sever diplomatic relations with the Nationalists, and at the same time request that it send a responsible representative to Beijing for talks on the establishment of diplomatic relations between China and Burma. The establishment of diplomatic relations should depend on the results of the talks. This procedure for the talks is absolutely necessary, and we must act in this way toward all capitalist countries. If some capitalist states publicly announce [a desire to establish] diplomatic relations with us, then we should also cable these states and ask them to send their representatives to China for talks on the establishment of diplomatic relations, and at the same time we can openly publish the main contents of these cables. This way the initiative always will be in our hands. [translators' omission]

4. Please ask [Hu] Qiaomu[4] to report [to me] briefly about the reaction to my visit to the Soviet Union inside the country and abroad.

5. Everything is all right with us here; the last few days we have been resting. I am awaiting your answer to my [Dec.] 18 cable.

SOURCE: JY, p. 193.

Doc. 19. Kovalev Report to Stalin re a Conversation with Mao, Dec. 20, 1949

To Comrade Stalin

Today, on December 20, Mao Zedong invited me to his place. [N. T.] Fedorenko also attended the meeting in his capacity as interpreter. Mao Zedong said the following:

1. He had already reported to the CCP Central Committee the contents of his talk with You on December 16 and is waiting the opinion of the Central Committee members on the questions touched on in the conversation with You.

2. Mao Zedong wants to have another meeting on about December 23 or 24.

3. Mao Zedong is intending to suggest for Your consideration two options for

[4]Hu Qiaomu then headed the News Department of the Central People's Government.

the program of future talks. The first option foresees a discussion of following questions: (1) a Soviet-Chinese treaty, (2) a loan agreement, (3) a trade agreement, (4) an agreement on the establishment of air [transport] communications, and (5) other questions, including the question of Burma's recognition of China.

Under this option, it is suggested that Zhou Enlai be summoned to Moscow for shaping and signing the agreements. Mao at the same time noted that he would use the time needed for Zhou Enlai's trip to Moscow for a tour to Stalingrad and Leningrad.

The second option essentially consists of a discussion of the same issues as the first but without formalizing them into agreements. In this case, there would be no need for Zhou Enlai to come to Moscow. For formalizing and signing agreements, Zhou could come some other time.

During the conversation, Mao Zedong stressed several times that in the resolving of all questions, including the questions of his rest and medical treatment in the Soviet Union, he is totally dependent on Your consideration.

4. Mao Zedong expressed a willingness to visit and to talk to the Central Committee of the Communist Party of the Soviet Union (Bolshevik)'s Politburo members [V. M.] Molotov, [N. A.] Bulganin, [A. I.] Mikoyan, and [M. N.] Shvernik.

5. Mao Zedong asked me to relay his requests to You for Comrades I. V. Kovalev and Fedorenko to be with him and accompany him at all times. Mao Zedong explained this request by the fact that a number of different questions have arisen for him about which he wishes to consult.

[I am] reporting that though he has been feeling in need of talks and advice, I have not visited him every day. He noted that he treated my absence as an unwillingness to provide him assistance with advice that he constantly needs.

At the same time, Mao Zedong expressed a wish for Kovalev and Fedorenko to be present with him at the ceremony and the reception for the 70th birthday of Comrade Stalin.

[I am] asking for Your instructions.

SOURCE: Kovalev's unpublished memoirs; partially reproduced in Kovalev, 2: 89–90. The latter source, p. 89, incorrectly gives Dec. 22 as the date of this document.

Doc. 20. *Mao Congratulatory Speech at the Ceremony in Honor of Stalin's Seventieth Birthday in Moscow, Dec. 21, 1949*[5]

Dear comrades, friends:

I am extremely pleased to have the opportunity at this time to participate in the ceremonies in honor of Stalin's seventieth birthday.

Comrade Stalin is a teacher and a friend of the people of the world; he is also a

[5]Mao Zedong's cable [from Moscow] dated Dec. 21, 1949, midnight, said: "At today's ([Dec.] 21) congratulatory meeting, besides the representatives of the Soviet republics, representatives of 13 countries made speeches. Among these 13 countries, I, representing China, was the first to deliver a speech, which was received with great enthusiasm. Three times everybody stood and applauded for a long time. When the Xinhua News Agency publishes the news, please let them write it in accordance with the text of the TASS release. Attached here is the text of my speech for release."

teacher and a friend of the Chinese people. He has developed the revolutionary theory of Marxism-Leninism and has made extremely outstanding and extremely broad contributions to the cause of the world Communist movement. The Chinese people in their bitter struggle against oppressors have deeply felt the importance of Comrade Stalin's friendship.

At this solemn gathering I, on behalf of the Chinese people and the Chinese Communist Party, would like to congratulate Comrade Stalin on his seventieth birthday, to wish him good health and a long life, to wish our great friend the Soviet state prosperity and strength under the leadership of Comrade Stalin, and at the same time to call for an unprecedented unity of the working class of the whole world under the leadership of Comrade Stalin.

Long live the great Stalin, leader of the working class of the whole world and of the international Communist movement!

Long live the Soviet Union, the stronghold of peace and democracy of the whole world!

SOURCE: JY, pp. 195–96.

Doc. 21. *Mao Cable from Moscow re Preparations for a Trade Agreement with the Soviet Union, Dec. 22, 1949, 0300*

Central Committee:

1. According to what [Wang] Jiaxiang has said, Poland, Czechoslovakia, and Germany want to do business with us. So, besides the Soviet Union, there are three more states that are on the eve of having trade relations with us. In addition, Britain, Japan, the United States, India, and other states are already doing business with us or will begin to do so pretty soon. For this reason, when preparing the trade agreement with the Soviet Union, you should proceed from a point of view that takes into account the whole situation. The Soviet Union, of course, occupies the first place, but at the same time, it is necessary to get ready to do business with Poland, Czechoslovakia, Germany, Great Britain, Japan, the United States, and other states. We must make a general evaluation of the scope and volume [of the transactions].

2. The cable dated [Dec.] 21 has been received. We have arranged with Stalin to have a talk on [Dec.] 23 or 24. After this talk, we will be able to define our guiding principles and will inform you about [the discussions] in a cable.

SOURCE: JY, p. 197.

Doc. 22. *Excerpts from Kovalev Report to Stalin, "Some Policies of the CCP Central Leadership and Practical Problems," Dec. 24, 1949*

. . . You recommended that the new government should not refuse to establish diplomatic relations with capitalist states, including America, if these states officially abandoned military, economic, and political assistance to Chiang Kai-shek and the Nationalist regime as a whole.

But until November 1949, Britain and America's continued active support of

Chiang Kai-shek notwithstanding, the CCP Central Committee leadership was infected with the illusion of a quick recognition of the People's Republic of China by those countries.

Reflecting this state of mind, Liu Shaoqi and Li Lisan opposed having Japan, India, and other countries under the control of or dependent on the Anglo-American bloc participate in the conference of trade unions of the Asian countries to avoid irritating America and England. . . .

In the same vein is the negative attitude of Zhou Enlai toward sending groups of Soviet specialists to Tianjin and Shanghai, since the huge economic interests of America and England are concentrated in those cities.

Such an attitude is the result of pressure exerted on the Central Committee by the bourgeois democrats and other capitalist elements inside the country, which were and are aspiring for the most rapid recognition of the new China by the United States and Britain, and so enable the Chinese bourgeoisie, relying on the imperialist states, to halt the further democratization of China and hinder the strengthening and broadening of friendship between China and the Soviet Union.

SOURCE: Kovalev, 2: 82–83.

Doc. 23. Mao Cable from Moscow re Sino-Soviet Cooperation, Dec. 29, 1949

Comrade [Liu] Shaoqi:[6]

The cable of [Dec.] 28 has been received.

1. I have passed a copy of your [Dec.] 24 cable, concerning the invitation of teachers to the People's University, to Stalin.

2. On the morning of [Dec.] 25, I asked Stalin about the question of repairing the Xiaofengman [hydroelectric station], and he told me that he had not yet received your cable. I am planning to give him a copy of your cable tomorrow (29).[7] [translators' omission].

SOURCE: JY, p. 199.

Doc. 24. Mao Interview with a TASS Correspondent, Jan. 2, 1950[8]

(Xinhua Agency dispatch, 2, Beijing). TASS Agency dispatch, Moscow, 2: Transcript of the TASS Agency correspondent's interview with Mr. Mao Zedong, Chairman of the Central People's Government of the People's Republic of China.

Correspondent's question: What is the situation in China at present?

[6][The addressee, Mao's then heir apparent Liu Shaoqi, was in charge of Party and state affairs in China during the Chairman's absence.—TRANS.]

[7]Here the phrase "tomorrow (29)" contradicts the date December 29 at the end of the cable; we suspect that this is a mistake in the original.

[8]This is the text of the news dispatch as published by TASS and then translated and released by the Xinhua News Agency. Mao Zedong, in a cable to Liu Shaoqi dated January 2, 1950, said: "My interview with the TASS correspondent will be published today (2). Please ask [Hu] Qiaomu and Chen Kehan to pay special attention to the translation and publication of the TASS dispatch."

Answer: The military situation in China is progressing smoothly. The CCP and the Central People's Government of the PRC are presently switching over to peaceful economic reconstruction.

Q. How long will you be staying in the Soviet Union, Mr. Mao Zedong?

A. I intend to stay for a few weeks. The length of my sojourn in the Soviet Union will be partly determined by the time required for resolving questions related to the interests of the PRC.

Q. Can you tell me what problems you are considering?

A. Among these problems, the problems of first importance are the existing Sino-Soviet Treaty of Friendship and Alliance [of 1945], the Soviet loan to the PRC, trade and a trade pact between the two countries, and others. In addition, I am thinking of visiting a number of localities and cities in the Soviet Union in order to gain a better understanding of economic and cultural construction in the Soviet state.

SOURCE: JY, p. 206

Doc. 25. Mao Cables from Moscow re Zhou Enlai's Departure for the Soviet Union to Participate in the Talks, Jan. 2, 1950, 2300; Jan. 3, 0400

1 [Jan. 2]

Central Committee:

1. There has been an important development in the work here during the last two days. Comrade Stalin has agreed to Comrade Zhou Enlai's arrival here and to the signing of a new Sino-Soviet Treaty of Friendship and Alliance, as well as agreements on credit, trade, civil aviation, and others. Yesterday, on January 1, the decision was made to publish my interview with the TASS correspondent; today (2), it is in the newspapers, and I think that you have already received it. Today at 2000, Comrades [V. M.] Molotov and [A. I.] Mikoyan[9] came to my place to have a talk and asked my opinion on the Sino-Soviet treaty and other matters. I immediately gave them a detailed review of three different versions [of what agreements we should reach in Moscow]:

A. To sign a new Sino-Soviet Treaty of Friendship and Alliance. By taking this action, we can gain enormous advantages. Sino-Soviet relations will be solidified on the basis of a new treaty; in China, workers, peasants, intelligentsia, and the left wing of the national bourgeoisie will be greatly inspired, so that we can isolate the right wing of the national bourgeoisie; and internationally we can acquire more political capital to counter the imperialist states and to look into the treaties that were concluded by China with the imperialist powers in the past.

B. To publish through the news agencies of the two countries a brief communiqué stating merely that the leaders of the two states have exchanged opinions on the old Sino-Soviet Treaty of Friendship and Alliance and other problems and have reached an identity of views on the important problems, without touching on the detailed contents [of the talks]. In fact this [step] would mean that we would be

[9]Molotov and Mikoyan were then the vice-chairmen of the Council of Ministers of the USSR.

delaying the problem for several years in order to return to it later. If we were to take this action, then it would certainly serve no purpose for Chinese Foreign Minister Zhou Enlai to come here.

C. To sign a statement that sets out the most important points in [our] bilateral relations but would not be a treaty. If this way is adopted, then Zhou Enlai also does not have to come.

After I had analyzed in detail the positive and negative sides of these versions, Comrade Molotov immediately stated that version A was good, and that Zhou may come. I asked again if we should replace the old treaty with a new one? Comrade Molotov answered: "Yes."

After that, we immediately began to figure out a timetable for Zhou's arrival and the signing of the treaty. I said that my cable would be in Beijing on January 3, and that Enlai would need five days for preparations and could depart from Beijing on January 9. It takes 11 days to go by train, so he could be in Moscow on January 19. The talks and the signing of the treaties would require 10 days, from January 20 until the end of the month, and Zhou and I would return home at the beginning of February.

At the same time, we also discussed the question of my sightseeing outside [my residence]. We decided that I shall visit Lenin's mausoleum, make a trip to Leningrad, Gorky, and other places, and also make tours of an ordnance factory, the metropolitan subway (these two places were suggested by Comrades Molotov and Mikoyan), a collective farm, and so on.

We also touched on the problem of [arranging my] discussions with various Soviet leading comrades. (Up to now, I have not had any chance to go out to speak face to face with any of them alone.)

2. Let me ask you to finish all the preparations [for Zhou's departure] in five days after you receive this cable. I hope that Enlai, together with the minister of trade and other necessary aides, and with all the necessary documents and materials, will depart from Beijing on January 9 for Moscow by train (not by plane). Comrade Dong Biwu[10] must assume the post of acting premier of the Government Administration Council. You must not publicize [the trip and Dong's appointment] openly; the news will be published only after Zhou's arrival in Moscow.

3. Let me ask you to think it over and report to me by return cable whether all the above-mentioned [proposals] are feasible, whether the preparations can be accomplished in five days' time or whether you will need one or two days more, and whether it is necessary for Comrade Li Fuchun[11] and other comrades to arrive together [with Zhou].

2 [Jan. 3]

Central Committee:

You must have received my cable of yesterday, 2300. [The decision] on Comrade Enlai's trip to the USSR must be approved at a meeting of the Government Admin-

---

[10]Dong Biwu was then a vice-premier of the Government Administration Council of the Central People's Government.

[11]Li Fuchun was then the vice-chairman of the Northeast People's Government.

istration Council. You must report [to the council as follows], that [the aim of] this trip is to conduct negotiations and to sign [these agreements]:

a new Sino-Soviet Treaty of Friendship and Alliance (in comparison to the old treaty, there will be a partial change concerning the problems of Lüshun and Dalian, but the concrete contents still have to be discussed;

the clauses about defense against possible aggression of Japan and its allies and the recognition of Outer Mongolia's independence, as before, constitute the basic spirit of the new treaty);

a credit agreement (we have proposed the sum of $300 million, which will be granted over a few years; the reason why we have not requested more is [simply] that at present and for several years it will be better for us to borrow less than to borrow more);

a civil aviation agreement (it is favorable for developing our own aviation industry);

and a trade agreement (the definition of the scope of the barter trade between the Soviet Union and us is favorable for both the course of development of our production and the conclusion of trade agreements with other countries).

Besides this, it is necessary to gather all the members of the [Central People's] Government Council now in the capital for a briefing, during which you should make the same report. During both meetings, you should stress that this move [i.e., the conclusion of a new treaty] will enable the People's Republic to gain an even more favorable posture. It will press the capitalist countries to play by rules that will be set by us, it will be favorable for the unconditional recognition of China by various countries, [it will lead to] the cancellation of the old treaties and the conclusion of new ones, and it also will deter the capitalist countries from reckless undertakings.

SOURCE: JY, pp. 211–13.

Doc. 26. *Mao Cable from Moscow re Zhou Enlai's Departure and Preparations for the Talks, Jan. 5, 1950, 0600*

Central Committee:

The cable dated January 4, 0730, has been received.

1. I have arranged for Zhou to come here with approximately 17 people; [he] really can come, there is no problem. I have also informed the authorities here that the train will depart from Beijing on the night of January 9.

2. It will be good if Burhan, Deng Liqun,[12] and the head of the trade department of the Ili [region of Xinjiang] arrive in Moscow two or three days later than Enlai, that is, January 21 or 22, or on the same day as Enlai, that is, on January 19. Please inform me immediately about your decision [on this matter]. Also please decide and report to me what kind of transportation Burhan and Deng Liqun will need to

[12]Burhan [Bao Erhan] was then the chairman of the People's Government of Xinjiang. Deng Liqun was then the secretary-general of the Xinjiang Branch of the Central Committee, and concurrently the head of both the Education and Culture Department and the Foreign Affairs Department of the People's Government of Xinjiang.

get here. Should we arrange for a plane here [Moscow] or can a plane sent by the air transport regiment now in Xinjiang perform this task? Please inform me immediately by cable about your decision.

3. Concerning the crucial points in the talks and preparatory work, all the points you have enumerated are certainly worth paying attention to, and preparations should be made accordingly. Since we shall be carrying on negotiations, we should certainly deliver [detailed] presentations, clearly explaining our point of view. I am asking the Central Committee to continue investigating [these problems] after Enlai's departure and to report its opinions at any time. As to the materials on trade, if you are not able to prepare them within five days, then you can continue working on them after Enlai's departure and report to us any time.

SOURCE: JY, p. 215.

Doc. 27. Mao Cable from Moscow re the Importance of Maintaining Secrecy on the Replacement of the 1945 Sino-Soviet Treaty, Jan. 5, 1950, 2100

Central Committee:

Please pay attention to two matters. 1. Please ask the people at the meetings of the Government Administrative Council and the [Central People's] Government Council to maintain secrecy after they have discussed the replacement of the [old] Sino-Soviet treaty by a new one. 2. Before Zhou [Enlai] and [his party of] more than 10 people depart or during their travel [to Moscow], it will be necessary to assemble all those people and to tell them that it is imperative to adhere to discipline, that undisciplined words and actions are prohibited, and that on every matter they must obey orders.

SOURCE: JY, p. 217.

Doc. 28. Mao Cable from Moscow re Export-Import Trade, Jan. 7, 1950

[Zhou] Enlai and the Central Committee:

Two cables on the settlement of the question of diplomatic relations with Great Britain and India and the cable on export-import trade, dated January 5, 0800, have been received. Concerning the question of export-import trade, please pay special attention to making a comprehensive calculation of the total varieties and volume of exports and imports with such states as the Soviet Union, Poland, Czechoslovakia, Germany, and Hungary, as well as Great Britain, France, the Netherlands, Belgium, India, Burma, Vietnam, Thailand, Australia, Japan, Canada, and the United States for the whole year of 1950, or otherwise we will find ourselves in a passive position. After Enlai's departure from Beijing, ask [Liu] Shaoqi, Chen Yun, and [Bo] Yibo[13] to pay attention to this matter.

SOURCE: JY, p. 218.

[13]Chen Yun was then a vice-premier of the Government Administration Council and the head of the council's Finance and Economics Committee. Bo Yibo was then the deputy head of the Finance and Economics Committee.

Doc. 29. Mao Cable from Moscow re an Official Statement Denying the Legitimacy of the Nationalist Government's Seat on the UN Security Council, Jan. 7, 1950

[Zhou] Enlai and Central Committee:

Today (7), 0100, [Foreign Minister A. Ia.] Vyshinskii came to my residence to talk about three matters:

1. It is possible to satisfy our demand for purchasing airplane fuel.

2. It is possible to satisfy our demand for looking into the question of repairing the Xiaofengman hydroelectric station. A letter with the answers on these two issues will be passed to me tomorrow (8).

3. [Vyshinskii] has proposed that our Ministry of Foreign Affairs publish a statement to the Security Council of the United Nations denying the legitimacy of giving Jiang Tingfu [Chiang Ting-fu], the representative of the former Nationalist government, China's seat in the Security Council. Vyshinskii said that if China publishes such a statement, the Soviet Union is ready to take action; that is, if Jiang Tingfu remains in the Security Council as a representative of China (and he reportedly even may become the president of the Security Council this year), then the Soviet Union will refuse to participate in the Security Council meetings. Vyshinskii asked my opinion. I immediately stated that the Ministry of Foreign Affairs of China could publish this declaration. I also said that my cable would be in Beijing on January 7, and the declaration of the Ministry of Foreign Affairs of China, signed by Minister Zhou Enlai, could be released on January 8 or 9. I asked him if it was necessary, besides the Security Council and the secretary general of the United Nations, to send [the same] cable to the Soviet Union, Great Britain, the United States, and France as permanent members of the Security Council. He said that this was possible, and that the Soviet Union would proceed with its action on the basis of the Chinese cable. He stated that he was acting as foreign minister when he asked for my opinion, and I officially expressed my agreement.

Let me ask you after receiving this cable to arrange this matter quickly, striving to send the cable with this declaration before Enlai's departure on January 9; in addition to the secretary general of the United Nations and the Security Council, send cables for information purposes to the foreign ministries of the Soviet Union, Great Britain, the United States, and France with the text of the cable to the United Nations attached. I am looking forward to a report about arrangements on this matter, as well as to your report on whether you will be able to send it on January 9.

SOURCE: JY, pp. 219–20.

Doc. 30. Mao Cable from Moscow with Draft Statement for the United Nations, Jan. 7, 1950, 2400

[Liu] Shaoqi, [Zhou] Enlai:

Here is a draft of the cable with Zhou's declaration to the president of the General Assembly, the secretary general, and the ten member states of the Security

Council of the United Nations (don't send it to Yugoslavia). Please dispatch the cable per this draft.[14]

SOURCE: JY, p. 221.

Doc. 31. Kovalev Report to Stalin re the Chinese Changchun Railway and Other Matters, Jan. 1950

TOP SECRET

To Comrade STALIN

[I am] reporting to You about the conditions under which the [foreign] concessions and the wholly owned enterprises of the capitalist countries [are allowed to] operate in China.

Comrades Mao Zedong, Liu Shaoqi, and Chen Yun (chairman of the Financial and Economic Committee of the government), with whom I have spoken many times, state that the democratic government of China has not yet created the apparatus for monitoring the entire economy of the country; consequently, it has almost no data about foreign capitalist enterprises, including the concessions, and no data on the conditions under which they are operating. Moreover, until now the government has not identified the enterprises that belong to the four biggest capitalist families of China and those of the capitalist bureaucracy that by the government's declaration are subject to nationalization. With respect to the inventory of capitalist enterprises and of the magnitude of their activities, they are only [now] planning to start their work.

All foreign capitalist enterprises, concessions, and trading companies continue to function according to the clauses of the previous agreements that have enslaved China and were concluded with them by the Chiang Kai-shek–Kuomintang authorities.

In talks with me on January 9, Mao Zedong expressed the opinion that they would nationalize only those foreign capitalist enterprises that harm China and would limit themselves to raising taxes on the rest. They are thinking of beginning the nationalization of the capitalist enterprises only after the completion of land reform (which they expect to accomplish after two or three years) and the solidifying of the national economy.

They plan to abrogate the China-enslaving trade treaty with America in the near future.

[14]The full text of Zhou Enlai's cable to the United Nations dated January 8, 1950, is as follows: "Lake Success, to Mr. [Carlos] Romulo, President of the General Assembly of the United Nations; to Mr. [Trygve] Lie, Secretary General of the United Nations; also to be passed to the member states of the United Nations Security Council—the Soviet Union, the United States, Great Britain, France, Ecuador, India, Cuba, Egypt, and Norway: The Central People's Government of the People's Republic of China is of the opinion that the presence of the representatives of the remnant Chinese Nationalist Party reactionary gang in the Security Council is illegal and holds that they must be expelled from the Security Council.

I am specially informing you about this matter by cable, in the hope that you will acknowledge this fact and act accordingly. Foreign Minister of the Central People's Government of the People's Republic of China, Zhou Enlai."

In all cases, when reconsidering treaties, Mao Zedong said, they would abide by the decisions that were endorsed by the Soviet side at the Teheran, Yalta, and Potsdam conferences.

Speaking in favor of the speediest possible conclusion of agreements with the Soviet Union on friendship and alliance, on a loan, on trade, and so on, Mao Zedong again stressed that these treaties would be the starting points on which democratic China would rely in renegotiating all the existing treaties concluded by the Chiang Kai-shek government with the capitalist countries.

In connection with this statement by him, [I am] reporting to You that Mao Zedong, Liu Shaoqi, Zhou Enlai, and Gao Gang have many times stated that the treaty on the Chinese Changchun Railroad is just and good, totally satisfying the interests of the Chinese people. However, on the eve of Zhou Enlai's departure for Moscow, acting on his instructions, the minister of railways of China, Deng Daiyuan, through the chief of the General Board of Railways of Manchuria, Yu Guangsheng, asked the manager of the Chinese Changchun Railroad, Comrade Zhuravlev, on what basis the Chinese Changchun Railroad would work in the future; answering Comrade Zhuravlev's question about their own thoughts on this matter, Yu Guangsheng conveyed the opinion of Deng Daiyuan that it would be desirable not to single out the Chinese Changchun Railroad from the railway system of Manchuria. Probably for this reason, the Chinese side until now has not nominated its leading representatives for the joint management of the railway (in accordance with the 1945 treaty). Nor, in connection with this, has any [financial] accounting for the activities of the Chinese Changchun Railroad [in its operations apart] from the [other] Manchurian railways been introduced. Since its restoration, the Chinese Changchun Railroad has in fact been managed by the Chinese, who are also in command of the railway's finances, while Soviet railway personnel, headed by the manager of the railway, all in all 277 people (excluding the Dalninskii region of the Chinese Changchun Railroad, which is totally managed by Soviet railway personnel and where 273 people are working), have found themselves in the positions of adviser-consultants.

Such behavior by Zhou Enlai can be explained by nothing else than pressure on the government of China from the right wing of the national bourgeoisie, which has pro-American inclinations, considers the treaty on the Chinese Changchun Railroad of 1945 unequal, and hopes for the railway's transfer as the exclusive property of China and for the Soviet side's exclusion from the territory of Manchuria.

For my own part, [I] consider that it is not in the interests of the Soviet Union to permit a change in the conditions of the 1945 treaty on the Chinese Changchun Railroad, and that the order for its use as defined by this treaty should be preserved.

At the same time, in order to strengthen the Soviet Union's rights and interests concerning the Chinese Changchun Railroad, [I] consider the following actions necessary:

1. To reiterate the treaty conditions on the management and use of the Chinese Changchun Railroad as settled in 1945.

2. To require the Chinese side to immediately nominate its representatives to

the Executive Board of the Society of the Chinese Changchun Railroad, to the Audit Committee of the society, and to the Management Department of the railway.

3. To create a Soviet-Chinese commission to draft the constitution of the board of the Railroad and identify the railway's property.

4. To introduce separate [financial] accounting on the operations of the railway within the limits of the treaty boundaries because the absence of such accounting every day brings losses to the economic interests of the USSR.

5. To put the port of Dalian and the Dal'dok plant under the single, already operating Society of the Chinese Changchun Railroad without creating a separate society for it.

Attached is a brief note on foreign investment in China.

SOURCE: Document from Kovalev's personal archives; #1101 ts (top secret). The first page of this document is reproduced in photo 22 of the photo section following p. 72, above.

Doc. 32. Mao Cable from Moscow re His Trip to Leningrad and Other Matters, Jan. 13, 1950[15]

Comrade [Liu] Shaoqi:

1. I'll depart for Leningrad today (13) in the evening and may be back to Moscow in two days.

2. I have arranged for Liu Yalou,[16] together with [chief] Soviet [military] adviser Kotov and two other men, to come here; please inform Nie Rongzhen[17] about it. [translators' omission]

SOURCE: JY, p. 234.

Doc. 33. Mao Cable from Moscow re Sending PRC Representatives to the United Nations and Other Matters, Jan. 13, 1950, 2200

Comrade [Liu] Shaoqi:

1. I agree with your cable dated January 13 about implementing the order to take over foreign barracks and also preparing for the expulsion from the country of all the former U.S. consulates.[18]

2. I agree that the Shanghai Military Control Committee has to confiscate or requisition immediately all the property of the U.S. Economic Cooperation Administration that was left in Shanghai.[19]

3. As to the problem of taking over the property left by the puppet government

[15][The omitted portion dealt with the appointment of Xiao Jingguang as commander of the navy. The JY compilers' gloss on him reads: "Xiao Jingguang was then the first deputy commander of both the PLA Fourth Field Army and the Central-South Military Region."—TRANS.]

[16]Liu Yalou was then the commander of the PLA air force.

[17]Nie Rongzhen was then the acting chief of the PLA General Staff.

[18][For the text of the proclamation of January 6 announcing Beijing's intention to confiscate the military barracks areas of foreign governments, see Department of State *Bulletin*, Jan. 23, 1950, p. 121.—TRANS.]

[19]That is, the goods stored in Shanghai by the China branch of the U.S. Economic Cooperation Administration for Chiang Kai-shek's use during the civil war.

in Hong Kong, please make a decision on the basis of the alternatives submitted by the Ministry of Foreign Affairs and the Central Finance and Economics Commission. I have no opinion on this matter.

4. Today in the evening [Foreign Minister A. Ia.] Vyshinskii came to my place for a talk and proposed that our country send a cable to the United Nations on the matter of sending our representative to the United Nations to replace the Nationalists' representative because right now there is a very severe struggle in the Security Council over the legitimacy of the Nationalists' representative. The Soviet Union is supporting our government's declaration about the expulsion of the Nationalists' representative; the United States, Great Britain, and the majority of the member states [of the Security Council] are against the expulsion. As a result, there is a need for a more forthcoming statement on the part of China. We can send our cable a week from now. I have agreed to his proposal. Let me ask the Central Committee to consider a nominee for the position of the head of our delegation [to the UN] and to report to me by cable. The decision will be made after [Zhou] Enlai's arrival here.

5. I will not go [to Leningrad] today; [the time] has been changed to tomorrow ([Jan.] 14), when I shall depart for Leningrad at 2200. On [Jan.] 15, I shall remain in Leningrad for one day, and on [Jan.] 16 I shall return. [Wang] Jiaxiang, [Chen] Boda, Shi Zhe, and Wang Dongxing[20] will accompany me. Ye Zilong[21] and the technical staff will [stay] to work in the residence [so] the Central Committee may send its cables as usual.

SOURCE: JY, pp. 235–36.

Doc. 34. Mao Cable from Moscow re Supporting the Cominform Bulletin's Criticism of the Japanese Communist Party Politburo Member Nosaka Sanzo, Jan. 14, 1950, 1600

Comrade [Hu] Qiaomu:

I shall depart for the tour to Leningrad today at 2100 and will not be back for three days. I still have not received the draft of the *Renmin Ribao* [People's Daily] editorial and the resolution of the Politburo of the Japanese Communist Party.

If you are inclined to wait until I can read it, then I will not be able to send a response by cable until [Jan.] 17; otherwise, it can be published after Comrade [Liu] Shaoqi has read it. Our Party should express our support of the criticism of Nosaka in the Cominform *Bulletin* and also express our disappointment over the Japanese Communist Party Politburo's inability to accept this criticism and our hope that the Japanese Communist Party will take appropriate steps to correct Nosaka's mistakes.

SOURCE: JY, p. 237.

[20]Chen Boda was then the deputy head of the CCP Central Committee's Propaganda Department and deputy head of the Institute of Marxism-Leninism. Shi Zhe then headed the Central Committee's Translation Section. Wang Dongxing then headed the Security Desk of the Central Committee's Administration Office.
[21]Ye Zilong was then Mao Zedong's secretary.

Doc. 35. Mao Cable from Moscow Approving the Establishment of Diplomatic Relations with the Democratic Republic of Vietnam, Jan. 17, 1950, 2200

Comrade [Liu] Shaoqi:

1. On the Vietnamese Government's request to establish diplomatic relations, we should consent to it by giving an immediate answer. I have worked out a draft for it. Please broadcast it tomorrow (18th) and cable it to Ho Chi Minh by internal transmitter.

2. Please direct the Ministry of Foreign Affairs to send the Vietnamese Government's announcement requesting the establishment of diplomatic relations with various countries to the Soviet Union and the new democracies.

[The following is Mao's draft reply to the Vietnamese Government's request to establish diplomatic relations with China.]

Foreign Minister of the Government of the Democratic Republic of Vietnam, Mr. Hoang Minh Gian:

It is my great honor to receive the esteemed minister's telegram of January 15, 1950, requesting the establishment of diplomatic relations with the People's Republic of China. Let me now inform the esteemed minister [of our decision]: The Central People's Government of the PRC holds that the Government of the Democratic Republic of Vietnam is a legal government by the will of the Vietnamese people. In order to consolidate the relations between the two countries and strengthen the friendship and cooperation between the two countries, the Central People's Government of the PRC is willing to establish diplomatic relations with the Government of the Democratic Republic of Vietnam and exchange ambassadors. This cable serves to affirm our response.

> Foreign Minister of the Central
> People's Government of the People's
> Republic of China, Zhou Enlai
> January 18, 1950

SOURCE: JY, pp. 238–39.

Doc. 36. Mao Cable from Moscow re Explaining the Confiscation of Foreign Barracks and Other Anti-Western Actions to Democratic Personages, Jan. 18, 1950

Comrade [Liu] Shaoqi:

The cable of January 17 has been received.

1. The fact that the United States is pulling out all [its] official personnel from China is extremely favorable for us, but those democratic figures suffering from the fear-of-the-United-States illness may be dissatisfied with the confiscation of the foreign military barracks and other actions. Please pay attention to explaining [the meaning of these actions to them].

2. Let me ask the Central Committee, together with the people from the Ministry of Foreign Affairs, to discuss what questions we should raise in the talks with the British chargé d'affaires [John C.] Hutchinson[22] when he arrives in Beijing; to define the guiding principles, position, and concrete contents [of the talks]; and to report to me in advance.

SOURCE: JY, p. 241.

Doc. 37. *Mao Cable from Moscow re the Nomination of Luo Fu (Zhang Wentian) as Head of the Chinese Delegation to the United Nations, Jan. 18, 1950, 1730*

Comrade [Liu] Shaoqi:

1. Today, at 1630, I had a telephone conversation with [Zhou] Enlai. (He has reached Sverdlovsk and will perhaps arrive in Moscow on January 20, at 1700.) [I] feel that Zhang Hanfu[23] lacks prestige, and so should be only a deputy. It would be appropriate to nominate Luo Fu[24] as head of the Chinese delegation to the United Nations. I have drafted a cable to the United Nations [reproduced below], and if the Central Committee agrees, I will ask you to dispatch it and publish it openly tomorrow, on the 19th.

2. As Enlai has said, Gao Gang and [Li] Fuchun[25] are both of the opinion that Luo Fu should be the diplomatic representative, and that the only problem is that we have not asked him in advance for his own views. Please send a cable to Luo Fu at the same time as you publish [the UN] cable, explaining that because of the lack of time, we were not able to seek his agreement, and asking him to excuse us. As for the time of his departure for the United Nations, we will inform him in a special cable.

3. We can wait for the 6th session of the [Central People's] Government Council to complete the procedure on his nomination. If you think it necessary, then tomorrow, [Jan.] 19, you can gather the vice-chairmen of the government and leading democratic political figures and have a talk with them.

4. Since Enlai will soon be in Moscow, the note must be signed by Li Kenong.

[22]Hutchinson, the then chargé d'affaires in China, was nominated by the British government to conduct talks with China on the establishment of diplomatic relations. [Great Britain had severed relations with the Nationalists on January 5 and formally recognized the PRC the next day. In his January 9 reply, Foreign Minister Zhou Enlai stated that the PRC accepted Hutchinson as the British representative in the "negotiations on the question of establishing diplomatic relations." When Zhou's message reached London, the Foreign Office decided to seek clarification on the meaning of such "negotiations." (See *China Weekly Review*, Jan. 14, Jan. 21, and Jan. 28, 1950, pp. 110–11, 130–31, 145, respectively.) It would be four years before the Chinese had even a chargé d'affaires in London (1954); the two governments did not exchange ambassadors until 1972.—TRANS.]

[23]Zhang Hanfu was then the vice-minister of foreign affairs of the PRC.

[24]Luo Fu (Zhang Wentian) was then a member of the CCP Politburo and a member of the Standing Committee of the CCP Central Committee's Northeastern Bureau. [The compilers routinely use Zhang after the first few occurrences of his name.—TRANS.]

[25][Gao Gang was then the secretary and Li Fuchun the deputy secretary of the CCP Central Committee's Northeast Bureau.—TRANS.]

5. After dispatching the cable, you must send this note in the same way as the previous one to the diplomatic corps of the Soviet Union, Czechoslovakia, Poland, Great Britain, France, the Netherlands, and others accredited in the capital.

6. In publishing the news, the Xinhua Agency must introduce Zhang Wentian as a member of the CCP Central Committee and as a participant in the 25,000-li Long March as well as in various kinds of revolutionary work.

7. I look forward to your report about the completion of this work.

The complete text of the cable to the United Nations is as follows:

To the President of the General Assembly of the United Nations, Mr. [Carlos] Romulo, [and the] Secretary General of the United Nations, Mr. [Trygve] Lie, to be transmitted to all delegations of the member states of the Security Council of the United Nations:

On the 8th of January, 1950, Minister of Foreign Affairs of the PRC Zhou Enlai sent a note to the United Nations demanding that the United Nations and the Security Council expel the illegitimate delegates of the Chinese Nationalist reactionary remnant clique. Judging from the return cable of Secretary General of the United Nations Mr. Lie, this note has been received and transmitted to all member states of the Security Council.

Mr. President and Mr. Secretary General, we are now informing you [of another action]: The Central People's Government of the PRC has appointed Zhang Wentian chairman of a PRC delegation [that is ready] to attend the meetings and participate in the work of the United Nations, including the meetings and the work of the Security Council.

I will also ask you, Mr. President and Mr. Secretary General, to answer the following two questions:

1. When will the illegitimate delegates of the Chinese Nationalist reactionary remnant clique be expelled from the United Nations and the Security Council? I consider the continued presence to this day of the illegitimate delegates of such a reactionary remnant clique in the United Nations and the Security Council completely unjustified. They must be expelled immediately.

2. When can the legitimate delegation of the PRC under the chairmanship of Zhang Wentian attend the meetings and participate in the work of the United Nations and the Security Council? I consider that this delegation should attend the meetings and participate in the work without delay.

An early reply to the above-mentioned points will be appreciated.

Vice-Minister of Foreign Affairs
of the People's Republic of China,
Li Kenong[26]

SOURCE: JY, pp. 242–43.

[26]When this cable was officially published, the signature was changed to that of Foreign Minster Zhou Enlai. Some minor changes in punctuation and wording were also made. The complete text is in *Renmin Ribao*, Jan. 20, 1950.

Doc. 38. Mao Cable from Moscow re the Release on U.S. Secretary of State Dean Acheson's Statement of Jan. 19, 1950, 0500

Comrade [Liu] Shaoqi; also for the information of [Hu] Qiaomu:

1

1. I have written an article under the name of Qiaomu; please publish it after careful scrutiny.
2. [Hu's] article "The Road (Toward the Liberation) of the Japanese People" is very well written. Right now it is being translated into Russian, and we are preparing to give it to Stalin to read.

2

(Xinhua Agency dispatch, Beijing, [Jan.] 20). The head of the Information Department of the Central People's Government, Hu Qiaomu, today gave an interview to the Xinhua Agency correspondent refuting the shameless slander of U.S. Secretary of State Acheson.

Department Head Hu Qiaomu states: U.S. Secretary of State Acheson has made all sorts of slander in his long speech before the National Press Club on January 12.[27] The fact that the officials of American imperialism, represented by such people as Acheson, are daily turning into utterly impotent political swindlers, who cannot survive without resorting to the most shameless slander, demonstrates to what extent the U.S. imperialist system has deteriorated in the spiritual realm. All through his speech, Acheson has camouflaged the aggressive nature of American policy by slandering [us]. For example, he said, "Our interests have been parallel to the interests of the people of Asia." When referring to China, he said, "there was not conflict but parallelism" in American and Chinese interests. "And so from the time of the announcement of the open door policy through the 9-power treaty to the very latest resolution of the General Assembly of the United Nations, we have stated that principle and we believe it." Here every word is a lie. Using all means to penetrate China and to turn it into an American colony—this is the basic policy of the United States. Using $600 million to help Chiang Kai-shek kill several million Chinese people during the past several years—these are so-called "nonconflictual and parallel" interests of the United States and the Chinese people.

Department Head Hu Qiaomu said: Yet the most shameless slander by Acheson of which we speak is not the above-mentioned [points] but has to do with Sino-Soviet relations.

Acheson has said that "the Soviet Union is detaching the northern provinces of China from China and is attaching them to the Soviet Union. This process is complete in outer Mongolia [the Mongolian People's Republic]. It also is nearly complete in Manchuria, and I am sure that in inner Mongolia and in Sinkiang [Xin-

[27][For the text of the speech, see Acheson, "Crisis," pp. 111–18. We have used the wording in this source in our translation of the Chinese text. Though the Chinese translation of Acheson's speech differs from the original English in important ways, we have no reason to assume that these differences were intentional.—TRANS.]

jiang] there are very happy reports coming from Soviet agents to Moscow. That is what is going on. It is the detachment of these whole areas, vast areas—populated by Chinese—the detachment of these areas from China and their attachment to the Soviet Union. . . . The fact that the Soviet Union is taking the four northern provinces of China is the single most significant, most important fact, in the relation of any foreign power with Asia."

The aforementioned words of the U.S. Department of State have their own history. There is no basis for the Soviet Union to help the Chinese Communist Party—those are the words spoken constantly by the lords in the U.S. Department of State before 1948, and this is because at that time, from the point of view of the lords in the Department of State, the U.S. gamble on the war in China still seemed promising. The Soviet Union is trying to control China—those are the words in the White Paper devoted to the problem of China published by the Department of State in 1949,[28] and this is because at that time, the lords at the Department of State were already feeling that they were going to totally lose their gamble very soon. The Soviet Union has occupied four regions of northern China—these are the words of January 12, 1950—and the reason is that the United States had by then completely lost its gamble on the Chinese mainland; only Taiwan remains, and it seems that they are trying to make something out of this. Thanks be to God that owing to the sweeping blows of the Chinese people and the People's Liberation Army, the American imperialists, besides making this kind of slander, now have no other better means [at their disposal]. Such impotent slander and insults as [the claim that] the Chinese Communist Party is the running dog of the Soviet Union, and [that] the Soviet Union has already annexed, right now is annexing, or will in the future annex China can have only these results: to raise the ire of the Chinese and Soviet people and strengthen Sino-Soviet friendship and cooperation.

Corrupted in the extreme and overloaded with contradictions, the American imperialist system has some interesting interpretations: two days after Acheson's speech, on January 14, 1950, the former American consul-general in Shenyang, [Angus] Ward, who was arrested, convicted, and expelled from the country by the Chinese People's Government, has unstoppered Acheson's ears. According to a TASS Agency dispatch from Washington dated January 14: "Former U.S. Consul-General in Shenyang Ward, on returning to the United States, had a talk with officials from the Department of State. After this talk, in response to [our] correspondent's question, he said that beyond the joint management of the [Chinese Changchun] railroad, rights for which are provided by treaty, he could see no signs of Soviet control over Manchuria. At the same time, Ward pointed out that there are no signs of a Soviet annexation of Manchuria. Answering the question whether the Communist authorities in Manchuria are under the control of Beijing, Ward stated that all Communist governments [in China's regions] are under a very highly centralized leadership. As far as he knows, Manchuria is a part of Communist China."

People can see what stories are appearing in the western hemisphere. One [of-

[28][U.S., Dept. of State, *United States Relations with China.*—TRANS.]

ficial] is saying that Manchuria is being annexed by the Soviet Union, the other is saying that he cannot see it at all, and both of them are important officials in the U.S. Department of State.

3

For the attention of the cipher clerk:

1. Use the [special] encrypted telegraphic code; do not use the standard telegraphic code.

2. Be extremely careful when proofreading; do not make any mistakes.

3. [The article] must be dispatched today (19), so that Comrade Liu Shaoqi can receive it tonight or tomorrow morning.

SOURCE: JY, pp. 245–48.

Doc. 39. Mao Cable from Moscow Approving the Indian Government's Proposal to Begin Talks on the Establishment of a Diplomatic Mission, Jan. 20, 1950, 0100

Comrade [Liu] Shaoqi:

1. The cable dated [January] 19 has been received. First, I agree with your idea of sending a cable to [Jawaharlal] Nehru[29] accepting in principle [the Indian representative's] coming to Beijing as a provisional representative for talks on the first steps and procedures for the establishment of a diplomatic mission. As for the answer to Great Britain, you should delay it. The comrades from the Ministry of Foreign Affairs do not understand the reason for the delays and are thus of the opinion that we shall "find ourselves in a deadlock." This is not right: here there is no deadlock; the initiative is always in our hands. Please decide on the length of the delay after consulting Li Kenong.

2. I agree with the draft statement on Tibet.

3. Concerning the air transport regiment, the answer will be given after consultations with Zhou [Enlai].

SOURCE: JY, p. 249.

Doc. 40. Mao Cable from Moscow re the Sino-Soviet Talks and the Drafting of the Treaty of Friendship, Jan. 25, 1950, 0500[30]

Comrade [Liu] Shaoqi:

1. Zhou [Enlai], Li [Fuchun], and others arrived here on [Jan.] 20. On [Jan.] 21, the 12 of us participated in the meeting in commemoration of Lenin. On [Jan.] 22, six of us, including Shi Zhe, had talks with Comrade Stalin and other comrades settling various questions of principle and methods of work. On [Jan.] 23, Zhou, Wang [Jiaxiang], and Li held talks with [A. I.] Mikoyan, [A. Ia.] Vyshinskii, and [N. V.] Roshchin on several concrete problems. On [Jan.] 24, we gave Vyshinskii

[29]Nehru was then the Indian prime minister and foreign minister.
[30]This treaty was drafted by Zhou Enlai under Mao Zedong's guidance.

our draft of the Sino-Soviet Treaty of Friendship, Alliance, and Mutual Assistance. Right now, we are drafting a second document—the agreement on Lüshun, Dalian, and the Chinese Changchun Railroad. The drafting work is supposed to be finished today, and we have decided to finish a third document, the Sino-Soviet barter agreement, within three days. Generally speaking, the work is proceeding fairly smoothly.

2. I am sending herewith the draft of the Sino-Soviet Treaty of Friendship, Alliance, and Mutual Assistance [omitted]. Please discuss it in the Central Committee and report to me by cable. Please do not transmit it anywhere outside [the Central Committee].

SOURCE: JY, p. 251.

Doc. 41. Mao Cable from Moscow re the Publishing of the Treaty, Feb. 10, 1950 Comrade [Liu] Shaoqi:

1. [translators' omission]

2. The first several phrases in the beginning of the credit agreement,[31] talking about China's compensation to the Soviet Union, must not be omitted.

3. Both sides are to publish the treaty and the agreements on the same day, and you will be specially informed about the date.

4. [Chen] Boda has written an editorial for the Xinhua Agency, which we will look over and be able to send to you by tomorrow. Please publish it simultaneously with the treaty after [Hu] Qiaomu has scrutinized it.

SOURCE: JY, p. 257.

Doc. 42. Mao Cable from Moscow Transmitting an Internal Party Cable on the Sino-Soviet Treaty and Agreements, Feb. 12, 1950, 0600

Comrade [Liu] Shaoqi:

Here is my draft of the internal Party cable. Please consider it as soon as you receive it and dispatch it quickly.

To all Central Committee Bureaus, Branch Bureaus, and Front-line Committees:

The new Sino-Soviet treaty and agreements will be signed and published in a day's time. As they are discussed collectively in different regions, and opinions are offered, it is essential to adhere to the position of the Xinhua Agency editorial and to avoid expressing any inappropriate opinions.

Central Committee
February 13, 1949

SOURCE: JY, p. 260.

[31][Translators' omission]. The first phrases of the document were as follows: "The Government of the Soviet Union agrees to satisfy the request of the Central People's Government of the PRC for a loan to be used in payment of the machines, facilities, and other matériel that the Soviet Union has agreed to provide to China."

Doc. 43. Mao Cable from Moscow re Revisions in the Editorial "A New Epoch in Sino-Soviet Friendship and Cooperation," Feb. 14, 1950, 0500

(Dispatch immediately to:) [Liu] Shaoqi, [Hu] Qiaomu:

Please immediately make the following changes in the Xinhua Agency's editorial, "The New Epoch in Sino-Soviet Cooperation," and then broadcast it tonight, together with the treaty.

1. In the first paragraph, the following 17 characters, "The Additional Agreement to the Sino-Soviet Treaty of Friendship, Alliance, and Mutual Assistance," have to be deleted; the 22 characters "exchange of notes between the foreign ministers of China and the Soviet Union, and the protocols connected with the above-mentioned agreements," have to be deleted; the 9 characters "and the Sino-Soviet Civil Aviation Agreement" have to be deleted; the 4 characters "and the supplements to them" have to be deleted; and the 7 characters "and the Civil Aviation Agreement" have to be deleted. All in all, 59 characters have to be deleted in the first paragraph.

2. In the second paragraph, of the 15 characters "and all the other agreements, protocols, and exchange of notes demonstrate" following the two characters "treaty" in the first phrase, 8 characters "all the" and "protocols, and exchange of notes" have to be deleted. Only the 7 characters "and other agreements demonstrate" are to remain.

3. In the third paragraph, the 19 characters "that is, the Sino-Soviet Treaty of Friendship and Alliance of the year 1945 and other exchange of notes" should be deleted, and in the phrase "this treaty and other exchange of notes," the two characters "exchange of notes" have to be changed to "agreements."

4. In the seventh paragraph, the 9 characters "and the Sino-Soviet Civil Aviation Agreement" have to be deleted, as do the 43 characters "China on its part will repay the Soviet Union for the Soviet loan with strategic raw materials lacking in the Soviet Union, and this point is also favorable to the Soviet Union."

5. In the eighth paragraph, the two characters "all the" have to be changed to the two characters "two."

6. All the ninth paragraph has to be deleted; that is, the 53 characters "The Additional Agreement to the Sino-Soviet Treaty of Friendship, Alliance, and Mutual Assistance is a necessary measure for guaranteeing the defense interests of the two states, and this measure will be beneficial for both China and the Soviet Union."

7. Concerning the above-mentioned changes, let me ask Qiaomu to be responsible for proofreading the editorial in strict accordance [with what I have written], and also let me ask Comrade Shaoqi to make a careful proofreading. The two of you must make absolutely no slips, so as to ensure that the statement is in full accord with the essence of the treaty and with the agreements that will be published by the Chinese and Soviet sides. Otherwise, discord will emerge, and the impact [of the discord] will be very negative. Pay attention. This is extremely important, extremely important!

SOURCE: JY, pp. 262–63.

Doc. 44. Communiqué on the Signing of the Treaty and Agreements Between the People's Republic of China and the Union of Soviet Socialist Republics, Feb. 14, 1950

In the recent past, negotiations have been held in Moscow between Mao Zedong, Chairman of the Central People's Government of the PRC, and Zhou Enlai, Premier of the Government Administration Council and Minister of Foreign Affairs of the PRC, on the one hand, and J. V. Stalin, Chairman of the Council of Ministers of the USSR, and A. Ia. Vyshinskii, Minister of Foreign Affairs of the USSR, on the other, in the course of which important political and economic questions concerning the relations between the PRC and the Soviet Union were discussed.

These negotiations, which proceeded in an atmosphere of cordiality and friendly mutual understanding, confirmed the desire of both parties to strengthen and develop their friendly cooperation in every way, and likewise confirmed their desire to cooperate for the purpose of ensuring peace and security for the peoples of all nations.

The negotiations concluded with the signing on February 14 in the Kremlin of the following: (1) a Treaty of Friendship, Alliance, and Mutual Assistance between the People's Republic of China and the Soviet Union; (2) an Agreement on the Chinese Changchun Railroad, Port Arthur [Lüshun], and Dairen [Dalian], according to which the Chinese Changchun Railroad is to be handed over in toto to the PRC and Soviet troops are to be withdrawn from Port Arthur, following the signing of a peace treaty with Japan; (3) an Agreement on the granting by the government of the Soviet Union of a long-term economic credit to be used by the government of the PRC to pay for deliveries of industrial and railway equipment from the USSR.

The aforementioned treaty and agreements were signed on behalf of the PRC by Zhou Enlai, Premier and Minister of Foreign Affairs, and on behalf of the USSR by A. Ia. Vyshinskii, Minister of Foreign Affairs.

In connection with the signing of the Treaty of Friendship, Alliance, and Mutual Assistance, and the Agreement on the Chinese Changchun Railroad, Port Arthur, and Dairen, Zhou Enlai, Premier and Minister of Foreign Affairs, and A. Ia. Vyshinskii, Minister of Foreign Affairs, exchanged notes to the effect that the respective Treaty and Agreements concluded on August 14, 1945, between China and the Soviet Union are now null and void, and also that both governments affirm that the independent status of the Mongolian People's Republic is fully guaranteed as a result of the plebiscite of 1945 and the establishment with it of diplomatic relations by the People's Republic of China.

At the same time, A. Ia. Vyshinskii, Minister of Foreign Affairs, and Zhou Enlai, Premier and Minister of Foreign Affairs, also exchanged notes on the decision of the Soviet government to transfer without compensation to the government of the PRC the property acquired in Manchuria from Japanese owners by Soviet economic organizations, and also on the decision of the Soviet government to transfer without compensation to the government of the PRC all the buildings in the former military compound in Peking.

SOURCE: *Sino-Soviet Treaty and Agreement* (Beijing, 1950) pp. 1–3; Chinese names are rendered in pinyin, and on names like the Chinese Changchun Railroad, we follow the usage of the main text.

Doc. 45. *Treaty of Friendship, Alliance, and Mutual Assistance Between the People's Republic of China and the Union of Soviet Socialist Republics, Feb. 14, 1950*

The Central People's Government of the People's Republic of China and the Presidium of the Supreme Soviet of the Union of Soviet Socialist Republics, fully determined to prevent jointly, by strengthening friendship and cooperation between the PRC and the USSR, the revival of Japanese imperialism and the resumption of aggression on the part of Japan or any other state that may collaborate in any way with Japan in acts of aggression; imbued with the desire to consolidate lasting peace and universal security in the Far East and throughout the world in conformity with the aims and principles of the United Nations; profoundly convinced that the consolidation of good neighborly relations and friendship between the PRC and the USSR meets the vital interests of the peoples of China and the Soviet Union, have towards this end decided to conclude the present Treaty and have appointed as their plenipotentiary representatives: Zhou Enlai, Premier of the Government Administration Council and Minister of Foreign Affairs, acting for the Central People's Government of the PRC; and Andrei Ianuarevich Vyshinskii, Minister of Foreign Affairs of the USSR, acting for the Presidium of the Supreme Soviet of the USSR. Both plenipotentiary representatives, having communicated their full powers and found them in good and due form, have agreed upon the following:

Article 1. Both Contracting Parties undertake jointly to adopt all necessary measures at their disposal for the purpose of preventing the resumption of aggression and violation of peace on the part of Japan or any other state that may collaborate with Japan directly or indirectly in acts of aggression. In the event of one of the Contracting Parties being attacked by Japan or any state allied with her and thus being involved in a state of war, the other Contracting Party shall immediately render military and other assistance by all means at its disposal.

The Contracting Parties also declare their readiness to participate in a spirit of sincere cooperation in all international actions aimed at ensuring peace and security throughout the world and to contribute their full share to the earliest implementation of these tasks.

Article 2. Both Contracting Parties undertake in a spirit of mutual agreement to bring about the earliest conclusion of a peace treaty with Japan jointly with other powers which were Allies in the Second World War.

Article 3. Each Contracting Party undertakes not to conclude any alliance directed against the other Contracting Party and not to take part in any coalition or in any actions or measures directed against the other Contracting Party.

Article 4. Both Contracting Parties, in the interests of consolidating peace and universal security, will consult with each other in regard to all important international problems affecting the common interests of China and the Soviet Union.

Article 5. Each Contracting Party undertakes, with a spirit of friendship and cooperation and in conformity with the principles of equality, mutual benefit, and mutual respect for the national sovereignty and territorial integrity and noninterference in the internal affairs of the other Contracting Party, to develop and consolidate economic and cultural ties between China and the Soviet Union, to render the other all possible economic assistance, and to carry out necessary economic cooperation.

Article 6. The present Treaty shall come into force immediately after its ratification; the exchange of instruments of ratification shall take place in Beijing.

The present Treaty shall be valid for thirty years. If neither of the Contracting Parties gives notice a year before the expiration of this term of its intention to denounce the Treaty, it shall remain in force for another five years and shall be further extended in compliance with this provision.

Done in Moscow on February 14, 1950, in two copies, each in the Chinese and Russian languages, both texts being equally valid.

> On the authorization of the Central People's Government
> of the People's Republic of China
> Zhou Enlai

> On the authorization of the Presidium of the Supreme
> Soviet of the Union of Soviet Socialist Republics
> A. Ia. Vyshinskii

SOURCE: Same as Doc. 44, pp. 5–8.

Doc. 46. Agreement Between the People's Republic of China and the Union of Soviet Socialist Republics on the Chinese Changchun Railroad, Port Arthur [Lüshun], and Dairen [Dalian], Feb. 14, 1950

The Central People's Government of the People's Republic of China and the Presidium of the Supreme Soviet of the Union of Soviet Socialist Republics record that since 1945, fundamental changes have occurred in the situation in the Far East, namely: imperialist Japan has suffered defeat; the reactionary Kuomintang government has been overthrown; China has become a People's Democratic Republic; a new People's government has been established in China which has unified the whole of China, has carried out a policy of friendship and cooperation with the Soviet Union, and has proved its ability to defend the national independence and territorial integrity of China and the national honor and dignity of the Chinese people.

The Central People's Government of the PRC and the Presidium of the Supreme Soviet of the USSR consider that this new situation permits a new approach to the question of the Chinese Changchun Railroad, Port Arthur [Lüshun], and Dairen [Dalian].

In conformity with these new circumstances, the Central People's Government of the PRC and the Presidium of the Supreme Soviet of the USSR have decided to conclude the present Agreement on the Chinese Changchun Railroad, Port Arthur, and Dairen:

Article 1. Both Contracting Parties agree that the Soviet government transfer without compensation to the government of the PRC all its rights to joint administration of the Chinese Changchun Railroad with all the property belonging to the Railroad. The transfer shall be effected immediately after the conclusion of a peace treaty with Japan, but not later than the end of 1952.

Pending the transfer, the existing Sino-Soviet joint administration of the Chinese Changchun Railroad shall remain unchanged. After this Agreement becomes effective, posts (such as manager of the Railroad, chairman of the Board, etc.) will be periodically alternated between representatives of China and the USSR.

As regards concrete methods of effecting the transfer, they shall be agreed upon and determined by the governments of both Contracting Parties.

Article 2. Both Contracting Parties agree that Soviet troops be withdrawn from the jointly utilized naval base Port Arthur, and that the installations in this area be handed over to the government of the PRC immediately on the conclusion of a peace treaty with Japan, but not later than the end of 1952. The government of the PRC will compensate the Soviet Union for expenses it has incurred in restoring and constructing installations since 1945.

For the period pending the withdrawal of Soviet troops and the transfer of the above-mentioned installations, the governments of China and the Soviet Union will each appoint an equal number of military representatives to form a joint Chinese-Soviet Military Commission which will be alternately presided over by each side and which will be in charge of military affairs in the area of Port Arthur; concrete measures in this sphere will be drawn up by the joint Chinese-Soviet Military Commission within three months after the present Agreement becomes effective and shall be put into force upon approval of these measures by the governments of both countries.

The civil administration in the aforementioned area shall be under the direct authority of the government of the PRC. Pending the withdrawal of Soviet troops, the zone for billeting Soviet troops in the area of Port Arthur will remain unaltered in conformity with existing frontiers.

In the event of either of the Contracting Parties becoming the victim of aggression on the part of Japan or any state that may collaborate with Japan, and as a result thereof becoming involved in hostilities, China and the Soviet Union may, on the proposal of the government of the PRC and with the agreement of the government of the USSR, jointly use the naval base Port Arthur for the purpose of conducting joint military operations against the aggressor.

Article 3. Both Contracting Parties agree that the question of Dairen harbor be further considered on the conclusion of a peace treaty with Japan. As regards the administration of Dairen, it is in the hands of the government of the PRC. All the property in Dairen now temporarily administered by or leased to the Soviet Union shall be taken over by the government of the PRC. To carry out the transfer of the aforementioned property, the governments of China and the Soviet Union shall appoint three representatives each to form a Joint Commission which, within three months after the present Agreement comes into effect, shall draw up concrete measures for the transfer of the property; and these measures shall be fully carried out in the course of 1950 after their approval by the governments of both countries upon their proposal of the Joint Commission.

Article 4. The present Agreement shall come into force on the day of its ratification. The exchange of instruments of ratification shall take place in Beijing.

Done in Moscow on February 14, 1950, in two copies, each in the Chinese and Russian languages, both texts being equally valid.

On the authorization of the Central People's
Government of the People's Republic of China
Zhou Enlai

On the authorization of the Presidium of the
Supreme Soviet of the Union of Soviet Socialist
Republics
A. Ia. Vyshinskii

SOURCE: Same as Doc. 44, pp. 9–13.

Doc. 47. Agreement Between the Central People's Government of the People's Republic of China and the Government of the Union of Soviet Socialist Republics on the Granting of Credit to the People's Republic of China, Feb. 14, 1950

In connection with the consent of the government of the Union of Soviet Socialist Republics to grant the request of the Central People's Government of the People's Republic of China for a credit to pay for the equipment and other materials which the Soviet Union has agreed to deliver to China, both governments have agreed upon the following:

Article 1. The government of the USSR grants to the Central People's Government of the PRC a credit which, in terms of American dollars, amounts to U.S. $300,000,000, taking 35 American dollars to one ounce of fine gold.

In view of the extraordinary devastation of China as a result of prolonged hostilities on its territory, the Soviet government has agreed to grant the credit at the favorable rate of interest of 1% per annum.

Article 2. The credit mentioned in Article 1 shall be granted over a period of five years starting January 1, 1950, in equal portions of one-fifth of the credit per year, to be used in payment for deliveries from the USSR of equipment and materials, including equipment for electric power stations, metallurgical and engineering plants, mining equipment for the extraction of coal and ores, railway and other transport equipment, rails, and other materials for the restoration and development of the national economy of China.

Types, quantities, prices, and dates of delivery of the equipment and materials shall be determined by special agreement of the two Parties. Prices will be determined on the basis of prices on the world markets.

Any part of the credit which remains unused in the course of one year may be carried over to the following year.

Article 3. The Central People's Government of the PRC shall repay the credit mentioned in Article 1, together with the interest thereon, in deliveries of raw materials, tea, gold, and American dollars. Prices for raw materials and tea and their quantities and dates of delivery shall be determined by special agreement, with prices to be determined on the basis of prices on the world markets.

The credit shall be repaid in ten equal annual installments—one-tenth of the total credit to be paid not later than December 31st of every year. The first repayment shall be made not later than December 31, 1954, and the last not later than December 31, 1963.

Interest on the credit, which will be computed for the amount actually used and from the date of use, is to be paid every six months.

Article 4. For clearance with regard to the credit provided for in the present Agreement, the State Bank of the USSR and the People's Bank of the PRC shall open special accounts and jointly establish the order of clearance and accounting under the present Agreement.

Article 5. The present Agreement comes into force on the day of its signing and is subject to ratification. The exchange of instruments of ratification shall take place in Beijing.

Done in Moscow on February 14, 1950, in two copies, each in the Chinese and Russian languages, both texts being equally valid.

On the authorization of the Central People's
Government of the People's Republic of China
Zhou Enlai

On the authorization of the Presidium of the
Supreme Soviet of the Union of Soviet Socialist
Republics
A. Ia. Vyshinskii

SOURCE: Same as Doc. 44, pp. 15–17.

Doc. 48. *Speech by Foreign Minister A. Ia. Vyshinskii, Feb. 14, 1950*

Mr. Chairman of the Central People's Government, Mr. Premier of the Government Administration Council, Gentlemen:

Today a new remarkable page has been added to the history of Soviet-Chinese relations. Today documents of tremendous historical importance have been signed—the Treaty of Friendship, Alliance, and Mutual Assistance, the Agreement on the Chinese Changchun Railroad, Port Arthur [Lüshun], and Dairen [Dalian], the Agreement on a long-term economic credit—the announced signing of which will be met with feelings of profound satisfaction not only by the whole of the Soviet people but also by all friends of peace, democracy, and progress.

The Treaty of Friendship, Alliance, and Mutual Assistance and the aforementioned agreements, based on respect for the principles of equality, state independence, and national sovereignty, seal the historical bonds between the peoples of the Soviet Union and China. The Soviet people have always entertained profound sentiments of friendship and respect for the Chinese people, for their heroic liberation struggle under the leadership of the leader of the Chinese people, Mao Zedong, against feudal and imperialist oppression. In their steady sympathy with this struggle, the Soviet people proceeded from a profound conviction that, as the leader of the Soviet people, J. V. Stalin, said back in 1925, "Truth and justice are fully on the side of the Chinese revolution." "This is why," J. V. Stalin said then, "we sympathize and shall sympathize with the Chinese revolution in this struggle for liberation of the Chinese people from the yoke of the imperialists and for uniting China in a single state."

The Soviet people have invariably demonstrated their sympathy with the cause of liberation of the Chinese people. The Treaty of Friendship, Alliance, and Mutual Assistance signed today between the Soviet Union and the People's Republic of China expresses the striving of both our peoples for eternal friendship and cooperation for the good of our countries, for strengthening the peace and security of nations.

Of great and important significance is the Agreement on the Chinese Changchun Railroad, Port Arthur, and Dairen. The Agreement points out that since 1945 radical changes have occurred in the situation in the Far East which permit a new approach to the question of the Chinese Changchun Railroad, Port Arthur, and Dairen. Every article of this agreement bespeaks high respect on the part of the Soviet Union for the national independence and national rights and interests of the Chinese people, bespeaks the grandeur of the principles of Soviet foreign policy.

Determination of our peoples to develop and consolidate economic and cultural ties between the Soviet Union and China and to render each other economic assistance formed the basis of the Agreement on the granting of a long-term economic credit by the Soviet Union to the People's Republic of China.

The treaty and agreements signed today between the USSR and the PRC constitute the biggest contribution to the cause of strengthening peace and democracy throughout the world.

Permit me, Mr. Chairman and Mr. Premier, to congratulate you on the signing of these historic documents sealing our alliance and friendship.

May the alliance and friendship between the peoples of the USSR and the PRC grow stronger and live forever!

SOURCE: Same as Doc. 44, pp. 19–21.

Doc. 49. *Speech by Premier and Foreign Minister Zhou Enlai, Feb. 14, 1950*

Mr. Chairman of the Council of Ministers of the USSR, Mr. Minister of Foreign Affairs of the USSR, Gentlemen:

The new Treaty of Friendship, Alliance, and Mutual Assistance, the Agreement on the Chinese Changchun Railroad, Port Arthur [Lüshun], and Dairen [Dalian], and the Agreement on granting credit to China have been signed today between the People's Republic of China and the Union of Soviet Socialist Republics and notes have been exchanged. The conclusion of the above treaty and agreements is based on the vital interests of the great peoples of China and the Soviet Union and indicates fraternal friendship and eternal cooperation between China and the Soviet Union. The conclusion of the treaty and agreements is a special expression of fervent assistance to the revolutionary cause of the Chinese people on the part of the Soviet Union directed by the policy of Generalissimo Stalin. There is no doubt that this close and sincere cooperation between China and the Soviet Union is of extremely profound historical importance and will inevitably have immense influence upon and consequences for the cause of peace and justice for the peoples of the East and the whole world.

The great friendship between our two Powers has been built up since the October Socialist Revolution. However, imperialism and the counterrevolutionary government of China hampered further cooperation between us. The victory of the Chinese people has brought about radical changes in the situation. The Chinese people, under the leadership of Chairman Mao Zedong, have set up the People's Republic of China and have formed a state having unprecedented unity, and this has made sincere cooperation possible between our two great states. Thanks to the meetings and the exchanges of opinions between Generalissimo Stalin and Chairman Mao Zedong, this possibility became a reality, and the friendship, alliance, and mutual assistance between China and the Soviet Union are sealed now with the signed treaty. The imperialist bloc headed by American imperialism has resorted to all kinds of provocative methods attempting to frustrate the friendship between our two nations, but these ignominious attempts have utterly failed.

The significance of the treaty and agreements between China and the Soviet Union is of particular importance for the newborn People's Republic of China. This treaty and these agreements will help the Chinese people to realize that they are not alone, and will help in the restoration and development of the Chinese economy. The Agreement between China and the Soviet Union on the Chinese Changchun Railroad, Port Arthur, and Dairen, the agreement on granting credit to China, and also the exchange of notes on transferring gratis to the Chinese government by the Soviet government the property acquired in Manchuria from Japanese owners and on transferring gratis buildings in the former so-called military compound in Beijing—constitute a demonstration of the great friendship on the part of the Soviet government and Generalissimo Stalin and will doubtlessly evoke the greatest enthusiasm among the Chinese people.

Permit me on behalf of the Chinese people to express gratitude to Generalissimo Stalin and the Soviet government for this great friendship.

China and the Soviet Union are effecting close cooperation for the sake of peace, justice, and universal security, and this cooperation represents not only the interests of the peoples of China and the Soviet Union but also the interests of all peoples of the East and the whole world who love peace and justice. I believe that our treaty and agreements will be supported not only by the peoples of China and the Soviet Union but also by progressive mankind throughout the world, while they will be regarded with enmity only by the imperialists and warmongers.

The unity of the nearly 700 million people of the two countries, China and the Soviet Union, will be an invincible force.

Long live permanent friendship and eternal cooperation between China and the Soviet Union!

SOURCE: Same as Doc. 44, pp. 23–25.

Doc. 50. Mao and Zhou cable from Moscow re Publishing the Regulations on the Land Reform and the Grain Tax in the Newly Liberated Areas, Feb. 17, 1950, 0700

Comrade [Liu] Shaoqi:

The cable concerning the draft of the regulations on the land reform and the grain tax has been received. Generally speaking, it is quite good and should be published quickly. Only the publication of the fourth part, dealing with the distribution of land itself, should be delayed. The reason is that when Comrade Stalin was listening to my report on the land reform policy, he proposed that the realization of the policy on distributing the lands of the landlords and rich peasants be divided into two comparatively long stages. Even in the case where the peasants demand that the excess land of the rich peasants be distributed, though we certainly cannot forbid it, there is still no need to approve it in advance by law. Even though we explained about the Chinese semifeudal rich peasants and noted that we are not confiscating [the lands] of the capitalist rich peasants at all, [Stalin] still gave the example of the Soviet Union after the October Revolution and insisted that we should regard [the issue of] opposing the rich peasants as a serious struggle. The core of his thinking is that at the time the landlord class is overthrown, the rich peasants should be neutralized, so there is no negative impact on production. A similar point was raised last year at the November meeting of the Politburo concerning the question of the cautious attitude towards the rich peasants to the south of the Yangtze River. Because it affects not only the rich peasants but also the national bourgeoisie, the land reform in the regions to the south of the Yangtze must differ from those in the north; [accordingly,] it is necessary to make amendments to the document of the year 1933 and the land law of the year 1947. For that reason, we are of the opinion that only the first three parts of the regulations on the land reform and grain tax in the newly liberated areas should be published, and the fourth part must be left for discussion until after we return. If it needs editing, then its publication can be delayed until April, when a special document on the land reform itself can be published. If you agree, you may explain to the democratic figures outside the Party that the fourth part only involved a policy that would not be implemented until after the autumn harvest; in order to give the matter further thought and discuss it later, it is better to take the decision to hold off publishing it until after Chairman Mao's return.

SOURCE: JY, pp. 264–65.

Doc. 51. Mao's Farewell Speech at the Moscow Railway Station, Feb. 17, 1950

Dear comrades and friends:

While in Moscow, I, Comrade Zhou Enlai, and [other] members of the Chinese delegation met with Generalissimo Stalin and responsible comrades from the Soviet government. It is hard to express in words the complete understanding and the profound friendship that have been formed on the basis of the fundamental interests of the peoples of the two great countries, China and the Soviet Union. Everybody sees that the unity of the great Chinese and Soviet peoples sealed by the treaty is lasting, inviolable, and unswerving. This unity will inevitably influence not only the flourishing of the two big countries—China and the Soviet Union—but also the future of all humanity and the victory of justice and peace the world over.

During our sojourn in the Soviet Union, we have visited a number of plants, collective farms, and other places. We have seen the great successes achieved by the workers, peasants, and intelligentsia of the Soviet Union in the construction of socialism; we have seen the style of combining revolutionary spirit with the pragmatic spirit of the Soviet people, a style developed through the instruction of Comrade Stalin and the All-Union Communist Party (Bolshevik). This confirms the conviction that Chinese Communists always had: experience in economic and cultural construction and in construction in other major spheres of the Soviet Union will serve as an example for the construction of the new China.

In the course of our sojourn in the capital of the USSR—Moscow—and in the city of the birth of the October revolution—Leningrad—we received warm hospitality. Leaving the great socialist capital, we especially express our heartfelt gratitude to Generalissimo Stalin, the Soviet government, and the Soviet people.

Long live the eternal friendship and eternal cooperation of China and the Soviet Union!

Long live the peoples of the Soviet Union!

Long live the teacher of revolutions the world over, the bosom friend of the Chinese people, Comrade Stalin!

SOURCE: We have based this English translation on the text of Mao's speech in *China Monthly Review*, Oct. 1950, supplement, pp. 8–9. We have changed the word "florescence" to "flourishing" in the first paragraph. For a Chinese text, see JY, pp. 266–67.

Doc. 52. Mao Cable from the Soviet Union re His Reception on the Way Home, Feb. 23, 1950

Ambassador Wang [Jiaxiang] to transmit to Comrades Liu Shaoqi and Gao Gang:

Having done some sightseeing along the way, we will reach Irkutsk today, on the 23rd. We are planning to arrive in Manzhouli on the 26th, and after that, we are planning to stay one to two hours or three to four hours each in Hailar, Qiqihar, Harbin, Changchun, Sipinjie, and Tieling, and to stay one or two days in Shenyang. We ask Comrade Gao Gang to inform responsible comrades in each place to maintain secrecy and to permit only a small number of the responsible cadres to be present at the receptions, not allowing many people to know and especially not to publish any news. After that, we shall be at Dahushan, Jinzhou, Shanhaiguan, Tangshan, Tanggu, and Tianjin, and in each will make some brief excursions. It is necessary to maintain secrecy everywhere. When we arrive in Beijing and leave the train, only a small number of people from the Party and from outside the Party (approximately 100 people) need to be at the station to participate in the meeting. Do not allow too many people to know; the news must be published only after our arrival in Beijing. Please arrange everything as per this cable.

SOURCE: JY, p. 268.

Doc. 53. Mao's Instructions and Added Comment on the Printing and Distribution of Zhou Enlai's Report on the Sino-Soviet Treaty, April 9, 1950

[I will] ask Zhou [Enlai] to print copies of this report and to do it today. Every one of the 170 to 180 people who are going to take part in the meeting of the Central People's Government Council has to receive a copy tomorrow.

Besides the four comrades, Zhou, Chen [Yun], Lin [Biao], and Deng [Xiaoping],[32] who are to make speeches at this meeting of the Government Council, it seems that we must give six [other] people [from among the democratic personages] a chance to speak: Zhang Zhizhong, Cheng Qian, Zhang Lan, Li Jishen, Huang Yanpei, and Guo Moruo. Please ask Zhou to let them know so that they can prepare. [translators' omission]

SOURCE: JY, pp. 288–89.

Doc. 54. Mao Speech at the 6th Session of the Central People's Government Council, April 11, 1950[33]

I

We have already pointed out that the exercising of the people's democratic dictatorship and unity with friends abroad are the two basic conditions for strengthening the victory of the revolution. The Sino-Soviet treaty and agreements signed at this time enabled the friendship between the two great countries of China and the Soviet Union to be strengthened through legal means and have gained us a staunch ally. All of this is beneficial for our full engagement in the work of internal construction and for [our] common resistance against possible imperialist aggression and [our] struggle for peace all over the world.

2

Since the formation of the Central People's Government of the PRC, our government has accomplished a very important task, the signing of the Sino-Soviet

[32]Lin Biao was then chairman of the Central-South Military Political Commission, and Deng Xiaoping was then the vice-chairman of the Southwest Military-Political Commission.

[33]Here Document 1 is the part of Mao Zedong's speech at the 6th session of the Central People's Government Council that was published in a news report, and Document 2 is a passage of the speech that he edited later. After the founding of New China, Stalin proposed that China and the Soviet Union jointly produce two documentary films, "The Victory of the Chinese People" and "Liberated China." Liu Baiyu and Zhou Libo participated in this work. Since this part of Mao Zedong's speech had to be used in the documentary "Liberated China," Liu Baiyu and Zhou Libo sent a cable to Mao from Moscow on July 27, 1950, asking for instructions. Mao Zedong edited this part of the speech, and on June 29, in a return cable, he said: "The cable dated June 27 has been received. The editorial changes to my speech at the Government Council are as follows. Let me ask you to change [the speech] if possible according to these changes; otherwise, [you may] leave it as it is. Please act accordingly." Afterward, a recording [Mao made] of this edited version of the speech was used in the documentary "Liberated China."

treaty. For our state, this is of tremendous importance. The people throughout the country have expressed this. Many of the comrades who are present here today have made speeches, and all spoke of the [treaty's] great significance. In what circumstances did we find ourselves at the time we signed this treaty? That is to say, [this was the time during which] we defeated the enemy, that is, the reactionaries inside the country, overthrowing the reactionary clique of Chiang Kai-shek supported by the reactionaries abroad. We also expelled the foreign reactionaries from the territory of our country; [that is,] basically expelled them. But other reactionaries still exist in the world, and these are the foreign imperialists. Inside the country there are still difficulties. . . . In circumstances such as this, we need to have a friend. . . . Our relations with the Soviet Union and our friendship with the Soviet Union had to be consolidated by a law, that is, by the treaty; and [we] used the treaty to consolidate the friendship between the two countries, China and the Soviet Union, and to establish the alliance relationship. . . . If the imperialists are preparing to strike at us, then we can invite [the help of] a good supporter. This treaty is a patriotic treaty. Comrades were saying this a few moments ago, and this is right. This treaty is also an internationalist treaty; it is internationalism. Premier and Foreign Minister Zhou Enlai and many of the council members here have already expressed [their] opinions, and all of these opinions were very good. Now, since nobody else wants to speak, we can proceed with the voting; that is, with the ratification of this treaty.

SOURCE: JY, pp. 290–91.

Doc. 55. *Mao Speech at the 8th Meeting of the Central People's Government Council, June 28, 1950*[34]

The Chinese people long ago declared that the affairs of the various countries of the entire world should be managed by the people of the various countries themselves and not by the United States. The U.S. invasion of Asia can only touch off the broad and resolute opposition of Asian people. On January 5, Truman said in an announcement that the United States would not intervene in Taiwan. Now his conduct proves that what he said was false.[35] Moreover, he shredded all international agreements related to the American commitment not to intervene in China's internal affairs. The United States thus reveals its imperialist nature in its true colors. It is useful for the Chinese people and the people of Asia [to draw a lesson from the U.S. policy toward Taiwan]. The United States is unable to justify in any way its intervention in the internal affairs of Korea, the Philippines, and Vietnam. The sympathies of the Chinese people and the vast people of the world lie with the countries that have been invaded, and by no means with the American imperialism.

[34]At the 8th session of the Central People's Government Council, Zhou Enlai gave a report on the current situation and issued his statement on U.S. President Truman's announcement. After a heated discussion of the matter among council members, Mao Zedong delivered this speech.

[35]On June 27, 1950, U.S. President Truman announced that the U.S. government had decided to prevent the Chinese government from liberating Taiwan. Shortly afterward, he ordered the U.S. Seventh Fleet to move to the Taiwan Strait.

[The people] will not be lured by imperialism or be terrified by imperialism's threat. Imperialism is outwardly strong and inwardly weak because it does not have the people's support. People throughout the nation and the world, unite and make full preparations for frustrating any provocation of American imperialism.

SOURCE: JY, p. 423.

Doc. 56. Mao Letter to Nie Rongzhen[36] re the Resolution Reached at the National Defense Conference, July 7, 1950, 2400

Comrade Rongzhen:

I agree to the items in the resolution[37] reached at the conference today. Please carry it out. I will preserve the original copy.

SOURCE: JY, p. 428.

Doc. 57. Military Commission Telegram to Gao Gang re Completing the Northeast Frontier Force's Combat Preparations, Aug. 5, 1950

Comrade Gao Gang,

I [Mao] have received your telegram of August 4.

1. Various units of the Frontier Force have been assembled. It is unlikely that they will have any operational tasks before the end of the month. However, we should prepare these units for battle by the first 10 days of September. Comrade Gao Gang is assigned to be in overall charge. Please convene a meeting of the cadres at the corps and division levels in the second 10 days of the month and there instruct them on the purpose and significance of the operation and its general direction. By the end of the month, various units should make full preparations and await orders to set off. You must solve [in time] the ideological problems of the troops so as to keep up their morale and have everything in readiness. We will tell Xiao Jingguang, Deng Hua, and Xiao Hua[38] to attend the meeting.

[36]Nie Rongzhen was then the acting chief of the General Staff of the People's Liberation Army.

[37]The resolution reached at the first conference of the [Central] Military Commission encompassed five items: (1) the movement and deployment of troops: by the end of July, four corps and three artillery divisions were to be deployed at Andong (now Dandong), Ji'an, and Benxi; (2) the organization of headquarters: Su Yu was appointed commander and political commissar of the Northeast Frontier Force Command, and Xiao Hua was appointed deputy political commissar; (3) preparations for logistic support; (4) preparations for bringing (the related military units) up to full strength: the General Logistics Department was charged with formulating relevant plans for implementation by the prescribed time; and (5) political mobilization: in general, political mobilization was to be conducted under the slogan of defending national security. The General Political Department was made responsible for working out a directive with concrete plans.

[38]Xiao Jingguang, then the commander of the PLA navy, was appointed in July 1950 as the deputy commander of the Northeast Frontier Force Command. Deng Hua was then the commander of the Thirteenth Army. Xiao Hua, then the deputy director of the General Political Department, was appointed in July 1950 as the deputy political commissar of the Northeast Frontier Force Command. The command was never formally created.

2. Based on the preceding guiding principles, you may arrange for the assembly and deployment of the troops at your discretion. You may redeploy the 38th Corps along the railroad near [the city of] Siping if that is of any advantage.

SOURCE: JY, pp. 454–55.

Doc. 58. *Mao Letter to Su Yu re Delaying His Assignment, Aug. 8, 1950*

Comrade Su Yu:

Comrade Luo Ruiqing[39] has passed your letter along to me. I worry about your serious illness. Currently, your new assignment does not seem very urgent. Just get better, and do not worry until you have fully recovered. You may remain in Qingdao if that is an appropriate place for your recuperation; you can also find a rest home in Beijing if Qingdao is inappropriate for your recuperation. Please use your own discretion.

With regards,

SOURCE: JY, p. 464.

Doc. 59. *Mao Telegram to Gao Gang re Hastening the Frontier Force's Combat Readiness, Aug. 18, 1950*

Comrade Gao Gang:

1. On August 15, I received your report to the meeting of the cadres of the Frontier Force. The report is correct.

2. Comrade Xiao Jingguang came to report on the various problems regarding the Frontier Force. All of these problems can be solved.

3. The deadline for the Frontier Force to complete its training and other preparatory work can be extended up to the end of September. Please supervise and speed up the preparations so that everything is wrapped up by September 30.

SOURCE: JY, p. 469.

Doc. 60. *Mao Telegram to Peng Dehuai[40] re the Need for 12 Corps, Aug. 27, 1950*

Comrade Dehuai:

To cope with the current situation, we must now assemble 12 corps for emergency use (four corps are already assembled). The decision, however, can be made at the end of September, when we will invite you to Beijing for face-to-face discussions.

SOURCE: JY, p. 485.

[39]Luo Ruiqing was then the head of the Ministry of Public Security.
[40]Peng Dehuai was then the vice-chairman of the People's Revolutionary and Military Commission, commander and political commissar of the PLA First Field Army, and commander of the Northwest Military Region headquarters.

Doc. 61. Mao Comment on the Ninth Army's Orders,[41] *Sept. 8, 1950*

By the end of October, the entire Ninth Army can move to the railroad line between Xuzhou and Jinan. In the second 10 days of November, the army can start training and consolidation.[42] During the period of training and consolidation, the army will still be under the jurisdiction of the East China [Military Region Command]; however, it is appropriate to put the [supply of] equipment and the formulating of the guiding principles and plans for training and consolidation under the direct administration of the [Central] Military Commission.

SOURCE: JY, p. 498.

Doc. 62. Excerpt from Zhou Enlai's Report to the Chinese People's Political Consultative Conference, Sept. 30, 1950[43]

The problem of establishing diplomatic relations with capitalist countries is more complicated than that of establishing trade relations. Here I may mention, especially, our long-drawn-out negotiations with Britain, out of which nothing has come yet. The reason for the fruitlessness of the negotiations is that the British government has made known its recognition of the People's Republic of China on the one hand while on the other it agrees to permit the so-called "representatives" of the reactionary rump of the Chinese Kuomintang clique to continue its illegal occupation of China's seat in the United Nations. This makes it difficult to commence formal diplomatic relations between China and Britain. Furthermore, Britain's extremely unjustifiable and unfriendly attitude toward Chinese residents in Hong Kong and other places cannot fail to draw the serious attention of the Central People's Government.

Throughout the Chinese people's war of liberation, the U.S. government sided with the enemy of the Chinese people, assisting the Kuomintang reactionaries with all its might in their attacks on the Chinese people. The enmity that the U.S. government harbors toward the Chinese people has increased since the founding of the People's Republic of China.

Despite the just criticisms of the Soviet Union, India, and other countries, the United States stubbornly obstructs the representatives of the PRC from attending the United Nations and its various organs, and shamelessly protects the seat of the so-called "representatives" of the Kuomintang reactionary rump. Similarly, the United States debars the Chinese representatives from attending the Allied Council for Japan and plots to exclude China and the Soviet Union in concluding a peace treaty with Japan, in order to rearm Japan and retain America's occupation troops and military bases in Japan.

[41]This comment was written on a report submitted by the PLA East China Military Region Command on September 5, 1950, on the northward movement of the Ninth Army.
[42]["Training and consolidation" translates *zhengxun*; by "consolidation," the Chinese normally mean "reorganizing for the purpose of strengthening."—TRANS.]
[43][For the full text of the foreign policy part of the report, see Zhou Enlai, "Foreign Policies," pp. 20–24.—TRANS.]

The United States deliberately concocted the assault of the Syngman Rhee gang against the Korean Democratic People's Republic in order to expand its aggression in the East and then, on the pretext of the situation in Korea, dispatched its naval and air forces to invade the Taiwan Province of China; [and] announced that the so-called problem of Taiwan's status should be solved by the American-controlled United Nations. Moreover, time after time, it sent its air force, which is invading Korea, to intrude into the air over the Liaodong Province of China, strafing and bombing; and sent its naval forces, which are invading Korea, to bombard Chinese merchant ships on the high seas.

By these frenzied and violent acts of imperialist aggression, the U.S. government has displayed itself as the most dangerous foe to the PRC. The U.S. aggressive forces have invaded China's borders and may at any time expand their aggression. [Gen. Douglas] MacArthur, commander-in-chief of American aggression against Taiwan and Korea, has long ago disclosed the aggressive design of the U.S. government, and is continuing to invent new excuses for extending its aggression.

The Chinese people firmly oppose the aggressive brutalities of America and are determined to liberate Taiwan and other Chinese territory from the clutches of the U.S. aggressors.

The Chinese people have been closely following the situation in Korea since she was invaded by the U.S.A. The Korean people and their People's Army are resolute and valorous. Led by Premier Kim Il Sung, they have scored remarkable achievements in resisting the American invaders and have won the sympathy and support of people throughout the world. The Korean people can surely overcome their many difficulties and obtain final victory, on the principle of persistent, long-term resistance.

The Chinese are peace-loving people. One hundred and twenty million Chinese have already signed their names to the celebrated Stockholm Appeal, and this signature movement is continuing to develop among the Chinese people. It is obvious that the Chinese people, after liberating the whole territory of their own country, want to rehabilitate and develop their industrial and agricultural production and cultural and educational work in a peaceful environment, free from threats. But if the American aggressors take this as a sign of weakness of the Chinese people, they will commit the same fatal blunder as the Kuomintang reactionaries. The Chinese people enthusiastically love peace, but in order to defend peace, they never have been and never will be afraid to oppose aggressive war. The Chinese people absolutely will not tolerate foreign aggression, nor will they supinely tolerate seeing their neighbors being savagely invaded by the imperialists.

Whoever attempts to exclude the nearly 500,000,000 Chinese people from the UN, and whoever sets at naught and violates the interest of this one-fourth of mankind in the world and fancies vainly to solve any Far Eastern problem directly concerned with China arbitrarily, will certainly break their skulls.

SOURCE: "Fight for the Consolidation and Development of the Chinese People's Victory," *China Monthly Review*, Nov. 1950, p. 104.

Doc. 63. *Mao Telegram to Stalin re the Decision to Send Troops to Korea, Oct. 2, 1950*

1. We have decided to send some of our troops to Korea under the name of [Chinese People's] Volunteers to fight the United States and its lackey Syngman Rhee[44] and to aid our Korean comrades. From the following considerations, we think it necessary to do so: the Korean revolutionary force will meet with a fundamental defeat, and the American aggressors will rampage unchecked once they occupy the whole of Korea. This will be unfavorable to the entire East.

2. Since we have decided to send Chinese troops to fight the Americans in Korea, we hold that, first, we should be able to solve the problem; that is, [we are] ready to annihilate and drive out the invading armies of the United States and other countries. Second, since Chinese troops are to fight American troops in Korea (although we will use the name Volunteers), we must be prepared for a declaration of war by the United States and for the subsequent use of the U.S. air force to bomb many of China's main cities and industrial bases, as well as an attack by the U.S. navy on [our] coastal areas.

3. Of these two problems, the primary problem is whether or not the Chinese troops can annihilate the American troops in Korea and effectively resolve the Korean issue. Only when it is possible for our troops to annihilate the American troops in Korea, principally the Eighth Army (an old army with combat effectiveness), can the situation become favorable to the revolutionary camp and to China, although the second problem (a declaration of war by the United States) is still a serious one. This means that the Korean issue will be solved in reality along with the defeat of American troops (in name it probably will remain unsolved because the United States most likely will not admit Korea's victory for a considerable period of time). Consequently, even if the United States declares war on China, the war will probably not be of great scope or last long. The most unfavorable situation, we hold, would result from the inability of the Chinese troops to annihilate American troops in Korea and the involvement of the two countries' troops in a stalemate while the United States publicly declares war on China, undermines the plans for China's economic reconstruction, which has already begun, and sparks the dissatisfaction of [China's] national bourgeoisie and other segments of the people (they are very afraid of war).

4. Under the current situation, we have reached a decision to order the 12 divisions stationed in advance in South Manchuria[45] to set off on October 15.[46] They will be deployed in appropriate areas in North Korea (not necessarily reaching to the 38th parallel). On the one hand, they will fight the enemies who dare to cross the 38th parallel. At the initial stage, they will merely engage in defensive warfare

[44]Syngman Rhee was then the South Korean president.
[45]South Manchuria is an old name for the areas to the southwest of Shenyang and to the east of the Shenyang–Dalian railroad line, embracing Liaozhong, Zhuanghe, Dandong, Tonghua, Linjiang, and Qingyuan.
[46]The schedule was later changed. These troops were ordered to set off on October 19.

to wipe out small detachments of enemy troops and ascertain the enemy's situation; on the other hand, they will wait for the delivery of Soviet weapons. Once they are [well] equipped, they will cooperate with the Korean comrades in counterattacks to annihilate American aggressor troops.

5. According to our intelligence to date, an American corps (composed of two infantry divisions and a mechanized division) has 1,500 guns of 70mm to 240mm caliber, including tank cannons and anti-aircraft guns. In comparison, each of our corps (composed of three divisions) has only 36 such guns.[47] The enemy dominates the air. By comparison, we have only just started training pilots. We shall not be able to employ more than 300 aircraft in combat until February 1951. Accordingly, we do not now have any certainty of success in annihilating a single American corps in one blow. Since we have made the decision to fight the Americans, we certainly must be prepared to deal with a situation in which the U.S. headquarters will employ one American corps against our troops in one [of the Korean] theaters. For the purpose of eliminating completely one enemy corps with a certainty of success, we should in such a situation assemble four times as many troops as the enemy (employing four corps to deal with one enemy corps) and firepower from one-and-a-half times to twice as heavy as the enemy's (using 2,200 to 3,000 guns of more than 70mm caliber to deal with 1,500 enemy guns of the same caliber).

6. In addition to the above-mentioned 12 divisions, we are moving 24 divisions from south of the Yangtze River and from Shaanxi and Gansu provinces to areas along the Xuzhou–Lanzhou, Tianjin–Pukou, and Beijing–Shenyang railroad lines. We plan to employ these divisions as the second and third groups of troops sent to aid Korea in the spring and summer of next year as the future situation requires.

SOURCE: JY, pp. 539–41.

Doc. 64. *Zhou Enlai Talk with Indian Ambassador K. M. Panikkar, Oct. 3, 1950*

Premier Zhou Enlai (hereafter called Zhou for short): The day before yesterday [Oct. 1] I received the letter from Prime Minister Nehru you forwarded, Mr. Ambassador. Thank you. The questions Prime Minister Nehru raised involved a wide range [of topics] and, therefore, it will take us time to review [them]. We acknowledge his kindness and appreciate his efforts [to preserve peace in Asia]. Of all the questions raised by Prime Minister Nehru, the issue of Korea is relatively urgent. U.S. troops are going to cross the 38th parallel in an attempt to extend the war. If the U.S. troops really do so, we cannot sit by idly and remain indifferent. We will intervene. Please report this to the Prime Minister of your country.

Ambassador Panikkar (hereafter called Panikkar for short): I have anticipated the possibility of such a situation. Accordingly, on September 26, I reported in a

---

[47]An American division then had 476 guns, consisting of 76 mortars of over 70 mm caliber, 120 recoilless guns, 72 howitzers, 144 tank cannons, and 64 anti-aircraft guns of various types. An American corps (three divisions) had 1,428 guns of various types. A CPV corps then had 198 guns: 126 mortars of over 70 mm caliber, 36 infantry guns, and 36 mountain guns.

cable to our government that the aftermath would be even worse than expected if the U.S. troops crossed the 38th parallel. Prime Minister Nehru thus wrote this letter to Your Excellency. As far as I know, he also signaled a warning in his official letters to the U.S. and British governments. At a press conference, in the Security Council, and in the UN General Assembly, the head of our country's delegation to the United Nations, Mr. [B. N.] Rau, has already read aloud the section on the Korean issue in Your Excellency's report of October 1.[48] Our government is doing its best to continue to exert pressure.

Zhou: We have exchanged points of view on the Korean incident. We favor a peaceful solution and the localization of the Korean incident. That is still our stand. I declared our government's attitude [toward the incident] in the October 1 report. We want peace and want construction in peacetime. During the past year, we made maximum efforts in this respect. The U.S. government is unreliable. Although an agreement reached at the meeting of the three foreign ministers [of France, Great Britain, and the United States in early September] stipulates that the 38th parallel cannot be crossed without the approval of the United Nations, there is some question whether the agreement is binding on the U.S. government.

Panikkar: Some signs suggest that the U.S. government will probably violate the agreement reached at the meeting of the three foreign ministers. [Gen. Douglas] MacArthur is exerting great pressure on the U.S. government. It was reported yesterday that South Korean troops had gone nine miles north of the 38th parallel.

Zhou: We have received the same information. [The crossing of the 38th parallel] reportedly happened on the eastern coast. It is also reported that troops under the command of [U.S.] General [Walton] Walker have crossed the 38th parallel. However, it has not been stated whether these troops were South Korean or American.

Panikkar: I will report to Prime Minister Nehru immediately. In addition to what you have told me, is there anything Your Excellency wants me to report? Are there any proposals?

Zhou: We need to review Prime Minister Nehru's letter. As to all other things, I will let you know [our view] when we meet next time.

Panikkar: Does the localization of the Korean incident, as Your Excellency said, mean confining the Korean armed conflict south of the 38th parallel? Or do you mean an immediate halt to the Korean armed conflict?

Zhou: The Korean armed conflict ought to stop immediately, and foreign troops ought to be withdrawn [from Korea]. This will be advantageous to peace in the East. Our idea for localizing the Korean incident is just to make efforts to keep the aggression of U.S. troops from expanding into an incident of worldwide dimensions.

Panikkar: The localization of the Korean incident currently contains two problems. First of all, U.S. troops are going to cross the 38th parallel. Accordingly, the localization of the Korean incident probably means the immediate withdrawal of

[48][For a complete text, see "Fight for the Consolidation and Development of the Chinese People's Victory."—TRANS.]

the U.S. troops that will have crossed the 38th parallel. Second, the Korean incident must be solved in a peaceful way. Various countries concerned, such as China and the Soviet Union, must participate in the discussion of this issue. So that I might write a relatively definitive report to Prime Minister Nehru, would you please let me know the contents of any proposals acceptable to China?

Zhou: There are two questions involved. First of all, U.S. troops are going to cross the 38th parallel in an attempt to expand the war. We will intervene. This serious situation is created by the U.S. government. Second, we advocate that the Korean incident be solved peacefully. Our position is that there must not only be an immediate halt to the Korean armed conflict and withdrawal of all aggressor troops from Korea, but also be negotiations on a peaceful solution by the concerned countries at the UN.

Panikkar: I am obliged to point out the problem of too little time. U.S. troops will probably cross the 38th parallel within 12 hours. However, the Indian government will not be able to take any effective action until 18 hours after the receipt of my cable. When the time comes, it probably will be too late for any peaceful plan to work.

Zhou: That is the Americans' business. The purpose of this evening's talk is to let you know our attitude toward one of the questions raised by Prime Minister Nehru in his letter.

SOURCE: Zhou Enlai, "We Will Intervene If U.S. Troops Cross the 38th Parallel," *Zhou Enlai Waijiao Wenxuan* [Selected Diplomatic Documents of Zhou Enlai] (Beijing, 1990), pp. 25–27.

Doc. 65. *Mao Directive Creating the Chinese People's Volunteers, Oct. 8, 1950*

Peng [Dehuai], Gao [Gang], He [Jinnian],[49] Deng [Hua], Hong [Xuezhi], Xie [Fang],[50] and leading comrades of various levels of the Chinese People's Volunteers:

1. In order to support the Korean people's war of liberation and to resist the attacks of U.S. imperialism and its running dogs, thereby safeguarding the interests of the people of Korea, China, and all the other countries in the East, I herewith order the name of the Northeast Frontier Force changed to the Chinese People's Volunteers and order the Chinese People's Volunteers to march speedily to Korea and join the Korean comrades in fighting the aggressors and winning a glorious victory.

2. The following units are put under the jurisdiction of the Chinese People's Volunteers: the 38th, 39th, 40th, and 42nd corps of the Thirteenth Army, and the headquarters of the Artillery Command of the [Northeast] Frontier Force and the 1st, 2nd, and 8th artillery divisions. The foregoing units should immediately get everything in readiness and await orders to set off.

[49]He Jinnian was then the deputy commander of the PLA Northeast Military Region Command.
[50]Hong Xuezhi was then the deputy commander of the Thirteenth Army. Xie Fang was then the chief of staff of the Thirteenth Army.

3. Comrade Peng Dehuai is appointed commander and political commissar of the Chinese People's Volunteers.

4. The Northeast Administrative Region is to be the general rear base for the Chinese People's Volunteers. Comrade Gao Gang, commander and political commissar of the Northeast Military Region Command, is responsible for handling affairs relevant to providing logistic support and aid to the Korean comrades.

5. While in Korea, the Chinese People's Volunteers must show fraternal feelings and respect for the people, the People's Army, the democratic government, the Workers' Party (namely, the Communist Party), and other democratic parties of Korea, as well as Comrade Kim Il Sung, the leader of the Korean people, and strictly observe military and political discipline. This is a most important political basis for ensuring the fulfillment of your military task.

6. You must fully anticipate possible and inevitable difficulties and be prepared to overcome them with great enthusiasm, courage, care, and stamina. At present, the international and domestic situation as a whole is favorable to us, not to the aggressors. So long as you comrades are firm and brave and good at uniting with the people there and at fighting the aggressors, final victory will be ours.

SOURCE: JY, pp. 543–44. Mao put his name to this with the formal title Chairman of the Chinese Peoples' Revolutionary Military Commission.

Doc. 66. Mao Telegram to Kim Il Sung re China's Entry in the War, Oct. 8, 1950

Comrade Kim Il Sung c/o Comrade Ni Zhiliang:[51]

1. In view of the current situation, we have decided to send volunteers to Korea to help you fight against the aggressors.

2. Comrade Peng Dehuai holds the posts of commander and political commissar of the Chinese People's Volunteers.

3. Comrade Gao Gang, commander and political commissar of the Northeast Military Region Command, is in charge of the rear service for the Chinese People's Volunteers and other arrangements in Manchuria to aid Korea.

4. Please immediately send Comrade Pak Il U[52] to Shenyang to discuss with Comrades Peng Dehuai and Gao Gang various problems regarding the operations of the Chinese People's Volunteers in Korea. (Comrades Peng and Gao will leave for Shenyang from Beijing today.)

SOURCE: JY, p. 545.

[51]Ni Zhiliang was then China's ambassador to the Democratic People's Republic of Korea. [China had only dispatched Ni to Korea two months before, on Aug. 13, 1950. —TRANS.]

[52]Pak Il U was then a member of the Standing Committee of the Politburo of the Workers' Party of Korea and head of the Ministry of Internal Affairs. [Pak was a member of the so-called Yan'an faction or Chinese-trained group in the North Korean government.—TRANS.]

*Doc. 67. Zhou Enlai Telegram Confirming Gao Gang's Responsibilities,
Oct. 9, 1950*

Ambassador Ni [Zhiliang] and Gao [Gang] c/o Ni:
  Your telegram of [Oct.] 8, 0100, has been received.
  1. The central leadership has assigned Comrade Gao Gang to be in charge of
all the affairs regarding aid to the Korean comrades. Please hereafter consult directly with Comrade Gao Gang about these affairs and let Gao give the answers.
Please ask Gao to handle the problems relevant to the Tank School and the Military
School.
  2. I agree with your idea on the location of the embassy.

SOURCE: JY, p. 546.

*Doc. 68. Excerpt from Mao Telegram to Kim Il Sung re Opening a Front
Behind Enemy Lines, Oct. 10, 1950*

Kim [Il Sung] c/o Ni [Zhiliang]; also inform Peng [Dehuai]:
  2. Currently, massive enemy troops are advancing northward. The enemy rear
is weakly defended. I suggest that the [Korean] People's Army units that cannot
withdraw to the north should remain in South Korea and open another front in the
enemy's rear areas. Strategically speaking, this will be necessary and useful. It will
be very helpful to the operations in the north if 40,000–50,000 troops of the
People's Army could remain in South Korea to undertake the assignment.

SOURCE: JY, p. 547.

*Doc. 69. Mao Telegram re the Lack of the Promised Air Cover, Oct. 11,
1950*

Peng [Dehuai]; also inform Gao [Gang] and Deng [Hua]:
  Your telegrams of October 9 and 10 have been received.
  1. I agree with your idea of dispatching all four corps and three artillery divisions and assembling them in the areas you have selected to await opportunities to
annihilate the enemy.
  2. In a telegram to [the] East China [Military Region Command], I have ordered an anti-aircraft regiment moved from Shanghai to Shenyang on October
14. Gao should pay attention to its transfer to other trains [on its arrival in Shen-
yang].
  3. I have already answered [your] other questions elsewhere. The [Soviet] air
force, however, cannot set off for the time being.

SOURCE: JY, p. 548.

Doc. 70. Mao Telegram to Chen Yi[53] re Moving the Ninth Army North Immediately, Oct. 12, 1950

Comrade Chen Yi:

Please order Song Shilun's[54] [Ninth] army to move directly northward for Northeast China ahead of schedule. Please let me know when the army is able to set off.

SOURCE: JY, p. 551.

Doc. 71. Mao Telegram Countermanding the Order to Send the Thirteenth Army to Korea, Oct. 12, 1950, 2000

Peng [Dehuai], Gao [Gang], Deng [Hua], Hong [Xuezhi], Han [Xianchu], Xie [Fang]:

1. For the time being, do not carry out the order issued on October 9. Various units of the Thirteenth Army should remain for training in the places where they were originally stationed. Do not set off [for North Korea].

2. Tomorrow or the day after tomorrow, Comrades Gao Gang and Peng Dehuai should come to Beijing for further discussions.

SOURCE: JY, p. 552.

Doc. 72. Central Committee Telegram Countermanding the Order to Move the Ninth Army and Other Units, Oct. 12, 1950

Rao [Shushi],[55] Chen [Yi]:

1. For the time being, do not carry out the order issued on October 9. Various units in Northeast China should remain for training and consolidation in the places where they were originally stationed. Temporarily, they should not set off.

2. Song Shilun's [Ninth] army should also remain for training and consolidation in the places where it was originally stationed.

3. Also do not give new explanations to the cadres and democratic personages.

SOURCE: JY, p. 553.

Doc. 73. Mao Telegram to Zhou Enlai in Moscow re the Advantages of Entering the War, Oct. 13, 1950

1. After discussion with comrades on the Politburo, we have reached a consensus that the entry of our army into Korea continues to be to our advantage. In the first phase, we can only fight the puppet [Republic of Korea] army. With a certainty of success in dealing with the puppet army, we can establish a base in the large

[53]Chen Yi was then the commander of the PLA East China Military Region. [He was also the commander of the PLA Third Field Army and the mayor of Shanghai.—TRANS.]
[54]Song Shilun was then the commander and political commissar of the PLA Ninth Army.
[55]Rao Shushi was then the political commissar of the PLA East China Military Region Command.

mountain area to the north of the Wonsan-Pyongyang line and thus encourage the Korean people. The Korean situation would change to our advantage if we could wipe out several divisions of the puppet army in the first phase.

2. The adoption of our active policy mentioned above is extremely favorable to China, Korea, the East, and the world. If we do not send troops [to Korea], the reactionaries at home and abroad will be swollen with arrogance when the enemy troops press to the Yalu River border. Consequently, it will be unfavorable to various parties and especially unfavorable to Northeast China. [In such a situation,] the entire Northeast Frontier Force will be tied down and the power supplies in South Manchuria will be controlled [by hostile parties].

In short, we hold that we should enter the war. We must enter the war. Entering the war is greatly to our advantage; it is greatly to our disadvantage if we do not enter the war.

SOURCE: JY, p. 556.

Doc. 74. Mao Telegram to Chen Yi re Assembling the Ninth Army in Taian and Qufu, Oct. 14, 1950, 0100

Comrade Chen Yi:

I have received your telegram sent at 2100, [Oct.] 12.

1. It is all right for the follow-up units of Song's [Shilun] [Ninth] army to leave the Shanghai-Changshu area between 1700 and 1900 on the 28th. As planned, Song's army should assemble in the area centered on Taian and Qufu for a period of training and consolidation and await orders to set off for the Northeast.

2. The anti-aircraft regiment still needs to be relocated to the Northeast.

3. Please let me know on which date the Shanghai People's Congress will be held.

SOURCE: JY, p. 557.

Doc. 75. Mao Telegram to Zhou Enlai in Moscow re the Current Status of the War, Oct. 14, 1950, 0300

Comrade Enlai:

A. Korean situation:

1. The U.S. 1st, 2nd, and 24th divisions, the British 25th Brigade, and the puppet [South Korean] 1st Division are assembling in the Kaesong-Kumchon area along the 38th parallel north of Seoul and making preparations for an attack on Pyongyang. It is reported today that the U.S. 2nd Division is to move toward Kumchon and gain a foothold. Judging from this, the United States has not made a final decision whether or when to attack Pyongyang.

2. The puppet Capital and 3rd divisions have reached Wonsan. The puppet 6th, 7th, and 8th divisions are moving toward the Wonsan area, where they will assemble and be resupplied by sea.

3. The U.S. Marine Corps 1st Division is in Seoul; the U.S. 25th Division is at the Taejon-Suwon front; and the U.S. 7th Division is at the Pusan-Taegu front. The headquarters of the U.S. Eighth Army is in Taejon. In South Korea, the advance of

two puppet divisions is being checked. In most parts of Korea, the enemy's rear is weakly defended.

4. Under Kim Il Sung's command, the various [North] Korean units that still have combat capability are resolutely resisting the enemy on the 38th parallel. The [Korean] People's Army has withdrawn about 50,000 soldiers from South [Korea] to areas north of the 38th parallel. Most of them still remain in the South. The People's Army has recovered the port of Ulchin [in South Korea].

. B. In Andong [Dandong], Comrade Peng Dehuai studied the [war] situation and holds that the following things will happen if our army can dispatch one corps to the mountainous areas in Tokchon County about 200 kilometers northeast of Pyongyang and deploy the three other corps and three artillery divisions to the Huichon-Chonchon-Kanggye area north of Tokchon. First of all, we can probably force the U.S. and puppet troops to think twice before continuing to advance north-ward and to protect the areas north of the Pyongyang-Wonsan front, at least the mountainous areas, from being occupied by the enemy. Thus, our army does not have to engage in fighting and can gain time to become well equipped and trained. Second, if the enemy at Pyongyang and Wonsan begins advancing northward and attacks the mountainous areas in Tokchon and other places, we can use our main forces to annihilate the puppet troops coming from the direction of Wonsan while employing adequate forces to pin down the enemy troops at Pyongyang. If we can completely wipe out one to two or even three puppet divisions, we can greatly change the [war] situation. Comrades Peng [Dehuai] and Gao Gang both hold that we are assured of success in fighting the puppet troops. Just as I do, they both hold that our entry into the war is necessary and advantageous.

C. Today Gao [Gang] will return to Shenyang to take an active part in arranging the preparations for our entry into the war. Peng will remain in Beijing temporarily to await your reply telegram.

SOURCE: JY, pp. 558–59.

Doc. 76. *Mao Telegram to Zhou Enlai in Moscow re the Plan of Attack, Oct. 14, 1950*

1. I have told Peng Dehuai to construct two or three defensive fronts in the areas north of the Pyongyang–Wonsan Railroad and south of the Tokchon–Yongwon road after he reaches Tokchon and studies the situation there. If the enemy launches an attack, we will break up [his units] into many pockets and wipe them out in front of our positions one by one. If the U.S. troops from Pyongyang and the [South Korean] puppet troops from Wonsan simultaneously launch attacks, we will con-centrate our efforts on fighting the enemy troops that are isolated and relatively weak. Now we are determined to fight the puppet troops and may also fight some isolated U.S. troops. Our troops will continue improving [their] defense works if they have enough time. If the enemy tenaciously defends Pyongyang and Wonsan and does not advance [north] in the next six months, our troops will not attack Pyongyang and Wonsan. Our troops will attack Pyongyang and Wonsan only when they are well equipped and trained, and we have clear superiority over the enemy

in both air and ground forces. In short, we will not talk about waging offensives for six months. [By holding off] we will have a certainty of success, and so it is in our interest to do that.

2. At present, the U.S. troops remain near the 38th parallel. It will take time for them to reach Pyongyang. It will take more time for them to attack Tokchon from Pyongyang. We estimate that it will be difficult for the puppet troops in Wonsan to launch an attack on their own if the U.S. troops do not attack Tokchon from Pyongyang. So this leaves time for the entry of our troops [into the areas around Tokchon] and for the construction of defense works and the organization of our defenses.

3. Our troops are to set off on October 19. It will take seven days for the advance corps to go by foot to Tokchon. They will spend a day or two resting there. They can arrive in the areas south of the Tokchon–Yongwon road on October 28, and then they will start constructing defense works there. It will take 10 days, until October 28, for all our troops, totaling 260,000 men, to cross the [Yalu] river.

4. So as to be prepared to win a victory when the enemy launches offensives against the Tokchon area in November, we still think that it is better for us to send all the 260,000 men (12 infantry divisions and three artillery divisions) to Korea. In the event they complete the construction of the defense works, and the enemy does not dare to launch attacks and confines himself to the defense of Pyongyang and Wonsan, we will transfer about half our troops [from Korea] back to China. The returned troops will engage in training and get grain supplies in China and will return to Korea if a big war should break out.

5. While half our troops are still entering [Korea] and constructing defense works, it will be useful to us for the Korean People's Army to continue its resistance and to do its best to pin down the U.S. and puppet troops.

SOURCE: JY, pp. 560–61.

Doc. 77. *Peng Dehuai Speech to Cadres of the Chinese People's Volunteers, Oct. 14, 1950*[56]

1. The U.S. imperialists are employing seven divisions and the lackey troops of Syngman Rhee in unbridled aggression against the Korean revolutionary government and people. Having crossed the 38th parallel, the enemy is continuing to advance northward with all his might. The current war situation in Korea is very serious. What attitude should we adopt when a fraternal party and the laboring people of a neighboring nation are suffering aggression and in a very difficult situation? After repeated discussions and careful consideration, the central leadership holds that we "cannot ignore it." That is to say, we will actively support the North Korean people to oppose the aggressors and help them strive for independence, freedom, and liberation. I think it extremely necessary and very correct for the central leadership to have made such a decision. However, there were differences of

[56]Peng delivered this speech in his capacity as the CPV's commander and political commissar at the headquarters of the Northeast Military Region in Shenyang. [The meeting was limited to cadres of division-level or above.—TRANS.]

opinion within the Party about this problem. All comrades here are Party members. If you have different opinions, you may put them forward for discussion.

Currently there are two opinions. One opinion is against or wants to postpone the dispatch of troops to Korea for the following reasons: (1) we have not healed the wounds of war; (2) we have not completed the work of land reform; (3) we have not rooted out all domestic bandits and special agents; (4) the preparation of military equipment and training has not been completed; and (5) some soldiers and civilians are war weary. In brief, [people with these opinions] do not favor sending troops for the time being because of inadequate preparations. The other opinion advocates dispatching troops immediately, based on the following considerations. Although we have not made adequate preparations, the enemy is not fully prepared either; the U.S. imperialists especially have not made adequate preparations. As the Central Military Commission has pointed out in a study, the U.S. army has 21 divisions in total. Seventeen [of these] divisions have combat capability. There are all together 1,460,000 people in the [U.S.] army, navy, and air force; [that is,] including the recently mobilized, there are one and a half million in all. By next June, an additional half million men will be conscripted. The total will be some two million. Thus, there will be 834,000 men in the army, 579,000 in the navy, 150,000 in the marine corps, and 584,000 in the air force. The British and French armed forces are even shorter of men. France has suffered many defeats in Vietnam. The Vietnamese recently liberated [the provincial capital] Cao Bang [in northern Vietnam] and other strongpoints and linked up the Sino-Vietnamese border. The French imperialists then became very nervous. Britain has even more difficulties.

Why does the imperialist bloc want to go into battle if it is not fully prepared? By waging war, the imperialists are attempting to consolidate their internal control, extend their influence, and win over some wavering countries. These are the true reasons for their adoption of a policy of war. The U.S. imperialists are making an empty show of strength in order to frighten those people who suffer from the fear-of-the-United-States illness. The relatively heavy blows the Korean People's Army inflicted [on the U.S. aggressors] in the initial stages [of the war] have greatly undermined their prestige. Therefore, they pieced together their forces in the Pacific to launch a desperate offensive. Having landed at Inchon and occupied Seoul, they are once again throwing their weight around. If we do not strike timely blows against them, a considerable number of wavering countries and strata will move toward U.S. imperialism. In reality, the active offensive of U.S. imperialism merely mirrors its worry about exposing its weak points.

Why has the belated economic crisis of the U.S. imperialists not broken out? They have temporarily relieved their economic crisis by giving [their economy] an injection of heart medicine. But a serious crisis still exists. One means adopted by the imperialists to avert economic crises is to raise the salaries of the masses slightly and put commodity prices under control. The other means to find a way out is to wage war. War is advantageous to a handful of big U.S. capitalists and disadvantageous to other classes and strata.

If we do not dispatch troops to actively support the Korean revolutionary government and people, the reactionaries at home and abroad will be swollen with arrogance and the pro-American people will be more active. We will be put under direct threat if U.S. imperialism should occupy all of Korea. Our country will be thrown into passivity, and our national defense and frontier defense will be placed in a disadvantageous position should U.S. imperialism transfer its forces to Vietnam and Burma and do mischief there. The impact on foreign affairs will also be bad because some countries will move closer to U.S. imperialism.

Would it be better for us to relax for a while and fight a war [against U.S. imperialism] three to five years from now? That surely would be better. However, we would still have to fight such a war three to five years from now. Such a war would destroy our small industry, whose construction will have taken us three to five years. At that time, it would be more difficult for us to check such an invasion because U.S. imperialism will have armed Japan, and Japan will be able to dispatch a relatively large number of troops. By that time, U.S. imperialism will probably also have armed West Germany. We should not neglect the huge output of iron and steel of West Germany. By that time, also, the revolution in other West European countries will probably have been suppressed, and the revolutionary forces weakened. After careful calculation, it is perhaps more advantageous for us to fight such a war now. Accordingly, we are not afraid of fighting a war right now.

But we hope that it will not be a big war and do not want to declare war against the United States. We shall merely support the Korean revolutionary war in the name of People's Volunteers. If we want to strive for peace, we will have to experience arduous and serious struggles. The worldwide revolutionary forces have gained the upper hand since the victory of our country's revolution. How pathetic for the world revolution [it would be] if we stood by with folded arms and did not actively help a neighboring nation struggle against aggression. On the other hand, it is impossible for us to strengthen our national defense and build [our] heavy industry [to the necessary extent] within a period of three to five years. We should not place excessive hopes [in achieving such a goal] within five years. Within such a short period as three to five years, it would be impossible for us to improve greatly the equipment of our army and air force, let alone the equipment of our navy. Therefore, it is better for us to fight an early war rather than a later one.

2. According to the available information, our enemies in Korea consist of seven U.S. divisions, each made up of 12,000 men whose morale is not high; seven puppet divisions that have some combat capability; one British brigade; and a few troops from other vassal countries. The U.S. troops are mainly deployed at Pusan, Taegu, and Seoul; the puppet troops are mainly deployed on the eastern coast. Three divisions have already occupied Wonsan. On October 1, both U.S. troops and the puppet troops crossed the 38th parallel. The enemy troops on the west are attacking Kumchon, about 100 *li* [50 km] from Pyongyang. If they continue launching offensives, the enemy forces will be dispersed. In addition, they will need to hold back some forces to deal with guerrilla forces. The enemy can release [only] three U.S. divisions and three puppet divisions for the northward advance. We can resist such forces. Although the U.S. air force has not used many [planes] in Korea, it still dominates the air. But the air force cannot decide the outcome of the war. The air

force has its own difficulties. In addition, the air force is not as fearsome as people think. The enemy's armored forces and artillery temporarily also hold a dominant position. In this regard, the enemy is stronger than we are.

But so long as we can construct good defense works and camouflage and conceal the movement [of our forces], we will be able to check the enemy's offensives and win victories. From the standpoint of tactical operations, we are better than the enemy. Our resolute and brave tactical operations consist in having the courage to fight close combat using dynamite, fighting the enemy with bayonets, and throwing hand grenades. The enemy is afraid of such operations. Our troops are of much higher political quality than the enemy's. The enemy's difficulties are increasing, and his superiority will not last long. The U.S. imperialists crossed vast oceans to fight a war. They have difficulties in the supply and transport [of weapons and equipment]. It takes them 38 days to complete the roundtrip [to and from the United States]. They fight a war for imperialism. [Their] people oppose war, and [their] soldiers are war weary; we receive the sympathy and assistance of the people of the world because we are fighting a just war for the liberation of oppressed people. These are the basic factors that will decide the outcome of the war.

[As for] our strength, the tentative operational plan calls for deploying four corps and three artillery divisions, totaling 250,000 men, on the first line; 150,000 men on the second line; and 200,000 men on the third line. The forces will total 600,000 in all. We will have eight air regiments by next month and 16 air regiments by the month after that. We will be able to equip 30 [infantry] divisions within six months. We do not have a problem in the supply of artillery pieces and shells.

Because of the enemy's situation and the topographical conditions of Korea, the mobile warfare of marching and retreating in big strides that we adopted in the civil war is not necessarily suited to the battlefield in Korea. Owing to the narrowness of Korea and some of the enemy's advantages, we must combine mobile warfare with positional warfare. We will resist the enemy and hold him in check when he launches an offensive; we will launch counterattacks, penetrate the enemy's rear area, and resolutely wipe out the enemy as soon as we discover his weak points. It is surely our task to defend territory, but it is more important for us to annihilate the enemy's effective strength. We will resolutely and thoroughly wipe out even [as little as] one battalion or one regiment whenever we have the opportunity to do so. Our tactical operations are flexible. We will not defend a certain position to the last; however, we will hold fast to our positions if need be. We will not devote ourselves to pure defense. We will consolidate our positions and defend territory only after we have seized the opportunity and annihilated a large number of the enemy. It will be best if we can wipe out the enemy as well as defend land. All of us should make specific adjustments to the situation as it develops on the battlefield.

As for positional warfare, we should adopt [the tactics of] defense in depth. Each squad should be divided into three or four teams. So as to ensure mutual support through cross-fire, these teams should be deployed in plum blossom—shaped pillboxes 20–30 meters apart. By constructing such defense works, we can reduce casualties from the enemy's bombing and shelling. We should deliberately build some camouflaged works to attract the enemy's fire and consume his shells. To deal with the enemy's tanks, our soldiers should conceal themselves in covered positions. When the tanks approach, our soldiers can launch surprise attacks and destroy them with explosives in close combat. Our artillery should also conceal itself by constructing covered positions and not expose itself. It takes time and labor to construct such pillboxes as the Nationalists used to build. It is easy for those pillboxes to be discovered and destroyed. They are inappropriate for us.

3. We are Communist Party members and internationalists. It is our duty to dispatch troops in support of the Korean people and a fraternal Party. The occupation of Korea by imperialism is a direct threat to our country's security. To aid Korea is to consolidate our victory, consolidate our national defense, and defend the industry in Northeast China. Therefore, we must under no circumstances be arrogant or take on the air of big-nation support troops. Do [take care to] respect the Korean Party, the People's Government, the People's Army, the [Korean] mass organizations, and the [Korean] broad masses. The Korean Party is still young. We should study its merits in all modesty, such as being very active and brave and not flinching from the difficulty of struggling resolutely against the enemy. It is inappropriate for us to criticize its shortcomings carelessly and still more so, to deliberately look for its shortcomings. As to seeking shortcomings, we have shortcomings ourselves. There is no need for us to have come [such] a long way for that purpose. I think that only by paying attention to others' merits and our own shortcomings can we make continuous progress. We can modestly pass on our merits to them and sincerely help them correct their shortcomings. Only when we become more modest and sincere can we unite with them and learn their merits. After we enter Korea, we should carry forward the glorious tradition of our Party. Every cadre should leave a good impression on the [Koreans] by his own exemplary behavior. I hope that the comrades will educate all officers and men to keep this in mind.

The question of discipline is more important when we fight a war in a foreign country. The Three Main Rules of Discipline and the Eight Points for the Attention of the Chinese People's Liberation Army have drawn the praise and support of the people of the whole country.[57] After we enter Korea, we must observe discipline in all earnest and not violate the interests of the masses. We must pay attention to the Korean people's customs and social conventions. Only by building good relations between the masses and ourselves and by obtaining help from the masses can we win victory in the war. Generally speaking, discipline might easily be violated under the following three conditions: (1) if we have just won a victory; (2) if we have just

[57][Mao Zedong set down the Three Rules of Discipline in 1928. He later expanded the list of Points for Attention that he set down at about the same time; the revised list was issued on Oct. 10, 1947. The Three Main Rules: (1) obey orders in all your actions; (2) do not take a single needle or piece of thread from the masses; (3) turn in everything captured. The Eight Points: (1) speak politely; (2) pay fairly for what you buy; (3) return everything you borrow; (4) pay for anything you damage; (5) do not hit or swear at people; (6) do not damage crops; (7) do not take liberties with women; and (8) do not ill-treat captives. (Mao [31], pp. 341–42.)—TRANS.]

suffered defeat; or (3) if we have met difficulties and hardships. We should pay special attention [to maintaining discipline] under those three conditions. We must not act proud after winning victories, lose heart after suffering setbacks, and complain when meeting difficulties. Under all circumstances, we must be modest and prudent, unite as one, overcome difficulties, and adopt a forward-looking attitude. Thus we can vanquish all enemies.

Our mission is an arduous but glorious one. We should make long-term plans, do careful research on the concrete situation, and devise more new methods. So long as we bring into full play the forces of the masses, we will successfully accomplish our mission.

SOURCE: Peng Dehuai, *Peng Dehuai Junshi Wenxuan* (Beijing, 1988), pp. 320–26.

Doc. 78. Mao Telegram re Moving Supplies Up to the Front, Oct. 15, 1950, 0100

Comrade Gao Gang, and Deng [Hua], Hong [Xuezhi], Han [Xianchu],[58] Xie [Fang]:

1. It has been decided that on October 18 or 19 at the latest, our People's Volunteers will begin crossing the [Yalu] river and moving forward. You should attach importance to the immediate delivery of grain and other supplies to the front. Be sure not to delay.

2. Today or tomorrow, Comrade Peng Dehuai will return to Andong.[59]

SOURCE: JY, p. 563.

Doc. 79. Mao Telegram re the Order of Attack, Oct. 15, 1950, 0500

Comrades Gao Gang, [Peng] Dehuai; also inform Deng Hua:

1. On the 13th, the U.S. troops, the British troops, and the puppet [South Korean] army that had been operating on the 38th parallel occupied Kimchon and continued preparing for an attack on Pyongyang. A U.S. Marine division is to land at Jinnampo [now Nampo] to join the attack on Pyongyang. Bits of information suggest that the puppet 6th and 8th divisions that were supposed to assemble in Wonsan will change direction and make Pyongyang their target.

2. One advance corps of our troops had better set off on the 17th and arrive at Tokchon on the 23rd. In order to hold its positions and await the fatigued enemy, the corps should start building defense works on the 25th after one day of rest. A second corps will set off on the 18th. Other units will set off successively thereafter. All of the units will cross the river within about ten days. Please settle the matter at your discretion.

3. Gao, please telegraph me whether you have started delivering grain and munitions across the river.

SOURCE: JY, p. 564.

[58]Han Xianchu was then the deputy commander of the CPV's Thirteenth Army.
[59]Andong was later renamed Dandong.

Doc. 80. Mao Telegram re the Date of the First Crossing, Oct. 17, 1950, 1700

Peng [Dehuai], Gao [Gang]; also inform Deng [Hua], Hong [Xuezhi], Han [Xianchu], Xie [Fang]:

1. Please have everything in readiness for the two advance corps to set off on the 19th. The formal order will be issued tomorrow (18th).

2. Please, Comrades Peng [Dehuai] and Gao [Gang], come to Beijing by plane for a discussion.

SOURCE: JY, p. 567.

Doc. 81. Mao Telegram Confirming the Scheduled Entry of the Volunteers, Oct. 18, 1950, 2100

Deng [Hua], Hong [Xuezhi], Han [Xianchu], Xie [Fang]; also inform Deputy Commander He [Jinnian]:

We are determined to move on schedule four corps and three artillery divisions to the northern part of Korea and commence military operations. Tomorrow evening, the 19th, [the first units] will start crossing the Yalu River between Andong and Ji'an. To keep the operation absolutely secret, the troops should start crossing the river every day at dusk and stop at 4:00 A.M. By 5:00 A.M., the troops should have taken cover, and you should keep a close watch on this. To gain experience, you should plan for two or three divisions to cross the river on the first night (the night of the 19th), and for more or less [the same number of] troops to cross the river on the second night. Thereafter, handle the matter at your own discretion. Gao Gang and [Peng] Dehuai will fill you in on the details face to face.

SOURCE: JY, p. 568.

Doc. 82. Mao Telegram Putting Senior Party Officials on Notice to Maintain a News Blackout on the Fighting in Korea, Oct. 19, 1950

Deng [Zihui], Tan [Zheng],[60] Rao [Shushi], Chen [Yi],[61] Liu [Bocheng], Deng [Xiaoping], He [Long],[62] Xi [Zhongxun], Ma [Mingfang]:[63]

Your telegram of October 13 has been received.

1. In order to defend China and aid Korea, we have decided to dispatch the Volunteers to the northern part of Korea still under control [of the Democratic

[60]Deng Zihui was then the third secretary of the South-Central Bureau of the CCP Central Committee and second political commissar of the South-Central Military Region. Tan Zheng was then a member of the bureau's Standing Committee and third political commissar of the military region.

[61]Rao Shushi and Chen Yi were then, respectively, the first and second secretaries of the East China Bureau of the CCP Central Committee.

[62]Liu Bocheng, Deng Xiaoping, and He Long were then, respectively, the second, first, and third secretaries of the Southwest Bureau of the CCP Central Committee.

[63]Xi Zhongxun and Ma Mingfang were then, respectively, the first and third secretaries of the Northwest Bureau of the CCP Central Committee.

People's Republic of Korea] today. There they will first get a firm foothold and then wait for opportunities to wage mobile warfare in support of the continued struggle of the Korean people. For several months, we will resort *only to action and no talk*, and we shall not reveal any information in the newspapers for propaganda purposes. We can only inform senior leading cadres within the Party of the matters [they need to know] to carry out [their] job assignments. Various central bureaus should make a point of this.

2. The 48th Corps may assemble next March. We will let you know if it is necessary to assemble [the corps] before then.

SOURCE: JY, p. 571.

NOTES

NOTES

For complete authors' names, titles, and publication on the works cited in short form in the Notes, see the References Cited, pp. 351–80. Three abbreviations are used in these Notes:

CPSU   Communist Party of the Soviet Union
FBIS   *Foreign Broadcast Information Service*
FRUS   *Foreign Relations of the United States*

Chapter One

1. V. M. Molotov, a Soviet leader who clearly grasped Stalin's foreign policy objectives, once put it this way: "It is good that Russian tsars had conquered so much land for us. Now it is easier for us to struggle against capitalism." *Sto Sorok Besed s Molotovym*, p. 14. For an analysis of Soviet relations with the Republic of China in this period, see Garver, Chap. 7.

2. See *Sto Sorok Besed s Molotovym*, p. 14; Molotov; "Speech," Feb. 7, 1946; Stalin; Voznesenskii; and "Address of the Central Committee," especially p. 3. We are indebted to David Holloway for providing these references.

3. On the traditional Chinese view of the world order, see the essays by John K. Fairbank, Lien-sheng Yang, and Wang Gungwu in Fairbank, pp. 1–62.

4. The Chinese Communists occupied Beiping (Northern Peace), as it was still called, on Jan. 31, 1949. With the founding of the PRC on Oct. 1, the city became their capital and was renamed Beijing (Northern Capital). *Cihai*, p. 331; Academy of Military Science, *Zhongguo Renmin Jiefangjun Liushi Nian Dashiji*, p. 447.

5. For a recent general analysis of U.S. views of postwar Soviet policy, see Leffler, Chaps. 1–4. On broader aspects of Soviet-Chinese relations in the immediate postwar years, see Levine, pp. 1–86.

6. The text of the Yalta agreement is in U.S., Dept. of State, *United States Relations with China*, pp. 113–14.

7. Lensen, pp. 150–52. Many Chinese historians concur with Zhu Jianhua, p. 6, who accuses "the Soviet Union of restoring the special rights and interests of Tsarist Russia in China" by signing the Yalta agreement.

8. For a common Chinese view of the Yalta agreement's impact on China's sovereignty, see Yang Yunruo, p. 75.

9. Garver, pp. 212–14, 229–30.

10. Unless otherwise cited, this and the following five paragraphs are based on Liang Chin-tung, pp. 382–90; Wu Jingping, pp. 176–90; Li Zhaoxin, pp. 4–9; and Shi Zheng, pp. 54–56.

11. The quotations in this paragraph are from the Victor Hoo Papers, Hoover Institution archives, Box 2, file "Sino-Soviet Relations, 1945–46," meetings of June 30, July 2 and 7, and Aug. 7 and 10, 1945. We are grateful to David Holloway for bringing this source to our attention. The reports on the Soong-Stalin conversations in FRUS 1945, 7: 910–14, 920–21, 926–28, 932–34, and 958–59, make no reference to Stalin's views on war.

12. For a discussion of Sino-Soviet negotiations, see U.S., Dept. of State, *United States Relations with China*, pp. 116–18; and Garver, pp. 214–28. Many of the relevant documents are in FRUS 1945, 7: 908–79.

13. Guo Tingyi, pp. 121, 126–27.

14. Truman, p. 315.

15. Precisely what Truman told Stalin about the bomb, and when, is a matter of some uncertainty, despite the later recollections of a number of people, including Molotov and Truman, whose memoirs were ghostwritten. Truman recalls, "On July 24 I casually mentioned to Stalin that we had a new weapon of unusual destructive force. . . . All [Stalin] said was that he was glad to hear it and hoped we would make 'good use of it against the Japanese.'" According to Charles E. Bohlen, who served as Truman's interpreter, this conversation took place only in the presence of a Soviet interpreter, and so "I have never been completely sure as to exactly how the President's remark came out to Stalin in Russian." The closest to contemporary references we have are by Charles Ross, the presidential press secretary, and Walter Brown, an aide to Secretary of State James Byrnes. Ross records asking Truman on Sept. 5, 1946, what he had said to Stalin. Truman replied that "he told Stalin that we had a bomb equal in power to twenty thousand tons of T. N. T. and that we would drop it on Japan within a week (Potsdam Conference ended August 2, 1945). The President did not tell Stalin the nature of the bomb." On July 14, Brown, who accompanied Byrnes to Potsdam, wrote in his notes, "Truman dropped over and nonchalantly told Stalin of atomic bomb. [Byrnes] thinks Stalin did not catch the significance. All Stalin said was 'That's great, let them have it.'" According to Molotov's recollections, "In Potsdam Truman decided to surprise us. As I remember, after the lunch given by the American delegation, he with secretiveness moved me and Stalin aside and stated that they have a kind of special weapon that never existed before, a kind of an unconventional weapon [*sverkhobychnoe oruzhie*]." Truman, p. 416; Bohlen to Feis, Jan. 25, 1960, Herbert Feis Papers, Box 14, Library of Congress; Ross Papers, Harry S. Truman Library; "W. B.'s Notes," file 602, Byrnes Papers, Robert Muldrow Cooper Library, Clemson University; *Sto Sorok Besed s Molotovym*, p. 81. We are grateful to Barton Bernstein for providing the American references.

16. Truman, pp. 423, 425.

17. Guo Tingyi, pp. 121, 126–27.

18. For Stalin's warning and its possible influence on the Nationalists, see Liu Likai and Yang Jinbao, p. 327.

19. On the renaming of the Manchurian railways, see Wu Jingping, p. 189; and *Cihai*, p. 1416.

20. Unless otherwise cited, the information in this paragraph is from Liang Chin-tung, pp. 382–90. Liang, a former justice of the Republic of China's Supreme

Court, has detailed how the agreements on Dalian, Port Arthur (Lüshun), and the Chinese Changchun Railroad exceeded the Yalta agreement.

21. The text of the treaty and notes relating to it are in U.S., Dept. of State, *United States Relations with China*, pp. 585ff. Wang Shih-chieh, who had succeeded T. V. Soong as Chinese foreign minister in early August, signed the treaty on behalf of China. Soong continued as president of the Executive Yuan, a position comparable to prime minister that he had held since May 31, 1945. Liang Chin-tung, pp. 388–90.

22. Garver, pp. 218, 220–21; Liu Likai and Yang Jinbao, p. 324.

23. Sung Tzu-wen, pp. 25–26.

24. On the Chinese view that the Yalta agreement caused Manchuria, Mongolia, and Xinjiang to become part of the Soviet "security belt," see Yang Yunruo, p. 75.

25. Snow, *Red Star*, p. 110. In 1954, when Khrushchev and Bulganin visited China, Mao formally requested that Outer Mongolia be returned to China. The Soviets flatly refused. In July 1964, Mao strongly condemned the Soviet Union for its annexation of Outer Mongolia, revealing a view on Yalta that he unquestionably held in 1945. Liu Likai and Yang Jinbao, p. 334; Mao [46], pp. 540–41.

26. Mao [18], pp. 327–28; Mao [19], p. 334.

27. Garver, p. 262. Recently published Chinese articles accuse Stalin of "selling out" the Communists in exchange for Soviet "special rights" in China. Shi Zheng, p. 56; Liu Likai and Yang Jinbao, pp. 323–26. See also Xue Qingchao, p. 4; Guo Xin, p. 4; and Wang Wenmu, p. 4.

28. During the Cultural Revolution, Zhou Enlai recalled that "many were frightened by the atomic bomb. At that time even Stalin was mentally shocked and was worried about the outbreak of World War III." Quoted in "Premier Chou's Criticism," p. 7. Mao's first known response to the bomb came on Aug. 13, 1945, when he said, "Some of our comrades . . . believe that the atom bomb is all-powerful; that is a big mistake." Mao [37], p. 21.

29. Rong Zhi, p. 92. The Chinese assessment of the Soviet position was summarized by Zhou Enlai in his instructions to Liu Xiao, the new ambassador to the Soviet Union, on the eve of Liu's departure for Moscow. Speaking about the immediate postwar period, Zhou said: "The Soviet Union was worried that a civil war in China could damage the sphere of influence defined at Yalta, provoke U.S. involvement, and threaten the Soviet Union. Stalin also was afraid of the outbreak of the Third World War. For Stalin, the starting point was to avoid a direct conflict with the United States strategically and to win time for peaceful construction." Liu Xiao, "Mission" (1987), p. 15; (1988), p. 360.

30. Chiang cabled Mao on Aug. 14, 20, and 23, 1945, inviting him to peace negotiations in Chongqing. "Chiang Kai-shek's Three Cables," pp. 6–8.

31. Mao replied to Chiang's invitation on Aug. 16, 22, and 24. His second cable stated that Zhou would be the one to go. Mao [8], pp. 4–5. On Mao's reluctance to go to Chongqing for talks with Chiang Kai-shek, see also Shi Zhe, "Mao Zedong," p. 10; and Xiong Xianghui.

32. Unless otherwise cited, the information in this and the following paragraph is from Shi Zhe, *Zai Lishi*, p. 308; Shi Zhe, "Mao Zedong," p. 10; Liu Yishun, p. 382; and Yang Kuisong, p. 22. See also on the Stalin cable in particular Wang Jinyu and Chen Ruiyun, pp. 681, 710; Li Ping and Fang Ming, pp. 614–15; and Borisov, *Iz Istorii*, p. 80.

33. The CCP Politburo's decision to send Mao to Chongqing to negotiate with Chiang Kai-shek was taken on Aug. 23. Li Ping and Fang Ming, p. 615; Wang Pei and Ren Qingguo, pp. 34–35; Yu Shumin, p. 51. Mao cabled his acceptance the next day. Mao [8], p. 5.

34. This is partially based on Borisov, *Iz Istorii*, p. 80. For the other sources, see above, n. 32.

35. P. P. Vladimirov, pp. 652–53.

36. *Ibid.*, pp. 645–47.

37. In 1958, Mao said: "The Chinese revolution achieved victory against Stalin's will. Imitation foreign devils did not permit us to carry out the revolution [to the end]." Mao [40], p. 164. In a novel by Lu Xun, one Chinese character who did not permit others to revolt was dubbed an "imitation foreign devil." Mao later repeated the charge, stating: "In 1945 Stalin attempted to hold back the progress of the Chinese revolution. He said that it was improper for us to fight a civil war and it was necessary for us to cooperate with Chiang Kai-shek. He even stated that otherwise the Chinese nation would perish. [Fortunately,] at that time we did not follow his instruction and won the revolution." Mao [41], p. 432. For a recent Soviet assessment of Mao's views at this time, see Meliksetov, pp. 45–56.

38. Interview with M. S. Kapitsa, former vice-minister of foreign affairs of the Soviet Union, April 3, 1992. From the late 1940s, Kapitsa played a key role in shaping Soviet policy toward China. He served in the Soviet embassy in Chongqing during the Second World War, and as a foreign ministry official, was part of the official reception party for senior Chinese delegations that visited Moscow in the 1940s and 1950s. He possesses one of the most important archives on Sino-Soviet relations.

39. See Shi Zhe, *Zai Lishi*, pp. 205–7.

40. *Ibid.*, pp. 213–15.

41. *Zhonggong Dangshi Jiaoxue*, 17:464–66. On Mao's general thinking about the shift to a civil war after the defeat of Japan, see Quan Yanchi, "Mao Zedong's Confidential Secretary," p. 43. The Soviets later pointed out that the Chinese Communists' peaceful stance toward the Nationalists in 1945–46, when Chiang was stronger than they and enjoyed U.S. support, had created the necessary conditions for accumulating force and, through diplomatic and political struggle, preparing the PLA for the forthcoming offensives. Borisov, *Iz Istorii*, p. 80.

42. On the determination of the new policy, see Du Shilin, p. 13.

43. On Aug. 20, 1945, the CCP Central Committee approved the plan of its Central China Bureau and the New 4th Army to launch an armed uprising in Shanghai and other cities. Wang Jinyu and Chen Ruiyun, p. 710. See also Wang Yaoshan et al.; and *Chen Yi Zhuan*, pp. 315–17.

44. Liu Xingjun, p. 24. On these events in general, see Tai Dong, pp. 46–48; Li Shiyu, p. 41; and Yang Shunren, p. 12.

45. On Aug. 14 and again on Aug. 21, the CCP Central Committee cabled the Central China Bureau to suspend the plans for armed uprisings in Nanjing and Shanghai. Li Shiyu, p. 42; Wang Jinyu and Chen Ruiyun, p. 710; Liu Xingjun, pp. 24–25.

46. *Zhonggong Dangshi Dashi Nianbiao Shuoming*, pp. 120–21.

47. Bi Jianzhong, pp. 25–26; Wang Yuannian et al., p. 20.

48. Bi Jianzhong, pp. 25–26; Meliksetov, p. 47.

49. The statement was made in a document entitled "Circular of the CCP Cen-

tral Committee on Peace Negotiations with the Kuomintang." Liu Xingjun, p. 25; Zhang Zhenglong, pp. 15–16.

50. Even the Chinese who served as senior officers in the Red Army were forbidden to disclose any information on Stalin's decision to the Chinese Communists. See Yang Kuisong, p. 222; Qu Xing, "Soviet Policy," p. 2; and Bi Jianzhong, p. 26.

51. Probably reflecting Stalin's viewpoint, Molotov stated, "Anyway, we can't take Manchuria. It is impossible. It is contradictory to our policy." *Sto Sorok Besed s Molotovym*, p. 101.

52. The total economic loss as a result of industrial equipment looted by the Red Army was $2 billion. Zhu Jianhua, p. 9. For Chinese comment on Soviet looting in Manchuria, see Peng Shi, p. 68; and Zhang Zhenglong, pp. 89–91. In negotiations, the Soviet side proposed the Sino-Soviet joint administration of 80% of heavy industrial enterprises in the Northeast. Dong Yanping, *SuE Ju Dongbei*, pp. 66–67. The Chinese Communist propaganda line at the time was that the Soviet actions helped the revolution by depriving the Nationalists of the means to oppose Mao's forces. Borisov and Koloskov, *Sovetsko-Kitaiskie Otnosheniia 1945–1977 gg.*, pp. 23–24. On the economic negotiations, see the documents in *Zhonghua Minquo Zhongyao Shiliao*, pp. 241–454.

53. Wang Yizhi, pp. 157–63. In 1940, Japanese troops had forced the remnants of the Anti-Japanese United Army, composed of Chinese and Koreans, to retreat from Manchuria into the Soviet Union. Moscow had harbored them in camps near Khabarovsk. *Ibid.*, p. 157. Some of these troops were incorporated into the 88th Brigade (on which see Chap. 5, n. 9). A detailed study of the relations between Moscow and the Northeast Anti-Japanese United Army then operating in the Soviet Union is *Dongbei Kangri*, pp. 437–72.

54. Peng Shilu, pp. 59, 60–61; Zhao Guoqin, p. 49; Wang Yuannian et al., p. 12; Zhu Jianhua, p. 3; Wang Yizhi, pp. 162–63.

55. Zhang Qianhua, p. 189; Yang Kuisong, p. 222. In Dec. 1945, Chiang Kai-shek sent his son Chiang Ching-kuo to discuss the Northeast issue with Stalin. Stalin flatly warned Chiang not to let a single American soldier set foot in China; otherwise, "it will be very difficult to solve the Northeast problem." Chiang Ching-kuo, "Talks" (1981), p. 113; Chiang Ching-kuo, *Fengyu*, p. 74. Despite the warning, the United States soon after dispatched two Marine divisions to China.

56. On Sept. 30, 1945, the CCP Central Committee ordered its forces in Manchuria to operate under the name of the Northeast People's Autonomous Army. Li Yunchang, pp. 175–76; Wang Yizhi, pp. 162–63; Yang Kuisong, p. 222; Bi Jianzhong, p. 26.

57. Interview with V. Ia. Sidikhmenov, 1991. An interpreter for the Red Army in Manchuria in 1945 and 1946, Sidikhmenov participated in most of the negotiations with the Chinese Communists there.

58. Unless otherwise cited, this and the next paragraph are based on Wu Xiuquan, "Liberation," pp. 154–55; Wu Xiuquan, "My Departure," pp. 30–35; Zeng Kelin, *Rongma*, pp. 228–30; Ning Zhiyi, pp. 8–9; Du Shilin, pp. 12–13; Li Yunchang, pp. 176–77; and Wang Yizhi, p. 164.

59. During his talks with CCP Politburo members, the Soviet representative asked the Communists to withdraw from Manchuria. When they refused, he proposed limits on their operating areas. Zeng Kelin, "Recollections," pp. 174–76; Zeng Kelin, "From Yan'an," p. 7; Du Shilin, p. 13; Tang Kai, p. 26. When Mao's forces later resisted the thought of withdrawing from the three cities, the Soviets

threatened to force them out of Shenyang. Wu Xiuquan, *Wo de Licheng*, pp. 172–73.

60. Even before the arrival of the Soviet military representative in Yan'an, Huang Kecheng, commander of the 3rd Division of the New 4th Army, had reportedly cabled the Politburo that the Communists should concentrate their forces in the Northeast to prepare for an inevitable decisive battle with the Nationalists. Hong Xuezhi, "Profoundly Mourn"; Liu Zhen et al.

61. Before leaving Yan'an for the Chongqing negotiations, Mao had assigned Liu Shaoqi to act for him as chairman of the CCP Central Committee. Liu helped the ailing Mao handle the committee's daily affairs until his full recovery in the autumn of 1947. Shi Zhe, "On the Eve," pp. 214–15. On Liu Shaoqi's career during the late 1940s, see Dittmer, pp. 26–27.

62. A CCP document drafted by Liu Shaoqi (issued on Sept. 19) stated, "So long as we place the Northeast and Jehol and Chahar provinces under our control . . . we will ensure the victory of the Chinese people." For the full text of the document, see Liu Shaoqi, "Current Task," pp. 9–11. The Republic of China's provinces of Jehol and Chahar are now part of Hebei, Liaoning, and Shanxi provinces and the Inner Mongolian Autonomous Region. On the revision of Communist strategy, see also Zeng Kelin, "From Yan'an," p. 6; Zeng Kelin, "Report," pp. 27–29; Wang Yuannian et al., pp. 21–22; Liu Xiaoqing, p. 46; and Luo Libin, pp. 516–17.

63. On the subsequent movement of Communist forces into Manchuria, see Chen Yun, "My Opinion," p. 3; Li Ping and Fang Ming, pp. 619–20; Zhu Jianhua and Zhao Yinglan, p. 198; Peng Zhen, p. 3; Zhu Xiangfeng and Wei Ziyang, p. 19; Xiao Jingguang, "My Mission," p. 19 (stating that by Nov. 1945, the CCP had moved more than 100,000 troops to Manchuria); Zeng Kelin, "Recollections," p. 177; and Zhang Zhenglong, pp. 21–22.

64. Zhu Jianhua, pp. 19–20; Wang Yuannian et al., p. 24. The four Politburo members were Peng Zhen, Chen Yun, Gao Gang, and Zhang Wentian. See Ren Jianshu, p. 283.

65. Shi Zhe, *Zai Lishi*, pp. 312–13.

66. See Du Yuming, "Whole Story," pp. 3, 5; Du Yuming, "Inside Story," p. 70; and Zhang Qianhua, p. 189. Du was then commander of the Nationalist forces in the Northeast.

67. *Voennaia Pomoshch*, p. 99; O. B. Vladimirov, p. 23.

68. Dong Yanping, "Disclosure," pp. 223–40; *Vneshniaia Politika*, p. 375.

69. Chen Yun, "Some Opinions," pp. 221–22. See also Xue Hui, p. 4.

70. Guo Tingyi, p. 128; Song Chun and Lou Jie, p. 205.

71. Yang Kuisong, pp. 220–21; Du Yuming, "Whole Story," pp. 7–8; Wang Yuannian et al., pp. 15–16; *Zhonghua Minguo Zhongyao Shiliao*, pp. 117–40.

72. Composed of five military enterprises and named the Dalian Jianxin Corporation, the munitions complex could mass-produce cannons and shells. He Changgong, pp. 409–11, 433; Wang Zhaoquan, pp. 48–50; Wang Jinyu and Chen Ruiyun, p. 686; Xiao Jingguang, *Xiao Jingguang Huiyilu*, 1: 339–40; Xiao Jingguang, "My Mission," pp. 27–28. Following the 1945 Sino-Soviet treaty, Lüshun, Dalian, Jin County, Haiyang and Changshan islands, and an area to the south of Shiheyi town were listed as Soviet-occupied areas. The 300,000 servicemen were recruited from these places. Gu Mingyi et al., p. 704.

73. He Changgong, pp. 409–11, 433. For an excellent historical analysis of the Huai-Hai campaign, see Clubb, "Chiang Kai-shek's Waterloo," pp. 389–99.

74. According to Molotov, Churchill's speech not only triggered Stalin's con-

cerns about a global confrontation with the West, but caused him to abandon the idea of retirement, something he had frequently talked of doing till then. *Sto Sorok Besed s Molotovym*, p. 86.

75. Dong Yanping, *SuE Ju Dongbei*, pp. 66–67. Chang Chia-ao, the chief Nationalist representative for economic affairs in the Northeast, advised Chiang Kai-shek to accept some of Stalin's demands in exchange for Soviet neutrality in the Nationalist-Communist conflict. See documents in *Zhonghua Minguo Zhongyao Shiliao*, pp. 394–97.

76. For information on Stalin's invitations to a Sino-Soviet summit and the motives that prompted Chiang to reject the idea, see Chiang Ching-kuo, "My Father," pp. 146–47; Peng Shi, pp. 60–61; and Song Chun and Lou Jie, p. 206.

77. Huang Kecheng, pp. 54–55; Song Chun and Lou Jie, p. 205; Kovtun-Stankevich, pp. 432–36.

78. Shi Zhe, *Zai Lishi*, pp. 319–20.

79. *Voennaia Pomoshch*, p. 102; Tao Wenzhao, p. 2. For a brief discussion of the Sino-U.S. commercial treaty, see U.S., Dept. of State, *United States Relations with China*, pp. 223–25; and Ren Donglai, pp. 16–22. For Mao's observations on the treaty, see Mao [5].

80. The Soviets signed other commercial contracts with the Chinese Communists in Manchuria on Feb. 27, 1948, and March 29, 1949. Yun Zhang and Xiao Chun, pp. 237–41; Sladkovskii, *Istoriia*, pp. 171–73. The Dec. 1946 agreement clearly violated the 1945 Sino-Soviet treaty, in which Moscow recognized the Nationalist regime as China's sole legitimate government.

81. Shi Zhe, *Zai Lishi*, p. 338. Ren Bishi was then a member of the CCP's Five-Man Central Secretariat.

82. Xia Lin'gen and Yu Xiyuan, p. 197.

83. Shi Zhe, *Zai Lishi*, pp. 345–47.

84. Academy of Military Science, *Zhongguo Renmin Jiefangjun Liushi Nian Dashiji*, p. 402; Peng Dehuai, *Memoirs*, pp. 458–61; Shi Zhe, *Zai Lishi*, pp. 346–48; Shi Zhe, "With Chairman Mao," pp. 146–47. The Chinese Communists launched the 50-day autumn counteroffensive in Manchuria on Sept. 14, 1947. Academy of Military Science, *Zhongguo Renmin Jiefangjun Dashiji*, p. 266. Mao conveys his general conclusions in Mao [42], pp. 141–46.

85. Shi Zhe, *Zai Lishi*, pp. 350–52.

86. The agreement of Oct. 27 provided relief assistance to China upon the expiration of the relief provided by the UN Relief and Rehabilitation Administration. The agreement is not mentioned in the U.S. Department of State's White Paper of 1949, and shortly after it was signed, the U.S. ambassador complained to Washington that it "evoked surprisingly little comment in China press." Stuart to Acheson, Nov. 4, 1947, in FRUS 1947, 7: 1357. On the Soviet response to the relief agreement, see Avarin, "New Stage," pp. 10–14.

87. See Yang Kuisong, pp. 222–23; and Liu Shitian, p. 49.

88. The information in this paragraph is from He Changgong, pp. 427–29; Yang Kuisong, p. 221; and Du Shilin, p. 12. On the Soviet decision to provide military aid to the Communists, see also Wu Xiuquan, *Wo de Licheng*, pp. 169–71; and Liudnikov, pp. 410–12.

89. Most of this matériel had been captured at the Japanese depot in Sujiatun, 15 km south of the city of Shenyang, and had been shipped on to Manzhouli for future delivery to the Soviet Union.

90. Wang Wenmu, p. 4; Yang Kuisong, p. 221. For other Chinese comments on

the Soviet military presence in the Northeast in the late 1940s, see Deng Xinghua, pp. 43–48; and Liu Shitian, p. 50.

91. This is the view of Shi Zhe, *Zai Lishi*, p. 418.

92. *Ibid*., p. 460.

93. Contact was first established in 1928–29 with a tie-up between the Comintern radio transmitter in Vladivostok and a Communist radio station in Shanghai. After a disruption of some years, communications were restored in 1936 via a Communist station in northern Shaanxi. In Feb. 1940, Ren Bishi brought a powerful new transmitter from Moscow, and by the end of the year, a special CCP department for "work in the countryside" was created to maintain regular communications with Moscow. It existed until 1944. Shi Zhe, *Zai Lishi*, pp. 200–204.

94. *Ibid*., pp. 208–12, 217–20, 315, 390.

95. Interviews with A. M. Ledovskii, Feb.-March, 1990.

96. *Ibid*.

97. Interview with S. L. Tikhvinskii, Nov. 1990; interviews with I. V. Kovalev, 1991–92.

98. The quote is from Li Yueran, *Waijiao*, p. 12; the information on the broken code is from interview with I. V. Kovalev, 1991.

99. Shi Zhe, *Zai Lishi*, pp. 390, 393, 420, 437–38.

100. *Ibid*., p. 455.

101. Mao [39], pp. 160–61; Yang Kuisong, pp. 216–20; Borisov, *Iz Istorii*, pp. 108–9.

102. Gittings, pp. 142–48.

103. Unless otherwise cited, the information in the following three paragraphs is from Mao [45], pp. 97–101; and Mao [26], pp. 50–51. Mao had earlier, in April 1946, tested out the ideas he expressed in his talk with Strong. See Mao [38], pp. 87–88. See also Shi Zhe, *Zai Lishi*, p. 351.

104. On the development of the "intermediate zone" theory and its application to China's foreign affairs, see Lu Lin, pp. 127–30.

105. Mao's interview came on the first anniversary of the atomic bombing of Japan. While we have no contemporary evidence about the Chinese attitude toward the bomb in 1946, reports from Soviet consulates in China during 1949–50 often mentioned widespread rumors that U.S. planes would soon use the bomb to destroy China's main cities. Information from a Soviet specialist, 1990. We believe this mood existed early and was one reason why Mao developed his "paper tiger" theory.

106. We have followed the analysis of Lu Lin, pp. 127–28.

107. Volkogonov, 2.2: 104–5.

108. Mao [16], pp. 119–27. On the Soviet side, see, for example, Avarin, "Political Situation," pp. 8–12.

109. On Oct. 10, 1947, the Soviet journal *Literaturnaia Gazeta* published Anna Louise Strong's biography of Mao Zedong, probably the first accurate biographic account of Mao's life in the Soviet mass media. It was not published for mass consumption in China until Feb. 19, 1948, when *Renmin Ribao*, then the official newspaper of the CCP North China Bureau, published a translation from the Russian, not from the English original.

110. In 1947, a Soviet reviewer of Chen Boda's book *Zhongguo Sida Jiazu* [China's Four Big Families] quoted Chen's conclusion, "The victory of the Chinese people is certain and inevitable." Avarin, "Four Clans," p. 31. At the beginning of

1948, the same author spoke of the impending Communist victory. Avarin, "Military Successes," p. 8. Even greater confidence in the Communist triumph was expressed in an article published a month later. Gamanin, p. 18.

111. Unless otherwise cited, the information in this and the next paragraph is from Djilas, p. 182.

112. Messer, p. 73; Gaddis, pp. 61–118.

113. Interview with M. S. Kapitsa, April 3, 1992. From the late 1940s, Kapitsa was one of the principal China specialists in the Soviet Ministry of Foreign Affairs. On several occasions, he served as interpreter in Stalin's talks with senior Chinese leaders.

114. For Mao's important articles on the Liaoxi-Shenyang, Huai-Hai, and Beiping-Tianjin-Zhangjiakou campaigns, see *Selected Works of Mao Tse-tung*, 4: 261–66, 279–82, 289–93.

115. "Facing the fact of the sharp deterioration in the military-political situation, the Nationalist leaders are turning to their American patrons again. In their heads all kinds of plans are appearing. [Chiang] is hoping to get direct military assistance from the future Dewey administration." Avarin, "New Offensive," p. 28.

116. In July 1948, Liu Shaoqi stated, "U.S. [armed] intervention also cannot prevent the Chinese Communist Party from winning victory even if the United States sends troops [to China]. It is impossible for the United States to send one or two million troops. Fewer troops won't work. If the United States sends one or two hundred thousand troops, the Americans can only occupy a few coastal cities. If you want to occupy them, just do it! China is such a big nation. Even if the Americans occupy a little bit, we will still be moving forward!" Liu Shaoqi, "Speech at Cadres Meeting," p. 14. See also Zhou Enlai, "Report," p. 323. In May 1949, Mao ordered his troops to be prepared to counter possible attacks by U.S. forces when crossing the Yangtze River. Mao [14], p. 337.

117. Shi Zhe, *Zai Lishi*, pp. 367–68.

118. *Ibid.*, p. 370.

119. Yu Zhan and Zhang Guangyou, pp. 19–20.

120. Djilas, pp. 82, 114.

121. *Ibid.*, p. 113.

122. Zhan Yizhi, pp. 43–44; Song Zhongfu, pp. 23–30.

123. Jiang Jin and Jiang Shipei, pp. 127–33.

124. Rong Zhi, p. 101; Wang Tingke, pp. 2–5.

125. "In the 1940s reliable information was given to Mao and Zhou [Enlai] about the affiliation with [U.S.] intelligence of several Americans who were staying in Yan'an and were receiving important information from there. Yet, in spite of the warnings, Mao and Zhou did nothing to isolate them." Borisov, *Iz Istorii*, p. 101. In the language of the Soviet secret police, "isolate" meant detention or worse. See also Shi Zhe, *Zai Lishi*, pp. 223–24, 319.

126. Qiao Mu, pp. 30–44.

127. Lu Dingyi, as reproduced in *United States Relations with China*, pp. 710–19. For a Chinese-language version, see *Qunzhong*, Jan. 30, 1947, pp. 3–6.

128. Borisov, *Iz Istorii*, pp. 113–17; Khrushchev, *Last Testament*, p. 243.

129. "Stalin greatly appreciated Gao Gang and specially presented him a car. Gao Gang every year on August 15 [the date of the announcement of the Japanese surrender] sent Stalin a cable of congratulations." Mao [39], p. 163.

130. Unless otherwise cited, this paragraph is based on Djilas, pp. 127–29; and

Volkogonov, 2.2: 95–96. On June 2, 1947, for example, the Soviet secret police issued a top-secret instruction to its agents to discredit and weaken the Eastern European governments, thereby increasing their dependence on Moscow. "Top Secret, Moscow," pp. 6–7.

131. Volkogonov, 2.2: 97–101.

132. Mao [33], pp. 171–73.

133. Mao [7], p. 220.

134. Mao and his lieutenants arrived in Chengnanzhuang, Fuping County, on April 11, 1948. Party History Research Section, p. 332. We know that Mao informed Stalin of his idea for a visit sometime before May 18, since he got Stalin's cabled response that day. Shi Zhe, "With Chairman Mao," pp. 150, 151. The Chinese Communists had created an "international route" from Yan'an via Mount Daqing (in Suiyuan Province) to Outer Mongolia (the Mongolian People's Republic) in 1941 and used it for many years. Worried about possible accusations of violations of the 1945 treaty with the Nationalists, the Soviets chose to pick up the Chinese Communists in Outer Mongolia rather than from such Soviet military bases in Northeast China as Dalian and Lüshun. *Jinsui Geming*, pp. 149–50; Mao [22], p. 271. Mao designated Yang Chengwu, a subordinate of Nie Rongzhen, to head an infantry division to escort him to the Sino-Soviet border. Yang Chengwu, "Call," p. 51.

135. Late in the anti-Japanese war, Mao had hopes of establishing economic ties with the United States after the war. For information on Mao's ideas for such ties, see Wang He, "Mao Zedong's Plans," pp. 15–19; and Wang He, "Plans of Mao Zedong and Zhou Enlai," pp. 7–11. On Mao's change in attitude toward the United States, see Xiong Xianghui; Wang Jisi, pp. 40–68; and He Di, "Evolution," 1989, pp. 40–43.

136. Li Yinqiao and Quan Yanchi, p. 59.

137. Shi Zhe, "Chairman Mao's First Visit," p. 8.

138. The quotations in this paragraph are from Min Li, "On the Eve," p. 14; and Shi Zhe, "I Accompanied Chairman Mao," p. 125. Mao received Stalin's cable after reaching Huashan, a village near Chengnanzhuang, Fuping County, on May 18. Abandoning the idea of a visit to Moscow, he left Huashan for Xibaipo on May 27. Shi Zhe, "With Chairman Mao," pp. 150, 151.

139. Nie Rongzhen, "With Comrade Mao Zedong," p. 5; Nie Rongzhen, *Nie Rongzhen Huiyilu*, p. 678.

140. Shi Zhe, "With Chairman Mao," pp. 146–47. In two letters written in mid-Nov. 1948, Mao says that he had only "minor problems" with his health, which in general was "much better than in Yan'an." Mao [23], pp. 290–91; Mao [25], p. 292. Throughout 1948, Mao did not mention any serious health problem in his letters.

141. According to Borisov, *Iz Istorii*, p. 91, "The Soviet doctor L. I. Melnikov, who at the request of the Chinese leadership treated Mao in the years of 1946–49, reported that in some cases Mao said he was ill to 'avoid making decisions on important matters.'"

142. On Stalin's decision to punish Tito, see Djilas, Chap. 3 ("Disappointments"). See also Girenko, pp. 234–89, which is based on substantial new material from the archives of the Soviet Ministry of Foreign Affairs.

143. Kovalev, "Stalin's Dialogue," 1: 84. At this writing, Kovalev's memoirs were still in press. We are grateful to him for sharing the unedited original with us.

144. Unless otherwise cited, the following five paragraphs are based on Kovalev, "Stalin's Dialogue," 1: 83–85, 2: 77.

145. These figures are from Kovalev. Wang Jinyu and Chen Ruiyun, p. 685, give much higher ones.

146. Ning Yi, "Tito," pp. 16–17; Ning Yi, "Newly Rising State," pp. 19–20; Wu Xiuquan, *Eight Years*, Chap. 4. The classic Western comparative analysis of the Chinese and Yugoslav revolutions is Johnson, *Peasant Nationalism and Communist Power*.

147. We have used Liu Shaoqi, *Lun Guojizhuyi*; and the Russian-language text in *Pravda*, June 7 and 8, 1949.

148. Mao [24], pp. 303–4.

149. Kovalev, "Stalin's Dialogue," 2: 86.

150. Document from the personal archive of I. V. Kovalev.

151. Zhang Xiaolu, p. 213.

152. Unless otherwise cited, this concluding section is based on Kovalev, "Stalin's Dialogue," 2: 83, 84.

153. For U.S. documents on the Ward affair, see FRUS 1948, 7: 825–49; and FRUS 1949, 8: 933–1051. On Ward's refusal specifically, see Ward to Acheson, Dec. 11, 1949, in FRUS 1949, 8: 1047. For a pro-Communist review of the events, see "Ward Case," pp. 104–6.

Chapter Two

1. Mao [29], pp. 255–320.

2. *Ibid.*, p. 281.

3. Salisbury, *New Emperors*, pp. 86–87.

4. Borisov, *Iz Istorii*, pp. 52–53, 81. This volume, written under the Borisov pen name by O. B. Rakhmanin (then deputy head of a Central Committee department, CPSU), was based on classified Soviet archives.

5. The information on the Soviet Politburo meeting in Dec. 1948 is from the manuscript of Kovalev's memoirs. The Kovalev sources are discussed in Chap. 1.

6. Mao [12], pp. 32–34.

7. The information in this and the next paragraph is from Bo Yibo, pp. 36–37.

8. *Ibid.*, p. 37.

9. Shi Zhe, *Zai Lishi*, p. 374.

10. Mao's secretary writes: "In May of the same year [1948], he [Mao] went to the village of Xibaipo in Pingshan County, where Stalin's representative was to have come to see him. Because of the fluid military situation, however, the visit was not so easy to arrange. Not until January 1949, when our troops had captured Tianjin and the enemy forces in the Baoding area had been wiped out, did Stalin's envoy finally come on his secret mission." Shi Zhe, "I Accompanied Chairman Mao," p. 126. Xibaipo is not far from the Shijiazhuang airfield, which Nie Rongzhen's troops put under tight security during Mikoyan's visit. Nie Rongzhen, *Nie Rongzhen Huiyilu*, p. 678.

11. Shi Zhe, "Chairman Mao's First Visit," p. 7; Shi Zhe, "With Chairman Mao," p. 153; Shi Zhe, "I Accompanied Chairman Mao," p. 126; Li Ping and Fang Ming, pp. 810–11; Lan Sou and Li Ding, pp. 17–18; Min Li, "On the Eve," pp. 18–19.

12. Shi Zhe, *Zai Lishi*, p. 375.

13. After the delegation returned to Moscow, E. F. (not Ivan) Kovalev, who accompanied Mikoyan as an interpreter, prepared a 90-page transcript of all the Chinese speeches. This document and an abridged summary were presented to Stalin. So far all attempts to find this document in the CPSU archives have failed. Interview with K. V. Shevelev, senior researcher of the Institute of Far Eastern Studies, Moscow, March 1992.

14. The discussion in this and the following six paragraphs is based on Shi Zhe, *Zai Lishi*, pp. 375–81.

15. On Mao's judgment that the U.S. would not intervene in the civil war, see also Li Yinqiao and Quan Yanchi, p. 62.

16. He Di, "Evolution," 1989, p. 46; Qu Xing, "Soviet Policy," p. 3.

17. Mao [36], pp. 369–70.

18. For Stalin's opinion on Hong Kong and the national bourgeoisie, see App., Doc. 3. Stalin's proposals for state building are contained in the unpublished part of his cable to Kovalev, cited in App., Doc. 4. The full text of the cable is in Kovalev's personal archive.

19. Khrushchev, *Khrushchev Remembers* (1970), p. 239.

20. Li Yinqiao and Quan Yanchi, p. 62.

21. Shi Zhe, *Zai Lishi*, p. 385.

22. Kovalev, "Stalin's Dialogue," 1: 86.

23. Qu Xing, "Soviet Policy," p. 3. Our reading of *Pravda* for the years 1948–49 supports this conclusion. From approximately March 1949 on, *Pravda* made predominant use of *Xinhua* dispatches. Previously, it had relied mainly on TASS dispatches.

24. Nie Rongzhen, *Inside*, p. 585; Nie Rongzhen, *Nie Rongzhen Huiyilu*, p. 679.

25. Mao's first known statement on the "Northern and Southern Dynasties" was made in the spring of 1949, when he said: "Some friends abroad half believe and half disbelieve in our victory. [They are] persuading us to stop here and make the Yangtze River a border with Chiang, to create the 'Northern and Southern Dynasties.'" *Zhonggong Dangshi Dashi Nianbiao Shuoming*, p. 133. In 1954, Zhou Enlai told Liu Xiao, the new ambassador to the Soviet Union, that Stalin had "sent a representative to Xibaipo principally for the purpose of understanding the situation in the Chinese revolution and the points of view from our side. . . . The Soviet Union was dissatisfied [with our intention to liberate all China] and demanded that we 'stop the civil war.' In fact the Soviet Union attempted to create the 'Northern and Southern Dynasties,' namely two Chinas." Liu Xiao, *Chushi*, p. 4; Liu Xiao, "Mission" (1987), p. 15. Mao referred to this same issue on April 11, 1957. Wang Fangming, p. 92; *Zhonggong Dangshi Dashi Nianbiao Shuoming*, p. 133.

26. Shi Zhe, "With Chairman Mao," pp. 152, 153.

27. March 1991 interview with Sergo Mikoyan, who plans to include the list of topics covered at Xibaipo in his father's memoirs.

28. Yu Zhan and Zhang Guangyou, pp. 15–21; Shi Zhe, "Chairman Mao's First Visit," p. 9. Nevertheless, some Chinese scholars still adhere to the traditional account. See, for example, Wang Fangming, p. 92; Xiang Qing, p. 61; Chen Guangxiang, p. 8; and Li Yinqiao and Quan Yanchi, p. 62. The historian Qu Xing has uncovered a memorandum in the French Foreign Ministry archives that indirectly supports their point of view. Dated 1954, it quotes a French diplomat as saying that in 1949 the Soviets were trying to stop the Chinese at the Yangtze; allegedly,

this information originated with one of the PRC's vice-foreign ministers. Qu Xing, "Evidence," p. 65.

29. Nie Rongzhen, *Nie Rongzhen Huiyilu*, p. 679.

30. During his visit to Xibaipo, Mikoyan reportedly told the Chinese to avoid a direct conflict with the United States in military operations against the Nationalist armies. Mikoyan's advice presumably reinforced Mao's suspicion that Stalin wanted the CCP forces to halt north of the Yangtze. Information from a well-informed Chinese specialist, Dec. 1989.

31. According to Chinese officials, Mao told Soviet ambassador P. F. Yudin in 1958 that he had been dissatisfied with Mikoyan's attitude: "During his visit to Xibaipo, Mikoyan had an air of complacency. He put on airs and treated us as his children." They further charge that Mikoyan "behaved like a scout" as he probed the Chinese for their stand on a variety of questions. Yu Zhan and Zhang Guang-you, pp. 16–17, 20–21.

32. Kovalev, "Stalin's Dialogue," 1: 85–86. The quoted portions of Stalin's cable in Kovalev's memoirs are undated, but in his text he indicates it was sent in June 1949. That date cannot be correct for two reasons. First, the cable mentions three governments then in existence: the Kuomintang governments in South China (at Guangzhou) and Central China (Nanjing) and the Communist government in the Northeast. In fact, the Nanjing government ceased to exist after the PLA crossed the Yangtze and seized Nanjing on April 23. Second, the cable gave instructions for organizing an offensive in the South that was by then already well under way.

33. Kovalev, "Stalin's Dialogue," 1: 86.

34. *Zhonggong Dangshi Dashi Nianbiao Shuoming*, p. 133.

35. A. M. Ledovskii, who was the most senior Soviet diplomat left in Nanjing after the evacuation of Ambassador Roshchin, provides an explanation for the decision to send Roshchin south: Moscow feared that the presence of foreign embassies in Nanjing might bring U.S. military intervention on the pretext of protecting foreign nationals and hoped that other missions would follow the Soviet lead. Ledovskii, "U.S.S.R. and China," pp. 107–8.

36. Clubb, *China and Russia*, p. 370. The talks in Xinjiang, which were not held in secret, did not end until May 1949.

37. Mao [30], pp. 415–17.

38. Shen Xiaoyun, p. 241. The author attributes the quote to a report by Consul General O. Edmund Clubb on U.S.-China conflicts in the years 1949–50.

39. *Ibid.*, pp. 240–44.   40. Mao [36], pp. 361–75.

41. Mao [29], p. 279.   42. Mao [36], pp. 363, 364, 372.

43. Stroganov, p. 19; Viktorov, "Concerning the Events," p. 12; Terskii, pp. 4–8; Martinov, pp. 3–7.

44. Svetlov, p. 23.

45. Stroganov, p. 19; "Great Victory," pp. 1–2.

46. "Historic Victory."

47. Zhukov, "Great October," pp. 14–18; Zhukov, "Historic Meaning," pp. 5–10; Astaf'ev, pp. 11–15.

48. G. Chang, pp. 9–10, 18–21. Bazhanov, pp. 37–38, argues that Mao deliberately tried to deceive such Americans as Edgar Snow and John Service about his real aims and interests.

49. Borisov, *Iz Istorii*, p. 81, criticizes Mao for his policies of cooperating with non-Communist elements and seeking accommodation with the Mongolian

People's Republic, even though Mao, as we have seen, attempted to bring those policies into line with Moscow's dictates. Bazhanov, p. 37, writes: "On several occasions, Stalin's dissatisfaction was caused by actions of the Chinese Communist Party leaders that were in fact aimed at realizing his own recommendations."

50. In 1949, for example, a leader of the Italian Communist Party passing through Moscow told the Soviet leaders: "Too much power has been given to Mao Zedong. If, in talks with the Chinese comrades, you have to point out some deficiencies, they as a rule would say that they are acting on orders from Mao Zedong. He is a leader of the Chinese people, but he does not have a clear perspective on his people, especially the working class, [and] there is a serious danger of a wholesale restoration of capitalism in the cities and in the countryside." Borisov, *Iz Istorii,* p. 99.

51. "After the victory of the revolution, [Stalin] again had concerns that China was Yugoslavia and that I would turn into a Tito." Mao [41], p. 432.

52. Han Yuhui, pp. 124–39.

53. Borisov, *Sovetskii Soiuz,* pp. 116–18.

54. The information in this paragraph is from Mao [36], pp. 370–71; and Han Nianlong, pp. 3–4.

55. Later on, in 1957, Mao expanded on these points: "It is relatively favorable for us if we wait for several years to establish diplomatic relations with the United States. In 1934, the Soviet Union established diplomatic relations with the United States, 17 years after the success of the 1917 revolution. . . . If we do not establish diplomatic relations with the United States in a hurry, it will not have any credibility either at home or abroad, and we will totally deprive it of its political capital and isolate it." Mao [44], p. 83. For some similar remarks on the advantages of nonrecognition, see Mao [43], p. 235.

56. Mao made the move on March 25, 1949, after a stay of more than 10 months in Xibaipo, Hebei Province. He Wenxun, pp. 44, 45; *Zhonggong Dangshi Dashi Nianbiao Shuoming,* p. 133; Shi Zhe, "With Chairman Mao," p. 153.

57. Pan Guangwei, p. 43.

58. Zhou Enlai, "Report," pp. 321, 322.

59. Shen Xiaoyun, p. 241; interview with a well-informed Chinese specialist, Dec. 1989.

60. Quoted in Shen Xiaoyun, p. 241. See also Zhang Xiaolu, pp. 215–16.

61. Tao Wenzhao, p. 5. See also Weng Zhonger, pp. 73–74.

62. One Chinese author, in trying to justify Mao's foreign policy at the time, imputes it to an array of convictions prevalent in Party circles: the Soviet Union was "pursuing an aggressive policy" toward China; Outer Mongolia was under Soviet control; the Northeast was a Soviet sphere of influence; the Sino-Soviet treaty of 1945 was unequal; the Soviet Union had plans to annex Lüshun and Dalian; Soviet aid to the Communists was just the same as U.S. aid to the Nationalists; China did not need foreign assistance if it sought independence; Soviet aid to China could not be unconditional; and the Soviet Union and the United States "were struggling for international influence" over China. Hai Fu, pp. 1–2.

63. Mao [30], pp. 415–23; Mao [17], pp. 62–64; Hai Fu, pp. 3–13; Huan Xiang, pp. 15–16. On the perceived U.S. threat, in April 1950, Mao in reporting on the just-completed treaty of alliance said: "If the imperialists are preparing to strike at us, we can invite a good supporter." App., Doc. 54.

64. For the Soviet perspective on the creation of NATO, see, for example, *Pravda,* April 10, 1949.

65. On Zhou's assignment, see Zhou Enlai, "Report," p. 322; and Wei Shiyan, pp. 3–5.

66. See App., Doc. 3.

67. Kovalev, "Stalin's Dialogue," 2: 84–85.

68. *Ibid.*, p. 82. For the relevant part of the April cable, see App., Doc. 4.

69. Kovalev, "Stalin's Dialogue," 2: 84.

70. Jing Shengzhi, p. 18.

71. Weng Zhonger, p. 74. In the spring and summer of 1949, the U.S. ambassador drew on the good offices of such prominent non-Communist politicians as Luo Longji, Ouyang Cheng, Zhou Yukang, and Chen Mingshu to convey U.S. intentions to the Communist regime. Jing Shengzhi, p. 18. These intermediaries, we believe, gave Mao the impression that the United States was ready to grant diplomatic recognition.

72. Mao designated the deputy political commissar of the 8th Army to handle the case. Wang Daming, p. 50; Jing Shengzhi, p. 18.

73. Weng Zhonger, p. 74.

74. Huang Hua, pp. 30–31. According to Huang, he did not give Stuart a written invitation; the one the ambassador got later was from the president of Yanjing University. On Stuart's view of the impact of the rejection on Mao and Zhou, see Stuart to Acheson, July 18, 1949, in FRUS 1949, 8: 791.

75. For a Chinese rationale for the Sino-American contacts from May to July, see Huang Hua, pp. 22–32; Jing Shengzhi, pp. 17–20; and Zhang Xiaolu, pp. 212–19.

76. He Di, "Evolution," 1989, pp. 44–46; Zhang Nan, pp. 52–53; Jing Shengzhi, p. 20.

77. Jing Shengzhi, p. 20; Zhang Xiaolu, p. 214; Shen Xiaoyun, pp. 243–46. U.S. documents make no mention of a meeting between a Chinese representative (Chen Mingshu in the Chinese sources) and Ambassador Stuart to discuss Mao's speech of June 30.

78. Shen Xiaoyun, p. 241.

79. Jing Shengzhi, p. 20.

80. Deng Xiaoping, p. 135.

81. A CIA source, cited by Buhite, p. 85, reported that on learning of Mao's American connection, Moscow sent a "special emissary" to Beiping, who pressed the Chairman to make this statement. Mao was reportedly so upset by this pressure that he almost fell ill.

82. For the Chinese text, see "Common Program of the Chinese People's Political Consultative Conference (Sept. 29, 1949)," pp. 578–83. An English version may be found in *Important Documents*, pp. 1–20.

83. Mao [6], pp. 15–18.

84. *Sto Sorok Besed s Molotovym*, p. 90. See n. 86, below.

85. Tucker is also of this opinion; see his paper "Prehistory."

86. In addition to the discussion in Chap. 1, see Dinerstein, Chaps. 1–3; Djilas, pp. 114, 115; Holloway, *Soviet Union*, p. 32; Holloway, "Stalin and Hiroshima," pp. 15–20; and *Sto Sorok Besed s Molotovym*, p. 90. For a discussion of Khrushchev's repudiation of Stalin's view on the inevitability of a third world war, see Holloway, *Soviet Union*, p. 32; and Dinerstein, Chap. 3.

87. *Sto Sorok Besed s Molotovym*, pp. 15, 16, 37–38, 92–94, 101, 102–4.

88. *Ibid.*, p. 81.

89. *Ibid.*, pp. 81–85.

90. For a brief discussion of Stalin's prenuclear thinking, see Holloway, *Soviet Union*, p. 36.

91. In 1946, Stalin ordered the 14th Airborne Army to the Chukotka Peninsula with instructions to attack Alaska in case of war. *Sto Sorok Besed s Molotovym*, p. 100.

92. "Stalin was heading for the victory of socialism and the annihilation of capitalism. . . . We needed peace, but according to the American plans, two hundred of our cities had to be bombed simultaneously." *Ibid.*, p. 90.

93. On the concept of encirclement in Soviet military thinking, see Garthoff, pp. 67–77.

94. Chiang Ching-kuo, "Account," p. 113.

95. Novikov, "Vneshniaia Politika"; the original is unascribed and is marked up by Molotov. See also Novikov, *Vospominaniia Diplomata*, p. 353. Excerpts of the report appear as App., Doc. 1. For an analysis and a full English translation, see Malkov, pp. 113–29. We are grateful to David Holloway for providing us with these important sources.

96. Novikov, *Vospominaniia Diplomata*, p. 394. By "these measures," Novikov was explicitly referring to the Truman Doctrine announced in March 1947, to Marshall's speech at Harvard University of June 5, 1947, and to Marshall's letter to Sen. Arthur H. Vandenberg of June 10, 1947.

97. Novikov characterized the Marshall Plan as a program that "in fact creates the conditions for the formation of an American–West European bloc with its spearhead aimed against the Soviet Union and the East European countries." *Ibid.*, p. 394.

98. Djilas, pp. 182–83.

99. Triska and Finley, pp. 293–98.

100. Unless otherwise cited, the information in this and the next three paragraphs is from Kovalev, "Stalin's Dialogue," 1: 86–88.

101. Liu Jianshi and Zou Bin, p. 171; Hou Dingyuan, p. 86. All three authors are former Nationalist officials.

102. Kovalev, "Stalin's Dialogue," 1: 87–88. The clearly troubled Forrestal resigned as defense secretary on March 1, 1949, and committed suicide in May.

103. On the growth of the U.S. arsenal and nuclear delivery capabilities during this period, see Rosenberg.

104. The incident occurred on April 20, 1949. For information on Mao's response to the incident and relevant Sino-British negotiations, see Kang Maozhao, pp. 33–47; and "I Am Tao Yong's Patron," p. 240.

105. Kovalev, "Stalin's Dialogue," 1: 87–88.

106. Unless otherwise cited, the information in this and the following five paragraphs is from *ibid.*, 2: 86, 88. See also Shi Zhe, *Zai Lishi*, pp. 390–92.

107. Mao reached the decision on the Liu mission in early May 1949. Shi Zhe, "On the Eve," p. 223; Shi Zhe, "I Accompanied Chairman Mao," p. 126.

108. For Mao's cable on the markers, see App., Doc. 2. On the Sino-Soviet negotiations on the border markers along the Amur River, see Li Ping and Fang Ming, p. 818.

109. Kovalev's unpublished memoirs.

110. The information in this and the next paragraph is from Kovalev, "Stalin's Dialogue," 2: 87.

111. For the pertinent part of the cable, see App., Doc. 5.

112. Kovalev, "Stalin's Dialogue," 2: 86; document from Kovalev's personal archive.

113. Shi Zhe, *Zai Lishi*, p. 395.

114. The Liu delegation quietly slipped out of Beiping by train. At Lüshun, it proceeded on by air via North Korea, arriving in Moscow on or about July 8. The delegation included Gao Gang, Wang Jiaxiang, Xu Jiefan, and Shi Zhe. Min Li, "On the Eve," p. 22; Zhu Yuanshi, pp. 76–79; Shi Zhe, *Zai Lishi*, pp. 395–96. According to Shi Zhe, the delegation was to arrive in Moscow on July 8 or 9, but a Kovalev document dated July 7 records, "soon after arrival in Moscow." See App., Doc. 8.

115. Shi Zhe, *Zai Lishi*, p. 425.

116. *Pravda*, July 6, 1949. Kapitsa, p. 342, notes that the Soviets also published Mao's speech as a special pamphlet.

117. Shi Zhe, "On the Eve," pp. 223–24; Shi Zhe, *Zai Lishi*, p. 408. Some Chinese sources put the number of meetings at five. See, for example, Huang Gangzhou, p. 160.

118. The following discussion is based on Shi Zhe, *Zai Lishi*, pp. 398–403.

119. *Ibid.*, p. 449.

120. *Ibid.*, p. 404.

121. The rest of this paragraph and the one that follows are based on *ibid.*, p. 405.

122. Kovalev, "Stalin's Dialogue," 2: 86.

123. Interview with M. S. Kapitsa, April 3, 1992.

124. Based on Kovalev's unpublished memoirs; and Kovalev, "Stalin's Dialogue," 2: 86.

125. For information on the meeting of July 27, see Kovalev, "Stalin's Dialogue," 1: 88–89; and Bo Yibo, p. 37.

126. Kovalev, "Stalin's Dialogue," 1: 89. The Soviet Union later reduced the number of republics to 15 by making the Karelo-Finnish Republic an administrative division of the Russian Soviet Federated Socialist Republic (the so-called Karel'skaia Autonomous Soviet Socialist Republic). In a published interview, Shi Zhe states that "Liu was the only spokesman" in the meetings with Stalin and that Gao had no opportunity to make any proposal on the status of the Northeast. Li Haiwen, p. 63. The problem is that Shi Zhe reports only that a banquet took place on "about July 27," suggesting that he did not attend the meeting that day. See below, n. 132.

127. Unless otherwise cited, the information in this and the next paragraph is from Kovalev, "Stalin's Dialogue," 1: 89. By gaining support from foreign countries, especially from Japan, Zhang Zuolin (Chang Tso-lin; 1875–1928) consolidated his personal power in Manchuria from 1919 on. He even extended his control over North China and his influence to the Yangtze River valley. For information on Zhang's career, see Chang Cheng.

128. Gao Gang left Moscow for Beiping on July 30. Bo Yibo, p. 37. According to Kovalev, on the same day, Stalin, in a conversation with Liu, said, "I was too severe toward Comrade Gao; you, too, and without any grounds. Please convey my opinion to Comrade Mao." Liu did so, thereby rescuing Gao from trouble. He remained the leader of the Northeast, and in conversations with Kovalev, Mao repeatedly stressed that he had always supported Gao Gang and had once even saved him from an attempt to eliminate him. Kovalev, "Stalin's Dialogue," 1: 89.

129. Kovalev, "Stalin's Dialogue," 2: 82. See also Shi Zhe, *Zai Lishi*, p. 405.

130. Document from Kovalev's personal archive. In his cables to Moscow before the departure of the Chinese delegation from Beiping, Mao repeatedly requested Stalin's air and naval support for the planned occupation of Taiwan.

131. Most of the information in this paragraph and the following one is from Kovalev, "Stalin's Dialogue," 1: 88; and Kovalev's unpublished memoirs.

132. Shi Zhe recollects only that on July 27 Stalin organized a grand reception at his dacha in Kuntsevo. Shi Zhe, *Zai Lishi*, pp. 410–11. According to Kovalev, the reception, during which the Soviet leader tried to restore relations between Gao Gang and the other Chinese, took place three days later. The information from Kovalev's unpublished memoirs seems more consistent with the flow of events, and we follow it here.

133. Bo Yibo, p. 37.

134. Kovalev, "Stalin's Dialogue," 1: 88; Kovalev's unpublished memoirs. Presumably Liu Shaoqi's report back to Mao and Zhou Enlai on Stalin's refusal to back PLA military action against Taiwan led to a CCP Politburo decision to withdraw the request for support.

135. Unless otherwise cited, the information in this and the next paragraph is from Deng Liqun, "On the Eve," pp. 143–44; Shi Zhe, *Zai Lishi*, pp. 407–8; Zhang Zhian, pp. 63–67; Zhu Peimin, "Whole Story," p. 197; Zhu Peimin, "Probing Some Problems," pp. 69–70; and Zhu Yuanshi, p. 79.

136. Stalin said: "Concerning sending combat aircraft to Xinjiang, that could be useful in fighting the cavalry of [the warlord] General Ma [Bufang]'s family; it is very easy to accomplish. We can send one of our air force regiments, 40–50 airplanes." Document from Kovalev's personal archive.

137. On Mao's original timetable, Xinjiang was to be occupied in 1950. In early August 1949, Mao instructed Peng Dehuai, commander of the 1st Field Army, to investigate the feasibility of occupying Xinjiang before the year was out. Peng Dehuai, "Peng Dehuai's Cable," p. 2.

138. For detailed information on Deng Liqun's activities in Xinjiang and the Soviet role in the takeover of Xinjiang, see Deng Liqun, "Selection of Cables," pp. 1–38.

139. This paragraph and the next are based on Shi Zhe, *Zai Lishi*, pp. 406–7.

140. Kovalev's unpublished memoirs.

141. Shi Zhe, *Zai Lishi*, p. 410; Zhu Yuanshi, pp. 76–77.

142. Kovalev, "Stalin's Dialogue," 1: 88.

143. Kovalev's unpublished memoirs; for related information, see Kovalev, "Stalin's Dialogue," 2: 79–80. For another statement in the same vein, see App., Doc. 6. This version of Stalin's speech in general corresponds to the version in Shi Zhe, *Zai Lishi*, pp. 412–13.

144. Interview with M. S. Kapitsa, April 3, 1992.

145. Unless otherwise cited, this and the next paragraph are based on Kovalev, "Stalin's Dialogue," 2: 79–80; and Shi Zhe, *Zai Lishi*, pp. 413–14. For Stalin's remarks on the Chinese entry into the Cominform, see App., Doc. 7.

146. On several other occasions, Stalin advanced the idea of China organizing such a union. For example, in May 1951, he made this proposal to Wang Jiaxiang, the Chinese ambassador to the Soviet Union. Lin Li, p. 213. In App., Doc. 7, Kovalev calls the organization the Union of East Asian Communist Parties, but in later documents he (like the Chinese) uses Union of Asian Communist Parties.

147. Shi Zhe, "What I Saw," pp. 27–28; Min Li, "On the Eve," pp. 24–26; Shi Zhe, "I Accompanied Chairman Mao," p. 126; Qu Xing, "Soviet Policy," p. 5.

148. Nie Rongzhen, *Nie Rongzhen Huiyilu*, p. 734; Shi Zhe, "What I Saw," pp. 28–31.

149. Shi Zhe, "I Accompanied Chairman Mao," p. 127.

150. Borisov, *Iz Istorii*, p. 55.

151. Kovalev, "Stalin's Dialogue," 2:78. Kovalev had made a handwritten 21-page transcript of Stalin's remarks. Here and in some other cases, we quote this document.

152. Yu Zhen, "On the Creation," p. 450; Li Ping and Fang Ming, p. 833.

153. Li Ke and Hao Shengzhang, p. 280. Additional information on the Soviet decision to assist in the development of the Chinese air force is in He Di, "Last Campaign," unpublished manuscript cited with the permission of the author; and Nie Rongzhen, *Nie Rongzhen Huiyilu*, pp. 734–35.

154. Shi Zhe, *Zai Lishi*, pp. 405–6.

155. For notes on Kovalev's report to Stalin on intelligence and counterintelligence, see App., Doc. 8.

156. Kovalev's unpublished memoirs; document in Kovalev's personal archive.

157. Deng Liqun, "On the Eve," p. 150.

158. Shi Zhe, "I Accompanied Chairman Mao," p. 127. Some Chinese sources state that the CCP leadership had already listed Oct. 1, 1949, as one of the appropriate dates for the founding of the People's Republic. See, for example, Huang Zhaokang, p. 4.

159. The first group of Soviet advisers in China totaled 200. The information in this and the next paragraph is from Li Yueran, *Waijiao*, pp. 4, 15; Qu Xing, "Soviet Policy," p. 5; and Shi Zhe, "I Accompanied Chairman Mao," p. 128. Other sources say there were 220 advisers in the first group. See, for example, Zhu Yuanshi, p. 79.

160. Shi Zhe, *Zai Lishi*, pp. 409, 416–17.

161. *Ibid.*, p. 406. See also Buhite, p. 87; Shi Zhe, "I Accompanied Chairman Mao," p. 126; and *Dongbei Ribao* [Northeast Daily], July 31, 1949. The first of the Soviet-CCP agreements on the Northeast was signed in 1946. By the autumn of 1949, such agreements had become almost routine. Yun Zhang and Xiao Chun, pp. 237–41; Borisov, *Sovietskii Soiuz*, pp. 29–31.

162. Shi Zhe, *Zai Lishi*, p. 424. Liu Yalou and Zhang Aiping, the commander of the Chinese air force and a senior naval officer, respectively, also stayed on in Moscow to discuss the matter of Soviet military advisers. Huang Gangzhou, p. 162.

163. See, for example, Zhu Yuanshi, p. 77.

Chapter Three

1. Zhou Enlai, "Memorandum," p. 5; "Cable from the Soviet Government," p. 6. Although the Soviet Union is officially held to be the first state to recognize the PRC, in fact the Yugoslav cable of recognition arrived before the Soviet message. To avoid infuriating Stalin, the Chinese did not accept Belgrade's offer of recognition. Kovalev's unpublished memoirs.

2. App., Doc. 9.

3. Qu Xing, "Soviet Policy," pp. 7, 8. Kovalev did not attend the banquet on the

founding of the PRC because he did not receive instructions to do so, thereby adding to the insult. Kovalev's unpublished memoirs.

4. *Pravda*, Sept. 25, 1949.

5. Holloway, *Stalin and the Bomb*, Chap. 12.   6. Malenkov, "Report."

7. *Pravda*, Nov. 9, 10, 1949.   8. Malenkov; Suslov.

9. See the text of Stalin's cable in *Pravda*, Oct. 14, 1949.

10. For excerpts from this report, see App., Doc. 22.

11. Kovalev, "Stalin's Dialogue," 2: 80. On the proper name of the Union, see Chap. 2, n. 146.

12. Liu Shaoqi, "Opening Speech," pp. 440–41.

13. Document from Kovalev's personal archive. See also Kovalev, "Stalin's Dialogue," 2: 80.

14. Kovalev, "Stalin's Dialogue," 2: 80.

15. Ershov, pp. 8–12. As early as July 1949, *Pravda* had emphasized that after the defeat in China, American capitalists would seek to make India the focus of their activities. Zhukov, "Colonial Appetites."

16. For information on Mao's decision to occupy Taiwan by the summer of 1950, see Xu Yan, *Diyi Ci*, pp. 12–13; and Yu Zhen, "On the Creation," p. 450.

17. Yang Guoyu, p. 41. For information on Mao's plan to attack Taiwan, see, for example, Zhou Jun, pp. 67–74; Zhao Wei, pp. 32–35; and Huang Shengtian, pp. 22–24.

18. During the four-day Quemoy campaign in October 1949, almost 10,000 members of the PLA's 28th Corps were killed or captured. Mao [3], p. 190; Xu Yan, *Jinmen*, pp. 44–93; Han Huaizhi and Tan Jingqiao, 1: 226–27, 233–37; Song Yijun, pp. 29–32; Sun Zhaiwei, pp. 27–31; Academy of Military Science, *Zhongguo Renmin Jiefangjun Dashiji*, p. 303.

19. On the very night (Oct. 25) that the General Staff pointed out in a report that "it is impossible to occupy Jinmen in the near future" without a stronger navy, Mao had written an instruction to that effect: "We must build a powerful navy capable of defending our coastal areas and guarding against possible aggression by the imperialists." Guo Fuwen and Cao Baojian, p. 74. For the impact of the failure of the Quemoy invasion on PLA morale, see Chen Yi, p. 9.

20. Mao [28], pp. 100–101; Xu Yan, *Diyi Ci*, p. 13.

21. See, for example, Durdin, "Formosa Invasion."

22. Simmons, pp. 65–66. During his Moscow visit, Mao asked that Roshchin be replaced. When informed of the request, Foreign Minister Andrei Vyshinskii said, "The Soviet Politburo, not Mao, will decide who is the right person to be Soviet ambassador to Beijing." Interviews with A. M. Ledovskii (Soviet consul general in Shenyang in the early 1950s), Nov. 1990, March 1991. All the while that Roshchin was in Beijing, Mao studiously ignored him. Kovalev's unpublished memoirs. Mao's formal reply on receiving Roshchin's credentials is in App., Doc. 10.

23. For another example of Stalin's signals, see the article by S. Toka, the first secretary of the regional Party Committee, praising the economic and cultural achievements of "Soviet" Tuva. Like the Nationalists before them, the Communists considered Tuva part of China and held that it had been illegally annexed by the Soviets during the war. Liu Likai and Yang Jinbao, pp. 303–4. Particularly offensive to the Chinese was a map in *Pravda* showing Tuva within the Soviet Union and the Mongolian People's Republic. See Kovyzhenko.

24. On the domestic situation in the country after the founding of the PRC, see Gurtov and Hwang, pp. 25–34.

25. Quan Yanchi, *Mao Zedong*, p. 96.

26. For example, in Aug. 1949, Gao Gang tried to demonstrate his special ties with Moscow and his loyalty to Stalin by going to meet a large group of Soviet advisers as they arrived in China with Liu Shaoqi. See Li Yueran, *Waijiao*, pp. 7–8.

27. Kovalev, "Stalin's Dialogue," 1: 89–90.

28. Qu Xing, "Soviet Policy," p. 77.

29. According to the U.S. consul general in Beiping, O. Edmund Clubb, Mao had told the leader of the China Democratic League that he was unable to accept American aid because it would arouse Soviet suspicions. Clubb to Acheson, Sept. 27, 1949, in FRUS 1949, 8: 538.

30. Hai Fu, pp. 82–87.

31. Li Yueran, *Waijiao*, p. 15; Li Yueran, "Recollections," p. 5.

32. Kovalev, "Stalin's Dialogue," 2: 88.

33. Shi Zhe, "I Accompanied Chairman Mao," p. 128.

34. Zhu Zhongli, *Liming*, pp. 354–55; Lu Hong, p. 49.

35. App., Doc. 11.

36. Unless otherwise cited, this paragraph is based on Shi Zhe, "I Accompanied Chairman Mao," pp. 128, 130; and Min Li, "On the Eve," pp. 32, 43.

37. Mao and Zhou had decided on this division of labor on Oct. 1, immediately after the founding ceremony of the PRC. Min Li, "On the Eve," pp. 9–10.

38. One celebrated example of face-saving dated back to 1139, when the Song Emperor designated his chancellor to kneel in his stead before the Jin Empire envoy. Goncharov, *Diplomatiia Imperatorskogo Kitaia*, pp. 198–206. Some Chinese authors contend that Mao decided to leave Zhou Enlai in Beijing during the initial stage of the talks purely for reasons of practical convenience. See, for example, Wu Xiuquan, *Eight Years*, pp. 10–11; and Min Li, "On the Eve," p. 9.

39. Mao took along just four men: Chen Boda, his political affairs secretary and the person in charge of drafting documents; Ye Zilong, chief secretary responsible for his daily life; Wang Dongxing, his chief bodyguard; and his interpreter and adviser on questions related to the Soviet Union, Shi Zhe, who was head of the Political Secretaries' Section and the Bureau of Compilation and Translation, both under the Central Committee. Three Soviet officials—Ambassador Roshchin, Kovalev, and N. T. Fedorenko of the embassy staff—accompanied the Chinese delegation. Li Yueran, *Waijiao*, pp. 5, 21, 136; Min Li, "On the Eve," p. 39; Shi Zhe, "I Accompanied Chairman Mao," p. 128; Fedorenko, pp. 135–36.

40. Unless otherwise noted, the information in this and the following two paragraphs is from Kovalev, "Stalin's Dialogue," 2: 88, 89.

41. For the request for medical assistance, see App., Doc. 12.

42. See, for example, Lei Zhongmin, pp. 96–101.

43. App., Doc. 13.

44. On Stalin's apparent change of attitude toward intervening in the decisions of the CCP, see Shi Zhe, "I Accompanied Chairman Mao," pp. 129–30; and Min Li, "On the Eve," pp. 25, 26, 28, 29, 30.

45. App., Doc. 14; Zhu Zhongli, *Nanyi*, pp. 33–34; Zhu Zhongli, *Liming*, p. 359.

46. At first, "Hunan lace and embroidery, china, tea, and salted bamboo

shoots" were selected as gifts for Stalin. At the insistence of Mao's wife, Jiang Qing, the Chinese delegation agreed to take along vegetables from Shandong as well, and on Dec. 1, 1949, the Central Committee sent a cable to the Shandong authorities instructing them to send the best radishes, cabbages, green onions, and pears to Beijing by a special plane. Shi Zhe, "I Accompanied Chairman Mao," p. 128; App., Doc. 16. Consul General Angus Ward was permitted to leave Shenyang the day after Mao departed; we do not believe there was any connection between the two events.

47. Shi Zhe, "What I Saw," p. 32.

48. Kovalev's unpublished memoirs; Kovalev, "Stalin's Dialogue," 2: 88. See also Bazhanov, p. 47. Acccording to Kovalev, on the eve of Mao's departure, he called Kovalev and described the country's desperate economic situation. Mao asked Kovalev to transmit his message to Stalin, and Kovalev assumed that Mao's purpose was to pave the way for the discussion of a loan.

49. Unless otherwise noted, this paragraph is based on Wu Xiangting and Han Xuejing, pp. 247–48; and an interview with S. L. Tikhvinskii, 1991. Tikhvinskii, then Soviet consul general in Beijing, accompanied Mao to the Soviet border.

50. Wu Xiuquan, *Wo de Licheng*, pp. 201–2; Ling Hui, "Description," p. 14.

51. According to Shi Zhe, the suspect arrested near Tianjin was held on a charge of carrying a grenade. Shi Zhe, "What I Saw," p. 32; Shi Zhe, "I Accompanied Chairman Mao," p. 128. On the anti-Mao activities of Nationalist intelligence during the trip to Moscow, see Ling Hui, "Cracking," pp. 71–73.

52. Kovalev, "Stalin's Dialogue," 1: 89, 90.

53. *Pravda*, Dec. 17, 1949.

54. Kovalev, "Stalin's Dialogue," 2: 89. Stalin had planned to have Mao stay in what had been a suburban residence for senior Nationalist diplomats, but on Kovalev's advice that this would be an insult, he put him up instead at a dacha of his own in Usachevka. Mao asked Kovalev and his wife to stay with him at the dacha, but Kovalev refused.

55. Shi Zhe, *Zai Lishi*, p. 433; Shi Zhe, "I Accompanied Chairman Mao," p. 129.

56. Kirk to Acheson, Dec. 21, 1949, in FRUS 1949, 8: 642. For the text of Mao's arrival speech on Dec. 16, see App., Doc. 17.

57. Unless otherwise cited, the account of this initial meeting is based on Shi Zhe, "Chairman Mao's First Visit," p. 4; Shi Zhe, *Zai Lishi*, pp. 435–36; Shi Zhe, "I Accompanied Chairman Mao," pp. 128–30; Min Li, "On the Eve," pp. 38, 42, 43, 47, 54; and Fedorenko, p. 137. The comments on the Soviet documents concerning the first Stalin-Mao meeting are based on an interview with a senior Soviet diplomat who has had extensive access to the archives, Aug. 1992.

58. Mao attempted to air his grievances several times during the talks, but Stalin always cut him off. Shi Zhe, *Zai Lishi*, pp. 451–52.

59. Years later, Mao explained what he had really meant by "both beautiful and tasty." "Beautiful" alluded to the replacement of the humiliating treaty of 1945 with a new treaty, "tasty" to the obtaining of credits. Quan Yanchi, *Mao Zedong*, p. 31.

60. According to Shi Zhe, "Chairman Mao did not want to state [his intentions] clearly because he believed that the Soviet side had more experience and had to propose assistance to us on its own initiative. [Otherwise], it would not be sincere." Shi Zhe, "Chairman Mao's First Visit," p. 4.

61. This paragraph is based on Wu Xiuquan, "Process," pp. 11, 12–13. Wu Xiuquan was in the Zhou Enlai entourage that arrived in Moscow on Jan. 20, 1950. He participated in the treaty negotiations in his capacity as director of the Department of Soviet and East European Affairs of the PRC Ministry of Foreign Affairs.

62. Shi Zhe, "I Accompanied Chairman Mao," pp. 129–30.

63. Zhu Zhongli, *Liming*, p. 362.

64. Since Wu did not attend this meeting, he is presumably quoting documents or the recollections of others. Wu Xiuquan, "My Diplomatic Career," p. 5; Min Li, "On the Eve," p. 58.

65. Liu Xiao, "Mission" (1987), p. 15.

66. Mao [41], p. 432.

67. Shi Zhe, "I Accompanied Chairman Mao," p. 130; Min Li, "Handshake," p. 44; Min Li, "On the Eve," p. 54.

68. Shi Zhe, "Chairman Mao's First Visit," pp. 4–5; Shi Zhe, *Zai Lishi*, pp. 437, 438.

69. *Sto Sorok Besed s Molotovym*, p. 114.

70. Kovalev, "Stalin's Dialogue," 2: 89.

71. App., Doc. 18.

72. Khrushchev, *Last Testament*, p. 240. Italics in original omitted.

73. Mao [41], p. 432.

74. Kovalev, "Stalin's Dialogue," 2: 89.

75. See App., Doc. 18.

76. Chinese sources state that Mao was forced to instruct Wang Jiaxiang to inform the Soviet side semiofficially and indirectly about his basic intentions. Zhu Zhongli, *Liming*, p. 362.

77. The information in this and the next paragraph is from Kovalev, "Stalin's Dialogue," 2: 89. Kovalev's report to Stalin on his Dec. 20 talk with Mao is in App., Doc. 19.

78. For a thoughtful analysis of this question, see Kirk to Acheson, Dec. 18, 1949, in FRUS 1949, 8: 637–38.

79. "Stalin was anxious to create the impression that we were on the best terms with Mao and firmly on the side of the Chinese people." Khrushchev, *Last Testament*, p. 240.

80. Volkogonov, 2.2: 78. See photograph of Mao sitting on Stalin's right during the celebrations in *Pravda*, Dec. 22, 1949. In his speech, Mao was lukewarm in his praise of Stalin, describing him as "great," as opposed to the glowing terms used by all the other foreign leaders: "genius," "genial thinker and leader," "genial teacher," and "genial warrior." The same attitude was even more evident in Chen Boda's article commemorating Stalin's birthday. In it, Chen emphasized that Mao had overcome his "dogmatist" rivals in the intra-Party struggle because he had correctly implemented Stalin's ideas while his opponents had perverted them. This was an indirect rebuff to the Soviet leader, who had in fact supported such "dogmatists" as Wang Ming. Chen Boda, p. 29.

81. Mao's speech is in App., Doc. 20. See also Shi Zhe, "I Accompanied Chairman Mao," p. 130. *Pravda*, Dec. 22, 1949, stated that the audience had applauded five times during the speech and then stood up and applauded loudly at the end.

82. Shi Zhe, *Zai Lishi*, p. 441.

83. App., Doc. 21.

84. Unless otherwise cited, the information in this and the following two paragraphs is from Bo Yibo, pp. 40–41; Kovalev's diary; and Kovalev's unpublished memoirs. Kovalev gives the full text of the report in his memoirs. Excerpts are in App., Doc. 22.

85. The dates of the three meetings are based on Mao's cables in App., Docs. 21, 23. With respect to the third meeting, Doc. 23 says only, "I am planning to give [Stalin] a copy of your cable tomorrow (29)."

86. Six of the original eight generators at Xiaofengman had been shipped to the Soviet Union after Japan's surrender; the other two were inadequate for the power needs of south Manchuria. Yao Xu, *Cong Yalujiang*, p. 21.

87. In his interview with a TASS correspondent on Jan. 2, 1950, Mao mentioned economic cooperation and loans as matters still to be settled. See App., Doc. 24.

88. App., Doc. 25.

89. Interview with a Soviet specialist who escorted Peng Zhen on his visit to the Soviet Union in Nov. 1956. On that visit, see Li Yueran, *Waijiao*, pp. 95, 99–107. On Mao's feeling of isolation during his visit to Moscow, see also Liu Ruizhe, p. 76. Liu exaggerates the span of time during which Mao failed to meet Stalin, claiming it was "tens of days."

90. Li Yinqiao and Quan Yanchi, pp. 63–64.

91. Kovalev's unpublished memoirs. See also Shi Zhe, "Chairman Mao's First Visit," p. 5; and Wu Xiuquan, "Process," p. 11.

92. See Shi Zhe, "What I Saw," p. 36; Shi Zhe, "I Accompanied Chairman Mao," p. 130; and Zhu Zhongli, *Liming*, p. 362.

93. Based on Shi Zhe, "What I Saw," p. 36; and Zhu Zhongli, *Liming*, p. 362. Mao Zedong stated that the decision to publish this interview was made on Jan. 1, 1950. Mao's cable, dated Jan. 2, is in App., Doc. 25.

94. For a Chinese analysis of the interview, see Shi Zhe, *Zai Lishi*, p. 439.

95. Interview with a well-informed Chinese specialist, Dec. 1989.

96. App., Doc. 24.

97. Based on Shi Zhe, "Chairman Mao's First Visit," p. 6.

98. "Good News," p. 5.

99. "Mao to Discuss Sino-Soviet Pact."

100. Shi Zhe, "What I Saw," p. 36, and Shi Zhe, "I Accompanied Chairman Mao," p. 130, may be the source of this error.

101. Unless otherwise cited, the information on the Molotov-Mikoyan talks is based on Mao's Jan. 2 cable (App., Doc. 25); and Shi Zhe, *Zai Lishi*, pp. 439–40.

102. Another indirect proof of this mood is Khrushchev's statement: "Rumors began reaching our ears that Mao was not at all happy, that he was kept under lock and key, and that everyone was ignoring him. Mao let it be known that if the situation continued, he would leave." Khrushchev, *Last Testament*, p. 240.

103. Both Mao and Stalin preferred to work at night. Pang Xianzhi, "Mao Zedong," p. 23; Quan Yanchi, *Mao Zedong*, pp. 26–27, 46; Fedorenko, p. 138. For Mao's Jan. 3 cable, see App., Doc. 25. In his memoirs, Shi Zhe mentions the cable sent at 11:00 P.M., Jan. 2, but not the one sent at 4:00 the next morning. Shi does say that Stalin phoned Mao after the Molotov-Mikoyan meeting. Shi Zhe, *Zai Lishi*, pp. 440–41.

104. Wu Xiuquan, "Process," pp. 13–14, notes, "Stalin was thinking about keeping Lüshun and Dalian as long as possible. Lüshunkou really was a very im-

portant naval base. The Soviet Union connected the stay of its troops in Lüshun and Dalian to the joint exploitation of the Chinese Changchun Railroad because it was moving provisions and matériel [for its troops there] via the railroad."

105. Rong Zhi, p. 103.

106. For additional information on Sino-Soviet trade issues, see App., Doc. 28.

107. App., Doc. 26. In this cable, Mao asked that Burhan (chairman of the Xinjiang People's Government) and Deng Liqun (secretary-general of the Xinjiang Branch of the Central Committee and head of the Foreign Affairs Division of the Xinjiang government) accompany Zhou. In his cable of Jan. 2 (Doc. 25), Mao had mentioned Li Fuchun (vice-chairman of the Northeast People's Government and deputy head of the Central Finance and Economics Commission).

108. Mao [39], p. 164.

109. App., Doc. 27.

110. See Shi Zhe, "Chairman Mao's First Visit," pp. 6–7.

111. Khrushchev, *Last Testament*, pp. 243–44. As noted, the editor of Khrushchev's memoirs incorrectly attributes Kovalev's report to Paniushkin. On Stalin giving Kovalev's report to Mao, see also Bo Yibo, p. 41. Stalin never told his agent in China that he had passed on the report. Kovalev only learned of it later, in Feb. 1950, from a confidential Chinese source. Kovalev, "Stalin's Dialogue," 1: 90–91; Kovalev's unpublished memoirs.

112. Shi Zhe, *Zai Lishi*, pp. 393, 438.

113. Zhu Zhongli, *Liming*, p. 362; Min Li, "On the Eve," pp. 54–56; *Pravda*, Jan. 12, 17, 1950.

114. At his news conference, Truman indicated that the United States had no desire to establish military bases on Taiwan and did not intend to pursue a course that would lead to American involvement in the Chinese civil war. "The Position of the United States with Respect to Asia" [NSC 48/2, Dec. 30, 1949] in FRUS 1949, 7.2: 1219; the text of the President's statement of Jan. 5 is in Dept. of State *Bulletin*, Jan. 16, 1950, p. 79. For U.S. press accounts and comment, see Hinton, "Senator Knowland"; White, "Acheson"; Krock; Durdin, "Chiang"; Reston, "Debate"; and "News of the Week." For a review of the history of NSC 48, see Cumings, 2: Chap. 5; and Schaller, *American Occupation*, Chap. 11.

115. "Texts of Statements."

116. White, "Congress."

117. Reston, "Debate"; "News of the Week." For an analysis of Washington's policy toward China and Taiwan in the context of the emerging Sino-Soviet alliance, see G. Chang, Chap. 2.

118. Hu Yuzhi, p. 4; Hu Shixian, pp. 16–18; Si Mu, "International Significance," pp. 19–21.

119. Si Mu, "Brief Discussion," p. 3; Deng Chao, "Establishment," pp. 10–11.

120. Hinton, "U.S. Recalls Aides." The Beijing Military Control Committee confiscated the American, French, and Dutch barracks in the city on Jan. 14 and 19. Feng Jing, p. 12. The British barracks were confiscated three months later, in April 1950. Han Nianlong, p. 18.

121. Kovalev, "Stalin's Dialogue," 2: 83.

122. "Secret Agreement"; "Secret U.S.-Nationalist Conference"; "People of Taiwan"; "United States Continues to Arm"; "New Assault." Some of these articles were reprints from Xinhua, and some were TASS originals.

123. Viktorov, "International Review." As early as Jan. 4, 1950, according to

Salisbury, "Soviet Backs Mao," *Krasnyi Flot* (Red Fleet) had come out in support of the PRC's right to liberate Taiwan and quoted a Soviet Central Committee message saying that this task had to be accomplished during 1950. On Jan. 7, only a day after British recognition, Moscow agreed to deliver airplane fuel to China, and on Jan. 13, Mao informed Liu Shaoqi that Moscow had agreed to the visit of Liu Yalou, commander of the Chinese air force, for negotiations on Soviet aid. See App., Doc. 32. In February and March, Moscow stationed one air division near Shanghai and other units near Xuzhou in northern Jiangsu Province. During the Nationalist air raids, Soviet-manned Soviet fighters shot down several Nationalist planes. Deng Lifeng, *Xin Zhongguo*, p. 82; Nie Rongzhen, *Nie Rongzhen Huiyilu*, p. 733; Borisov and Koloskov, *Sovetsko-Kitaiskie Otnosheniia, 1945–1980 gg.*, p. 53.

124. Xiao Jingguang, *Xiao Jingguang Huiyilu*, 2: 29; Zhou Jun, p. 70.

125. Interview with a Chinese specialist who was well informed about the Stalin-Mao talks, 1989.

126. For an insightful treatment of how Britain's policy toward the PRC was shaped by its concerns about the security of Hong Kong, see MacDonald, passim.

127. App., Docs. 29, 30.

128. "Peiping Urges"; "Peiping U. N. Drive"; Hamilton, "Russian Quits"; Rosenthal; Hamilton, "Malik Again Quits"; "Soviet Walks Out."

129. Hamilton, "Russian Quits." For a later scholarly analysis that reached almost the same conclusion about the Soviet walkout, see Shulman, p. 142.

130. Interview with V. P. Tkachenko, former head of the Korean section of the Central Committee, CPSU, March 30, 1992.

131. Acheson, "Crisis," pp. 111–18. The quote is from p. 115. For an exhaustive examination of the background and possible meaning of the speech, see Cumings, 2: Chap. 13. Here we concentrate on how the speech was read by Stalin and Mao, not on Acheson's intent or broader policies.

132. Waggoner, "Acheson."

133. In Dec. 1949, Su Yu, deputy commander of the 3rd Field Army, in reporting on invasion plans for Taiwan, said, "American imperialism at most can only interfere in the war indirectly, such as mobilizing Japanese 'volunteers' to come to the bandit Chiang's rescue." Responding that "direct involvement of American imperialism in China's civil war is detrimental to its interests politically and militarily," Mao expressed confidence that U.S. forces would not intervene. Xu Yan, *Diyi Ci*, pp. 11–12.

134. *Cankao Xiaoxi* (Reference News), as translated in *Posolstvo SSSR*, pp. 3–6. A note in *Cankao Xiao*, a publication that ran translations of articles from the Western press, concluded, "[The U.S.] statements are full of fear over the results of the future U.S. policy in the Far East. . . . Major newspapers of reactionary persuasion suggest either deploying American troops on Formosa, recognizing the Chinese [that is, the PRC] government, treating Formosa as Japanese territory, or putting it under a trusteeship of the United Nations." In the analytical foreword to the Russian edition, a Soviet diplomat stated that there were "only a few suggestions to recognize China" in the American press at the moment.

135. Zhou Jun, p. 71.

136. Su Yu, "Report on the Problem of Liberating Taiwan" (Jan. 27, 1950), cited in He Di, "Last Campaign."

137. App., Doc. 33.

138. "State Department's Statement"; Hinton, "U.S. Recalls Aides."

139. App., Doc. 36. Mao left Leningrad on Jan. 16 and got back to Moscow the next day. "Chairman Mao and Premier Zhou," p. 1110.

140. On Jan. 20, Mao approved opening talks with India on the establishment of diplomatic relations but ordered a delay, for tactical reasons, in the talks with Britain. App., Doc. 39.

141. App., Doc. 33. One sign of the importance Stalin attached to Acheson's statement is the manner in which the Soviet denunciation of it was released. Usually official statements were simply published by *Pravda* or *Izvestia*, but in this case, French journalists were summoned to the Kremlin at one o'clock in the morning and given copies. Salisbury, "Vyshinskii Assails Acheson Remarks."

142. App., Doc. 37.

143. Shi Zhe, *Zai Lishi*, pp. 454–55.

144. App., Doc. 38. Mao cautioned his cipher clerks to send the telegram in encrypted form, not in standard code and to be "extremely careful when proof-reading; do not make any mistakes."

145. "Statement of USSR Minister of Foreign Affairs"; "Statement of the Head of the News Department" (*Renmin Ribao*).

146. Both documents concentrated on disproving Acheson's point that the Soviet Union was "detaching" lands from China and "attaching them to the Soviet Union." Both quoted from statements by the former U.S. Consul General at Shenyang, Angus Ward, rebutting the notion of detachment. See "Ward Feels Russia Won't Annex Land."

147. Based on Shi Zhe, *Zai Lishi*, pp. 454–55.

148. Waggoner, "Connally"; Durdin, "Sino-Soviet Talks."

149. Sulzberger, "Vast Issues."

150. Durdin, "Sino-Soviet Talks." On the date of Zhou's arrival in Moscow, see Lu Hong, p. 51; Zhu Zhongli, *Liming*, p. 362; and Min Li, "On the Eve," p. 58.

151. Acheson to Bruce, Jan. 25, 1950, in FRUS 1950, 6: 294–96.

152. Waggoner, "State Department"; "Text of the U.S. 'Background' on China"; "Acheson Backing."

153. The information on this meeting and its aftermath is from Shi Zhe, *Zai Lishi*, pp. 456–59.

154. "Statement of the Head of the News Department" (*Pravda*) Maevskii.

155. Borisov, *Iz Istorii*, pp. 55–56.

156. Shi Zhe, "I Accompanied Chairman Mao," p. 131; Shi Zhe, "What I Saw," pp. 38–39.

157. Interview with M. S. Kapitsa, April 3, 1992.

158. Shi Zhe, *Zai Lishi*, p. 459. Yudin was later Soviet ambassador to China.

159. *Pravda*, Jan. 4, 1950.

160. Baranov; Pospelov.

161. See, for example, Salisbury, "Full Asia Victory."

162. Our description of the Nosaka affair is based on Gittings, pp. 160–62.

163. App., Doc. 34. Mao had originally been scheduled to leave the night before (Jan. 13). See Doc. 32. On Jan. 12, Kovalev sent Stalin the following report: "To Comrade Stalin. Reporting to You. MAO ZEDONG [*sic*] has asked me to report to you that he wants to visit Leningrad and to stay there no more than one day. He is ready to depart any time." Document from Kovalev's personal archive. Mao spent the day of the 15th there. Zhu Zhongli, *Liming*, p. 362.

164. See "Road Toward Liberation." See also Li Chunqing, pp. 10–11; and "On the Situation," pp. 886–87.
165. App., Doc. 38.
166. Gittings, p. 162.
167. App., Doc. 35.
168. Ho Chi Minh arrived in Beijing sometime in late January. Mao [1], p. 254. On Ho's request for aid, see Wang Xian'gen, p. 38.
169. Mao [1], p. 254.
170. Mao [2], p. 198.
171. App., Doc. 35.
172. See Leffler, pp. 277–86, 317–23; the quotation is on p. 322.
173. Wang Xian'gen, p. 223.
174. "Soviet Union and Vietnam," pp. 1–2.
175. Wu Xiuquan, *Eight Years*, p. 19. Khrushchev, *Glasnost Tapes*, pp. 154–56, relates the story of Ho Chi Minh's visit to Moscow and reveals how Stalin deliberately insulted the Vietnamese revolutionary leader.
176. "Indo-China"; Sulzberger, "Red Blow"; Sulzberger, "Asian 'Spain' "; "Soviet Strategy"; "Jessup Cites Risk."
177. "U.S. Recognizes Viet Nam"; Hailey; Durdin, "Indo-China."
178. Hamilton, "Soviet Held Trying to Stall"; Waggoner, "Issue."
179. Knowles.
180. Interview with M. S. Kapitsa, April 3, 1992.
181. Personal communication from David Holloway, Dec. 1991. His conclusions are based on evidence presented in his forthcoming book *Stalin and the Bomb*.

Chapter Four

1. *Pravda*, Jan. 23, 1950.
2. The other participants in the talks were Li Fuchun and Wang Jiaxiang, on the Chinese side, and Gromyko and Roshchin on the Soviet side. Unless otherwise cited, the information in this paragraph is from Shi Zhe, "Visits of New China's Premier," p. 416; Shi Zhe, "I Accompanied Chairman Mao," p. 130; Lu Hong, p. 51; Wu Xiuquan, *Eight Years*, p. 12; and Zhu Zhongli, *Liming*, p. 363.
3. Shi Zhe, "I Accompanied Chairman Mao," p. 130; Min Li, "On the Eve," p. 54.
4. Min Li, "Handshake," p. 44, "On the Eve," p. 63, claims that after Zhou's arrival, Mao did not stay at the dacha but moved to the Kremlin at Stalin's request.
5. Zhu Zhongli, *Liming*, p. 363; Lu Hong, p. 51. Other authors give the date of the Stalin-Mao-Zhou meeting as Feb. 8. See, for example, Min Li, "On the Eve," p. 65. This paragraph is based on App., Docs. 40 and 41.
6. For the full texts of the treaty, other agreements signed on Feb. 14, and the relevant officially released speeches and communiqué, see App., Docs. 44–49.
7. The Jan. 22 talks between Mao and Stalin are based on Shi Zhe, *Zai Lishi*, pp. 405, 445.
8. Kapitsa, pp. 321–23.
9. App., Doc. 31.
10. The information on this issue is contradictory. According to the compilers of *Jianguo Yilai*, "The draft of this treaty was prepared by Zhou Enlai under the

guidance of Mao Zedong." Mao [20], p. 261. See also Mao's cable in App., Doc. 40. However, both Wu Xiuquan and Zhu Zhongli state that the initial draft was presented by the Soviet side. Wu Xiuquan, *Eight Years*, p. 12; Wu Xiuquan, "My Diplomatic Career," p. 5; Zhu Zhongli, *Liming*, p. 364. According to Shi Zhe ("Chairman Mao's First Visit," pp. 5–6), the Soviets wrote the first draft, which the Chinese revised. This Chinese version became the working draft.

11. Wu Xiuquan, *Eight Years*, pp. 12–13.

12. "Treaty of Friendship, Cooperation, and Mutual Assistance Between the Union of Soviet Socialist Republics and the People's Republic of Bulgaria," "Treaty of Friendship, Cooperation, and Mutual Assistance Between the Union of Soviet Socialist Republics and the Hungarian Republic," "Treaty of Friendship, Cooperation, and Mutual Assistance Between the Union of Soviet Socialist Republics and the People's Republic of Romania," in *Sbornik*, pp. 15–17, 17–19, 20–23, respectively.

13. App., Doc. 45.

14. See, for example, *Pravda*, Feb. 17 and March 18, 1950. The first article said: "Never throughout all history has our Motherland possessed such just and well-established state boundaries. . . . Our defense in the Far East has been strengthened too."

15. Molotov, "Speech," March 11, 1950.

16. See the speech by N. M. Shvernik in *Pravda*, March 3, 1950. The relations with China and the Sino-Soviet treaty were also discussed in detail by the head of the secret police, L. P. Beria, at about this time. *Pravda*, March 10, 1950.

17. App., Doc. 54.

18. "New Epoch." On the instructions for publishing this editorial, see App., Docs. 41, 43.

19. Zhou Enlai, "Speech," p. 22. Zhou's expression "unity of more than 700 million people" was picked up by *Novoe Vremia* in "Treaty of Eternal Soviet-Chinese Friendship," p. 3.

20. One of the few Chinese articles in which the matter of buffer zones is mentioned in detail is Si Mu, "New Sino-Soviet Alliance," p. 4.

21. *Sbornik*, p. 16. See also *ibid.*, pp. 19, 21.

22. Bukharkin, pp. 84–89.

23. App., Doc. 45, Art. 4.

24. On the steps the Chinese leaders took to preserve independence and flexibility in the foreign policy domain, see Liu Simu, pp. 78–79, 83–85.

25. App., Doc. 45, Art. 5.

26. Shi Zhe, "I Accompanied Chairman Mao," p. 131; Shi Zhe, "Visits of New China's Premier," pp. 416–17. See also Min Li, "On the Eve," p. 67.

27. Li Zhaoxin, pp. 7–8.

28. App., Doc. 45, Art. 1.

29. "Treaty of Friendship and Alliance," in U.S., Dept. of State, *United States Relations with China*, p. 586.

30. Wu Xiuquan, *Eight Years*, p. 13.

31. Liu Simu, p. 86; Han Nianlong, p. 27. Similarly, "the Soviet Union was not bound by any legal obligation to help the Chinese in [the Taiwan Strait crisis of 1958]; if some help was rendered, it was not made because of the treaty but because of the spirit of internationalism." From the speech of a senior Soviet diplomat, 1989.

32. App., Doc. 46.

33. Wu Xiuquan, "Process," p. 14.

34. *Ibid.*

35. Shi Zhe, *Zai Lishi*, p. 450; Wu Xiuquan, *Huiyi*, pp. 240–41.

36. Shi Zhe, *Zai Lishi*, p. 450.

37. App., Doc. 44.

38. Wu Xiuquan, *Huiyi*, p. 241.

39. On the Chinese perception of the Western reaction to the treaty, see *ibid.*, pp. 248–49.

40. Mao implied the existence of the Additional Agreement in a speech he made in March 1958 (see Mao [39], p. 164), but Goncharov, "From Alliance Through Animosity," p. 14, was the first open mention of it.

41. Han Nianlong, pp. 30–31.

42. Interview with a senior Soviet diplomat stationed in Beijing during the 1950s, Dec. 1990.

43. Mao [39], p. 164. In an attempt to avoid mentioning the Additional Agreement, some Soviet writers have interpreted Mao's "two colonies" as a reference to the Sino-Soviet joint enterprises in Xinjiang and the Northeast. See Borisov, *Iz Istorii*, p. 73; and Bazhanov, p. 50.

44. The quotations in this and the next paragraph are from Shi Zhe, *Zai Lishi*, p. 446.

45. Interview with M. S. Kapitsa, April 3, 1992.

46. App., Doc. 41.

47. App., Doc. 42.

48. The editorial did not carry Chen Boda's by-line; see "New Epoch." This and the following four paragraphs are based on App., Doc. 43.

49. For the text of the revised editorial "New Epoch," see *ZhongSu Youhao Guanxi Xuexi Shouce*, pp. 21–24.

50. Clubb to Acheson, Dec. 23, 1949, in FRUS 1949, 8: 644; Acheson to Bruce, Jan. 25, 1950, in FRUS 1950, 6: 295.

51. Sulzberger, "Secret Codicils." In January, according to *Pravda* (Feb. 1, 1950), U.S. newspapers reported that a secret "Harbin agreement" and a secret "Moscow agreement" had been concluded in October that gave the Chinese the right to pass through North Korea enroute to the Soviet Union, gave permission for the Chinese to establish a pilot training school in the Soviet Union, set aside special regions in China for stationing Korean troops, and permitted the deployment of Soviet troops in Xinjiang and Manchuria.

52. Sun Siding, pp. 9–10; Deng Chao, "Imperialism," pp. 14–15.

53. Shi Zhe, *Zai Lishi*, pp. 446–47.

54. *Ibid.*, p. 446; Wu Xiuquan, *Huiyi*, p. 241.

55. App., Doc. 46.

56. Unless otherwise cited, the information in this and the next paragraph is from a well-informed Soviet specialist, 1990. The text of the 1945 "Agreement Between the Republic of China and the U.S.S.R. Concerning the Chinese Changchun Railway" is in U.S., Dept. of State, *United States Relations with China*, pp. 593–96.

57. App., Doc. 31.

58. Shi Zhe, *Zai Lishi*, p. 210.

59. Gromyko, *Pamiatnoe* (1988), 2: 128–29. See also Gittings, p. 153.

60. Shi Zhe, *Zai Lishi*, p. 465.

61. App., Doc. 52.

62. See the reports in *Pravda*, Feb. 24–27, 1950. Perhaps not without a certain irony, Stalin assigned Vice–Foreign Minister A. I. Lavrentev to accompany Mao to Beijing. As ambassador to Yugoslavia, Lavrentev had played a prominent role in Tito's split with Moscow.

63. Shi Zhe, *Zai Lishi*, p. 471.

64. *Ibid.*, p. 451.

65. In 1956, at a CCP Politburo meeting, Mao chided Peng Dehuai, his defense minister, for not understanding that the collapse of the Sino-Soviet alliance was inevitable. Quan Yanchi, *Mao Zedong*, p. 119.

66. Mao designated 10 people to give speeches at the meeting. Four were Party bigwigs (Zhou Enlai, Chen Yun, Lin Biao, and Deng Xiaoping), and six "democratic figures." For their names and Mao's comment, see App., Doc. 53.

67. For the text of the speech, see App., Doc. 54.

68. Deng Liqun, "On the Eve," p. 149, for example, argues that at this time the Additional Agreement expelling "imperialist forces" from Xinjiang and the Northeast was "favorable for us; it also coincided with our political course."

69. Interview with a well-informed Soviet specialist, 1989.

Chapter Five

1. Hao Yufan and Zhai Zhihai, p. 100.

2. The quotation is from Merrill, *Korea*, pp. 26–27, which is based on the original tapes of the Khrushchev memoirs. Merrill has shown that there are serious omissions in the English transcripts about the events surrounding the Korean War. One especially misleading example he points to is *Khrushchev Remembers* (1970), pp. 368–69. We will use the full Russian text of Khrushchev's memoirs on the war published in *Ogonëk* (Khrushchev, "Korean War," pp. 27–28) and, where necessary, will compare that text with the English version. In his published memoirs, Shi Zhe does not mention the Stalin-Mao discussion of Kim Il Sung's intention to attack the South during Mao's visit. According to Chen Jian, a Chinese scholar who read the original manuscript of Shi's memoirs, Shi said: "Stalin told Mao Zedong, 'Kim Il Sung came. He wants to move against the South. Kim is young and brave; however, he overestimates the favorable factors and underestimates the unfavorable ones.' Stalin asked for Mao Zedong's opinion." Interview with Chen Jian, Aug. 1992.

3. Among recent studies on the origins of the Korean War adding to an already vast literature on this subject, see Cumings, 2 vols.; and Foot, *Substitute for Victory*. In our judgment, the best summary of the "competing explanations" of the war's origins is Merrill, *Korea*, Chap. 1; and the most intellectually interesting effort to examine who started the war is Cumings, 2: Chap. 18. See also G.-D. Kim, "Who Initiated the Korean War?," pp. 33–50; and H. Kim, pp. 326–70.

4. "Top Secret, Copying Prohibited," p. 213. At this time, the NKVD was no more. Before its successor, the KGB, was established, the secret police operated under the Ministry of Internal Affairs.

5. Interview with the Soviet Korean specialist Vasilii Mikheev, May 1991. According to Syn Song-Kil and Sin Sam-Soon, pp. 242–43, there are no documents on the decisions leading to the Korean War in either the Soviet Ministry of Foreign

Affairs or the Soviet Ministry of Defense archives. (This is a pseudonymous article written by a former high official in the North Korean Foreign Ministry now living in Moscow and a Russian expert on Korea.) According to one report, a Central Committee–ordered search for documents on the war in the Ministry of Foreign Affairs archives in 1989 turned up only one item—a transcript of a conversation between Mao and Mikoyan in April 1956, in which Mao recalled his Moscow talks with Stalin on Korea. But we now know that those archives contain other relevant documents, though they are scattered and mostly still classified. Interview with a former Soviet military adviser to North Korea, who claims to have had access to these archives, as well as to those of the military, Dec. 1991. For a discussion of the archival materials that are becoming available, see the Preface.

6. For a useful discussion of the historiography of the war, see H. Kim, pp. 335–68.

7. See, for example, Whiting, pp. 42–43.

8. On the history of Korean communism in general, see Scalapino and Lee, 2 vols; for the Soviet role in this development specifically, see 1: Chap. 5.

9. The unit is variously called the 88th International Independent Brigade (Wang Yizhi, p. 157; Yoo Sung Chul, interview of April 13, 1992); the 88th Special Independent Ambush Brigade or the 88th Special Sharp-shooting Brigade (Yoo Sung Chul, "My Testimony," Nov. 15, 1990, pp. 21, 22); or the 88th Special Sharp-shooting Patrol Brigade (*Chungang Ilbol*, Seoul, June 15, 1992, in FBIS: East Asia, June 17, 1992, p. 16). According to Wang Yizhi, the 88th was formally created on Aug. 1, 1942. The *Chungang Ilbol* article, purportedly based on a Soviet Ministry of Defense document, gives these details: the brigade was ordered into creation by Stalin in June 1942, was under the command of a Chinese officer, Senior Col. Zhou Baozhong, consisted of 400 Chinese and Koreans and 150 Russians and Nanai tribesmen, and was attached to the Soviet Far Eastern Army.

10. Unless otherwise cited, the information in this and the next paragraph is from Morosov, p. 10. This article is based on an interview with Col. Grigorii Kuzmin, the pen name of a well-informed Soviet military historian who served as a senior military adviser in North Korea and had access to closed Soviet military archives. See also Maksimov, p. 4. Kuzmin kindly granted us an interview as well, and we are grateful to him for sharing such important materials as the files on the 66 officers of the 88th Brigade on condition that his real name not be revealed.

11. Interview with Kang Sang Ho, Yoo Sung Chul, and Chung Sang Chin, April 13, 1992. The quote is from Yoo, who spent three years in the 88th Brigade. Yoo should have said "liberation," not "unification," given the early date.

12. Cho Man-sik, a highly respected nationalist, treated the Soviet forces in Korea as occupiers who differed little from the Japanese. His attitude was noted by Col. Gen. T. Shtykov, co-chairman of the Allied negotiations on Korean unification and one of the most influential officers in the Soviet military administration in the North. Shtykov reported to Moscow that Cho was "nationalistic," "anti-Soviet," and "not loyal to Stalin's policy." Because of this report, Stalin agreed to Cho's removal and ordered his representatives to find a new leader who would be more subservient to Soviet interests. Morosov, p. 10; interviews with Kuzmin, April–July 1991. For a detailed account of the Soviet role in the formation of the North Korean regime, see Lan'kov, pp. 104–12.

13. For important new information on the life of Kim Il Sung, see Yoo Sung Chul, "My Testimony," passim. During the Korean war, Yoo was the director of

the Operations Bureau of the KPA. When his memoirs on the war were translated, some of the most senior Soviet military advisers who had been stationed in North Korea told us they were angered that Yoo had "sold out state secrets" but basically confirmed the validity of his information. The material on the selection of Kim is from Kang Sang Ho. Interview with Kang, Yoo Sung Chul, and Chung Sang Chin, April 13, 1992. A Soviet diplomat interviewed by John Merrill stated, "Stalin himself gave Kim the nod—saying, 'Korea is a young country. It needs a young leader.'" John Merrill, personal communication, March 2, 1992.

14. Morosov, p. 10; interviews with G. Kuzmin, April–July 1991, and with a former high-ranking Soviet military adviser to Korea, June 1991.

15. For the text of Zhu De's order to the Koreans, see *Zhonggong Zhongyang Wenjian Xuanji*, p. 121. See also Cumings, 2: Chap. 11.

16. Interview with Kang Sang Ho, Yoo Sung Chul, and Chung Sang Chin, April 13, 1992.

17. Petukhov, pp. 93–94, 96, 107–8.

18. *Ibid.*, pp. 101–12; interviews with G. Kuzmin, April-July 1991.

19. The monumental study of the unrest in the South is Cumings, especially 2: Chaps. 7, 8. See also Heo, pp. 311–12.

20. Interviews with G. Kuzmin, April–July 1991.

21. Interview with Kang Sang Ho, Yoo Sung Chul, and Chung Sang Chin, April 13, 1992.

22. Interviews with G. Kuzmin, April–July 1991.

23. *Ibid.*

24. Sladkovskii, *Znakomstvo*, p. 357.

25. Petukhov, p. 155. In July 1946, the CCP Northeast Bureau had set up an office (*banshichu*) in Pyongyang, and part of its mission was trade liaison. In March 1949, the office was upgraded and renamed the Trade Delegation of the Northeast Administrative Committee. Ding Xuesong et al., pp. 625–26.

26. See, for example, Cumings, 2: 355–69. Cumings uses no Chinese sources to substantiate his conclusion that "veterans of the China fighting, not Soviet-aligned Koreans, dominated the Korean People's Army" (p. 361). The claim rests almost entirely on contemporary U.S. intelligence reports. Cumings does highlight the largely unknown role of Koreans in the Chinese civil war and the importance of the Chinese experience to many of the soldiers in the KPA.

27. Interviews with G. Kuzmin, April–July 1991.

28. Zhang Zhenglong, p. 574; Chai Chengwen and Zhao Yongtian, 1989, pp. 39–40, 44; Xu Yan, *Diyi Ci*, p. 21; Yang Zhaoquan, p. 431.

29. Lim Un, p. 182. Lim obtained most of the materials for this book from Yoo Sung Chul and Lee Sang Jo. Interview with Kang Sang Ho, Yoo Sung Chul, and Chung Sang Chin, April 13, 1992.

30. Kim Il Sung arrived in Moscow on March 4 and departed on April 7. The visit was extensively covered by *Pravda* (for example, March 4, 13, 21, and 25, and April 10 and 12), but the paper did not mention any talks with Stalin, speaking merely of an agreement on economic and cultural cooperation. For a brief discussion of the trip, see Merrill, *Korea*, pp. 143–44.

31. Morosov, p. 11. The man who acted as interpreter was Anatolii Kulikov (Shabshin), the Soviet vice-consul in Seoul in the mid-1940s. On his return to Moscow, Kulikov served as the Central Committee's specialist on Korean affairs. Another participant in the talks, Marshal Meretskov, in a later conversation with Kuz-

min, generally supported Kulikov's statement. Interviews with G. Kuzmin, April–July 1991.

32. In a Dec. 1991 interview, a former Soviet military adviser to North Korea, who claims to have had access to his country's foreign ministry and military archives, stated that Stalin disapproved of an all-out assault against the South. Yoo Sung Chul bears him out. During the talks in the spring of 1949, Yoo says, "First, they [Stalin and Kim] discussed the economic agreement. By the end of the talks, Kim Il Sung spoke about the possibility of war, but Stalin at this time did not agree with him." Interview with Kang Sang Ho, Yoo Sung Chul, and Chung Sang Chin, April 13, 1992.

33. Interviews with G. Kuzmin, April–July 1991.

34. Merrill, "Origins," p. 2.

35. *Ibid.*, pp. 2–3.

36. Heo, pp. 314–15.

37. Interviews with G. Kuzmin, April–July 1991.

38. Merrill, "Origins," p. 3. Heo, pp. 315–16, states, "Unlike what is generally supposed, the guerrillas were not annihilated. Many guerrillas survived and they continued to participate as support troops throughout the Korean War. They were not incapable of going on the attack."

39. Interview with Kang Sang Ho, Yoo Sung Chul, and Chung San Chin, April 13, 1992. The quote is from Yoo.

40. Merrill, *Korea*, pp. 187–88. On the guerrilla activity in this period, see *ibid.*, Chaps. 4–6; and Cumings, 2: Chaps. 7–8.

41. Interview with a former high-ranking North Korean diplomat now living in the Soviet Union, June 1991. See also Bak, pp. 257–60, quoted in Heo, pp. 317–18.

42. Lim Un, p. 168; Syn Song-Kil and Sin Sam-Soon, p. 249.

43. Interview with a senior Soviet diplomat who has had extensive access to the relevant archives, Aug. 1992; Hao Yufan and Zhai Zhihai, p. 100.

44. Interviews with M. S. Kapitsa, April 3, 1992, and V. P. Tkachenko, March 30, 1992. Yoo Sung Chul, "My Testimony," Dec. 27, 1990, pp. 25–26, states: "We also were equipped with modern military equipment transferred to us by the Soviet forces, who withdrew in 1948. Unsatisfied with this, Kim Il-song made two trips to the Soviet Union in 1949, concluding a treaty of friendship with Stalin and receiving military aid in heavy weaponry such as tanks and field guns, further strengthening the KPA." On the February trip, see Kobayashi, pp. 22–26. Kobayashi's source, Gen. Dmitrii Volkogonov, cited documents from the Soviet archives. The March–April trip is confirmed by V. P. Tkachenko, interview, March 30, 1992; Syn Song-Kil and Sin Sam-Soon, p. 250; and Hao Yufan and Zhai Zhihai, p. 100. From the details Syn and Sin give on this visit, it is clear that one of the authors either participated in or was briefed on it.

45. Interview with M. S. Kapitsa, April 3, 1992. See also Yoo Sung Chul, "My Testimony," Dec. 27, 1990, p. 26.

46. Hao Yufan and Zhai Zhihai, p. 100.

47. Khrushchev's account appears to combine information from two separate visits. As Merrill has shown, after telling about the first talks, Khrushchev says, "In my opinion, either the date of his return was set, or he was to inform us as soon as he finished preparing all of his ideas. Then, I don't remember in which month or year, Kim Il-sung came and related his plan to Stalin." Merrill, *Korea*, p. 25. Mer-

rill's account, which is based on the Khrushchev tapes, does not appear in Khrushchev, "Korean War." There he writes (p. 27), "I want to tell those things to which I was an eyewitness. It seems to me in 1950, when I had already begun to work in Moscow, or a little bit earlier before arriving in Moscow, Kim Il Sung came with his delegation." Khrushchev became the first secretary of the Moscow Municipal Party Committee in Dec. 1949. Adzhubei, p. 29.

48. Yoo Sung Chul, "My Testimony," Dec. 27, 1990, p. 25.

49. Interview with M. S. Kapitsa, April 3, 1992.

50. Hao Yufan and Zhai Zhihai, p. 100.

51. The Communist leaders might well have discussed Korea before Truman and Acheson gave their speeches (on Jan. 5 and Jan. 12, respectively).

52. Interview with M. S. Kapitsa, April 3, 1992.

53. Interview with Kang Sang Ho, Yoo Sung Chul, and Chung Sang Chin, April 13, 1992. The information is from Kang.

54. Interview with V. P. Tkachenko, March 30, 1992.

55. Interview with Kang Sang Ho, Yoo Sung Chul, and Chung Sang Chin, April 13, 1992.

56. Nie Rongzhen, *Inside*, pp. 642–43; Deng Lifeng, *Xin Zhongguo*, p. 60. Nie's translator uses the term "long war," but the Chinese original says "a large-scale war." Nie Rongzhen, *Nie Rongzhen Huiyilu*, p. 748. With the outbreak of war, Kim Kwang Hyop was appointed army chief of staff. Scalapino and Lee, 1: 392, and 2: 997–98. Three divisions of the 4th Field Army—the 164th, 165th, and 166th—contained some 40,000 ethnic Koreans. Virtually all of these men served in the Korean War. The Koreans in the 164th and 166th had already gone to Korea in 1949. The all-Korean 165th Division contained 13,500 officers and men plus a cadre brigade of 1,500; these are the "14,000" men referred to by Nie. This force was in Korea by the end of March 1950. Xu Yan, "Tortuous Course."

57. Interview with Kang Sang Ho, Yoo Sung Chul, and Chung Sang Chin, April 13, 1992. The quote is from Kang.

58. Gen. Dmitrii Volkogonov, head of the Institute of Military History in Moscow and author of the biography *I. V. Stalin: Triumf i Tragediia*, as cited in Kobayashi, pp. 22–26; and article citing interview with Dr. Gavriil Korotkov of the same institute, *Korean Herald*, Aug. 30, 1992.

59. Interview with V. P. Tkachenko, March 30, 1992.

60. Khrushchev, "Korean War," p. 28. Khrushchev uses the verb *zaprosit'*, which normally means to request information in written form.

61. Shi Zhe, *Zai Lishi*, pp. 466, 472. The article on Korotkov (n. 58) gives the date as Feb. 27.

62. The information in this and the next paragraph is from the interview with Kang Sang Ho, Yoo Sung Chul, and Chung Sang Chin, April 13, 1992. On the South Korean Workers' Party and its reorganization in 1948, see Merrill, *Korea*, pp. 87–90. For a discussion of the Chirisan guerrillas, see *ibid*., pp. 119–22, 145–46, 154–55.

63. Lim Un, p. 181.

64. Scholars continue to debate both the intent of Truman's and Acheson's remarks and how they were perceived in other capitals. The historian Bruce Cumings, for example, argues that Acheson included South Korea in the defense perimeter and was so understood by both prominent U.S. journalists and leaders in Moscow and Pyongyang. But according to Michael Schaller, it was clear as early as Sept.

1947 that the Joint Chiefs of Staff "had little strategic interest in maintaining the present troops and bases in Korea." Moreover, even the Far Eastern commander, Gen. Douglas MacArthur, "gave very little public indication [before June 1950] that he considered Korea especially vital to the United States." Schaller accepts the view that Acheson had excluded Korea from the U.S. defense perimeter, though in his speech he promised Korea aid and, if attacked, military support through the United Nations. The political scientist John Merrill adds that when the Acheson speech was "widely interpreted as a sign that the United States had decided to distance itself from the Rhee government," U.S. spokesmen attempted to downplay its significance. Merrill cites a report that Kim Il Sung was "greatly excited to learn of the speech." Cumings, 2: 423–28; Schaller, *Douglas MacArthur*, pp. 161, 163, 172; Merrill, *Korea*, pp. 166–67. For balanced assessments of some of the issues involved, see Bernstein, pp. 417–18; and George and Smoke, pp. 146–49.

65. Interview with M. S. Kapitsa, April 3, 1992.

66. Khrushchev, "Korean War," p. 28.

67. *Ibid.*

68. Interview with V. P. Tkachenko, March 30, 1992.

69. Interview with Generals Kang Sang Ho, Yoo Sung Chul, and Chung Sang Chin, April 13, 1992.

70. Syn Song-Kil (pseud.) in Syn and Sin Sam-Soon, pp. 250–51. Yoo Sung Chul has identified Syn as a former vice-minister in the North Korean government who was heavily involved in the decision-making on the war. Interview with Kang Sang Ho, Yoo Sung Chul, and Chung Sang Chin, April 13, 1992.

71. Interview with Kang Sang Ho, Yoo Sung Chul, and Chung Sang Chin, April 13, 1992. According to Yoo, "My Testimony," Dec. 27, 1990, p. 28, "our southern invasion plan ended with the occupation of Seoul after four days."

72. Syn Song-Kil and Sin Sam-Soon, p. 250.

73. Lim Un, p. 168. Though Lim's dating of this visit to early March is almost certainly wrong, we consider his information on the whole reliable.

74. On the purge of Pak Hon Yong in Dec. 1955, see Scalapino and Lee, 1: 447–52.

75. Yoo Sung Chul, "My Testimony," Dec. 27, 1990, p. 26. We attribute this account to Kim's April visit based on Yoo's statements that the invasion was approved shortly after Kim returned home, and that Kim handed the approved battle plan to his chief of staff in May.

76. Interview with M. S. Kapitsa, April 3, 1992.

77. Interview with He Di, June 23, 1992. He Di had interviewed Shi Zhe in 1990. Both M. S. Kapitsa and the former North Korean generals we interviewed doubt that such a visit ever took place. The latter believe the poor relations between Kim and Mao argue against it. Yoo Sung Chul notes, "I personally think that Kim did not visit Beijing after meeting with Stalin. It is improbable because until 1951 relations between Kim and Mao were not so good. . . . At the beginning of 1950, Korean officers who had served in the PLA—in the 8th Route Army—arrived in Korea. They did not respect Kim Il Sung too much. They always said, 'Mao Zedong, Mao Zedong.' Because of that, I heard, Kim Il Sung was so jealous that at almost every Supreme Officers' Meeting, he would say, 'Mao Zedong is Mao Zedong and Kim Il Sung is Kim Il Sung.' He was implying that it was his country, and he was the boss there." Interview with Kapitsa, April 3, 1992; interview with Kang Sang Ho, Yoo Sung Chul, and Chung Sang Chin, April 13, 1992.

78. Hao Yufan and Zhai Zhihai, p. 100. One entry in the chronological notes V. P. Tkachenko kept for reference reads: "April 7–26—[Kim Il Sung's] visit to the USSR (China)." Interview with Tkachenko, March 30, 1992.

79. Hao Yufan and Zhai Zhihai, p. 100; interview with Tkachenko, March 30, 1992. See the fn., p. 136, which summarizes a document from the Soviet archives; this and other documents date the visit from May 13 to 16.

80. Unless otherwise cited, the information in this paragraph is from an interview with a well-informed Chinese specialist, Oct. 1991; and a senior Soviet diplomat, Aug. 1992.

81. Hao Yufan and Zhai Zhihai, p. 100.

82. Interview with M. S. Kapitsa, April 3, 1992.

83. Information from a well-informed Chinese specialist, Oct. 1991, based on interviews with Shi Zhe and Lei Yingfu.

84. Interview with Kang Sang Ho, Yoo Sung Chul, and Chung Sang Chin, April 13, 1992. The quote is from Chung. Cumings, 2: 447–48, argues on the basis of a contemporary CIA report that the supply of Soviet weapons had not been "geared to an invasion in June 1950" or any other specific time. Chung's statement appears to contradict Cumings. Interview with a former Soviet military adviser to Korea, Dec. 1991.

85. Interviews with G. Kuzmin, April–July 1991; Plotnikov, p. 41.

86. An example of the Soviet thinking on the superiority needed for offensive operations is *Istoriia Velikoi*, 5: 57, cited in Werth, p. 953. The example is for the offensive drive from Warsaw to Berlin. See also Evangelista, p. 120, n. 33.

87. This paragraph is based on Mao [20], pp. 256, 257, 259, 271, 282. On Mao's plan to attack Taiwan, see Zhou Jun, p. 72; Zhao Wei, pp. 32–35; and *Gongfei Gongtai*.

88. The PLA totaled 5,300,000 men before April 1950, when the Politburo decided on a cut of 1,400,000. Tang Qun and Li Bing, p. 673. A total cut of 1,500,000 was ordered on June 30. Academy of Military Science, *Zhongguo Renmin Jiefangjun Liushi Nian Dashiji*, pp. 488–89. On the three reasons for Mao's demobilization decision, see Xu Yan, *Jinmen*, p. 124.

89. Unless otherwise cited, this paragraph is based on Mao [20], pp. 310, 319, 322, 336, 357.

90. N. B. Tucker, pp. 56–58.

91. The 32nd Corps was originally under the jurisdiction of the Shandong Military District Command. As part of the military buildup opposite Taiwan in 1950, the Central Military Commission moved the corps to Nanping County, Fujian Province, and put it under the 10th Army. See Academy of Military Science, *Zhongguo Renmin Jiefangjun Liushi Nian Dashiji*, p. 453.

92. The details on Zhou Enlai's cable and the Central Committee's instruction discussed in the next paragraph are from Zhou Jun, p. 70. On Zhou's role in the Central Ordnance Commission and the creation of China's defense industry, see Lewis and Xue, *China's Strategic Seapower*, Chaps. 2, 4.

93. The information in this and the following five paragraphs is from Lim Un, pp. 171–72; Yoo Sung Chul, "My Testimony," p. 26, Dec. 27, 1990, and interview with Kang Sang Ho, Yoo Sung Chul, and Chung Sang Chin, April 13, 1992 (the long quotation is from Yoo).

94. Interview with a high-ranking Soviet diplomat who formerly held one of the leading positions in the Soviet Ministry of Foreign Affairs archives, Feb. 1991.

95. Connally. For State Department comments on this statement, see Rusk to Webb, May 2, 1950, in FRUS 1950, 7: 64–65.

96. Quoted in G.-D. Kim, "Legacy," p. 285.

97. Acheson, "United States Policy," pp. 467–72. The quote is on p. 468.

98. Rusk to Acheson, April 17, 1950, in FRUS 1950, 6: 330. On the strongly pessimistic reactions to the invasion of Hainan Island as a portent of the fate of Taiwan, see Strong to Acheson, April 27, 1950, in FRUS 1950, 6: 335–39.

99. G. Chang, p. 70. Our analysis here closely follows Chang, pp. 69–76. The text of NSC 68 is in FRUS 1950, 1: 234–92.

100. See, for example, "U.S. China Policy Called Confusing"; and Reston, "Asia." At the beginning of the war, Chinese leaders appear to have concluded that given a choice between losing Korea and losing Taiwan, the American administration would become vastly more exercised over the loss of Korea. See, for example, Ye Mang.

101. Xu Yan, *Jinmen*, p. 124; Zhou Jun, p. 72. On Mao's resolve to proceed against Taiwan, see his report to the 3rd plenum of the 7th Party Congress (June 6, 1950). Mao [15], pp. 391, 394. This report is also in Mao, *Selected Works of Mao Tsetung* (Beijing, 1977), 5: 26–32.

102. Mao [35], pp. 410–11. On Mao's plan for a sweeping demobilization of the PLA, see Mao [4], p. 310.

103. Zhou Jun, p. 69; He Di, "Last Campaign"; interview with a well-informed Chinese specialist, Oct. 1991.

104. Hao Yufan and Zhai Zhihai, p. 100; interview with Kang Sang Ho, Yoo Sung Chul, and Chung Sang Chin, April 13, 1992. See also Lim Un, p. 186: "To our knowledge they [the Chinese] did not have any prior consultation nor did they consent to starting a war."

105. Yoo Sung Chul, "My Testimony," Dec. 27, 1990, p. 26.

106. Interview with Kang Sang Ho, Yoo Sung Chul, and Chung Sang Chin, April 13, 1992.

107. Interview with V. P. Tkachenko, March 30, 1992.

108. Interview with He Di, April 9, 1992.

109. Interview with Kang Sang Ho, Yoo Sung Chul, and Chung Sang Chin, April 13, 1992.

110. *Ibid.*

111. *Ibid.*

112. *Ibid.*; interview with former KPA major Ju Young Bok, April 13, 1992. Yoo Sung Chul seems to waver on whether the first stage of the Korean operations plan allowed for three days or four in his published article. See Yoo Sung Chul, "My Testimony," Dec. 27, 1990, pp. 26, 28, and Dec. 28, 1990, p. 13. In our interview with him, he insisted the total plan was for three days, but a former Soviet adviser states the first stage of the month-long plan was to end after three days with the seizure of Seoul. Interview, Dec. 1991.

113. Interview with Kang Sang Ho, Yoo Sung Chul, and Chung Sang Chin, April 13, 1992. The quotation is from Yoo.

114. U.S., Dept. of State, Office of Intelligence Research, Estimates Group, "Korea," June 25, 1950, in FRUS 1950, 7: 150.

115. For details on high-level Department of State thinking at this time, see Acheson, *Present at the Creation*, Chaps. 44–45.

116. U.S., Dept. of State, Office of Intelligence Research, Estimates Group, "Korea," in FRUS 1950, 7: 153. For an illuminating history of the policy of weakening the Sino-Soviet alliance, see G. Chang.

117. Annex to Jessup memo, June 25, 1950, in FRUS 1950, 7: 161.

118. Editorial note, in *ibid.*, p. 143.

119. MacArthur memo, June 14, 1950, in *ibid.*, p. 161.

120. Nolting to Matthews, June 30, 1950, in *ibid.*, p. 258.

121. Jessup memo, Nov. 28, 1950, in *ibid.*, p. 1243. Secretary of State Dean Acheson's statement agreeing with Marshall's assessment is in *ibid.*, p. 1246.

122. According to a report of the Chinese military attaché in Pyongyang, the North Koreans suffered 40% casualties (that is, more than 50,000 killed and wounded) in their drive to the Naktong River, at the Pusan perimeter. The report was circulated at a meeting of the Central Military Commission on Aug. 6. Spurr, p. 61.

123. U.S. analysts, of course, monitored the spate of Chinese articles denouncing the war. These are reviewed in Whiting, Chap. 4.

124. For an early, lucid examination of all the evidence then available, see *ibid.*, especially Chap. 4.

125. "Victorious Future."

126. Acheson to Certain Diplomatic and Consular Offices, July 6, 1950, in FRUS 1950, 7: 310. See also the Army Dept. memo of that date on p. 311.

127. App., Doc. 55.

128. See Wu Xiuquan, "Wu Xiuquan's Speech," p. 208; and Guo Binwei and Tan Zongji, p. 35.

129. At the National Conference on Finance on Feb. 24, 1950, PLA commander Zhu De proposed that the PLA reduce its personnel by 2,000,000 men. It was partly on the basis of this report that the Politburo decided to sharply reduce the number of PLA troops. Xu Xiaolin, p. 12.

130. The Central Military Commission reported directly to the Politburo and was responsible for all military affairs. Chen Ping, p. 28. For short but authoritative histories of that body, see Lei Yuanshen, pp. 218–35; Zhi Shaozeng, pp. 50–54; Yan Jingtang, pp. 50–59; and Song Ke, pp. 62–64. Ultimately, this scheduled scaling back of the PLA from some 5,500,000 men to 4,000,000 did not take place because of the outbreak of the Korean War. By the end of 1950, only 935,000 old, weak, sick, and disabled soldiers had been demobilized. But in June of the next year, when the situation in Korea had become relatively stable, the Politburo was ready to go forward with an even more substantial cut, of 2,000,000 men. Jiang Naiwen, p. 12. The Central Demobilization Commission was eventually renamed the Central Commission for Military-Civilian Transfers. Deng Lifeng, *Xin Zhongguo*, p. 110.

131. He Di, "Last Campaign," p. 19.

132. Zhou Jun, p. 72.

133. Xiao Jingguang, *Xiao Jingguang Huiyilu*, 2: 26. As commander of the navy, Xiao Jingguang was charged with transporting the combat units of the 3rd Field Army for the landing on Taiwan. Zhou Jun, p. 67.

134. At that time, the commission formally notified Su Yu, deputy commander of the 3rd Field Army, that the liberation of Taiwan was being postponed against the possibility of reversals in the Korean War. Yang Guoyu, p. 41.

135. The delay to 1952 was proposed in the first instance by Chen Yi, commander of the 3rd Field Army. Zhou Jun, p. 72. For Mao's order on the slogans, see Mao [21], p. 536.

136. For a discussion of the impact of the Korean War on Mao's plan to attack Taiwan, see, among others, Zhou Jun, pp. 67–74.

137. Wu Xiuquan, "Wu Xiuquan's Speech," pp. 205–6; Hu Guangzheng, p. 35; "Background," pp. 94–95, 108.

138. Xiao Jianning, p. 170. This is a scholar's assessment; we have no direct evidence on the two questions.

139. From then on, according to Nie Rongzhen, *Inside*, p. 643, "the traffic there continued to flow almost uninterruptedly despite innumerable U.S. bombing raids."

140. One official Chinese source justifies the North's initiation of the war: "The Korean Workers' Party was determined to lead the Korean people to wage a revolutionary war of liberation in order to achieve the unification of Korea and build it into a socialist country of independence, freedom, and democracy." Hu Guangzheng, p. 34.

141. There is evidence of Mao's worry about the possible consequences of the Korean War as early as July 6, when an official editorial declared that the military involvement of the United States, Britain, Australia, and other countries in Korea "would certainly postpone the victory of the Korean people. The Korean people have to get ready for longer and fiercer battles." See "Victorious Future." Nie Rongzhen in his capacity as acting chief of the General Staff frequently handled minor military affairs without notifying the Chairman. Mao became angry and ordered Nie to keep in daily contact with him. Li Yinqiao and Quan Yanchi, pp. 92–93.

142. Shen Zonghong and Meng Zhaohui, p. 7; Huang Yi, "Zhou Enlai," 1: 9; Chen Yan et al., p. 12.

143. Most of the soldiers of the 4th Field Army had been conscripted from the Northeast and had fought there during the civil war. Hong Xuezhi, *KangMei*, pp. 1–2.

144. The resolution is summarized in a footnote to Mao's cover letter (see App., Doc. 56) to the acting chief of the General Staff, Nie Rongzhen.

145. Resolution S/1588, passed at the Security Council's 476th meeting. For the text, see *Yearbook of the United Nations*, 1950 (New York, 1951), p. 230. Yao Xu, *Cong Yalujiang*, p. 14, connects the Chinese and UN resolutions.

146. "The Soviet absence from the UN Security Council was a grave mistake, one of the biggest in Soviet diplomacy. It was motivated by a quite different reason, the absence of China from the UN." Interview with M. S. Kapitsa, April 3, 1992. For Chinese and Korean comment, see Yao Xu, *Cong Yalujiang*, p. 11; Chai Chengwen and Zhao Yongtian, 1989, p. 11; and Syn Song-Kil and Sin Sam-Soon, p. 251. The information on the level of the decision is from a veteran Soviet diplomat stationed in the UN at this time, Dec. 1991.

147. Gromyko (1990), pp. 249–50. The quotation is on p. 250. A former Soviet military adviser to Korea (interviewed, Dec. 1991) likewise maintains that Stalin knew that the lack of Soviet representation on the Security Council would ensure both North Korea's being branded the aggressor and the UN's endorsement of U.S. actions in Korea.

148. Chai Chengwen and Zhao Yongtian, 1989, p. 13.

149. Yao Xu, "Wise Decision," pp. 7–8; Chen Mingxian et al., p. 30; Zhang

Hui, p. 36. As noted, this unit had till then been stationed in Henan Province. The 38th Corps had been based in Xinyang, the 39th in Luohe, and the 40th in Luoyang. Du Ping, *Zai Zhiyuanjun Zongbu*, pp. 7, 11; Hong Xuezhi, *KangMei*, p. 2; Zhang Hui, p. 36; Xu Yan, *Diyi Ci*, p. 16.

150. The 42nd, the newest of the 4th Field Army's corps, was scheduled for demobilization before the outbreak of the Korean War. Huang Yi, "Zhou Enlai," 1: 10; Xu Yan, *Diyi Ci*, pp. 16, 17.

151. Liao Guoliang et al., p. 355.

152. Because the headquarters of the NFF was never formally established, the 13th Army ultimately assumed the actual command of the units assigned to the force. The 1st, 2nd, and 8th were among China's finest artillery divisions. Xu Yan, *Diyi Ci*, p. 17; "Frontier Force"; Hong Xuezhi, *KangMei*, p. 2; Shen Zonghong and Meng Zhaohui, pp. 7–8; Chen Yan et al., p. 12.

153. The 42nd Corps was stationed right on the border, the other NFF units in the nearby locales. These deployments took place over the three-day period July 24–26. Du Ping, *Zai Zhiyuanjun Zongbu*, p. 17; Du Ping, "Wise Decision," p. 9; Shen Zonghong and Meng Zhaohui, p. 8; Han Huaizhi and Tan Jingqiao, 1: 450; Huang Yi, "Zhou Enlai," 1: 9; Nie Rongzhen, *Inside*, pp. 633–34; Chai Chengwen and Zhao Yongtian, 1989, p. 33.

154. Xu Yan, *Diyi Ci*, pp. 18, 19; Du Ping, *Zai Zhiyuanjun Zongbu*, pp. 28–29.

155. Unless otherwise cited, the information in this paragraph is from Chai Chengwen and Zhao Yongtian, 1989, pp. 33, 67.

156. On Sept. 27, 1949, the First Session of the Chinese People's Political Consultative Conference (CPPCC) adopted a transitional constitution (the Common Program of the CPPCC) and a series of laws establishing the basic organs of the Central People's Government. For the relevant documents, see *Important Documents*. Under regulations promulgated in Dec. 1949, seven administrative regions were created, in four cases with military and administrative committees. The exceptions were North China, the Northeast, and Inner Mongolia, where "People's Governments" had been established. In the Northeast, a separate "People's Government" had been created on Aug. 27, 1949. The regional system was changed in 1952; on the revised system, see Zhou Fang; Xu Yuandong et al., p. 8; and Wu Lanfu. Theoretically, the Northeast Administrative Committee, which was established in 1946, was abolished with the creation of the Northeast People's Government, but in Chai Chengwen and Zhao Yongtian, 1989, p. 33, the reference is to the committee.

157. Nie Rongzhen, *Inside*, p. 634.

158. Interview with a well-informed Chinese specialist, Oct. 1991.

159. Lim Un, p. 198. According to Hao Yufan and Zhai Zhihai, pp. 101–2, instead of heeding Mao's warning, Stalin "approved Kim's tactic of 'hot pursuit,' leaving his rear unguarded and empty." They cite Yao Xu, *Cong Yalujiang*, p. 22, as their source, but there is no mention of this on p. 22 or anywhere else in the Yao book.

160. On July 22, Zhou Enlai and Nie Rongzhen proposed that Gao Gang take command of all forces assembled in the Northeast, and Mao agreed. Huang Yi, "Zhou Enlai," 1: 10. Unless otherwise cited, the information in this and the next paragraph is from App., Doc. 57.

161. On the Force's original mission of frontier defense, see Academy of Mili-

tary Science, *Zhongguo Renmin Jiefangjun Liushi Nian Dashiji*, p. 489; and Hong Xuezhi, *KangMei*, pp. 1–2. On the Chinese government's initial attitude toward intervening in the war, see Chen Hanbo, p. 21.

162. Nie Rongzhen, *Inside*, p. 634.

163. Army Dept. memo, Aug. 30, 1950, in FRUS 1950, 7: 659. The report put the Chinese troop strength near Andong (Antung) at 80,000 and the total regular forces in the Northeast (Manchuria) at "246,000 comprising nine armies of 37 div[ision]s." A U.S. military intelligence estimate of Jan. 1950 set the PLA total at 2,570,000 men, organized into 62 armies and 214 divisions. The bulk of these forces were in the South, Southwest, East, and Northwest, "destroying the remaining Nationalist forces on the mainland." The (North) Korean People's Army had 56,000 men, organized into three infantry divisions plus several smaller units (including a tank regiment), and "15,000 Korean troops of the Chinese Communist forces." U.S., Joint Intelligence Committee, pp. 9, 11.

164. For the American side of the story, see, for example, Dingman, pp. 50–91; and Calingaert, pp. 176–202. Ryan, *Chinese Attitudes*, deals with some aspects of the U.S. decision-making in this respect but concentrates mainly on what has been available from Chinese sources. He concludes (p. 29), "there is only scattered evidence specifically relating to how the possibility of a U.S. nuclear response may have been factored into the Chinese decision to enter the war." Most of the evidence deals with the Chinese decision to end the war. In addition to Ryan, Chap. 7, see Lewis and Xue, *China Builds the Bomb*, pp. 13–16; and Foot, "Nuclear Coercion."

165. See, for example, Shi Xiaochong, p. 10; and Bin Fu, p. 18.

166. On the Chinese Communists' judgment that the United States was unlikely to use the atomic bomb, see, for example, Wang Hanming, pp. 12–13.

167. "Great Political Significance," p. 2; this article is discussed in Ryan, p. 27.

168. Zhu Guangya, pp. 24–25; Xing Shi, p. 177.

169. Du Ping, *Zai Zhiyuanjun Zongbu*, pp. 23–24.

170. In the latter half of 1950, the Chinese press published numerous articles belittling the role of atomic bombs in a large-scale war. For information on these articles, see, for example, *KangMei YuanChao Ziliao Mulu*, pp. 292–96.

171. Chiang's statement appears in Carlyle, pp. 657–58. For official, classified comment on MacArthur's statements in Taiwan, see Acheson to Sebald, Aug. 1, 1950, and Strong to Acheson, Aug. 3 and 4, 1950, in FRUS 1950, 6: 405, 411, 417–18.

172. Spurr, pp. 53–65. The quotation appears on p. 62.

173. The Politburo's conclusion was reaffirmed in a directive of Oct. 26, 1950. See Central Committee, Chinese Communist Party, *Guanyu Shishi*. For the text of the directive, see *Zhonggong Dangshi Jiaoxue*, 19: 211–13. Unless otherwise cited, the information in this and the following four paragraphs is from Wang Hanming, pp. 12–13; and a Chinese specialist, 1990. Chinese official publications later reflected the Politburo's point of view on the question of whether the United States would use nuclear weapons against the Chinese. See, for example, "Introduction to the 'Paper Tiger,'" pp. 29–30; "Why Can't the Atomic Bomb Decide the Outcome of War?," pp. 54–66; and "How to Recognize the United States," p. 684.

174. When the war began, Mao pronounced the Soviet possession of atomic bombs sufficient to deter a U.S. nuclear strike. In addition to the sources in the preceding note, see Lin Yunhui et al., p. 180. However, after assessing the results

of the war, Mao held that the Soviet nuclear umbrella was unreliable. See Quan Yanchi, *Mao Zedong*, pp. 97, 119.

175. Du Ping, *Zai Zhiyuanjun Zongbu*, pp. 19–20.

176. Zhang Xi, "On the Eve," pp. 125–26.

177. Lin's statement is from the memoirs of Lei Yingfu, deputy head of the Operations Department of the General Staff, who attended the meeting of the military commission. Quan Yanchi, "Profound Reminiscences," p. 111; Xu Yan, *Diyi Ci*, pp. 23–24.

Chapter Six

1. For an analysis of Soviet policy during the first months of the war, see Ulam, pp. 517–34; and Shulman, Chap. 6. A general analysis of the period is found in Whiting, Chap. 5.

2. Zhang Hui, p. 36; Tan Jingqiao, p. 18; Han Huaizhi and Tan Jingqiao, 1:450.

3. Joint Chiefs of Staff to MacArthur, June 29, 1950, in FRUS 1950, 7:240–41.

4. CIA memo, Aug. 18, 1950, in *ibid.*, pp. 600–603.

5. See *ibid.*, pp. 574, 593, 599–600, 613–14, 721–22. Here the town of Najin (spelled Rajin in North Korea) is referred to as Rashin.

6. Lay memo, Sept. 1, 1950, in FRUS 1950, 7:685–93 passim. The quotation is on p. 687.

7. Acheson to Embassy, Seoul, Sept. 11, 1950, in FRUS 1950, 7:723. For the Secretary of State's reply, see U.S., Dept. of State, *Bulletin*, Sept. 18, 1950, p. 460. For details on the Inchon landing and subsequent offensives, see Appleman, pp. 488ff.

8. The relevant documents are in FRUS 1950, 7:731ff.

9. Matthews to Burns, Sept. 16, 1950, in *ibid.*, p. 731.

10. Henderson to Acheson, Sept. 20, 1950, in *ibid.*, p. 742.

11. See, for example, documents in *ibid.*, pp. 756, 760, 765, 768.

12. Kirk to Acheson, Sept. 26, 1950, in *ibid.*, pp. 779–80. As late as July, as we have noted, economic reconstruction was still the PRC's priority over the Korean War. Chai Chengwen and Zhao Yongtian, 1989, p. 33.

13. Henderson to Acheson, Sept. 27, 1950, in FRUS 1950, 7:791.

14. Merchant memo, Marshall to Truman, both Sept. 27, 1950, in *ibid.*, pp. 792–95.

15. Merchant memo, Sept. 27, 1950, in *ibid.*, p. 794.

16. See documents in *ibid.*, pp. 795–832.

17. See footnote to Marshall to MacArthur, Sept. 29, 1950, in *ibid.*, p. 826.

18. See, for example, *ibid.*, pp. 271–730 passim; and Acheson, *Present at the Creation*, pp. 540–52. See also Panikkar.

19. Xu Yan, *Diyi Ci*, pp. 18–19; Chai Chengwen and Zhao Yongtian, 1989, p. 67. Following Mao's order of early August, Zhou interviewed Nationalist generals who had fought alongside U.S. units in Burma against the Japanese. These generals noted the heavy American dependence on logistical support. Zheng Dongguo, pp. 22–23.

20. App., Doc. 59; Nie Rongzhen, *Inside*, p. 634. Luo Ronghuan, director of the PLA General Political Department, had recommended Deng Hua's appoint-

ment as commander of the 13th army on July 7, and he was confirmed in the position in early August, shortly after the army's arrival in the Northeast from Henan Province. Du Ping, *Zai Zhiyuanjun Zhongbu*, p. 14; Hong Xuezhi, *KangMei*, p. 3.

21. Unless otherwise cited, the information in this paragraph is from Sun Baosheng, p. 13; "Mao Zedong Predicted"; and Xu Yan, *Diyi Ci*, pp. 18–19.

22. Because of his correct prediction, Lei Yingfu was later made deputy head of the Operations Department of the General Staff. But he remained on as Zhou Enlai's military secretary, and Mao later gave him special permission to attend Politburo meetings. Quan Yanchi, "Profound Reminiscences," pp. 108–20; Zhang Qinghua, pp. 412, 414. At the outbreak of the Cultural Revolution, Lin Biao charged Lei with conspiring against Yang Chengwu, acting chief of the General Staff, and ousted him from his positions.

23. Some Chinese believe that MacArthur formally decided on the Inchon landing on the very day (Aug. 23) that Mao told Zhou to report Lei's prediction to Kim Il Sung. Xu Yan, *Diyi Ci*, p. 19.

24. Lee Sang Jo, pp. 171–72. Lee, then DPRK vice-minister of foreign trade, had been sent to Beijing to ask the Chinese leaders for winter clothing for the KPA and more broadly, to probe their attitude toward the war. Interview with Kang Sang Ho, Yoo Sung Chul, and Chung Sang Chin, April 13, 1992.

25. Interview with Kang Sang Ho, Yoo Sung Chul, and Chung Sang Chin, April 13, 1992.

26. Ni Wei, p. 53. As early as July 14, Zhou Enlai ordered the first of a series of emergency measures in connection with the logistical problems of moving the Strategic Reserve to the Northeast. But these orders did not clarify the specific financial responsibilities, and the Northeast officials were unable to cope with the huge influx of men and matériel. Huang Yi, "Zhou Enlai," 1: 10–11.

27. The 4th Field Army was given a budget to fund the NFF's peacetime operations and maintenance, and the central government would directly fund all wartime operations. The Northeast People's Government was to supply the NFF with rations, forage for the cavalry, and coal. Zhou Enlai, "On Logistic Support," pp. 433–34; Huang Yi, "Zhou Enlai," 1: 11.

28. App., Doc. 60. See also Zhang Xi, "On the Eve," p. 120.

29. Chai Chengwen and Zhao Yongtian, 1989, p. 66; Xu Yan, *Diyi Ci*, pp. 18, 19.

30. At this point, by the end of August, the field hospitals and first-aid stations in the Northeast were equipped to care for 60,000 men. Yao Xu, "Wise Decision," p. 7. The information in this paragraph is based on Liao Guoliang et al., p. 354; Xu Yan, *Diyi Ci*, p. 19; Yu Ruping, p. 13; Shen Zonghong and Meng Zhaohui, p. 8; and Zhang Hui, p. 37.

31. Chai Chengwen and Zhao Yongtian, 1989, pp. 66; Han Nianlong, p. 36.

32. Chai Chengwen and Zhao Yongtian, 1992, p. 58.

33. According to some sources, including Ma Kaijun, p. 50, the 50th Corps was not moved from Hubei Province until the last 10 days of September. We believe this is incorrect. Unless otherwise cited, this paragraph is based on Shen Zonghong and Meng Zhaohui, p. 8; Liao Guoliang et al., p. 355; Xu Yan, *Diyi Ci*, pp. 19, 20; and Zhang Hui, p. 39.

34. App., Doc. 61. (This document is a comment Mao wrote on a report sub-

mitted by the East China Military Region Command on Sept. 5.) The 9th Army, part of the 3rd Field Army, had been assigned to the invasion of Taiwan. Zhou Jun, p. 67; Xie Youfa, p. 234.

35. Nie Rongzhen, *Inside*, pp. 634–35; Hu Guangzheng, p. 34; Guo Binwei and Tan Zongji, p. 34. According to Lim Un, p. 189, Zhou Enlai was among those who opposed entry into the war on the grounds that it would delay economic reconstruction.

36. Unless otherwise cited, the information in this paragraph is from Chai Chengwen and Zhao Yongtian, 1989, p. 79; and Li Jukui, p, 265.

37. The commanders of the NFF made two additional proposals; the first, for Beijing to ascertain Moscow's willingness to provide air cover, and the second, for Beijing to provide two more armies as a reserve force. Du Ping, *Zai Zhiyuanjun Zongbu*, pp. 21–22.

38. Shen Zonghong and Meng Zhaohui, p. 8; Tan Jingqiao, p. 18; Chen Yan et al., p. 13.

39. Chai Chengwen and Zhao Yongtian, 1989, p. 77. Unless otherwise cited, the information in the next paragraph is from this source.

40. Pak Il U was a member of the standing committee of the Politburo of the Korean Workers' Party and head of the Ministry of Internal Affairs. App., Doc. 66, n. 52; Scalapino and Lee, 1: 380, 410. Mao later made Pak deputy commander and deputy political commissar of the Chinese People's Volunteers (CPV) and deputy secretary of the CPV's Party Committee. Qi Dexue, p. 55. Years later, Kim Il Sung sentenced him to death as part of a general purge.

41. Wang Ming, "Polveka." On orders from high-ranking officials in the CPSU Central Committee, the material on this cable was deleted when Wang's manuscript was published in 1975; see Wang Ming, *Polveka KPK*, pp. 206–7. We are grateful to Wang Ming's son, Wang Danzhi, for allowing us to read and quote the original typewritten manuscript. According to Wang Danzhi, his father learned this and other details of the decision-making process that brought China into the war from Liu Shaoqi during his visit to Moscow in Nov. 1952. Wang Ming, who had been ousted as Mao's rival for Party leadership in 1938, frequently related the story of Mao's concessions. Wang Ming's information is indirectly supported by Shi Zhe, *Zai Lishi*, pp. 492–93, who says Stalin sent a cable to Mao after the Inchon landing asking about the PLA's deployments along the Shenyang–Dandong Railroad and about Beijing's intentions toward Korea.

42. Yao Xu, *Cong Yalujiang*, p. 25; Zhang Xi, "On the Eve," p. 147.

43. Syn Song-Kil and Sin Sam-Soon, p. 251.

44. Mao's statement to this effect was deleted from the published version of Wang Ming's work; see n. 41.

45. See Wang Ming, *Polveka KPK*, pp. 206–7. For later reflections on why Mao was reluctant to enter the war at this time, see Choudhury, pp. 271–72.

46. Yoo Sung Chul, "My Testimony," Dec. 28, 1990, p. 16.

47. Huang Yanpei, vice-premier of the Government Administration Council, suggested the term volunteers, because "supporting forces" might still be considered official. "Origin of the Name"; Quan Yanchi, "Profound Reminiscences," pp. 111–12; Xu Yan, *Diyi Ci*, p. 27.

48. Nie Rongzhen, *Inside*, p. 635; Yang Zhaoquan, p. 430. For the relevant portion of Zhou Enlai's speech, see App., Doc. 62.

49. MacArthur's quote and details on the crossing of the 38th parallel are found in Appleman, pp. 608, 615. On Kim's interview, see Chai Chengwen and Zhao Yongtian, 1989, p. 80.

50. For the full text of the urgent message, see Ye Yumeng, *Heixue*, pp. 49–51. See also Qi Dexue, pp. 46–47; Li Zhongzhi and Wang Li, p. 44; and Zhang Liyao, p. 313. A Chinese specialist on the Korean War confirms the authenticity of this text but disputes some other parts of Ye's account; interview, July 1992.

51. Liu Shaoqi told Wang Ming that these enlarged meetings took place daily through the first half of October. Zhou Guoquan et al., p. 466. See also Chai Chengwen and Zhao Yongtian, 1989, p. 81; *Nie Rongzhen Yuanshuai*, p. 162; and Qi Dexue, p. 49.

52. Unless otherwise cited, the information in this and the following two paragraphs is from Zhang Xi, "On the Eve," pp. 125–27; Xu Yan, *Diyi Ci*, p. 23; Peng Dehuai, *Peng Dehuai Zishu*, p. 257; and Hu Guangzheng and Bao Mingrong, p. 60.

53. The title *zong* was normally given to PLA officers of field army commander level or higher.

54. On Su Yu's background, see Ju Kai, p. 531. On his sickness and Mao's letter, see App., Doc. 58; Zhang Zhen, p. 51; Zhang Jian, p. 522; Liu Xiangshun, p. 16; and Ju Kai, p. 531.

55. Soon thereafter, Mao alleged that Lin Biao worried that he would be no match for MacArthur, and that a defeat in Korea would damage his military reputation. Nie Rongzhen, *Inside*, pp. 635–36; Deng Hua et al., p. 123; Zhang Xi, "On the Eve," p. 135. For additional confirmation of Lin's refusal to serve in Korea from a highly suspect source, see Central Committee, Chinese Communist Party, "Report," p. 114.

56. Zhang Xi, "On the Eve," p. 127.

57. Zhang Hui, p. 37; Tan Jingqiao, p. 18; Li Jukui, p. 265; Yao Xu, "Wise Decision," p. 8; Chai Chengwen and Zhao Yongtian, 1989, p. 80.

58. The cable makes it clear that Mao adopted a very Chinese approach to remind Stalin indirectly of his promise to provide air cover.

59. App., Doc. 63. The compilers' notes are omitted here.

60. For information on Mao's thinking on this issue, see Quan Yanchi, "Profound Reminiscences," pp. 111–12.

61. Interview with a former senior Soviet official, 1989.

62. Chai Chengwen and Zhao Yongtian, 1989, pp. 80–81; Xu Yan, *Diyi Ci*, p. 23. See also, Snow, *Other Side*, pp. 88–89; for Snow's conclusions, see pp. 714–15.

63. App., Doc. 64. In conveying his warning, Zhou asked his interpreter, Pu Shouchang, to find an accurate English term for *guan*, by which he meant "legitimately" intervene. Li Yueran, "Part of Recollections," p. 97. The U.S. consideration of Zhou's warning is recorded in FRUS 1950, 7: 848–52; relevant British documents are in Yasamee and Hamilton, pp. 162–67.

64. Interview with a well-informed Chinese specialist, Oct. 1991.

65. Qi Dexue, p. 49; *Chen Yi Zhuan*, p. 486.

66. Peng Dehuai, *Memoirs*, pp. 472–74; Zhang Liyao, pp. 313–14; Hong Xuezhi, *KangMei*, pp. 18–19; Hu Guangzheng and Bao Mingrong, p. 60; Zhang Xi, "On the Eve," pp. 130–36.

67. Zhang Xi, "On the Eve," p. 132.

68. Lin Biao's disagreement with Mao's decision for war has been noted. On

the others named in the text, see Miao Changqing, pp. 50–51; "Chen Yun Is a Master Schemer," p. 30; Zhang Yuwen, p. 19; Zhou Guoquan et al., pp. 464–65, 466; and Central Committee, Chinese Communist Party, "Report," p. 114.

69. Lin Yunhui et al., p. 179; Chen Mingxian et al., p. 33; Zhang Xi, "On the Eve," p. 132.

70. On the national sentiment against war, see Yao Xu, *Cong Yalujiang*, p. 20; Hu Zhixing, p. 84; Hu Sheng, p. 280; and Xu Yan, *Diyi Ci*, p. 22.

71. Nie Rongzhen, *Inside*, pp. 634–35.

72. From the eve of the PLA's campaign to force its way across the Yangtze River, Mao had held that an armed conflict with the Americans was almost inevitable and had called for full preparations for the impending fighting. Ye Fei, pp. 6–7; Zhang Zhen, p. 49.

73. He Di, "Evolution," 1987, p. 18; Xiong Xianghui. On Mao's army dress, see Quan Yanchi, "Everyday Life," p. 5.

74. For the details on these arguments, we draw heavily on Zhou Enlai, "Resist," pp. 28–33; and Central Committee, Chinese Communist Party, *Guanyu Shishi*.

75. Wu Xiuquan, "Wu Xiuquan's Speech," p. 208; Guo Binwei and Tan Zongji, p. 35.

76. Zhou Enlai, "Resist," p. 30. See also Chen Geng's diary entry, Nov. 5, 1950, in Xu Peilan and Zheng Pengfei, p. 602.

77. Zhou Enlai, "Resist," pp. 30, 33; Hao Sheng, pp. 6–7.

78. Yao Xu, *Cong Yalujiang*, p. 22; Hao Sheng, pp. 6–7; "Why We Can't Ignore the American Invasion"; Liu Hongxuan, p. 61; Yao Xu, "Wise Decision," p. 10; Chen Mingxian et al., p. 28.

79. The count of "hostile elements" took in 2,000,000 "political bandits," 600,000 Nationalist "special agents," and 600,000 "core members of the reactionary Kuomintang and the San-min Chu-i Youth League." Lin Yunhui et al., p. 138; Chen Mingxian et al., p. 6. On revolts, see, for example, Jing Song, p. 229; and "Inside Information."

80. Ren Jianshu, p. 382; Hu Zhixing, p. 85; Lin Yunhui et al., p. 139.

81. By the autumn of 1950, "hostile elements" had allegedly killed almost 40,000 Communists and pro-Communists. *Zhongguo Gongchandang Jianshi Jiangyi*, p. 246; Wang Xuebao, pp. 48–53; Wang Yu, pp. 50–52.

82. Lin Yunhui et al., p. 139.

83. Bo Yibo, pp. 134–35.

84. App., Doc. 73.

85. Information from a Chinese specialist on the Korean War, July 1992.

86. Spurr, p. 62. The PRC often uses this saying to characterize Sino-Korean strategic relations in its official publications. See, for example, Hao Sheng, p. 6.

87. Xiao Jianning, p. 173; Xue Mouhong, p. 41. The Chinese government still holds that the Sino-Soviet treaty dissuaded the Americans from extending the war to China. See Han Nianlong, p. 27.

88. App., Doc. 73; Lin Yunhui et al., p. 180. In 1959, Mao pointed out at the Lushan Plenum that his decision to enter the Korean War "partly was based on [the weak combat capability of] the South Korean puppet army. . . . We made our living by . . . [annihilating] puppet armies." Li Rui, p. 224.

89. Yao Xu, "Wise Decision," pp. 11, 12 (the quotation is from p. 11); Hu Guangzheng, p. 36.

90. Mao [13], pp. 352–53. For similar admissions by one of Beijing's leaders, see Peng Dehuai, *Peng Dehuai Zishu*, p. 262.

91. Peng Dehuai, "Speech," p. 322; Zhou Enlai, "Resist," p. 33; Du Ping, *Zai Zhiyuanjun Zongbu*, p. 25; Hu Guangzheng, p. 36.

92. In Chinese, "not resigned to advanced age" is *bu fu lao*. Most of the military commanders in China at the time were in their thirties or forties. The information in this paragraph is from Peng Dehuai, *Memoirs*, pp. 472–74; Zhang Xi, "On the Eve," pp. 130–36; Nie Rongzhen, *Inside*, p. 636; Hong Xuezhi, *KangMei*, pp. 18–19; and Hu Guangzheng and Bao Mingrong, p. 60.

93. Zhang Xi, "On the Eve," pp. 137–38. Mao Anying, whose Russian name was Sergei, died in a U.S. bombing raid on Nov. 25, 1950. For information on his death and Mao Zedong's response to it, see Zhou Enlai, "Sacrifice," p. 446.

94. At the meeting of Oct. 6, Lin Biao expressed his doubts one more time on sending troops to Korea. Zhou criticized Lin and stressed that the participants should only discuss how to implement the Politburo's decision of Oct. 2. Xu Yan, *Diyi Ci*, pp. 23–24; Zhang Xi, "On the Eve," p. 139.

95. Tan Jingqiao, pp. 16, 430; Shen Zonghong and Meng Zhaohui, p. 10; Hong Xuezhi, *KangMei*, p. 13; Sun Qitai, p. 162; Han Nianlong, p. 37; Chai Chengwen and Zhao Yongtian, 1989, p. 82; Zhou Enlai, "Resist," p. 29.

96. Unless otherwise cited, the information in this and the next paragraph is from Yao Xu, *Cong Yalujiang*, pp. 20–21; Yao Xu, "Wise Decision," pp. 9–10; Hu Guangzheng, p. 35; Xu Yan, *Diyi Ci*, p. 25; Ding Xuesong et al., p. 630; and Chen Li and Jin Ruishen, pp. 25, 27.

97. On Mao's assessment of U.S. military pressure on the Northeast, see also Zhou Enlai, "Resist," p. 30; Hu Guangzheng, p. 35; and Yao Xu, *Cong Yalujiang*, p. 21.

98. Lim Un, p. 189.

99. The following, from Mao [20], pp. 543–44 (and reproduced in App., Doc. 65), is the full text of Mao's order. The official version in Mao's *Selected Works* (Mao [32]) is much abridged: part of paragraph 1 and all of paragraphs 2–4 are deleted, with paragraphs 5 and 6 of the full text becoming paragraphs 2 and 3. We have accepted the translation from the official version with some minor corrections based on the original. Li Tao, head of the Operations Department of the PLA General Staff, who wrote the first draft, used the term "supporting forces." Mao replaced it with "volunteers" and added the fifth and sixth paragraphs. Information from a Chinese specialist on the Korean War, July 1992.

100. See App., Doc. 65. For the background of Hong Xuezhi and Xie Fang and their roles in the Korean War, see Hong Xuezhi, *KangMei*; Hong Xuezhi, "Logistics Work," pp. 3–8; He Maozhi, pp. 5–7; Sun Yaosheng and Cui Jingshan, pp. 247–56; and Wang Wanli, pp. 171–79.

101. App., Doc. 66.

102. Zhang Xi, "On the Eve," p. 142.

103. We have been unable to locate the actual text of the operational order issued on Oct. 9. Mao's telegram to Ni Zhiliang is in App., Doc. 67; it was sent in the name of Zhou Enlai. On the temporary relocation of the Chinese embassy from Pyongyang to Huichon and the capital of North Korea from Pyongyang to Tokchon, see Zhao Yongtian and Zhang Xi, p. 42; and Xu Yan, *Diyi Ci*, p. 24. U.S. intelligence incorrectly reported that the "emergency North Korean capital" had moved to Sinuiju; see Smith to Truman, Nov. 1, 1950, in FRUS 1950, 7: 1025.

104. App., Doc. 68.

105. *Zhonggong Dangshi Dashi Nianbiao*, p. 239; Ni Zhongwen, p. 110; Ren Jianshu, p. 383; Yao Xu, *Cong Yalujiang*, p. 85. The formal title of the order was "Directive Concerning Correcting the Right Deviation in Suppressing Counterrevolutionary Activities."

106. According to Liu Shaoqi's "Report of the Politburo to the Fourth Plenary Session of the CCP Seventh Central Committee," the campaign swept up 3,230,000 people all told. Of these, 710,000 were executed, 1,290,000 were jailed, and 1,230,000 were put under public surveillance. See Sun Kejia, p. 5; Yao Xu, *Cong Yalujiang*, p. 84; and Ni Zhongwen, p. 110. In 1959, Mao admitted at the Lushan Plenum that 1,000,000 "counterrevolutionaries" had been executed in the campaign. Li Rui, p. 333.

107. Shi Zhe, *Zai Lishi*, p. 495; Zhang Xi, "On the Eve," pp. 147, 148.

108. The information in this paragraph is from Huang Jijun, pp. 467–69; Li Jukui, pp. 264–66, 273; Chen Zhiliang, p. 244; Huang Yi, "Zhou Enlai," 2: 34; Hong Xuezhi, *KangMei*, pp. 181–84; Hong Xuezhi, "Logistics Work," p. 4; and Tan Jingqiao, p. 437.

109. Hong Xuezhi, *KangMei*, p. 20; Zhang Xi, "Peng Dehuai," p. 3; Hu Guangzheng and Bao Mingrong, p. 60.

110. On the Oct. 9 order, see App., Doc. 71.

111. Li Jukui was the original head of the Logistics Department when it was set up by order of Nie Rongzhen on Aug. 7, 1950. Initially, this department was in charge of CPV logistics in both the Northeast and North Korea, but this responsibility was to change several times during the course of the war.

112. Qi Dexue, p. 65; Yao Xu, "Wise Decision," p. 9; Yao Xu, *Cong Yalujiang*, p. 25.

113. Yao Xu, "Wise Decision," p. 9; Zhang Xi, "Peng Dehuai," p. 3; Hong Xuezhi, *KangMei*, pp. 21–22; Nie Rongzhen, *Inside*, pp. 636–37.

114. Hong Xuezhi, *KangMei*, pp. 22–23. See also Yang Chengwu, "66th Corps' Entry," pp. 55–58.

115. App., Doc. 69. Though Mao did not say "Soviet air force," this could be the only meaning because the PRC at this time had no air force of any consequence.

116. Zhang Xi, "On the Eve," pp. 147, 148. Though Zhang puts the date of Zhou's cable as the 10th, this is surely incorrect, as we shall see. On the reversal of Moscow's attitude toward offering air cover for the CPV, see also Hong Xuezhi, *KangMei*, pp. 24–26; Hao Yufan and Zhai Zhihai, p. 110; and Zhang Xi, "Peng Dehuai," p. 3. We highlight the Chinese *kongjun* because the term, which normally translates as "air force," can also mean "aircraft and pilots."

117. Shi Zhe, *Zai Lishi*, p. 496. The Soviet officials who attended the Stalin-Zhou negotiation on the Black Sea were G. Malenkov, L. Kaganovich, L. Beria, A. Mikoyan, N. Bulganin, and V. Molotov—all senior Communist Party leaders close to Stalin. Zhang Xi, "On the Eve," p. 147.

118. Shi Zhe, *Zai Lishi*, p. 496.

119. Interview with Kang Sang Ho, Yoo Sung Chul, and Chung Sang Chin, April 13, 1992. Yoo was a member of a North Korean delegation, headed by Pak Hon Yong, that went to Beijing on Oct. 18. On the way back home, the delegation met with Gao Gang, who told the Koreans about the talks between Stalin and Zhou, as well as about the CCP Politburo's discussions concerning China's entrance into the war.

120. Shi Zhe, *Zai Lishi*, p. 496.

121. The information in this and the following paragraph is from *ibid.*, pp. 496–97.

122. This and the following four paragraphs are based on *ibid.*, pp. 497–99; Zhang Xi, "On the Eve," pp. 147–48; Zhao Yongtian and Zhang Xi, p. 42; Hao Yufan and Zhai Zhihai, pp. 110–11; and Chai Chengwen and Zhao Yongtian, 1989, p. 83. Most of the quotations in these paragraphs are from Shi Zhe. As we have noted, Lin Biao was an early opponent of the intervention. On Sept. 8, in an interview with Chai Chengwen, Lin asked, "Are [the leaders of the Korean Workers' Party] prepared to go into the mountains and wage guerrilla warfare? . . . If we don't send troops, is it possible for them to go into the mountains and wage guerrilla warfare?" Chai Chengwen and Zhao Yongtian, 1992, p. 59.

123. The information in this paragraph is from Shi Zhe, *Zai Lishi*, pp. 498, 499; and Zhang Xi, "On the Eve," p. 148.

124. Some Chinese sources state that Zhou departed for Moscow on Oct. 10. See, for example, Zhang Xi, "On the Eve," p. 148. We believe this is incorrect.

125. This paragraph is based on the recollections of Kang Yimin, a confidential secretary from the CCP Central Committee's Administration Office who accompanied Zhou to Moscow. See Qi Dexue, pp. 62–63.

126. See Ledovskii, *Delo*, pp. 72–73. This previously classified book is based entirely on documents from the archives of the Soviet Ministry of Foreign Affairs; Ledovskii was the Soviet consul general in Shenyang during the Korean War (and had close relations with Gao Gang).

127. Khrushchev, "Korean War," p. 28. This paragraph is missing in the English translation of Khrushchev's memoirs.

128. Interview with Kang Sang Ho, Yoo Sung Chul, and Chung Sang Chin, April 13, 1992. This statement was made by Chung.

129. We should note the well-known account by Ye Yumeng (*Heixue*, pp. 107–8) on this incident. Ye reportedly has said that his verbatim account of Mao's statement on this occasion is largely fiction.

130. For an example of Chinese comment on Stalin's conclusion, see Zhang Xi, "On the Eve," p. 148.

131. Hong Xuezhi, *KangMei*, p. 26; Xu Yan, *Diyi Ci*, p. 24.

132. Quan Yanchi, "Mao Zedong's Entry," p. 4; Xu Yan, *Diyi Ci*, pp. 20–21; Yan Chi, p. 9; Hao Yufan and Zhai Zhihai, p. 111; Ruan Ming, p. 36.

133. Zhang Xi, "On the Eve," pp. 146–47, 148–49; Xu Yan, *Diyi Ci*, p. 24. Zhang states that Nie called Peng at 1:00 A.M. on the 11th, but according to Wang Yazhi, Nie's staff officer, the call was made at 1:00 A.M. on the 12th. Information from a Chinese specialist on the Korean War, July 1992.

134. App., Doc. 70.

135. Xu Yan, *Diyi Ci*, p. 24; Hong Xuezhi, *KangMei*, p. 26; Zhang Xi, "On the Eve," p. 149. As noted, the Oct. 9 order implemented Mao's broad directive of the 8th.

136. App., Doc. 71. See also Hong Xuezhi, *KangMei*, p. 24; and Zhang Xi, "On the Eve," p. 149.

137. App., Doc. 72. Rao Shushi was political commissar of the East China Military Region.

138. Based on Peng Dehuai, *Memoirs*, pp. 472–73; Hu Guangzheng, p. 34; Du Ping, "Wise Decision," p. 10; and Hong Xuezhi, *KangMei*, p. 18.

139. App., Doc. 72. In telling his commanders not to "give new explanations," Mao apparently foresaw a reaffirmation of the Oct. 9 order. New explanations would have cast doubt on the order and created problems when it was activated.

140. Hong Xuezhi, *KangMei*, p. 24; Zhang Xi, "On the Eve," p. 149. On the Politburo's emergency session, see also Zhang Xi, "Peng Dehuai," p. 3; Mao's telegram to Zhou, App., Doc. 73; and Xu Yan, *Diyi Ci*, p. 24.

141. Zhou Enlai, "Resist," p. 30; Chai Chengwen and Zhao Yongtian, 1989, p. 73.

142. For Kim's statement on the 11th, see Zhang Xi, "On the Eve," pp. 149–50.

143. For Mao's final deliberations on the advantages and disadvantages of going to war, see Chen Mingxian et al., p. 32; Zhou Guoquan et al., p. 466; and Zhang Xi, "On the Eve," pp. 149–51.

144. App., Doc. 73.

145. Unless otherwise cited, the information in this and the next paragraph is from Shi Zhe, *Zai Lishi*, pp. 501–2.

146. Yao Xu, "Wise Decision," p. 10, quoting Marshal Chen Yi speech of April 16, 1964.

147. Shi Zhe, *Zai Lishi*, p. 502.

148. Chinese official sources later revealed Mao's worry about the threat of U.S. Korean operations to China's security. See, for example, "Statement of the Foreign Ministry's Spokesman," p. 29; "Why Can't We Ignore the Korean War?"; "Why Can't We Ignore the War of Aggression?"; and "Why Can't We Ignore the American Invasion?"

149. Unless otherwise cited, the information in the rest of this paragraph and the one that follows is from App., Docs. 74–76.

150. See also Cui Xianghua and Chen Dapeng, pp. 388–90; Zhang Tinggui, p. 4; and Deng Lifeng, *Xin Zhongguo*, p. 146.

151. The high command's original operational plan called for an alternate use of positional warfare and mobile warfare. Wang Chengguang, p. 10; Zhang Xi, "On the Eve," p. 151.

152. Mao [34], especially pp. 121–29.

153. Mao [9], pp. 367–70; Mao [10], pp. 361–66; Mao [11], pp. 375–79.

154. App., Doc. 78.

155. App., Doc. 79.

156. We believe that Peng Dehuai visited the Anshan Steel and Iron Complex and the Shenyang Ordnance Factory on Oct. 15, as stated in Hong Xuezhi, *KangMei*, p. 27; Zhang Xi, "On the Eve," p. 152, not on the 16th or 17th, as some sources claim. See, for example, Hu Guangzheng and Bao Mingrong, p. 60.

157. Liao Guoliang et al., p. 357; Zhang Xi, "On the Eve," pp. 153–54, 157; information from a Chinese specialist on the Korean War, July 1992.

158. App., Doc. 80; Hong Xuezhi, *KangMei*, p. 30; Zhang Xi, "On the Eve," pp. 157–58.

159. Xu Yan, *Diyi Ci*, p. 25; Du Ping, *Zai Zhiyuanjun Zongbu*, p. 40; Zhang Xi, "On the Eve," p. 157.

160. Zhang Xi, "On the Eve," p. 158; Qi Dexue, pp. 66–67; Liao Guoliang et al., p. 357.

161. Ledovskii, *Delo*, p. 73.

162. Lim Un, p. 189. Mao and Kim Il Sung met and agreed on the terms of the

Joint Command on Dec. 3. Kim Ung and Pak Il U were selected as the deputy commander and deputy political commissar, respectively. Ye Yumeng, *Hanjiang*, pp. 3–8.

163. Lim Un, p. 187. Yoo Sung Chul, "My Testimony," Dec. 28, 1990, p. 16, writes: "Even today I distinctly recall this meeting. The reason I can is that Mao Zedong used his unique body movements to convey various advice regarding the KPA's military strategy."

164. App., Doc. 81; Hong Xuezhi, *KangMei*, p. 30.

165. App., Doc. 82. This is a cable Mao sent to Deng Zihui and Tan Zheng, second and third political commissars of the Central-South Military Region, among others; they were instructed to pass the orders on to leaders of various regional Party bureaus.

166. During the Korean War, the city of Andong (Dandong) became a strategic gateway between China and Korea and a key link in the CPV's communication line. Feng Fangzhu and Ye Zhi, p. 31.

167. Unless otherwise cited, this paragraph is based on Hong Xuezhi, *KangMei*, pp. 29–32, 46; Xu Yan, *Diyi Ci*, p. 40; Tan Jingqiao, pp. 25, 28; Du Ping, *Zai Zhiyuanjun Zongbu*, p. 44; Zhang Hui, p. 38; Deng Lifeng, *Xin Zhongguo*, pp. 136–37; Xu Zhongjing and Dai Yifang, p. 33; Yang Chengwu, "66th Corps' Entry," pp. 55–58; Yang Zhihua, p. 55; Ma Kaijun, p. 50; and Zhang Tinggui, p. 3.

168. Han Huaizhi and Tan Jingqiao, 1: 455–56; Tan Jingqiao, pp. 34–41.

169. For concise discussions of the five major campaigns, see Nie Rongzhen, *Inside*, pp. 638–39; Cai Tianfu, pp. 30–31; Zhang Tinggui, pp. 3–5; Jing Yu, pp. 16–25; Zhang Liyao, pp. 313–14; and Chen Yan et al., p. 12.

170. These dates are from Academy of Military Science, *Zhongguo Renmin Jiefangjun Dashiji*, pp. 320–29, and *Zhongguo Renmin Jiefangjun Liushi Nian Dashiji*, pp. 498–510. Other Chinese sources, though ambiguous, basically accept this periodization. See Song Shilun, pp. 631–37; Nie Rongzhen, *Inside*, pp. 639–41; and Peng Dehuai, *Memoirs*, pp. 474–84.

171. Lobov, pp. 33–34; interviews with G. Kuzmin, April–July, 1991. Air Force Lt. Gen. (Ret.) G. Lobov was the commander of the 64th and a Hero of the Soviet Union. For further details on the activities of this unit, see *Aviatsiia i Kosmonavtika* [Aviation and Cosmonautics], No. 11–12, 1990, and No. 1–5, 1991.

172. Lobov, p. 33.

173. Interviews with G. Kuzmin, April–July, 1991.

174. Unless otherwise cited, this paragraph is based on Deng Lifeng, *Xin Zhongguo*, pp. 144, 145; and interviews with G. Kuzmin, April–July, 1991.

175. For brief Soviet descriptions of Soviet armed forces in Korea itself, see Borisov and Koloskov, *Sovetsko-Kitaiskie Otnosheniia, 1945–1977 gg.*, p. 53; and the transcript of an interview with the chairman of the Korean Group of the Soviet Veterans Committee, Moscow Radio, March 20 and 21, 1990, in FBIS: Soviet Union, March 27, 1990, pp. 17–19.

176. Clubb to Rusk, Nov. 1, 1950, in FRUS 1950, 7: 1024.

177. Volkogonov, 2.2: 109. Mao himself believed that his actions in Korea had won Stalin's trust. See, for example, Mao [39], p. 165.

178. On Mao's characterization of his relations with Stalin, see Mao [40], p. 183.

179. For Chinese evaluations of the role of Soviet military aid in the war, see

Zhang Zongxun, pp. 436–37; Yang Chengwu, "Preparations," p. 47; and Deng Lifeng, *Xin Zhongguo*, pp. 144, 145.

180. Hong Xuezhi and Hu Qicai; Yao Xu, *Cong Yalujiang*, p. 64. Many of the Soviet weapons and equipment were shipped per an agreement worked out during Chief of the General Staff Xu Xiangqian's visit to Moscow in May 1951. According to Marshal Xu, many of the weapons were old and could not be used. Xu Xiangqian, pp. 798–99.

181. Unless otherwise cited, the information in this and the next paragraph is from Xu Yan, *Diyi Ci*, pp. 30, 31, 32; Li Ke and Hao Shengzhang, p. 280; and Yao Xu, *Cong Yalujiang*, p. 64.

182. Rong Zhi, p. 103; Shi Zhe, *Zai Lishi*, p. 502.

183. Xu Yan, *Diyi Ci*, p. 32; Li Yueran, *Waijiao*, p. 38.

184. The first Sino-American air battle of the war occurred on Jan. 21, 1951. Liu Zhen, pp. 347, 357; Wang Dinglie, p. 199; Yao Xu, *Cong Yalujiang*, pp. 63, 64, 166. The maximum number of air divisions under the CPV's jurisdiction was 15. Xiao Shizhong, p. 52. For information on the Sino-American air battles in the war, see Yu Zhen, "CPV's Air Force."

185. Xu Yan, *Diyi Ci*, p. 31. According to Lobov, p. 32, by the end of the summer of 1951, the Chinese had two divisions of MiG-15s operating from two airfields in the Northeast.

186. Zhou Enlai, "Comintern," p. 300.

187. Lewis and Xue, *China Builds the Bomb*, pp. 7–10.

188. The lessons of the Korean War were reviewed and summarized by a special committee set up by the People's Liberation Army. *KangMei YuanChao Zhanzheng*, pp. 107–20.

Chapter Seven

1. Mao's favorite novel was *Dongzhou Lieguo Zhi* [The History of Various Kingdoms Under the Eastern Zhou Dynasty]. Intrigue and turbulence dominated the Warring States period (475 B.C.–221 B.C.) of that era. Unless otherwise cited, the information in this paragraph is from Chen Dunde, p. 421; a Chinese specialist, Dec. 1989; and Pang Xianzhi, "Description," pp. 203–4.

2. For studies on Mao's strategic thinking, see Yang Yanpu, pp. 3–7; Lei Zhongmin, pp. 96–101; Zhang Jian and Jin Shi, pp. 117–21; and Zhang Quanqi and Wang Shengyu, pp. 122–25. *Zongheng baihe* is a phrase that dates to the Warring States period. In literal translation, it means "over the length and breadth make trouble and settle disputes," but it is usually translated as simply "maneuver among various political groupings."

3. See the bibliography on just one period of the relationship in Garver, pp. 278–94.

4. Fedorenko, pp. 136, 137, 140.

5. Mao [30], p. 416.

6. Arkhipov had two stints as chief economic adviser to the Government Administration Council (later the State Council), in 1950–51 and 1953–58. Untitled interview with Arkhipov, in *USSR-China in the Changing World*, pp. 39–51; Li Yueran, *Waijiao*, pp. 22–23.

7. Interview with a Soviet specialist with ties to senior advisers in China, 1990.

8. Untitled interview with Arkhipov, in *USSR-China in the Changing World*, pp. 43, 47.

9. According to a well-informed Chinese author, Mao in 1958 expressed dissatisfaction that the imperialists had the atomic bomb and China did not. When a colleague pointed out that the Soviet Union also had the atomic bomb, Mao replied, "it is undependable." Quan Yanchi, *Mao Zedong*, p. 97.

10. Lewis and Xue, *China Builds the Bomb*, pp. 60–72.

11. Quan Yanchi, *Mao Zedong*, p. 119.

12. See, among others, Liao Guoliang et al., pp. 481–85.

References Cited

References Cited

Chinese romanizations are not provided for newspaper or journal articles. English names are given in brackets for all journals, newspapers, and books except the most frequently cited ones:

Dangshi Yanjiu [Studies on Party History]
Junshi Lishi [Military History]
Junshi Shilin [Military History Circles]
Novoe Vremia [New Times]
Pravda [Truth]
Renmin Ribao [People's Daily]
Shehui Kexue Zhanxian [Social Science Front] (Changchun)
Shijie Zhishi [World Knowledge]
Zhonggong Dangshi Yanjiu [Studies on CCP History]

Unless otherwise stated, all Chinese-language journals and newspapers are published in Beijing and all Russian-language journals and newspapers are published in Moscow. We use one abbreviation in this list: NYT for the *New York Times*.

Academy of Military Science. *Zhongguo Renmin Jiefangjun Dashiji (1927–1982)* [Chronicle of Major Events of the Chinese People's Liberation Army (1927–1982)]. Beijing, 1983.

———. *Zhongguo Renmin Jiefangjun Liushi Nian Dashiji (1927–1987)* [Chronicle of Major Events of the Chinese People's Liberation Army over the Past 60 Years (1927–1987)]. Beijing, 1988.

"Acheson Backing in China View Seen," NYT, Jan. 30, 1950.

Acheson, Dean. "Crisis in Asia—An Examination of U.S. Policy," Department of State *Bulletin*, Jan. 23, 1950.

———. *Present at the Creation: My Years in the State Department*. New York, 1969.

———. "United States Policy Toward Asia," Department of State *Bulletin*, March 27, 1950.

"Address of the Central Committee of the All-Union Communist Party (Bolshevik)," *Bol'shevik*, No. 2, 1946.

Adzhubei, Aleksei. *Te Desiat' Let* [Those Ten Years]. Moscow, 1989.

Appleman, Roy E. *South to the Naktong, North to the Yalu*. Washington, D.C., 1961.

Astaf'ev, G. "The Economic Problems of China," *Novoe Vremia*, No. 16, 1950.

Avarin, V. "Four Clans of the Chinese Plutocracy," *Novoe Vremia*, No. 49, 1947.

———. "Military Successes of Democratic China," *Novoe Vremia*, No. 1, 1948.

———. "New Offensive of the People's Liberation Army of China," *Novoe Vremia*, No. 44, 1948.

———. "The New Stage of American Interference in China," *Novoe Vremia*, No. 46, 1947.

———. "The Political Situation in China," *Novoe Vremia*, No. 2, 1947.

"Background of the Civil War in Korea," *China Weekly Review*, July 8, 1950.

Bak, Gab-dong. *Bak Hon-Yong: A Reevaluation of Modern History as Seen from His Life and Times*. Seoul, 1984.

Baranov, L. "About the Functions of Proletarian Dictatorship, Fulfilled by the People's Dictatorship," *Pravda*, Jan. 5, 1950.

Bazhanov, E. P. *Kitai i Vneshnii Mir* [China and the Outside World]. Moscow, 1990.

Bernstein, Barton J. "The Truman Administration and the Korean War," in Michael Lacey, ed., *The Truman Presidency*. London, 1989.

Bi Jianzhong. "A New Exploration into the Strategic Guidelines for the Nationwide Liberation War," *Zhonggong Dangshi Yanjiu*, No. 4, 1990.

Bin Fu. "The Peace Signature Drive and the Atomic Bomb," *Shijie Zhishi*, June 16, 1950.

Bo Yibo. *Ruogan Zhongda Juece yu Shijian de Huigu Shangjuan* [A Look Back to Several Key Decisions and Main Events], Vol. 1. Beijing, 1991.

Borisov, O. B. [O. B. Rakhmanin]. *Iz Istorii Sovetsko-Kitaiskikh Otnoshenii v 50kh Godakh (K Diskussii v KNR o Mao Tsedone)* [From the History of Soviet-Chinese Relations in the 1950s (Toward the Discussion in the PRC About Mao Zedong)]. Moscow, 1981.

———. *Sovetskii Soiuz i Manzhurskaia Revoliutsionnaia Baza (1945–1949)* [Soviet Union and the Manchurian Revolutionary Base (1945–1949)]. Moscow, 1985.

Borisov, O. B., and B. T. Koloskov [B. T. Kulik]. *Sovetsko-Kitaiskie Otnosheniia, 1945–1977 gg.* [Soviet-Chinese Relations, 1945–1977]. Moscow, 1977.

———. *Sovetsko-Kitaiskie Otnosheniia, 1945–1980 gg.* [Soviet-Chinese Relations, 1945–1980]. 3d enlarged ed. Moscow, 1980.

Buhite, Russell D. *Soviet-American Relations in Asia, 1945–1954*. Norman, Okla., 1981.

Bukharkin, Igor. "Torn to Pieces," *Vestnik* [Herald] (Moscow), April 1990.

"Cable from the Soviet Government," in *Zhonghua Renmin Gongheguo Duiwai Guanxi Wenjian Ji (1949–1950)* [Collection of Documents on the Foreign Relations of the People's Republic of China (1949–1950)], Vol. 1. Beijing, 1957.

Cai Tianfu. "The Experiences and Lessons in the 5th Campaign of the War to Resist America and Aid Korea," *Junshi Lishi*, No. 5, 1990.

Calingaert, Daniel. "Nuclear Weapons and the Korean War," *Journal of Strategic Studies*, 11.2 (June 1988).

Carlyle, Margaret, ed. *Documents on International Affairs, 1949–1950*. London, 1953.

Central Committee, Chinese Communist Party. *Guanyu Shishi Xuanchuan de Zhishi* [Instructions Concerning Propaganda on Current Events (Oct. 26, 1950)] (Beijing, 1950).

———. "Report on the Investigation of the Counterrevolutionary Crimes of the Lin Piao [Biao] Anti-Party Clique," *Zhongfa* [Central Committee Distribution] 34, 1973. Reproduced in Michael Y. M. Kau, *The Lin Piao Affair: Power Politics and Military Coup.* White Plains, N.Y., 1975.

Chai Chengwen and Zhao Yongtian. *Banmendian Tanpan* [The Panmunjom Negotiations]. Beijing, 1989. Revised, Beijing, 1992.

"Chairman Mao and Premier Zhou Enlai in the Soviet Union," *Xinhua Yuebao* [New China Monthly], March 15, 1950.

Chang Cheng, chief ed. *Zhang Zuolin* [(The Biography of) Zhang Zuolin]. Shenyang, 1981.

Chang, Gordon H. *Friends and Enemies: The United States, China, and the Soviet Union, 1948–1972.* Stanford, Calif., 1990.

Chen Boda. *Stalin and the Chinese Revolution: In Celebration of Stalin's Seventieth Birthday.* Beijing, 1953.

Chen Dunde. *Guigen Li Zongren yu Mao Zedong Zhou Enlai Woshou* [The Return of Li Zongren to China: Shaking Hands with Mao Zedong and Zhou Enlai]. Beijing, 1991.

Chen Guangxiang. "Stalin Persuaded Our Party Not to Cross the Yangtze River," in *Dangshi Yanjiu Ziliao* [Research Materials on Party History], Vols. 7–8. Chengdu, 1989. Excerpted in *Zhonggong Dangshi Tongxun* [CCP History Newsletter], No. 2 (Jan. 25, 1990).

Chen Hanbo. "Whether China and the Soviet Union Should Participate in the [Korean] War?," *Shijie Zhishi*, July 14, 1950.

Chen Li and Jin Ruishen, chief eds. *KangMei YuanChao Yundong zhong de Dongbei yu Chaoxian Tuji* [Pictures of the Northeast and Korea Collected in the Campaign to Resist America and Aid Korea]. Shanghai, 1951.

Chen Mingxian et al., eds. *Xin Zhongguo Sishi Nian Yanjiu* [Research on the 40-Year History of New China]. Beijing, 1989.

Chen Ping. "Our Practice and Experiences in Building Up the Quality of the Army in the 1950s," *Junshi Lishi*, No. 6, 1989.

Chen Yan et al. "Some Points of Enlightenment from the Experiences in the War to Resist America and Aid Korea for Guiding Local Wars Hereafter," *Junshi Shilin*, No. 5, 1987.

Chen Yi. "The First Visit to Guangzhou," *Dajiang Nanbei* [On Both Sides of the Yangtze River] (Nanjing), No. 1, 1990.

Chen Yi Zhuan [The Biography of Chen Yi]. Beijing, 1991.

Chen Yun. "My Opinion on the Writing and Editing of *LiaoShen Juezhan*," in *LiaoShen Juezhan* [The Liaoxi-Shenyang Campaign], Vol. 1. Beijing, 1988.

———. "Some Opinions on Our Work in Manchuria" [Nov. 30, 1945], in *Chen Yun Wenxuan (1926–1949)* [Selected Works of Chen Yun (1926–1949)]. Beijing, 1984.

"Chen Yun Is a Master Schemer Against Our Great Leader Chairman Mao," *Beijing Gongshe* [Beijing Commune], Aug. 14, 1967. Reprinted in *Zhanwang* [Look Ahead] (Hong Kong), May 1, 1979.

Chen Zhiling. "Li Fuchun in the Northeast," *Shehui Kexue Zhanxian*, No. 1, 1992.

Chi Aiping. "Mao Zedong's Strategic Guidance for New China's Foreign Affairs," *Dang de Wenxian* [Party Documents], No. 1, 1992.

Chiang Ching-kuo. "Account of the Talks During the Visit to the Soviet Union," in *Zhonghua Minguo Zhongyao Shiliao Chubian Dui Ri Kangzhan Shiqi Di Qi*

Bian Zhanhou Zhongguo (I) [Important Historical Materials on the Republic of China During the War of Resistance Against Japan, Vol. 7: Postwar China (Part I)]. Taipei, 1981.

———. *Fengyu zhong de Ningjing* [Tranquility in the Wind and Rain]. Taipei, 1967.

———. "My Father," in *Zongtong Jianggong Aisi Shilu* [The True Record of Our Grief over President Chiang (Kai-shek)]. Taipei, 1975.

———. "The Talks During My Visit to the Soviet Union," in *Zhonghua Minguo Zhongyao Shiliao Chubian Dui Ri Kangzhan Shiqi Di Qi Bian Zhanhou Zhongguo (I)* [Important Historical Materials of the Republic of China During the Period of the War of Resistance Against Japan, Vol. 7: Postwar China (Part I)]. Taipei, 1981.

"Chiang Kai-shek's Three Cables to Comrade Mao Zedong," in *Chongqing Tanpan Ziliao* [Materials on the Chongqing Negotiations]. Chengdu, 1980.

Choudhury, Golam W. "Reflections on the Korean War (1950–1953): The Factors Behind Chinese Intervention," *Korea and World Affairs* (Seoul), 14.2 (Summer 1990).

Cihai [A Sea of Words (Dictionary)]. Shanghai, 1979.

Clubb, O. Edmund. "Chiang Kai-shek's Waterloo: The Battle of the Huai-Hai," *Pacific Historical Review*, 25.4 (Nov. 1956).

———. *China and Russia: The "Great Game."* New York, 1971.

"Common Program of the Chinese People's Political Consultative Conference (Sept. 29, 1949)," in *Zhonggong Dangshi Jiaoxue*, Vol. 18, listed below.

Condit, Kenneth W. *The History of the Joint Chiefs of Staff: The Joint Chiefs of Staff and National Policy*, Vol. 2: 1947–1949. Wilmington, Del., 1979.

"Congratulations on the Jubilee," *Gudok* [Whistle], June 28, 1991.

Connally, Tom. "World Policy and Bipartisanship," *U.S. News & World Report*, May 5, 1950.

Cui Xianghua and Chen Dapeng. *Tao Yong Jiangjun Zhuan* [Biography of General Tao Yong]. Beijing, 1989.

Cumings, Bruce. *The Origins of the Korean War*, 2 vols. Princeton, N.J., 1981, 1990.

Deng Chao. "The Establishment of Diplomatic Relations Between China and Britain and the Colombo Conference," *Shijie Zhishi*, Jan. 27, 1950.

———. "Imperialism Is Caught in a Dilemma After the Signing of the New Sino-Soviet Treaty," *Shijie Zhishi*, March 10, 1950.

Deng Hua et al. "Cherish the Memory of Comrade Peng Dehuai, an Excellent Ex-Leader of the Chinese People's Volunteers," in *Hengdao Lima Peng Jiangjun* [The Extraordinarily Brave General Peng]. Beijing, 1979.

Deng Lifeng. "A General Description of the Struggle to Suppress Bandits Right After the Founding of the Republic," *Junshi Lishi*, No. 1, 1991.

———. *Xin Zhongguo Junshi Huodong Jishi (1949–1959)* [The True Records of New China's Military Affairs (1949–59)]. Beijing, 1989.

Deng Liqun. "On the Eve of and After the Peaceful Liberation of Xinjiang: One Page of Sino-Soviet Relations," *Jindai Shi Yanjiu* [Modern History Studies], No. 5, 1989.

———. "A Selection of Cables Sent and Received by the 'Liqun Transceiver,'" in *Zhonggong Dangshi Ziliao* [Materials on CCP History], Vol. 36. Beijing, 1990.

Deng Xiaoping. "The Way to Break the Imperialist Blockade" [July 19, 1949], in *Deng Xiaoping Wenxuan (1938–1965)* [Selected Works of Deng Xiaoping (1938–1965)]. Beijing, 1989.

Deng Xinghua. "My Point of View on the Dispatch of Soviet Troops to the Northeast," *Junshi Shilin*, No. 5, 1989.

Dinerstein, H. S. *War and the Soviet Union: Nuclear Weapons and the Revolution in Soviet Military and Political Thinking.* Westport, Conn., 1962.

Ding Xuesong et al. "Our Reminiscences of the Office of the Northeast Bureau in Korea During the Northeast Liberation War," in *LiaoShen Juezhan* [The Liaoxi-Shenyang Campaign], Vol. 1. Beijing, 1988.

Dingman, Roger. "Atomic Diplomacy During the Korean War," *International Security*, 13.3 (Winter 1988/89).

Dittmer, Lowell. *Liu Shao-ch'i and the Chinese Cultural Revolution: The Politics of Mass Criticism.* Berkeley, Calif., 1974.

Djilas, Milovan. *Conversations with Stalin.* Tr. Michael B. Petrovich. New York, 1962.

Dongbei Kangri Lianjun Douzheng Shi [The History of the Northeast Anti-Japanese United Army's Struggle]. Beijing, 1991.

Dong Yanping. "Disclosure of the Process of Occupation of the Northeast by the Russian Troops," in *Zhonghua Minguo Zhongyao Shiliao Chubian Dui Ri Kangzhan Shiqi Di Qi Bian Zhanhou Zhongguo (I)* [Important Historical Materials of the Republic of China During the Period of the War of Resistance Against Japan, Vol. 7: Postwar China (Part I)]. Taipei, 1981.

———. *SuE Ju Dongbei* [The Occupation of the Northeast by the Soviet Russia]. Taipei, 1966.

Du Ping. "A Wise Decision," *Xinghuo Liaoyuan* [A Single Spark Can Start a Prairie Fire], No. 6, 1985.

———. *Zai Zhiyuanjun Zongbu* [At the Headquarters of the (Chinese People's) Volunteers]. Beijing, 1989.

Du Shilin. "The Pioneers in the Creation of the Northeast Base Area," *Dangshi Wenhui* [Collection on Party History] (Taiyuan), No. 5, 1987.

Du Yuming. "Inside Story of the Scheme of the United States and Chiang Kai-shek to Seize the Northeast," in Wang Dikang et al., eds., *Dongbei Jiefang Zhanzheng Jishi* [True Records on the Liberation War in the Northeast]. Beijing, 1988.

———. "The Whole Story of Chiang Kai-shek's Plan to Jeopardize Peace and Attack the Northeast," in *Wenshi Ziliao Xuanji* [Selected Materials on Literature and History], Vol. 42. Beijing, n.d.

Durdin, Tillman. "Chiang Holds Formosa in an Uncertain Grip," NYT, Jan. 8, 1950.

———. "Formosa Invasion Seen Set by Spring," NYT, Dec. 21, 1949.

———. "Indo-China Called Key Anti-Red Base," NYT, Feb. 19, 1950.

———. "Sino-Soviet Talks Held Near Climax," NYT, Jan. 22, 1950.

Ershov, T. "Imperialistic Intrigues in Tibet," *Novoe Vremia*, No. 49, 1949.

Evangelista, Matthew A. "Stalin's Postwar Army Reappraised," *International Security*, 7.3 (Winter 1982/83).

Fairbank, John K., ed. *The Chinese World Order.* Cambridge, Mass., 1968.

Fedorenko, N. T. "The Stalin-Mao Summit in Moscow," *Far Eastern Affairs* (Moscow), No. 2, 1989.

Feng Fangzhu and Ye Zhi. "Port Dandong: The Northernmost Seaport in Our Country," *Jianchuan Zhishi* [Naval and Merchant Ships Knowledge], No. 11, 1990.

Feng Jing. "The Final Reckoning with the Imperialist Aggression Against China," *Shijie Zhishi*, Jan. 27, 1950.

Foot, Rosemary. "Nuclear Coercion and the Ending of the Korean Conflict," *International Security*, 13.3 (Winter 1988/89).

———. *A Substitute for Victory: The Politics of Peacemaking at the Korean Armistice Talks.* Ithaca, N.Y., 1990.

"The Frontier Force Created at the Earliest," *Jiefangjun Bao* [Liberation Army Daily], Nov. 14, 1988.

Gaddis, John Lewis. "The Strategic Perspective: The Rise and Fall of the 'Defensive Perimeter' Concept, 1947–1951," in Dorothy Borg and Waldo Heinrichs, eds., *Uncertain Years: Chinese-American Relations, 1947–1950.* New York, 1980.

Gamanin, D. "Inside the Nationalists' Rear," *Novoe Vremia*, No. 4, 1948.

Garthoff, Raymond L. *Soviet Military Policy: A Historical Analysis.* New York, 1966.

Garver, John W. *Chinese-Soviet Relations, 1937–1945: The Diplomacy of Chinese Nationalism.* New York, 1988.

George, Alexander L., and Richard Smoke. *Deterrence in American Foreign Policy: Theory and Practice.* New York, 1974.

Girenko, Iu. S. *Stalin-Tito.* Moscow, 1991.

Gittings, John. *The World and China, 1922–1972.* New York, 1974.

Goncharov, Sergei N. *Diplomatiia Imperatorskogo Kitaia: Otnosheniia Mezhdu Imperiiami Jin yi Sung v 1127–1142 Godakh* [Diplomacy of Imperial China: Relations Between the Song and Jin Empires During the Years 1127–1142]. Moscow, 1986.

———. "From Alliance Through Animosity Toward Good-Neighborly Relations: 40 Years of Soviet-Chinese Relations," *Literaturnaia Gazeta* [Literary Newspaper], Oct. 4, 1989. Translated and reprinted in *Cankao Ziliao* [Reference Materials], Oct. 30, 1989.

Gongfei Gongtai Zuozhan Jihua [The Communist Bandits' Operational Plan to Attack Taiwan]. Taipei, 1950.

"Good News from Moscow," *Shijie Zhishi*, Jan. 13, 1950.

"The Great Political Significance of the 'One-Week Campaign to Oppose the American Imperialist Invasion of Taiwan and Korea,'" *Shijie Zhishi*, July 21, 1950.

"The Great Victory of the Chinese People," *Novoe Vremia*, No. 42, 1949.

Gromyko, Andrei A. *Pamiatnoe* [Memoirs], 2 vols. Moscow, 1988. 2d, enlarged ed., Book 1. Moscow, 1990.

Gu Mingyi et al., eds. *Riben Qinzhan Lüda Sishi Nian Shi* [The 40 Years of the Japanese Occupation of Lüshun and Dalian]. Shenyang, 1991.

Guo Binwei and Tan Zongji. *Zhonghua Renmin Gongheguo Jianshi Shang* [A Guide to the History of the People's Republic of China], Vol. 1. Changchun, 1988.

Guo Fuwen and Cao Baojian. "Advance Toward the Pacific Ocean," *Hainan Jishi* [Record of Events (Hainan)] (Haikou), No. 7, 1989.

Guo Tingyi. *E Di Qinlüe Zhongguo Jianshi* [A Concise History of Imperialist Russia's Aggression Against China]. Taipei, 1958.

Guo Xin. "General Description of the Sixth Scholarly Conference on the Problem of the Relationship Between the Soviet Union, the Communist International, and the Chinese Revolution," *Zhonggong Dangshi Tongxun* [CCP History Newsletter], No. 2, 1990.

Gurtov, Melvin, and Byong-Moo Hwang. *China Under Threat: The Politics of Strategy and Diplomacy*. Baltimore, 1980.

Hai Fu. *Weishenme Yibiandao?* [Why Should We Lean to One Side?]. Shanghai, 1950.

Hailey, Foster. "Indo-China Has Become Vital Cold War Front," NYT, Feb. 12, 1950.

Hamilton, Thomas J. "Malik Again Quits Council as Chinese Ouster Is Beaten," NYT, Jan. 14, 1950.

———. "Russian Quits U.N. Council on China Recognition Issue; Acheson Is Firm on Policy," NYT, Jan. 11, 1950.

———. "Soviet Held Trying to Stall U.S. Recognition of Peiping," NYT, Jan. 20, 1950.

Han Huaizhi and Tan Jingqiao, chief eds. *Dangdai Zhongguo Jundui de Junshi Gongzuo* [Military Affairs of the Contemporary Chinese Army], Vols. 1, 2. Beijing, 1989.

Han Nianlong, chief ed. *Dandai Zhongguo Waijiao* [Contemporary China's Foreign Affairs]. Beijing, 1987.

Han Yuhui. "How Did China Manage to Abolish Unequal Treaties During the Anti-Japanese War?," *Jindai Shi Yanjiu* [Modern History Studies], No. 5, 1986.

Hao Sheng. "To Aid Korea Is Indispensable for Resisting America," *Shijie Zhishi*, Nov. 4, 1950.

Hao Yufan and Zhai Zhihai. "China's Decision to Enter the Korean War: History Revisited," *China Quarterly*, No. 121 (March 1990).

He Changgong. *He Changgong Huiyilu* [Memoirs of He Changgong]. Beijing, 1987.

He Di. "The Evolution of the Policy of the Chinese Communist Party Toward the United States from 1945 to 1949," *Lishi Yanjiu* [Historical Studies], No. 3, 1987.

———. "The Evolution of the Chinese Communist Party's Policy Toward the United States, 1944–1949," in Harry Harding and Yuan Ming, eds., *Sino-American Relations, 1945–1955: A Joint Reassessment of a Critical Decade*. Wilmington, Del., 1989.

———. " 'The Last Campaign to Unify China': The CCP's Unmaterialized Plan to Liberate Taiwan, 1949–1950." Unpublished article, n.d. Cited with the permission of the author.

He Maozhi. "General Hong Xuezhi," *Yanhuang Zisun* [The Chinese], No. 6, 1989.

He Wenxun. "[Mao's] Last Rural Headquarters in China's War of Liberation," *Junshi Shilin*, No. 4, 1990.

Heo, Man-Ho. "From Civil War to an International War; A Dialectical Interpretation of the Origins of the Korean War," *Korea and World Affairs* (Seoul), 14.2 (Summer 1990).

Hinton, Harold B. "Senator Knowland, Just Back from Far East, Calls for Support of Chiang," NYT, Dec. 31, 1949.

———. "U.S. Recalls Aides in China as Peiping Seizes Offices; Foes Demand Acheson Quit," NYT, Jan. 15, 1950.

"The Historic Victory of the Chinese People," *Pravda*, Oct. 5, 1949.

Holloway, David. *The Soviet Union and the Arms Race.* 2d ed. New Haven, Conn., 1984.

———. *Stalin and the Bomb.* Forthcoming.

———. "Stalin and Hiroshima." Unpublished paper, April 1989.

Hong Xuezhi. *KangMei YuanChao Zhanzheng Huiyi* [Recollections of the War to Resist America and Aid Korea]. Beijing, 1990.

———. "Logistics Work in the War to Resist America and Aid Korea," *Junshi Lishi*, No. 1, 1987.

———. "Profoundly Mourn Comrade Huang Kecheng," *Jiefangjun Bao* [Liberation Army Daily], Jan. 9, 1987.

Hong Xuezhi and Hu Qicai. "Mourn Marshal Xu with Boundless Grief," *Renmin Ribao*, Oct. 16, 1990.

Hou Dingyuan. "What We Saw and Heard About Chiang Kai-shek's Return to Xikou Town After Being Forced to Relinquish Power," in *Wenshi Ziliao Xuanji* [Selected Materials on Literature and History], Vol. 66. Beijing, 1979.

"How to Recognize the United States," in *Weidade KangMei YuanChao Yundong* [The Great Campaign to Resist America and Aid Korea]. Beijing, 1954.

Hu Guangzheng. "On the Decision to Send Troops to Participate in the War to Resist America and Aid Korea," *Dangshi Yanjiu*, No. 1, 1983.

Hu Guangzheng and Bao Mingrong. "Corrections of Some of the Historical Facts in 'On the Wise Decision to Resist America and Aid Korea,'" *Dangshi Yanjiu*, No. 3, 1981.

Hu Sheng. *Zhongguo Gongchandang de Qishi Nian* [The 70 Years of the Chinese Communist Party]. Beijing, 1991.

Hu Shixian. "A Retrospect on the International Situation in 1949," *Shijie Zhishi*, Jan. 1, 1950.

Hu Yuzhi. "The Place of People's China in the World," *Shijie Zhishi*, Jan. 1, 1950.

Hu Zhixing. "Our Party's United Front Works in the Campaigns to Perform Land Reform, to Resist America and Aid Korea, and to Suppress Revolutionaries," *Lilun Tantao* [Theoretical Evaluation] (Harbin), No. 6, 1988.

Huan Xiang. "Changes in Our Country's Foreign Policy and Contemporary International Relations," in *Guoji Zhengzhi Jiangzuo (Xubian)* [Lectures on International Politics], Vol. 2. Beijing, 1987.

Huang Gangzhou. *Zhang Aiping yu Haijun Gongheguo Haijun Chuchuang Jishi* [Zhang Aiping and the Navy: True Records on the Creation of the Republic's Navy]. Beijing, 1991.

Huang Hua. "Several Contacts Between Stuart and Me During the Initial Period After the Liberation of Nanjing," in *Xin Zhongguo Waijiao Fengyun* [Main Diplomatic Events of New China]. Beijing, 1990.

Huang Jijun. *Li Jukui Jiangjun Zhuan* [Biography of General Li Jukui]. Beijing, 1989.

Huang Kecheng. "From North Jiangsu Province to the Northeast," in Wang Dikang et al., eds., *Dongbei Jiefang Zhanzheng Jishi* [True Records on the Liberation War in the Northeast]. Beijing, 1988.

Huang Shengtian. "Zhang Aiping After the Creation of the East China People's Navy," *Dajiang Nanbei* [On Both Sides of the Yangtze River] (Nanjing), No. 3, 1990.

Huang Yi. "Zhou Enlai: A Leader and Organizer of the Strategic Logistics in the War to Resist America and Aid Korea," 2 parts, *Junshi Shilin*, Nos. 5, 6, 1989.

Huang Zhaokang. "The Founding of New China in 1949 Had Nothing to Do with Stalin," in *Dangshi Yanjiu Ziliao* [Research Materials on Party History] (Chengdu, 1990), Vol. 12. Excerpted in *Zhonggong Dangshi Tongxun* [CCP History Newsletter], No. 8 (April 25, 1991).

"I Am Tao Yong's Patron," in Jia Sinan, ed., *1915–1976: Mao Zedong Renji Jiaowang Shilu* [True Records on How Mao Zedong Got Along with People (1915–1976)]. Nanjing, 1989.

Important Documents of the First Plenary Session of the Chinese People's Political Consultative Conference. Beijing, 1949.

"Indo-China Viewed as Key Asia Point," NYT, Jan. 24, 1950.

"Inside Information on the Struggle to Suppress Bandits," *Sichuan Ribao* [Sichuan Daily], April 25, 1990.

"An Introduction to the 'Paper Tiger'—U.S. Imperialism," in *Fensui Meiguo Diguozhuyi de Qinlüe* [Shatter the U.S. Imperialist Invasion]. Beijing, 1950.

Istoriia Velikoi Otechestvennoi Voiny Sovetskogo Soiuza [History of the Soviet Union's Great Patriotic War], Vol. 5. Moscow, 1963.

"Jessup Cites Risk in Indo-China Blow," NYT, Feb. 7, 1950.

Jiang Jin and Jiang Shipei. "Concerning the Comintern's Influence on the Great Revolution in China," *Shehui Kexue* [Social Science] (Shanghai), No. 1, 1981.

Jiang Naiwen. "On the Basic Situation of Our Army's Construction in the 17 Years After the Founding of the Republic," *Junshi Shilin*, No. 1, 1988.

Jing Shengzhi. "The Inside Information on Stuart's Stay in Nanjing," *Minguo Chunqiu* [The History of the Republic of China] (Nanjing), No. 2, 1991.

Jing Song. "On the Historic Significance of the Victory in the Struggle to Suppress Bandits in Sichuan in the Early Days After the Founding of the Republic," in Shao Chengye, chief ed., *Huigu Zhanwang Tantao* [Retrospect, Prospect, and Exploration]. Chengdu, 1987.

Jing Yu. "Consideration of Our Army's Combat Experience in the War to Resist America and Aid Korea," *Junshi Shilin*, No. 3, 1988.

Jinsui Geming Genjudi Dashiji [Chronicle of Major Events of the Shanxi-Suiyuan Revolutionary Base]. Taiyuan, 1989.

Johnson, Chalmers A. *Peasant Nationalism and Communist Power: The Emergence of Revolutionary China, 1937–1945*. Stanford, Calif., 1962.

Ju Kai. "Kind Guidance, Memorable Recollection," in *Yidai Mingjiang Huiyi Su Yu Tongzhi* [A Famous General: Reminiscences About Comrade Su Yu]. Shanghai, 1986.

Kang Maozhao. "Incident with the British Warship *Amethyst*," *Xin Zhongguo Waijiao Fengyun* [Main Diplomatic Events of New China]. Beijing, 1990.

KangMei YuanChao Zhanzheng de Jingyan Zongjie (Caogao) [Summing Up the Experiences of the War to Resist America and Aid Korea (Draft)], ed. Editorial Commission on Summing Up the Experiences of the Chinese People's Volunteers in the War to Resist America and Aid Korea, Vol. 1. Beijing, 1956.

KangMei YuanChao Ziliao Mulu [Catalogue of the (Propaganda) Materials on the War to Resist America and Aid Korea]. Beijing, 1950.

Kapitsa, M. S. *Sovetsko-Kitaiskie Otnosheniia* [Soviet-Chinese Relations]. Moscow, 1958.

Kennan, George. *Memoirs, 1950–1963*. New York, 1972.

Khlebodarov, N. "Special Missions of General Kovalev," *Socialisticheskaia Industriia* [Socialist Industry], May 9, 1985.

Khrushchev, Nikita. *Khrushchev Remembers*. Tr. and ed. Strobe Talbott. Boston, Mass., 1970.

———. *Khrushchev Remembers: The Glasnost Tapes*. Tr. and ed. Jerrold L. Schecter with Vyacheslav V. Luchkov. Boston, Mass., 1990.

———. *Khrushchev Remembers: The Last Testament*. Tr. and ed. Strobe Talbott. Boston, Mass., 1974.

———. "The Korean War," *Ogonëk* [Small Fire], No. 1 (Jan. 1991).

Kim, Gye-Dong. "The Legacy of Foreign Intervention in Korea: Division and War," *Korea and World Affairs* (Seoul), 14.2 (Summer 1990).

———. "Who Initiated the Korean War?," in James Cotton and Ian Neary, eds., *The Korean War in History*. Atlantic Highlands, N. J., 1989.

Kim, Hakjoon. "International Trends in Korean War Studies: A Review of the Documentary Literature," *Korea and World Affairs* (Seoul), No. 2, 1990.

Knowles, Clayton. "Korea, Formosa Aid Is Passed by House in Reversing Stand," NYT, Feb., 10, 1950.

Kobayashi, Keiji. "Who Was the Instigator of the Korean War? [An Interview with General Volkogonov]," *Aera* (Tokyo), June 19, 1990.

Kolko, Joyce, and Gabriel Kolko. *The Limits of Power: The World and United States Foreign Policy, 1945–1954*. New York, 1972.

Kovalev, I. V. "The Rails of Victory," *Nash Sovremennik* [Our Contemporary], No. 5, 1985.

———. "Stalin's Dialogue with Mao Zedong," 2 parts, *Problemy Dal'nego Vostoka* [Problems of the Far East], No. 6, 1991, No. 1–3, 1992.

Kovtun-Stankevich, A. I. "Commandant of Mukden," in *Na Kitaiskoi Zemle: Vospominaniia Sovetsikh Dobrovoltsev, 1925–1945* [On Chinese Soil: Memoirs of the Soviet Volunteers, 1942–1945]. Moscow, 1977.

Kovyzhenko, V. "The Successes of the PLA," *Pravda*, Nov. 3, 1949.

Krock, Arthur. "Bases of Hands-Off Policy Toward Formosa," NYT, Jan. 6, 1950.

Lan Sou and Li Ding. "The Days and Nights Before the Birth of the New China," *Dangshi Wenhui* [Collection on Party History] (Taiyuan), No. 5, 1989.

Lan'kov, A. "North Korea, 1945–1948: From Liberation to Foundation," *Problemy Dal'nego Vostoka* [Far Eastern Affairs], No. 6, 1991.

Ledovskii, A. M. *Delo Gao Gana–Rao Shushi* [The Case of Gao Gang and Rao Shushi]. Moscow, 1990.

———. "The USSR and China, 1937–1949 (Notes of a Soviet Diplomat)," *Novaia i Noveishaia Istoriia* [Modern and Contemporary History], No. 5, 1990.

Lee Sang Jo. "Now the Truth About the Korean War Is Exposed," *Bungei Shunju* [The Spring and Autumn of Literature and Art] (Tokyo), April 1990.

Leffler, Melvyn P. *A Preponderance of Power: National Security, the Truman Administration, and the Cold War*. Stanford, Calif., 1992.

Lei Yuanshen. "The Evolution of the Central Military Commission," in *Zhonggong Dangshi Ziliao* [Materials on CCP History], Vol. 34. Beijing, 1990.

Lei Zhongmin. "An Exploration into Mao Zedong's Strategic Thinking," *Mao Zedong Sixiang Yanjiu* [Studies on Mao Zedong's Thought] (Chengdu), No. 2, 1988.

Lensen, George A. "Yalta and the Far East," in John L. Snell, ed., *The Meaning of Yalta: Big Three Diplomacy and the New Balance of Power*. Baton Rouge, La., 1956.

Levine, Steven I. *Anvil of Victory: The Communist Revolution in Manchuria, 1945–1948.* New York, 1987.

Lewis, John W., and Xue Litai. *China Builds the Bomb.* Stanford, Calif., 1988.

———. *China's Strategic Seapower: The Politics of Force Modernization in the Nuclear Age.* Stanford, Calif., forthcoming.

Li Chunqing. "Nosaka's Mistakes," *Shijie Zhishi,* Jan. 20, 1950.

Li Haiwen. "A Distortion of History: An Interview with Shi Zhe About Kovalev's Memoirs," *Chinese Historians,* No. 2, 1992.

Li Jiagu. "Sino-Soviet Intercourse on the Mongolian Question," *Sulian Lishi Wenti* [Problems of Soviet History], No. 2, 1987. Excerpted in *Guoji Gongchanzhuyi Yundong* [International Communist Movement], Nos. 5–6, 1987.

Li Jukui. *Li Jukui Huiyilu* [The Memoirs of Li Jukui]. Beijing, 1986.

Li Ke and Hao Shengzhang. *Wenhua Dageming zhong de Renmin Jiefangjun* [The People's Liberation Army in the "Great Cultural Revolution"]. Beijing, 1989.

Li Ping and Fang Ming, chief eds. *Zhou Enlai Nianpu* [Chronicle of Zhou Enlai's Life]. Beijing, 1990.

Li Rui. *Lushan Huiyi Shilu* [A True Record on the Lushan Plenum]. Beijing, 1989.

Li Shiyu. "Hidden in the Enemy Camp for 15 Years," Part 2, *Zongheng* [Talk Freely], No. 6, 1986.

Li Yinqiao and Quan Yanchi, eds. *Mao Zedong Weishizhang Zaji* [Memoirs of Mao Zedong's Chief Bodyguard]. Hong Kong, 1989.

Li Yueran. "Some Recollections from When I Was Working at the Side of Premier Zhou Enlai," in *Xin Zhongguo Waijiao Fengyun* [Main Diplomatic Events of New China]. Beijing, 1990.

———. "Recollections of [My Experience as] an Interpreter for Chairman Mao," *Shijie Bolan* [World Review], No. 4, 1990.

———. *Waijiao Wutai shang de Xin Zhongguo Lingxiu* [New China's Leaders on the Diplomatic Scene]. Beijing, 1989.

Li Yunchang. "Reminiscences on the Entry of Our Troops into the Northeast from the Hebei-Jehol-Liaoning Border Region," in *LiaoShen Juezhan* [The Liaoxi-Shenyang Campaign], Vol. 1. Beijing, 1988.

Li Zhaoxin. "The Birth of New China and the Pattern of International Politics," *Jinan Xuebao* [Jinan University Bulletin] (Guangzhou), No. 1, 1986.

Li Zhongzhi and Wang Li, chief eds. *Zhonghua Renmin Gongheguo Sishi Nian Shilüe* [A Survey of the 40-Year History of the People's Republic of China]. Shenyang, 1990.

Liang Chin-tung. "The Sino-Soviet Treaty of Friendship and Alliance of 1945: The Inside Story," in Paul K. T. Sih, chief ed., *Nationalist China During the Sino-Japanese War, 1937–1945.* Hicksville, N. Y., 1977.

Liao Guoliang et al. *Mao Zedong Junshi Sixiang Fazhan Shi* [The Evolution of Mao Zedong's Military Thought]. Beijing, 1991.

Lim Un. *The Founding of a Dynasty in North Korea: An Authentic Biography of Kim Il-song.* Tokyo, 1982.

Lin Li. "Comrade Jiaxiang's Revolutionary Character and Morals Will Be Imprinted Forever on the Mind of Later Generations," in *Huiyi Wang Jiaxiang* [Reminiscences About Wang Jiaxiang]. Beijing, 1985.

Lin Yunhui et al. *1949–1989 Nian de Zhongguo Kaige Xingjin de Shiqi* [China's Triumphant March from 1949 to 1989]. Zhengzhou, 1989.

Ling Hui. "Cracking a Hidden All-Purpose Transceiver," *Zongheng* [Talk Freely], No. 3, 1986.

———. "A Description of Yang Qiqing, Former Vice-Minister of the Ministry of Public Security," *Mingren Zhuanji* [Biographies of Famous People], No. 2, 1988.

Liu Hongxuan. "A Summary of the Theoretical Symposium on the 40th Anniversary of the War to Resist America and Aid Korea," *Junshi Shilin*, No. 6, 1990.

Liu Jianshi and Zou Bin. "A General Description of the Shanghai Campaign," in *Wenshi Ziliao Xuanji* [Selected Materials on Literature and History], Vol. 66. Beijing, 1979.

Liu Likai and Yang Jinbao. "Soviet Policy Toward China in the Second World War," in *Dangshi Yanjiu Ziliao* [Research Materials on Party History], Vol. 6. Chengdu, 1985.

Liu Ruizhe. "Chinese Legend of 1958–1960: Research on the History of the Great Leap Forward," *Hainan Jishi* [Record of Events (Hainan)] (Haikou), No. 2, 1989.

Liu Shaoqi. "The Current Task and Strategic Deployment" [Sept. 19, 1945], in *LiaoShen Juezhan* [The Liaoxi-Shenyang Campaign], Vol. 1. Beijing, 1988.

———. *Lun Guojizhuyi yu Minzuzhuyi* [On Internationalism and Nationalism]. Shanghai, 1949.

———. "Opening Speech at the Conference of Asian-Australian Trade Union Representatives" [Nov. 21, 1949], *Xinhua Yuebao* [New China Monthly], Dec. 15, 1949.

———. "Speech at the Cadres Meeting on July 1, 1948," *Dangshi Yanjiu*, No. 3, 1980.

Liu Shitian. "On Several Questions Concerning the Dispatch of Soviet Troops to the Chinese Northeast," *Junshi Shilin*, No. 1, 1990.

Liu Simu. *Zenyang Xuexi Guoji Shishi* [How to Study Current International Events]. Beijing, 1951.

Liu Xiangshun. "General Su Yu Spent His Remaining Years Writing His War Memoirs," *Junshi Lishi*, No. 4, 1991.

Liu Xiao. *Chushi Sulian Ba Nian* [Eight Years in the Soviet Union as Ambassador]. Beijing, 1986.

———. "A Mission to the Soviet Union," in Gao Ge, chief ed., *Lishi Neimu Jishi* [True Records on the Background of History], Vol. 1. Lanzhou, 1988.

———. "A Mission to the Soviet Union," Part 1, *Shijie Zhishi*, No. 3, 1987.

Liu Xiaoqing. "Several Important Proposals Army General Huang Kecheng Made During His Military Career," *Junshi Shilin*, No. 1, 1990.

Liu Xingjun. "The Shift of Our Party's Strategic Guiding Principle on the Eve of and After the Victory of the War of Resistance Against Japan," *Shehui Kexue Zhanxian*, No. 3, 1991.

Liu Yishun. "A Concise Description of the Soviet Attitude Toward China's Liberation War," *Jiaoxue Cankao* [Teaching Materials], No. 5, 1986. Excerpted in Liao Gailong, chief ed., *1986 Nian Zhonggong Dangshi Wenzhai Niankan* [Yearbook of Excerpted Essays from the CCP's History (Published in) 1986]. Beijing, 1988.

Liu Zhen. *Liu Zhen Huiyilu* [Memoirs of Liu Zhen]. Beijing, 1990.

Liu Zhen et al. "Cherish the Memory of Our Leader Comrade Huang Kecheng," *Jiefangjun Bao* [Liberation Army Daily], Jan. 19, 1987.

Liudnikov, I. I. "Internationalist Assistance," in *Na Kitaiskoi Zemle: Vospomi-*

naniia Sovetskikh Dobrovoltsev, 1925–1945 [On Chinese Soil: Memoirs of the Soviet Volunteers, 1925–1945]. Moscow, 1977.

Lobov, G. "In the Sky of North Korea," *Aviatsiia i Kosmonavtika* [Aviation and Cosmonautics], No. 10, 1990.

Lu Dingyi. "An Explanation of Several Basic Questions Concerning the Postwar International Situation," *Jiefang Ribao* [Liberation Daily] (Yan'an), Jan. 4, 5, 1945. Reproduced in U.S. Department of State, *United States Relations with China*, Washington, D.C., 1949; and in *Qunzhong* [Masses] (Hong Kong), Jan. 30, 1947.

Lu Hong. "Wang Jiaxiang: Our Country's First Ambassador to the Soviet Union," *Dangshi Wenhui* [Collection on Party History] (Taiyuan), No. 1, 1989.

Lu Lin. "A Preliminary Study on the Evolution of China's Strategic Thinking on International Issues," *Mao Zedong Sixiang Yanjiu* [Studies on Mao Zedong's Thought] (Chengdu), No. 3, 1987.

Luo Guibo. "Comrade Shaoqi Sent Me to Vietnam," in *Mianhuai Liu Shaoqi* [Cherish the Memory of Liu Shaoqi]. Beijing, 1988.

Luo Libin. *Ba Nian Fenghuo Zhan Lugou* [The 8-Year Anti-Japanese War]. Nanning, 1989.

Ma Kaijun. "A Brief History of the 50th Corps of the Chinese People's Liberation Army," *Junshi Lishi*, No. 4, 1991.

MacDonald, Callum. *Britain and the Korean War*. Oxford, 1990.

Maevskii, V. "International Review," *Pravda*, Jan. 24, 1950.

Makhov, Alexander. "Stalin Had Approved Kim Il Sung's Order, States the Former DPRK Ambassador to the USSR," *Moskovskie Novosti* [Moscow News], July 8, 1990.

Maksimov, M. "The Great General Is Leading the Battle; Our Correspondent Talks With the Military Historian Grigorii Kuzmin About the Korean War and Its Protagonists," *Komsomolskaia Pravda* [Communist Youth League *Pravda*], June 25, 1991.

Malenkov, G. M. "Report at the Solemn Meeting of the Moscow Soviet," *Pravda*, Nov. 7, 1949.

Malkov, V. "Documents of the Early Cold War Period," *International Affairs* (Moscow), No. 12, 1990.

"Mao to Discuss Sino-Soviet Pact with Kremlin; New Treaty Seen," NYT, Jan. 2, 1950.

Mao Zedong [Mao Tsetung] (all works published in Beijing unless otherwise noted; the nonhyphenated form of Tsetung, adopted in Vol. 5 of the *Selected Works*, is used throughout. The collections in entries [20] and [27] are shortened to *Jianguo Yilai* and *Mao Zedong Tongzhi* in this list. Only those documents from *Jianguo Yilai* not reproduced in the Appendix are given.

[1]. "Cable from Mao Zedong and Zhou Enlai to Liu Shaoqi on the Greetings to Ho Chi Minh" [Feb. 1, 1950], in *Jianguo Yilai*.

[2]. "Cable on Preventing the Former Nationalist Troops from Penetrating into Vietnam and Burma" [Dec. 29, 1949], in *Jianguo Yilai*.

[3]. "Cable to Lin Biao on Amphibious Operations and Other Problems" [Dec. 18, 1949], in *Jianguo Yilai*.

[4]. "The Central Directive on the Demobilization of the Troops" [April 21, 1950], in *Jianguo Yilai*.

[5]. "The Chiang Kai-shek Government Is Besieged by the Whole People" [May 30, 1947], in *Selected Works of Mao Tsetung*, Vol. 4. 1961.

[6]. "The Chinese People Have Stood Up!" [Sept. 21, 1949], in *Selected Works of Mao Tsetung*, Vol. 5. 1977.

[7]. "A Circular on the Situation" [March 20, 1948], in *Selected Works of Mao Tsetung*, Vol. 4. 1977.

[8]. "Comrade Mao Zedong's Three Cables in Reply to Chiang Kai-shek," in *Chongqing Tanpan Ziliao* [Materials on the Chongqing Negotiations]. Chengdu, 1980.

[9]. "The Concept of Operations for the Huai-Hai Campaign" [Oct. 11, 1948], in *Selected Military Writings of Mao Tsetung*. 1963.

[10]. "The Concept of Operations for the Liaohsi-Shenyang Campaign" [Sept. and Oct. 1948], in *Selected Military Writings of Mao Tsetung*. 1963.

[11]. "The Concept of Operations for the Peiping-Tientsin Campaign" [Dec. 11, 1948], in *Selected Military Writings of Mao Tsetung*. 1963.

[12]. "Current Situation and the Task of the Party in 1949" [Jan. 8, 1949], in *Wenxian he Yanjiu 1984 Nian Huibianben* [Documents and Essays Collected in 1984]. 1985.

[13]. "Currently We Should Encircle Small Numbers of American and British Troops for Winning Minor Battles of Annihilation" [May, 26, 1951], in *Mao Zedong Junshi Wenxuan (Neibuben)* [Selected Military Writings of Mao Zedong (Volume for Internal Circulation)]. 1981.

[14]. "The Deployment for Occupying the Whole Nation" [May 23, 1949], in *Mao Zedong Junshi Wenxuan (Neibuben)* [Selected Military Writings of Mao Zedong (Volume for Internal Circulation)]. 1981.

[15]. "Fight for a Fundamental Turn for the Better in the Nation's Financial and Economic Situation" [June 6, 1950], in *Jianguo Yilai*.

[16]. "Greet the New High Tide of the Chinese Revolution" [Feb. 1, 1947], in *Selected Works of Mao Tsetung*, Vol. 4. 1961.

[17]. "Instructions Given at a Meeting of Some Delegates to the First Conference of the Second All-China Association of Industry and Commerce" [Dec. 8, 1956], in *Mao Zedong Tongzhi*.

[18]. "Interview with the Correspondent of *Dagong Bao*" [Sept. 5, 1945], in *Mao Zedong Ji* [Collected Works of Mao Zedong]. Tokyo, 1971, Vol. 9.

[19]. "Interview with Reuters Correspondent" [Aug. 28, 1945], in *Mao Zedong Ji* [Collected Works of Mao Zedong], Vol. 9. Tokyo, 1971.

[20]. *Jianguo Yilai Mao Zedong Wengao Diyi Ce* (1949.9–1950.12) [Mao Zedong's Manuscripts After the Founding of the Republic, Vol. 1: Sept. 1949–Dec. 1950]. Beijing, 1987.

[21]. "Letter to Hu Qiaomu on Not Mentioning in Propaganda the Schedule for Attacking Taiwan and Tibet" [Sept. 29, 1950], in *Jianguo Yilai*.

[22]. "Letter to Nie Rongzhen and Wang Jiaxiang" [May 19, 1946], in *Mao Zedong Shuxin Xuanji* [Selected Letters of Mao Zedong]. 1983.

[23]. "Letter to Wu Yuzhang" [Nov. 18, 1947], in *Mao Zedong Shuxin Xuanji* [Selected Letters of Mao Zedong]. 1983.

[24]. "Letter to Wu Yuzhang" [Aug. 15, 1948], in *Mao Zedong Shuxin Xuanji* [Selected Letters of Mao Zedong]. 1983.

[25]. "Letter to Zhang Shushi" [Nov. 18, 1947], in *Mao Zedong Shuxin Xuanji* [Selected Letters of Mao Zedong]. 1983.

[26]. "Mao Zedong on the World Situation (Talks with Mrs. Strong) [Aug. 1946], in *Mao Zedong Ji* [Collected Works of Mao Zedong], Vol. 10. Tokyo, 1971.

[27]. *Mao Zedong Tongzhi Shi Dangdai Zui Weida de MaLiezhuyizhe* [Comrade Mao Zedong Is the Greatest Marxist-Leninist of the Contemporary Era]. Beijing, 1969.

[28]. "The Military Commission's Circular on the Lessons Drawn from the Defeat of Attack on Jinmen" [Oct. 29, 1949], in *Jianguo Yilai*.

[29]. "On Coalition Government" [April 24, 1945], in *Selected Works of Mao Tsetung*, Vol. 3. 1965.

[30]. "On the People's Democratic Dictatorship" [June 30, 1949], in *Selected Works of Mao Tsetung*, Vol. 4. 1961.

[31]. "On the Reissue of the Three Main Rules of Discipline and the Eight Points for Attention—Instruction of the General Headquarters of the Chinese People's Liberation Army" [Oct. 10, 1947], in *Selected Military Writings of Mao Tsetung*. 1963.

[32]. "Order to the Chinese People's Volunteers" [Oct. 8, 1950], in *Selected Works of Mao Tsetung*, Vol. 5. 1977.

[33]. "The Present Situation and Our Tasks" [Dec. 25, 1947], in *Selected Works of Mao Tsetung*, Vol. 4. 1961.

[34]. "Problems of Strategy in China's Revolutionary War" [Dec. 1936], in *Selected Military Writings of Mao Tsetung*. 1963.

[35]. "Remarks on and Corrections to Nie Rongzhen's Draft Report on Military Matters" [June 15, 1950], in *Jianguo Yilai*.

[36]. "Report to the 2d Plenary Session of the 7th Central Committee of the Communist Party of China" [March 5, 1949], in *Selected Works of Mao Tsetung*, Vol. 4. 1961.

[37]. "The Situation and Our Policy After the Victory in the War of Resistance Against Japan" [Aug. 13, 1945], in *Selected Works of Mao Tsetung*, Vol. 4. 1961.

[38]. "Some Points in Appraisal of the Present International Situation" [April 1946], in *Selected Works of Mao Tsetung*, Vol. 4. 1961.

[39]. "Speech at the Chengdu Conference" [March 1958], in *Mao Zedong Tongzhi*.

[40]. "Speech at the Conference in Hankou" [April 6, 1958], in *Mao Zedong Tongzhi*.

[41]. "Speech at the 10th Plenum of the 8th Central Committee of the Chinese Communist Party" [Sept. 24, 1962], in *Mao Zedong Tongzhi*.

[42]. "Strategy for the Second Year of the War of Liberation" [Sept. 1, 1947], in *Selected Works of Mao Tsetung*, Vol. 4. 1961.

[43]. "Summary of Speech at the Supreme State Conference" [Sept. 5, 1958], in *Mao Zedong Tongzhi*.

[44]. "Summary Report at the Conference of Secretaries of the Party Committees of [Several] Provinces and Cities" [Jan. 1957], in *Mao Zedong Tongzhi*.

[45]. "Talk with the American Correspondent Anna Louise Strong" [Aug. 1946], in *Selected Works of Mao Tsetung*, Vol. 4. 1961.

[46]. "Talks with Japanese Guests" [July 10, 1964], in *Mao Zedong Tongzhi*.

"Mao Zedong Predicted a Possible U.S. Landing at Inchon," *Jiefangjun Bao* [Liberation Army Daily], Nov. 14, 1990.

"Mao Zedong's Four Talks and Statements Concerning the Guiding Principles for Foreign Affairs," *Dang de Wenxian* [Party's Documents], No. 1, 1992.

Martinov, A. "Combat Activities in China," *Novoe Vremia*, No. 32, 1949.

Meliksetov, A. V. *Pobeda Kitaiskoi Revoliutsii, 1945–1949* [The Victory of the Chinese Revolution, 1945–1949]. Moscow, 1989.

Meng Zhaohui. "The Application and Development of Mao Zedong's Military Thought in the War to Resist America and Aid Korea," *Junshi Lishi*, No. 1, 1991.

Merrill, John. *Korea: The Peninsular Origins of the War*. Newark, Del., 1989.

———. "The Origins of the Korean War: Unanswered Questions," Paper presented at the Second International Conference on the Korean War, June 14–15, 1990, Seoul.

Messer, Robert L. "Roosevelt, Truman, and China: An Overview," in Harry Harding and Yuan Ming, eds., *Sino-American Relations, 1945–1955: A Joint Reassessment of a Critical Decade*. Wilmington, Del., 1989.

Miao Changqing. "A Look Back to the Gao-Rao [Gao Gang–Rao Shushi] Affair," *Lilun Xuekan* [Theoretical Bulletin] (Jinan), No. 6, 1990.

Min Li. "The Handshake of Giants," *Dangdai Qingnian* [Modern Youth], No. 7, 1989.

———. "On the Eve of and After the Mao Zedong–Stalin Talks in Moscow," in Min Li et al., *Mao Zedong Sidalin Mosike Huiwu Qianhou* [On the Eve of and After the Mao Zedong–Stalin Talks in Moscow]. Chengdu, 1989.

Molotov, V. M. "Report at the Solemn Meeting of the Moscow Soviet," *Pravda*, Nov. 7, 1945.

———. "The Speech of Comrade V. M. Molotov at the Meeting of the Electorate of the Molotov Electoral District in the City of Moscow," *Pravda*, Feb. 7, 1946.

———. "The Speech of Comrade V. M. Molotov at the Meeting of the Electorate of Molotov Electoral District in the City of Moscow," *Pravda*, March 11, 1950.

Morosov, Igor. "'The War Has Not Begun Yet . . .'; Interview with the Military Historian Grigorii Kuzmin," *Pereval* [Mountain Pass], March 1991.

"A New Assault by Nationalist Airplanes Against Shanghai," *Pravda*, Jan. 13, 1950.

"A New Epoch in Sino-Soviet Friendship and Cooperation," *Renmin Ribao*, Feb. 15, 1950.

"The News of the Week in Brief: Problem of Asia," NYT, Jan. 8, 1950.

Ni Wei. "Some Recollections About Zhou Enlai," in *Huainian Zhou Enlai* [Cherish the Memory of Zhou Enlai]. Beijing, 1986.

Ni Zhongwen, chief ed. *Zhonghua Renmin Gongheguo Jianguo Shi Shouce* [Manual on the History of China After the Founding of the People's Republic]. Beijing, 1989.

Nie Rongzhen. *Inside the Red Star: The Memoirs of Marshal Nie Rongzhen*. Beijing, 1988.

———. *Nie Rongzhen Huiyilu* [Memoirs of Nie Rongzhen], Vol. 3. Beijing, 1986.

———. "With Comrade Mao Zedong in Chengnanzhuang," in *Nanwang de Huiyi Huainian Mao Zedong Tongzhi* [Unforgettable Reminiscences: Cherish the Memory of Comrade Mao Zedong]. Beijing, 1985.

Nie Rongzhen Yuanshuai [Marshal Nie Rongzhen]. Beijing, 1989.

Ning Yi. "A Newly Rising State," *Qunzhong* [Masses] (Hong Kong), Aug. 7, 1947.

———. "Tito and the New Yugoslavia," *Qunzhong* [Masses] (Hong Kong), Sept. 4, 1947.

Ning Zhiyi. "Liu Shaoqi's Contributions to the Party Central Leadership's Decisions on Military Strategy," *Mao Zedong Sixiang Yanjiu* [Studies on Mao Zedong's Thought] (Chengdu), No. 2, 1989.

[Novikov, Nikolai V.], "Vneshniaia Politika SShA V Poslevoennii Period" [The USA's Foreign Policy in the Postwar Period], Sept. 27, 1946, AVP SSSR [USSR Foreign Policy Archive], F. 06, Op. 08, d. 45, pp. 759ff.

———. *Vospominaniia Diplomata, Zapiski 1938–1947* [Memoirs of a Diplomat, Notes for 1938–1947]. Moscow, 1989.

"On the Situation in Japan," *Xinhua Yuebao* [New China Monthly], Feb. 15, 1950.

"The Origin of the Name 'Chinese People's Volunteers,' " *Jiefangjun Bao* [Liberation Army Daily], Nov. 2, 1990.

Pan Guangwei. "A Talk Between Mao Zedong and Zhang Zhizhong 40 Years Ago," *Shulin* [The Forest of Books], No. 3, 1989.

Pang Xianzhi. "A Description of How Mao Zedong Studied Books on Culture and History," in Gong Yuzhi et al., *Mao Zedong de Dushu Shenghuo* [Mao Zedong's Life of Reading Books]. Beijing, 1986.

———. "Mao Zedong and His Secretary Tian Jiaying," in Dong Bian et al., eds., *Mao Zedong he Tade Mishu Tian Jiaying* [Mao Zedong and His Secretary Tian Jiaying]. Beijing, 1989.

Panikkar, K. M. *In Two Chinas: Memoirs of a Diplomat*. London, 1955.

Party History Research Section, CCP Beijing Municipal Committee. *Beijing Gemingshi Dashiji (1919–1949)* [Chronicle of Major Events of the Revolutionary History of Beijing (1919–1949)]. Beijing, 1989.

"Peiping U.N. Drive Pushed by Soviets," NYT, Jan. 10, 1950.

"Peiping Urges U.N. Oust Nationalists," NYT, Jan. 9, 1950.

Peng Dehuai. *Memoirs of a Chinese Marshal: The Autobiographical Notes of Peng Dehuai (1898–1974)*. Beijing, 1984.

———. *Peng Dehuai Zishu* [The Autobiography of Peng Dehuai]. Beijing, 1981.

———. "Peng Dehuai's Cable to Mao Zedong on the Schedule of Occupying Xinjiang," in *Zhonggong Dangshi Ziliao* [Materials on CCP History], Vol. 36. Beijing, 1990.

———. "Speech at the Meeting to Mobilize the Cadres of the Chinese People's Volunteers at the Division Level and Above" [Oct. 14, 1950], in *Peng Dehuai Junshi Wenxuan* [Selected Military Writings of Peng Dehuai]. Beijing, 1988.

Peng Min, chief ed. *Dangdai Zhongguo de Jiben Jianshe* [Contemporary China's Capital Construction], Vol. 1. Beijing, 1989.

Peng Shi. *SuE zai Zhongguo Xiangjie* [A Detailed Explanation for (Chiang Kai-shek's) *Soviet Russia in China*]. Taipei, 1958.

Peng Shilu. "Return to Our Motherland for Which We Had Longed Day and Night," in Wang Dikang et al., eds., *Dongbei Jiefang Zhanzheng Jishi* [True Records on the Liberation War in the Northeast]. Beijing, 1988.

Peng Zhen. "The First Nine Months of the Liberation War in the Northeast" [Nov. 1988], *Dang de Wenxian* [Party Documents], No. 1, 1989.

"The People of Taiwan Protest Against the Aggressive Plans of the U.S. Imperialists," *Pravda*, Jan. 9, 1950.

Petukhov, V. I. *U Istokov Borby za Edinstvo I Nezavisimost Korei* [At the Origin of the Struggle for the Unity and Independence of Korea]. Moscow, 1987.

Plotnikov, G. K. "The Patriotic Liberation War of the Korean People (Overview of the Combat Activities)," in *Za Mir Na Zemle Korei: Vospominaniia i Stat'i* [For Peace on Korean Soil: Memoirs and Articles]. Moscow, 1985.

Posolstvo SSSR v Narodnoi Respublike Kitaia: Ezhednevnii Biulleten' Pressy, #8, 10 Ianvaria 1950 God [Soviet Embassy in the People's Republic of China: Daily Press Bulletin, #8, Jan. 10, 1950], pp. 3–6. [This bulletin re-translates and analyzes articles from the Western press published in *Cankao Xiaoxi* (Reference News).]

Pospelov, P. N. "Under the Great and Invincible Banner of Lenin and Stalin Toward the Triumph of Socialism," *Pravda*, Jan. 22, 1950.

"Premier Chou's Criticism of Liu Shao-ch'i," *Wenge Tongxin* [News Reports on the Cultural Revolution], Oct. 9, 1967, in *Survey of China Mainland Press* (Hong Kong), No. 4060 (Nov. 15, 1967).

"Proclamation of [the] Central People's Government" [Oct. 1, 1949], in *China Monthly Review*, Oct. 1950, supplement.

Qi Dexue. *Chaoxian Zhanzheng Juece Neimu* [New Insights into Decision-Making During the Korean War]. Shenyang, 1991.

Qi Shengping. "A Description of Marshal Liu Bocheng, the Prime Mover of the Military Academy," *Xinghuo Liaoyuan* [A Single Spark Can Start a Prairie Fire], No. 2, 1985.

Qiao Mu. *Lun Shijie Maodun* [On World Contradictions]. Hong Kong, 1946.

Qu Xing. "Evidence of the CPSU Leadership's Intervention in the Chinese Revolution," *Guoji Gongchanzhuyi Yundong* [International Communist Movement], No. 2, 1988.

———. "Soviet Policy Toward New China on the Eve of and After Its Creation," *Guoji Gongyun* [International Communist Movement], No. 6, 1986.

Quan Yanchi. "Everyday Life of Mao Zedong," *Yanhuang Zisun* [The Chinese], No. 2, 1989.

———. *Mao Zedong yu Heluxiaofu* [Mao Zedong and Khrushchev]. Changchun, 1989.

———. "Mao Zedong's Confidential Secretary, Gao Zhi, Talks About Mao Zedong," *Wenhui Yuekan* [Encounter Monthly] [Shanghai], No. 4, 1989.

———. "Mao Zedong's Entry into Beijing: The Recollections of Mao's Chief Bodyguard," in Hua Lin, ed., *Mao Zedong he Tade Zhanyou Men* [Mao Zedong and His Comrades-in-Arms]. Beijing, 1990.

———. "Profound Reminiscences of Lei Yingfu, Zhou Enlai's Military Adviser," in Quan Yanchi, *Lingxiu Lei* [The Tears of the Leader]. Beijing, 1990.

Reischauer, Edwin O. *The United States and Japan*. 3d ed. Cambridge, Mass., 1965.

Ren Donglai. "On the Sino-U.S. Treaty of Friendship, Commerce, and Navigation of 1946," *Zhonggong Dangshi Yanjiu*, No. 4, 1989.

Ren Jianshu, chief ed. *Zhongguo Gongchandang Qishi Nian Dashi Benmo* [Major Events in the 70-Year History of the Chinese Communist Party]. Shanghai, 1991.

Reston, James. "Asia Need Pressed at Senate Hearing by Acheson, Jessup," NYT, March 30, 1950.

———. "Debate over China Shows Seven Misconceptions," NYT, Jan. 8, 1950.

"The Road Toward the Liberation of the Japanese People," *Renmin Ribao*, Jan. 17, 1950.

Rong Zhi. "On the Postwar Soviet Foreign Policies," in *Guoji Zhengzhi Jiangzuo (Xubian)* [Lectures on International Politics], Vol. 2. Beijing, 1987.

Rosenberg, David Alan. "U.S. Nuclear Stockpile, 1945 to 1950," *Bulletin of the Atomic Scientists*, May 1982.

Rosenthal, A. M. "Russian Maneuver Carefully Staged," NYT, Jan. 11, 1950.

Ross, Steven T. *American War Plans, 1945–1950*. New York, 1988.

Ruan Ming. "Hu Yaobang and I," Part 1, *Zhongguo Shibao Zhoukan* [China Times Weekly] (Taipei), May 4–10, 1991.

Ryan, Mark A. *Chinese Attitudes Toward Nuclear Weapons: China and the United States During the Korean War*. Armonk, N. Y., 1989.

Salisbury, Harrison E. "Full Asia Victory Is Seen in Moscow," NYT, Jan. 22, 1950.

———. *The New Emperors: China in the Era of Mao and Deng*. Boston, 1992.

———. "Soviet Backs Mao on Formosa Claim," NYT, Jan. 5, 1950.

———. "Vyshinskii Assails Acheson Remarks on China as False," NYT, Jan. 21, 1950.

Sbornik Deistvuiushchikh Dogovorov, Soglashenii i Konventsii, Zakluchennykh SSSR s Inostrannymi Gosudarstvami, Vip. XIII: Deistvuiushie Dogovory, Soglasheniia i Konventsii, Vstupivshie v Silu mezhdu 1 Ianvaria 1947 Goda i 31 Dekabria 1948 Goda [Collection of the USSR's Valid Treaties, Agreements, and Conventions with Foreign States, Vol. 13: Valid Treaties, Agreements, and Conventions That Came into Effect Between January 1, 1947, and December 31, 1948]. Moscow, 1956.

Scalapino, Robert A., and Chong-sik Lee. *Communism in Korea*, 2 vols. Berkeley, Calif., 1972.

Schaller, Michael. *The American Occupation of Japan: The Origins of the Cold War in Asia*. New York, 1985

———. *Douglas MacArthur: The Far Eastern General*. New York, 1989.

Schonberger, Howard B. "The Cold War and the American Empire in Asia," *Radical History Review*, Vol. 33 (1985).

———. "The Japan Lobby in American Diplomacy, 1947–1952," *Pacific Historical Review*, 46.3 (Aug. 1977).

"The Secret Agreement Between the United States Government and the Nationalists," *Pravda*, Jan. 5, 1950.

"The Secret U.S.-Nationalist Conference on the Philippines," *Pravda*, Jan. 6, 1950.

Shen Xiaoyun. "An Analysis of the Readjustment of U.S.-China Relations in the Late 1940s," *Jindai Shi Yanjiu* [Modern History Studies], No. 5, 1989.

Shen Zonghong and Meng Zhaohui, chief eds. *Zhongguo Renmin Zhiyuanjun KangMei YuanChao Zhanshi* [History of the Chinese People's Volunteers in the War to Resist America and Aid Korea]. Beijing, 1988.

Shi Xiaochong. "The Forces of the Peace Camp Are Invincible," *Shijie Zhishi*, March 17, 1950.

Shi Zhe. "Chairman Mao's First Visit to the Soviet Union," in *Xin Zhongguo Waijiao Fengyun* [Main Diplomatic Events of New China]. Beijing, 1990.

———. "I Accompanied Chairman Mao," *Far Eastern Affairs* (Moscow), No. 2, 1989.

———. "Mao Zedong on the Eve of and After the Chongqing Negotiations," *Zhonghua Yinglie* [China's Heroes and Martyrs], No. 6, 1989.

———. "On the Eve of New China's Birth," in *Mianhuai Liu Shaoqi* [Cherish the Memory of Liu Shaoqi]. Beijing, 1988.

———. "The Visit of New China's Premier Zhou Enlai to Moscow," in *Bujinde Sinian* [Boundless Recollections]. Beijing, 1987.

———. "What I Saw and Heard During Mao Zedong's Visit to the Soviet Union," in Zheng Yi and Jia Mei, eds., *1946–1976 Mao Zedong Shenghuo Shilu* [True Records of Mao Zedong's Daily Life, 1946–1976]. Nanjing, 1989.

―――. "With Chairman Mao from Yan'an to Beiping," *Renwu* [Personages], No. 5, 1989.

―――. *Zai Lishi Juren Shenbian Shi Zhe Huiyilu* [Beside Great Historical Figures: The Memoirs of Shi Zhe]. Beijing, 1991.

Shi Zheng. "The Negotiations Between Stalin and T. V. Soong in Moscow," *Hainan Jishi* [Record of Events (Hainan)] (Haikou), No. 6, 1989.

Shulman, Marshall D. *Stalin's Foreign Policy Reappraised.* Cambridge, Mass., 1963.

Si Mu. "A Brief Discussion of the British Decision to Establish Diplomatic Relations with Us," *Shijie Zhishi*, Jan. 13, 1950.

―――. "The International Significance of the Victory of the Chinese People's Revolutionary War," *Shijie Zhishi*, Jan. 1, 1950.

―――. "The New Sino-Soviet Alliance Treaty and World Peace," *Shijie Zhishi*, March 3, 1950.

Simmons, Robert R. *The Strained Alliance: Peking, P'yongyang, Moscow and the Politics of the Korean Civil War.* New York, 1975.

The Sino-Soviet Treaty and Agreements. Beijing, 1950.

Sladkovskii, M. I. *Istoriia Torgovo-Ekonomicheskikh Otnoshenii SSSR s Kitaem (1917–1974)* [History of Trade and Economic Relations Between the USSR and China (1917–1974)]. Moscow, 1977.

―――. *Znakomstvo s Kitaem i Kitaitsami* [Coming to Know China and the Chinese]. Moscow, 1984.

Snow, Edgar. *The Other Side of the River: Red China Today.* New York, 1961.

―――. *Red Star Over China.* Rev. and enlarged ed. New York, 1968.

Song Chun and Lou Jie. "On the Evolution of the Nationalist Policy Toward the Soviet Union During the War of Liberation," *Shehui Kexue Zhanxian*, No. 3, 1991.

Song Ke. "An Organizational Introduction to the Central Military Commission Before the War to Resist Japan," *Dangshi Yanjiu*, No. 4, 1981.

Song Shilun, chief ed. *Zhongguo Dabaike Quanshu Junshi* [Chinese Encyclopedia of Military Affairs], Vols. 1, 2. Beijing, 1989.

Song Yijun. "Some Ideas on the Pluses and Minuses of Our Army's Landing Operations on Jinmen, Hainan, and Other Coastal Islands," *Junshi Shilin*, No. 6, 1989.

Song Zhongfu. "An Investigation of the Recognition of the Notion: 'The Chinese Revolution Was Part of the World Revolution,'" *Xibei Shiyuan Xuebao* [Northwest Normal Institute Bulletin] (Lanzhou), No. 3, 1986.

Soong, T. V., *see* Sung Tzu-wen.

"Soviet Strategy in Asia," NYT, Feb. 3, 1950.

"The Soviet Union and Vietnam," *Novoe Vremia*, No. 6, 1950.

"Soviet Walks Out at U.N. 15th Time on China Issue," NYT, Jan. 24, 1950.

Spurr, Russell. *Enter the Dragon: China's Undeclared War Against the U.S. in Korea, 1950–51.* New York, 1989.

Stalin, Joseph. "The Speech of Comrade J. V. Stalin at the Meeting of the Electorate of the Stalin Electoral District in the City of Moscow," *Pravda*, Feb. 10, 1946.

"State Department's Statement on Seizure of U.S. Consulate Property," NYT, Jan. 15, 1950.

"The Statement of the Head of the News Department of the PRC Government Administration Council, Hu Qiaomu," *Pravda*, Jan. 22, 1950.

"The Statement of the Head of the News Department of the PRC Government Administration Council, Hu Qiaomu," *Renmin Ribao*, Jan. 21, 1950.

"The Statement of USSR Minister of Foreign Affairs A. Ia. Vyshinskii on U.S. Secretary of State Acheson's Statement," *Pravda*, Jan. 21, 1950.

"Statement of the Foreign Ministry's Spokesman on the UN General Assembly's Adoption of the Eight Countries' Motion" [Oct. 10, 1950], in *Weidade KangMei YuanChao Yundong* [The Great Campaign of Resisting America and Aiding Korea]. Beijing, 1954.

Sto Sorok Besed s Molotovym: Iz Dnevnika Feliksa Chueva [140 Talks with Molotov: From the Diary of Feliks Chuev]. Moscow, 1991.

Stroganov, A. "From Yan'an to Harbin," *Novoe Vremia*, No. 3, 1949.

Stueck, William. "The Soviet Union and the Origins of the Korean War," *World Politics*, 28.4 (July 1976).

Sulzberger, C. L. "An Asian 'Spain' Threatened in Soviet Recognition of Ho," NYT, Feb. 1, 1950.

———. "Red Blow to West in Indo-China Seen," NYT, Jan. 28, 1950.

———. "Secret Codicils to Sino-Soviet Pact Said to Give Russia Key Peiping Posts and Large Force of Chinese Labor," NYT, Feb. 16, 1950.

———. "Vast Issues Face Peiping, Moscow," NYT, Jan. 14, 1950.

Sun Baosheng. "Mao Zedong Predicted a Possible U.S. Landing at Inchon," *Junshi Shilin*, No. 5, 1990.

Sun Kejia. "New Development of Mao Zedong's People's War Concept During the War to Resist America and Aid Korea," *Junshi Lishi*, No. 5, 1990.

Sun Lizhong. *Peng Zong Zai Guowai* [Chief Peng Abroad]. Beijing, 1990.

Sun Mei. "An Introduction to the Various Armies of the People's Liberation Army," Part 2, *Junshi Shilin*, No. 4, 1988.

Sun Qitai. "A Brief Introduction to the Campaign to Resist America and Aid Korea," in *Zhonggong Dangshi Ziliao* [Materials on the CCP's History], Vol. 36. Beijing, 1990.

Sun Siding. "Several Questions About the New Sino-Soviet Treaty," *Shijie Zhishi*, March 10, 1950.

Sun Yaosheng and Cui Jingshan. "General Xie Fang in the War to Resist America and Aid Korea," *Shehui Kexue Zhanxian*, No. 4, 1990.

Sun Zhaiwei. "On the Defeat of the Landing Operations on Jinmen Island," *Junshi Shilin*, No. 2, 1989.

Sung Tzu-wen [T. V. Soong]. "Prime Minister T. V. Soong's Cabled Report to Chairman Chiang on His Talk with the U.S. President About the Problems Facing China in the Postwar Period" [Aug. 18, 1945], in *Zhonghua Minguo Zhongyao Shiliao Chubian Dui Ri Kangzhan Shiqi Di Qi Bian Zhanhou Zhongguo (I)* [Important Historical Materials of the Republic of China During the Period of the War of Resistance Against Japan, Vol. 7: Postwar China (Part I)]. Taipei, 1981.

Suslov, M. "Defense of Peace and Struggle Against Warmongers: Report at the Conference of the Information Bureau of the Communist Parties in the Second Half of November 1949," *Pravda*, Dec. 3, 1949.

Svetlov, Yu. "In Manchuria," *Novoe Vremia*, No. 7, 1949.

Syn Song-Kil and Sin Sam-Soon [pseuds.]. "Who Started the Korean War?," *Korea and World Affairs* (Seoul), 14.2 (Summer 1990).

Tai Dong. "Feng Shaobai's Four Missions in Shanghai," *Renwu* [Personages], No. 6, 1987.

Tan Jingqiao, chief ed. *KangMei YuanChao Zhanzheng* [The War to Resist America and Aid Korea]. Beijing, 1990.

Tang Kai. "The Push Deep into the Northeast After the Japanese Surrender," *Zongheng* [Talk Freely], No. 6, 1986.

Tang Qun and Li Bing. "Introduction to the 3d Plenum of the 7th Central Committee of the Chinese Communist Party," in *Dangshi Yanjiu Ziliao* [Research Materials on Party History], Vol. 3. Chengdu, 1982.

Tao Wenzhao. "A Comment on Our Country's Research in the 1980s on Sino-U.S. Relations During the Liberation War Period," *Shijie Shi Yanjiu Dongtai* [Developments in World History Studies], No. 5, 1990.

Terskii, F. "Events in China," *Novoe Vremia*, No. 22, 1949.

"Text of the U.S. 'Background' on China," NYT, Jan. 26, 1950.

"Texts of Statements on China," NYT, Jan. 7, 1950.

Toka, S. "Five Years of Soviet Tuva," *Pravda*, Oct. 11, 1949.

"Top Secret, Copying Prohibited; Must Be Returned to the CPSU Central Committee Chancellery; Stenographic Transcript of the CPSU Central Committee Plenary Meeting, July 1953," in *Izvestiya CK KPSS* [CPSU Central Committee Information (Bulletin)], No. 1, 1991.

"Top Secret, Moscow (June 2, 1947): Top Secret, K.AA/SS 113 Order NK (003) 47," in *Demokraticheskaia Rossiia* [Democratic Russia], No. 4, 1990.

"A Treaty of Eternal Soviet-Chinese Friendship," *Novoe Vremia*, No. 8, 1950.

Triska, Jan F., and David D. Finley. *Soviet Foreign Policy*. London, 1968.

Truman, Harry S. *Memoirs*, Vol. 1: *Year of Decisions*. Garden City, N.Y., 1955.

Tucker, Nancy Bernkopf. *Patterns in the Dust: Chinese-American Relations and the Recognition Controversy, 1949–1950*. New York, 1983.

Tucker, Robert C. "The Prehistory of the First Détente: Stalin and the Soviet Controversy over Foreign Policy, 1949–53," paper presented at Columbus, Ohio, seminar on U.S.-Soviet relations, Oct. 1988.

Ulam, Adam B. *Expansion and Coexistence: Soviet Foreign Policy, 1917–73*. 2d ed. New York, 1974.

United States, Department of State. *Bulletin*, 1950.

———, ———. *Foreign Relations of the United States*. Washington, D.C., vols. for the years 1945, 1947–50.

———, ———. *United States Relations with China*. Washington, D.C., 1949.

———, Joint Intelligence Committee, Joint Chiefs of Staff. "Note by the Secretaries to the Joint Intelligence Committee on Soviet Capabilities and Intentions in the Far East in the Event of a Major War in 1950," J. I. C. 500 (Jan. 13, 1950).

"The United States Continues to Arm the Nationalists," *Pravda*, Jan. 12, 1950.

"U.S. China Policy Called Confusing," NYT, March 30, 1950.

"U.S. Recognizes Viet Nam, Two Other Indo-China States," NYT, Feb. 8, 1950.

USSR-China in the Changing World. Moscow, 1989.

"The Victorious Future of the Korean People's Liberation War," *Renmin Ribao*, July 6, 1950.

Viktorov, Ia. "Concerning the Events in China," *Novoe Vremia*, No. 6, 1949.

———. "International Review," *Pravda*, Jan. 8, 1950.

Vladimirov, O. B. *Nezabyvaemye Stranitsy Istorii i Maoistskie Falsifikatory* [Unforgettable Pages of History and the Maoist Falsifiers]. Moscow, 1971.

Vladimirov, P. P. *Osobyi Raion Kitaia, 1942–1945* [A Special Region of China, 1942–1945]. Moscow, 1973.

Vneshniaia Politika Sovetskogo Soiuza, 1945 God.: Dokumenty i Materialy [Documents and Materials on the Foreign Policy of the Soviet Union in the Year 1945], Part 1. Moscow, 1952.

Voennaia Pomoshch SSSR v Osvoboditelnoi Borbe Kitaiskogo Naroda [USSR Military Assistance in the Liberation Struggle of the Chinese People]. Moscow, 1975.

Volkogonov, Dmitrii. *I. V. Stalin: Triumf i Tragediia* [Stalin: Triumph and Tragedy], 2 2-part vols. Moscow, 1989.

Voznesenskii, N. A. "The Five-Year Plan for the Reconstruction and Development of the USSR's National Economy for the Period 1946–1950," *Pravda*, March 16, 1946.

Waggoner, Walter H. "Acheson Says U.S. Counts on Chinese Anger at Soviet for Land Seizures in North," NYT, Jan. 13, 1950.

———. "Connally Assails Vyshinskii's Words," NYT, Jan. 22, 1950.

———. "Issue of Recognition Has Many Complexities," NYT, Jan. 29, 1950.

———. "State Department Details Its Charge on Soviet in China," NYT, Jan. 26, 1950.

Wang Chengguang. "A General Description of Peng Dehuai's Military Theory," *Junshi Lishi*, No. 1, 1991.

Wang Daming. "The Yangtze Crossing Campaign: The Liberation of Shanghai," *Fujian Dangshi Yuekan* [Party History Monthly (Fujian)] (Fuzhou), No. 4, 1989.

Wang Dinglie, chief ed. *Dangdai Zhongguo Kongjun* [Contemporary China's Air Force]. Beijing, 1989.

Wang Fangming. "We Do Not Dance to the Baton of Others," in Guo Simin, ed., *Wo Yanzhong de Mao Zedong* [Mao Zedong in My Eyes]. Shijiazhuang, 1990.

Wang Hanming. "A Brief Study of Sino-American Relations in the Korean War," *Junshi Lishi*, No. 4, 1989.

Wang He. "Mao Zedong's Plans for Economic Cooperation with the United States in the Later Stage of the Anti-Japanese War," *Mao Zedong Sixiang Yanjiu* [Studies on Mao Zedong's Thought] (Chengdu), No. 4, 1986.

———. "The Plans of Mao Zedong and Zhou Enlai to Visit the United States in the Later Stage of the Anti-Japanese War," *Mao Zedong Sixiang Yanjiu* [Studies on Mao Zedong's Thought] (Chengdu), No. 2, 1988.

Wang Jinyu and Chen Ruiyun, chief eds. *Zhongguo Xiandai Zhengzhi Shi (1919–1949)* [Contemporary Chinese Political History (1919–1949)]. Harbin, 1990.

Wang Jisi. "American Policy Toward China (1945–55) and Its Results," *Meiguo Yanjiu* [American Studies], No. 1, 1987.

Wang Ming. "Polveka KPK i Predatel Mao Zedona" [Half a Century of the CCP and the Traitor Mao Zedong], manuscript, published under the title *Polveka KPK i Predatelstvo Mao Zedona* [Half a Century of the CCP and the Treachery of Mao Zedong]. Moscow, 1975.

Wang Pei and Ren Qingguo. "The Question of China's Developmental Path After the Victory of the Anti-Japanese War," *Zhonggong Dangshi Yanjiu*, No. 4, 1988.

Wang Tingke. "The Soviet Union and China's Anti-Japanese War," *Wenshi Zazhi* [Literature and History Magazine], No. 4, 1987.

Wang Wanli. "General Xie Fang in His Youth and the 'Tianjin Incident,'" *Shehui Kexue Zhanxian*, No. 2, 1985.

Wang Wenmu. "Why Our Party Agreed to the Signing of the 'Sino-Soviet Treaty,'" *Dangshi Zongheng* [Explorations into Party History]. Excerpted in *Zhonggong Dangshi Tongxun* [CCP History Newsletter], No. 26 (Jan. 25, 1990).

Wang Xian'gen. *KangMei YuanYue Shilu* [The True History of Resisting America and Aiding Vietnam]. Chengde, 1990.

Wang Xuebao. "A True Record of the 1950 Revolutionary Armed Rebellion in Ji-shan [County, Shanxi Province]," *Dangshi Wenhui* [Collection on Party History] (Taiyuan), No. 1, 1990.

Wang Yaoshan et al. "In Commemoration of the 20th Anniversary of the Death of Comrade Liu Changsheng," *Renmin Ribao*, Oct. 15, 1987.

Wang Yizhi. "The Northeast Anti-Japanese United Army on the Eve of and After 'August 15,'" in *LiaoShen Juezhan* [The Liaoxi-Shenyang Campaign], Vol. 1. Beijing, 1988.

Wang Yu, chief ed. *Zhonggong Dangshi Jianbian* [Concise History of the CCP]. Beijing, 1988.

Wang Yuannian et al. *Dongbei Jiefang Zhanzheng Chujian Jiaofei Shi* [History of Eliminating Traitors and Suppressing Bandits During the Northeast Liberation War]. Harbin, 1990.

Wang Zhaoquan. "The Creation of the Dalian Jianxin Corporation and Its Support for the Huai-Hai Campaign," *Junshi Lishi*, No. 1, 1991.

"The Ward Case," *China Weekly Review*, Jan. 14, 1950.

"Ward Feels Russia Won't Annex Land," NYT, Jan. 15, 1950.

Wei Shiyan. "Zhou Enlai's Diplomatic Thinking," *Zhonggong Dangshi Yanjiu*, No. 2, 1988.

Weng Zhonger. "An Analysis of Sino-American Relations on the Eve of and After the Founding of New China," *Liaocheng Shifan Xueyuan Xuebao* [Liaocheng Normal Institute Bulletin] (Liaocheng), No. 2, 1990.

Werth, Alexander. *Russia at War, 1941–1945*. New York, 1964.

White, William S. "Acheson to Reply to China Aid Critics," NYT, Jan. 5, 1950.

———. "Congress Divided on British Action," NYT, Jan. 7, 1950.

Whiting, Allen S. *China Crosses the Yalu: The Decision to Enter the Korean War*. New York, 1960.

Whitson, William W. *The Chinese High Command: A History of Communist Military Politics, 1927–71*. New York, 1973.

"Why Can't the Atomic Bomb Decide the Outcome of War?," in *Fensui Meiguo Diguozhuyi de Qinlüe* [Shatter the U.S. Imperialist Invasion]. Beijing, 1950.

"Why Can't We Ignore the American Invasion of Korea?," *Renmin Ribao*, Nov. 6, 1950.

"Why Can't We Ignore the Korean War?," *Guangming Ribao* [Bright Daily], Oct. 31, 1950.

"Why Can't We Ignore the War of Aggression by U.S. Imperialism Against Korea?," *Tianjin Ribao* [Tianjin Daily], Nov. 4, 1950.

Wu Jingping. "The United States and the Sino-Soviet Negotiations of 1945," *Lishi Yanjiu* [Historical Studies], No. 1, 1990.

Wu Lanfu. "Inner Mongolia in the Past Ten Years," *Renmin Ribao*, April 30, 1957.

Wu Xiangting and Han Xuejing. *Gensui Mao Zedong Jishi* [Reminiscences About Mao Zedong]. Taiyuan, 1991.

Wu Xiuquan. *Eight Years in the Ministry of Foreign Affairs (January 1950–October 1958)—Memoirs of a Diplomat*. Beijing, 1985.

———. *Huiyi yu Huainian* [Recollections and Reminiscences]. Beijing, 1991.

———. "The Liberation of the Northeast in Cooperation with the Soviet Army," in *LiaoShen Juezhan* [The Liaoxi-Shenyang Campaign], Vol. 1. Beijing, 1988.

———. "My Departure from Yan'an by Airplane," in Wang Dikang et al., eds., *Dongbei Jiefang Zhanzheng Jishi* [True Records on the Liberation War in the Northeast]. Beijing, 1988.

———. "My Diplomatic Career," *Chunqiu* [Spring and Autumn] (Wuhan), No. 3, 1987.

———. "The Process of Concluding the Sino-Soviet 'Treaty of Friendship, Alliance, and Mutual Assistance,'" in *Xin Zhongguo Waijiao Fengyun* [Main Diplomatic Events of New China]. Beijing, 1990.

———. *Wo de Licheng (1908–1949)* [My Career (1908–1949)]. Beijing, 1984.

———. "Wu Xiuquan's Speech at the Security Council" [Nov. 28, 1950], in *Zhonghua Renmin Gongheguo Duiwai Guanxi Wenjian Ji (1949–1950)* [Collection of Documents on the Foreign Relations of the People's Republic of China (1949–1950)], Vol 1. Beijing, 1957.

Xia Lin'gen and Yu Xiyuan, chief eds. *ZhongSu Guanxi Cidian* [A Glossary of Sino-Soviet Relations]. Dalian, 1990.

Xiang Qing. "My Point of View on Stalin's Attempt to Persuade the Liberation Army Not to Cross the Yangtze River," 2 parts, *Dang de Wenxian* [Party Documents], Nos. 1 and 6, 1989. Excerpted in *Junshi Lishi*, No. 3, 1990.

Xiao Jianning. "An Analysis of U.S. Policy Toward China on the Eve of the Outbreak of the Korean War and After," *Dangshi Yanjiu*, No. 6, 1987.

Xiao Jingguang. "My Mission to the Northeast," in Ge Fulu et al., eds., *Dongbei Zhanchang Fengyun Lu* [Records of the Decisive Battles in the Northeast]. Beijing, 1988.

———. *Xiao Jingguang Huiyilu* [Memoirs of Xiao Jingguang], 2 vols. Beijing, 1987, 1988.

Xiao Shizhong. "Source Materials on the Korean War," Part 3, *Junshi Lishi*, No. 1, 1991.

Xie Youfa. "Comrade Xiao Hua in the Rectification Movement and the War to Resist America and Aid Korea," in *Huiyi Xiao Hua* [The Reminiscences of Xiao Hua]. Beijing, 1988.

Xing Shi, ed. *Muqian Shishi Wenti Xuexi Ziliao* [Materials for Studying the Questions on the Current Situation]. Beijing, 1950.

Xiong Xianghui. "My 12-Year Underground Work and Zhou Enlai," Part 4, *Renmin Ribao*, overseas ed., Jan. 11, 1991.

Xu Peilan and Zheng Pengfei. *Chen Geng Jiangjun Zhuan* [The Biography of General Chen Geng]. Tianjin, 1988.

Xu Xiangqian. *Lishi de Huigu* [A Look Back in History]. Beijing, 1987.

Xu Xiaolin. "Zhu De and the Ideology for Dual Military-Civilian Production," *Mao Zedong Sixiang Yanjiu* [Studies on Mao Zedong's Thought] (Chengdu), No. 2, 1989.

Xu Yan. *Diyi Ci Jiaoliang KangMei YuanChao Zhanzheng Lishi Huigu yu Fansi* [The First Trial of Strength: Historical Retrospection and a Review of the War to Resist America and Aid Korea]. Beijing, 1990.

———. *Jinmen zhi Zhan* [The Jinmen Campaign]. Beijing, 1992.

————. "The Tortuous Course of Decision-Making [with Respect to] Sending Troops to Resist America and Aid Korea," *Zhonggong Dangshi Yanjiu Ziliao* [Research Materials on CCP History], No. 3, 1991.

Xu Yuandong et al. *Zhongguo Gongchandang Lishi Jianghua Xubian* [A Guide to the History of the Chinese Communist Party], Vol. 2. Beijing, 1988.

Xu Zhongjing and Dai Yifang. "What We Have Gained from Studying the Initial Concept of Operations for the War to Resist America and Aid Korea," *Junshi Shilin*, No. 3, 1988.

Xue Hui. "General Description of the Sixth Scholarly Conference on the Problems of the Relations Between the Soviet Union, the Communist International, and the Chinese Revolution," in *Zhonggong Dangshi Tongxun* [CCP History Newsletter], No. 18 (Sept. 25, 1990).

Xue Mouhong. *Meidi zai Xiou de Beizhan* [U.S. Imperialist War Preparations in West Europe]. Beijing, 1951.

Xue Qingchao. "Appraisal of the 1945 'Soviet-Chinese Treaty,'" *Henan Dangshi Yanjiu* [Studies on Party History (Henan)], No. 6, 1990. Excerpted in *Zhonggong Dangshi Tongxun* [CCP History Newsletter], No. 47 (Dec. 10, 1990).

Yan Chi. "Mao Zedong's Arrival in Beijing," *Yanhuang Zisun* [The Chinese], No. 3, 1989.

Yan Jingtang. "A Brief Introduction to the Evolution of the Central Military Commission," *Dangshi Yanjiu*, No. 2, 1983.

Yang Chengwu. "A Call on Chairman Mao," *Dangshi Yanjiu yu Jiaoxue* [Studies and Teachings on Party History] (Fuzhou), No. 5, 1990.

————. "Preparations for Going to Battle," *Dangshi Yanjiu yu Jiaoxue* [Studies and Teachings on Party History] (Fuzhou), No. 4, 1990.

————. "The 66th Corps' Entry into the Korean War," *Dangshi Yanjiu yu Jiaoxue* [Studies and Teachings on Party History] (Fuzhou), No. 2, 1990.

Yang Guoyu, chief ed. *Dangdai Zhongguo Haijun* [Contemporary China's Navy]. Beijing, 1987.

Yang Kuisong. "Several Problems Concerning Relations Among the Comintern, the Soviet Union, and the Chinese Communist Party During the Sino-Japanese War," *Zhonggong Dangshi Yanjiu*, No. 6, 1987.

Yang Shunren. "His Transition from a Major General in the Military Bureau of Investigation and Statistics to a Revolutionary Martyr," *Dajiang Nanbei* [On Both Sides of the Yangtze River] (Nanjing), No. 4, 1989.

Yang Yanpu. "An Exploration into Mao's Decision-making Thinking," *Hebei Xuekan* [Hebei Bulletin] (Shijiazhuang), No. 1, 1987.

Yang Yunruo. "The Evolution of Sino-Soviet-American Relations on the Eve of and After the Soviet-German War and the Pacific War," *Zhonggong Dangshi Yanjiu*, No. 6, 1988.

Yang Zhaoquan. *ZhongChao Guanxi Shi Lunwen Ji* [A Collection of Essays on Sino-Korean Relations]. Beijing, 1988.

Yang Zhihua. "A Brief History of the Chinese People's Liberation Army," *Junshi Lishi*, No. 1, 1991.

Yao Xu. *Cong Yalujiang dao Banmendian* [From the Yalu River to Panmunjom]. Beijing, 1985.

————. "The Wise Decision to Resist America and Aid Korea," *Dangshi Yanjiu*, No. 5, 1980.

Yasamee, H. J., and K. A. Hamilton. *Documents on British Policy Overseas*, Series 2, Vol. 4: *Korea, 1950–1951* (London, 1991).

Ye Fei. "The Liberation of Fujian and the Struggle on the Fujian Front," Part 1, *Fujian Dangshi Yuekan* [Party History Monthly (Fujian)] (Fuzhou), No. 8, 1989.

Ye Mang. "U.S. Imperialism's Crime of Invading Taiwan," *Shijie Zhishi*, July 7, 1950.

Ye Yumeng. *Hanjiang Xue Chubing Chaoxian Jishi zhi Er* [The Blood on the Bank of the Han River: The Actual Record of the Decision to Send Troops to Korea], Vol. 2. Beijing, 1990.

———. *Heixue Chubing Chaoxian Jishi* [Black Snow: The Actual Record of the Decision to Send Troops to Korea]. Beijing, 1989.

Yoo Sung Chul [Yu Song-chol]. "My Testimony," 5 parts, *Hanguk Ilbo* [Korea Daily] (Seoul), Nov. 1, 3, 9, 11, 13, 1990. The translations in *Foreign Broadcast Information Service: East Asia*, Nov. 15, Dec. 4, 27, 28, 1990, are cited in the Notes.

Yu Ruping. "An Exploration into the Strategic Guiding Principles for the War to Resist America and Aid Korea," *Junshi Lishi*, No. 4, 1987.

Yu Shumin. "The Party Line on Achieving Peace, Democracy, and Unification After the Victory in the Anti-Japanese War and Its Historic Role," *Kaituo* [Open Up] (Chengdu), No. 1, 1987.

Yu Zhan and Zhang Guangyou. "An Investigation of the Question Whether Stalin Advised Us Not to Cross the Yangtze River," in *Xin Zhongguo Waijiao Fengyun* [Main Diplomatic Events of New China]. Beijing, 1990.

Yu Zhen. "The CPV's Air Force in the Korean War," 2 parts, *Junshi Shijie* [Military World] (Hong Kong), Nos. 4, 6, 1989.

———. "On the Creation and Development of the Air Force in Modern China," in Liang Juxiang, chief ed., *Zhongguo Jindai Junshi Lunwen Ji* [Collected Essays on Chinese Military History in Modern Times]. Beijing, 1987.

Yun Zhang and Xiao Chun. "On the Foreign Trade of the Northeast Base Area During the Liberation War Period," *Shehui Kexue Zhanxian*, No. 3, 1990.

Zeng Kelin. "From Yan'an to Shenyang Via Shanhaiguan: My Reminiscences on Making Contacts with the Soviet Army," in *ZhongE Guanxi Wenti Huabei Diqu ZhongE Guanxi Yanjiuhui* [The Issues on Sino-Russian Relations Discussed at the Sino-Russian Symposium in North China]. Beijing, No. 28 (Oct. 1990).

———. "Recollections on Comrade Liu Shaoqi's Strategic Decision-making on the Contention in the Northeast [Between Our Party and the Nationalists]," in *Mianhuai Liu Shaoqi* [Cherish the Memory of Liu Shaoqi]. Beijing, 1988.

———. "Report on the True Situation in the Northeast to the Party's Central Leadership," in Wang Dikang et al., eds., *Dongbei Jiefang Zhanzheng Jishi* [True Records on the Liberation War in the Northeast]. Beijing, 1988.

———. *Rongma Shengya de Huiyi* [Reminiscences of the War Years]. Beijing, 1992.

Zhan Yizhi. "The Soviet Socialist Road and Its Influence on Mao Zedong," *Mao Zedong Sixiang Yanjiu* [Studies on Mao Zedong's Thought] (Chengdu), No. 4, 1988.

Zhang Hui. "The Strategic Decision-making Contest Between China and the United States," *Dangshi Wenhui* [Collection on Party History] (Taiyuan), No. 6, 1988.

Zhang Jian. "I Worked at the Side of Chief of the General Staff Su Yu," in *Yidai Mingjiang Huiyi Su Yu Tongzhi* [A Famous General: Reminiscences About Comrade Su Yu]. Shanghai, 1986.

Zhang Jian and Jin Shi. "A Comparison of the Strategic Concepts of Mao Zedong and the Westerners," *Mao Zedong Sixiang Yanjiu* [Studies on Mao Zedong's Thought] (Chengdu), No. 3, 1983.

Zhang Liyao. "The War to Resist America and Aid Korea and Peng Dehuai," in Wang Ping and Zhang Liyao, chief eds., *Zhongguo Jinxiandai Fengyun Lu* [Main Events in Modern and Contemporary Chinese History]. Shanghai, 1988.

Zhang Nan. "What Was Leighton Stuart Doing in Nanjing?," *Renwu*, No. 6, 1986.

Zhang Qianhua. "The Political Study Faction's Wishful Thinking in the Takeover of the Northeast," in *Wenshi Ziliao Xuanji* [Selected Materials on Literature and History], Vol. 42. Beijing, n.d.

Zhang Qinghua. "[Zhou Enlai] Wisely Dealt with Enemies in Chongqing and Made Great Contributions to China's War of Liberation," in *Huainian Zhou Enlai* [Cherish the Memory of Zhou Enlai]. Beijing, 1986.

Zhang Quanqi and Wang Shengyu. "On the Characteristics of Mao Zedong's Strategic Thinking," *Mao Zedong Sixiang Yanjiu* [Studies on Mao Zedong's Thought] (Chengdu), No. 3, 1983.

Zhang Tinggui. "An Introduction to the War to Resist America and Aid Korea," *Dangshi Yanjiu yu Jiaoxue* [Studies and Teachings on Party History] (Fuzhou), No. 6, 1988.

Zhang Xi. "On the Eve of and After Peng Dehuai's Assignment to Command [in the War] to Resist America and Aid Korea," in *Zhonggong Dangshi Ziliao Xuanji* [Selected Materials on the CCP's History], Vol. 31. Beijing, 1989.

———. "Peng Dehuai in the War to Resist America and Aid Korea," *Xinghuo Liaoyuan* [A Single Spark Can Start a Prairie Fire], No. 6, 1985.

Zhang Xiaolu. "Efforts at a Crucial Moment: An Analysis of CCP Policy Toward the United States in 1949," *Shehui Kexue Zhanxian*, No. 4, 1990.

Zhang Yuwen. "Inside Information on the Decision to Send the CPV to Korea and on Lin Biao's 10-Year Plea of Illness," *Baokan Huicui* [Anthology of Articles Published in Newspapers and Periodicals] (Xi'an), Feb. 1990.

Zhang Zhen. "The Third Field Army Forced Its Way Across the Yangtze River," in *Zhonggong Dangshi Ziliao* [Materials on CCP History], Vol. 36. Beijing, 1990.

Zhang Zhenglong. *Xuebai Xuehong* [White Snow and Red Blood]. Hong Kong, 1991.

Zhang Zhian. "Some Ideas on the Reasons for the Peaceful Liberation of Xinjiang," *Shishi Qiushi* [Seek Truth Through Facts], No. 1, 1988.

Zhang Zongxun. *Zhang Zongxun Huiyilu* [Memoirs of Zhang Zongxun]. Beijing, 1990.

Zhao Guoqin. "The Whole Story of Creating a Training Brigade in the Soviet Union for the Northeast Anti-Japanese United Army," *Junshi Lishi*, No. 5, 1990.

Zhao Wei. "The Planned Attack on Taiwan by the Third Field Army of the Chinese Communists," *Kaifang* [Open] (Hong Kong), No. 5, 1991.

Zhao Yongtian and Zhang Xi. "Corrections to Some Facts in 'Black Snow: The Actual Record of the Decision to Send Troops to Korea,'" *Junshi Lishi*, No. 6, 1989.

Zheng Dongguo. "Mao Zedong and Zhou Enlai Showed Concern for and Educated Me," *Liaowang* [Outlook], No. 15, 1992.

Zheng Xiaoguo. "The Emergence and Change of the Foreign Guiding Principle of 'Leaning to One Side,'" *Zhonggong Dangshi Yanjiu*, No. 1, 1991.

Zhi Shaozeng. "Essentials of the Evolution of the Central Military Commission," *Junshi Lishi*, No. 6, 1989.

Zhonggong Dangshi Dashi Nianbiao [Chronological Table of Major Events in CCP History]. Beijing, 1987.

Zhonggong Dangshi Dashi Nianbiao Shuoming [Explanation for Chronological Table of Major Events in the CCP History]. Beijing, 1983.

Zhonggong Dangshi Jiaoxue Cankao Ziliao [Reference Materials for the Teaching and Study of CCP History], Vols. 17–19. Beijing, 1985, 1986.

Zhonggong Zhongyang Wenjian Xuanji [Selected Documents of the CCP Central Committee], Vol. 13. Beijing, 1987.

Zhongguo Gongchandang Jianshi Jiangyi [Teaching Materials on the Concise History of the CCP]. Guangzhou, 1985.

Zhonghua Minguo Zhongyao Shiliao Chubian Dui Ri Kangzhan Shiqi Di Qi Bian Zhanhou Zhongguo (I) [Important Historical Materials on the Republic of China During the War of Resistance Against Japan. Vol. 7: Postwar China (Part I)]. Taipei, 1981.

ZhongSu Youhao Guanxi Xuexi Shouce [Handbook on the Friendly Relations Between China and the Soviet Union]. Shanghai, 1950.

Zhou Enlai. "The Comintern and the Chinese Communist Party" [July 14, 15, 1960], in *Zhou Enlai Xuanji* [Selected Works of Zhou Enlai], Vol. 2. Beijing, 1984.

———. "The Foreign Policies of the People's Republic of China (Sept. 30, 1950)," in *Zhou Enlai Waijiao Wenxuan* [Selected Diplomatic Documents of Zhou Enlai]. Beijing, 1990.

———. "Memorandum from Foreign Minister Zhou Enlai to the Governments of Various Countries on Chairman Mao Zedong's Declaration of the Establishment of the Central People's Government of the People's Republic of China," in *Zhonghua Renmin Gongheguo Duiwai Guanxi Wenjian Ji (1949–1950)* [Collection of Documents on the Foreign Relations of the People's Republic of China (1949–1950)], Vol. 1. Beijing, 1957.

———. "On Logistic Support to the Frontier Force and Its Supply by the Northeast—a Report to Chairman Mao" [Aug. 24, 1950], in *Zhou Enlai Shuxin Xuanji* [Selected Telegrams and Letters of Zhou Enlai]. Beijing, 1988.

———. "Report on the Problems Concerning the Peace Talks" [April 17, 1949], in *Zhou Enlai Xuanji* [Selected Works of Zhou Enlai], Vol. 1. Beijing, 1980.

———. "Resist America and Aid Korea, Defend Peace" [Oct. 24, 1950], in *Zhou Enlai Waijiao Wenxuan* [Selected Diplomatic Documents of Zhou Enlai]. Beijing, 1990.

———. "The Sacrifice of Mao Anying Is Glorious—[A Letter] to Mao Zedong and Jiang Qing" [Jan. 2, 1951], in *Zhou Enlai Shuxin Xuanji* [Selected Telegrams and Letters of Zhou Enlai]. Beijing, 1988.

———. "The Speech of Premier and Foreign Minister Zhou Enlai at the Signing Ceremony," *Shijie Zhishi*, Feb. 24, 1950.

Zhou Fang. "Explaining the Changes in the Organic Structure and Function of the

People's Governments in the Administrative Regions," *Guangming Ribao* [Bright Daily], Dec. 25, 1952.

Zhou Guoquan et al. *Wang Ming Pingzhuan* [A Critical Biography of Wang Ming]. Hefei, 1989.

Zhou Jun. "A Study on the Reasons why the PLA Aborted Its Plan to Attack Taiwan Soon After the Founding of the New China," *Zhonggong Dangshi Yanjiu*, No. 1, 1991.

Zhu Guangya. "My Experiences in Promoting the Propaganda Work on [the Might of] the Atomic Bomb," in *Beida KangMei YuanChao Yundong Teji Disi Ji* [Beijing University's Special Collection of Information on the Campaign to Resist America and Aid Korea], Vol. 4. Beijing, 1951.

Zhu Jianhua. *Dongbei Jiefang Zhanzheng Shi* [History of the Northeast Liberation War]. Harbin, 1987.

Zhu Jianhua and Zhao Yinglan. "The History of the Creation of the Northeast Revolutionary Base in the Liberation War," *Shehui Kexue Zhanxian*, No. 3, 1984.

Zhu Peimin. "Probing into Some Problems Concerning the Peaceful Liberation of Xinjiang," *Shehui Kexue* [Social Science] (Ürümqi), No. 5, 1989.

———. "The Whole Story of the Peaceful Liberation of Xinjiang," in *Zhonggong Dangshi Ziliao* [Materials on CCP History], Vol. 32. Beijing, 1989.

Zhu Xiangfeng and Wei Ziyang. "Chen Yun in the Liberation War in the Northeast," *Dongbei Difangzhi Yanjiu* [Northeast Local History Studies] (Shenyang), No. 4, 1989.

Zhu Yuanshi. "Liu Shaoqi's Secret Visit to the Soviet Union in 1949," *Dang de Wenxian* [Party Documents], No. 3, 1991.

Zhu Zhongli. *Liming yu Wanxia* [Dawn and Sunset]. Beijing, 1986.

———. *Nanyi Wangque de Zuotian Wang Jiaxiang Xiaozhuan* [The Unforgettable Yesterday: Profile of Wang Jiaxiang]. Xiamen, 1987.

Zhukov, E. "Colonial Appetites of the American Monopolies," *Pravda*, July 9, 1949.

———. "The Great October Socialist Revolution and China," *Novoe Vremia*, No. 46, 1949.

———. "The Historic Meaning of the Victory of the Chinese People," *Novoe Vremia*, No. 3, 1950.

Index

In this index an "f" after a number indicates a separate reference on the next page, and an "ff" indicates separate references on the next two pages. A continuous discussion over two or more pages is indicated by a span of page numbers, e.g., "57–59." *Passim* is used for a cluster of references in close but not consecutive sequence.

Library of Congress Cataloguing-in-Publication Data

Goncharov, S. N. (Sergei Nikolaevich)
  Uncertain partners : Stalin, Mao, and the Korean War / Sergei N.
Goncharov, John W. Lewis, Xue Litai.
    p.   cm. — (Studies in international security and arms control)
  Includes bibiliographical references and index.
  ISBN 0-8047-2115-7 (cl.) : ISBN 0-8047-2521-7 (pbk.)
    1. China—Foreign relations—Soviet Union. 2. Soviet Union—
Foreign relations—China. 3. Korean War, 1950–1953. 1. Lewis, John
Wilson, 1930– . 11. Xue, Litai, 1947– . 111. Title. 1v. Series.
DS740.5.S65G66 1993
327.51047—dc20   93-23971
                                                                  CIP